Value(s)

Value(s)

Building a Better World for All

MARK CARNEY

PUBLICAFFAIRS

New York

To Sasha, Amelia, Tess and Cleo

PublicAffairs
Hachette Book Group
1290 Avenue of the Americas, New York, NY 10104
www.publicaffairsbooks.com
@Public_Affairs

Printed in the United States of America

Originally published in 2021 by William Collins in Great Britain.

First US Edition: May 2021

Published by PublicAffairs, an imprint of Perseus Books, LLC, a subsidiary of Hachette Book Group, Inc. The PublicAffairs name and logo is a trademark of the Hachette Book Group.

The Hachette Speakers Bureau provides a wide range of authors for speaking events. To find out more, go to www.hachettespeakersbureau.com or call (866) 376-6591.

The publisher is not responsible for websites (or their content) that are not owned by the publisher.

Print book interior Typeset in Sabon MT

Library of Congress Control Number: 2021931634

ISBNs 978-1-5417-6870-3 (hardcover), 978-1-5417-6871-0 (e-book)

LSC-C

Printing 1, 2021

Contents

PART III – RECLAIMING OUR VALUES

Introduction

HUMANITY DISTILLED

The car weaves silently through the City. When it reaches St Michael's Lothbury, it waits momentarily while security guards swing open giant steel gates, and it then rolls into the bullion yard. I get out, pass through an alarmed door, by enormous vaults, and up a granite staircase. I rub the nose of the lion adorning a brass portal as I enter the inner sanctum. I bid good morning to the pink-jacketed stewards, walk by portraits of my predecessors and step into the office of the Governor of the Bank of England.

Everything I see evokes the history of the Bank and the permanence of its mission. The entrance hall echoes the style of British imperial capitals. The corridors are lined with mosaics showing images of Roman coins and Mercury, the god of commerce. Lions – the traditional guardians of treasure – populate the gilded stair wells and front the doors.

The Governor's office is much as it has been over the centuries. The desk has been in continual use since it was crafted by Sir John Soane in the eighteenth century. One wall is dominated by a gigantic Canaletto, depicting the Thames in the late seventeenth century. Floor-to-ceiling glass doors open on to a tranquil courtyard that preserves the seventeenth-century churchyard of St Christopher-le-Stocks.

There are symbols of money and value everywhere. Mulberry trees outside the windows allude to the earliest paper currency that was fashioned out of their bark. Mercury's winged head oversees the magnificent Court room where griffons guard the portals as steadfastly as they did the mythical pile of gold at the centre of the earth.

There's real gold at the centre of the Bank. Beneath my feet, nine vaults with three-foot steel walls are filled with 5,500 tons of bullion that the market values at over $180 billion. That's 5 per cent of all the gold ever mined since the dawn of humanity.

Everything appears solid, safe, permanent.

But all is not what it seems. The Empire is gone. The Union is under threat. Permanence is temporary. And value is an illusion.

Of Soane's original Bank of England – an architectural master-piece designed to stand for a millennium – only the exterior walls, the state rooms and the desk remain. The Canaletto is now recognised as being 'of the school' not 'by the master'.

The gold lies pointlessly in our vaults, a vestige of a bygone era when it backed the value of money – a link that became a cross, inspiring booms before triggering busts. Financial markets value gold for its perceived safety not for its revealed beauty. The gold price surges with fears of financial distress or geopolitical conflict. In such times of turbulence, faith in a commodity replaces trust in institutions.

Gold's gyrations are a reminder that the permanence of the Bank of England relies on its values. And that value is built on values.

For over twelve years, I had the privilege and challenge of being a G7 governor, first in Canada and latterly in the UK. During this time I saw kingdoms of gold rise and fall. I led global reforms to fix the fault lines that caused the financial crisis, worked to heal the malignant culture at the heart of financial capitalism and began to address both the fundamental challenges of the Fourth Industrial Revolution[1] and the existential risks from climate change. I felt the collapse in public trust in elites, globalisation and technology. And I became convinced that these challenges reflect a common crisis in values and that radical changes are required to build an economy that works for all.

Whenever I could step back from what felt like daily crisis management, the same deeper issues loomed. What is value? How is it grounded? Which values underpin value? Can the very act of valuation shape our values and constrain our choices? How do the valuations of markets affect the values of our society? Does the narrowness of our vision, the poverty of our perspective, mean we undervalue what matters to our collective wellbeing?

These are the questions that this book seeks to explore. It will examine how our society came to embody Wilde's aphorism – knowing the price of everything but the value of nothing. How by elevating belief in the market to an inviolable truth we moved from a market economy to a market society. And how we can turn this around.

In many respects, this book is a belated response to a question posed a few summers ago when a range of policymakers, business people, academics, labour leaders and charity workers gathered at the Vatican to discuss the future of the market system.

Pope Francis surprised us by joining the lunch and sharing a parable. He observed that:

> Our meal will be accompanied by wine. Now, wine is many things. It has a bouquet, colour and richness of taste that all complement the food. It has alcohol that can enliven the mind. Wine enriches all our senses.
>
> At the end of our feast, we will have grappa. Grappa is one thing: alcohol. Grappa is wine distilled.

He continued:

> Humanity is many things – passionate, curious, rational, altruistic, creative, self-interested.
>
> But the market is one thing: self-interested. The market is humanity distilled.

And then he challenged us:

> Your job is to turn the grappa back into wine, to turn the market back into humanity.
>
> This isn't theology. This is reality. This is the truth.

This book draws on my experience in the private sector and public policy to examine the relationship between value and values. How they shape each other, and how, by doing so, they can determine our livelihoods, identities and possibilities. And how, once we recognise these dynamics, we can turn grappa back into wine.

The book is divided into three parts. Part I examines various concepts of value and their roots in political philosophy and, more recently and narrowly, in economic theory and financial practice. It uses a series of valuation paradoxes from art to the environment to illustrate the potential disconnects between valuations in markets and the values of society.

Values and value are related but distinct. In the most general terms, values represent the principles or standards of behaviour; they are judgements of what is important in life. Examples include integrity, fairness, kindness, excellence, sustainability, passion and reason. Value is the regard that something is held to deserve – the importance, worth or usefulness of something. Both value and values are judgements. And therein lies the rub.

Increasingly, the value of something, of some act or of someone is equated with their monetary value, a monetary value that is determined by the market. The logic of buying and selling no longer applies only to material goods but increasingly governs the whole of life from the allocation of healthcare to education, public safety and environmental protection.

When we decide that certain goods and services can be bought and sold, we decide that they can be treated as commodities, as instruments of profit and use. And we assume, again at least implicitly, that the values of society will remain unchanged in the process. But as Part I shows, when everything is relative, nothing is immutable.

To draw out the relationship between value and values, Chapters 3 and 4 explain how money is used to measure value and what gives money its value. The historic formal backing of money by gold is contrasted with its current informal backing by institutions like central banks. It reveals how the value of such fiat money is grounded in underlying values of trust, integrity and transparency.

Chapter 5 then looks forward, exploring key questions about the future of money including whether cryptocurrencies could be solutions to the mistrust of central authorities and how trust scores in social media (and the surveillance state) could 'monetise' social capital.

Chapter 6 shows that our deepest challenges are rooted in the narrowing of our values to market fundamentalism, and it explains how this is contributing to the growing exclusivity of capitalism and the rise of populism. In particular, it argues that, just as all ideologies are prone to extremes, capitalism loses its sense of moderation when the belief in the power of the market enters the realm of faith. In the decades prior to the financial crisis, such radicalism came to dominate economic ideas and became a pattern of social behaviour.

In short, we have moved from a market economy to a market society, and this is now undermining our basic social contract of relative equality of outcomes, equality of opportunity and fairness across generations.

Part II explores the three most significant crises of the twenty-first century – of credit, Covid and climate.

In each case, it examines the underlying causes and describes policy responses. The book argues that, when taken together, these events were driven by a common crisis of values, and that our response could begin to recast the relationship between values and value, providing the basis for the strategies for individual, companies, investors and countries that are described in Part III.

As Chapter 7 shows, market fundamentalism contributed directly to the global credit crisis, in the form of light-touch regulation, a belief that bubbles cannot be identified and a misplaced confidence in a new era. Authorities and market participants fell under the spell of the three lies of finance, believing that 'this time is different', that 'markets are always right' and that 'markets are moral'.

Rather than reinforcing social capital, we consumed it. Banks were deemed too big to fail, operating in a 'heads I win, tails you lose' bubble. Equity markets blatantly favoured technologically empowered institutions over retail investors. With too few market participants feeling responsible for the system, bad behaviour went unchecked, proliferated and eventually became the norm.

In such an environment, means and ends conflate all too easily. Value becomes abstract and relative, and the pull of the crowd overwhelms the integrity of the individual. The resulting unjust sharing of risk and reward widens inequalities and corrodes the social fabric on which finance depends.

Chapter 8 reviews my experience leading the G20's efforts to create a safer, simpler and fairer financial system. It argues that in order for financial reforms to rebuild social capital they must balance the tension between free-market capitalism, which reinforces the primacy of the individual at the expense of the system, and social capital, which requires from individuals a sense of responsibility for the system. In other words, a sense of self must be accompanied by a sense of solidarity.

Chapter 9 describes the causes and dynamics of Covid-19 which has wrought twin crises of health and economics, both unprecedented in our lifetimes. This global pandemic has moved with alarming speed and virulence because of deep global interconnectedness, but its severity has been magnified by our failure to prepare adequately despite ample and varied warnings. For too long, we undervalued resilience and have been forced to pay the heaviest costs. The economic shock has resulted in deep recessions and enormous jobs losses, and it now threatens to widen the fissures of inequality in the years to come.

Despite these tragedies, as Chapter 10 outlines, this crisis could help reverse the causality between value and values. When pushed, societies have prioritised health first and foremost, and then looked to address the economic consequences. We have acted as Rawlsians and communitarians, not as utilitarians or libertarians. Cost–benefit analyses, steeped in calculations of the Value of Statistical Lives, have mercifully been overruled, as the values of economic dynamism and efficiency have been joined by those of solidarity, fairness, responsibility and compassion.

Basing our response on objectives derived from these values, and not on an economic determination of where the net benefit lies, will be the key to building back better. This is completely achievable;

our limited historical experience with such epochal events is that afterwards the aspirations of society focus not just on the rate of growth but also on its direction and its quality. In the aftermath of the health crisis, it's reasonable to expect public demands for improvements in the quality and coverage of social support and medical care, for greater attention to be paid to managing tail risks and for more heed to be given to the advice of scientific experts.

How we address the climate crisis will be the test of these new values. After all, climate change is an issue that i) involves the entire world, from which no one will be able to self-isolate, ii) is predicted by science to be the central risk tomorrow, and iii) we can address only if we act in advance and in solidarity.

Climate change is the ultimate betrayal of intergenerational equity. It imposes costs on future generations that the current generation has no direct incentives to fix. As Chapter 11 explains, we face the 'tragedy of the horizon' in which the catastrophic impacts of climate change will be felt beyond the traditional perspectives of most business, investors, politicians and central bankers. In other words, once the physical effects of climate change become the defining issue for a critical mass of decision makers, it could be too late to stop their catastrophic effects.

Like the financial crisis, the tragedy of the horizon represents a crisis of valuation and values. Compare the valuations of Amazon and the Amazon region. Amazon's $1.5 trillion equity valuation reflects the market's judgement that the company will be very profitable for a very long time. In contrast, it is only once the rainforest is cleared and a cattle herd or soya plantation is placed on the newly opened land that the Amazon region begins to have market value. The costs to the climate and biodiversity of destroying the rainforest appear on no ledger.

Chapter 11 highlights how changes in climate policies, new technologies and growing physical risks will prompt reassessments of virtually every financial asset. Firms that align their business models with the transition to a net-zero carbon economy will be rewarded handsomely; those that fail to adapt will cease to exist. To address the climate crisis we need innovation on every front, and Chapter 12 on climate change details how the financial system can be retooled to make the markets a part of the solution. With comprehensive climate disclosure, a transformation in climate risk management by banks and the mainstreaming of sustainable investment, we can ensure that every financial decision takes climate change into account.

This new sustainable finance can work alongside private innovation and aggressive government action to help deliver net zero. The importance of this goal cannot be overstated: the task is large, the window of opportunity is short and the risks are existential. How our economy conceptualises value has been standing in the way.

Both the climate and Covid crises demonstrate the value of society forging a consensus around common goals, and then letting market dynamism determine how to achieve them rather than pursuing a trade-off between what society values and optimising current financial values as priced in the market.

Part III of the book builds on the responses to the three crises to draw out common themes and to create action plans for leaders, companies, investors and countries. It concludes with a new platform-based approach to managing the global commons in the wake of the demise of the rules-based international order.

To rebuild an inclusive social contract, it is essential to recognise the importance of values and beliefs in economic life. Economic and political philosophers from Adam Smith (1759) to Friedrich Hayek (1960) have long stressed that beliefs are part of inherited social capital, which provides the social framework for the free market. The experience of the three crises suggests that the common values and beliefs that underpin a successful economy are:

- *dynamism* to help create solutions and channel human creativity;
- *resilience* to make it easier to bounce back from shocks while protecting the most vulnerable in society;
- *sustainability* with long-term perspectives that align incentives across generations;
- *fairness*, particularly in markets to sustain their legitimacy;

- *responsibility* so that individuals feel accountable for their actions;
- *solidarity* whereby citizens recognise their obligations to each other and share a sense of community and society; and
- *humility* to recognise the limits of our knowledge, understanding and power so that we act as custodians seeking to improve the common good.

These beliefs and values are not fixed. They need to be nurtured. Just as any revolution eats its children, unchecked market fundamentalism devours the social capital essential for the long-term dynamism of capitalism itself. Markets on their own will never be adequately incentivised to build social capital, which requires a sense of purpose and common values among individuals, companies, investors and countries. Conversely, values are like muscles that grow with exercise. The book therefore turns to the imperatives of how to recognise and reinforce these essential social foundations of the common good.

Chapter 13 on leadership examines the traits and behaviours necessary for leaders to catalyse change, help their colleagues realise their potential and encourage their organisations to fulfil their missions. To inspire the confidence and trust for their initiatives to be most effective, leaders must engage, explain and emote. Leaders must continually earn their legitimacy, and to maximise the impact of their organisation they must stay true to its purpose – a purpose grounded in the objectives of clients, colleagues and community. Great leadership isn't just effective, it's also ethical, building both value and virtue through its exercise.

How purposeful companies create value is the focus of Chapter 14. It reviews the evidence of the alignment between purpose and long-term value creation – dynamism – from the perspectives of both companies and societies. The chapter then describes various strategies for purposeful corporations to benefit all stakeholders. True corporate purpose drives engagement with stakeholders, including employees (by being a responsible and responsive employer), suppliers and customers (through honest, fair and lasting relationships in the supply chain) and communities (as good

corporate citizens that make full contributions to society).
Corporate purpose embeds solidarity at local, national and supranational levels, and recognises the paramount need for sustainability
across generations. By uniting broader interests behind a common
purpose, purposeful companies can be more impactful, dynamic
and profitable.

Chapter 15 then outlines how investors can both reinforce these
initiatives and be rewarded by them. A critical element of rebalancing value and values will be developing and embedding
comprehensive and transparent approaches to measuring stakeholder value creation by companies. The chapter shows how best to
measure sustainable and financial value, the dynamic relationship
between these two sources of value and the strategies investors can
pursue to maximise both.

Sustainable investing is developing into an essential tool to bring
the values of the market into line with those of society. It improves
the measurement of what society values from workplace diversity
to the Sustainable Development Goals, the SDGs. It is being
deployed to increase shareholder value through multiple channels
by helping companies to attract and retain the best people, to
increase their resilience, improve efficiency, align better with stakeholders and maintain social licence. When social needs – such as
climate change – are tackled with a profitable business model, the
answers to many of the most deeply rooted problems we face
become scalable and self-sustaining.

The many policy strands discussed in the book are brought
together in Chapter 16 to develop a framework for countries to
build value for all. This is built on traditional foundations of strong
institutions, and investments in physical and human capital. Given
the far-reaching changes wrought by new technologies from artificial intelligence to bio-engineering, there must be a heavy emphasis
on mandatory workforce training, universal skills development, the
balancing of rights of all stakeholders, incentives to promote an
enterprise society, and free trade for small and medium-sized
enterprises.

Country strategies must make existing markets work better and
build new markets. But markets alone won't solve our most intracta-

ble problems. We need political processes to define our goals and objectives – to set our values. Markets can then be marshalled to help discover and drive solutions in a form of mission-oriented capitalism. As we shall see, however, given that the marketisation of society has created some of our problems, the market simply cannot be the answer to every question.

The nation serves an essential economic role, but it is much more than a collection of marketplaces or a trade negotiator. The state embodies collective ideals such as equality of opportunity, liberty, fairness, solidarity and sustainability. We must build consensus around national goals, such as a just transition to a net-zero economy, combating Covid or universal skills training so that all can reap the rewards of the Fourth Industrial Revolution. And we must strive to achieve those goals in ways that serve the common good so that all benefit.

A deeper sense of national values could lead to more focused, constructive international engagement. Using a values-based approach, it is possible to build a more inclusive, resilient and sustainable globalisation. Though we cannot agree binding global rules to tackle the challenges we face, multilateralism can still be powerful. The chapter shows how we can build on the lessons from how the international community responded to the financial crisis, creating a form of cooperative internationalism that is more compatible with the complexities of the problems we face and people's demands for both sovereignty and results.

RESTORING HUMANITY IN A SOCIETY THAT VALUES WHAT MATTERS

An overarching theme that runs through this book is that we cannot take the market system – which produces such plenty and so many solutions – for granted. Markets are essential to progress, to finding solutions to our most pressing problems, but they don't exist in a vacuum. Markets are social constructs, whose effectiveness is determined partly by the rules of the state and partly by the values of society. If left unattended they will corrode those values. We must concentrate on rebuilding social capital to make markets work. To do so, individuals and their firms must rediscover their sense of solidarity and responsibility for the system. More broadly, by rebasing valuation on society's values, we can create platforms of prosperity.

My experience in the private and public sectors accords with Pope Francis' parable. Value in the market is increasingly determining the values of society. We are living Wilde's aphorism at incalculable costs to our society, to future generations and to our planet.

This book will argue that, once we recognise these dynamics, we can turn grappa back into wine, and channel the value of the market back into the service of the values of humanity.

PART I

THE RISE OF THE MARKET SOCIETY

1

Perspectives of Value – Objective Value

Consider these paradoxes of value. Great minds from Plato to Adam Smith have pondered why water – which is essential for life – is virtually free, and diamonds – which have limited utility beyond their beauty – are so expensive.

During the Covid crisis, the extraordinary values of public service, dedication and heroism of healthcare workers across the world were celebrated. As the sounds of applause and saucepan drums rang from doorsteps and raised spirits, few recalled the arguments made by economists that the wages of these workers (wages that generally consigned them to long commutes to work on risky public transportation) reflected their marginal contribution to society. Instead there was, for a time, recognition that some values cannot be priced. And yet assessments soon emerged that compared the value of people's lives to the economic costs of the lockdown in order to chart an exit strategy.[1]

Why is Amazon rated as one of the world's most valuable companies by financial markets, but the value of the vast geographical region of the Amazon rainforest appears on no ledger until it is stripped of its foliage and converted into farmland? Who can calculate the value of the species being lost for ever in the Sixth Mass Extinction?

To explore whether value must be priced in order to be valued, let's begin with concepts of value.

* * *

Concepts of value are rooted in philosophy and more recently – and narrowly – in economic and financial theory.

Value and values are related but distinct. In the most general sense, values represent principles or standards of behaviour. They are judgements of what is important in life, determining what actions are best to do or what ways are best to live (a field of study called normative ethics). Examples include integrity, fairness, responsibility, sustainability, dignity, reason and passion.

Value is the regard that something is held to deserve – its importance, worth or usefulness. The verb to value is 'to consider someone or something to be important or beneficial; to have a high opinion of' or 'to estimate the monetary worth of something'.[2] Value is not necessarily constant but specific to time and situation. Consider Shakespeare's Richard III who in battle cries despairingly, 'A horse, a horse, my kingdom for a horse,' or the value people have placed on basic daily essentials and healthcare workers during the pandemic.

These examples emphasise that the economic value of a good or service is generally[3] depicted as relative – 'how much' of a desirable condition or commodity would be given up in exchange for another. When expressed in monetary terms, this is known as the 'exchange value'. The distinctions between exchange value, use value and intrinsic value have been sources of intense debate in economics.

It is increasingly common to equate the monetary estimate of something with its worth and, in turn, that worth with society's values. The subjective (or price) theory of value – once contentious – now goes largely unchallenged in economic teaching, is taken as given in business schools and frequently determines society's perception of its deeper values.

To begin to draw out the consequences of the convenient shorthand of price equalling value, it is helpful to consider a brief history of the theory of value in economic thought.

A BRIEF HISTORY OF VALUE

One of the most fundamental questions in economics has been what determines the value of a good or service. By the turn of the last century, 'in the language of the craft "economic theory" had come to mean value theory'.[4]

But with what does economic value theory properly concern itself? After all, value is also a property of literature, art, education and religion. At their core, economic theories of value seek to explain why goods and services are priced as they are and how to calculate their *correct* price, if such a value is thought to exist. As we shall see, however, the reach of economic thinking about value has extended widely from this narrow remit, and the profession's discipline in restricting economic thinking to economic value has been relaxed considerably.

Much of historical thinking about economic value concentrates on the process of value creation, with different conceptions of value rooted in the socioeconomic and technological conditions of the time. Many value theorists give heavy consideration to distributional consequences, and distinguish between productive and unproductive activities, with the aim of increasing the 'wealth of the nation'. In these regards, historical approaches to economic value embody values relating to 'what is important in life'.

The various approaches to value also usually differentiate between value creation and value extraction, or rent seeking. Value creation results from combining different types of resources (human, physical and intangible) to produce new goods and services. Value extraction can be thought of as the product of 'moving around existing resources and outputs and gaining disproportionately from the resulting trade'.[5] 'Rent' is the return to this activity, and it has been at best viewed as unearned income or, at worst, theft.

These distinctions between productive and non-productive activities, between value creation and extraction and between just returns and rents are critical because they guide public policy, and in turn influence growth and welfare.

Over the centuries there have been two broad schools of thought regarding the determinants of economic value: objective and subjective.

In objective theories of value, value is determined by the production of goods and services. Objective approaches contend that, although the price of a product results from supply and demand, its underlying value is derived from how that product is produced and how that production affects wages, profits and rents. In objective theories, value is tied to the nature of production, including the time required, the quality of labour employed and the influence of new technologies and ways of working. Proponents span Aristotle to Adam Smith and Karl Marx.

In contrast, subjective theories of value place greater weight on how exchange value (the price of goods and services in the market) reveals underlying value. In subjective theories, value is in the eyes of the beholder, driven by preferences and to a lesser extent scarcity. This approach is most clearly associated with neo-classical economists of the nineteenth century, such as William Jevons and Alfred Marshall, and it is dominant in our time. This has a variety of consequences, especially the implication that something which is not priced is neither valued nor valuable; it is as if the price of everything is becoming the value of everything.

EARLY OBJECTIVE THEORIES OF VALUE

The Greek philosophers, notably Aristotle (384–322 BC), held that the source of value was based on need, without which exchange of goods and services would not take place. Aristotle was the first to distinguish between the dual uses of an article (an idea that is taken up with enthusiasm by the classicists of the nineteenth century who distinguished between value and price):[6]

Of everything we possess there are two uses: both belong to the thing as such, but not in the same manner, for one is the proper, and the other the improper or secondary use of it. For example, a shoe is used to wear and is used for exchange; both are uses of the shoe.[7]

Aristotle's considerations of value were incidental to his primary concern, 'justice'. Value takes the form of utility (in use value) and is measured by labour. Aristotle's 'just price' was the exchange of equal values in terms of labour, with differences in labour quality taken into account.[8] He made no attempt to explain how commerce worked or therefore how prices were determined in a 'positive theory of value'.

In the Middle Ages, the 'canonists' were philosopher theologians who, like their Aristotelian forebears, regarded economics as integral to ethical and moral philosophy. Their economic approach therefore cannot be divorced from their systems of social philosophy which were aspects of ecclesiastical jurisprudence, whose ultimate objective was achieving God's grace.

In this context, canonist thinking on value centred on two aspects. First, a normative approach – what value should be – instead of what actually is revealed in markets through exchange. And second, addressing the practical problem of establishing prices in accord with ecclesiastical justice; in other words, how to justify earthly commerce before God.

The canonists advanced the concept of a 'just price', although its precise definition was open to interpretation, interpretations that were, of course, adjudicated by the Church. Consistent with Aristotle, labour costs were important. Albertus Magnus (c.1200–80) counsels that goods 'containing the same amount of labour and expense' should be exchanged. In his *Summa Theologica*, St Thomas Aquinas (1225–74) distinguished the 'just price' of a good from the 'wrong price' that results from greed or other moral ills.

There were few moral ills worse than usury. In Dante's *Inferno*, usurers are consigned to the seventh circle of hell because they make money not from productive sources (nature or art), but from speculative charges in interest rates. This theme of the evil of rent-seeking finance is prominent in most theories of value before neo-classicism.

Aquinas allowed variations from the 'just price', but only as payment for the merchant's labour, and only to degrees that would be sufficient to allow the merchant their accustomed standard of living, a concession that in practice could allow considerable tolerance of different prices and profits.

A century after Aquinas, St Antonino (1389–1459) justified prices on the basis of a concept of disutility:

> The case when a man needs something, the loss of which will be a grave inconvenience to the owner. The latter may in these circumstances demand a higher price, not looking to the value of the thing in itself, but its value to him, i.e. not looking to the thing, but to the inconvenience its loss will occasion him.[9]

St Antonino rationalised interest with similar logic, pointing out that the money involved could have secured capital, and the capital could have earned a profit; therefore, the loss of profit could justly be charged as interest. But he held throughout that gains were not ends, merely means to the ultimate spiritual object of all activity.

When divining the value theorems of the canonists (or for that matter the Greek philosophers) it is critical to recognise the extent to which their value theories and economics were unified aspects of a much larger world (indeed heavenly) view.[10]

For our purposes, it is sufficient to conclude that the canonists prioritised a welfare with an other-world content over temporal wealth, they subordinated profit to moral ends and they insisted that economic offices be discharged consistent with a doctrine of stewardship.[11] In this last respect, they provide some of the foundations for modern ideas of corporate purpose and stakeholder capitalism (albeit without the vibrant financial sector or the sense of secular duty to make a profit).

The canonist influence over economic conduct waned with the Reformation and the growing separation of religious doctrine and economic activity. Their heirs were, in turn, the mercantilists and the physiocrats, both of whose value systems favoured real-world political economy over higher conceptions of value and welfare.

The fifteenth and sixteenth centuries brought new technologies and modes of organisation that gave rise to commercial society. Maritime trade grew with the new navigational instruments; farming began to lose its feudal characteristics; and the economy moved towards large, organised markets, under guilds and the great trading companies (such as the East India Company) that were monopolistically controlled under official protection.

In response, a new economic doctrine – mercantilism – was born. At its heart, mercantilism was the view that maximising net exports was the best route to national prosperity, and that a country's wealth was measured by gold, the by-product of these surpluses.

The significance of mercantilism lay largely in its substitution of the national competitive state for the moral order of the canonists. As will be discussed in Chapter 3, the legitimacy of the monarch was shifting from being grounded in divine right to being the Hobbesian protector first against the scourges of the age and gradually of new trade routes and commercial opportunities. The common good was redefined in national political terms, beginning the quest for value theories that determined how best to advance the wealth of nations. Despite such lofty aims, however, the mercantilist literature was primarily intended to advance the fortunes of a select group of individuals and corporations, whose pursuit of personal gain was clothed in a larger national purpose.

Attitudes towards what constituted rent seeking changed during the mercantilist era. During this age of European conquest of the so-called New World and the plunder of its gold and silver, value was assigned to activities that developed and protected trade routes and accumulated precious metals. As Thomas Mun, a director of the East India Company, declared, national wealth was enhanced by selling 'more to strangers yearly than we consume of theirs in value'.[12] Moving things around came to be viewed as value creation rather than value extraction.

Perceptions of value changed accordingly. In his *Lecture on Money*, the Florentine merchant and historian Bernardo Davanzati (1529–1606) constructed a theory of value based on utility that focused on the drivers of the demand for goods, a natural consequence of valuing merchants who controlled trading not production processes.[13] Davanzati also distinguished 'value in exchange' from 'value in use', identifying the 'paradox of value' in the process.[14] He argued that gold has no value in use but great value in exchange because it can be used to command other goods.

Around the same time, an influential approach to value was developed by Sir William Petty (1623–87), an anatomist, physician and Member of Parliament, who had been a tax administrator in Ireland under Oliver Cromwell's Commonwealth government. With his training as a physician and heavily influenced by the scientific advances of his era, Petty searched for natural and intrinsic laws of reality – including 'natural value'. According to Petty, 'natural value' was determined by the factors of production – land and labour – and the market price ('actual price') of any commodity would fluctuate around its natural value ('natural price'). Petty simplified his theory of value to one based on labour, by solving for a 'par' value for land in terms of labour.[15] That labour value, in turn, was determined by a form of subsistence wage, which was the unit of measure consisting of 'The easiest-gotten food of the respective countries of the world'.[16] In this respect, Petty foreshadows the labour theories of value of Adam Smith, David Ricardo and Karl Marx.

But while he dabbled in value theory, Petty was more concerned with being the first to calculate the nation's total output or wealth, rather than with how that output came about, and it was through these statistical breakthroughs that he made his most lasting contributions.[17] To measure the nation's production, he formed a series of judgements about which activities were productive and which were not. To him, the only expenditures worth counting were those devoted to necessities such as food, housing and clothes, and, consistent with mercantilist thought, those that promoted merchant trade. The professions – including the law, clergy and finance – were mere facilitators.

By explicitly identifying a productive sphere of the economy, Petty implicitly defined what was valuable. Moreover, by creating the practice of calculating national accounts, which would form the basis for GDP, Petty created a framework to which governments (and societies) still default as the measure of national wealth, and which they use as a compass to steer their economic policies.[18]

Mercantilism contained little that can be clearly recognised as value theory.[19] Labour was presented as the source of value, although there was no consensus that it was the measure of value. Money was viewed as a store of value but not necessarily as the measure of revealed utility as would be argued by neo-classicists like Jevons and Marshall in the late nineteenth century and as is generally accepted today (see the next chapter). Mercantilism purported to be a theory of how a nation became rich, though it was, in practice, a justification for what today we would term crony capitalism.

In the eighteenth and nineteenth centuries, deeper inquiries into the sources of value focused on the key factors of production: first, the physiocrats identified land (understandably in predominantly agrarian societies) and then, as economies industrialised, the classicists like Smith and Ricardo concentrated on labour.

The physiocrats were French enlightenment philosophers who founded a scientific approach to economic analysis and developed the first formal land theory of value. Their name, derived from the Greek for 'government by nature', alluded to a 'natural order', a term that appealed to ideas of both a natural social contract and unchanging laws governing economic processes. From the latter and consistent with the coining of the phrase '*laissez faire, laissez passer, le monde va de lui-même*' by their most prominent member, François Quesnay (1694–1774), the physiocrats were wary of government intervention – a radical position in a mercantilist age living under an absolute monarchy.

In contrast to the mercantilist focus on a positive trade balance and the accumulation of gold, the physiocrats believed that the wealth of nations derived solely from agriculture, and that the production of manufactured goods was equivalent to the consumption of the agricultural surplus. Rents were the returns to absentee owners of the land on which the agricultural production took place.

The most revolutionary contributions of the physiocrats arose from their methodological approaches to the economy and value creation. In these regards, they are considered by some as the first economists; they were certainly the first to view the economy as a system.

In the mid-eighteenth century, Quesnay, King Louis XV's physician and adviser, formulated the first systematic theory of value that
also classified which economic activities were and were not productive (Petty's classifications in his national accounts had not been
linked to any underlying theory). In his seminal work *Tableau
Économique*, published in 1758, Quesnay showed on a single page
how value was created and circulated in the economy by using a
metabolic analogy, with pumps introducing new value and tubes
removing value from the system. Quesnay's model demonstrated
how an entire economy could grow based on the value generated by
a small group of its members.

The subject of value looms large in physiocratic thought, but
practical, political ends still influenced their categories of productive and unproductive industrial activities.[20] Quesnay identified
farmers as the small group of value creators and highlighted the
enormous pressures on them. Agriculture was highly taxed both by
absentee and licentious nobles and by a central government engaged
in frequent wars. Further burdens were imposed by mercantilist
policies that suppressed the prices of agriculture goods in favour of
an export-oriented manufacturing sector that could secure gold and
therefore it was thought increase the national wealth.

Quesnay's *Tableau* supported farmers against the mercantilists, as
it showed that all value arose from the land.[21] His classification over-
turned the mercantilist approach which had placed exchange and
what was gained from it – gold – at the centre of value creation. Now
value was linked inextricably with production, albeit only agricultural production.[22] In Quesnay's tableau, as long as what is produced
is greater than what is consumed, the resulting surplus could be reinvested, and the economy would grow. Conversely, if value extraction
by unproductive sectors exceeds value creation by agriculture, the
economy would decline. This conception of surplus and reinvestment
driving the economy forward would be adopted by the classicists.

Quesnay's depiction of the economy was comprehensive, but his
view of what constituted productive activities was exceptionally
narrow. His contemporary A. R. J. Turgot also saw wealth as coming
solely from land but saw usefulness in artisans who prepared the
materials produced by cultivators. Landowners remained a 'dispos-

able class' who merely collected rents, though Turgot acknowledged that members of the disposable class may offer services, such as the administration of justice or assisting in war efforts, that respond to the general needs of society.

The approach of the physiocrats complemented the land theory of value of their Irish-born contemporary Richard Cantillon (1680–1734). Cantillon was briefly a successful speculator in France, and later published one of the early great works of economic theory, *Essai sur la Nature du Commerce en Général*. It is one of few texts that spans both the objective and subjective schools of value. With respect to the former, Cantillon began with a labour-and-land theory of value like Petty, but then reduced the determinants of intrinsic value to land by assuming constant returns to scale and equating the value of a labourer with that of twice the produce of the land they consume, while allowing for variations in the skills and status of labourers. He also discovered how resources were allocated between different markets when the market price diverges from his intrinsic 'land' value. With respect to the latter, Cantillon's pioneering of a two-stage general equilibrium model of the economy and his careful description of a supply-and-demand mechanism for the determination of short-run market price (albeit not long-run natural price) made him a forefather of the nineteenth-century marginalist revolution.

The physiocrats' main contributions to the understanding of value and value creation were their emphasis on the economy as a system, their exploration of the different sources of income and their explicit consideration of its distribution. Although it seems arcane today, Quesnay's *Tableau Économique* showed the economy as a complex organism that needed to be analysed, understood and nurtured – much like the human body. The economy could not simply be bent to suit the wills of the merchant class or an absolute monarch. The Comte de Mirabeau, an important figure during the French Revolution, considered Quesnay's *Tableau* to be one of the world's three great discoveries – equalled only by the invention of printing and the discovery of money.[23]

That judgement has not, however, stood the test of time, perhaps because the physiocrats' conclusion that land is the source of all value soon came into question as economies industrialised rapidly and production processes changed radically. Only one year after Quesnay died, Richard Arkwright filed his grand patent to mechanise weaving, and Boulton and Watt founded their firm to manufacture steam engines. The British Industrial Revolution was moving into full swing.

THE CLASSICISTS

By the end of the eighteenth century, the economic, social and political consequences of the Industrial Revolution brought new economic theories of value from a succession of outstanding thinkers. These individuals, who would become known as the 'classicists',[24] included three giants whose influence persists to this day: Adam Smith, David Ricardo and Karl Marx.

The focus of the classicists was political economy, with the study of economics integral to their study of society. Their approach centred on the development of markets and placed the growth and distribution of value squarely in the context of the enormous social and technological changes then underway. They worked during an unprecedented period of growth, urbanisation, industrialisation and globalisation. The classicists would have found profoundly alien the view – widespread today – that economics is a neutral technical discipline which can be pursued in isolation from such dynamics.[25]

Although their views differed in many respects, the classical economists shared three basic ideas.

- First, the value of goods and services is determined by the value of inputs that produced them, principally labour.
- Second, economies are fundamentally dynamic and the relations between workers, landlords and industrialists change with new technologies and methods of production. This process promotes value creation and changes its distribution.
- Third, the process of exchange is central to both the distribution and creation of value. For example, Ricardo

focused on the gains from the exchange of goods in foreign trade and Marx on the exchange value of work and the distribution of income.

Smith, in contrast, was concerned with exchange across the entire economic and social spheres. To Smith, all of human life involved exchange, with the consequence that we can no more extricate his theories of markets and value creation from their broader social context than we could separate the views on value of the canonists from their systems of social philosophy and ecclesiastical jurisprudence.

Adam Smith was born in Kirkcaldy, Fife in 1723. His father, who died two months before Adam's birth, had been a senior solicitor, judge advocate and the local comptroller of customs. Adam's mother was born Margaret Douglas, daughter of the landed Robert Douglas of Strathendry, also in Fife. Smith was close to his mother, who encouraged him to pursue his scholarly ambitions. He was educated locally, studied social philosophy at the age of fourteen at the University of Glasgow, and then Balliol College, Oxford. As his biographer Jesse Norman notes, Smith was unhappy at Oxford as his college 'was Jacobite, Tory, factional, costly and Scotophobic; and Adam Smith was Presbyterian, Whiggish, sociable, impecunious and a Scot'.[26]

After graduating, Smith delivered a successful series of public lectures at the University of Glasgow, obtained a professorship in moral philosophy at Glasgow and began a lifelong collaboration and friendship with David Hume. In later life, he took a tutoring position (with the son of the Duke of Buccleuch, the richest landowner in Scotland) that allowed him to travel throughout Europe, where he met other intellectual leaders of his day including Quesnay and, once back in the British isles, Benjamin Franklin.

Smith published two magisterial works, *The Theory of Moral Sentiments* in 1759 and *An Inquiry into the Wealth of Nations* in 1776. The latter is the most purchased, the most often cited and, arguably, the least read book in economics. To understand the totality of Smith's thinking, it should not be considered in isolation from its predecessor.

Widely viewed as the father of economics, Smith's enduring relevance is a testament to the power and breadth of his scholarship. For example, during my time at the Bank of England, we frequently drew on his insights to address issues ranging from the future of money in the age of crypto-assets to how to rebuild the social foundations of financial markets following the financial crisis in 2008 – subjects for later in this book. In doing so, we were inspired by Smith the sage of politics, morality, ethics and jurisprudence, not Smith the market fundamentalist of legend and political expediency of both the right and left. Indeed, Smith's writings warn of the mistakes in equating money with capital and divorcing economic capital from its social partner – errors that can arise from reading only a few, admittedly brilliant, pages of *The Wealth of Nations*. This caricature of Smith as 'the father of *laissez faire*' grossly devalues this most considered and catholic of the worldly philosophers; the phrase 'invisible hand' appears only once in that book and but three times in Smith's collected works.[27]

In an effort to explain why Scotland had been able to make such an incredible transformation during his lifetime to become a centre of the European enlightenment, Smith concentrated on the cultural, economic and social implications of the evolution of commercial society – that moment when people move away from dependence on one person or another to a world of commercial interaction, a world where every person is a merchant who lives by exchange.[28]

He also had a deeper project. He looked at all major aspects of human life – philosophy, religion, political economy jurisprudence, arts, the sciences, and languages – in order to devise a science of man that could serve as the basis for every other branch of human knowledge. In keeping with the scientific method, Smith's conclusions were based on observation and experience, not dogma.

The central concept that links all of Smith's works is the idea that continuous exchange forms part of all human interactions. This is not just the exchange of goods and services in markets, of meanings in language and of regard and esteem in the formation of moral and social norms. Humans are social animals who form themselves in action and interaction with each other across all spheres of their existence.

Smith's goal in writing *The Theory of Moral Sentiments* was to explain the source of humankind's ability to form moral judgements, given that people begin life with no moral sentiments. He believed that we form our norms (values) as a matter of social psychology by wishing 'to love and to be lovely' – that is, to be well thought of or well regarded. Smith proposes a theory of 'mutual sympathy', in which the act of observing others and seeing the judgements they form makes people see how others perceive their behaviour (and therefore become more aware of themselves). The feedback we receive from perceiving (or imagining) others' judgements creates an incentive to achieve 'mutual sympathy of sentiments' that leads people to develop habits, and then principles, of behaviour which come to constitute their conscience.

So moral sentiments are not inherent. To use the modern terminology of Richard Dawkins, they are social memes that are learned, imitated and passed on. Like genetic memes, they can mutate, in behavioural cascades and tipping points.

It is in this context that Smith was the first to put markets at the centre of economics, a move that fundamentally reoriented political economy. Specifically, *The Wealth of Nations* is built on the exchanges in markets that are at the centre of commercial society. His most famous passage describes this 'invisible hand' in action:

> It is not from the benevolence of the butcher, the brewer, or the baker, that we expect our dinner, but from their regard to their own interest. We address ourselves, not to their humanity but to their self-love, and never talk to them of our own necessities but of their advantages.[29]

Again, Smith's conception of markets must be seen in a broader social context. He emphasised that they may come into being because of private purpose but they are part of an evolving social order and must have a public value. Smith would not have recognised the disembodied mathematical constructs of markets that characterise modern economics and policymaking. Rather markets are living institutions, embedded in the culture, practice, traditions and trust of their day. This is the genius of his first work, *The Theory of Moral Sentiments*.[30]

Smith also saw that markets are far from monolithic or benevolent, and that while they have common features, they are as different as all humans are. Smith was well schooled in how markets actually work from the market for corn to the market for bills of exchange, so he was careful to distinguish the workings of the markets for land, labour, financial assets and commercial products.

Smith addressed too the question of what happens when markets go wrong. He was well aware of the damage that monopolies could do, and he viewed a free market as one that was free of rent. He included a searing attack on mercantilists – or what we would now refer to as crony capitalists. Like Quesnay, he argued that mercantilist policies restricted competition and trade, and undercut industry, which was the true source of value creation in the economy.

Smith's contributions to our understanding of value follow from this analysis.

First, he demonstrated that markets, properly grounded in social trust, are engines of prosperity. His famous description of the division of labour in pin factories revealed a ground-breaking understanding of how the combination of competition and changes to the organisation of work could drive productivity, growth and 'general plenty'.[31]

Second, although Smith adopted the same systematic approach to economic growth as the physiocrats, he widened the concept of the productive sphere of the economy from agriculture to include industry. In both systems, growth arises because of surpluses that are reinvested in productive activities (in Smith's case manufacturing) rather than in unproductive consumption of luxuries or rent seeking.

Third, Smith was wary of the dangers of capture of government by business. He consistently warned of the collusive nature of business interests, including fixing the highest price 'which can be squeezed out of the buyers'. He cautioned that a business-dominated political system would allow a conspiracy of industry against consumers, with the former scheming to influence politics and legislation.[32] Consistent with this view, he promoted free trade to break

the power of the mercantilists and increase the share of manufacturers in a competitive market.

While his understanding of markets and industrial organisation
was original, Smith's attempts to develop a formal theory of value
were less successful. He believed that industrial workers in commercial society – not, as for Quesnay, farmers in an agrarian one – were
at the heart of a productive economy. Manufacturing labour, not
land, was the main source of value, with total value creation
proportional to the amount of time spent by workers on
production:

> The value of any commodity, therefore, to the person who
> possesses it, and who means not to use or consume it himself,
> but to exchange it for other commodities, is equal to the
> quantity of labour which it enables him to purchase or
> command. Labour, therefore, is the real measure of the
> exchangeable value of all commodities.[33]

Smith acknowledges that differences in labour quality mean that
simply measuring the hours of work that went into producing an
object is not equivalent to the effort. And he highlights the ways in
which a good's 'real' value (determined by labour) can be distinct
from the money price of the good, which he calls its 'nominal' price:
'Labour alone, therefore, never varying in its own value, is alone the
ultimate and real standard by which the value of all commodities
can at all times and places be estimated and compared. It is their
real price; money is their nominal price.'[34]

In a barter economy, Smith argues, goods could be more easily
traded at ratios that directly reflect the labour required to produce
them, as in his famous example: 'If among a nation of hunters, for
example, it usually costs twice the labour to kill a beaver which it
does to kill a deer, one beaver should naturally exchange for or be
worth two deer.'[35]

In a world where almost all exchanges are transacted using
money, however, the price of a good is an 'estimate' of the ultimate,
real value of that good, which is determined by labour. Smith didn't
resolve what drives gaps between market prices and labour value,

leaving it to Ricardo and Marx to advance his thinking on the labour theory of value.

Although Smith emphasised that effective market functioning requires particular sentiments – trust, fairness and integrity – he didn't recognise the paradox of how the act of valuing can change those sentiments. As we will see in later chapters, this can set in train a dynamic process that undermines market functioning while changing society's values.

Arguably the greatest economist of his time, Ricardo was born in London near the current Liverpool Street Station in 1772, the third of six sons in a family that would number fifteen grown children. His father was a Sephardic Jew from Portugal who had settled in England after a spell in Holland. Ricardo followed his father into the City where he made a fortune (worth over £100 million in today's money), principally by speculating on government debt. After betting on the right outcome in the Battle of Waterloo (allegedly on false information), he retired an extremely wealthy man to his Gloucestershire estate where he pursued an interest in political economy that had originally been prompted by his reading *The Wealth of Nations* at the turn of the century.

David Ricardo's writings on political economy were slightly less ambitious than Smith's (in that he didn't aspire to the full science of man), but his ideas have been just as influential. Ricardo advanced key elements of Smith's work by making at least two stunning contributions to economic thought. First, he put forward a compelling and original case for free trade through the theory of comparative advantage, which would become a central tenet of economic liberalism. And second, he formalised the labour theory of value, which would become a cornerstone of Marxism.[36]

In 1815 a controversy arose in England over the proposed Corn Laws, which were designed to regulate the import and export of grain, and in the process protect the economic interests of domestic landlords. The prospect of tariffs on wheat imports and the resulting higher domestic prices on grain prompted Ricardo to publish his influential *Essay on the Influence of a Low Price of Corn on the Profits of Stock* (1815). In it, he argued that raising tariffs on grain imports would increase the rents of landlords, decrease the profits of manufacturers and slow economic growth.

Ricardo's opposition was part of a more general aversion to mercantilism that he shared with Adam Smith. Smith had recognised that trade was a two-way exchange, and that imports could help countries increase exports and boost economic growth. Consumers, Smith argued in *The Wealth of Nations*, should buy products from where they were cheapest. All protection did was create monopolies, which were 'a great enemy to good management'.

Ricardo took Smith's ideas further. First, he articulated what came to be known as the 'law of diminishing marginal returns', one of the most important in economics. It holds that as more and more resources are combined in production with a fixed resource – for example, as more labour and machinery are used on a fixed parcel of land – the incremental increase in output will diminish. Restricting foreign imports would bring more marginal land into production, raising grain prices, increasing rents to landlords, reducing the profits of manufacturers and, as a consequence, lessen their capacity to invest in new production. As we shall see in the next chapter, the analogue on the demand side is diminishing marginal utility, which holds that the more of a good one consumes – such as ice cream on a sunny day – the less the enjoyment derived from each additional scoop.

Ricardo's main argument against the Corn Laws specifically and mercantilism in general was based on his formulation of what became known as the law of comparative advantage (which he originally called 'comparative costs'). He showed that even if one country was absolutely superior to another in the production of all goods there could still be gains from trade based on differences in the relative efficiency of production between them. These gains arise from each country specialising in producing the good for which its comparative (domestic) cost is lower. It is better for the country to exchange on more advantageous terms with its trading partner than within its own economy with its own labour. As the great Paul Samuelson once quipped, 'comparative advantage is one of the few things in economics that is true, but not obvious'. The Appendix to this book details this non-obvious truth.

Ricardo began his most famous work, *Principles of Political Economy and Taxation* (1817), with his labour theory of value:

> The value of a commodity, or the quantity of any other commodity for which it will exchange, depends on the relative quantity of labour which is necessary for its production, and not on the greater or less compensation which is paid for that labour.[37]

He distinguished between the price of a good or service and its underlying value. Like Aristotle and Adam Smith, he held that the relative values between two goods are determined by the relative quantities of labour needed to make them.

Under this pure theory of labour value, if it took twice as much labour to produce a bottle of wine as a loaf of bread, the wine would be twice as valuable. Actual prices could fluctuate in the short run with wages and profits but in the long run they would return to their natural values anchored by the amount of labour employed to produce them. Ricardo generalised this theory by adding returns to land (rent) and capital (profit), and then concentrated on how the distributions of the returns to the factors of production varied.

He used time as a measure of labour quantity, accommodated the different skills of labour by comparing wages to productivity and assumed that capital's influence on value was neutralised since it was merely stored up in labour. He added a theory of land rent, arguing that rent is determined by the price of goods (rather than determining the price of goods) and provided reasons why profits had varying effects on value (such as different capital intensities of industries).[38]

In *Principles of Political Economy and Taxation*, Ricardo set out laws determining the distribution of everything produced by the 'three classes of the community' – landlords, labour and the owners of capital. He viewed the distribution of wages as the issue that ultimately regulates the rate of growth and wealth of a nation.

He believed that returns to labour would tend towards a subsistence wage anchored by the price of food, which in turn would reflect the marginal land brought into production (this would become known as the iron law of wages). As wages rose and fell in line with the cost of necessities, profits would vary inversely. Ricardo also determined that rents would increase as population grows, owing to the higher costs of cultivating more food because of diminishing returns. As he observed in his *Essay on Profits*, 'Profits depend on high or low wages, wages on the price of necessaries, and the price of necessaries chiefly on the price of food.'

Ricardo's theory of growth and accumulation follows from this. As profits grow, capitalists invest and expand production, which creates more jobs and raises wages. This encourages population growth, pushing wages back to subsistence as more land is drawn into production. This in turn increases profits (and rents) and continues the cycle. As the economy grows, more and more people earn the subsistence wage.

With the price of food ultimately regulating wages, the more productive that agriculture becomes, the lower the prices of food and therefore wages, and the higher the profits to manufacturing. These profits can be reinvested in further growth in manufacturing (productive consumption). If agriculture is less productive, there is no surplus to reinvest and no growth. Rents are a draw on the surplus and therefore a drag on economic growth.

Ricardo's approach has two major shortcomings. First, his analysis tended to concentrate on monetary and fiscal factors and to underweight the importance of the organisation of production and of the centrality of economic institutions.[39] Most curiously, despite his careful reading of Smith, there is no mention of the division of labour as the fundamental institution of economic organisation.

Second, Ricardo's derivation of his labour theory of value had a fundamental flaw: how to account for differences in the time horizon of the returns to the various factors of production. To solve for labour as the single determinant of value, he needed to establish a relationship between capital and labour (as he had between land and labour based on the price of food and the subsistence wage). His solution was to treat capital as accumulated labour (by observing that there were so many person hours required to make a machine). But this approach came unstuck when he realised that the time horizon for the returns to work (that is, daily or weekly or

monthly wages) was much shorter than that for the returns on physical capital, which would normally stretch out over years.[40]

It was left to Karl Marx to square the circle by focusing on labour
power, the dynamics of wage bargaining and what he saw as the
inherent instability of capitalism.

Marx was a German philosopher, political economist and revolutionary. Born in Trier in 1818, he studied law and philosophy at the
universities of Bonn, Berlin and Jena. He became radicalised at
university as a member of the Young Hegelians. Hegel's metaphys-
ics had a profound influence on Marx. He adopted with enthusiasm
Hegel's 'dialectic approach' in which alternative truths were revealed
through the process of criticising concepts and their relations,
inclusions and omissions. The combination of that writing style,
Marx's prodigious output and his frequent revisions of texts has
spawned a wide range of interpretations of his writings, which –
like Smith's – are often mined by commentators for support of their
previously held positions.

Due to his politics, Marx – with his wife and children – for
decades lived in exile in London, where he continued to develop his
thought in collaboration with Friedrich Engels, often researching in
the reading room of the British Museum. His best-known works are
The Communist Manifesto (1848) and the three-volume *Das Kapital*
(1867), although there were numerous other pamphlets and studies
and he left voluminous notes which have occupied scholars and
adherents ever since. Only twelve people attended his funeral, though
now thousands visit his grave in Highgate cemetery every year.

Marx's political and philosophical thought have had enormous
influence on subsequent intellectual, economic and political history,
and his name remains an adjective, a noun and a school of social
theory. From the perspective of value, Marx made several
contributions.

First, like Smith, the canonists and Aristotle, he placed value in a
social and political context, and as a consequence it is difficult to
extricate his approach from his broader theoretical framework. He
was concerned with the progress of social history, generally derid-
ing the classicists for their inadequate historical perspective. He

stressed that economic processes did not exist in a social vacuum but are conditioned by time, place and the past.

> The categories of bourgeois society provide an insight into the structure and relations of production of all formerly existing social relationship, and the ruins of these social relations were used in the creation of bourgeois society, so too could the ruins of bourgeois society provide the elements of a new scientific political economy.[41]

Marx was even more explicit than Smith in his insistence that production is a social activity that depends on the prevailing form of social organisation and techniques of production. He stressed that the nature of productive activities and the distribution of value changed over time.

Second, Marx asserted that, despite this ever changing economic structure, there was one constant: the value of every good and service was determined by the labour that went into its production. To develop this conclusion, he continued the tradition of objective theories of value that goes back to Aristotle and posits that every good has two values, of use and exchange. Marx then added a definition of value (or worth) that is determined by the amount of 'socially necessary labour' to produce it, with socially necessary labour defined as the average skill and intensity of labour, utilising the most advanced technology. Surplus value is the difference between the (exchange) value of a product when it is sold and the exchange value of the inputs in its production (that is, labour and the labour 'embedded in machines').

So, like Smith and Ricardo, Marx took the view that labour is the sole source of use value, or intrinsic value. But, unlike them, he was able to solve for the invariant standard of value by which the value of all other products could be determined. This solution to the problem that had bedevilled Ricardo (of the differing time horizons of the returns to labour and capital) was central to Marx's theory of economic and political dynamics.[42]

Marx argued that his 'law of labour' (what is now referred to as his labour theory of value) could explain the value of all commodities, including the commodity that workers sell to capitalists, labour power, or their capacity to work. Marx's distinction between labour expended in production and 'labour power' is critical. At a minimum, workers need to work for long enough to regenerate their labour power: receiving an amount equivalent to a subsistence wage. But their labour power is such that they can work longer and, if they do, surplus value is created. The genius of capitalism is to make this happen, and for capitalists to then pocket the vast majority of the associated surplus value, paying workers only a wage sufficient for workers to buy commodities like food and housing to restore their strength to work.

Marx asserted that the class struggle determines who receives the surplus. That is, the relative power of the workers and the capitalists who employ them determines workers' wages and the returns to the various forms of capital. If wages increase above the subsistence level necessary to restore labour power, capitalists would substitute more machines for workers. Discipline on labour power would also be exerted by what Marx termed a 'reserve army of labour'.

And what of capital, the subject of Marx's *magnum opus*? Marx identifies several types, each of which receive portions of the surplus value created by labour (see the Appendix for more detailed relationships). Assuming the capitalists have sufficient power – and Marx saw substantial evidence that they did – these dynamics explained how the economy moved forward. Capitalists appropriated most, if not all, of the labour surplus creating profits, an excess return on their constant capital. Capitalists would then reinvest the net proceeds (after any calls on them from interest-bearing and commercial capital) in new machines, expanding production. To Marx, productive activities did not depend on the sector. Services as well as manufacturing could be productive provided their labour produced a surplus that was reinvested in capitalist production.

Marx foresaw several reasons why capitalism, unlike the previous systems of feudalism and mercantilism, would be in a constant state of flux and fundamentally unstable. One central contradiction was that the reinvestment of profits would increase mechanisation, which would displace labour and reduce the only source of profits, labour power. The potential responses would intensify the class struggle by attempting to reduce the exchange value of the labour power through increasing the reserve army of labour or otherwise reducing the bargaining power of labour.

Marx also saw that the growing general commercialisation and financialisation of the economy could ultimately undermine the growth of production. In his view, commercial and speculative financial firms do not add value to capitalist production. By capturing an increasing share of the surplus, they diminished the profit in the economy available for reinvestment.

Finally, the social dimension of capital would feed instability. Capital gives capitalists their power over workers who cannot realise their labour power in isolation from the means of production. Workers become alienated from their work because they do not own the means of production, and the surplus they create is taken away from them. For Marx as for Aristotle and Aquinas, the exchange of value, or more appropriately the exchange of 'just' value, had moral as well as economic implications.

Smith, Ricardo and Marx each redrew the production frontier to include industry and focused on the implications of the new production processes of the Industrial Revolution for the returns to labour and capital. They shared the ideas that value was derived from the production costs, particularly labour, and that any subsequent activities, such as finance, did not in themselves create value.

Although Marx used the classical concepts of value, he applied his vast philosophical and sociological knowledge to reach conclusions in *Capital* that diverged radically from them. It would demand a response from more orthodox value theorists. They did not wait long.

As we will see in subsequent chapters, that response set in train a process that has fundamentally changed perceptions of value from intrinsic to the good or activity that is produced to external and in the eye of the beholder that consumes. We equate the market prices of goods, activities and labour with their worth and that worth with what society values. If left unacknowledged, this could have profound implications for how successfully society addresses the large structural changes now being wrought by the combination of the Fourth Industrial Revolution and the Covid crisis.

2

Perspectives of Value – Subjective Value

If beauty is in the eye of the beholder, what about value?

A few years ago, a new record was set for the sale of a painting at public auction when a mystery buyer paid $450 million for a rediscovered Leonardo da Vinci portrait of Christ, *Salvator Mundi*. How do you value a fifteenth-century canvas so badly damaged that most of the work was painted by the restorer? And why is this depiction of the 'saviour of the world' who taught that 'blessed are the poor' now in the private collection of one of the world's richest people, its value to the world obscured as its scarcity value is maximised?

Around the same time as that auction, I received a visit from the artist Damien Hirst. He wanted to create his own money in the form of 2,000 virtually identical paintings of dots, 8 inches by 12 (they would be distinguished by the names of songs on their backs). The paintings would be sold and then a market would be set up so that they could be traded. The art would be in the process of exchange – they would literally have exchange value! Hirst was on to something. As befits one of the most commercially successful artists of this age, his art was at the intersection of modern value and the value of money. The very act of valuing had artistic – and commercial – value.

But what happened to 'art for art's sake'? Moved by the Covid crisis, Frances Morris, the Director of the phenomenally successful Tate Modern, warned of the danger that blockbuster exhibitions, while enabling the museum to thrive, 'crowd out other things that are equally important and valuable such as the work of our learning and community teams, or the great collections of British and international art Tate holds in trust for the nation. These tangible and intangible assets cannot be measured in numbers or cash returns.'[1]

Morris's plea was that we should 'privilege what we really value': environmental sustainability, local community, education and engagement. If realised, her vision would rebalance the values of a superstar museum born from the legacy of a nineteenth-century British industrialist, Henry Tate. Tate was a contemporary of the group of economists who launched the neo-classical revolution,[2] and it is the effects of that economic school on value and values that contribute to Tate Modern's current struggle for art 'as a social space not a marketplace'.[3]

The neo-classicists launched an upheaval in value theory comparable to the Copernican revolution in science. Whereas Copernicus transformed astronomy by moving its axis from the earth to the sun, the neo-classicists shifted the axis of value theory from objective factors of production to the subjective perceived value of goods to the consumer.

As we have seen, in objective theories of value, the value of the inputs, such as labour, determines the value of the output. With the neo-classicists, that causality is reversed. People value final goods that satisfy specific wants, and it is because those final goods are valued that the inputs that went into making them also have value. Labour does not *give* goods value; labour is valued because the final good it helps create is valuable. In its simplest variant, value flows from consumption to production, not in the opposite direction. The value of inputs is *derived from* the value we attribute to the outputs.

The neo-classicists explained the value of a product through differences in utility (or usefulness) to the consumer. These economists tended to conceptualise utility in keeping with the utilitarianism of Jeremy Bentham rather than the welfarism of John Stuart Mill, a distinction with a difference as we shall see in subsequent chapters.

The core of neo-classicism is embodied in William Jevons' statement that 'value depends entirely upon utility'.[4] In this, he was building on a long tradition. Early thinkers on the topic, such as

Aristotle and Thomas Aquinas, acknowledged the importance of demand – and thus utility – in setting value, though they never brought the concept into the centre of their analysis as they were more concerned with ethical considerations and the normative determination of a 'just price'. As a consequence, their observations on demand and the utility of goods are scattered throughout their writings and offer only hints of Jevons' insight.

Centuries after Aquinas, Davanzati connected value and utility in his 'Discourse on Coins'. Davanzati argued that no matter what costs were incurred in producing a good, when it arrived on a market its value would depend solely on the utility the buyer expects to receive. Merchants set the prices only because they take the time to inform themselves carefully of the desires of their customers.

Likewise, the English thinker Nicholas Barbon (1640–98) antici-pated subjective utility theory by suggesting that the natural value of goods was represented by their market price: 'the value of all wares arise[s] from their use; things of no use, have no value, as the English phrase is, they are good for nothing'.[5]

Not long afterwards, the Italian cleric and diplomat Ferdinando Galiani (1728–87), borrowing from Davanzati among others, devel-oped a utility theory of value and scarcity sufficiently insightful to earn him the title 'grandfather of the marginal revolution'. While at the court of Versailles, he became a scourge of the physiocrats, whose ideas he viewed as unrealistic and dangerous.

Another contemporary of the physiocrats, the Scot John Law (1671–1729), made an important advance in the theory of value by combining supply and demand. In his *Essay on a Land Bank*, Law described the famous water–diamond paradox of value. His insight was to combine utility with scarcity. It may seem painfully obvious in retrospect but his emphasis on the joint role of supply and demand in determining value broke with his predecessors. Unfortunately for the development of value theory, this dualistic analysis was suppressed for almost 200 years, until its resurrection by the neo-classicists.

The British philosopher and political economist John Stuart Mill (1806–73) gave up the classical–Ricardian search for absolute value for his belief that 'The value which a commodity will bring in any market is no other than the value which, in that market, gives a demand just sufficient to carry off the existing supply.'⁶ Mill also recognised the effects of demand on the supply in different time periods, and he contributed the idea that supply and demand have a tendency to reach an equilibrium. In these respects, his work anticipated the approaching neo-classical school. He would have been uncomfortable, however, with their enthusiasm for value functions based on utility rather than welfare.

Jean-Baptiste Say (1767–1832) disavowed the labour theory of value and attempted a direct demonstration of how utility was reflected in price. In his *Treatise on Political Economy*, published in 1803, Say stated that utility is the capacity to satisfy wants and that value originates in utility. He went on to show that price is the measure of value and that value is the measure of utility. Hence, price measures utility, from which it originated. This was more tautology than proof but nonetheless kept the idea of utility-based value alive.

The decisive breakthrough for subjective value theory came when the neo-classicist economists introduced another revolutionary concept, marginalism, to explain economic decision making. In the 1870s, William Jevons (1835–82) in England, Leon Walras (1834–1910) in Switzerland and Carl Menger (1840–1921) in Austria all argued, in different ways, that value was determined 'on the margin', depending not on the total supply of a good but on the particular unit that was being considered for purchase or sale at a given time and place.

Take for example, a consumer who is willing to buy a pair of shoes to wear to work for $100 even though the retail price is only $60. In addition, they are willing to buy an extra pair of the same shoes to wear on the weekend, but are only willing to pay $80 for this second pair because overall they offer less additional benefit given they already have one pair. This consumer receives a total utility of $180 from the two purchases but only pays $120. This $60 difference is considered the 'consumer surplus'.

If the consumer was willing to buy a third pair of shoes (as a back up for when one wears out) but valued this pair at only $60, the total value of the shopping spree would rise to $240 and payment would rise to $180. Consumer surplus, however, would remain at

$60 as the third pair was purchased for the exact amount at which the consumer valued them.

The value of each subsequent pair of shoes is its 'marginal value' and is different from the average total value of the purchases as each pair of shoes is valued differently. Subjectivism says that utility is based on the preferences of the consumer at a given time and place. And diminishing marginal utility means that additional utility decreases with the additional amount consumed or held. As Menger writes,

> Value is thus nothing inherent in goods, no property of them,
> nor an independent thing existing by itself. It is a judgment [that]
> economizing men make about the importance of the goods at
> their disposal for the maintenance of their lives and well-being.
> Hence value does not exist outside the consciousness of men.[7]

So, the neo-classicists argue, value is subjective, in that it is a function of our 'judgment' and 'consciousness', and marginal, in that value depends upon the 'goods at [our] disposal' not on their total stock.

Consider how the combination of marginalism and subjectivism resolves the water–diamond paradox. As Law had observed almost two centuries prior, part of the reason for the difference in the value of water and diamonds was relative scarcity, which when combined with diminishing marginal utility of goods means that value decreases the more that the goods are held or consumed. But this is inseparable to preferences, which depend on individuals, time and circumstances. In a desert, water is exceptionally valuable and diamonds virtually useless.

'Thinking on the margin' has become core to the economic way of thinking. Facing a choice, we consider not the total benefits or costs of the good or service in question, but the benefits and costs of this particular unit in this specific context. When deciding whether to buy a pair of shoes, we don't consider the total benefits of owning any footwear at all in our decision. Instead, we consider the benefits of adding the specific pair of shoes in question to our wardrobe. It's the marginal utility not the total utility that matters. When I was at graduate school, our college bar advertised itself as 'marginally better than the Westgate', the local pub. That endorsement was compelling to the economists who would pack it nightly, but curiously not to the sociologists or political scientists. As we shall see, such tribal reinforcement causes economists some blind spots, such as when they apply the maximisation of marginal utility by rational agents too widely when thinking about real-world issues.

Jevons' *Theory of Political Economy* and Menger's *Principles of Economics* both developed the new tool of marginal analysis in 1871 as a means of understanding value. But they erred in trying to find a simple one-way cause-and-effect relationship between utility and value. Walras and Alfred Marshall (1842–1924) would see that the cost of production (supply) and utility (demand) were interdependent and mutually determinant of each other's values.

Walras independently discovered the concept of marginal utility, but unlike Jevons and Menger he saw a complex interrelated economic system. In his *Elements of Pure Economics*, Walras created his theoretical model of general equilibrium as a means of integrating the effects of both the demand- and supply-side forces in the whole economy. This mathematical model of simultaneous equations concluded that 'In general equilibrium everything depends upon everything else.'[8]

Meanwhile, Marshall combined the best of classical analysis with the new tools of the marginalists in order to explain value in terms of the simultaneous interaction of supply and demand. One of his many insights was that market dynamics would vary over time, because of technological diffusion and competition.

Marshall divided his analysis into four time periods. First, in the market period where time is short and supply is therefore fixed, the value of a good is determined solely by demand. Second, in the short run when firms can change their production runs but not their plant size, supply and demand jointly determine value. Third, in the medium term, where plant size itself can be altered, the effects of supply on value depend on whether the industry of a particular good has constant, increasing or decreasing costs to scale. Finally, in the long run in which technology and population vary, the supply-side conditions dominate.

To Marshall, taking into account the time and interdependence of economic variables as well as technological changes resolves any controversy over whether the cost of production or utility determines value: 'we might as reasonably dispute whether it is the upper or under blade of a pair of scissors that cuts a piece of paper, as whether value is governed by utility or costs of production'.[9]

In the century since the neo-classicists, subjective value theory has gone mainstream. The invisible hand of Adam Smith, with our wants satisfied by exchanges in markets, has been generalised and formalised into the First Fundamental Theorem of welfare economics. This theorem demonstrates mathematically that competitive markets can lead to optimal equilibrium outcomes in which no one can be made better off (known as 'Pareto optimality'). All marginal benefits and costs are equalised. It is sometimes forgotten that this result holds only in an idealised world, namely under the strict conditions of perfect competition (no monopolies or oligopolies), complete markets, no transaction costs, perfect information and preferences that are 'non-satiated'.

The combination of subjective value theory – in which price equals value – and a cursory understanding of the invisible hand – in which markets yield optimal outcomes under idealised conditions and supported by unseen social capital – promotes a view that all market outcomes equal value creation, and with them the growth of the wealth and welfare of nations.

Before turning to some of the potential consequences of this consensus, it is important first to reflect a little more deeply on the meaning of utility that the economy is purported to be maximising.

The subjective or marginal theory of value depicts all income as a reward for productive undertakings. This reward is equal to its price which is equal to value. In other words, the return for a good or service is equal to the utility that it provides to the purchaser. Under the strict conditions of a competitive market, the sum of all these utility-maximising transactions in the economy realises the 'greatest happiness of the greatest number of people'.

This is the economic manifestation of the utilitarian project pioneered by Jeremy Bentham, John Stuart Mill and Henry

Sidgwick in the nineteenth century. Utilitarianism holds that the most ethical choice will produce the greatest good for the greatest number of people. 'Utility' is broader than 'usefulness', the common conception that we have been using thus far, but it is arguably a narrower concept than is consistent with welfare or wellbeing. Bentham defines utility as:

> That property in any object, whereby it tends to produce benefit, advantage, pleasure, good or happiness, (all this in the present case comes to the same thing) or (what comes again to the same thing) to prevent the happening of mischief, pain, evil, or unhappiness to the party whose interest is considered.[10]

The very idea of happiness needs to be defined. People care about more than 'happiness', including meaning, dignity and a sense of purpose. Purely hedonic measures of welfare, focused only on pleasure and pain, are inadequate. People seek meaning as well as pleasure. Some things – tools, money – principally have use value. Others – friendship, knowledge – are valued for their own sake. In the words of Mill,

> Nor is it only the moral part of man's nature. In the strict sense of the term – the desire of perfection, or the feeling of an approving or of an accusing conscience – that he overlooks; he but faintly recognizes, as a fact of human nature, the pursuit of any, other ideal end for its own sake. The sense of honour and personal dignity – that feeling of personal exaltation and degradation which acts independently of other people's opinion, or even in defiance of it; the love of beauty, the passion of the artist, the love of order, of congruity, of consistency in all things, and conformity to their end; the love of power, not in the limited form of power over other human beings, but in abstract power, the power of making our volitions effectual; the love of action, the thirst for movement and activity, a principle scarcely of less influence in human life than its opposite, the love of ease … Man, that most complex being, is a very simple one in [Bentham's] eyes.[11]

In the experience of Cass Sunstein, one of the world's most sophisticated regulators and academics, the actual practice of cost–benefit analysis attempts to implement Mill's conception of welfarism not Bentham's utility. Sunstein helped pioneer the development of modern cost–benefit analysis and oversaw its use in the Obama White House as the Head of the Office of Information and Regulatory Affairs. By law, US regulations must be rigorously assessed to see whether they make people's lives better, and it is not as simple as seeing whether the increase in aggregate 'happiness' outweighs any rise in aggregate 'unhappiness'. From his experience, cost–benefit analysis operates in a much broader domain than Benthamite utility:

> It does not only focus on pleasure and pain, important as those are. Cost-benefit analysis includes everything that matters to people's welfare, including such qualitatively diverse goods as physical and mental health, freedom from pain, a sense of meaning, culture, clean air and water, animal welfare, safe food, pristine areas, and access to public buildings.[12]

One of the great challenges of evaluating public policies is how to compare these concepts which are generally not priced, a challenge referred to as the 'knowledge problem'. Policymakers have developed a range of tools to address this issue including randomised control trials, retrospective analysis and strategies to 'measure and react'. All of these strategies seek to assign a monetary value to 'what money can't buy' in order to make a comprehensive assessment of policy on welfare. Their efforts to show that the knowledge problem can be overcome underscore the reality that there are many values that people hold that are not valued in the market. The sum of all market values does not equal total welfare.

One example of value without a market price is that of life itself. The experience of Covid-19 has brought to the fore the practice of valuing life on both an absolute and a quality-adjusted basis. This can occur when making difficult health decisions such as triaging patients or allocating scarce treatments in overwhelmed hospitals. It can also be applied in regulatory decisions about safety measures, and about critical decisions that balance health and economic considerations such as when and how to end lockdowns and whether to reimpose them.[13] We explore these issues in Chapter 10 but their prevalence shows the importance of society knowing its values.

To recap, economic theories of value went from objective, with value tied to factors of production and how production takes place, to subjective, with value being in the eye of the beholder and determined by preferences. Today, it is widely assumed that there is no underlying, intrinsic or fundamental value that isn't already reflected in the price. The market determines value, and the intersection of supply and demand reveals it. It is increasingly common to equate that worth with society's values.

This is a departure. Throughout history, value theories have been rooted in the socioeconomic circumstances and political economy of their day, adapting to reflect what the society of the time values. That's why proto-economists distinguished between activities that were productive and unproductive, or those that were value creating and rent extracting. Today, the concepts of unproductive activities and rent extraction have been largely discarded. All returns in the market are portrayed as just rewards for value creation; all that is priced can be (mis)characterised as advancing the wealth (and welfare) of nations.

The concept of value – synonymous with economic theory a century ago – is now barely discussed. In her magisterial book *The Value of Everything*, the economist Mariana Mazzucato makes the case forcefully that we need a 'contested debate on value'.[14] In particular, she emphasises the importance of focusing on the process of value creation, examining the distribution of its spoils and considering the contributions of activities to welfare.

Tellingly, Mazzucato warns of the dangers of 'performativity' – how we talk about things affects our behaviour – and argues that the sources of value creation in the economy are modern myths. So pharmaceutical companies practise 'value-based pricing', and financial speculation has moved from 'semi-parasitic' to value creating.[15] Mainstream corporate governance promotes shareholder value by portraying shareholders as the biggest risk takers, while downplaying the risks that workers take with their careers or the benefits of public and social infrastructure. To Mazzucato, in a world where the concept of value is 'incredibly fuzzy', anyone can call themselves 'a value creator'.

There are a variety of consequences of the dominance of the subjective approach to value and the widespread ignorance of both its limitations and its impacts. These can be grouped into four categories: market failures, human frailties, the welfare of nations and the theory of market sentiments.

Market failures. All economic theories are based on a number of assumptions, and many of their conclusions hold only in very specific circumstances of which Keynes' 'madmen in authority' are usually unaware. Subjective value theory is no different. As we have seen, at its core, subjective theory assumes an idealised world of perfect competition, commodity goods and complete markets, a world in which consumers are rational agents.

The realities of markets can mean that there are many cases where these assumptions do not hold, and this can drive a wedge between private and social value. For example,

- When there are *oligopolies or monopolies*, marginal benefits exceed marginal costs in equilibrium. In other words, when companies have market power, prices are too high and production is too low. Often that market power exists because of rules, regulation or the structure of markets (for example, network externalities in social media). Recall Smith's warnings against government capture by business, and his view that a free market was one that was free of rent.
- When there are externalities, costs (or benefits) are incurred (or received) by third parties, over which they have no control. These *externalities* are not reflected in market prices leading to equilibria with too much or too little production for socially optimal purposes. Negative externalities are some of the most important causes of the climate crisis. Although externalities can explain the limitations of property rights in achieving socially optimal outcomes, the failure of private

actors to take into account the harm their actions are causing others is also broadly a question of values.

– Or when there are *incomplete markets*, there may be multiple equilibria, many of which are inconsistent with welfare maximisation. In finance, complete markets are often assumed, for example for the hedging of risks. When their absence is exposed under stress, widespread damage can be caused. As we will see in Chapter 7, this can lead to huge fluctuations in market values and adverse economic outcomes for people who are otherwise unconnected with financial dealings.

As subsequent chapters explain, such real-world issues have been core causes of crises in areas ranging from finance to climate.

Subjective value theory also abstracts from the deeper conditions for markets to be fair and effective. As Smith stressed, markets are living institutions, embedded in culture, practices and traditions. As we shall see, values of trust, integrity and fairness are critical to effective market functioning. They should not be assumed or taken for granted. After all, Smith stressed that the practices, mores and values of society are established and reinforced by the process of mutual sympathies. Social capital needs to be nurtured for economic capital to grow.

Human frailties. Whereas consumers in subjective value models are rational and forward looking, behavioural science has demonstrated the many frailties we exhibit when making decisions, including commitment biases, availability biases and tendencies to hyperbolic discounting. In plain English, we tend to support our past decisions even if new information suggests they are wrong, we tend to think that examples that come readily to mind are more common than they are, and we are irrationally impatient.

In this context, it is important to recall that subjective values are time and situation specific. Ice cream on a hot summer afternoon is more valuable than on a winter morning. Water in a desert is essential, as are healthcare workers, ventilators and testing capacity in a pandemic. If we have high discount rates (we value the present much more than the future), then we are less likely to make necessary investments today to reduce risks tomorrow. This is particularly true under uncertainty, when the timing and magnitude of those risks cannot be precisely foreseen.

The examples of how these human realities affect value and revealed values are legion. We didn't invest adequately in either pandemic preparedness or the capacity of our healthcare systems or care homes. If people are well informed, rational, forward looking, this would suggest to some economists a value on human life that was considerably lower than society's revealed preference once the virus struck. Society did not choose laissez-faire, but rather supported lockdowns and economic privations to save lives at valuations well above those generally assumed in cost–benefit models. To take another example, despite a history of financial crises that stretches back eight centuries, banks did not build up adequate rainy-day buffers in advance of the global financial crisis. And today society is underinvesting in addressing climate change, even though action today will be far less costly than in the future.

These tragedies of the horizon are manifestations of how yawning gaps between value and values can develop. They arise from human realities and will not be closed by addressing market imperfections alone. The next Part of the book begins to outline some broader values-based approaches that hold greater promise.

The welfare of nations. Different theories of value cannot be separated from the social, technological and political dynamics of their time. Aristotle's economics were integral to his ethical and moral philosophy and to his primary concern, justice. The canonists' economic approach was part of their social philosophy and theology. The classicists focused on political economy, at a time of unprecedented growth, urbanisation, industrialisation and globalisation. To varying degrees, all these historical approaches to value recognised that the changing nature of production and trade determine the returns to the factors of production, and in particular the distribution of income and wealth in our society.

An essential motivation of these theories has been to advance the wealth and welfare of nations. Approaches to value have helped define the activities that society viewed as productive, and as a consequence influenced public policies and set private priorities. The mercantilists supported commerce, the physiocrats extolled agriculture and the classicists backed industry. Over the centuries, what has been considered productive has widened considerably and it now includes many activities, such as finance, that were previously viewed as rent seeking. Now at the advent of the Fourth Industrial Revolution, the consideration of which activities are productive and unproductive, value creating and rent seeking should naturally again come to the fore.

An advantage of the subjective approach to value is that it is neutral. Everything that is priced can be compared by means of a common, widely available standard, the market price. But from the perspective of welfare, it creates several issues.

First, with basically everything priced counted as GDP[16] – the shorthand widely used as a measure of national prosperity – there is a risk that the relative value of the future drivers of prosperity is obscured. Objective-based theories of value were careful to make the judgements concerning what was productive. But all that is valued today – that is, what has a market price – is not equally productive or important to future value creation. Moreover, what is considered productive versus unproductive becomes self-fulfilling, as being included in GDP is a marker of productiveness itself. For example, the economist Diane Coyle notes that the view that finance is a strategically important sector of the economy developed alongside changes in statistical methodology that designated it part of national production.[17]

Second, whereas economic infrastructure and economic capital are usually priced, social infrastructure and social capital generally are not. This can lead to underinvestment in what matters for well-being. In standard GDP accounting, government contributes no value added beyond public sector salaries. Measurement of (unpriced) outputs would better reflect both living standards and economic performance.[18] What captures performance during the crisis? A healthcare worker's salary or their heroic efforts at saving lives?

Third, extensive research on the science of wellbeing finds that a wide range of determinants of human happiness (I will use these terms wellbeing and happiness interchangeably) are not priced. These include mental and physical health, human relationships, community and general social climate. This reality means that, even if markets were perfectly competitive and complete, information were equally shared, there were no transaction costs and people were rational, then the sum of their individual utility-maximising transactions would not maximise welfare.

Fourth, consistent with the focus of value theorists down the ages, distribution matters for welfare, and these benefits may not always be captured by monetary figures (and their proxies). When there are large benefits for disadvantaged groups and only small costs for others, a policy may be welfare enhancing despite what market values suggest.[19] The allocation (or 'incidence') of costs and benefits matters, and even 'if losers lose more than gainers gain in monetary terms, we cannot exclude the possibility that the losers lose less than the gainers gain *in welfare terms*'. Or in other words, an extra £1,000 means less to Mark Zuckerberg than £500 does to someone on the dole. In part, this can be explained by the diminishing marginal utility of money. There is widespread evidence that, above certain thresholds, small additional monetary gains or losses are relatively immaterial from a welfare perspective, whereas for the least well off they are material.[20]

The theory of market sentiments. Consider again the core message of Smith's *Theory of Moral Sentiments* in which people form their norms (and values) as a matter of social psychology by wishing to be well thought of or well regarded. What if what's measured influences perceptions of value and values? Subjectivism does not distinguish between productive and non-productive activities, creative and rent seeking. If society values activities that are value extracting, our sentiments could adjust accordingly.

Could it even imply that anything that is not priced is not valuable? Any assessment of the costs and benefits of a new policy must try to address this issue, but how reasonable is it for people to conduct such complicated assessments? Or is it possible that, with time and observation, market value increasingly becomes the measure of all things?

Relatedly, if that which is not in a market is not valued, will that encourage bringing more goods and activities into markets, and could that affect perceptions of their value particularly when they relate to broader values ranging from awe to human dignity?

Future chapters will explore whether by changing how we value, by extending the price system and defaulting to a market economy, we may be changing our values. Or, in the language of value theory, could the dominance of subjectivism corrode intrinsic value? The paradox is that effective market functioning requires other sentiments, such as trust, fairness and integrity. Whatever its broader merits, if it is allowed to dominate, subjective value theory could sow the seeds of its demise by turning moral sentiments into market sentiments.

To explore these issues, let's turn to the measure of value in our age – money.

3

Money, Gold and the Age of Consent

Today, 5,500 tons of gold lie in the bank of England's vaults – more than 190 million ounces. Think of the futility. The raw ore is scraped from the depths of the South African Transvaal or the Canadian Arctic. It is then refined, assayed and shipped across the oceans to be brought through the Bank of England's Lothbury gates to be buried once again.

Once, when reflecting on gold's fate, the sculptor Sir Antony Gormley conceived of bringing that journey to life. He would return both the gold and the observer to their origins by creating a sculpture made from the gold in the vaults. A solitary clay human figure on top of a carpet of gold on which people could walk, sedimented into the earth from whence they and the gold came. I suggested to him that the sculpture was unlikely to be seen, given the security requirements. Understanding the true nature of value, he was relaxed. The value was in the creation. In the act, not the witness.

The gold held in the vaults of the Bank of England has a market 'value' of around $180 billion, though part of that market price is explained by the view that this gold – held by central banks – will never be sold but to other central banks. The gold is a vestige of a bygone era when gold backed money and an even earlier time when gold was money.

Today, the Bank of England still holds the second largest gold stores in the world (most of it for other central banks after it sold the majority of its own reserves at the turn of the millennium). London remains the centre of the private gold market. These superlatives are the product of an age when the Bank of England had an iron-clad commitment to convert its currency on demand into gold and the pound was the very centre of the international monetary system.

The United Kingdom's own gold reserves now represent the equivalent of 17 per cent of notes and coins in circulation, and less than 1 per cent of the total money supply. Whereas once it was compared to a crown of thorns pressed down on the brow of labourers (as the demands of the gold peg would often force their wages down to restore competitiveness), today gold is a relic, shorn of its barbs.[1]

The story of how gold became money and then lost its crown reveals much of how money is used to measure value and something of the relationship between value and values. And it raises the question: if gold no longer backs money, what does?

THE ROLE OF MONEY

Money is used to measure value. Money – rather than some direct measure of utility, like the fictitious utils of the introductory economics textbooks – is the unit of account for prices (and therefore subjective value in equilibrium). Money allows comparisons between different goods and between the same goods across different times and circumstances.

Without money the decentralised exchange of Smith's invisible hand could not operate. Money unlocks the specialism of labour in the pin factory and 'the great increase in the quantity of work that results'.[2] Only money can solve the coincidence of wants between the butcher, the brewer and the baker to produce our dinner.[3] The alternative, barter, is inefficient if not wholly impractical because we are unlikely to have what the other party wants, in the right proportions at the same time every time for every transaction.

But if money is used to measure value, which values give money its value? The answer begins with its role. Money is defined by what it does. In *The Wealth of Nations*, Adam Smith defines money by how well it serves as:

- a store of value with which to transfer purchasing power
  from today to some future time;
- a medium of exchange with which to make payments for
  goods and services; and
- a unit of account with which to measure the value of a
  particular good, service, saving or loan.

These functions of money operate in a hierarchy. There are many assets that people view as stores of value – houses, for instance – that are not used as mediums of exchange. By comparison, an asset can act as a medium of exchange only if at least two people are prepared to treat it as a store of value, at least temporarily. And for an asset to be considered a unit of account, it must be able to be used as a medium of exchange across a variety of transactions over time between several people.[4]

This hierarchy points to the reality that money is a social convention. We accept that a token has value whether made of metal, polymer or code because we expect that others will also do so readily and easily. Money is like an IOU that applies to everyone: 'we all owe you'.[5]

Before examining the history of money, it is useful to begin with where that history has led: the three forms of modern money.

First, banknotes issued by central banks, such as the Adam Smith £20s. In the UK, these account for just 3 per cent of the stock of money and only about one-quarter of all consumer transactions.[6] When I was born (admittedly some time ago), most workers in the UK were paid weekly in cash and three-quarters of people did not have a bank account. Cash's share of transactions has fallen steadily with the revolution in e-commerce and payment technologies. Its descent accelerated during the pandemic with fears that currency's new role as a 'shared surface' brought the potential to transmit the disease.

Next is electronic central bank money in the form of the reserves that commercial banks hold with their central bank, including to settle transactions with one another. This means that every transaction in the economy effectively settles with the central bank,

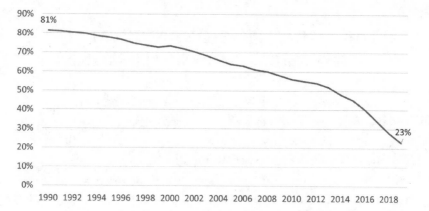

Figure 3.1 Number of cash payments in the UK as a share of
total payments 1990–2019

ensuring finality of payment such that payments once made are
irrevocable and people can transact with confidence.

Finally, and most significantly, the electronic deposits that commercial banks create when they extend loans to borrowers, accounting
for fully 80 per cent of money in the system.[7] This is the product of
'fractional reserve banking', a practice pioneered in the seventeenth
century by wealthy European families like the Medicis and developed
in fits and starts in tandem with quasi-public institutions like
Sweden's Riksbank (which would become the world's first central
bank). Fractional reserve banking is still the heart of modern finance.

In fractional reserve banking, banks take deposits but keep only
a fraction of their assets in gold, cash or liquid securities, with the
balance used to fund loans and investments. This improves the efficiency of the financial system in that a well-run bank can extend
credit to businesses and households on a scale that can be multiples
of its loss-absorbing capital. If concerns about a bank's solvency
emerge, however, depositors can withdraw more funds than the
bank can readily meet, not least because its loans cannot be immediately called in (they aren't *liquid*). Repeated crystallisations of
this vulnerability over the centuries would eventually prompt the
creation of both institutions of public oversight of private money
(like banking supervision) and public safety nets (like depositor
insurance and the central banks' core role as 'lenders of last resort').

PUBLIC INSTITUTIONS AND VALUES
ULTIMATELY UNDERWRITE MONEY

Over the centuries, central banks have developed this critical role as lenders of last resort to backstop solvent banks against such liquidity crises. In other words, when depositors or other creditors of a bank begin to grow concerned about a bank's solvency, the central bank, with its superior real-time information and unlimited resources in its own currency, can step in to bridge a temporary liquidity squeeze. The key is that the bank must actually be 'well run'; getting this right is one of the toughest judgements in finance.

In the modern financial system, the private financial sector creates most of the money in circulation. The reality of how that happens is different from the standard textbook depictions in ways that are important to maintaining money's value. Textbooks often state that money is created by new deposits. In this world, the 'saving' decision of households creates new money, which banks then lend out. But these deposits have to come from somewhere, and when a household chooses to deposit at a bank, those savings come at the expense of purchases of goods and services of companies (who would then in turn deposit the money in their bank, meaning no net money creation).[8]

The principal way banks create money is by making a loan. When the bank decides a borrower is creditworthy (that they are likely to pay the loan back), it credits their deposit account for the amount of the loan and new money enters circulation. In making that lending decision, the bank relies on a degree of trust, which after all is the meaning of the Latin *credere*, the root of our word for credit. Supplementing that trust is the bank's due diligence of the borrower's information as well as prudent assessment of the risk. In the words of Mikhail Gorbachev, 'Trust, but verify.'[9]

Banks cannot create money without limit but are disciplined by competition, constrained by prudential regulation (that is, overseen by central banks) and limited by decisions of households and companies that can reduce the stock of money (by, for example, repaying their existing debts). Monetary policy is the ultimate limit on money creation because, by changing interest rates, it directly influences the price of money and other financial assets and therefore the demand for the money created by the private sector.[10]

This form of money creation, known as fountainpen money in the age of banking clerks and electronic money today, is a far cry from the physical tokens that have represented money over the millennia. These have taken many forms, from cowry shells in ancient times to cigarettes during the Second World War and mobile-phone minutes in modern Kenya.

When I was at the Bank of Canada, at the centre of our entrance foyer, which curiously doubled as a giant tropical terrarium in the middle of the world's second coldest capital city, was a four-ton limestone doughnut. This was a Rai stone, the world's largest monetary token, a cash behemoth and precursor of the distributor ledger from the Micronesian island of Yap.[11] The ownership of the Rai stone is recorded through oral history, an early form of consensus mechanism.

More conventional monetary tokens, and much easier to carry, are of course banknotes. These were first issued in China in the seventh century, fashioned from the bark of mulberry trees. Private banknotes began to circulate in Europe during the Renaissance and became increasingly prevalent in the eighteenth and nineteenth centuries. Today, they are almost always issued by a central bank. Note issuance was a core function of the Bank of England from its inception in 1694. Initially, the Bank fulfilled its mission 'to promote the good of the people' by issuing handwritten banknotes, exchangeable into gold, in order to finance King William III's war with France.

Most forms of money, past and present, have nominal values that far exceed their intrinsic ones (it costs only a few pence to make a £20 polymer banknote). And this gap has meant that money has a long and sorry history of debasement. 'Money for nothing' almost always proves too tempting a prospect. Throughout history, governments would often betray the trust of their citizens. The silver content of Roman coins fell by 25 per cent in the century between the reigns of Augustus and Marcus Aurelius.[12] There were debasements in Florence in the fourteenth century, Castile and Burgundy in the fifteenth. In the 1540s, Henry VIII issued coins with a face value of £4.4 million that was twice the value of the underlying metal. The French did the same with their silver coins around the same period. By the seventeenth century, there were hundreds of coins of varying metallic content circulating in Europe, increasing the costs of commerce and reducing the opportunities for governments to raise revenues through the surprise inflation created by debasement.

The record of private money has been at least as bad. Over the ages, the various forms of private money, such as the notes issued by European banks and American banks in the eighteenth and nineteenth centuries, have inevitably succumbed to oversupply and eventual collapse. Initially strong commitments to back their value, by pledging assets and establishing 'binding' rules for their issuance, have given in to temptations to increase profits by relaxing these strictures and drawing on credibility built up over time. The decline in public trust and with it the value of the private currency comes, as Hemingway once wrote about bankruptcy, 'gradually and then suddenly'.[13]

Through this cycle of promise, trust and disillusionment over the centuries, the foundations of monetary value have developed. This at times painful progress involved experiments with unbacked private money, the purity of the money backed by gold and, after trial and error, the successful model of fiat money that was ultimately backed by an independent authority, a central bank, operating under constrained discretion (a model we will examine in more detail in the next chapter). The effectiveness of these public and private institutions in maintaining the value of money depends in turn on their underlying values – a lesson that is worth learning before moving on to considering the future of money in Chapter 5.

A good place to begin exploring the values underpinning sound money is the history of the Bank of Amsterdam. The Bank of Amsterdam was initially an innovative solution to the problem of determining what can give money its value, before it succumbed to the temptations of unsupervised private money creation. The bank gained prominence in the wake of the Thirty Years War (1618–48), involving small German states of the Holy Roman Empire and neighbouring regional powers. The war brought one of the most severe economic crises ever recorded, with rampant hyperinflation and the breakdown of trade and economic activity. The crisis became known as the *Kipper-und Wipperzeit* (the clipping times), after the practice of clipping coins (shaving metal from their circumference) and sorting good coins from bad.[14]

The Bank of Amsterdam offered a service that brought debasement under control and in the process helped advance modern money. The bank allowed people to deposit their coins, credited at fair and standardised rates depending on their metallic value (minus a small fee), and then issuing deposit notes that people could then use as a form of currency (known as 'bank money'). In effect, the bank pioneered the system of cheques and direct debits that we take for granted today.[15] People used bank money to conduct trade free from concerns of theft, loss or damage since the notes were recorded in the Bank of Amsterdam's accounts. Confidence was maintained because the deposit accounts were backed by gold and silver.

And so it continued for more than a century and a half.[16] The Bank of Amsterdam's excellent reputation even allowed it to depart from its charter from time to time to provide liquidity assistance to market participants through overdrafts, again anticipating a future role of a central bank as the lender of last resort. By the late 1770s, however, it began lending more and more to its largest customer, the Dutch East India Company. Once it became public knowledge in 1790 that its creditworthiness had declined, so too did public trust in its account-based money, leading to a run and the Bank of Amsterdam's collapse. The bank failed because it deviated from its core mission and began taking on risks of fractional reserve banking without proper oversight or transparent disclosure. Discovery of those facts led to suspicions about the quality of governance, the quality of its balance sheet and the soundness of 'bank money'. In matters of money, there is no room for doubt.

The history of the Bank of Amsterdam illustrates some of the important values behind money: a sense of purpose, good governance, transparency and accountability. Money, whether issued publicly or privately, is a public good. Those who create, manage and store it; and those who facilitate and record its transactions all bear special responsibilities to maintain trust in the system, for loss of confidence in one part of the system can undermine trust in the whole.

In the Free Banking Era in the United States (from 1837 to 1863), numerous private banks issued currencies without any oversight by federal authorities.[17] This was a chaotic period of 'wildcat banking' in which private banknotes of varying reputations circulated at different prices in different places, making transactions complicated. With supervision largely absent, banks would eventually reduce the amount of gold or silver backing of their notes, debasing their values. There were frequent banking panics and periodic deflations that destroyed livelihoods and disrupted economic activity. Ultimately, the Federal Reserve System was established to oversee the system in 1913, and instituted consistent prudential rules.

In the UK, the failure of note-issuing banks was commonplace, putting pressure on the Bank of England to act as an (informal) lender of last resort. Consider the contrasting fortunes of the Austen siblings, one who represents sound money and the other who participated in its debasement. The celebrated author Jane Austen currently graces the £10 note. This is fitting because £10 is what she was paid for *Pride and Prejudice*, the equivalent to about £1,000 in today's money. This is not, however, the first time that the Austen name has appeared on a banknote. Jane's brother Henry set himself up as a banker with interests in Hampshire as well as in London. At that time many banks were small and local, and could issue their own banknotes. The British Museum holds a £10 note from Henry Austen's bank in Alton, on which are listed the names of the partners in the bank: Austen, Gray and Vincent.

Unfortunately, while Jane Austen wrote in an early work that 'when a man has once got his name in a banking house he rolls in money', that turned out not to be the case for her brother Henry. Banking was for a time profitable, but unwise lending led to the collapse of the Alton bank, followed by the collapse of Henry's London bank and his personal bankruptcy in 1816. Depositors in these banks, including Jane Austen herself, were left out of pocket.

While this sorry tale had a familiar ring in the failures of other note-issuing banks in eighteenth- and nineteenth-century England, it should be a comfort that part of the Bank of England's job now is to protect the value of money, including the Jane Austen note. Maintaining confidence in currency is the fundamental responsibility of a central bank. That extends to maintaining its value, protecting against counterfeiting and also ensuring that the choice of character on the notes commands respect and legitimacy. We will explore in the next chapter how central banks like the Bank of England do so, and what they need to do to maintain those roles.

Given the experiences of private banks issuing notes on the basis of 'their good name', most observers would agree that laissez-faire is not a good foundation for sound money. There have been two approaches to maintaining public confidence in money and guarding against debasement: i) backing by a commodity, principally gold (and occasionally land or oil) and ii) backing by institutions led by independent central banks. Before reviewing the second in the next chapter, we will consider the lessons that gold can teach about the values behind money.

WHAT BACKS MONEY?
THE GOLD STANDARD

The origins of the gold standard stretch back in time. For thousands of years, precious metals have been used as currency. The earliest coins date from 600 BC and were found in the Temple of Artemis, near İzmir in modern-day Turkey. By Roman times, gold, silver and bronze coins were produced stamped with an image of the emperor of the day on one side and Romulus and Remus on the other.[18] So embedded are these coins in our history that their names live on today: the English pound and penny derive from the Roman libra and denarius.

The system in which gold coins circulated as money, usually in parallel with silver ones, was known as the gold specie standard. Silver coins have usually been more prevalent because gold was too light when cast into coins of values convenient for everyday transactions. Gold coins, such as florins in Florence and ducats in Venice, were generally used to settle large transactions.

With the invention of paper money, coins were eventually supplanted by banknotes, creating the gold bullion standard, under which authorities agreed to exchange the circulating currency for gold on demand at a fixed price. Importantly, banknotes could be either fully or partially backed by gold.

The system of metal-backed money was plagued by reliance on the unpredictable supply of precious metal. Shortages of silver helped explain why the Roman system of coinage endured to outlive the Roman Empire so that prices were still quoted in denarii in Charlemagne's time at the beginning of the ninth century. The Spanish conquest of the New World led to the opposite problem. Such was the plunder of gold and silver that the sixteenth century saw a huge monetary stimulus that spread across Europe, pushing up prices sevenfold between the 1540s and the 1640s during the so-called 'price revolution'.[19] The Spanish learned the hard way that acquiring money did not make you rich; the value of precious metals was not absolute. If its supply increased, its purchasing power would fall.

The spillovers from the Spanish monetary expansion reached England where the price level rose by a then unprecedented rate. But even once that surge subsided in the middle of the seventeenth century, English financial problems persisted. In this age of mercantilism, England's relatively primitive financial system was allowing the Dutch to steal a march in global trade. Such lost opportunities were compounded by domestic currency shortages, chronic underfinancing of the state and, not unrelatedly, very real merchant fears of expropriation of gold. That would change in the wake of the Glorious Revolution of 1688–9, which some scholars argue was triggered as much by financial envy as by religious enmity.[20]

Towards the end of the seventeenth century, a series of developments in the UK would heavily influence the evolution of money and the monetary system, and would in turn impart several lessons for how to maintain the value of money.

The first was the founding of the Bank of England in 1694. The new bank combined the right to issue banknotes with a role in financing the state. Its status as a joint-stock company added to its effectiveness, and its focus on its core financial role insulated it from the type of errors that contributed to the collapses of the French Banque Royale (in 1720) and the English South Sea Bubble. The Bank's role would grow considerably with the sophistication of the financial system.

Second, a rare miscalculation in 1717 by Sir Isaac Newton in his role as Master of the Royal Mint had the effect of driving silver coins out of circulation and putting Britain on a gold standard. Under bimetallism, gold and silver coins circulated in parallel, with the authorities setting a ratio between the two that determined their relative value. This meant that whenever there were material discoveries of either precious metal, the ratio would need to be changed or people would have an incentive to swap the overvalued coins for the undervalued ones.

Newton's error in setting too low a gold price for silver caused all silver to disappear from circulation, putting what would become the world's most important trading nation and its financial superpower on the path to a purely gold specie standard. This *de facto* regime would be formalised in the UK a century later, widely adopted throughout its Empire and subsequently on the European continent. Other countries, particularly the United States, continued to operate under bimetallism until the gold exchange standard took effect in the latter half of the nineteenth century.

Third, in nineteenth-century England, an intense debate developed over the backing of banknotes, eventually leading to the hardening of the gold bullion standard. In 1797, fears of a French invasion contributed to the failures of a number of private banks and imperilled even the Bank of England. With the Bank's reserves draining at an alarming rate, on 25 February 1797 the Prime Minister William Pitt the Younger suspended convertibility of banknotes into gold by an Order in Council. This act prompted an MP to describe the Bank as 'an elderly lady in the City who had unfortunately fallen into bad company'. To this day, the Bank is known as the Old Lady of Threadneedle Street.

Throughout the period of the Napoleonic Wars, a robust dispute raged over the merits of reinstating convertibility. The Bullionist group – led by David Ricardo and Sir Henry Parnell – argued that if banks were not required to convert into gold, they would issue too many notes, causing inflation and the debasement of money. These arguments anticipated many of those of the monetarist school of economics.

The opposing side appealed to the 'Real Bills Doctrine', associated with John Law, Adam Smith and James Stuart. They argued that the banknotes would be credible provided the assets that backed them were creditworthy. At this time, those assets were largely gold and bills of exchange (which were used by companies for trade). Since the demand for bills of exchange would be dictated by the activities of commercial firms, it was contended that there would not be excess note issuance, and if any temporary one occurred it would be quickly mopped up. Conversely, if the money supply were restricted to the available gold, it could prove too meagre for commercial activity.

The Bullionists eventually won the day. Convertibility to gold was restored in 1821, and full parity of note issuance to gold became law in 1844 and was generally maintained until the First World War.[21] This hardening of the gold standard in the UK would influence the international monetary system during a period of flourishing international trade and capital flows. It was notable that the quantity of Bank of England notes grew more slowly than its gold reserves from the mid-1890s to the First World War. It was only the expansion of new (joint-stock) deposit-taking banks that permitted the expansion of private finance needed to support commerce.[22]

The stature and importance of the Bank of England grew over the course of the nineteenth century as it assumed many of the core roles of a central bank. Restrictions on note issuance by competing private banks were gradually tightened and in 1844 the Bank was granted a monopoly in England and Wales.[23] In parallel, as the sophistication of the private banking system increased, the Bank became the lender of last resort, intervening to finance solvent private banks at times of market stress. As we shall see, the addition of these prudential responsibilities created conflicts for the Bank such as when balance of payments pressures demanded higher interest rates but domestic banking problems required lower ones. The difficulties in choosing between external and internal balance would fatally undermine the gold standard and continues to represent one of the greatest challenges to achieving monetary and financial stability.

THE INTERNATIONAL GOLD STANDARD: COMMITMENT WITHOUT CONSENT

The final major development was adoption of the international gold exchange standard. By the third quarter of the nineteenth century pressures on the hybrid system of currencies, with some on the gold standard and others on bimetallic standards, were becoming intense. The tipping point was the Franco-Prussian War of 1870–1 during which France, Russia, Italy and the Austro-Hungarian Empire all suspended convertibility. With war's end and with Britain an island of monetary stability and the world's leading financial and commercial power, most of the world adopted Britain's gold standard.[24]

There is a high degree of path dependence in international monetary affairs, with the international monetary arrangements that a country prefers depending heavily on those adopted by others, particularly the most powerful nations: so 'Britain's "accidental" adoption of the gold standard in the eighteenth century could place the system on a trajectory where virtually the entire world adopted the same standard within a century and a half.'[25] The move to the gold exchange standard ushered in several decades of monetary stability before the shortcomings of the system were laid bare in the aftermath of the First World War. In this respect, the current discussions in the US and China on the future of money could set the standard for the next century.

David Hume first described the workings of the gold standard more than a century before it fully came into being. Each time goods were exported, the exporter received payment in gold, which was brought to the mint to be coined. Each time an importer bought a good, they made a payment by exporting gold. For a country with a trade deficit, gold flowed out on net, setting in train a self-correct-ing mechanism of falling domestic prices because less gold was chasing the same amount of goods. In the foreign country, prices rose because there was more gold chasing the same amount of goods. With imports more expensive, people would consume less of them and more of the now cheaper domestic produce. The trade deficit would shrink and balance would be restored.

In an era of banking and large capital flows there were additional complications. The flows would initially be in currency rather than gold, with the currency received by the exporter in turn presented to the central bank for gold. In the countries with trade deficits, the money supply would contract (because more would flow out than come in), interest rates would rise, domestic prices and wages would fall and export competitiveness would eventually be restored. Central banks could anticipate these pressures by changing interest rates in advance, affecting the availability of domestic credit and restoring the balance of payments without gold flows taking place.

The gold exchange standard generally worked because the major central banks at its centre – the Bank of England, the Banque de France, the German Reichsbank – all had high degrees of commitment and credibility. Financial markets could anticipate their reactions and there was a general absence of speculative attacks.[26] Trust was essential.

This trust wasn't a product of the system's design, with its fixed exchange rate into gold. As monetary history shows, there is no magic rule that in itself can guarantee that money will keep its value. There have always been incentives to relax 'temporarily' monetary rules, strictures and disciplines. In the absence of a strong social consensus, eventually these pressures will overwhelm. Trust in the gold standard could be maintained only as long as social, political and economic conditions resembled those when it came into being. As conditions changed, the ability of the authorities to honour their commitments waned and the breakdown of the system became inevitable.

There were three factors in particular that reinforced the effectiveness of the system in its early years.

First, the UK's position as the financial and commercial hegemon created large, self-reinforcing synergies. The UK was the main exporter of capital goods (that is, machinery), it provided much of the financial capital to fund those imports by the emerging economies of the day (from Argentina through to Canada) and it bought much of their produce. In essence, the UK economy and financial system were oriented to recycle gold back into the global economy for productive investment.

Second, with banking systems relatively underdeveloped, central banks initially faced relatively few conflicts between the requirements of external and internal stability.

Third, the system was backed by a strong consensus of those active in politics. The cornerstone of the gold standard was the priority that governments attached to stability and maintaining convertibility. Initially, there was no doubt that those countries at the centre of the system would 'do whatever it takes' to keep the system stable (does that sound familiar?). With the right to vote limited and labour poorly organised (recall the class struggle), workers who suffered the most from the measures needed to defend currencies were poorly positioned to influence those policies.[27] As a consequence, central banks could raise interest rates to encourage gold inflows and exert downward pressures on prices and wages that would eventually restore competitiveness and external balance. It helped that wages and prices were relatively flexible, meaning that the required reduction in domestic spending could be delivered primarily through falls in domestic prices and costs rather than increases in unemployment.[28]

Pressures on the system built up because all of these factors changed. By the end of the nineteenth century, global economic power was becoming more dispersed and the gold standard therefore tougher to manage. As international trade and financial integration steadily grew, the UK economy became relatively less important. At the same time, an inherent flaw of the system – its dependence on new supplies of gold – exerted a renewed deflationary bias that put pressure on domestic wages, prices and banks across the membership of the international gold standard.

When the supply of gold grew more slowly than the economy, the price level needed to fall to restore equilibrium in purchasing power. This was starkly illustrated when a number of countries adopted the gold standard in quick succession in the 1870s. With less money chasing more goods, the system was highly deflationary, with the British price level falling by more than one-third between 1873 and the end of the century.[29] An environment of sharply falling prices and wages would increase the real burden of debts and make it more difficult for banks to remain solvent.

Although deflationary pressures were temporarily eased by large gold discoveries in South Africa, Australia and Alaska in the 1890s, once their effects began to fade, downward pressures on prices resumed. To combat them, the system increasingly relied on (unbacked) foreign exchange reserves. This reduced the credibility of the gold pegs and increased the potential for destabilising banking and balance of payments crises.

As financial systems grew more complex, the self-equilibrating nature of the system became less evident. Central banks found themselves conflicted between their responsibilities as lender of last resort and their commitment to convertibility. As the nineteenth century progressed, fractional reserve banking grew in importance (for example, demand deposits increased by five times compared to a 3.5 times rise in gold reserves).[30] This meant more frequent tensions between the requirements of external balance (that is, convertibility) and internal balance (that is, the domestic financial system and economy). Bank runs meant the withdrawal of funds, demands for gold and pressures on the Bank of England to provide emergency liquidity. However, the provision of liquidity – more money at potentially lower interest rates – ran directly counter to the rules of the game of the gold standard. Moreover, if financial markets sensed a weakening resolve of the central bank to maintain external balance, then a self-fulfilling run on the currency would ensue.

In such an environment, international cooperation was at a premium.[31] As Keynes once put it, the Bank of England had been the 'conductor of an international orchestra'. By following its cue, different central banks coordinated adjustments to international credit conditions, helping to manage excesses in the flows of gold. But as incidents requiring international cooperation grew in number and severity, particularly due to financial instability, the audience began to detect some false notes. The Barings crisis in 1890, triggered by a default by the Argentine government, forced the Bank of England – the lynchpin of the system – to borrow gold from the central banks of France and Russia. A string of US financial crises in the early 1900s required similar loans. Survival of the system increasingly depended on cooperation rather than on Hume's automatic adjustment mechanism.

Political pressures began to emerge as suffrage was extended, labour began to organise and political parties representing the working classes began to gain popularity. A single-minded focus on convertibility to the exclusion of the impacts on the domestic economy, particularly on wages and employment, became increasingly untenable. This undermined the credibility of the system, emphasising that the gold standard was 'a socially constructed institution whose viability hinged on the context within which it operated'.[32] Indeed, the original gold standard had been adopted before the development of paper banknotes and fractional reserve banking. It presupposed a political setting in which governments were shielded from political pressure to direct policy to other ends, such as domestic activity, wages or financial stability. In short, it had been created in a climate in which governments could value currency and exchange rate stability above all else.

THE GOLD STANDARD FELLED BY VALUES

The gold standard would ultimately fail because its values were not consistent with those of society. It prioritised international solidarity over domestic solidarity. Its emphasis on external stability conflicted with domestic financial prudence. And once workers gained greater influence, the adjustments required were politically more difficult and took longer, with the burden falling ever more heavily on employment. In short, the system became increasingly unsustainable.

The system finally broke down with the First World War. Efforts to resurrect it began soon after hostilities ceased, only to face stiff challenges because the changes that had been underway before the war had accelerated. Britain's industrial and commercial pre-eminence was over, with many of its foreign assets having been sold off during the hostilities. On the eve of the war, the US economy was more than double the size of the UK economy, which had also fallen behind Germany and Russia.[33] By the inter-war years, the differences in the scale and timing of US business and financial cycles would severely hamper the functioning of the gold standard. The US was not necessarily willing to follow the same tune but neither was it yet ready to conduct the orchestra.

During this inter-war period, the financial sectors grew more complex and more central banks had to assume the role of lender of last resort. The spread of trade unionism meant that wages no longer responded as rapidly. Political suffrage had widened considerably, changing the balance between domestic and international priorities. And the mystique of invincibility of the golden peg had been shattered.

This was not as clear to the bankers and economists of the time as it seems to us now. Indeed, when the Mansion House Merchants and Bankers Dinner resumed in 1920, the Governor of the Bank of England, Montagu Norman, emphasised in his speech the unity that the City needed in order to return to normal. The unity to which he referred was around 'the policy' proposed by the Bank of England. He believed 'the policy was the one and only policy which ultimately would place the City and the country again on that eminence which it occupied before the war'.

Such was his confidence that Norman mentioned only once, in passing, that 'the policy' in question was to 'attempt to regain the gold standard', and he spent no time at all explaining what, apart from normalcy, would be achieved by it. In retrospect, it appears obvious that an elliptical speech at a white-tie dinner to City grandees was a poor way to establish political consensus around returning to golden fetters, but this was the era of 'never elaborate, never explain'.

This complacent attempt to return to the past would eventually plunge the country into deflation and a deep recession. The old policy was not suited to the new post-war normal and the UK was forced to abandon it a few years later having suffered a disastrous recession that hastened the end of sterling as the global reserve currency. Clinging to old certainties would prove the UK's undoing. By the time it abruptly abandoned the peg to gold in September 1931, unemployment had doubled to 15 per cent and the economy had not grown in aggregate since 'the policy' was readopted in 1926.

I was reminded of how an obsession with gold had plunged the UK into crisis on my first day as Governor of the Bank of England. Conscious of my predecessor's chequered history, I decided to remove one of the thirteen paintings of Montagu Norman from the Governor's room for meeting external guests. Within a few hours, the Chancellor, George Osborne, called me. 'Hmm,' I thought, 'the Bank appears to be a somewhat leaky institution.'

George asked to borrow the painting of Norman. 'Sure but why?' I naively responded.

'To hang it in the dining room of 11 Downing Street, because that's where Montagu Norman convinced Winston Churchill [when he was Chancellor in the 1920s] to go back on the gold standard at the pre-war parity,' came the reply. The painting would, Osborne said, remind him 'never to listen to the advice of the Governor of the Bank of England'.

I duly shipped it over, along with a portrait of the man who took the other side in that 1920 debate, John Maynard Keynes. Legend has it that Keynes had been unwell that evening when the decision was made and didn't do his case (or the UK economy) justice. In choosing sides in the gold debate, it turns out that George Osborne, the Prince of Austerity, was a Keynesian at heart.

LESSONS FROM THE GOLD STANDARD FOR THE VALUES BEHIND MONEY

The first lesson from the experience with the gold standard is familiar: trust is essential for any form of money to be adopted and sustained. For a time, under certain circumstances, that trust can be supported by a simple rule such as strict convertibility at the heart of the gold standard. This had created a self-equilibrating mechanism in which flows of gold lead to changes in interest rates, prices and wages and to the re-establishment of an equilibrium.

But credibility and trust cannot be maintained without political support. This in turn requires public understanding, which is built through transparency and accountability, and it requires consent which is grounded in solidarity, including a fair sharing of the burdens of adjustments.

These foundations of money were shaken as the adjustments required to maintain the gold standard grew larger. The world became multipolar and international solidarity grew in importance relative to domestic solidarity. Domestic financial systems became more complex and conflicts between internal and external balance more frequent. This could bring financial prudence into conflict with the commitment to convertibility into bullion. Finally, wages and prices became less downwardly flexible as labour power increased. This would increase the duration of the adjustment to any shock, calling into question the sustainability of the system.

These developments made the political economy of the gold standard untenable. The history of the gold standard teaches that the values underpinning the value of money extend well beyond trust to include transparency, accountability, solidarity and resilience. All of these must be respected for a monetary system to support a dynamic economy.

With the wisdom born from experience, most countries have now settled on centralised, public fiat money backed by robust institutions in order to provide the public with money that is both highly trusted and easy to use. But as we shall see in the next chapter, those institutional foundations, central banks, will prove as fragile as golden rules if they too are not grounded in the right values.

4

From Magna Carta to
Modern Money

The history of money shows that sound money is a social convention that endures because of the backing of public institutions that act consistently with society's values.

Modern money is backed by a series of institutions, most of which are housed in central banks. Its value rests on confidence. The value of money requires not just the belief of the public at a point in time but, critically, the consent of the public at all times. That dictates not just what the central bank does to maintain the value of money but how it does it, how it accounts for its actions and how it takes responsibility for any mistakes. In just this way, the effectiveness of the gold standard was ultimately determined by how long it was accepted. When it comes to money, the consent and trust of the public must be nurtured and maintained.

The paradigm of strict banking regulation and supervision and central banks overseeing the financial and monetary system that has emerged over the last century has proven the most effective way to avoid the instability and high economic costs associated with the proliferation of private and public monies. It helped usher in the enormous improvements in global living standards through the third wave of globalisation in which we live, but it is now being severely tested by the combination of economic crisis and technological change.

To understand the antecedents of this powerful institutional framework, it helps to go back in time to well before the development of the gold exchange standard and the establishment of the

Bank of England. A few years ago, the United Kingdom marked the anniversary of a truly historic event. The celebrations of some scrawls on a weathered piece of vellum brought me from Salisbury to Lincoln to the vaults of the British Library and to the grand offices of the High Court. By participating in those commemorations, I saw how a society reinforces and lives its values, and I developed a better understanding of the constitutional principles underpinning the value of money.

It was a time of surging inflation. A crisis in the public finances. Public sector bailouts. Infighting in Europe. Not some eight years ago, but eight hundred. This was the economic context for the striking of Magna Carta.

To many, Magna Carta is a document of profound, almost mythical, significance. It is seen as the cornerstone of the United Kingdom's constitutional arrangements and as a blueprint for the constitutions of many other nations, including the United States. It is credited with establishing the foundations of parliamentary democracy, creating a framework for the rule of law, protecting individual liberty, defending the rights of the innocent and limiting the role of the state.

It is undoubtedly true that Magna Carta – or more correctly the idea of Magna Carta – has played a central role in political developments in Britain and beyond over the centuries, not least as a banner under which those seeking liberty from oppression have rallied. But many modern scholars argue that its significance has been overstated. They characterise Magna Carta as a pragmatic political document that was a product of its time, including the difficult economic circumstances that then prevailed. As usual with historical arguments, the answer lies somewhere in between.

The enduring legacy of Magna Carta is how its strictures on unconstrained power are still reflected in our systems of political and economic governance. These constitutional and pragmatic perspectives remain relevant to modern central banking and to maintaining the value of money. Specifically, the costs of inflation were among the key economic catalysts of Magna Carta, and its core constitutional legacy – namely the importance of delegated authority, with clear lines of public accountability – is at the heart of the Bank of England's institutional arrangements. This approach has been widely adopted by other jurisdictions.[1]

In the spirit of Magna Carta, central banks, like the Bank of England, have been given great responsibilities to deliver monetary and financial stability, operating under constrained discretion in that pursuit and accountable to the people for their performance.

THE ECONOMIC AND POLITICAL CONTEXT OF MAGNA CARTA

The political background to Magna Carta is one of nearly constant conflict within the dysfunctional 'English' monarchical family, as well as conflict with France over control of Normandy and the rest of Henry II's continental empire.[2]

The England of the 1200s was far from being a unitary state. Most matters were administered by local barons, with the King acting as an arbiter in the event of a dispute. The relationship between local (baronial) and central (monarchical) authority was much less deferential, and much more arm's-length (and arms-bearing) than it is today. Indeed, the early Plantagenet kings of England spent most of their time living at home in Normandy or Anjou, allowing the English barons a considerable degree of autonomy. It was only after King John lost Normandy to the French in 1204 that the King resided full-time in England, breathing down the necks of the barons, who did not much like the closer observation of their activities and the eyeing of their stockpiles of silver that this proximity entailed.

The relationship between the barons and King John broke down in part because of unsustainable public finances, with John imposing an intolerably heavy and arbitrary tax burden in order to pay for royal extravagance, for infighting, for wars with the French and for crusades. The royal judicial system, whose tendrils extended ever deeper into the barons' lives, was used to extort cash and as an instrument of royal control, rather than to ensure 'justice'.

The King's finances had become unsustainable due to many factors. First, and most obviously, the King's need to pay for constant military protection for the Normandy estates created what modern-day macroeconomists would think of as an enormous structural deficit. If John had let his expulsion from the continent be the end of the matter this financial burden would have extinguished itself. But he did not. His folly was a series of vain attempts to reconquer Normandy, efforts which finally ended on the eve of Magna Carta.[3]

Second, the monarchic finances had taken a colossal hit in 1193 because of the need to fund a gigantic public sector bailout. Richard I had managed to get himself caught in Germany on his way back from the Holy Land and was held to ransom for £66,000 in silver. Being 'too big to jail', the equivalent of two to three times annual Crown income was needed to bail him out. In comparison, the government's peak cash support to UK banks in 2007–10 amounted to a trifling one-quarter of annual UK government revenues.

This would have been bad enough on its own. What was even worse was that it had come only five years after the collection of the 'Saladin Tithe', a windfall tax of a similar amount, in order to pay for a campaign to wrestle Jerusalem out of the hands of Salahuddin Ayubi, who had captured it in 1187. That cost the barons one-tenth of all their revenues and movable property.

Third, the need to raise additional cash for the public finances was made much more problematic by the strain of inflation, which accelerated in the early years of the thirteenth century.[4] The problem was that a large proportion of regular Crown income came in the form of 'farms', which were fixed rental payments for leases to use the King's land for agriculture. These farms were fixed by custom in nominal terms, whereas the King's expenditures were not. The King's finances were unhedged.

The preferred way of hedging the risk was to kick the leaseholders off the land and bring it into direct demesne management.[5] This is what the barons themselves had been doing with their own landholdings. By bringing it into demesne control, instead of receiving a fixed nominal rent, the lord of the manor could take receipt of the real output of the land, which could be consumed, traded or sold for silver at the going spot price. The consequence was that the richer the baron, the more land he had to exploit and the greater his potential profits.

The effect was to create a massively wealthy elite, now breaking free both of the middling ranks of the gentry at one end and of the hard-pressed King (or public sector) at the other. In all of this, the option of demesne management was unfeasible for the King, likely because it would have involved destabilising relations with the administrative class of sheriffs and other royal officials upon whom the King's political stability depended.

Given the countless other abuses of authority that were going on at the time, one wonders why it was so problematic for the rents simply to be 'renegotiated' periodically. In part, custom dictated that this was not the done thing. In part, the problem lay with the sheriffs in each of England's counties.[6]

Forget royal infighting, wars or the whiff of revolution, it is inflation that really sets the pulses of central bankers racing. And for good reason because closer inspection suggests that inflation may have been a significant catalyst to Magna Carta.

Historians estimate that prices were rising sharply in the early 1200s. The prices of agricultural goods, including wheat and oxen, probably doubled in that period.[7] Evidence suggests that prices of linen, wax, lead and even palfreys – the Toyota Prius of medieval horses – were also rising rapidly.

Wages were rising as well – and to a greater extent than if the increase had just been the consequence of medieval real-wage resistance. King John was paying his knights almost three times as much as his father Henry II had done.[8] The daily rate for foot soldiers had doubled. And limited evidence suggests the wages of skilled labourers on the Crown estates probably increased by a similar proportion.[9] With pay growth approaching 20 per cent a year, wages really were fizzing.[10]

The underlying causes of this inflation are debated among historians, but the most convincing argument is that the inflation was a monetary one, albeit with a twist. Not surprisingly, the quantitative information on the thirteenth-century money supply is of poor quality, imputed, as it has been, from archaeological finds of cash hoards.[11]

Paul Latimer notes that 'between the middle of the twelfth century and the middle of the thirteenth century there was an enormous increase in the quantity of silver coins in England'.[12] As well as the possibility of a general increase in the European silver supply (especially with the opening up of the Harz silver mines in eastern Germany), it is likely that silver inflows to England in particular were boosted as the counterpart to a sizeable private trade surplus – probably resulting, especially, from the success of the wool trade with Flanders. Over several decades, these silver inflows were likely to have more than offset the 'public sector deficit' as silver leaked out to pay for the protection of Normandy as well as the occasional trip to the Holy Land. As a result, the balance of payments was probably in surplus for years, with the consequent increase in the silver money supply going unsterilised.

Even to a thirteenth-century Englishman, global monetary conditions mattered. Would Britain's constitutional history have been different had King John lamented, 'A central bank! A central bank! My kingdom for a central bank!'? He needed one because other factors reinforced monetary developments, including the usual suspect – financial innovation. Specifically, developments in the common law made land an increasingly liquid asset, and therefore one capable for the first time of being used as a store of wealth.[13]

This set a medieval financial accelerator in train (about 750 years before Ben Bernanke coined the term)[14] by providing an alternative to storing one's wealth in silver coin (prone to being whisked away by the King). This led to a reduction in the demand for silver money balances. An increase in money velocity would have followed and with it, all else being equal, price inflation until the transactions demand for silver had risen sufficiently to equal its supply. At the very least, the existence of an alternative store of wealth provided an environment in which money velocity *could* take off, were it to be nudged in that direction.

One possible nudge was the anticipation of the recoinage of 1204.[15] Recoinages were good for the King because he benefited from the fees paid to have coins melted down and reminted. They were bad for cash holders both because of those fees and because they had to exchange their clipped coins for what they were actually worth based on their metallic value, rather than their face value (a medieval haircut – some of which were appalling). Consequently, there was a strong incentive not to be the one holding the old-issue coins when the music stopped.[16]

To sum up: a fiscal squeeze exacerbated by accelerating inflation combined with monarchical ambition and incompetence to stretch and then break relations with the barons.

MAGNA CARTA'S ENDURING CONSTITUTIONAL SIGNIFICANCE

In that context, Magna Carta was a desperate (and probably disingenuous) attempt at a peace treaty that failed almost immediately. Brokered by the Church, and issued by King John in June 1215, the Charter sought to placate the disgruntled barons. It is doubtful that John ever intended to uphold his side of the bargain, with all the constraints on his authority that this implied. Indeed, within a few months of its agreement, by the end of August 1215, John had convinced Pope Innocent III to annul the Charter on the grounds that it had been issued under duress.[17] So the 1215 Magna Carta was never enacted, and England slipped into the First Barons' War.

Charters of this type were not uncommon at that time. It had been fairly routine, in fact, for English kings to attempt to curry favour with the nobles upon whom the stability of their realm depended by rubbishing the reputations of their predecessors and issuing 'coronation charters' that demonstrated how virtuous and peace-loving they were by comparison. It was also fairly routine for kings to renege on the promises in those charters, creating fertile ground to begin the cycle anew.[18]

What was novel about Magna Carta was that (a) it was longer and more detailed than its predecessors, and (b) it was issued not at John's coronation, but under compulsion from a true political opposition, sixteen years into his reign and evidently too late to serve its purpose.[19]

This brings a second observation. Obnoxious and tyrannical as he might have been, King John was not solely to blame for the aristocratic discontent that had led to Magna Carta. His predecessors had reneged on their promises, mismanaged the realm and imperilled its finances. John's administrative and military incompetence was merely the straw that broke the camel's back.

If Magna Carta was such a product of its time, how did it become to be so venerated? And once we cut through the legend, what is its significance for economic governance today?

The revisionist interpretation of Magna Carta as a timeless statement of natural rights and liberties became imprinted on to the minds of the English-speaking world only in the seventeenth century. In large part, this was due to the work of Edward Coke. As well as being an enormously influential jurist, Coke was also the author of popular English legal textbooks that exported his views around the world. Finding words of old to suit his times, he resurrected the long-forgotten Magna Carta from 400 years of obscurity by appealing to its spirit in order to resist the absolutist tendencies of the Stuart kings James I and his son Charles I – themselves inspired by the continental European model of monarchic divine right. The Charter, Coke argued, could trace its lineage from an ancient constitution that harked back not just to the time of pre-Norman King Edward the Confessor, but (somewhat implausibly) to King Arthur himself: an ancient constitution that was now being imperilled – and with it the Englishman's rightful way of life – by the tyrannical behaviour of the Stuarts.

Despite the efforts of Coke and others, Charles I's rejection of all attempts to constrain his authority led to the English Civil War and to the King's beheading in 1649. Meanwhile, Coke's unstoppable Magna Carta redux had been set in motion.

In contradiction to their behaviour at home, James and Charles had been busily granting royal charters promising the liberties of Englishmen to the American colonists. Coke himself had been involved in the drafting of the first charter of the Virginia Company in 1606, and similar English liberties were extended in the charters of Massachusetts, Maryland, Connecticut, Rhode Island and Carolina over the next sixty years.

Some have argued that references to Magna Carta, however irrelevant its provisions might by then have been, were used as a way of inspiring New World settlers. To this day, twenty-five US states have extracts from Magna Carta on their statute books; a further seventeen have the full text. Goodness knows how the latter intend to enforce the removal of '[a]ll fish-weirs ... from the Thames, the Medway, and throughout the whole of England, except on the sea coast' (Clause 33). Of course, American extraterritoriality sometimes literally knows no bounds.

Coke's romantic resurrection of Magna Carta transformed it into part of the backdrop to the American Revolution, with his influence clearly evident in the drafting of the US Constitution.

MAGNA CARTA'S GENERAL PRINCIPLES AND ITS SPECIFIC INJUNCTIONS

We have seen how the economic forces and political developments of the time played a crucial part in the mounting hostilities between King John and the barons that led to Magna Carta and the First Barons' War. Given that background, it is not as shocking as it first seems that Magna Carta is very largely taken up with the parochial interests of the rich. It is dominated by three basic themes: taxes; abuses of the 'judicial system' with the aim of raising revenue; and the protection of the barons' mercantile interests.

Given how irrelevant those specific concerns now seem, it is hardly surprising that almost all of the Charter's clauses that survived the 1225 reissue (and therefore made it into the law in the first place) have since been repealed. In fact, only four clauses of the original sixty-six remain. These stand out as different in character from the others. They are much more general, universal and time-less. They are:

- Clause 1: Freedom for the Church.
- Clause 13: Protection for the 'ancient liberties' of the City of London.
- Clause 39: No wrongful imprisonment. Perhaps the most famous clause. 'No free man shall be seized or imprisoned, or stripped of his rights or possessions, or outlawed or exiled, or deprived of his standing in any way, nor will we proceed with force against him, or send others to do so,

except by the lawful judgment of his equals or by the law of
the land.'
– Clause 40: Justice is not for sale.

Added to that, the spirit of Clause 12 of the 1215 Magna Carta
(dropped from all later reissues), that 'no "scutage" or "aid" may be
levied in our kingdom without its general consent', is clearly what
would later become 'no taxation without representation': to establish a council (the embryonic embodiment of what would later
become Parliament) to agree whatever new taxes the King might
demand.

Whatever their purpose at the time, the more universal clauses
that remain on the statute book resonate today. They encompass the
ideas of the rule of law and of due process as a means of ensuring
justice. It is tempting, therefore, to think of these clauses as the
enduring legacies of Magna Carta, while at the same time to
patronise the juxtaposition of these apparently fundamental principles alongside so much antiquated gibberish about fish weirs, the
obligation to construct bridges and the theft of wood for building
castles.

This would be a mistake. The specificity of the clauses animates
the general principles of the treaty. It is because they are detailed
and targeted the concerns of the time that they are genuine attempts
to place a boundary on the King's authority, rather than relying on
vague platitudes.[20] And this, we shall see, is the case with the modern
'constitutions' that govern money.

Magna Carta was nowhere near the first attempt to encapsulate
ideas of justice and good government, nor was it the last. Indeed, it
was a spectacularly unsuccessful attempt – and it was anyway
concerned only with the interests of a very small segment of society.
But, largely because King John's heirs were forced into a tight corner
and therefore obliged to reissue the Charter again and again after
1215 (in 1216, 1217, 1225, 1234, 1253, 1265, 1297 and 1300, to cite
only the more famous reissues), Magna Carta has become the icon
of the principle that the exercise of authority requires permission
from those subject to that authority – and that, once granted, this
permission can just as easily be withdrawn.

In the monetary sphere, it has taken societies centuries to determine the relevant powers and permissions. The gold standard assumed consent and was undermined when the society refused to be ruled by an arbitrary fixed peg. In the ensuing decades, countries searched for a new political order to ensure that money retains its value. They would find that the most successful approach, constrained discretion, adopted the values of Magna Carta.

TOWARDS A CONSTITUTIONAL ORDER FOR MODERN MONEY

At its most idealised, Magna Carta makes clear that power derives from the people and constrains the authority of the state. The state can in turn devolve power to regions and independent bodies, but their power must remain in check. Constitutional law theorists have grappled with the delegation of authority for centuries, and the issue has reached a new zenith today with the expansion of the administrative state.

In order to function within a democracy, the authority of independent bodies must be constrained, allowing them to do only that which is necessary to pursue specific objectives, and they must be accountable to the people for their performance.[21] It took three centuries for the Bank of England's constitution to embody these principles fully – a delay that explains some of the UK's historical challenges with maintaining the value of money.

This imprecision has meant that various answers have been given over time to the simple question 'What is the Bank of England for?' The Bank's founding charter of 1694 explains that its original purpose was to 'promote the publick Good and Benefit of our People'. What that meant in practice at the time was pithily summarised by the diarist John Evelyn, who recorded the event more than 300 years ago in the following terms: 'A publick bank ... set up by Act of Parliament ... for money to carry on the war'. The war in question was against France, and in return for the monies raised the Bank received both income and banking privileges: it was soon the only bank allowed to be constituted as a joint-stock company, and had an effective monopoly of the note issue in the London area.

By the first half of the nineteenth century, the Bank had become the core of the financial infrastructure. Its notes were the accepted means of settlement between banks, with the Bank effectively acting as the banker to other banks. Commercial banks held Bank of England notes in place of gold, relying on the Bank's credibility for ultimate convertibility.[22]

Despite the Bank's founding aim of public service, it was criticised as late as the mid-nineteenth century on the grounds that, at times of financial stress, it would act in its own rather than the public interest by protecting its gold reserves to the detriment of its customers. That criticism faded as the Bank gradually assumed the role of lender of last resort (see Chapter 3), adopting essayist and economist Walter Bagehot's principle that it should lend freely against good collateral at penalty rates in times of crisis.[23]

By the end of the nineteenth century the Bank of England had informal responsibility for a broad range of policy areas. It remained the fiscal agent for the government. It maintained monetary stability through the operation of the gold standard. And it promoted financial stability through its role as the effective lender of last resort, and more generally – through the judicious exercise of the Governor's eyebrows – as the institution which managed and resolved financial crises.[24]

The Bank of England was brought into public ownership in 1946. As former Governor Eddie George remarked, for the half-century that followed 'the Bank operated under legislation which, remarkably, did not attempt to define our objectives or functions'. They were, instead, 'assumed to carry over from [the Bank's] earlier long history'.[25] In that regard, the Bank's 'constitution' resembled that of the United Kingdom, comprising a rich history of law, principle and convention.

While the Bank's responsibilities varied over the following decades, they remained broad and largely informal until 1997. During this period, the value of money suffered a precipitous decline, with the devaluations of the 1950s and 1960s, followed by the high and volatile inflations of the 1970s and 1980s. There were

a series of banking crises and cycles of booms and busts in the housing market. Sterling suffered a series of foreign exchange crises and
was devalued in 1949 and 1967 before the break-up of the Bretton
Woods system in 1971. Periodic balance of payments crises would
follow, with acute strains in 1976, in 1985 and following the 'Black
Wednesday' ejection in 1992 from the Exchange Rate Mechanism
of the European Union. In the half-century from the nationalisation
of the Bank of England until the granting of monetary policy independence, cumulative inflation was 2,200 per cent.

Quite simply, money was losing its value.

Although the government had formal responsibility for monetary
policy during this period, the credibility of all authorities, including
the Bank of England, suffered during the period of high and volatile
inflation. The experience demonstrates the growing complexity and
interconnectedness of modern money, and the need for a comprehensive, transparent and accountable approach to maintaining its
value.

Modern money is not backed by gold, land or some other 'hard'
asset. Modern money is all about confidence. Confidence that:

- the banknotes that people use are real not counterfeit;
- money will hold its value and that it will not be eroded away
  by high inflation;
- the burden of debt won't skyrocket because prices and wages
  fall in a deflation;
- money will be safe in banks and insurance companies, and
  that it won't disappear even if there's a depression, a
  financial crisis or a pandemic.

People want to be confident in money so they can worry about more
important things, like saving for a new home, to pay for their children's education or to secure their retirement.

Maintaining that confidence requires both sound institutions and
broad public acceptance. That confidence can be shaken by any
surprise or disappointment. A failed bank. High and volatile inflation. Counterfeits. Operational failures in public authorities

including central banks. Confidence is drained by mystique and secrecy.

Modern money is backed by the actions of central banks not by the gold that lies within them. The tried, trusted and robust way to maintain confidence in public money is an independent central bank. This means legal safeguards and clear goals together with democratic accountability to ensure broad-based public support and legitimacy. While not fully immune from the temptation to cheat, central banks have proven the most effective safeguards of society's economic and political interests in a sound currency.

I learned early on as a governor that a central bank might be effective but it wasn't sexy. The first spring when I was Governor of the Bank of Canada, I began to hear a tour bus every forty-five minutes outside my window. The guide would say, 'That's the Bank of Canada – they have the world's second biggest gold reserves in there,' and I would think, 'No we don't, we sold our gold in the 1990s.' After a few days of this, I thought I had better set the record straight in case there was a growing number of Canadians who might inquire about all of the gold that 'disappeared' under my watch. So I asked a colleague to call the tour company to let them know that our money was backed not by gold but by 'the Bank of Canada's conduct of an independent monetary policy to deliver low, stable and predictable inflation'. I never heard the bus pass by again. No amount of carefully considered technocratic decisions have the allure of gold. Even though they are more than worth its weight.

Central banks have two broad objectives both central to the value of money: monetary and financial stability.

Monetary stability means ensuring that money's value can be depended on. It is achieved by producing the highest-quality bank-notes that people can use with confidence. That's why polymer banknotes contain sophisticated counterfeit protections ranging from holographic images to ultraviolet features. And it is achieved by keeping inflation low, stable and predictable. This price-stability objective is currently defined by the 2 per cent inflation target.

Financial stability means ensuring that the financial system can support the nation's households and businesses in bad times as well as good. That requires the financial system, which creates most of the money that we actually use, to be resilient enough to continue lending to households and businesses when economic shocks occur. And it means that macroeconomic downturns are not made worse because of unsustainable debt burdens.

It requires:

- ensuring the safety and soundness of the banks and building societies that hold people's money;
- maintaining the resilience of the financial system as a whole;
- ensuring that any failures of institutions are orderly and do not affect the system more broadly;
- providing a wide range of liquidity to banks and other financial institutions in order to promote the continuous functioning of the financial system during shocks; and
- operating the core of the payments system, RTGS, which processes over £600 billion worth of bank-to-bank payments per day to the highest standards of efficiency and resilience;[26] every purchase from an app to a home ultimately settles through the Bank of England every day.

To illustrate why it can be difficult to achieve the objectives of monetary and financial stability, recall that the gold standard failed when political constraints overrode the measures needed to restore external balance and therefore to maintain gold convertibility. The UK's experience with inflation is a stark example of what can happen when short-term political considerations coincide with tough decisions required by monetary authorities.

Prices in the UK were anything but stable during the 1970s and 1980s. With the collapse of the Bretton Woods system in 1971, UK monetary policy lost its nominal anchor. There followed a series of botched experiments, with targets for incomes, monetary aggregates and the exchange rate. The costs of such failures were enormous, with prices rising by 750 per cent in the twenty-five years to 1992, more than over the previous 250 years combined.[27] This distorted price signals, inhibited investment, damaged the productive potential of the economy and hurt those least well-off. Unemployment was high (averaging just under 8 per cent) and volatile (with a standard deviation of 2.8 per cent).

Although the value of low and stable inflation was widely recognised, delivering it proved challenging. Even if the economic situation was not quite as fraught as in 1215 when the Magna Carta was struck, it was serious enough to lead eventually to a change to the monetary constitution that could prove as enduring in that sphere as the Magna Carta has proven to be in the political one.

This was because the instrument that affects inflation most powerfully – monetary policy – also affects output and employment, at least in the short run. This tempted authorities, influenced by governments, to promise low inflation in the future, but then to renege, lowering interest rates in order to boost activity. Electoral cycles reinforced this predisposition. Firms and households began to anticipate these incentives, and eventually pre-empt them.

This time inconsistency was resolved by first having society choose the preferred rate of inflation, and then delegating operational responsibility to the monetary authority to take the necessary monetary actions to achieve that objective. By 'tying the hands' of authorities, better outcomes for both inflation and unemployment became possible.

Removing political considerations from the conduct of monetary policy makes possible a credible commitment to low inflation. But they require strong accountability mechanisms and transparency to legitimise that independence and maintain its public consent. In the 1990s, led by New Zealand and Canada, a number of countries adopted inflation-targeting frameworks in independent central banks that embodied these approaches.

THE NEW UK FRAMEWORK FOR THE BANK OF ENGLAND

The Bank of England Act in 1998 represented the most comprehensive adoption of these insights.[28] The Act clarified the Bank's responsibilities and granted independence to the Bank for the operation of monetary policy. In delegating authority to a new independent body, the Monetary Policy Committee (MPC), the Act ensured that the Bank would operate under 'constrained' rather than 'unfettered' discretion.[29] The Act gave the MPC a clear remit to achieve the inflation target over the medium term, and delegated to it the decisions regarding how to achieve it.[30] The MPC was made accountable to Parliament for operating the instruments of monetary policy to achieve the objectives of monetary policy, as determined by the government.[31]

At last, the spirit of the Magna Carta had made it to monetary policy.

The operational independence of the Bank of England is an example of power flowing from the people via Parliament within carefully circumscribed limits. Independence in turn demands accountability in order that the Bank commands the legitimacy it needs to fulfil its mission. By publishing its analysis, giving testimony and delivering speeches, the Bank explains how it is exercising its powers to achieve its clearly defined policy remits. Under constrained discretion, the Bank takes its orders from the remit and is accountable to Parliament and the people for its performance.

The gains from independence have been enormous. In the two decades that followed independence, inflation averaged just under 2 per cent compared with over 6 per cent in the preceding two. It's been one-fifth as volatile. Crucially, independence allowed monetary policy to respond boldly and effectively to the biggest financial crisis in a century. And it leaves the Bank well placed to address a range of possible developments around Brexit.

The experience of the past few decades has taught a few important lessons.

First, it has underscored the importance of flexibility in inflation targeting. A major improvement to the inflation-targeting framework itself was to confirm explicitly (beginning with the 2013 remit) that the MPC is required to have regard to trade-offs between keeping inflation as the target and avoiding undesirable volatility in output. In other words, the MPC can use the full flexibility of inflation targeting in the face of exceptionally large shocks to return inflation to target in a manner that provides as much support as possible to employment and growth or, if necessary, promotes financial stability. For example, even though monetary policy could not prevent the weaker real income growth likely to accompany the transition to new trading arrangements with the EU, it can influence how this hit to incomes is distributed between job losses and price rises.

The second lesson is more fundamental. The changes in 1997 reflected the belief that price stability was the best contribution a central bank could make to macroeconomic stability and by extension to the broader public good. This represented a narrowing of central banks' focus and a deconstruction of the old model of central banking.

While there were enormous innovations of enduring value during this period, the reductionist vision of a central bank's role that was adopted around the world was fatally flawed. A healthy focus on price stability had become a dangerous distraction. While inflation remained under control, financial vulnerabilities built inexorably during the 2000s and then crashed with the debacle of the global financial crisis.

The global financial crisis was a powerful reminder of the imperative of financial stability. Advanced economies were in the midst of an era known as the Great Moderation: a long period of uninterrupted growth combined with low, stable and predictable inflation. The crisis made it obvious that central banks had won the war against inflation during this time only to lose the peace.

The costs were enormous. The complete loss of confidence in private finance that occurred in 2008 could be arrested only by public support that totalled $15 trillion in bailouts, government guarantees of bank liabilities and special central bank liquidity schemes. In the UK, real wages experienced their weakest decade of real growth since Karl Marx wrote the *Communist Manifesto* in the mid-nineteenth century. Trust in the system collapsed.

As shocking as the crisis was, it was hardly unique. These pressures have meant that across 800 years of economic history financial crises occur roughly once a decade. That's because of systemic problems in maintaining the value of money.

Financial policy decisions are subject to the same time-inconsistency problems as monetary policy. Financial lobbies are strong, and the temptations of a dash for growth are powerful. Lighter-touch regulation can provide a powerful boost to near-term activity, a temptation that is reinforced by governments motivated by electoral cycles and the complacency curve of the financial cycle. In the long run, the cost of such indulgence is financial and macroeconomic instability, lower growth and higher unemployment.

Conversely, there are no obvious or immediate rewards to the tough decisions necessary to avoid future crises. The costs of macroprudential interventions can be felt today but their benefits are often realised far into the future. These benefits – moderating downturns and avoiding crises – are not directly observable. The bad outcomes that macroprudential policies prevent have to be estimated. But counterfactuals are difficult to sell: 'it could have been worse' doesn't quite have the ring of 'you've never had it so good'.

All these complexities and uncertainties make it challenging to implement the right prudential policies and harder to communicate the rationales for them. Over time, and particularly during good times, these challenges can feed a bias towards inaction. As memories of the last crisis fade, complacency sets in and pressures to ease policies re-emerge. When it comes to financial stability, success is an orphan.

A lesson from the financial crisis is that trust can be undermined not just through a loss of certainty about the future value of money, but also through a loss of confidence in banks or even a loss of faith in the financial system itself. In other words, both monetary stability and financial stability are essential to maintaining public confidence in money.

Central banks have a primordial responsibility to act as the guarantors of trust and confidence in money because of their status as monopoly issuers of currency. This naturally gives them control over the quantity of money and interest rates – monetary policy. It also means that a core part of financial stability policy – acting as lender of last resort to private financial institutions at times of financial stress – falls to them.

It has now been recognised that they have a core responsibility to prevent the build-up of vulnerabilities in the first place. That means maintaining the safety and soundness of banks and insurers by ensuring they are adequately capitalised and have resilient funding and liquidity. And it means safeguarding the stability and resilience of the financial system as a whole both by managing the financial cycle and by addressing structural risks in financial institutions and markets.

That's why, in the wake of the 2008 financial crisis, a number of central banks were given increased responsibilities for addressing risks in the financial system. For example, the Bank of England was radically overhauled, reuniting responsibilities for monetary and financial stability under the direction of three independent committees: the MPC, the Financial Policy Committee (FPC) with responsibility for setting macroprudential policy, and the Prudential Regulation Committee (PRC) with responsibility for maintaining financial stability and the safety and soundness of banks and insurers.[32] The Bank has been given clear remits by Parliament for these responsibilities, has operational independence to use its powers to achieve them and is accountable to Parliament and the people for its performance.

ACCOUNTABILITY, TRANSPARENCY AND LEGITIMACY

Delegating responsibility to an independent central bank to take the tough decisions necessary to support the value of money is well supported in both theory and practice. But, as the Magna Carta makes clear, these central banks can never forget from whence their power came or to whom they are responsible. Their authority is limited to what's necessary to achieve monetary and financial stability, and they are accountable to the people for their performance. To support the value of money they need the values of resilience and trust. To maintain the value of money they need the values of accountability, transparency and legitimacy.

Just as the gold standard failed when it lost public confidence, the effectiveness of independent central banks will not stand the test of time without continual public support. As became apparent when I started at the Bank of England, that support must be nurtured. On my first day, I learned of a growing controversy over the lack of diversity of the characters on our banknote. With the selection of Winston Churchill to replace the prison reformer Elizabeth Fry on the £5 note, there would be only male characters on the Bank's suite of four notes (apart from Her Majesty the Queen who graces one side of each note).

A public campaign led by the author and activist Caroline Criado Perez rightly pointed out that this was hardly representative of British society and presented a petition to have a female character replace Charles Darwin on the £10. I gathered the Bank's team of experts to discuss what I had assumed would be a relatively straightforward decision. I was told triumphantly that the Bank couldn't be legally found to have discriminated because the characters on the notes were chosen from the deceased and 'you cannot discriminate against dead people'. Leaving aside the dubious legal merits of this interpretation of the European Human Rights Act, many of my colleagues and I felt this rather missed the point. Money that doesn't reflect the diversity of the society it serves will divide rather than unite. So one of the greatest writers in English literature, Jane Austen, was quickly chosen to appear on the £10 note.

And we went further by abolishing the old system in which the Governor alone chose the character in favour of a public process for nominations supplemented by advice from an expert panel and guided by criteria that stressed that the banknotes that people carried every day should celebrate the full diversity of great British historical figures and their contributions in a wide range of fields. We recognised that it wasn't enough that the Bank was committed to that objective. We needed people to have confidence in our commitment to diversity. A few years later it was natural that, after a process in which we received almost a quarter of a million public nominations for scientists and mathematicians, we chose Alan Turing for the £50 note.

Turing's accomplishments were legion. His 'indispensable' code-breaking contributions at Bletchley Park during the Second World War arguably helped shorten that conflict by a few years, saving countless lives.[33] The advances he made in cryptanalysis then – including co-inventing the Bombe computer for solving ciphers and applying statistical techniques to speed up rates of decryption – were pivotal in cracking the hitherto unbreakable German Enigma code. Turing devised the foundations of computer science,[34] played a vital role in the development of early electronic computers after the war[35] and founded the field of morphogenesis in biology (the study of how plants and micro-organisms develop their shapes). A visionary as well as a revolutionary, he recognised that 'This is only a foretaste of what is to come and only the shadow of what is going to be.'[36]

Both Austen and Turing represent the best of the United Kingdom. Austen's writing is still extraordinarily popular over 200 years after her death. Current advances in computer science, artificial intelligence and even future forms of money stand on Turing's giant shoulders. Austen and Turing also represent those in the UK whose accomplishments and potential were not recognised in their lifetimes. Austen published her works anonymously as female writers were not valued, and only found acclaim decades after her death. In 1952, Turing was convicted of gross indecency for his private relationship with a man, avoiding prison only by submitting to chemical castration. The conviction ended his career and he died shortly thereafter from cyanide poisoning.

THE FOUNDATIONS OF MONEY

Placing figures such as Austen and Turing on banknotes is one way of rectifying past wrongs and bestowing recognition on those who deserve it. But it is more than that. The value of money and the legitimacy of the Bank come from people's trust and their belief in the fairness and integrity of the system. Large segments of the UK population have been treated unfairly throughout history, including by institutions like the Bank of England. Today the Bank must work on gaining and maintaining the trust of the people of the United Kingdom. Committing to diversity and inclusivity is essential to putting the right values behind the value of money.

The effectiveness of the Bank of England's monetary and financial policies rests on good governance, transparent conduct of policy and clear accountability to Parliament and the public. The expectations of the public have changed dramatically since former Governor Montagu Norman's remark in 1930 when pressed by the Macmillan Committee to explain the Bank's actions: 'Reasons, Mr Chairman? I don't have reasons, I have instincts.'

That was not a response I would have dared to venture during my fifty-odd parliamentary testimonies. The age of informal responsibilities, nods, winks, secrecy and instinct is long past. The need for the Bank to be open and accountable is greater than ever, not only because of the growing distrust of institutions and the 'experts' who reside within them, but also because better public understanding makes our policies more effective.

Since operational independence was granted to the Bank, there have been a raft of improvements to its communications. Transparency has steadily increased with initiatives ranging from publishing detailed assumptions underlying forecasts *ex ante* to assessing their accuracy *ex post* as well as the simultaneous release of monetary policy summaries, minutes and inflation reports. Layered communications have been introduced with simpler, more accessible language and graphics to reach the broadest possible audience.

The Bank conducts extensive outreach to improve accountability and maintain public consent. It publishes all relevant information for each policy decision on the day it is released, discloses the key judgements underlying its forecasts and accounts for differences when they occur. The Bank also meets with thousands of businesses every year and tens of thousands of people who attend town halls and public forums, and hundreds of thousands more through social media.

During my time as Governor, these were simultaneously the most challenging and most enjoyable parts of the job. Challenging because meeting with the public meant shedding the safety of technical jargon, statistics and coded references. Challenging because people ask the most basic questions, such as 'what is money?' or 'when am I going to get a pay rise?'

When I was contemplating joining the Bank of England, one of my reservations was whether the UK public would accept a foreigner in such a prominent role. I was reassured that 'Once you go north of Birmingham, the Governor of the Bank of England is an alien creature. No one will know the difference.' This struck me as odd, and I was pleased to see that the Bank had an extensive and growing programme of regional visits. I would find that these were when I would feel most at home.

It was clear we could do more than meet with local businesses. So we substantially extended those visits to include meetings with third sector groups to get a better sense of the impact of the weak recovery on people and to hear their concerns. We instituted town hall meetings and citizens panels to hear directly from those far removed from the concepts of monetary and financial stability and constrained discretion but directly affected by their applications. And we visited a huge range of schools, aided by the creation of a teaching module for economic decision making that has now reached one in five state schools across England and Wales.

I was particularly struck by the school visits. Lots of them were in deprived areas where half the children were on free school meals and many were coming from families in which no one had worked for three generations. The younger children were wide-eyed and optimistic, while the teenagers were inquisitive and wanted to know how much money I made ('not as much as a footballer'), what kind of car I drove (disappointingly a Ford Galaxy) and why we don't all just use Bitcoin ('because it doesn't work': see the next chapter).

My core objectives in these visits were to explain that the Bank's job was to maintain confidence in money, to make the world of finance seem less alien and to advise the students that if they pursued their interests they were likely to be successful on their own terms. My example was personal: I had gone to state school like theirs, in a part of my country that was also far away from its centres of business, media and government. I had studied economics because I was interested in understanding better how the world works, and I had worked at the intersection of the public and private sectors to try to make it work better. I had never set out to be the Governor of the Bank of England (and if I had sought the post out

I would never have achieved it). I was there because of an accident of history, but that accident was possible because I was doing something I loved. And if a clown like me from the far north of Canada could become the Governor of the Bank of England, there was no reason why they couldn't as well.

Afterwards, I would wonder how much of that message sank in, beyond the bit about my being a clown with which they clearly agreed. Then, a few days after one such visit to a secondary school in the north-east, I received a letter from a mother telling me that her son had returned from the talk with new enthusiasm for his studies and plans for the future. She scrawled at the end of the note in large capitals, 'Such visits change lives.'

That is a clue to what gives money its value: resilience, solidarity, transparency, accountability and trust.

The Future of Money

Bliss was it in that dawn to be alive;
but to be young was very heaven!
*William Wordsworth, 'The French Revolution as it
Appeared to Enthusiasts at its Commencement'*

To its advocates, the wave of innovation sweeping through the world of financial technology promises nothing short of revolution. Fintech heralds the dawn of narrow banking and portfolio optimisation. It will change the nature of money,[1] shake the foundations of central banking and deliver nothing less than a democratic revolution for all who use financial services.

It would be foolish to dismiss such claims out of hand when new general-purpose technologies are transforming a host of industries from retail to media and education. Incumbents seldom anticipate the scale or pace of change. By their nature, revolutions become conventional wisdom only in retrospect.

Consider a previous new dawn. In marvelling at the possibilities that the combination of technology and finance had created at the start of the twentieth century, Keynes remarked that:

> The inhabitant of London could order by telephone, sipping his morning tea in bed, the various products of the whole earth … he could at the same moment and by the same means adventure his wealth in the natural resources and new enterprises of any quarter of the world … or he could decide to couple the

security of his fortunes with the good faith of the townspeople of any substantial municipality in any continent that fancy or information might recommend.[2]

Such global portfolio management was made possible by technological developments stretching back decades, ranging from the 'pantelegraph' of the 1860s – capable of transmitting signatures to verify bank deposits – to the cable buried deep beneath the Atlantic that could transmit eight words a minute. Such remote trade confirmation and low latency made the 'flash boys' of the day possible.

The financial globalisation these innovations enabled was built on a much earlier, simpler and more profoundly transformational development: the ledger. For there is no finance without the ability to record transactions, compare balances and assess obligations. Money and credit, the universal instruments of commerce, could not exist without this most fundamental of financial technologies, which allows debits and credits to be netted off; debt to circulate as currency; money to replace memory; and, with it, trade to expand exponentially.

How much have we progressed since Keynes' bed-ridden globalisation?

Replace 'telephone' with a 'tablet' and 'tea' with a 'soy latteccino' and you have the start not of the twentieth century but of the twenty-first, a century in which opportunities are no longer limited to men or denizens of the City. The second great wave of globalisation is cresting. The Fourth Industrial Revolution is just beginning. And a new economy is emerging, driven by immense changes in technology, the reordering of global economic power and the growing pressures of climate change.

The Covid crisis has added to the disruption. Supply chains are becoming more local and resilient. Digital integration is accelerating. And the resulting 'great reset' of company and national strategies offers renewed opportunity to tackle climate change and promote the transition to a net-zero economy.

The extent to which finance continues to democratise and transform depends on superficially arcane, but fundamentally vital, enabling technologies. The emergence of mobile telephony, the ubiquity of the internet, the availability of high-speed computing, advances in cryptography and innovations in machine learning could combine to enable rapid changes in finance – just as they have in other areas of the economy.

THE NATURE OF MONEY
ALWAYS EVOLVES

It would be hubris to think that the current model of independent central banks represents the end of monetary history.

There has been a series of monetary innovations over the centuries. Most have failed, succumbing to the age-old temptations of debasement, but a few have changed the nature of money for the good. Both outcomes are now possible as a result of the current flurry of innovation around money and payments systems. The trick will be determining which innovations to support and which to suppress in the pursuit of value.

Throughout history, the most promising monetary innovations have originated in the private sector to serve the changing nature of commerce. The first-known banknotes were developed in seventh-century China during the Tang and Song dynasties, in order to allow merchants and wholesalers to avoid carrying heavy copper coins in large commercial transactions. Marco Polo introduced the concept to Europe in the thirteenth century, and notes would become increasingly common, though not without problems in retaining their value, in the seventeenth and eighteenth centuries.

Banking adapted to support growing cross-border trade during the Renaissance. Italian banking dynasties in fourteenth- and fifteenth-century Florence, like the powerful Medici, were foreign exchange dealers for the currencies of varying quality that circulated through the trade routes of Europe. After rising from humble beginnings operating a money-changing stall outside Cavalcanti Palace to become bankers to the Vatican, the real coup of the Medicis was to pioneer bills of exchange as a way of managing burgeoning medieval trade. These promises to pay that were passed from one merchant to another could be used as payments in their own right or sold to the bank to raise cash.

Fractional reserve banking developed to provide the capital needed to expand trade and industry from the seventeenth century onwards. Its core skills of information gathering, credit judgement and loan monitoring broadened the application of Smith's invisible hand at the price of greater risks to financial stability. To maintain the value of money central banks would have to become increasingly involved as supervisors of the private banks and, *in extremis*, as their lenders of last resort.

Today, private money is created in the non-bank sector (not least by pensions, insurers and various asset managers) and it can help individuals to manage their risks and grow their savings. However, as we will see in Chapter 7, the non-bank financial sector today is in much the same position as fractional reserve banking was in the nineteenth century. Good practices are mixed in with the bad, resilient institutions interconnected with the fragile, such that non-bank finance can itself become a source of risk to value in society.

Into this tradition of change comes the fintech revolution in money and payments. It is being driven by several factors.

First, money is changing in response to the fundamentally transformative technical innovations, such as advances in cryptography and artificial intelligence, as well as the powerful network effects in social media. After all, if 'likes' are the social currency of this generation, could they be the economic currency of the next?

More fundamentally, monetary innovations are responses to the broader reorganisation of the economy and society into a series of distributed peer-to-peer connections across powerful networks.[3] People are increasingly forming connections directly, instantaneously and openly, and this is revolutionising how they consume, work and communicate. Yet the financial system continues to be arranged around a series of hubs and spokes like banks and payments, clearing and settlement systems. Even if the current generation of money-like substitutes, such as cryptocurrencies and stablecoins, are not the answer, they are throwing down the gauntlet to the existing payment systems, which now need to evolve to meet the demands of fully reliable, real-time, distributed transactions.

Public authorities need to create the right environment to support such private dynamism.

The new economy is placing new demands on finance. Consumers and businesses increasingly expect transactions to be settled in real time, checkout to become a historical anomaly and payments across borders to be indistinguishable from those across the street. Money and payments could be organised to exploit the greater efficiency and resilience made possible by smart contracts. The system could be adapted, according to personal preferences and societal norms, either to increase privacy surrounding financial transactions or alternatively to realise greater opportunities from pooling personal data.

And yet, for all the hype, the innovations in everyday payments in western countries have thus far been more apparent than real. Most of the changes have happened around payment initiation – the methods used to make a purchase – which has switched to contactless credit cards, smartphone mobile wallets and banking apps. The underlying payments infrastructure is basically the same – transactions run on credit card or banking 'rails' and they involve digital money.

That money is created by private banks (as we saw in Chapter 4). To the extent that people think about it (and most naturally don't), they take comfort from the facts that the banks are regulated by central banks and that any deposits they have in private banks are insured by the state up to a certain limit (currently £85,000 in the UK and over $100,000 in Canada).

This system is convenient but relatively expensive, with costs running at between 0.5 and 2 per cent of the transaction value. It also can be slow, with payments taking up to three days to reach a merchant. Cross-border payments can cost as much as ten times more, discouraging competition and limiting consumer choice.

But the beginnings of more transformative innovations are also apparent. Ant Financial, the Chinese payments giant has a billion customers – five times more than the largest US bank. Together with WeChat Pay (an affiliate of Tencent), it handles almost 90 per cent of all mobile payments globally. Paytm, an Indian payments platform, has well over 300 million clients, many of them small businesses. The next stage will be to integrate these private payment systems with public ledgers and backstops.

In addition, the fastest-growing lenders to small and medium-sized businesses are online marketplaces and digital payments providers, like Stripe and Shopify, which can improve credit scoring and speed of lending decision through their access to superior customer data.

THE GROUNDING OF PRIVATE MONETARY INNOVATIONS

At this time of intense innovation, the public custodians of money must be both constructive and vigilant. Constructive means providing a platform for private innovation. Central banks should be as open to new providers as they are to traditional players. This means equal access to key central bank facilities like real-time wholesale payments systems, the ability to place deposits and access short-term liquidity.[4] But it also means the same regulation for the same activities, irrespective of whether the provider is primarily a bank, a non-bank financial services company or a tech company. That consistency is part of being vigilant, so that the new money is as secure, reliable and trusted as the old money.

Central banks must also be alive to the possibility that the rise of private money-like alternatives could mark the beginnings of a shift in public confidence in response to a series of crises. As the saying goes, 'trust takes years to build, seconds to break and forever to repair'.[5] The financial crisis undermined public trust in the private financial system and raised questions about the effectiveness of public oversight. The enormous expansion of public debt in response to the Covid crisis coupled with large-scale purchases by central banks – unprecedented in peacetime – could create the conditions to shake public confidence in money.

Indeed, this book will argue that one of the important contributions of rebalancing values will be to maintain the value of public money. That doesn't mean holding back the tide of innovation. Rather it means supporting it in a way that reinforces the core values behind money. The future of money must be trusted, resilient, fair, inclusive, transparent, accountable and dynamic. Fundamentally, the public response to private innovation must ensure that the new system serves the public. That means the new system of money and payments must meet a number of requirements.

It must be resilient and trustworthy. New forms of money and payments must be as resilient as the existing system while offering better services to customers. When economic shocks hit, the new money should hold its value (monetary stability) and all the institutions that touch it should remain reliable (financial stability). Money must also be operationally resilient, robust in response to unusual events and never prone to technical outages.

It must be accountable and transparent by protecting privacy and preserving customer data sovereignty. Cash is anonymous, and there is an expectation that private banking details will remain private, within the constraints of the laws that guard against money laundering, the financing of illicit activities or terrorism. New electronic forms of money will need to define the boundary between anonymity and customer-sanctioned access to private information in order to provide improved services.

It is simply untenable in democracies that the core of the monetary system could be based on forms of electronic private money whose creators control large blocks of the currency, like Bitcoin, would have privileged access to customer data or payments systems (like some stablecoins) or whose backing is prone to the types of debasement that has, eventually, consistently occurred with private money such as note-issuing banks like the Bank of Amsterdam.

As we saw in the previous chapter, transparency and accountability are essential for maintaining public support (and ultimately consent) for policies necessary to maintain monetary and financial stability. These can neither be run by algorithm nor be the ultimate responsibility of the private sector.

It must improve fairness by increasing financial inclusion and promoting solidarity. New forms of money and payments must make good on their potential to democratise financial services by opening access to all. That means dramatically lowering the costs of payments, banking and cross-border transactions including remittances. And it means promoting competition for customer services. All network externalities in new forms of money should accrue to the benefit of the public.

Promoting solidarity means never going back to forms of money, like the gold standard, where the burden of adjustment falls most heavily on one class, labour. Rather, it means taking full advantage of new technologies to create a more flexible economy that makes more regular, smoother adjustments, instead of building large imbalances and vulnerabilities that are then brutally resolved.

It must support economic dynamism by offering new services and providing cheap, efficient and secure payments. New services could include pooling data for more efficient access of small business to growth capital, integrating with smart contracts to improve efficiencies from finance to commercial trade and making cross-border commerce indistinguishable from domestic activity. New payment systems must be scalable. After all, money is a social convention, a network. The more people that use it, the more useful it is. To be effective, the forms of money must be at least as efficient at large scale as they are at smaller ones. At present, this is a marked deficiency of most crypto-substitutes.

BUILDING ON PUBLIC FOUNDATIONS

It is fair to say that central banks will not imagine the possibilities that could be opened up by the current wave of financial innovation. Instead, they should create as level a playing field as possible for private innovation while ensuring that the new system respects the core values underpinning money: trusted, resilient, fair, inclusive, transparent, accountable and dynamic.

This means two things. First, the core of the system must continue to be public money, even though the nature of its connection to private money may change radically. The promise on UK banknotes to 'pay the bearer' carries the unconditional backing of the state, something no current form of retail electronic payment can claim.[6]

The backstop of the current system of private electronic money is that users can always shift their holdings into cash. These new forms of money should mimic the use of cash for physical transactions by delivering cash-like certainty. This means finality of payments such that when a payment is made it is irrevocable. If someone hands over a £10 note for a round at the pub, their debt is instantly settled, the publican has the cash in hand and can immediately use it for another transaction as they see fit. It is one of the jobs of central banks to ensure finality of payments so that businesses and customers can transact with full confidence.

Second, for the new system to maintain the values of sound money, central banks will continue to provide a series of public backstops to maintain public trust in money. Specifically that means: securing underlying money in the form of (electronic) cash or the unit of account; ensuring finality of payments; providing support for scalability in times of stress by proving liquidity needed for the system to function; and overseeing the payments system as a whole because it will only be as strong as its weakest link.

EVALUATING THE THREE CURRENT OPTIONS

Everyone can create money;
the problem is to get it accepted.
Hyman Minsky[7]

Consider how well three major innovations – cryptocurrencies, stablecoins and central bank digital currencies (or CBDCs) – stack up when measured against these core functions and fundamental values.

As we shall see, the electronic pretenders to the monetary crown currently fall short on most criteria, but the revolution they have launched will overthrow the old regime. This disruption can be embraced because, provided we maintain our focus on the values that underpin sound money, the future of money will support a more dynamic and inclusive economy.

First, some definitions. There are two types of money: account based and token based. Token-based money includes familiar examples ranging from Yap stones to banknotes. The intrinsic value of the token is basically worthless, but the power of social convention brings widespread acceptance. For that to endure requires the right institutional backing.

Account-based money started to take off when deposit banks, like the Bank of Amsterdam, became widespread in seventeenth-century Europe. It uses intermediaries, typically banks, to complete transactions when the account of the payer is debited and that of the payee is credited. These can be at the same bank or different ones, with the final settlement at the central bank. Account-based money is how most (over 95 per cent) of our money is held.

These bank balances are digital currency in the sense that they are electronic entries in a ledger maintained by our bank, but this is basically the same architecture of account-based money as existed in the seventeenth century, even if the speed and convenience of payments has vastly improved.[8] This is also true for forms of account-based money on innovative payment apps from non-bank payment service providers, such as Apple Pay, Venmo or Stripe.

The current system of electronic money is two-tiered. At the lower tier, as we have seen in the discussion of fractional reserve banking in the previous chapters, banks create private money by making new loans. These loans are supported by the banks' capital and funded by deposits.[9] Transactions between banks settle in the upper tier in central bank reserves, which is account-based money that the private banks hold at the central bank.

This system has several advantages. It ensures finality of payments. It facilitates core central bank activities such as providing liquidity to the financial system during times of stress, acting as lender of last resort and engaging in asset purchases through quantitative easing.

Elements of this system could be adapted to help deliver the promise of the fintech revolution. For example, central bank reserves are electronic public money, but they are not available to the wider public. One option for the future of money is to make them so (under a variant of a CBDC). Another is to allow private currencies to become the medium of exchange.

The first unapologetic challengers to the old monetary regime are cryptocurrencies. Cryptocurrencies are token-based digital assets rather than currencies because it is far from clear that they fulfil the functions of money. These digital assets are based on networks that are distributed across large numbers of computers, which allow them to exist outside the oversight of governments and central authorities. The word 'cryptocurrency' is derived from the encryption techniques that are used to secure the network. Techniques that, as we saw in the previous chapter, have their origins in some of the work conducted by the 'face' of the next £50 Bank of England physical note, Alan Turing.

In the depths of the global financial crisis, the coincidence of technological developments and collapsing confidence in some banking systems sparked the cryptocurrency revolution. Its advocates claim that a decentralised cryptocurrency, such as Bitcoin, is more trustworthy than centralised fiat money because:

- its supply is fixed and therefore immune from the age-old temptations of debasement;
- its use is free from risky private banks; and
- those who hold it can remain anonymous and therefore free from the ravenous eyes of tax authorities or law enforcement.

Some also argue that cryptocurrencies could be more efficient than centralised fiat money because the underlying distributed ledger technology cuts out intermediaries like central banks and financial institutions and allows payments to be made directly between payer and payee.*

---

* Whereas banks hold records of most fiat money and are entrusted to ensure its validity, with digital currencies, the ledger containing all transactions by all users is publicly available. Rather than placing trust in central institutions – such as banks (and by extension the centralised authorities like the Bank of England that supervise them) – reliance is placed on the network and the rules to update the ledger reliably.

In this spirit of dystopian fear and libertarian optimism, the message accompanying the first or genesis Bitcoin block read: 'The Times 3 Jan 2009 Chancellor on brink of second bailout for banks.'

CRYPTOCURRENCIES AND THE ROLES OF MONEY

How well cryptocurrencies fulfil the roles of money has to be judged against the functioning of the entire cryptocurrency ecosystem which extends beyond the currencies themselves to the exchanges on which cryptocurrencies can be bought and sold, the 'miners' who create new coins and verify transactions and update the ledger, and the wallet providers who offer custodian services.

The charitable answer is that cryptocurrencies act as money, at best, only for some people and to a limited extent, and even then only in parallel with the traditional currencies of the users.[10]

Cryptocurrencies are proving volatile short-term stores of value, exhibiting price fluctuations that can lead to gains or losses of 50 per cent within months. Over the past five years, the daily standard deviation of Bitcoin was ten times that of sterling. And Bitcoin is one of the more stable cryptocurrencies.

This extreme volatility reflects in part the fact that cryptocurrencies have neither intrinsic value nor any external backing. Their worth rests on beliefs regarding their future supply and demand – ultimately whether they will be successful as money or as a hedge against the debasement of other forms of money.

The most fundamental reason to be sceptical about the longer-term value of cryptocurrencies as money is that it is not clear how they will ever become effective media of exchange and therefore they are unlikely to become units of account. In short, few retailers accept cryptocurrencies. Transactions are very slow and highly carbon intensive. Ultimately, the scalability of cryptocurrencies will likely rely on the netting of transactions within digital wallets, a framework that, as described below, is better suited to central bank digital currencies.

Unlike every other successful money in history, crypto-assets are not the liability of any individual or institution nor are they backed by any authority. Bitcoin is backed by an algorithm. Many are beset by governance issues, such as the concentration of ownership that makes them prone to manipulation. Even though they were set up in opposition to it, cryptocurrencies piggyback on the same institutional infrastructure that serves the overall financial system and therefore on the trust that it provides. This reflects their difficulties in establishing their own trust in the face of cyber-attacks, loss of customer funds, limits on transferring funds and inadequate market integrity.

Finally, cryptocurrencies, when used as money, raise a host of issues around consumer and investor protection, market integrity, money laundering, terrorism financing, tax evasion and the circumvention of capital controls and international sanctions. To the extent that they are used for transactions rather than speculation, many cryptocurrencies seem more attractive to those active in the black or illegal economy. This adds to their trust deficit and means that once they are brought into the regulatory net – as all forms of money eventually are – their attractiveness as money will diminish.

Cryptocurrencies are not the future of money. But that is not to dismiss them. Some could be valued for their fixed supply (to the extent they can resist debasement) and low correlations with other assets. That is how some view Bitcoin. If enough people take the subjective view that Bitcoin is a safe haven against inflation, uncertainty or shocks, then there will be demand for it as an asset rather than as money per se. Its high volatility and relatively low correlation with traditional assets, such as stocks and bonds, create a hedge similar to that of gold. To the extent that a social convention forms behind this type of digital gold, however, it would be a convention subject to the risks of a regime switch to a different safe haven, a switch that could be triggered by governance challenges, new regulation or future innovations in digital money. Time will tell whether such a coordinated view of the subjective value of Bitcoin holds.

More immediately, the core technologies behind cryptocurrencies are already having an impact on the future of money. Indeed, crypto-assets help point the way to the future of money in three respects:

- by suggesting how money and payments will need to adjust to meet societies' changing preferences, particularly for decentralised peer-to-peer interactions;
- through the possibilities their underlying technologies offer to transform the efficiency, reliability and flexibility of payments; and
- by means of the questions they raise about whether central banks should provide a CBDC accessible to all.

STABLECOINS

The revolution launched by cryptocurrencies has spawned private stablecoins, which, although their initial designs have some serious flaws, could significantly advance the future of money.

Unlike cryptocurrencies which are backed by nothing more than an algorithm, stablecoins are cryptocurrencies that are pegged to (and therefore backed by) another underlying asset, such as gold or oil, or a fiat currency like the US dollar or euro. Stablecoins combine several technical elements of cryptocurrencies, including their token-based form and the use of distributed ledger technology for transaction verification, but they are enhanced by the credibility of the underlying asset. The highest-profile examples of stablecoins, such as Libra, are best thought of as payments systems rather than money *per se* since they derive their moneyness from the underlying sovereign currencies.

Even if stablecoins are not money, they could change its nature. By stabilising the price of the 'coin' through the link to an underlying asset, stablecoins are much more capable of serving as a means of payment and stores of value than cryptocurrencies. Therefore, they could help create global payment systems that are faster, cheaper and more inclusive. Stablecoins could integrate with digital wallets and smart contracts, making real-time distributed, low-cost peer-to-peer transactions a reality. And they create the possibility of an alternative payment system outside of the banking or credit-card-based systems, while substantially lowering the costs of cross-border payments.

The welfare gains could be huge. Despite significant improvements in recent years, current payment systems still have two major failings: lack of universal access to financial services for a large share of the world's population and inefficient cross-border retail payments. Globally, 1.7 billion adults do not have access to a transaction account, even though 1.1 billion of them have a mobile phone.[11] As transaction accounts are gateways to additional financial services such as credit, saving and insurance, the lack of access to such accounts impedes financial inclusion.[12] Already, mobile wallets and mobile money, like Kenya's M-Pesa, have demonstrated the potential step-change in financial inclusion.

Stablecoins are at their heart payments systems, but by creating money-like instruments for transactional purposes, people might be encouraged to hold them as stores of value outside of the conventional financial system, for example in digital wallets. In that case, authorities should apply the principle of the same risk/same regulation to ensure that stablecoins meet the same standards as commercial bank money with respect to stability of value, the robustness of legal claim, the ability to be redeemed in full (at par) in the underlying fiat currency and the resilience of the payments ecosystem.

Moreover, if a stablecoin like Libra (rebranded Diem), linked to the world's dominant social media platform Facebook with over 2.5 billion users, went mainstream, much of the money in the economy could end up outside of the formal banking system. This would fundamentally change the supply of credit to the real economy and the dynamics of monetary and financial stability.

One of the biggest issues with stablecoins is the nature of their backing. For those backed by a currency, such as the dollar or sterling, to meet the standards of fiat money this backing must be absolute, irrevocable and risk-free for all time. It is hard to see how this could be accomplished without the full cooperation of the central bank that issues the underlying fiat currency.

As Agustín Carstens stresses, private stablecoins should heed the governance lessons from the failure of the Bank of Amsterdam.[13] With time, 'binding rules' for private money are almost inevitably loosened unless governance is robust, transparency complete and public oversight vigilant. The Bank of Amsterdam went from one-to-one backing of 'bank money' with gold to making surreptitious loans. What would stop stablecoins backed with a fiat currency from gradually taking on interest rate, credit, counterparty or even currency risk? Absolute clarity and legal certainty on these aspects are essential. In addition, stablecoins would need to address significant issues, including who would provide liquidity under stress, the appropriate protection of data privacy and addressing potential for money laundering, terrorist financing and other forms of illicit finance.

CBDC

Ultimately, it is highly likely that only a publicly accountable institution could fulfil the governance, liquidity and operational requirements for a stablecoin to work consistently through time. In this respect, the credibility of central banks is compelling. The most likely future of money is a central bank stablecoin, known as a central bank digital currency or CBDC.

A CBDC would be an electronic form of central bank money that could be used by the public to make digital payments. Currently when we make payments with our debit cards or mobile phones we are using private money originally created by banks. Our only access to the ultimate risk-free asset of the central bank is when we use physical cash. Its use is declining rapidly, and this is creating new opportunities and risks. The possibility now exists to combine the convenience of digital payments with the ultimate safety of central bank money.

If properly designed, a CBDC could serve all the functions to which private cryptocurrencies and stablecoins aspire while addressing the fundamental legal and governance issues that will, in time, undermine those alternatives. It could open up new possibilities with the 24/7 availability of payments, different degrees of anonymity, peer-to-peer transfers or scope for paying interest on a currency.

It is likely that the best structure for a CBDC would be a two-tiered system, where consumers have an indirect claim on the

CBDC via an intermediary, which can be a bank or a digital wallet (such as Apply Pay or Facebook's Calibra). This would improve the efficiency because the vast majority of payments could be crossed within and between the wallets. A two-tiered system would also improve resilience if the 'narrow banks/wallets' that held the indirect CBDCs were supervised by the central bank. And it would create opportunities for private innovation including integration into smart contracts and, depending on consumer preference, the pooling of data to improve digital services to them.

One important consideration is the public's direct access to the CBDC, which would be the ultimate risk-free asset, the true digital equivalent of cash. At present, people can convert their commercial bank deposits into cash (though of course fractional reserve banking means that not everyone can do this at the same time). In a wholly digital world, if they had the same right, depending on the design, it could lead to instant bank runs. A two-tiered structure would eliminate the financial stability risk of a run to the CBDC (either if customers had direct access to central bank accounts as would be the case in a one-tier account-based system or if they had seamless access to a token-based retail CBDC).

But if people couldn't convert their holdings, would the state be providing them with adequate financial protection? A compromise would be a form of hybrid structure which allowed people access to a certain amount of CBDC, perhaps akin to current deposit insurance thresholds.

Other design issues include whether interest should be paid on the CBDC. It would obviously reinforce the attractiveness of holding money in digital cash and thereby increase the fragility of the banking system. Conversely, it would also give the central bank the ability to charge negative interest rates, something which is currently limited by the fact that cash yields zero (actually slightly negative once the cost of storage is taken into account).

Who should take responsibility for the enforcement of Know Your Customer and anti-money-laundering regulation? Under what terms could customer data be accessed? Would it be for the benefit of better targeting customer services with their consent? Or would it be used to balance privacy rights with the extent to which the information in a CBDC could be used to fight terrorism and economic crime?

A major concern is that, if not properly designed, a CBDC could lead to the central bank crowding out the private sector in both the gathering of deposits and the allocation of credit. Once again, that argues for limiting the scale of direct access by the public. If not, a general-purpose CBDC could mean that central bank balance sheets could grow so large that they disintermediate commercial banks in normal times and run the risk of destabilising flights to quality in times of stress.[14]

A revolution in the future of money has begun. Its origins are driven by fundamentals: new technologies which make new forms of payments possible and a new economy which creates tremendous demands for change. Public authorities need to channel this energy and innovation so that new money serves people better. They must be guided by the enduring values that have underpinned sound money through the ages.

SOCIAL INTERACTION AS CREDIT

A few years ago, the Bank of England had a competition in which schoolchildren were asked what money meant to them. The response was fantastic, but one submission in particular caught my attention. It was a video from Charles Darwin secondary school in Kent – appropriately since Darwin had appeared on the £10 a few years back. But the young woman who submitted the work had anticipated an evolution of a different sort, a kind of natural selection of money. The imagery was of idyllic nature scenes, with a squirrel husbanding resources. Naturally, there were selfies of the characters participating that were then posted. Each member of the cast racked up followers, bringing a smile to the videographer's face, and prompting her to go shopping. The stores in this future world accept only followers, while the indigent on the street beg for someone to follow them.

Initially I thought, 'Of course, I remember high school: to a teenager that's what's valued – the approval of their peers. Popularity.'

But on reflection I realised that followers were akin to what Adam Smith defined as the process of human interaction and exchange through which we develop our moral sentiments. In Smith's theory of 'mutual sympathy', the act of observing others and seeing the judgements they form makes people see how others perceive their behaviour (and therefore become more aware of themselves). The feedback we receive from perceiving (or imagining) others' judgement creates an incentive to achieve 'mutual sympathy of sentiments' that leads people to develop habits, and then principles, of behaviour, which come to constitute their conscience.

In Smith's day, 'likes' established social mores. Now, 'likes' can be monetised. Those who compile widely followed Spotify playlists are well rewarded. Well-liked Instagrammers and YouTubers turn their proven popularity into lucrative advertising dollars, creating their own crowded trades in trending goods, new styles and popular memes. Moral sentiments are market sentiments. Likes and traffic are used by social media companies to target ads, to improve services. We are liked and this boosts validation.

And social interaction measured by data is being used to shape moral (or at least normative) behaviour. China is piloting the tracking of social behaviour via the Social Credit System to create a form of a national reputation system. The initiative builds unified data records of individuals, businesses and governments that can be tracked and evaluated on their trustworthiness. There are multiple variants, with some rating reputations numerically and other having simple white and black lists. Social credit scores have been used to restrict access to air and rail transportation, or conversely to reduce waiting times at hospitals and government agencies.

Supporters of the Credit System claim that it helps improve social behaviour and enhance 'trustworthiness' including timely payment of taxes and bills and the more general promotion of moral values. Critics claim that it infringes the legal and privacy rights of individuals and organisations, diminishes personal dignity and could be used for surveillance.

So money is going full circle. Once based on trust, trust is becoming money.

*   *   *

The experience of money down the ages shows that, for any form of money to endure, trust must be grounded in much more than a simple rule or tradition, however long-lasting.

From the early clipping of coins to the Bank of Amsterdam to Bitcoin, time and time again the temptations to cheat and debase have proven too great. From the banking dynasties of the Medicis to the monetary triumphs of the Great Moderation, time and again success has bred complacency, and complacency has brought crisis. Shocks to the system must be met with tough decisions that trade off short-term pain for longer-term gains. Sound money ultimately needs, at the core of the system, the public institutions to take these decisions in the pursuit of monetary and financial stability. This will mean that some private innovations are eventually drawn into the public sphere and adapted to serve broader public aims.[15]

From the Magna Carta to the gold standard, we have learned that the ability of authorities to take those tough decisions will lack the essential credibility if public institutions are not properly grounded and public consent is not maintained.

For money to be sound it must be trusted. It must hold its value and be part of a financial system that maintains confidence by being resilient to shocks. Resilience requires the right institutional backing, institutions with clear mandates, the right tools to achieve them and the political and public accountability. The key institutions behind the value of money, particularly central banks, need to nurture and maintain the consent of the public. As Hobbes argued, people will cede some of their freedoms to the state in return for their protection. If it fails to provide that protection, the state loses the right to rule. That bargain has been clear with respect to Covid-19. With fear on the march, people were willing to surrender to Hobbes' 'Leviathan' such basic rights as the freedom to leave their homes.

And so it is with money. People will support the delegation to independent central banks of the tough decisions that are necessary to maintain the value of money provided the authorities deliver monetary and financial stability. And they must do so transparently and fairly. And they must be held accountable for their actions.

If these values are kept at the forefront, the future of money holds great promise. It can support both greater economic inclusion and renewed economic dynamism. New forms of finance will always develop to try to meet the changing needs of the economy and to take advantage of new technologies. Many of these innovations will be old wine in new bottles, but a few will be truly vintage. Authorities must know how to spot the difference, and then they need to adapt the institutions backing money so that the economy benefits from dynamism, while money remains trusted, reliable and resilient. Indeed, so important is the value of money that nothing central to its functioning can remain long outside of some form of public supervision.

If money is resilient, responsible, transparent, dynamic and trusted, it will be valued. And then it can be used to value. Determining the scope and terms under which a monetary price affects our values is the subject of the next chapter.

6

The Market Society and
the Value of Nothing

At some point, every North American child learns a sentimental story by the American writer O. Henry. It tells the tale of a newlywed couple one Christmas Eve. Virtually penniless and desperate to find a gift for her husband Jim, Della Young sells her long tresses of hair and uses the proceeds to buy a platinum chain for his beloved watch. When they are reunited that evening for dinner in their small, draughty apartment, she discovers that Jim has just sold his watch to buy a set of combs for her hair. Although they are left with gifts that neither can use, the Youngs realise how far each was willing to go to show their love for each other, and how priceless their love really is.

When I first heard the story, it had its desired effect. I momentarily forgot about the hockey stick I had been coveting and thought more about my mother's need for new slippers. It is in the giving that we receive. Of course, I was only eight and hadn't yet learned the true economic meaning of Christmas.

To many economists, gift giving is fraught with inefficiencies of which the Youngs' 'coordination failure' is only an extreme example. For example, Joel Waldfogel's analysis of the 'deadweight loss of Christmas' calculates a primitive loss in utility that results from 'imperfect' gifts in kind rather than efficient gifts in cash.[1] He attributes the practice of presents over payments to 'the stigma over cash giving'.[2] If only the Youngs could have overcome this stigma, they could have efficiently swapped $20 notes so each could buy what they really wanted.[3]

No consideration is given by Waldfogel or his editors of the prestigious economics journal the *American Economic Review* or at the Princeton Press to the idea that the 'stigma' against monetary gifts may reflect 'norms worth honouring and encouraging like attentiveness and thoughtfulness'.[4] Perhaps they never reached the end of O. Henry's tale: 'But in a last word to the wise of these days let it be said that of all who give gifts these two were the wisest. Of all who give and receive gifts, such as they are wisest. Everywhere they are wisest. They are the magi.'[5]

This juxtaposition of magi and merchant captures much of the story of value thus far. In economics, the combination of subjective value and marginalism changed the perceptions of value from the intrinsic characteristics of a good or service to its exchange value, its price in the market. In the process, the importance of distribution of income and the distinctions between productive and unproductive activities were downplayed, and, with them, corporate purpose and national ideals were devalued.

Today, this economic approach to value has spread widely. Market value is taken to represent intrinsic value. And if a good or activity is not in the market, it is not valued. We are approaching the extremes of commodification as commerce expands deep into the personal and civic realms. The price of everything is becoming the value of everything.

What impact will this have on the values of society, its ability to create value, and more precisely to improve the welfare of its citizens?

A SOCIAL CONTRACT FOR INCLUSIVE GROWTH

Market-based economies have generally relied on a basic social contract comprised of relative equality of outcomes, general equality of opportunity, and fairness across generations. Different societies have placed different weights on these elements but few omit any of them. Societies aspire to this trinity of distributive justice, social equity and intergenerational equity for at least three reasons.

First, there is growing evidence that relative equality is good for growth. More equal societies are more resilient, they are more likely to invest for the many not the few, and to have robust political institutions and consistent policies.[6] And few would disagree that a society that provides opportunity to all of its citizens is more likely to thrive than one which favours an elite, however defined.

That symbiosis between just and economic outcomes is increasingly backed by hard evidence. For example, a comprehensive OECD study using data from the period 1970–2010 covering thirty-one OECD countries measured at five-year intervals finds that inequality has a statistically significant negative impact on economic growth.[7] In particular, it estimates that for a number of countries including the US and UK cumulative growth between 1990 and 2010 would have been more than one-fifth higher had income disparities not widened. In contrast, the data suggests that decreases in inequality in Spain, France and Ireland over the time period helped increase the GDP per capita in all three countries. On the other hand, greater equality helped increase GDP per capita in Spain, France and Ireland prior to the crisis.

Similar results are obtained by IMF researchers who find that existing rates of inequality are harmful for growth, even when controlling for redistribution.[8] There is a strong negative relation between the level of net inequality and growth in income per capita over the subsequent period. In addition, inequality has a statistically significant negative relationship with the duration of spells of growth.[9] A one-Gini-point increase in inequality is associated with a 6 percentage point higher risk that the spell will end the next year.[10] While some studies have found a short-term positive relationship between economic growth and inequality,[11] a wide range of research has found that inequality is associated with both slower and less durable growth particularly over the long term.[12] This holds for rates of growth over long periods of time,[13] the level of income across countries and the duration of growth spells. The few exceptions to these findings tend to pick up ambiguous short-run correlations.[14]

The channels through which greater inequality slows growth are not limited to weaker and more volatile aggregate demand but extend to a meaningful drag on overall growth from higher inequalities of opportunity. The evidence backs the intuition that greater inequality can be self-reinforcing and growth limiting, with fewer investments in their skills by those who are less well-off and less public investment in education and infrastructure to benefit the many.[15] Moreover, these negative effects of inequality on growth are self-reinforcing. Income inequality exerts a greater drag on growth in economies characterised by low equality of opportunity (as measured by intergenerational mobility).[16]

Second, research suggests that inequality is an important determinant of relative happiness and that a sense of community is a critical determinant of wellbeing.[17] Extensive analyses across countries and over time have found that the most important contributors to whether people are flourishing, enjoying their lives and feeling fulfilled are:

- their mental and physical health;
- the quality of their human relationships;
- the sense of community;
- their work;
- their incomes; and
- the general social climate (including freedom, quality of government, peace etc.).[18]

The relationship between income and happiness is complicated. Although it is less important than community and mental and physical health, absolute and relative income are still significant. More importantly, it is non-linear in that above a certain threshold (about $75,000 in the US) more money doesn't make people happier.[19] But a little bit of extra money to the least well-off can make a significant difference to the individual's happiness and society's aggregate welfare.

There has certainly been no improvement in happiness alongside the spread of markets into more walks of human interaction, and there is no definitive relationship between growth and happiness.[20] While there is a variety of potential explanations for these results, one plausible candidate is the steady expansion of the competitive sphere into our lives. Richard Layard bemoans the increasing prevalence of the testing of children and the ranking of education and health professionals. These are approaches that make success personal and individualistic rather than the result of improving the happiness and welfare of others. Evidence suggests that it breeds stress and dissatisfaction, even among the 'winners'.

Third, recalling that economics is part of a broader ethical and moral system, the trinity of inclusive capitalism appeals to a fundamental sense of justice.[21] The American philosopher, John Rawls conducted a thought experiment by asking people what type of society they would construct if their choice were made behind a 'veil of ignorance' about their place in it. He settled on a version of the golden rule that can be found at the heart of many of the world's religions: do unto others as you would wish to have done to yourself.

As we shall discuss in Chapters 9 and 10, societies have given close consideration to how we treat the most vulnerable among us when tackling the threat of Covid-19. When pushed, from a health perspective, we have been Rawlsian, with the values of economic dynamism and efficiency joined by those of solidarity, fairness, responsibility and compassion.

From an economic perspective, more generally, who behind a veil of ignorance – not knowing their future talents and circumstances – wouldn't want to maximise the opportunities and welfare of the least well-off?

THE ECONOMIC CONTRACT

The social contract comprising relative equality of outcomes, absolute equality of opportunity and intergenerational equity seeks to maximise social wellbeing. It has moral as well as economic dimensions. In many cases, these are aligned; for example, policies to grow employment increase both income and the dignity of work. But tensions can arise, especially when economic policies do not acknowledge them.

Although economics has become the arbiter of value, many economists seek to portray it as being values neutral. To quote the popular book *Freakonomics*, 'morality represents the way we would like the world to work and economics represents how it actually does work', and that economics 'simply doesn't traffic in morality'.[22] Is it really that simple? Do the policy prescriptions of modern economic analysis really not have an underlying moral philosophy? And do economic relationships, particularly as they encroach on new spheres, really not affect 'the way the world does work' possibly in ways that 'we may not like' or predict?

As Tony Atkinson observed, in the tradition from Aristotle to Smith 'economics is a moral science' and economics journals 'are replete with welfare statements'.[23] When ethical considerations are taken into account in economic problems, a utilitarian approach to social justice is usually adopted (even if it is often not acknowledged). As discussed in Chapter 2, it matters whether the utilitarian approach is the simpler variant of Bentham in which individual utilities are added up on an unweighted basis as opposed to the welfarist approach of John Stuart Mill which more closely approximates the religious and secular traditions of maximising aggregate happiness.

The quotation from Mill with which Cass Sunstein begins his book on *The Cost-Benefit Revolution* makes the point in language that both evokes scripture and anticipates Rawls:

> I must again repeat, what the assailants of utilitarianism seldom have the justice to acknowledge, that the happiness which forms the utilitarian standard of what is right in conduct, is not the agent's own happiness, but that of all concerned. As between his own happiness and that of others, utilitarianism requires him to be as strictly impartial as a disinterested and benevolent spectator. In the golden rule of Jesus of Nazareth, we read the complete spirit of the ethics of utility. To do as you would be done by, and to love your neighbour as yourself, constitute the ideal perfection of utilitarian morality.[24]

Sunstein underscores the importance of a broad concept of welfare: 'People care about other things, including a sense of meaning or purpose. A good life is not merely "happy".'[25] He uses a series of real-world examples to demonstrate how a simple but common economic application of utilitarianism that focuses on maximising net monetary benefits (and thereby equating money with value) may be inconsistent with net welfare benefits, as a result, for example, of:

– the distribution (or incidence) of the gains and losses (recall the non-linear contribution of income to happiness), or
– unpriced benefits and costs related to the dignity of life, the avoidance of mental anguish and the hedonic benefits of increased convenience.[26]

New approaches to welfare look to expand the scope of the social contract, reversing the trend in which the pursuit of happiness has become equated with the pursuit of prosperity. Richard Layard appeals for a secular revolution guided by a new ideology of happiness. In his view, the objective of society should be 'to produce the greatest happiness we can – especially the least misery'. This requires a great deal of altruism, and a culture that encourages and grows this basic human trait.

The question in this chapter is related but more immediate: whether the expansion of the market is changing the underlying social contract on which it has been based. Has the emphasis on the individual over the community, our selfish traits over our altruistic ones, imperilled both the market's effectiveness in determining value and ultimately society's values? In short, in moving from a market economy to a market society, are we consuming the social capital necessary to create economic and human capital?

The risks to the market functioning should not be underestimated. We simply cannot take the market system, which produces such plenty and so many solutions, for granted. In recent decades, its widespread adoption has lifted billions of people out of poverty and helped extend life expectancy. And it is driving breakthrough technologies from genomics to artificial intelligence that could transform for the better the way we work, connect and live.

The genius of the market rests on a series of attributes that share what John Kay calls the disciplined pluralism of capitalism. This starts with the familiar invisible hand with prices as signals acting as far superior guides to resource allocation than central planning. And it extends to two other key, but less widely acknowledged, qualities. First, markets are *forces of discovery* via the chaotic process of experimentation through which the market adapts to change. Markets facilitate a process of trial and error where the successful ventures thrive and the unsuccessful are terminated. Second, markets diffuse political and economic power such that entrepreneurial energy is focused on the creation of wealth rather than its appropriation from others.

The market is essential to progress, but it doesn't exist in a vacuum. It is a social construct whose effectiveness is determined partly by the rules of the state and partly by the values of society. It requires the right institutions, a supportive culture and the maintenance of social licence. If left unattended or allowed to capture the political sphere, the market will corrode those values essential to its effectiveness.

As discussed in Chapter 16, sustained economic progress depends on inclusive economic institutions that allow and encourage the great mass of people to take part in economic activities that make the best use of their talents and skills. To be inclusive, economic institutions must include secure private property, an unbiased system of law and the public services that provide a level playing field in which people can exchange and contract. Education must be both of high quality and open to all, and people must be able to choose their own careers and be free to open new businesses. Even a passing familiarity with economic history reveals that these institutions which underwrite prosperity require investments in social as well as economic capital.

Social capital refers to the links, shared values and beliefs in a society which encourage individuals not only to take responsibility for themselves and their families but also to trust each other and work collaboratively to support each other. Social capital is the product of both institutions and culture. It includes what the Nobel laureate Douglass North referred to as 'incentives embodied in belief systems'.[27] It is possible that rising market supremacy has begun to squeeze out, corrode or (in the words of Pope Francis) distil broader values.

The examples are legion. As we saw in previous chapters, the value of money does not rely on a simple rule or even on a complex legal framework. It is ultimately grounded in the beliefs and consent of society, which must be first obtained and then nurtured. As we will see in the next chapter, when individuals and their firms do not have a sense of responsibility for their clients and the broader financial system, disaster awaits. And for the leading economies, an open and competitive political process is an essential complement of inclusive economic institutions. Capture brings failure.

THE SHIFTING BALANCE BETWEEN STATES AND MARKETS

The balance between the market and the state has shifted over time, with the markets gaining in stature, prominence and influence in recent decades. Although often wilfully misunderstood and widely derided, Francis Fukuyama's bold prediction in the wake of the fall of the Berlin Wall in 1989 that the world had reached the End of History is proving at least half right. Fukuyama's thesis did not anticipate the end of historical events, such as wars or financial crises, but suggested rather that the process of historical inevitability would culminate, not in Marx's predicted communist utopia, but in the combination of capitalism and liberal democracy as the best way of organising society.

As the economist Branko Milanović concludes, virtually every economy organised under capitalist terms (in the parsimonious definition of Marx and Weber) features modes of production privately owned, labour being hired and the coordination of production decentralised.[28] The world has moved well beyond the classical capitalism in which there are three distinct classes: landlords (as a purely rentier class that does not work), capitalists (who own the machinery of production and do not work) and workers (who work but own neither land nor machinery). But it is clearly organised on capitalist lines that can be grouped into two main camps: political, authoritarian capitalism and liberal, meritocratic capitalism.

The most prominent examples of political or authoritarian capitalism are China and Russia, though it also appears in parts of Asia, Europe and Africa. With 80 per cent of its industrial production from the private sector and the vast majority of its prices liberalised, China is clearly a capitalist, market-based system. It does not share, however, either the inclusive economic and political institutions or the liberal meritocratic order with which those in the west would be familiar.

A political capitalist system has three main characteristics: 1) an efficient technocratic and merit-based bureaucracy; 2) the absence of consistent application of the rule of law; and 3) the ultimate autonomy of the state. The system's legitimacy rests on its ability to deliver consistent growth which requires maintaining a difficult balance between a degree of legal and regulatory consistency and arbitrary rent seeking or outright corruption.

Many of the world's economies aspire to forms of liberal or meritocratic capitalism. That means meritocratic in that there is no legal constraint on people earning an income or having a position in society. And they are liberal through attempts to correct for initial differences in endowments through widespread education and in some cases inheritance taxes.

It is significant that the market is the organising framework not only for economies but also, increasingly, for broader human relations. In the west, the reach of markets has extended well into civic and family life, such that 'the whole of society is becoming the factory'.[29] In parallel, the social constraints on unbridled capitalism – religion and a tacit social contract – have been steadily eased.

The past is always sedimented in the present. Legacies of religious beliefs shape current social capital as recognised by thinkers from Adam Smith to Weber and Hayek. Marx argued that past modes of production coloured nineteenth-century relations between the working classes and bourgeoisie. And, as will be discussed in greater detail in Chapter 16, the relative positions of the state and markets today are the products of four revolutions in government each driven by new ideas, new technology and new threats.[30]

First, Thomas Hobbes helped inspire the development of the competitive nation state. In the seventeenth century when Hobbes wrote his masterpiece *Leviathan*, life was in his famous words 'solitary, poor, nasty, brutish and short',[31] punctuated by wars, revolutions and disease. As a consequence, added Hobbes, 'fear and I were born twins together'.[32] A state that could ease those fears deserved the people's support, much more than one that derived its legitimacy from the divine right of kings. Monarchies imposed order on the feudal barons, while the struggle for mastery in Europe improved their effectiveness. They used new technologies in ships and weaponry to expand their influence in search of mercantilist glory building far-flung colonial empires and launching commercial society.

The second revolution was the rise of the liberal state, inspired by Adam Smith and John Stuart Mill who argued that corrupt monarchical privilege should give way to liberal efficiency. Government shrank and became more efficient, not least as it was populated by a professional class of civil servants. The time of Gladstone in the nineteenth century was one of small government (no more than 20 per cent of GDP), free flows of trade and capital, limited domestic regulation and primitive labour market institutions. It was also a time of strong cultural institutions and the apogee of the Protestant work and social ethics.

The third development was the expansion of the doctrine of state protection that led to the creation of the welfare state. The watchword again was security but this time against maladies, misfortunes and inequalities. This would eventually spark the development of European social democracy and produce Lyndon Johnson's Great Society. The growth of the welfare state was spurred by new technologies (such as mass production and electrification) and new ideas about social justice.

Some, such as John Micklethwait and Adrian Wooldridge, argue that the challenge of Thatcher and Reagan to the welfare state represented a 'half revolution', during which Leviathan only 'paused to digest rather than go on a diet', and is now a 'grumpy, unloved compromise in which people who pay for it think it gets too much, but those who use its services think it gives them too little'.[33] They believe that in the west both the left and right have lost their way, with the former more loyal to the institutions of the welfare state, such as teachers' unions, than to their objectives, the quality of education; and the right captured by interest groups using small-state arguments to shower boondoggles on favoured industries.

There is much insight in such analysis about how to increase the effectiveness and efficiency of the state which we will examine in Chapter 16. However, fixating on the size of the western state risks missing its change in orientation. The institutions and culture of the state have become increasingly pro-market, particularly in the determination of value, with profound implications for both competitiveness and welfare.

The Thatcher–Reagan revolution fundamentally shifted the dividing line between markets and governments. To be clear, this change of direction was long overdue following the steady encroachment of the state into market mechanisms including the control of interest and exchange rates, the widespread use of incomes policies (extending at times to wage and price controls), widespread state ownership of commercial businesses and a steady proliferation of rules, regulations and bureaucratic red tape across large swathes of the economy.

The Thatcher–Reagan reforms reversed these trends and unleashed a new dynamism. Administrative controls were lifted. Exchange rates were freely floated, financial sectors were liberalised, and large swathes of the state were privatised. Taxes, particularly on investment, were cut. Perverse incentives discouraging work and entrepreneurialism were removed. After an initial period of adjustment, productivity growth picked up and aggregate incomes rose, but inequality also soared and values changed.

The political and social impact of the economic success of these measures was reinforced by the fall of communism at the end of the 1980s. By the time the political opponents of Thatcher and Reagan gained power (Clinton and Blair), pro-market ideas were central to their approaches to a range of economic and social issues. As time went on, these ideas graduated to conventional wisdom.

I realised this when, as a new Deputy Governor of the Bank of Canada having recently moved from the private sector, I met an urbane, deeply experienced Italian policymaker, Tommaso Padoa-Schioppa. At the time, he was a member of the Governing Board of the European Central Bank. He would later rise to be the Italian Minister of Finance and Chair of the IMF's powerful International Monetary and Financial Committee (IMFC) before his untimely death in 2010. I have met few individuals as wise.

I first encountered him at a breakfast of the G7 deputies while attending the IMF/World Bank Annual Meetings in Dubai in the fall of 2003. This group styled themselves as the informal steering committee of the global economy, heirs to the architects of the Louvre and Plaza exchange rate accords in the 1980s. But the discussion in a small, airless room in the Dubai conference centre was far removed from pacts hammered out in luxury settings and then bestowed on grateful financial markets. When our discussion shifted to exchange rates and Tommaso held forth on how the dollar was misaligned, a colleague interrupted, 'Misaligned to what? The dollar is priced in the world's deepest market.'

Tommaso drew in a short breath and lamented how far the received wisdom of market efficiency had come. The doctrine held that if a market is deep and liquid, it should always move towards equilibrium, or, said another way, 'it was always right'. The policymakers have nothing to tell the market, they had only to listen and learn. If markets move sharply away from a range that seems appropriate, the policymakers must humbly admit that there must be something they are missing that causes the market 'in its infinite wisdom' to behave the way that it does. But as Tommaso observed, 'when we grant an entity infinite wisdom, we enter the realm of faith'.

Faith can guide life but blind policy. This exchange took place during a time when the mindsets of public policymakers had fully absorbed pro-market radicalism in academia, in the discourse of political leaders and in patterns of social life where 'industry' and private finance were held up as 'masters of the universe'. This cognitive capture led to 'the self-cancellation of the policymaker's judgement: only the market knows'.[34] Such trust in the market reigned in the years following our G7 breakfast, unbridled faith which dictated that the only solutions to market failures were to add more markets or to reduce further regulation. As bubbles grew from housing to derivatives, the miracles of securitisation and synthetic risk sharing were extolled. We will explore the enormous costs of the ensuing crisis in the next chapter.

Shortly before his death with the crisis still raging, Tommaso warned of the immense challenge and the stakes in the struggle between states and markets.

> It took centuries to define and set up the appropriate
> constitutional relationship between the state and the church.
> The process was so long because politics and religion are linked
> and separate at the same time and both aspire to capture that
> totality of the person. They must be kept apart because they
> have to do with fundamentally different aspects of human
> experience – power and faith – and when the two contaminate
> each other, both deprave.
>
>   Political and economic activity too are linked and separate at
> the same time. They too are corrupted by contamination, but
> need to relate to each other. Power and wealth are two
> fundamentally different categories, and yet each may determine
> the fate of the other. The present crisis is not only a powerful
> reminder that the relationship between markets and government
> is still largely unsettled, it is also an event that may disrupt
> economic prosperity and democratic freedoms.[35]

And in the years since he spoke, the market has extended its scope and this mutual reliance has become dangerously unbalanced.

There has been a steady commodification of assets and activities – putting them up for sale – including of our free time.[36] Activities as diverse as cooking, essay writing, gardening and child-rearing can now be hired in the gig economy. This is the latest phase in the historical progression of commodification: first agriculture through the commercialisation of surplus production, then manufacturing, then industry and now services, with many people encouraged to do many jobs flexibly. The logical extreme predicted by Paul Mason, in his book *Postcapitalism*, is that the whole of society becomes the factory.

Michael Sandel takes a similar view that market values and market reasoning are increasingly reaching into spheres of life previously governed by non-market norms: procreation, child-rearing, health and education, sports and recreation, criminal justice, environmental protection, military service, political campaigns, public spaces and civic life.

While this greater commodification has made our lives better in many cases, it has often weakened personal ties and undermined social and civic values. The change in personal and civic relations is drawing on social capital and altering the social contract. The question is whether we will reach Milanović's predicted endpoint of 'a utopia of wealth and a dystopia of personal relations'.[37]

THE SOCIAL CONTRACT IS
BREAKING DOWN

There is a growing sense that this basic social contract is breaking down. That unease is backed up by hard data. Within societies, virtually without exception, inequality of outcomes both within and across generations has demonstrably increased.

The big drivers of technology and globalisation are magnifying market distributions. Technology's impact on inequality is felt across all economies, while globalisation's contribution is principally felt in advanced economies.[38] Moreover, returns in a globalised world are amplifying the rewards of the superstar and, though few of them would be inclined to admit it, the lucky. Milanović argues that these forces are being reinforced by the structure of modern capitalism, in which the wealthy have both labour and capital income, earn higher returns on their capital, have better access to top schools (social mobility) and can influence the political class.[39]

Now is the time to be famous or fortunate. As Michael Lewis remarked to the Princeton graduating class, 'Success is always rationalised. People don't like to hear success explained away as luck – especially successful people. But you are lucky to live in the richest society the world has ever seen, in a time when no one actually expects you to sacrifice your interests to anything.'[40]

There is also disturbing evidence that equality of opportunity has fallen, with the potential to reinforce cultural and economic divides. For example, social mobility has declined in the US, undercutting the sense of fairness at the heart of American society. Miles Corak finds that the elasticity of a son's adult earnings with respect to his parents' earnings – the intergenerational elasticity – rose from 0.3 to 0.55 between 1950 and 2000 in the US. Corak also shows that intergenerational earnings elasticity tends to be higher in more unequal countries, a phenomenon termed the 'Gatsby Curve' by Alan Kruger.[41]

Intergenerational equity is similarly strained across the advanced world. Social welfare systems designed and enjoyed by previous generations will prove, absent reform, unaffordable for future ones. As discussed in Chapter 11, the climate crisis grows remorselessly. And Chapter 9 shows that the Covid crisis has further imperilled the prospects of the young by disrupting their education and stealing their jobs.

WHY IT MATTERS: UNDERMINING THE FUNCTIONING OF THE MARKET

To maintain an inclusive social contract, it is necessary to recognise the importance of values and beliefs in economic life. Economic and political philosophers from Adam Smith (1759) to Friedrich Hayek (1960) have long recognised that beliefs are part of inherited social capital, which provides the social framework for the free market. As discussed in the previous chapters, even money, the token used to measure value, must be underpinned by values of resilience, transparency, accountability, solidarity and trust.

So what values and beliefs provide the foundations of inclusive capitalism?

- Clearly to succeed in the global economy, *dynamism* is essential.
- To align incentives across generations, a long-term perspective is required, *sustainability*.
- For markets to sustain their legitimacy, they need to be not only effective but also *fair*. Nowhere is that need more acute than in financial markets; finance has to be *trusted*.
- Individuals must feel *responsible*, and be *accountable*, for their actions.
- To value others demands engaged citizens who recognise their obligations to each other. In short, there needs to be a sense of *solidarity*.

These beliefs and values are not necessarily fixed. They must be nurtured. An essential point is that, just as any revolution eats its children, unchecked market fundamentalism devours the social capital essential for the long-term dynamism of capitalism itself. All ideologies are prone to extremes, and capitalism loses its sense of moderation when the belief in the power of the market enters the realm of faith. In the decades prior to the crisis, such radicalism came to dominate economic ideas and became a pattern of social behaviour.

In the financial system, market fundamentalism – in the form of light-touch regulation, the belief that bubbles cannot be identified and that the market is always right – contributed directly to the financial crisis and the associated erosion of social capital.[42] These will be explored more thoroughly in the next chapter.

What the crisis revealed further strained trust in the financial system:

- major banks were deemed too big to fail, operating in a privileged 'heads I win, tails you lose' bubble;
- there was widespread rigging of market benchmarks for personal gain; and
- equity markets demonstrated a perverse sense of fairness, blatantly favouring the technologically empowered over the retail investor.

Such practices widen the gap between insider and outsider returns and challenge distributive justice. More fundamentally, the resulting mistrust in market mechanisms has both reduced happiness and impaired social capital. More generally, as Kay stresses, if too little emphasis is given to the pluralism of markets, policies can become pro-business rather than pro-market, and this in turn can undermine the social and political legitimacy of the market economy.

Indeed, there is considerable evidence of this erosion of trust in the market economy, and in the experts that preside over it, with a resulting fall of support for both (see Chapter 13). We will explore in Part III how leaders, companies and governments can earn that trust in an environment which combines democratised information and social media algorithms that reinforce existing preferences.

WHY IT MATTERS: COMMODIFICATION CORRODES VALUES

There are several reasons why the extreme spread of market mechanisms may change society's values.

First, there is a demonstration effect of a purely commercial society in which social hierarchies are based on wealth. This naturally leads people to focus on acquiring it, the systematic pursuit of wealth that Max Weber defined as the key sociological determinants of capitalism.[43] Boom! The status sphere built on money![44] Adam Smith feared that such a single-minded pursuit could encourage amoral behaviour. In this he vehemently disagreed with the seventeenth-century social theorist Bernard Mandeville's conclusion from his parable of the bees in which the pursuit of private vices by the bees leads to the prosperity of the hive, making them public virtues. It is telling that economists have sided with the bees, adopting them as the symbol of the Royal Economic Society.

Yet when the means – money – become the ends, society suffers. Marx saw greed as a stage of social development. In other words, it was neither intrinsic nor natural. Money is an accelerant giving greed an abstract hedonism because the pursuit of its accumulation 'possesses all pleasures in potentiality'.[45] Greed itself is reinforced by the commodification of life as there is more and more that money *can* buy. Milanović observes that when money becomes the sole criterion by which success is judged, society sends the message that 'being rich is glorious' and 'the means used to achieve glory are largely immaterial – as long as one is not caught doing something illegal'.[46]

Second, the risks of growing market fundamentalism are amplified by the weakening of the traditional constraints on behaviour. For thousands of years, religion was able to preserve the entrepreneurial spirit necessary for the flourishing of commercial society while internalising certain forms of acceptable behaviour. Protestantism eschewed ostentation, limiting the consumption of the elites and their displays of wealth.[47] This in turn encouraged the necessary reinvestment in social and economic capital, as profits were to be used for God and the community or to pursue further gain as was God's will. To quote Weber: 'the inevitable practical result is obvious: accumulation of capital through ascetic compulsion to save. The restraints which were imposed upon the consumption of wealth naturally served to increase it by making possible the productive investment of capital.'[48] This moderating force was complemented by what Rawls termed a tacit social contract which reaffirms in its daily actions the main beliefs of society.[49]

Neither of these constraints binds today. The steady decline of religion in the west is well documented. From a commercial perspective, it has reached the point that the Archbishop of Canterbury, the Pope and Rabbi Jonathan Sacks have all sought to reinforce ethical considerations in business life.[50] As Rabbi Sacks put it:

> The big question is: how do we learn to be moral again?
> Markets were made to serve us; we were not made to serve markets. Economics needs ethics. Markets do not survive by market forces alone. They depend on respect for the people affected by our decisions. Lose that and we lose not just money and jobs but something more significant still: freedom, trust and decency, the things that have a value, not a price.[51]

The tacit social contract has also been loosened in a hyper-capitalist globalised world because individuals are unmoored from their social settings. 'Our actions are no longer monitored by the people amongst whom we live. People live in one place and work in another.'[52] The 'citizens of nowhere' haven't been transcending their polity to rise to the level of humanity but detaching from it and atomising into themselves. It is possible that the Covid-driven location restrictions will re-establish some sense of community among the formerly footloose.

In the absence of these traditional internal constraints, there is a greater reliance on external ones, in the form of laws and regulation. In the harsh assessment of Milanović, 'Morality has been gutted out and fully externalised. It has been outsourced from ourselves to society at large.'[53] So people walk a fine line or game the system. Cheating in sports is grudgingly admired, with Thierry Henry's blatant use of his hand to gain France a spot in the football World Cup just part of the tradition of Diego Maradona's 'hand of God' to win a key World Cup match a couple of decades earlier. Tech companies repeat the mantra of 'paying all the taxes that are due' while inventing sham companies to abrogate their fiscal responsibilities in the countries where they are most active and make their greatest profits. Financial settlements spread amorality, as wrongful behaviour is given a price. Fines become viewed as fees.

Third, the spread of markets can lead to more unequal exchanges, in which there are in effect forced sellers. This undermines human dignity. It should be fairly obvious that it matters if the exchange is unequal such as when someone who is desperately poor sells a kidney.

Fourth, commodification – putting a good up for sale – can corrode the value of the activity being priced. As we move from a market economy to a market society, both value and values change. Increasingly, the value of something, of some act or of someone is equated with their monetary value, a monetary value that is determined by the market. The logic of buying and selling no longer applies only to material goods but increasingly governs the whole of life from the allocation of healthcare to education, public safety and environmental protection. As Sandel argues, 'When we decide that certain goods and services can be bought and sold, we decide, at least implicitly, that it is appropriate to treat them as commodities, as instruments of profit and use.'[54] And we assume, again at least implicitly, that the values of society will remain unchanged in the process.

Most goods are not changed by being in the market,[55] but, as we shall see, putting a price on every human activity erodes certain moral and civic goods. It is a moral question how far we should take mutually advantageous exchanges for efficiency gains. Should sex be up for sale? Should there be a market in the right to have children? Why not auction the right to opt out of military service? Why shouldn't universities sell admission to raise money for worthy causes?

Standard economic reasoning is that the spread of market exchanges increases economic efficiency without moral cost. The canonical position was set out by Nobel laureate Kenneth Arrow in 1972. Put simply, the economic argument is that commodifying a good does not alter its character, and ethical behaviour is a commodity that needs to be economised. Neither proposition is convincing, and it is an indictment of the economics profession that the consequences of these views are not taken more seriously.

As markets reach into spheres of life traditionally governed by non-market norms, the notion that markets never taint the goods or activities they touch becomes increasingly implausible. Consider three examples with respect to children.

The first is the famous case of a day-care centre in Israel, where it was decided to introduce fines for parents who were picking up their children late and inconveniencing the day-care staff who had to stay late.[56] In response, the incidence of late pick-ups rose sharply. The fine was viewed as a fee, removing the social stigma of making teachers wait. Instead, parents were covering the cost and optimised *their* time accordingly.

The second (referenced by Sandel) is giving in to the temptation to pay a child to read a book. This not only puts a relative price on reading compared to staying on their mobile phone but also signals that reading is a chore that must be compensated for rather than an intrinsic good to be enjoyed. When everything becomes relative, nothing is immutable.

The third is paying children to raise money for charity. Building on their observations at the day-care centre, the economists Uri Gneezy and Aldo Rustichini conducted an experiment to determine the impact of financial incentives on student motivations.[57] They divided high-school students into three groups. The first was given a motivational speech about the good cause they would be supporting as they canvassed their neighbourhood for money. The second and third received the same speech but were offered incentives (paid by a third party, so with no impact on net proceeds) of 1 per cent and 10 per cent of proceeds raised, respectively. Not surprisingly, the group with the higher incentive was more motivated and raised more money than the lower-paid cohort. But the group that responded only to charitable and civic virtue raised the most. Money had crowded out civic norms.

These examples suggest that, before putting a price on a good, consideration should be given to whether this will alter its meaning. Economics has generally avoided this question in part because it purports to be a value-neutral subject. This position is untenable.

There is extensive evidence that, when markets extend into human relationships and civic practices (from child-rearing to teaching), being in a market can change the character of the goods and the social practices they govern. This is known as the commercialisation effect, and there is a growing body of work in social psychology that offers a possible explanation for the difference between intrinsic motivations (such as moral convictions or interest in the task at hand) and external ones (such as money or a reward). As Sandel concludes, when people are engaged in an activity that they see as intrinsically worthwhile, offering them money may weaken their motivation by depreciating or crowding out their intrinsic interest or commitment.[58] There are many aspects of social life in which the introduction of a monetary incentive is not additive but corrosive.

One of the best-known examples was documented by Richard Titmuss in his comparative study of blood-donation systems in the US and the UK, *The Gift Relationship*. Titmuss demonstrated that,

in economic and practical terms, the UK system of voluntary donations was superior to the US system which paid for donations. He
added an ethical argument that turning blood into a commodity
diminished the spirit of altruism and eroded people's sense of obligation to donate blood to support others in their community.[59]
Sandel provides numerous other examples from how payments
diminished people's sense of civic responsibility for addressing
nuclear waste in Switzerland to the degradation of the US democratic process by paying people to secure 'free access' to
Congressional hearings.

These lessons extend to the nature of commerce and the effectiveness of the market. As we shall see in the next chapter, for
example, when bankers became detached from the end users of
financial products, their only reward was money. But purely financial remuneration ignores the non-pecuniary value of employment,
such as satisfaction from helping a client or colleague succeed. This
reductionist view of the human condition is a poor foundation for
ethical financial institutions needed to support long-term prosperity. The global financial crisis was as much a crisis of culture as of
capital. Central to the action plans for leaders and companies in
Chapters 13 and 14 is the reality that the daily practice of values
reinforces personal identity, corporate purpose and social
responsibility.

This underscores the second moral error of many mainstream
economists, which is to treat civic and social virtues as scarce
commodities, despite there being extensive evidence that public
spiritedness increases with its practice. Commenting on Arrow's
claim that virtue must be rationed, Sandel observes, 'This way of
thinking about the generous virtues is strange, even far-fetched. It
ignores the possibility that our capacity for love and benevolence is
not depleted with use but enlarged with practice … Similar questions can be asked of social solidarity and civic virtue.'[60]

Civic virtue and public spirit atrophy with disuse and grow like
muscles with regular exercise. According to Aristotle in the
Nicomachean Ethics, virtue is something we cultivate with practice:
'We become just by doing just acts, temperate by doing temperate
acts, brave by doing brave acts.'[61] Rousseau held a similar view,

summed up by Sandel: 'The more a country asks of its citizens, the greater their devotion to it ... Civic virtue is built up not spent down.'[62]

These observations are familiar from the civic response to Covid. None of the voluntary groups that spontaneously formed were paid for the makeshift PPE and protective masks they created and donated. A call for volunteers to help those in the National Health Service was met with over a million people within days. No citizen drew on a government payment to help elderly neighbours or the homeless in their communities.

Conversely, the spread of the market undermines community, which is one of the most important determinants of happiness. When we outsource civic virtues to paid third-party providers, we narrow the scope of society and encourage people to withdraw from it.

THE RISE OF THE MARKET SOCIETY AND THE DECLINE OF VALUE(S)

The economic historian John Fagg Foster concluded in his review of the history of value theory, 'Economic value is the degree of technological efficiency. It is as simple as that.'[63] Like many other economists, he strips value from any relationship to its social and political context. But while such reductionism may be satisfying, economics does not rest apart from the world.

In the pursuit of efficiency by expanding the market space, economics makes moral choices. It is doing so blindly because it assumes that values are merely subjective preferences not open to reasoned argument and that the act of pricing an activity or good does not change its underlying nature. To the extent that economics recognises civic or social virtues, it generally assumes that price incentives complement, or reinforce, the intrinsic values which already encourage that behaviour. It doesn't anticipate that intrinsic and monetary incentives are at best substitutes and that there are circumstances where commodifying the social space, putting a price on values, can corrode those values.

When markets erode non-market norms we need to ask whether the efficiency gains are worth the cost both in the specific situation and in the broader sense of maintaining the social capital necessary for market functioning and societal wellbeing. As Tony Atkinson stresses, efficiency only matters insofar as it makes society better off.[64] When economists promote policies solely on the grounds of efficiency, they are making moral assessments. But the judgement of whether a policy initiative is right for society often requires more than the simple utilitarian add-up favoured by economists of costs and benefits that are priced in the market. At a minimum, it requires the highly complex assessments advocated by Sunstein that take into account estimates of a wide range of non-priced attributes, such as mental health, human dignity and agency.

The issue extends and goes deeper by affecting values themselves. Altruism, generosity, solidarity and civic spirit are not like commodities with fixed supplies that are depleted with use. In contrast, they grow stronger with exercise. Alternatively, by shrinking the social space and expanding the reach of the market into the heart of what had been family life, the market undercuts community, atomises the family and affects mental health by turning more of life into a scorecard competition.

As we shall see in subsequent chapters, the final corrosion of the drift from moral to market sentiments is how the spread of subjective value flattens values when we make decisions. An advantage of the subjective approach is that it is neutral. Most things can be compared by a common, widely available standard, the market price. The disadvantage is that it sets in train a process in which welfare is interpreted as simply the sum of all prices.

This flattens, adding them up with no hierarchy or consideration of their distribution. As we will see, this encourages trade-offs of growth today and crisis tomorrow, of health and economics, and of planet and profit.

These dynamics have led to a series of crises of value that will be explored in Part II. The crises of finance, health, climate and identity are not merely the product of shortcomings in the ability of markets to value, they are also the result of how the encroachment of the market has changed our values.

In my experience, the upheaval the world has been experiencing demonstrates that it is vital to rebalance the essential dynamism of capitalism with our broader social goals. This is not an abstract issue or a naive aspiration. Part II draws out some initiatives to reinforce the core values needed for the fair and efficient markets and the broader social capital we need to truly live our values.

PART II

THREE CRISES
OF VALUE(S)

7

The Global Financial Crisis:
A World Unmoored

It's hard to remember how different things were in August 2007. The New World (Economic) Order promoted by the US, in its role as the G1, had delivered seemingly effortless prosperity. The Washington consensus – centred on free markets, free trade and open capital markets – reigned supreme. Many countries were experiencing their longest economic expansions since the Second World War. The UK was experiencing fourteen years – fifty-six straight quarters – of uninterrupted output growth. Inflation was quiescent, and central banks were congratulating themselves on delivering the Great Moderation. Borders were being erased, with emerging economies, led by China, integrating into the world trading system, and countries clamouring to join the EU.

In the financial sector, bankers saw themselves as masters of the universe. Risk was thought to have been spread evenly across the globe through the miracle of subprime securitisation. And light-touch regulation protected trusting, if somewhat envious, citizens.

Yet even then the most perceptive could feel the first tremors of profound change. North Korea launched its first nuclear test, the SNP won its first Scottish election and a panel of international scientists suggested that global warming might be man-made. And in my world, a couple of obscure European synthetic credit funds stopped dancing to the music. The Canadian ABCP market began to crack, and though few recognised it at the time, the worst financial crisis since the Great Depression had begun.

Jean-Claude Trichet, then President of the European Central Bank (ECB), was fond of telling a story of a fellow central banker taking their long-scheduled walking holiday at this time in Scotland. With his BlackBerry having run dry and anxious for news, he went into a local shop and asked the women behind the counter, 'Do you have the *Financial Times?*'

'Yes sir. Would you like yesterday's or today's?' she replied.

'Well, Madame, I would very much prefer today's ...'

'Then come back tomorrow ...'

Trichet's colleague didn't wait but went straight back to Frankfurt to join the ECB's initiative, unprecedented at the time, to pump billions of euros of liquidity into their money markets because he sensed that by tomorrow all would have been lost.

That same weekend, on one of those sweltering August days when the heat and humidity briefly make Ottawa feel like Georgia, I was relaxing in my backyard, watching my children play, when my phone rang. Although it seems commonplace now, it felt a bit odd for a long weekend when most of the country was taking a break. After all, Canada was participating in the same bout of global prosperity, growth had averaged 3.8 per cent over the previous decade, unemployment was 5.2 per cent, summer was here and the living felt easy. I wasn't minded to pick the call up until I saw that it was a senior banker from Toronto's Bay Street, Jamie Kiernan. I knew he wasn't checking on my welfare.

As would become a pattern over the next two years, I answered a call to hear palpable fear on the other end of the line. Jamie told me that the Canadian asset-backed commercial paper market was freezing up and might not reopen the following Tuesday. There were margin calls and the liquidity backup lines would need to be activated. If they weren't, the whole market would crash and the carnage would spread quickly to London and New York. The government of Canada needed to *do something.*

With this cold bucket of water applied, I felt my summer ending, even if his story made about as much sense to me then as it probably does to many reading these words now. It wasn't that the banker was speaking a foreign language to me. I was working at Canada's Department of Finance, after a long career on Wall Street and in the

City. I had started out in commercial paper, a sleepy backwater where new recruits can learn the ropes of credit risk and market liquidity without causing too much damage. Commercial paper wasn't generally known for drama, and for it to interrupt a weekend with talk of market panic suggested a small tail was trying to wag a very big dog.

Commercial paper, or CP, is short-term debt, usually maturing in three to six months, issued by highest-quality companies to institutional investors. Traditionally, the CP market plays an important but straightforward role financing the short-term business needs of companies (such as helping them maintain inventories of their products) with the excess funds of banks, insurance companies and other investors. Asset-backed commercial paper was the more sophisticated end of this market, but it too was relatively straightforward. Or at least it used to be, last time I'd checked.

I knew from experience that few people got rich working in CP. Provided they did their homework, the benefits were that they could count on sleeping soundly at night and enjoy long uninterrupted weekends. So talk of margin calls, bankruptcies and a looming panic in London seemed totally foreign. Jamie didn't know all the details, he was only hearing things and he wasn't himself in the middle of the transactions. But I knew he wouldn't waste my time, so once we had said goodbye I began to ring around to find out more.

To put it in context, the Canadian CP market was small. Jamie was talking about a $30 billion corner, dwarfed by the $500 billion government debt and $1.5 trillion equities. The links to London and New York were obscure. Why this couldn't wait until work began again on Tuesday and why the government should step into the middle of a series of private transactions between supposedly sophisticated institutions was unexplained. The only clarity was urgency.

WHEN SOMETHING DOESN'T
MAKE SENSE …

Early on in my career in finance, I was taught an invaluable rule by Bob Hirst, one of the partners at Goldman Sachs: 'If something doesn't make sense, it doesn't make sense.' Beneath the Popeye-esque tautology was real wisdom. Bob's point was that if someone explains something to you in finance – such as a flashy new product or why a company's valuation should be orders of magnitude higher than others in their sector – and it doesn't make sense, ask the person to repeat the rationale. And if following that response, it still doesn't make sense, you should run.

Run because in finance you should never buy simply on trust, just to go along with the crowd, or least of all to pretend that you understand something for fear of looking foolish. Run because there are really only two possibilities. The first is that you're being sold something that really doesn't make sense. It's merely a form of financial alchemy in which debt is being turned into equity, the newest version of the mythical risk-free return, or the latest variant of the four most expensive words in the English language, 'This time is different.'

Over time, I have learned that a second explanation is distressingly common. Something doesn't make sense because the person promoting the new idea doesn't themselves understand it. Too often in finance, decisions are made on the basis that someone else has been successful in an area, that it's a hot sector or even that people just don't want to admit they don't understand. It really is the case that the only dumb questions in finance are the ones that are never asked. It's this reason – when feigned knowledge masks real ignorance – that leads to panic when the scales fall from people's eyes.

That's not to suggest people can't be in the dark and also get lucky for a while. After all, a rising tide lifts all boats. In a bull market, people can do well for a time just following a trend or copying a strategy. Banks can cut and paste the new products of their rivals without fully understanding them. In a bull market, when everything seems to be going fine, the fear of missing out is skyrocketing and a brave new dawn seems to have broken, the dumb questions pile up fast.

Eventually they must be answered.

A quick tug on the thread Jamie provided me that August afternoon revealed that the Canadian ABCP market was unravelling because it just didn't make sense. If what follows over the next few pages doesn't make sense to you, don't worry. The more complex the structures became, the fewer people in the market really understood how they worked, and hardly anyone grasped either how dependent markets and institutions had become on them or what would happen when the economy started to turn down.

FROM CAUTION TO CRISIS

As with many things in finance, the Canadian ABCP market started with the prudent application of a reasonable concept. Banks would develop long histories of lending to certain sectors or types of individuals. The performance of these loans was relatively predictable, particularly if they were assembled in pools so that any idiosyncrasies would largely cancel each other out. This observation that a diversified pool of assets was less risky than single exposure or a group of identical types of loans (say mortgages in one city) led to the development of securitisation, where assets were combined in pools and sold as securities to investors.

And so it was in ABCP, where banks would pool their short-term assets, like credit card receivables, and sell them to an off-balance-sheet structured investment vehicle, or SIV.[1] The SIV was really little more than a shell company that would fund the purchase by issuing commercial paper. Provided the total interest paid on the credit cards (after adjusting for any defaults) was higher than the interest costs on the commercial paper, everyone would be happy. The bank could sell the credit card receivables and get cash up front to make new loans. The SIV owners would make money on the spread between the payments on the credit cards and the interest costs of the CP. And the investors would be paid a bit more in interest than they would for CP of companies of similar credit quality (in return for the extra time and analysis they would have to undertake to ensure that it all made sense).

Whether it made sense for investors to buy ABCP boiled down to two risks. The first, liquidity risk, refers to the ability to sell an asset or to borrow against its value. In deep markets, sales by individual investors will have a minimal impact on the asset's price, and in many cases the asset can even be turned into cash by borrowing against its value. But when markets are thin or shallow, it can be tough for investors to realise cash when they need it. In the extreme, liquidity risk is the market analogue of a bank run, except that in markets there are no lenders of last resort like central banks and investors aren't protected by a safety net, whereas retail depositors in banks benefit both directly from deposit insurance and indirectly from central bank facilities that help banks to weather storms.

In rising markets, liquidity is pretty much taken for granted, with investors confident that they could sell their commercial paper whenever they need cash. As backup, companies that issue commercial paper have other sources of liquidity including bank lines that they can draw on in case the market shuts or their creditworthiness deteriorates to the extent that investors no longer want their paper. In Canadian ABCP, the former was viewed as highly unlikely and the latter was expected to change only gradually. After a long period of tranquil market functioning, investors had forgotten that markets can turn quickly from deep to shallow, liquid to illiquid, robust to fragile.

The second risk that the investors in Canadian ABCP faced was credit risk – that is, whether enough of the credit cards could actually be paid off. The investors should have been monitoring the quality of the assets in the SIV that they were backing with their money, but, as I mentioned, commercial paper was a sleepy backwater, so they generally relied on the reputation of the SIV and independent rating agencies who assessed their creditworthiness.

By the summer of 2007, those lines of defence had weakened. The managers of the SIVs usually made their credit judgements by relying on the track record of the bank that was selling them the assets. Although the credit-rating agencies conducted due diligence on the assets going into a SIV, it's obvious in retrospect that they hadn't really considered either what would happen to the quality of those assets once banks no longer owned them or whether banks would be less careful when they gave out new loans and expected to sell them quickly into the market. An example of how the existence of a market can corrode.

In other words, the investors in the commercial paper of the SIVs were far removed from the end borrowers, such as people buying goods with their credit cards. No one was asking the tough questions; everyone was relying on everyone else. The SIVs were acting like banks but had outsourced the basic roles of banking to the rating agencies and the banks who were selling them the assets. The banks were relying on markets to take their loans off their books. These relationships called into question what banks were really for and whether they could be reliably replaced by markets.

WHAT ARE BANKS REALLY FOR?

Commercial banks perform several key functions. To begin with, they are a critical part of the payments system – the pipes through which financial transactions occur. By facilitating Adam Smith's decentralised exchange, the payments system is critical to the functioning of a market economy. It passes unnoticed unless it breaks down, and it's one of the jobs of central banks to oversee systemic elements of the payments system to ensure its reliability. As we saw in Chapter 5 on the future of money, the payments system could soon be disrupted by new technologies and forms of private money.

The second important role of banks is to transform the maturities of assets and liabilities. Banks take short-term liabilities, usually in the form of deposits, and transform them into long-term assets, such as mortgages or corporate loans. Households and businesses can therefore do the reverse, holding short-term assets and longer-term liabilities. This helps them to plan for the future and to manage risks arising from uncertainties over their cash flows.

Banks also provide liquidity to their customers by allowing rapid access to those same short-term assets. Indeed, by transacting at a wide range of maturities, banks provide arbitrage which increases the efficiency of financial markets. This allows borrowers to obtain the lowest rate of interest appropriate to their risk characteristics.

The social value of maturity transformation is without question. However, by definition, it also leads to a maturity mismatch that creates a fundamental risk for banks. Banks hold liquid reserves that are only a fraction of their outstanding obligations. If a depositor wants their money back, this isn't a problem because banks maintain sufficient liquidity to meet typical demands and can borrow from other banks if the shock is larger than anticipated. But if many depositors want their money back at the same time, there is a tipping point when liquidity problems become self-fulfilling runs.

To manage this risk, banks rely on two crucial supports. First, deposit insurance gives depositors the comfort that their funds will be there when they need them, and central banks act as lenders of last resort to solvent but illiquid institutions. These support mechanisms are carefully crafted to discourage banks from taking inappropriate risks while still providing the necessary support, and they are accompanied by a robust regulatory framework. Bankers accept a social contract that gives them these safety nets in times of a stress in return for regulation of their behaviour at all times.

Banks perform a third essential role of credit intermediation, channelling funds from savers to investors in the real economy. This allows savers to diversify their risk and all of us to smooth our consumption over time. Young families can borrow to buy a house, students can pay for university. People can invest in low-risk, interest-bearing accounts for our retirements, and businesses can finance working capital and investment.

It is critical to remember that banking is not an end in itself, but a means to promote investment, innovation, growth and prosperity. Banking is fundamentally about intermediation – connecting borrowers and savers in the real economy. Yet in the run-up to the crisis too many in finance saw it as the apex of economic activity. Banking became more about banks connecting with other banks. Clients were replaced by counterparties, and banking was increasingly transactional rather than relational. As we shall see, these attitudes developed over years as new markets and instruments were created. The initial motivation was to meet the credit and hedging needs of clients in support of their business activities. Over time, however, many of these innovations morphed into ways to amplify bets on financial outcomes.

BANKS AND MARKETS BECOME LOCKED IN A FATAL EMBRACE

Banks are not the only game in town. In the run-up to the crisis, in many countries, markets became as important as banks for the financing of companies and households. From a financial system perspective, the deepening of markets is generally welcome because it can make the system more robust and increases competition, which disciplines banking activity. That is provided it's done right: which means sufficient transparency, sound liquidity management, aligned incentives and appropriate separation between banks and markets.

While markets expand the choices and lower the prices available to financial consumers, they function differently from banks. Unlike banks, markets rely more completely on confidence for liquidity. That confidence can disappear quickly.

A key advantage of banks is their relationships with their customers. Banks follow borrowers over time and monitor their payment history and reliability. When performing their roles properly, banks tailor their products to the borrower, imposing higher or lower standards as appropriate.

In contrast, the lifeblood of markets is transactions. Markets act as intermediaries between savers and borrowers but maintain relationships with neither. Consequently, market instruments are more robust when the underlying product is more standardised. Determining whether an activity is best financed through a bank or a market depends on the relative benefits to that activity of specialisation versus standardisation.

In response to rising competitive pressures from markets, banks increasingly became direct participants in them, in ways that ultimately sowed the seeds of the crisis.

First, banks relied more and more on short-term markets to fund their activities and, in the process, substantially boosted their leverage. This made banks dependent on continuous access to liquidity in money and capital markets. That reliance was brutally exposed when markets turned in the autumn of 2007.

Second, banks used securitisation markets, like ABCP, to straddle relationship banking and transactional market-based finance. Under the originate-to-distribute business model, banks originated a set of loans, repackaged them as securities and sold them to investors. In essence, banks took specialised loans and sold them in standardised packages. While securitisation promised to diversify risks for banks, this risk transfer was frequently incomplete. Banks often sold securities to arm's-length conduits, like SIVs, that they were later forced to re-intermediate or they held on to AAA tranches of complex structures that proved far from risk-free.[2]

This originate-to-distribute business model was taken to a ridiculous extreme by Northern Rock, the UK mortgage lender which would collapse a few weeks after my summer phone call. Northern Rock was founded in 1965 as a building society, a mutual savings institution whose primary purpose was to provide mortgages to its members, with those mortgages largely funded by other member deposits. By the mid-1990s Northern Rock had expanded into other traditional banking activities – made possible by the financial deregulation of the Thatcher era – and in 1997 Northern Rock Building Society demutualised, listed its shares on the stock market and became the Northern Rock Bank. Responsible now to shareholders not to its members, the new bank pursued an ambitious growth strategy based on an originate-to-distribute model. Rather than holding the mortgages of members to maturity and lending out only what the size of its member deposits would allow, Northern Rock would underwrite mortgages to meet demand, funding them in the short-term money markets, until they could be repackaged and sold off as securitised bonds.

By 2007, Northern Rock was Britain's fifth-largest mortgage provider. It was highly over-leveraged and wholly dependent on the wholesale debt market for mortgage-backed securities. When that dried up with the intensifying crisis in American subprime mortgages, the flaws of the bank's business model became brutally apparent, leading to the first bank run in Britain in over a century.

The financial crisis exposed the fundamental incentive problems that can occur with securitisation. In the originate-to-distribute model, the incentives of the originating institution were no longer aligned with those of the risk-holders. Once that relationship was severed, the underwriting standards for new loans and their ongoing monitoring both deteriorated from responsible to reckless. However, pricing and risk management did not reflect these changes until it was too late. As clients became counterparties, any form of solidarity between them and bankers fell away. Values affected value.

The third embrace of markets by banks was the expansion of many retail and commercial banks into investment banking. This allowed banks to package traditional lending with higher value-added agency business, to undertake market-making activities and, increasingly, to engage in proprietary trading. The push by banks into markets helped spur the proliferation of over-the-counter derivative products, which created counterparty and investment risks that were difficult to identify and control.

Incentive problems also plagued this transition. In many banks, a culture that rewarded innovation and opacity over risk management and transparency undermined organisations more than originally thought. As we shall see, by that time the more junior traders who had assumed the risks had already been paid, largely in cash. Many large, complex banks learned too late that there can be principal–agent problems within firms, as well as between firms and their shareholders.

Just as banks began doing what markets traditionally did best, markets moved into banking. But without either a safety net or proper oversight. More and more of the traditional functions of banks – including maturity transformation and credit intermediation – were conducted through a broader range of intermediaries and investment vehicles, which have been collectively referred to as the 'shadow banking' system. Shadow banks included investment banks (in other countries), mortgage brokers, finance companies, structured investment vehicles (SIVs), hedge funds and other private asset pools.

The scale of these developments was remarkable. During this decade, banking assets grew enormously, to anywhere from one and a half times to six times national GDP in Canada, the United States, the United Kingdom and Europe. In all countries besides Canada, much of this growth was financed by increased leverage.[3]

In the final years of the boom, when complacency about access to liquidity reached its zenith, the scale of the shadow banking system exploded. The value of SIVs, for example, tripled in the three years to 2007. The growth in financial activity and the increasingly complex array of financial players created a dramatic increase in claims *within* the financial system, as opposed to between the financial system and the real economy. That meant risks were difficult to identify and manage. More fundamentally, it showed the extent to which the financial system had drifted from its role serving the real economy.

Financial institutions, including many banks, came to rely on high levels of liquidity in markets. In the United States, the total value of commercial paper rose by more than 60 per cent and the ABCP market by more than 80 per cent in the three years before the crisis. In essence, the shadow banking system practised maturity transformation without a safety net – that is, it was wholly reliant on the continuous availability of funding markets. The collapse in market liquidity that began in August 2007 crystallised these risks.

The regulatory system neither appreciated the scale of this activity nor adequately adapted to the new risks created by it. The shadow banking system was not supported, regulated or monitored in the same fashion as the banking system. With hindsight, the shift towards the shadow banking system was allowed to go too far for too long.

FROM SIMPLE TO STUPID:
ABCP STOPS MAKING SENSE

Like many financial innovations, the original securitisation structures were carefully assembled. They made sense. The best assets were selected, and they either had short maturities so they could be quickly unwound if something started to go wrong or long-term investors whose horizons matched the underlying assets. Big margins of error to absorb potential losses were built into the structures in terms of capital cushions and overcollateralisation.

The Canadian ABCP market was a tiny corner of what had become a huge global asset class. Securitisation of debt had been expanding for decades, with corporate debt, credit card debt and mortgages all being packaged into securities and sold to market. This growth accelerated sharply in the years preceding the financial crisis, with the value of outstanding securitisations rising from $5 trillion to $17 trillion between 2000 and 2007.[4] Securities that were further removed from the underlying asset grew at an even faster rate in the same period. Issuance of collateralised debt obligations (CDO) – securities composed of pooled collections of various debt – grew sixfold, while issuance of CDO-squared – pooled collections of other CDOs – grew elevenfold.[5]

The buyers of these securities were investment banks, hedge funds, investment funds, money market funds and of course SIVs, like the issuers of Canadian ABCP. By the mid-2000s these shadow banking operations financed around $8 trillion in assets in the United States, making it about as large as the real banking system itself.[6]

By this point a combination of complacency and greed was taking over such that much of shadow banking stopped making sense. Complacency – in the forms of relying overly on past performance and relying on others – weakened each line of defence. Financiers abdicated responsibility. Greed prompted those who ran the SIVs to view the interest spread the SIV earned as a little modest, so they worked to increase their returns, by adding riskier assets to the portfolio, like subprime mortgages. Unlike credit cards that were to be paid back monthly, these long-term mortgages made the ABCP SIVs more like banks as they increased their maturity transformation – a core role of banks – which substantially increased their liquidity risks.

After all, if a bank like Northern Rock with thousands of employees, capital, depositor protection and the supervision of authorities could be subject to a bank run, why couldn't a shell company with a handful of employees, little capital, no depositor protection and no supervision be subject to a buyers' strike in the CP market? The prospect of such a pullback was made more likely by the addition of subprime mortgages. Their creditworthiness heavily relied on the securitisation's ability to reduce the overall risk of a pool of assets by combining uncorrelated risky assets. In this case, the risk of the whole is less than the sum of its parts. But subprime hadn't been tested in a downturn, and it was arguably the area most susceptible to the incentive problems in the originate-to-distribute model.

To compound these risks, the managers of the Canadian ABCP vehicles also began to put the assets on the SIVs' balance sheet to use while waiting for people to pay back their credit card debts. This was a time when the miracle of securitisation was being turbocharged by the explosion in synthetic derivatives. Mimicking developments in New York and London, some of the Canadian SIVs began to sell credit derivatives to investment banks based in London for a fee. The SIVs would back up their promises to pay by pledging a portion of their assets as collateral.

Now I recognise that this is starting to get pretty complicated but derivatives are where much of shadow banking including Canadian ABCP really lost the plot. And they did so in a way that was representative of problems across the global financial system in the run-up to the crisis.

To be clear, derivatives serve many essential functions. As financial instruments that 'derive' their value from the value of other underlying variables, they can be used to transfer financial risks from one entity to another that is better able to bear them. A farmer, for instance, can agree in the spring to sell their crop in the autumn for a set price, providing some peace of mind in a challenging profession. The farmer's income is locked in by the contract and protected against uncertain outcomes, but the extent to which the recipient of the crop benefits from or is harmed by the deal depends on the price of the crop at that future date. In Ancient Mesopotamia, farmers engaged in such transactions by specifying a price and future sell date on clay tablets.

Moving forward several millennia, the use of derivatives has dramatically expanded. In addition to protecting farmers and those who produce commodities, derivatives are used to insulate home-owners, pension holders and businesses from all types of risk. By the mid-2000s, derivatives were being deployed in a wide range of markets, with underlying assets ranging from mortgages to individual company credits (known as CDS) and baskets of company credit exposures (known as CDX). The notional value of the global over-the-counter derivative market grew from under $100 trillion in 2000 to over $500 trillion by the summer of 2007.[7]

As we were to discover in the autumn of 2007, derivatives had created an enormous inverted pyramid of risk on the backs of homeowners, with the users of derivatives increasingly far removed from the underlying assets. Long gone were the simple days when I had worked at a retail bank in Edmonton and would be sent out to double-check the property valuations we had received. As explained in Chapters 4 and 5, the ability of conventional banks to grant mortgages, to create money, was governed by their risk appetite and constrained by their capital and liquidity requirements. By the summer of 2007, the ability of many banks to underwrite new mortgages was largely constrained by how quickly they could sell off the asset in a securitised pool. The buyer could then pool those pools of mortgages into CDO2 or hedge out their risk with credit derivatives. Each step moved further and further away from the homeowner. Nobody ever checked on the house or the homeowner. Finance was increasingly abstract, and not only did people buy and sell mortgage exposures without asking enough questions, they didn't even know who to call.

In particular, investment banks began to use credit derivatives to 'insure' their own balance sheets. For example, if a bank owned a portfolio of mortgages, they could buy a derivative that would pay them if mortgage defaults rose, so that at least some of what they lost on the mortgages would be made back on the derivatives. Of course, this depended on whether the supplier of the derivative could pay out when mortgages went bad. To protect themselves in case that derivative supplier itself defaulted just when the mortgage market went badly, the bank would ask for collateral, also known as margin. The riskier the position, the more collateral they would require.

Are you still with me? If so, you'd be ahead of 99 per cent of the market, the rating agencies, the purchasers of the commercial paper, the buyers of the credit default swaps. And almost all of the managers and shareholders. Most in the market saw only a portion of what was going on. The vast majority assumed that someone else – the banks, the rating agencies, big investors, the owners of the SIVs, or the regulators who had trusted the wisdom of the market – had asked the right questions and done the hard work. Few connected the markets that grew on top of markets. No one calculated the size of the exposures and relatively small changes could destabilise the whole edifice.

THINGS FALL APART

And then in the summer of 2007 loose threads began to appear in a few structured credit funds. Pulling on those threads unravelled not just a single sweater but the whole wardrobe. And it wasn't any wardrobe. It was a walk-in closet, positively Kardashian in its expanse. To put this into context, at the time my August holiday weekend ended, the Canadian ABCP market was around C$32 billion in size. The assets broadly matched the liabilities, but the market was growing nervous because some of the assets were US subprime loans, and the first inkling of trouble in that market was beginning to be felt. The cautious CP investors wanted out; after all one of the benefits of working in commercial paper was supposed to be a quieter life.

But there was a problem. Unbeknown to most, many of these assets had been pledged as collateral for credit insurance. How much credit had been insured? As we dug in, the numbers grew and grew until they reached more than ten times the size of the outstanding commercial paper! Investment banks in London were holding Canadian 'insurance' on more than $200 billion in total credit exposures. And this exposure was part of a broader credit stack totalling over $600 billion, more than half the size of the Canadian economy. And because as surprisingly big as the derivative exposures to Canadian ABCP ultimately were, they were dwarfed by similar structures in the UK, Europe and the US.

Without grasping the extent of this, in the late summer of 2007 the banks which had bought credit insurance from the Canadian ABCP vehicles were getting concerned. The market value of subprime mortgages was under pressure, and a few credit funds were discovering that there was no market price for their products. Instead they argued that value should be based on a model of the underlying credit.

Unwittingly, they had switched their allegiances from subjective to objective value!

With these developments, those holding credit insurance from Canadian ABCP wanted more collateral. But the Canadian ABCP providers could provide more collateral only if they could issue more CP and buy more assets, but that's exactly what the now wide-awake Canadian market didn't want. The London banks knew that if their margin calls weren't met, they would instantly have enormous exposure to the credits on their balance sheets that they thought they had magically and cheaply insured away. And that this explosion in the size of their balance sheets would happen just at the time that their investors and creditors were starting to ask tough questions about their exposures.

By the middle of August, the tensions in markets were beginning to spill over. A few funds in France and the US (sponsored by BNP Paribas and Bear Stearns, respectively) suspended redemptions, ruining the European central bankers' Scottish holiday. The plumbing of the financial system began to malfunction, prompting the ECB and Bank of Canada to intervene. Questions began to pile up. And my phone began to ring.

With this house of cards tumbling, we did something so extraordinary that I still cannot fully believe it happened. Through the force of personality of Henri-Paul Rousseau, who ran the Caisse de Dépôt et Placement du Québec which was the largest investor in the sector, and the collective weight of the Governor of the Bank of Canada, David Dodge, and the Canadian Department of Finance, we were able to engineer a standstill with the London, NY and Canadian banks and the major investors, stopping both the margin calls and the issuance of new commercial paper. Within days of that summer phone call, everyone was locked in, and a nail-biting work-out began.

If events in the Canadian ABCP market had been allowed to run their course during those few days in August, it would have brought on a Lehman-style crisis. As it was, the freeze averted disaster in the short term and created the possibility of a permanent solution. A solution negotiated with the help of Purdy Crawford, a legendary Canadian lawyer, who never once complained that his agreeing to my request for a 'little help' turned into eighteen months of constant brinksmanship. At the darkest moments over the next eighteen months it looked like the investors might receive only 20 cents per dollar invested, whereas in the end they received more than 90 cents. Yes, in financial markets there can be very large differences between intrinsic value and subjective value!

From that August long weekend on, I lived with a sense of foreboding. My colleagues and I realised that if this was happening in relatively staid Canada on this scale, it must be rampant in the world's largest financial centres. The global securitisation and derivative markets were dead men walking. Collectively they could bring the entire financial system down. And eventually they would.

THE PROXIMATE CAUSES OF THE GLOBAL FINANCIAL CRISIS

The problems at the heart of the Canadian ABCP market were representative of the fault lines that plagued the global financial system.

As all financial crises do, this one started with new-era thinking. From the Great Moderation of the economic cycle, the new economics of home ownership through subprime mortgages, the spreading and reduction of risk through new financial products, a series of beliefs promoted an enormous rise in borrowing that, for a time, fuelled growth and fed complacency before leading to misery. Many of the ideas were sound in moderation but became toxic when applied without discretion.

There was leverage everywhere. The unregulated securitisation vehicles were profitable mainly because they had higher leverage than the regulated banks. Not satisfied with that, they added even more leverage through derivatives like the credit insurance written by the Canadian ABCP companies. In the run-up to the crisis, the reported balance sheets of UK and US banks went from 15x to 40x. Their actual leverage was even greater because they had offloaded assets to SIVs like those in Canada, and they had appeared to have hedged many of the risks that were still technically on their balance sheets through derivatives. Once the crisis hit, risks crashed back on to their balance sheets and their leverage ballooned.

If you think this doesn't make sense, you would be right.

A decade ago, this complex of shadow banking masked enormous leverage in the system, including large contingent exposures and interconnections between banks. Opaque securitisations, like Canadian ABCP, gave rise to imperfect credit risk transfer, which collapsed when margin calls couldn't be met. Monoline credit insurers supported unsustainable debts, and banks became overly reliant on fragile short-term funding from money markets, which themselves were major purchasers of suddenly risky asset-backed commercial paper. As the complex chains in shadow banking unravelled, a spiral of asset fire sales and liquidity strikes followed, threatening the stability of the entire system and withdrawing access to credit from millions of households and businesses.

The system developed markets on top of other markets, spreading the risk through synthetic derivatives, so that in theory, even if something did go wrong, a lot of people would lose only a little money. In reality, everything was connected. Banks to SIVs which bought their assets. SIVs to banks whose credits they insured. Banks to other banks through a web of derivatives and short-term funding.

When sentiment turned, markets collapsed on to each other, and risks that the banks thought had flown to the four winds came home to roost. This is what happens when unbridled faith in markets collides with their limits. These are the consequences of trying to solve market failures by adding more markets.

When the markets turned, these opaque structures, the complexity, the lack of transparency all bred panic. I knew from conversations in the autumn of 2007 that many bank CEOs were belatedly realising that risks they had thought had been sold off had only been 'insured' by the equivalent of a Canadian shell company or by a counterparty that had enormous exposure to the now collapsing US subprime market. While that was concerning enough, what about their competitors? And what did that mean for their own banks' exposures to them? There was a rush for the exit, which helps explain why $200 billion of credit losses in US subprime mortgages (actual defaults) bred $1 trillion of market losses. Value which had become disconnected from reality on the way up did so again on the way down.

At the core of the problems were a series of issues around incentives. This was a time when the value of the present was everything and of the future nothing. As we worked through the ABCP mess, we discovered something troubling but typical: the incentives of those working within the banks were seriously misaligned. Mid-level traders would take credit exposure buying the debts of companies in the bond market. So far so natural. Then they would hedge out the risks of a basket of them by buying credit insurance from a Canadian AAA. They would then be paid a cash bonus on the projected spread between the costs of the insurance and the interest on the debt over the life of the debt (often out to ten years). Their incentive was to add these exposures that stretched well into the future, especially because they weren't going to be around to bear the consequences.

We have already touched on the second set of incentives problems that plagued securitisation. When those who make decisions to grant loans are doing so only in order to sell them on, their duty of care diminishes. In the run-up to the crisis, underwriting criteria moved from careful to careless, responsible to reckless. As the quality of underwriting diminished, so did the ethical foundations of finance.

This was an age of disembodied finance, when markets grew far apart from the households and businesses they ultimately served. In most professions, people see the 'real' impact of their work: teachers witness the growth of their students, farmers that of their crops. When bankers become disconnected from their ultimate clients in the real economy, they have no direct view of the impact of their work. The Libor setter sees only the numbers on the screen as a game to be won, ignoring the consequences of their actions on mortgage holders or corporate borrowers. Value was relative and values suffered. Markets on markets were not just financially but ethically fragile.

And when the music stopped, these masters of the universe turned to the state. I remember that, once I became Governor of the Bank of Canada in early 2008, I would receive delegations of investors in ABCP or bankers that were exposed to the mess. Their requests had the benefit of being consistent – consistently self-interested. They would argue that it was the responsibility of the Bank of Canada to take on their risks. We shouldn't be unduly worried: the market had momentarily taken leave of its senses.

They left out the bit about why Canadians, who had never had a chance to ask the questions unvoiced by these masters of the financial universe, should take on the burden. And they left out the implications such behaviour would have for moral hazard in the system, for if banks and markets were bailed out from their mistakes, then what was to stop them from taking on greater risks in the future – a continuation of 'heads they win, tails we lose' finance? How would that promote the values of responsibility, accountability, prudence and trust that are essential to sustainable finance?

At the same time, with financial sectors imploding, economies were in free fall. We didn't have the luxury of wishing things had been done differently. The crisis had to be gripped.

LESSON IN CRISIS MANAGEMENT

During the following year, I would learn a great deal about financial crisis management from Ben Bernanke, Tim Geithner, Hank Paulson, Christine Lagarde, Mario Draghi and Jean-Claude Trichet. There are five lessons that stick with me.

First, the market can be wrong longer than you can stay solvent. Appeals to fundamental values in a panic fall on deaf ears. Not least because people find it tough to hear when they're screaming. This causes a number of challenges. When markets collapsed in the autumn of 2008, markets were hoist on their subjective value petards. If the market was always right and the market said subprime was worth one-third of its former value, then the balance sheets of many US and European banks were insolvent, even if most of the mortgagees were making their payments. The big institutions that lent to banks in the capital markets began to perform such mark-to-market calculations, and then withdrew their funding, turning liquidity problems into solvency ones overnight.

Second, hope is not a strategy and to quote Tim Geithner's refrain *plan beats no plan*. And a plan that is actually executed is the best one of all. Searching endlessly for the best is the enemy of the good.

We applied this lesson at the Bank of England in the run-up to the Brexit referendum. With markets pricing a Remain vote as the most likely outcome, our job was straightforward: plan for the opposite. In the weeks before the vote, we developed a playbook hundreds of pages long for what to do in different market scenarios; we rehearsed what could go wrong and what could be done to mitigate the risks. We recognised that we couldn't anticipate every contingency, so we underwrote the whole package by having the banks pre-position collateral with the Bank. This would enable us to lend up to £250 billion to the banks, equivalent to more than four times their total lending to the businesses and households the previous year. On the morning after the vote to leave and immediately following the Prime Minister's resignation, with the currency in free fall and markets under huge pressure, I was able to make a simple declaration on behalf of the Bank: 'We are well prepared for this.' Once we backed that up with £250 billion, the market knew it was true and stabilised.

Third, communicate clearly, frequently and honestly. You can't spin your way out of a crisis. The truth will out. During the harrowing eighteen months following that August call, I would hear from Ben Bernanke, Chair of the Federal Reserve, regularly and always in advance of any major initiative by the Fed, so there would be no surprises and we could coordinate if helpful. I knew that we had to be straight with Canadians about both our strengths and our weaknesses. If you don't mention the latter, the former aren't credible.

Fourth, just as there are no atheists in foxholes, there are no libertarians in financial crises. Financial crises expose brutally the limits of markets. I remember when, as Governor of the Bank of Canada, I attended a meeting of the G7 in the spring of 2008. We had dinner with a collection of CEOs of the world's largest banks that evening in the gilded Cash Room of the US Treasury. Towards the end of the dinner, the call came from Dick Fuld, the CEO of Lehman Brothers, for us to 'shut the hedge funds down'. The free market was over.

Within a few months, a combination of hubris, opacity and leverage meant that Lehman itself rather than any hedge funds was on the verge of collapse. A little over a year after the ABCP crisis erupted, I took another call on a Sunday afternoon, this time from Ben Bernanke. He was in the New York Federal Reserve, where the US authorities had tried and were failing to arrange a private sector rescue of Lehman Brothers. As I listened, my then two-year-old daughter was wrapped around my leg; she seemed more upset than Ben, who as always was calm under immense pressure. With the private sector rescue failing and Lehman going down, we discussed what could be done to help market functioning the next day. It was really little more than 'foam on the runway' in the words of Tim Geithner. This crash was going to hurt, but at least the free market was going to have its day.

As Congressman Barney Frank later quipped, it was appropriate to call it 'free-market day' because it only lasted twenty-four hours. By Tuesday, the resulting carnage prompted a public rescue package to stabilise the giant insurer AIG, which stood atop the credit-derivative pyramid that stretched from Montreal to mayhem. Within hours every major bank was under immense pressure. The dominoes were set up to fall in quick succession. I spent the next few days fielding calls from panicked bankers and their investors, demanding that something somewhere be done. I knew that the US authorities now recognised the need for major action, but not wanting to give their game away, I concentrated on the strength of the Canadian banks. In this game of dominoes, the Canadian banks – who had kept their leverage down and steered clear of subprime lending, big securitisations, risky proprietary trading and esoteric derivatives – would be the last to fall. I assured the callers that Canadian banks were the last stop before the barter economy. I left out my estimation that this was only weeks away.

The Lehman debacle demonstrated that the financial system cannot be fixed in the middle of a crisis, particularly when a web of interconnections mean that failure of one bank can pull down its competitors. In warning against the 'moral hazard fundamentalists', Larry Summers observed that 'the prospect that people may smoke in bed is not usually taken as an argument against the existence of a fire department'.[8] When there is the prospect of contagion – if the fire started by the tired smoker could quickly spread to adjoining buildings – the case for dousing the flames is strengthened. In the wake of the failure of Lehman and the rescues in quick succession of Merrill Lynch and AIG, there could be no doubt that this was a five-alarm fire. Although it was unpalatable to put out the flames caused by negligence on a planetary scale, it had to be done. And if it has to be done, it was best that it was done quickly.

This leads to the final lesson I learned about managing crises: the importance of *overwhelming force*. Fighting a financial fire with half-measures is futile. Whether it was Hank Paulson's $750 billion bazooka in 2008, or Mario Draghi's 'whatever it takes' pledge a few years later at the height of the euro crisis, effective crisis-fighting measures need to be massive, institutionally grounded and credible. Ultimately, overwhelming force can only come from the state. This is when public values come into their own. Resilience, responsibility and solidarity. Taking tough action in the public interest was essential to restoring confidence.

I learned this most clearly in the weeks following the Lehman collapse. Canada was in the midst of a federal election, with the Conservative minority government of Prime Minister Stephen Harper seeking to return to power. With what in hindsight proved spectacularly poor timing, the campaign began a few days before the crisis erupted. The government was campaigning on the positive economic outlook. After Lehman fell, this was still true in relative terms – Canada would perform less badly than everyone else – but a future that was only really bad instead of outright awful wasn't so compelling. Election campaigns in Canada are relatively short, and the government didn't do much to adjust their message (at one point they suggested that the free fall in the markets was a buying opportunity). To many voters the stance was beginning to look like indifference.

And so it was about ten days before the election date. I knew that some of the world's largest financial institutions were on the brink of collapse. The UK government was injecting enormous capital into a number of its banks and all but nationalising the largest one, RBS. In discussions with Ben Bernanke, then Bank of England Governor Mervyn King and Jean-Claude Trichet, we formed the view that central banks needed to conduct an unprecedented coordinated 50-basis-point interest rate cut to bridge the system through to the weekend when there would be a G7 meeting and we might be able to act with overwhelming force to arrest the free fall. The case for action was clear (by this point, a global recession in advanced economies was assured), but I was concerned. What if the Bank of Canada's action laid bare that the government's position on the economy was untenable? Could the actions of an independent, apolitical central bank influence an election?

But on reflection I realised that not acting would be political. With the financial sector now imploding, we needed to provide immediate liquidity to the financial system. And with the global economy grinding to a halt, the Canadian economy would need major stimulus to preserve as many jobs as possible. Moreover, we needed to show markets that there was a 'pilot in the plane' – that the authorities recognised the gravity of the situation and would act with overwhelming force.

So that afternoon the Bank of Canada Governing Council agreed to conduct an emergency interest rate cut first thing the next morning alongside the Fed, ECB, Bank of England, Riksbank and the Swiss National Bank. Around 7pm, I called the Finance Minister Jim Flaherty, a brilliant, hard-nosed career politician, who had appointed me as Governor only a year before. After I had told him our plans, he asked whether the Bank had ever done something like this before. 'Only after 9/11,' I replied. There was a sharp intake of breath, and then after a long pause, 'Good luck.'

It turned out the rate cut was lucky for Flaherty, whose party would see their poll numbers bounce, as Canadians appeared relieved to see action taken in the public interest. Yet he and I knew we would need more than luck for the weekend's meeting when the world economy was on the brink. We needed a plan.

BUILDING A NEW SYSTEM FROM THE RUINS OF THE OLD

A few days later we were back in the Cash Room of the US Treasury with the other G7 finance ministers and central bank governors. We had barely made it to the weekend, and there wasn't yet a plan. Going into the meeting all we had was a long, garbled communiqué written in opaque and ultimately toothless G7-speak. I knew because I used to slave over such documents as a deputy. They had their place, but this was definitely not it.

Comparing what has been written about that meeting to my contemporaneous notes, the length and eloquence of the interventions seem to grow with the years. From my perspective, it was 'full, frank and focused'. Arguments that markets had overshot and would self-equilibrate were crushed. The German Finance Minister, Peer Steinbrück, remarked that he had met a woman that week in the former East Germany who told him that 'she had seen the fall of communism, and now she was witnessing the fall of capitalism'. The few remaining moral-hazard fundamentalists were told they'd have their day once we began reforming the system so that large banks could fail without pulling down the economy. The focus turned to the only thing that mattered: saving what was left of the financial system to prevent a depression.

A consensus was forged that governments and central banks would unequivocally backstop our banking systems with liquidity and capital, if necessary. The draft communiqué was discarded and a new one of five spare, clear bullet points was crafted. We had a plan, based on overwhelming force, and it was going to be clearly communicated. Finally, all the lessons of crisis management were being applied.

Afterwards as I walked down the steps of the US Treasury, I thought back to my first G7 meetings when as a finance deputy I had the privilege of sitting next to Chair of the Federal Reserve Alan Greenspan. This was a time when the Washington Consensus reigned supreme – the belief that free markets, free trade, floating exchange rates and liberalised capital flows would promote global prosperity. The G20 was a young forum to socialise these pillars of globalisation across the membership. And for a time it worked. Markets were liberalised and the global economy became increasingly integrated. Hundreds of millions of people rose out of poverty and global inequality began to fall. Greenspan understood far earlier than most how globalisation and technology were driving a productivity boom in the US, and he correctly predicted that these forces would be disinflationary. There really was a new era. But new eras always bring risks alongside opportunities.

At the same time imbalances within and between economies began to grow. Inequality fell globally but rose sharply in many advanced economies. The US became heavily dependent on foreign borrowing to fund its consumer spending and housing booms. The window to address these vulnerabilities was limited. By 2005, most indicators of financial stress were flashing amber, but few steps were taken.

It wasn't because the Chair of the Federal Reserve was the market fundamentalist of caricature. Exceptionally well versed in the nature of financial cycles, Greenspan had seen evidence of irrational exuberance in equity markets in the 1990s and described a 'conundrum' in the bond market in 2005 when longer-term yields hadn't risen in tandem with recent interest rate hikes. But while he recognised that markets could over- and undershoot, he doubted that authorities could identify those cases with sufficient confidence to act. Moreover, Greenspan took the view that it was more efficient to 'clean up' after a bubble had burst than to lean into a potential one as it appeared to be developing. He had successfully argued against extending regulation and stopped vital improvements in the mechanics of the rapidly expanding derivative markets, the very markets that would bring down Lehman. He twice refused to allow the Fed to take on oversight of the massive GSEs (Government Sponsored Enterprises in the US such as Fanny Mae and Freddy Mac) whose increasingly reckless behaviour stoked the US housing

bubble. And he relied on the self-interest of financial market participants to limit excessive risk taking.

They were to disappoint him bitterly. In his famous Congressional
testimony on 23 October 2008, Greenspan issued a *mea culpa*:
'Those of us who have looked to the self-interest of lending institutions to protect shareholders' equity – myself especially – are in a
state of shocked disbelief.' He went on to state that he had been
'partially' wrong to hold that some complex trading instruments,
such as credit default swaps, did not need oversight. When the
committee chair asked him, 'You found your view of the world,
your ideology, was not right, it was not working?', Greenspan
replied, 'Absolutely, precisely,' before adding, 'You know, that's
precisely the reason I was shocked, because I have been going more
than 40 years or more with very considerable evidence that it was
working considerably well.'

As described by his biographer, Sebastian Mallaby, Alan
Greenspan was *The Man Who Knew*. He understood more than
most the limits of market rationality. That's why he had intervened
forcefully following major financial and economic shocks from the
1987 stock market crash to 9/11. But he was equally sceptical of
regulation, so he hadn't intervened to bolster resilience. Nor did he
favour using monetary or other policies to address the build-up of
systemic risks. He saw the G20, which had been formed in the wake
of the Asian crisis of the late 1990s, as an effective forum for spreading common understanding of such approaches as the underpinning
of open global markets.

As I headed into a hastily convened meeting of the G20, I knew that
such light-touch, laissez-faire thinking was dead. With the economies in the emerging world sideswiped by the implosion of the
financial systems in advanced economies, we would need to forge a
new consensus.

G20 finance ministers and central bank governors were hastily
convened around a large table to endorse the G7 decision to backstop their entire financial systems. Treasury Secretary Paulson and
Chair Bernanke were at the head separated by an empty chair. Early
on, as Jean-Claude Trichet was speaking, the room began to buzz,

and I turned my head to see President Bush stride in, sit down and begin to listen. The Brazilian Finance Minister Mantega, who had been highly critical of the US handling of Lehman Brothers, was the next person due to speak. He offered to pass not least because his English was not that good. 'No, go ahead,' the President replied, 'mine's worse.' It helped cut the tension.

When Bush addressed us, he spoke well, admitting the mistakes the US had made, vowing to fix things, committing to strengthening the US banking system and then asking for our help. 'We need you too to get behind this. We will be stronger together,' he emphasised. Humility. Responsibility. Resilience. Determination. Solidarity. By checking the right values, it was clear when he had finished that he had won the room.

Thus reassured, as I walked out with a much more experienced and much wiser colleague, Mario Draghi, I told him how impressed I was with how the President had handled the meeting. Mario told me of the time that he had met Mikhail Gorbachev, back in the early 1990s when the Soviet Union was asking the G7 for advice on economic reform.

At that time Mario, a G7 deputy finance minister, looked at the General Secretary of the Supreme Soviet and thought, 'What's a guy like that doing meeting a guy like me? These Russians must be in more trouble than I thought.' He continued, 'Mark, you know what? Right now I'm thinking exactly the same thing about the Americans.'

The world had moved from G1 to G0. Could the system survive without a hegemon? Only if it could rediscover its values.

8

Creating a Simpler, Safer, Fairer Financial System

Following the meeting with President Bush, the G20 was empowered to lead the reform of the global financial system. The goal wasn't just to address the causes of the crisis but to make the financial system simpler, safer and fairer. It charged a new body, the Financial Stability Board, with these tasks and had it report directly to G20 leaders, thereby providing the essential political backing. It was my privilege to help lead those efforts as the successor to the FSB's first chair, Mario Draghi. In taking up our task, we knew we had to rebalance the relationships between banks and markets, between the market and the state, and between economic and social capital.

While many elements of the new approach have been technical, the essential changes could not be found in any formula. They went well beyond the conventional instincts of economists, who after all suffer from physics envy. We covet its neat equations and crave its deterministic systems. This inevitably leads to disappointment. The economy isn't deterministic. People aren't always rational. Human creativity, frailty, exuberance and pessimism all contribute to economic and financial cycles.

As the great physicist Sir Isaac Newton lamented, 'I can calculate the motions of celestial bodies, but not the madness of people.' Newton's exasperation came after he had lost a fortune investing in the South Sea Company, or more precisely after he had speculated on a bubble that didn't make sense.[1] Newton's experience is common throughout history. Something that starts as fundamentally innovative ends up being pushed to ridiculous extremes. Belief turns to madness. Momentum is everywhere. Value loses touch with fundamentals, and everything becomes relative. Eventually the bubble bursts with dire financial consequences.

And so it was in the run-up to the global financial crisis. The new-era thinking in the first decade of the millennium was grounded in the very real boosts to prosperity from global integration and technological innovation. Financial innovations increased financial inclusion and had the potential to reduce risks, if applied appropriately. But initial successes bred complacency.

Faith in markets reigned supreme. Risks in the financial system were increasingly ignored. Few masters of the universe were focused on the longer-term consequences of their actions. The future arrived with a bang: from Great Moderation to Great Recession, from boom to bust, from confidence to mistrust.

The consequences were severe.

A lost decade. Real household incomes in the United Kingdom did not grow at all over the ten years following the fall of Northern Rock (Figure 8.1). This was the worst performance since Karl Marx was scribbling the *Communist Manifesto* in the British Library. Are current political developments so surprising?

Growing fragmentation of the global economic system. The third wave of globalisation crested with the financial crisis. Over the

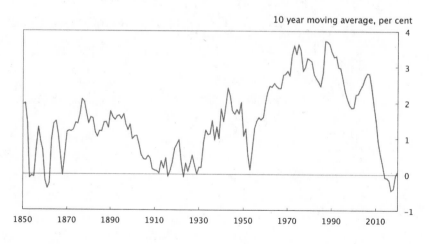

Figure 8.1 Changes in UK real wages 1850–2015

previous decade, trade and cross-border capital flows had been growing at 8 per cent and 20 per cent per year, respectively. Since the crash, trade growth slowed to 2 per cent (pre-Covid) and cross-border capital flows had still not recovered their pre-crisis levels. For the first few years afterwards, G20 countries managed, in the words of their communiqués, to 'resist protectionism',[2] but as economic difficulties mounted, trade restrictions have begun to multiply, most prominently in the trade war that erupted between the US and China. The restrictions prompted by the Covid crisis will, at a minimum, make these trends harder to reverse, and could intensify them.

Growing mistrust of the elites. The financial crisis was arguably one of the main causes of the marked decline in trust in experts.[3] A financial system, lauded by most economists and policymakers as well as by *all* bankers, came crashing down on the heads of ordinary people, some of whom are still suffering the consequences. They, like Queen Elizabeth, wondered, 'Why did no one notice it?'[4] The answer, according to a letter addressed to Her Majesty and signed by thirty-three distinguished economists, 'was a failure of the collective imagination of many bright people, both in this country and internationally, to understand the risks to the system as whole'.[5]

The key fault lines that those experts missed were outlined in the previous chapter. Too much debt. Excessive reliance on markets for liquidity. Byzantine complexity in derivative markets. Huge regulatory arbitrage with institutions, like ABCP vehicles, acting like banks without a safety net. The misaligned incentives that cut across banks and their imitators.

But there were deeper causes. This was a crisis of values as well as value. On the positive side of the ledger, financial innovations at the turn of the millennium were initially designed to increase financial inclusion, and for a while they did. Home ownership in the US increased sharply. And for a while the rapid expansion of leverage helped fuel stronger growth, and greater economic dynamism. But much of this growth would prove ephemeral largely because, in the process, finance lost track of its core values of fairness, integrity, prudence and responsibility.

THE FSB AND RADICAL
FINANCIAL REFORM

In the few years following that fateful weekend when President Bush spoke to finance ministers and governors in Washington, the G20 pursued a radical programme of reforms that have made the global financial system safer, simpler and fairer. These initiatives were possible because the gravity of the economic and financial challenges in the wake of the 2008 crisis was so great that countries were spurred to collective action. As we have seen, they formed a new body, the Financial Stability Board (FSB), and charged it with fixing the fault lines that had caused the crisis. The FSB brought together the heads of the central banks, securities regulators and treasuries from the world's largest economies along with those running the major standard-setting bodies.

Under the skilful and energetic leadership of Mario Draghi, the FSB had an immediate impact in giving shape to a more resilient global financial system. Over the course of the next decade, it would develop a comprehensive programme of over 100 reforms. By the time I succeeded Mario as Chair, I learned from his example what is required for multilateralism to succeed in a G0 world.

First, it is vital to have a clear mission with political backing. G20 leaders in Pittsburgh charged the FSB with identifying and addressing the risks to global financial stability. This mission is simple yet hard, but the annual cycle of summits and the scrutiny of G20 leaders and the public have kept the FSB focused on results. The FSB enjoys delegated, carefully circumscribed authority. It develops proposals but they must be endorsed by the G20 before countries choose whether to implement them.

Second, get the right people around the table. The FSB isn't a large international bureaucracy. Its secretariat has just thirty people. Its strength lies in its membership: the group of central banks, regulators, finance ministries and standard setters. They bring their expertise and a sense of shared objectives, working closely together to find global solutions to common problems.

Third, the FSB process of developing reforms builds consensus to instil ownership. The standards agreed at the FSB do not have direct force in any member jurisdiction. Moreover, some of the mistrust in globalisation arises from what Dani Rodrik termed an impossible trinity – a trilemma – between economic integration, democracy and sovereignty.[6] Common rules and standards are required for trade in goods, services and capital, but those rules cede, or at best pool, sovereignty. To maintain legitimacy, the process of agreeing those standards must be rooted in democratic accountability.

The FSB process squared that triangle. No country has to implement any new reform, even though it is in the interests of every country that everyone does since financial risks easily spill across borders. The process of developing new measures through shared analysis and the building of consensus instils ownership of new reforms, and leads, in most cases, to their timely and comprehensive implementation at the national level.

THE THREE LIES OF FINANCE

The comprehensive programme of financial reforms is creating a system that can serve households and businesses in bad times as well as good. The performance of the financial sector during the Covid crisis is a case in point. Despite an economic shock to rival the Great Depression, finance has been part of the solution not the cause of the problem. If the spirit of the financial reform programme is sustained, further changes can be pursued that will deepen financial inclusion, better meet the needs of ageing populations and help fund the transition to a low-carbon economy.

But all these gains will be forfeit if policymakers and financiers rest on their laurels. Financial history rhymes all too frequently, with enormous costs to our citizens. As already noted, 800 years of economic history teaches that financial crises occur roughly once a decade – a frequency that reflects, in part, the short institutional memories in finance. Lessons painfully learned during busts are gradually forgotten as 'new eras' dawn and the financial cycle begins anew.

A major bank CEO once told his daughter a financial crisis is 'something that happens every five to seven years'.[7] In no other aspect of human endeavour do people not strive to learn and improve. And in no other industry would such weary fatalism be tolerated. This depressing cycle of prudence, confidence, complacency, euphoria and despair reflects the power of the three lies of finance: this time is different, markets always clear, and markets are moral. To break their seductive power, we need to reinforce the underlying values required for the financial system to fulfil its role as a servant, rather than master, of society.

Consider the first lie, which is the four most expensive words in the English language: 'This time is different.'[8]

This misconception is usually the product of an initial success, with early progress gradually building into a blind faith in a new era of effortless prosperity. For example, it took a revolution in macroeconomic policy to help win the battles against the high and unstable inflation, rising unemployment and volatile growth of the 1970s and 1980s.

As we saw in Chapter 4, stagflation was tamed by new regimes for monetary stability that were both democratically accountable and highly effective. Clear remits. Parliamentary accountability. Sound governance. Independent, transparent and effective policy-making. These were the great successes of that time and their value endures today.

But these innovations did not deliver lasting macroeconomic stability. Far from it. Price stability was no guarantee of financial stability. An initially healthy focus became a dangerous distraction. Against the serene backdrop of the so-called Great Moderation, a storm was brewing as total non-financial debt in the G7 rose by the size of its GDP.

Several factors drove this debt super-cycle, including demographics and the stagnation of middle-class real wages (itself the product of technology and globalisation). In the US, households had to borrow to increase consumption. 'Let them eat cake' became 'let them eat credit.'[9] Financial innovation made it easier to do so. And the ready supply of foreign capital made it cheaper. Most importantly – and this is the lie – complacency among individuals and institutions, fed by a long period of macroeconomic stability and rising asset prices, made this remorseless borrowing seem sensible.[10]

As described by the economist Hyman Minsky, a prophet not heard in his own town, this cycle typically starts with a fundamentally positive development, such as new markets or a new technology of broad application. The ensuing period of prosperity and macroeconomic stability leads borrowers and lenders to make increasingly optimistic assumptions about the future such as 'house prices can only go up' or 'financial innovation has reduced risk'. Debt and asset prices build, reinforcing each other for a time.

The resulting vulnerabilities are only exposed when economic conditions turn. When they do, lenders hastily revise their expectations for the future – the 'Minsky moment' – and pull back on lending. Borrowers reduce spending or, *in extremis*, default. These responses make the economic downturn much deeper and more prolonged.

When the crisis broke, policymakers quickly dropped the received wisdoms of the Great Moderation and scrambled to relearn the lessons of the Great Depression. Minsky went mainstream.[11]

A deep-seated faith in markets lay beneath the new-era thinking of the Great Moderation. Captured by the myth that finance can regulate and correct itself spontaneously, authorities retreated from their regulatory and supervisory responsibilities, just as Tommaso Padoa-Schioppa had foreseen in that Dubai conference room.

The second lie is the belief that 'markets always clear'. That is, the supply of whatever is traded will always equal demand for it, and at the 'right price' there will never be excess supply or demand.

This belief that markets always clear has two dangerous consequences. First, if markets always clear, they can be assumed to be in equilibrium – or, said differently, 'to be always right'. If markets are efficient, then bubbles cannot be identified nor can their potential causes be addressed. Second, if markets always clear, they should possess a natural stability. Evidence to the contrary must be the product of either market distortions or incomplete markets.[12] Such thinking dominated the practical indifference of policymakers to the housing and credit booms before the crisis.

Such naivety is striking given the ample evidence of disequilibria in markets for goods and labour. In goods markets, there is 'sluggishness everywhere'. Left to themselves, economies can go for sustained periods operating above or below potential, resulting in either excessive or deficient inflation. Yet efficient market forces 'should' bring about changes in prices sufficient to equate demand with potential, leaving inflation as a purely monetary phenomenon.

In labour markets, there is 'rigidity everywhere'. Rather than fluidly adjusting to equate the demand for labour with its supply, periods of deficient labour demand can persist, sustaining mass unemployment and joblessness. Yet efficient market forces 'should' eliminate these disequilibria by having wages adjust to ensure full employment always and for ever. Monetary policy is not only a response to these rigidities; it is made effective by them.

Much of financial innovation springs from the logic that the solution to market failures is to build new markets on old ones.[13] An attempt at progress through infinite regress.

During the Great Moderation, this view became an organising principle for financiers and policymakers. The latter pursued a light-touch regulatory agenda in a quest for a perfect real world of complete markets first described as abstract theory by Arrow and Debreu. This is a coherent world of self-interested, atomistic agents, coolly calculating odds over all future possible states of the world, writing and trading contracts with each other, all frictionlessly enforced, all achieving mutually beneficial – indeed socially optimal – outcomes.[14]

Of course, markets only clear in textbooks. In reality, as Newton learned to his cost, people are irrational and economies imperfect. When such imperfections exist, adding markets can sometimes make things worse.

Take synthetic credit derivatives, which were supposed to complete the market in default risk and thereby improve the pricing and allocation of capital – a financial alchemy that appeared to have distributed risk, parcelling it up and allocating it to those who wanted most to bear it.[15] However, the pre-crisis system had only spread risk, contingently and opaquely, in ways that ended up increasing it. Once the crisis began, the markets for ABCP, securitisations and credit derivatives all seized up, risk quickly concentrated on the balance sheets of intermediaries that were themselves capital constrained. And with the fates of borrowers and lenders tied together via hyper-globalised banks and markets, problems at the core spread violently to the periphery.

A truth of finance is that the riskiness of an asset depends on who owns it. When markets don't clear, agents may be surprised to find what they own and for how long. When those surprises are – or are thought to be – widespread, panic ensues.

The impossibility of completing markets was not the only practical problem with the pre-crisis approach. Even if markets could be perfected, nature itself is unknowable. Newtonian mechanics breaks down at the subatomic level, and the search for the grand unifying theory of everything that matters persists to this day. Recall that the Arrow–Debreu world relies on people being able to calculate the odds of each and every possible scenario. Then they can trade contracts and insure each other against risks they are unwilling to bear.

Even a moment of introspection reveals the absurdity of these assumptions compared to the real world. More often than not, even describing the universe of possible outcomes is beyond the means of mere mortals, let alone ascribing subjective probabilities to each of those outcomes. This is genuine uncertainty, as opposed to risk, the distinction made by Frank Knight in the 1920s.[16] And it means that market outcomes reflect individual choices made under a pretence of knowledge.[17]

The swings in sentiment that result – pessimism one moment, exuberance the next – reflect not only nature's odds but also our own assessments of them, inevitably distorted by human behaviour. In his *General Theory*, Keynes mused on how rational agents would treat a hypothetical contest to choose the most beautiful faces from a hundred photographs. The winning strategy:

> is not a case of choosing those [faces] that, to the best of one's judgment, are really the prettiest, nor even those that average opinion genuinely thinks the prettiest. We have reached the

third degree where we devote our intelligences to anticipating what average opinion expects the average opinion to be. And there are some, I believe, who practise the fourth, fifth and higher degrees.[18]

As a successful speculator himself, Keynes argued that similar behaviour was at work within financial markets, with people pricing shares based not on estimates of their fundamental value but rather on what they think everyone else thinks their value is, or what everybody else would predict the average assessment of that value to be. It is the derivative of the derivative of subjective utility. The CDO2 of welfare. In a Minsky cycle, market valuations can become seriously detached from fundamental values.

Cass Sunstein's work on social movements could help explain why (what appear to have been) widely held beliefs can be subject to sudden reappraisals. There is considerable evidence that changes in social norms, like reported attitudes to same-sex marriage or even political revolutions, often happen suddenly.

Sunstein identifies several factors that explain this phenomenon. These include preference falsification, which is when what we are willing to say publicly diverges from what's inside our heads, and interdependencies, which is when what we are willing to say or do depends on others. These characteristics mean that once conditions ripen, a critical mass of new opinions can form quickly, sometimes with brutal consequences. And so it is with financial markets. As the Minsky cycle progresses, value increasingly becomes relative. When stocks are generally expensive, buying the ones with the greatest momentum becomes attractive, based on hope that there will be a greater fool who will buy them before the crash. But this 'devil take the hindmost' approach eventually overestimates what the true opinion of the average opinion of the average opinion really is.

But how do markets become disconnected from value in the first place? In behavioural-science trials, if people learn about a *new or emerging* social norm (such as taking up veganism) they are more likely to behave in accordance with that norm. The latter could help explain how new-era thinking takes off. For his part, Keynes famously emphasised the role of animal spirits in driving markets away from fundamental value:

> Even apart from the instability due to speculation, there is the instability due to the characteristic of human nature that a large proportion of our positive activities depend on spontaneous optimism rather than on a mathematical expectation, whether moral or hedonistic or economic. Most, probably, of our decisions to do something positive, the full consequences of which will be drawn out over many days to come, can only be taken as a result of animal spirits – of a spontaneous urge to action rather than inaction, and not as the outcome of a weighted average of quantitative benefits multiplied by quantitative probabilities.[19]

These dynamics can afflict not just sophisticated investors, but mortgage lenders and homebuyers, especially during a 'new era'. If house prices can only go up, it is possible to borrow large multiples and pay off future obligations with the capital gains that will follow.

Such 'rational' behaviour fuelled the credit binge that ultimately led to the global crisis. And, in the end, belief that 'markets are always right' meant that policymakers didn't play their proper roles moderating those tendencies in pursuit of the collective good.

The third lie – that 'markets are moral' – takes for granted the social capital that markets need to fulfil their promise. In financial markets, means and ends can be conflated too easily. Value can become abstract and relative. And the pull of the crowd can overwhelm the integrity of the individual.

Consider the example of fixed income, currencies and commodities markets (FICC) which have historically relied heavily on informal codes or understandings. They have also, over the centuries, been beset by poor behaviour. A comprehensive review of financial misconduct by the Fixed Income, Currencies and Commodities Markets Standards Board (FMSB) found consistent fraudulent behaviour over the past 200 years.[20] The commodity squeeze of rye in 1868 is similar to the squeezes on ice in 1900, oats in 1951 and cocoa in 2010. The so-called 'wash trades' used to boost the sales price on Manhattan Electrical Supply in 1930 were employed by TeraExchange in 2014 for the same purpose. Planted rumours to boost share value are a recurring phenomenon, delivered via telegraph in the nineteenth century and social media in the twenty-first. Technology evolves and new legislation gets passed, but at its core the misconduct remains the same.[21]

Repeated episodes of misconduct in the run-up to the global financial crisis – including the Libor and FX scandals – called into question the social licence that markets need to innovate and grow. Financial market participants were found to have knowingly missold to clients products that were inappropriate or even fraudulent. Professionals across firms manipulated key interest rate and foreign exchange benchmarks to support trading positions within their firms while costing retail and corporate clients who relied on those benchmarks billions. One of the most striking things about the transcripts of the chatroom discussions that orchestrated these outrages is how detached they are from those businesses and households in the real world which they were affecting.

Rather than being professional and open, critical markets – such as those for bonds, currencies and derivatives – became informal and clubby. Rather than competing on merit, participants colluded online. Rather than everyone taking responsibility for their actions, few were held to account.

The scale of misconduct impaired banks' ability to function fairly and effectively. A decade after the crisis, global banks' misconduct costs had exceeded $320 billion, capital that could otherwise have supported around $5 trillion of lending to households and businesses.[22] And in a system where trust is fundamental, only 20 per cent of UK citizens thought banks were run well after the crisis, compared to 90 per cent in the 1980s.[23]

The crisis reminded us that real markets don't just happen; they depend on the quality of market infrastructure for their effectiveness, resilience and fairness. That means both hard infrastructure – the structure of markets themselves such as the design of financial market benchmarks – and soft infrastructure – like regulations, codes and culture that govern behaviour in them.

It is critical to get this infrastructure right because financial markets serve the real economy. By financing firms to hire, invest and expand, markets help drive growth and create jobs. By opening up cross-border trade and investment, our markets create new opportunities for businesses and savers. And by transferring risks to those most willing and able to bear them, our markets help UK households and businesses insure against the unexpected.

Much of this activity depends on fixed income, currency and commodity markets – like the markets for corporate bonds, for commercial paper, for derivatives and for foreign exchange. These FICC markets establish the borrowing costs of households, companies and governments. They set the exchange rates we use when we travel or buy goods from abroad. They determine the costs of our food and raw materials. And they help companies manage the financial risks they incur when investing, producing and trading.

Markets have become ever more important to people as they bear increasing responsibility for financing their retirements and insuring against risks. The suitability of those decisions will depend heavily on FICC markets. It is therefore vital that they work well. And that they are seen to do so.

Though they can be powerful drivers of prosperity, FICC markets can go wrong. Left unattended, they are prone to instability, excess and abuse. Markets without the right standards or infrastructure are like cities without building codes, fire brigades or insurance. Poor infrastructure allowed the spark of the US subprime crisis to light a powder keg under UK markets, triggering the worst recession so far in our lifetimes:

- poor 'soft' infrastructure such as codes of conduct that too few read and too many ignored;
- faulty 'hard' infrastructure like interest rate and foreign exchange benchmarks that were quite literally fixed; and
- weak banks whose light capital and heavy reliance on short-term funding created a tinderbox.

Central banks shared in these failings, operating a system of fire insurance whose ambiguity was anything but constructive when global markets were engulfed in flames. In the run-up to the crisis, the general approach of central banks was consistent with the attitude of FICC markets, which historically relied heavily on informal codes and understandings. That informality was well suited to an earlier age. But as markets innovated and grew, it proved wanting.

Most troubling were the numerous incidents of misconduct that exploited such informality. These undercut public trust and threatened systemic stability. Mistrust between market participants raised borrowing costs and reduced credit availability. Falling confidence in market resilience meant companies have held back productive investments. And uncertainty meant people hesitated to move jobs or homes.

These effects are not trivial, and they have reduced the dynamism of our economy in the post-crisis years.[24] Widespread mistrust has also had deeper, indirect costs. Markets are not ends in themselves, but powerful means for prosperity and security for all. As such they need to retain the consent of society – a social licence – to be allowed to operate, innovate and grow. Everyone has been let down by these repeated episodes of misconduct. And everyone in finance, in the public and private sectors, shares responsibility for fixing them.

So this time is no different. Markets don't always clear. And we can suffer from their amorality. What to do with such knowledge? And how to retain it?

The answer starts with the radical programme of G20 reforms that is creating a safer, simpler and fairer financial system. A financial system that can better serve households and businesses in bad times as well as good. A system that can help support greater inclusion and the transition to a net-zero carbon economy. These pro-market reforms are vital but they are not sufficient.

Regulation alone won't break an eight-century cycle of financial boom and bust. Recent gains will be lost if we once again fall under the spell of the three lies of finance. To resist their siren calls, policymakers and market participants must bind themselves to the mast. That ultimately means recognising the limits of markets and rediscovering our responsibilities for the system.

ADDRESSING THE CONSEQUENCES OF 'MARKETS THAT DON'T ALWAYS CLEAR'

There have been major reforms to make markets less complex and more robust. Their core objective has been to rebuild real markets. Real markets are resilient, fair and effective. They maintain their social licence. Real markets don't just happen; they depend on the quality of market infrastructure.

Robust market infrastructure is a public good in constant danger of under-provision, not least because the best markets innovate continually. This risk can be overcome only if all market actors, public and private, recognise their responsibilities for the system as a whole.

A decade ago, over-the-counter (OTC) derivative trades were largely unregulated, unreported and bilaterally settled. When Lehman Brothers fell, the uncertainty about such exposures sparked panic. Since then, reforms have made these markets safer and more transparent, not least by requiring trade reporting and by encouraging central clearing of OTC trades. As a result, 90 per cent of new OTC single-currency interest rate derivatives are now centrally cleared in the US. And an additional $1 trillion of collateral is now held globally against all derivative trades.[25]

A decade on from the financial crisis, a series of measures are eliminating the toxic forms of shadow banking at the heart of the crisis, like Canadian ABCP – with their large funding mismatches, high leverage and opaque, off-balance-sheet arrangements. Other, more constructive forms of market-based finance, including money-market funds and repo markets, are subject to new policy measures that reduce their risks and reinforce their benefits.

As the old fault lines close in advanced economies, however, they are widening in some emerging market economies. For example, while China's economic miracle over the past three decades has been extraordinary, its post-crisis performance has relied heavily on a large build-up of debt and an associated explosion of shadow banking. The non-bank finance sector has increased from around 10 per cent of GDP a decade ago to over 100 per cent now, with developments echoing those in the pre-crisis US such as off-balance-sheet vehicles with large maturity mismatches, sharp increases in repo financing and large contingent liabilities of borrowers and banks.

More broadly, a potentially major new vulnerability has emerged across the G20. This risk starts, as is often the case, with a positive development. Global assets under management have grown from around $50 trillion a decade ago to around $90 trillion today, and have accounted for all the increase in foreign lending to emerging market economies since the crisis. This is bringing welcome diversity to the financial system.

However, more than $30 trillion of assets are held in funds that promise daily liquidity to investors despite investing in potentially illiquid underlying assets.[26] This liquidity mismatch creates an advantage to investors who redeem ahead of others, particularly in stress. This 'first-mover advantage' could prompt a destabilising rush for the exits, not only in the market where problems first occur, but also across markets with analogous risks. Fund suspensions, a widely available tool, exacerbate the issue.

In other words, they are built on the lie that markets always clear.

Outflows from open-ended funds are indeed more sensitive to fund performance when funds hold more illiquid assets and when market conditions are worse. Although risks have, so far, crystallised only within some niche managers and smaller markets, and their impact has been contained, these risks have the potential to become systemic if funds' holdings of less liquid assets continue to grow.

As is the case for banks, the institutions at the heart of market-based finance, particularly open-ended investment funds, must prudently manage their leverage and liquidity. Mismatches between redemption terms and the liquidity of some funds' assets means there is an advantage to investors who redeem ahead of others, particularly in stress. This has the potential to become a systemic risk as first-mover advantage could prompt a destabilising rush to the exits.

In response, the Bank of England and the Financial Conduct Authority (FCA) decided that there should be greater consistency between the liquidity of a fund's assets and its redemption terms (Figure 8.2). Specifically:

- the liquidity of funds' assets should be assessed either as the price discount needed for a quick sale of a vertical slice of those assets or as the time period needed for a sale to avoid a material price discount;
- investors who redeem should receive a price for their units that reflects the discount needed to sell the required proportion of a fund's assets in the specified redemption notice period; and
- redemption notice periods should reflect the time needed to sell the required proportion of a fund's assets without discounts beyond those captured in the price received by redeeming investors (Figure 8.3).

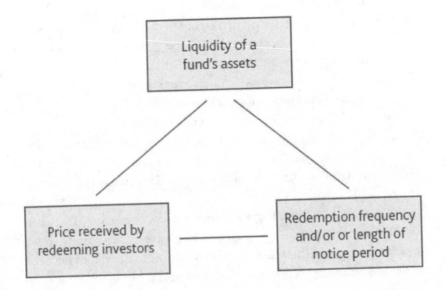

Figure 8.2 The FPC's principles for resilience of mutual fund design

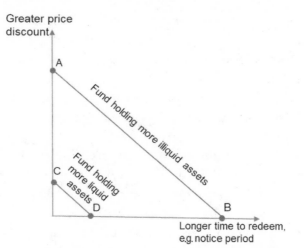

Figure 8.3 Stylised combinations of price discounts and notice periods
needed to reduce incentives to redeem ahead of others

During the crisis, liquidity dried up, particularly in the interbank market, as cash-rich banks hoarded excess funds. In parallel, a 'run on repo', triggered by increased haircuts on collateral to guard against counterparty risk, pushed the shadow banking sectors in advanced economies into collapse. In the euro area, the sovereign debt crisis compounded these problems, causing some markets to splinter along national lines.

Global reforms have addressed the fault lines that caused this fiasco. New global standards for liquidity regulation are now in place including the Liquidity Coverage Ratio and Net Stable Funding Ratio. Bank capital standards now take into account exposures to shadow banks, including step-in risk, and through-the-cycle margining prevents Minsky cycles in secured lending. These reforms are transforming banks' approach to liquidity management and building the resilience of the system as a whole. For example, liquid assets – relative to liabilities that can readily run – are tenfold higher than before the crisis.[27]

However, in recent years, volatility in US dollar repo markets suggest there are still frictions that need to be addressed. In 2020 when strains emerged in these markets, banks did not step in to lend cash, viewing the profit opportunity to be insufficient to offset the impact on *perceived* regulatory liquidity requirements. The Federal Reserve's open-market operations eventually calmed the markets, but longer-term repo rates remained elevated, as dealers priced in a higher likelihood of similar spikes in the future. This was one of a series of incidents, including tantrums in the US and German government bond markets, that indicate broader problems of discontinuous market liquidity in stress.

The solution is not to unwind post-crisis liquidity regulation, a recidivism that would only recreate, with time, the enormous systemic risks of the past. Moreover, the limited systemic conse-quences of these events should be noted. After all, the riskiness of an asset depends on who holds it. What feels like a 'crisis' in periph-eral markets is a bad day for those operating in them; whereas a bad day in the core of the banking system is an *annus horribilis* for the real economy.

As we saw in previous chapters, central banks developed over the centuries formal roles as lenders of last resort to banks in order to prevent temporary liquidity shortages from turning into solvency crisis. Every central banker grows up learning Bagehot's dictum, 'To avert panic, central banks should lend early and freely, to solvent firms, against good collateral and at a high rate.'[28] Would that it were so simple.

Putting Bagehot into practice, a central banker encounters several challenges. The first is the difficult judgement of whether a firm is solvent, not least because the scale of bank leverage means that if the market is against an institution whose assets are otherwise sound, 'the market can be wrong, longer than the bank can stay liquid', and for a bank staying liquid is the equivalent of staying solvent.

The second is the question of what constitutes good collateral. A prudent central banker would always want to lend secured by the highest-quality assets such as government bonds, but this isn't much of a service, and it became apparent during the crisis that doing so would have only limited knock-on effects on liquidity in markets, such as asset-backed securities, that had become vital to the func-tioning of the system. Banks have tended to hoard the liquidity they receive, rather than flowing it through to improve market functioning. A lender-of-last-resort function that only serves banks increasingly does not serve society.

The third challenge is that the high or penalty rate itself can cause problems. It is designed to avoid moral hazard, so that banks don't run with low liquidity on the assumption that they can outsource their liquidity management. However, borrowing at a high rate carries stigma – it signals distress. And that means that banks are unlikely to come early to the central bank; in fact, by the time they come it may already be too late.

This is closely related to another factor: a conflict of values. Traditional central banking operated in the shadows. Emergency lending could take place on the sly. This practice is not sustainable in an era of democratic accountability. Huge sums of taxpayer money are being put at risk. But disclosure can bring on the very risk of a bank run that emergency liquidity is designed to avoid.

The combination of these factors has meant that the lender-of-last-resort function of central banks has changed almost beyond recognition. The emphasis is on transparent auctions of liquidity to a wide range of counterparties including banks, broker-dealers and financial market infrastructure like central counterparties (who lie at the heart of derivative markets). The experience of the past few years suggests that it needs to expand further still.

One of the potential problems underlying the repo market stress is that what may look to be sufficient liquidity in aggregate can prove too little if it is asymmetrically distributed either across institutions or across national boundaries. This suggests that central banks should provide more liquidity in aggregate, including by widening access to their balance sheets.

For example, prompted by the potential risks that come with Brexit, the Bank of England began running weekly auctions in sterling, US dollars and euros that could be used to absorb pressures if they arose. It also has a contingent term repo facility that could be activated at a higher frequency if needed; and the Bank of England – like the ECB – can lend to a very broad range of counterparties against a wide range of collateral.

Central banks and regulators must also be clear that liquidity facilities and buffers are there to be used. For example, the Bank clarified its supervisory expectations to re-emphasise its commitment to providing liquidity in the ordinary course of business. The Bank does not expect firms to justify any usage, nor is there any presumption they would use their own buffers before the Bank's facilities.

Increased central clearing would be a capital-efficient way to further improve repo market liquidity; this would be most effective if smaller institutions participated directly. And a more holistic approach by firms to internal capital management would make them more agile, including not applying the leverage ratio at the desk level.

There is a strong argument for widening access to central bank facilities to include a broad range of financial market participants such as asset managers. Experience of the last decade is that banks do not pass on sufficient liquidity under stress to improve market functioning. This has a knock-on effect of exacerbating market swings, which may prompt more extraordinary central bank interventions including the asset purchase programmes in corporate and high-yield debt that are conducted more for financial stability reasons than to meet monetary policy objectives.

ADDRESSING 'THIS TIME IS DIFFERENT'

If the experience of the financial and Covid crises teaches us anything, it's humility. We cannot anticipate every risk or plan for every contingency. But we must, and can, plan for failure. That means creating an anti-fragile system that is robust to both the intensification of known risks and the crystallisation of Rumsfeldian unknowns.

Perhaps the most severe blow to public trust was the revelation that there were scores of too-big-to-fail banks at the heart of finance. A decade ago, large complex banks operated in a 'heads I win, tails you lose' bubble. They privatised profits in the run-up to the crisis before socialising the losses when the music stopped. The complete loss of confidence in private finance that crystallised in the autumn of 2008 could be arrested only by public support over the following year that totalled $15 trillion in bailouts, government guarantees of bank liabilities and special central bank liquidity schemes.

That unjust sharing of risk and reward contributed directly to inequality but – more importantly – has had a corrosive effect on the broader social fabric on which finance relies. By replacing the implicit privilege of powerful banks with the full discipline of the market, social capital can be rebuilt and economic dynamism increased. That's why it is imperative to create an anti-fragile system – one that can thrive even in the face of shocks and disorder.

To that end, bank capital requirements are now ten times higher than the pre-crisis standard. A decade ago, banks were woefully undercapitalised. Some were levered over fifty times once off-balance-sheet vehicles collapsed on to them, compared to the fifteen to twenty times leverage that history shows is prudent, and with complex business models that relied on the goodwill of markets and, ultimately, taxpayers. With capital requirements for the largest that are ten times higher, banks have raised more than $1.5 trillion of capital. And they are disciplined by a new leverage ratio that guards against risks that seem low but prove not to be.

The financial system is simpler in part because, a decade on, banks are less complex and more focused. Business strategies that relied on high-leverage, risky trading activities and wholesale funding are disappearing, as intended. Trading assets have been cut in half, and interbank lending is down by one-third. Banks lend more to households and businesses, and less to each other.

To bring back the discipline of the market and end the reliance on public funds, G20 standards help ensure that globally systemic banks can fail safely in the future. Banks have had to make themselves easier to resolve, by writing 'living wills' and reorganising themselves so that they can continue to serve households and businesses, even if there is severe strain in their investment banking businesses. Most importantly, they must now hold sufficient debt such that, in the event one fails, its successor can be recapitalised to support the continued operation of its most important activities. As a consequence, market discipline is back, with the public subsidy enjoyed by the UK's largest banks having fallen by 90 per cent. The system is fairer with banks and their management treated like other businesses in that they will bear the consequences of any failure.

While past crises had their roots in financial losses, in our digital era systemic shocks can also come from non-financial sources, including cyber-attacks. To improve firms' cyber defences, the UK largest banks are now subject to cyber penetration tests. In parallel, we are literally planning for failure, including by setting standards for how quickly critical financial institutions must restore vital services following a successful cyber-attack.

A macroprudential approach encourages authorities to meet the next challenge, not simply fight the last war. They must explore 'what could happen?' rather than seek the false comfort of being ready for what's most likely to happen. A macroprudential approach brings to life the response to the Queen: it means looking for the risks across the system as a whole.

The raison d'être of macroprudential policy is to ensure that the financial system supports the *economy*. A macroprudential framework is countercyclical, building resilience when risks are increasing and drawing on that resilience when risks crystallise. The specific objective of macroprudential policy – financial stability – is most easily defined in its absence. It is the opposite of the instability of bust, crises and panics. A positive definition of financial stability is when the financial system is capable of a sustainable provision of financial services in bad times as well as good, and there is confidence that the system can withstand future shocks without major disruption to those services.

Supporting the economy in bad times as well as good requires the financial system to be strong enough to continue lending to households and businesses when economic shocks occur. And it means that macroeconomic downturns are not made worse because of unsustainable debt burdens.[29]

To accomplish these goals, macroprudential authorities concentrate on systemic risks – that is, those large enough to impact growth materially. Such systemic risks fall broadly into two camps: cyclical and structural. Cyclical risks are the tendencies for financial conditions to loosen and debt to build up over time when the economy strengthens and people become more complacent – the extreme is the classic Minsky cycle. Structural risks are systemic risks that do not vary with the cycle. They generally relate to interconnections and concentrations within the financial system but can also arise from the structure of financial contracts or regulations.

For example, if financial institutions have a web of exposures to each other through derivatives, a problem at one bank can set off a chain reaction through the system. Or if several firms are exposed to the same market, problems in that market can be amplified because of how these firms react. Risks will also be higher if structurally weak investment vehicles, prone to fire-sale their assets, play a meaningful role in important markets. And structurally deficient market infrastructure increases the complexity and opaqueness of markets, making risks harder to identify.

Over the past decade, a flurry of macroprudential policy actions have been taken to address the fault lines that caused the crisis including raising bank capital minima and buffers, introducing liquidity buffers for banks, reducing bank interconnectedness and improving their resolvability, targeted restrictions on mortgage lending, transforming fragile OTC derivative markets and winding down the toxic forms of shadow banking and building up more resilient market-based finance.

The focus on improving the system and the widespread support for doing so reflected in part the very raw experience that people had with the costs of financial crises.

A clear framework for macroprudential policy, as described in Chapter 4, can help to break this dreary complacency curve of the financial cycle, guide policymakers and improve the understanding and effectiveness of macroprudential policy. It can promote self-reinforcing behaviour within the private financial sector. And improve the transparency and accountability of the central bank to Parliament and the people it serves.

Ultimately, the true test of the effectiveness of macroprudential policy is how well the financial system responds to shocks. Covid was as large a test as could be imagined. Major UK banks passed. Their resilience contributes to a high degree of financial sector preparedness for the current crystallisation of what had previously been an unknown unknown risk.

This strength hadn't been built up for its own sake. It was there to be used when needed. This was prudence with a purpose. Resilience with a reason, and that reason is the ultimate objective that unifies the Bank of England's monetary and financial functions – the meaning of the central banker's life which can be found in the opening sentence of the 1694 Charter – 'to promote the good of the people of the United Kingdom'.

RESTORING MORALITY TO MARKETS

A series of scandals have called the social licence of finance into question. This malaise in corners of finance can be remedied only by a combination of regulatory measures and true cultural change.

Multiple factors contributed to a tide of ethical drift in financial markets. Market standards were poorly understood, often ignored and always lacked teeth. Too many participants neither felt responsible for the system nor recognised the full impact of their actions. Bad behaviour went unchecked, proliferated and eventually became the norm.

In the cycle of scandal, response, integrity, drift and new scandal, potential solutions have oscillated between the extremes of light-touch regulation and total regulation. There are problems with each.

By undervaluing the importance of infrastructure to real markets, light-touch regulation led directly to the financial crisis.

Yet a system reliant on total regulation and large *ex post* sanctions is similarly bound to fail because it promotes a culture of complying with the letter of the law, not its spirit, and because authorities will inevitably lag developments in fast-changing markets.

A more comprehensive, lasting solution combines public regulation with private standards to restore the accountability of individuals for their own actions and for the system. There are three components:

- aligning compensation with values;
- increasing senior management accountability; and
- renewing a sense of vocation in finance.

A lesson of the crisis was that compensation schemes that delivered large bonuses for short-term returns encouraged individuals to take on excessive long-term and tail risks. In short, the present was over-valued and the future heavily discounted.

To align better incentives with the long-term interests of their firm – and, more broadly, society – compensation rules in the banking, insurance and asset-management industries in the UK now defer a significant proportion of compensation for up to seven years.[30] The UK has also introduced a system of regulatory references to address the issue of people with conduct and compliance violations who move firms without disclosure. Financial firms are now required to share information on breaches of individual conduct rules, their fitness and propriety assessments, and outcomes around subsequent disciplinary hearings. This means that the histories of such 'rolling bad apples' will be known to anyone hiring them who can then make their own judgements.[31]

The deferral of bonuses means they can be forfeit if evidence emerges of employee misconduct, errors, failures of risk management or unexpectedly poor financial performance by the individual, their team or company. In the UK, under the Senior Managers Regime (SMR) these provisions apply to employees who are judged culpable directly and to those who could reasonably have been expected to identify and manage risks or misconduct but didn't take steps to do so, as well as to senior executives who could reasonably be deemed responsible by establishing the culture and strategy of the organisation. Where problems of performance or risk management are pervasive, bonuses can be adjusted for whole groups of employees.

These measures reinforce the responsibilities of individuals for the longer-term consequences of their actions and make them accountable. They also establish clearly the responsibilities of senior managers for training their employees and overseeing their performance; this creates the right sense of solidarity within the organisation. Although for some the financial sector bonuses are equated with 'excessive' compensation, having a substantial proportion of compensation at risk is essential for aligning reward with risks. Compensation should depend not just on performance during the year for which a bonus is granted but also on how the key decisions taken during that year play out over time. For instance, the traders at the London banks who bought credit insurance from shell companies that subsequently disappeared hardly deserved to be paid cash bonuses up front. In the UK, deferred compensation (bonuses) can now be forfeit and, if there is misconduct, clawed back after it has been paid out (in the most severe cases in the UK this ability extends out a decade).

Such horizons concentrate the mind, encouraging individuals to consider the longer-term implications of their actions. The effectiveness of this approach explains why, when I was Governor of the Bank of England, we opposed the European bonus cap. Although it sounded appealing to those uncomfortable with the very high compensation levels in financial services, it had the perverse effect of reducing at-risk, performance-related compensation – thereby blunting accountability and responsibility – while leaving total compensation unchanged. Or in some cases, increased.

Of course, no compensation package can fully internalise the impact of individual actions on systemic risks, including on trust in the system. To do so, market participants need to become true stakeholders. That is, they must recognise that their actions affect not merely their personal rewards, but also the legitimacy of the system in which they operate.

Many banks have rightly developed codes of ethics or business principles, but, given their generality, is it fair to wonder whether all traders will absorb their meaning? If it isn't realistic for traders to apply Aristotelian principles to fast-moving money markets, a complementary approach to restoring trust in markets is to rely on traders' intuitive understanding of what constitutes a true market.

To guide that understanding, we developed principles of fair and effective markets for FICC markets.[32]

Fair markets are those which:

1) have clear, proportionate and consistently applied standards of market practice;
2) are transparent enough to allow users to verify that those standards are consistently applied;
3) provide open access (either directly or through an open, competitive and well-regulated system of intermediation);
4) allow market participants to compete on the basis of merit; and
5) provide confidence that participants will behave with integrity.

Effective markets are those which also:

1) allow end users to undertake investment, funding, risk transfer and other transactions in a predictable way;
2) are underpinned by robust trading and post-trade infrastructures enabling participants to source available liquidity;
3) enable market participants to form, discover and trade at competitive prices; and
4) ensure proper allocation of capital and risk.

Drawing on a lesson from Magna Carta, that having the right principles is essential, it can be invaluable to have practical examples to make them tangible. New codes and standards designed by the private sector bring to life the principles of fair markets. To recreate fair and effective markets, authorities have encouraged market participants to develop standards of market practice that are well understood, are widely followed and, crucially, keep pace with market developments. Important examples include the Global FX Code and a series of standards for FICC markets that have been developed by the private sector FMSB.[33]

Of course, codes are of little use if nobody reads, follows or enforces them. This is where measures like the UK Senior Managers Regime come in. The SMR gives teeth to voluntary codes by incentivising firms to embed them. By requiring the identification of the most senior decision makers and their responsibilities, the SMR re-establishes the link between seniority and accountability, strengthens individual accountability and reinforces collective responsibility.

Under the SMR, the most senior decision makers of banks, insurers and major investment firms are now held individually accountable if they fail to take reasonable steps (including training or proper oversight) to prevent regulatory breaches in their areas of responsibility. Whether actions taken by a senior manager were reasonable can be determined by reference to select voluntary codes that the FCA has publicly recognised. And under the related Certification Regime firms must annually assess and certify the fitness and propriety of a wide range of risk-taking employees. Adoption of this approach is spreading, with some international firms adopting elements of the SMR's certification requirements to strengthen their global operations. A number of jurisdictions (like Hong Kong, Australia and Singapore) are applying the principles and many features of the SMR. And elements have been included in the FSB's toolkit on governance.[34]

The right compensation and conduct regimes are essential. And there have been huge strides in better aligning compensation with risk and conduct in the UK that other jurisdictions, particularly the US, would do well to emulate. Similarly, the Senior Managers Regime embeds best practice of senior manager accountability and responsibility across the financial system. But ultimately integrity can be neither bought nor regulated. It must come from within and be grounded in values.

A strong banking culture requires sustained commitment from the industry. Initiatives, like the Banking Standards Review Council (BSRC), are designed to create that sense of vocation in banking by promoting high standards of competence and behaviour across the UK industry. A prime objective of the BSRC is to help individual banks improve standards of behaviour and competence through a process of internal and external assessment. This requires a process of continuous improvement, with regular assessments of culture, competence and workforce development, and customer outcomes. As discussed in Chapter 6, like muscles these values need to be exercised.

People who run major financial institutions should have clearly defined responsibilities and behave with integrity, honesty and skill. And they should recognise their roles upholding the values of the financial system. They must have a sense of solidarity.

All market participants, large and small, should recognise that market integrity is essential to fair financial capitalism. Confidence in the integrity of those markets needs to be reinforced alongside genuine competition to ensure that the needs of end customers are properly and effectively served.

As we will see in Part III, this process begins with boards and senior management defining clearly the purpose of their organisations and promoting a culture of ethical business throughout them. Employees must be grounded in strong connections to their clients and their communities.

The G20 reforms have created a stronger, simpler and fairer financial system. It has proven resilient through the Covid crisis, and it could, with time and continued service of households and businesses, regain people's confidence.

We know we cannot rest on our laurels. Financial history rhymes, all too frequently, with enormous costs to our citizens. We must remain vigilant, resist the three lies of finance and reinforce some core financial truths.

Because the next time won't be different, authorities and market participants must try to anticipate new risk from cyber to crypto. But because we cannot anticipate every shock, we need to maintain an anti-fragile system to address those that we don't see.

Because markets don't always clear, central banks need to adapt their role as lenders of last resort, but they also must recognise and address the consequences of markets that aren't always right and can overshoot in both directions.

And because markets aren't inherently moral, they can distort value and corrode values if they are left unattended. We need to promote the values of accountability, responsibility, solidarity, integrity and prudence as best we can through compensation, codes and regulation while recognising that these can be fully developed and lived only through culture and practice.

So while authorities must put in place the hard and soft infrastructure to make markets work, there is no simple formula to break the cycle of financial history. Physics can help but it won't save finance. Promoting a system in which all its participants live society's core values will.

9

The Covid Crisis:
How We Got Here

At the end of February 2020, I sat in a gilded chair in the ornate Al Yamamah palace in Riyadh at what would be my last meeting of the G20 Finance Ministers and Central Bank Governors. After attending these gatherings for more than fifteen years, I was familiar with their rhythms. The heads of the international organisations would warn of the vulnerabilities from unbalanced growth, increased inequality and chronic environmental unsustainability, yet, as memories of the global financial crisis faded, ministers would appear indifferent. They were increasingly scripted, rattling off talking points prepared by their officials, with the combination of jet lag, the immediacy of domestic politics and slavish devotion to social media meaning that few paid full attention when they weren't speaking.

That day, however, something was different. Several ministers spoke in agitated tones, with alacrity and force, of an impending catastrophe. Heads snapped up from iPads. Everyone around the table was familiar with the coronavirus that was then thought to be confined to parts of Asia. Some even could name its strain, Covid-19. But few were prepared for what would be required in just a few weeks in their countries. And no one imagined how the professional and personal lives of everyone they knew – everyone on the planet – would be transformed.

The ministers from Singapore and South Korea described the measures their countries were taking to control the virus, including testing and track-and-trace regimes that would soon become the envy of other governments around the table. The Italian Finance Minister Gualtieri spoke of a growing threat from the disease in Lombardy just days before the incidence of cases and deaths would explode.[1]

Although they listened more attentively, few ministers saw what was coming and none was truly prepared. We now know that, at this point, there were about twenty cases each in the UK and Canada and around sixty in the US.[2] In these three countries, there were virtually no travel restrictions,[3] no localised quarantines, no stock-piling of vital equipment or expansion of healthcare capacity. Their publics were being advised that the threat to them was low.

When I returned to the UK, shaken by what I had heard, I called Peter Piot, one the world's most esteemed epidemiologists. I had met Peter several years earlier at a conference where he had described his experience leading the fight against Ebola and the looming threat of another pandemic. We had since kept in touch socially rather than professionally as the Bank of England has many respon-sibilities, but pandemic preparedness is not one of them. I knew that the Bank would, however, now be a critical part of the response to the economic and financial fallout. Given the pace of events, my concerns were growing that we might need to act soon – possibly even before the end of my term in two weeks' time – notwithstand-ing the reassuring words of officialdom.

Affable, concise and exceptionally well prepared, Peter answered my basic questions about the virus and did so with a clarity and foreboding that only heightened my fears. He offered to share his team's modelling of the disease with Bank colleagues so that we could gauge the potential economic and financial impacts and begin to think through the policy response. What we found over the next few days was shocking. Our head of economic forecasting, Jamie Bell, came to me with some of the central estimates of disease impact: 250,000 deaths if Covid-19 were left to run its course towards the soon-to-be-notorious 'herd immunity'. The economic impacts of preventative measures, including school closures and lockdowns, were at first hard to comprehend: our models suggested that GDP could fall by 10 per cent within weeks (it ended up drop-ping by twice that). The economy would have to be put on life support in order to support lives.

At the start of March, we immediately began preparing contingency plans to draw on the strength of the financial sector to support businesses and households. We cancelled all social gatherings and freshened up our contingency plans for home working. We created new liquidity facilities just in case financial markets seized up, and modelled potential monetary stimulus packages that might be needed. I intended to hand over to my successor, Andrew Bailey, a Bank that was well prepared for any eventuality over the coming months.

Within ten days, all those plans would be activated, and work would begin on new facilities to provide even greater support. With calm determination and remarkable speed, Andrew and his colleagues would forcefully deploy these measures (and more) in the weeks that followed. The combination of the scale of the Bank's actions and its institutional credibility would mean not only that disaster was averted but also that the strength of the entire financial system was deployed on behalf of the people it was meant to serve. Unlike during the financial crisis, this time when the UK financial system was subject to a severe test, it passed.

The challenge for the broader health response was even greater, not least because that system did not draw on existing protocols or clear institutional credibility. Once the scale of the threat was finally appreciated, the immediate action was the lockdown of the whole population. This was an extreme example of the state fulfilling its duty to protect by using its coercive powers. The effectiveness of these actions was ultimately determined by the legitimacy of the state, with the sacrifices demanded of people being an emergency response of unprepared societies.

The approach of most governments around the world has been to prioritise the health emergency and then to try to address the resulting economic consequences. This initially resulted in deep falls in economic activity, enormous job losses and widespread destruction of financial values. With time pressure has grown for explicit trade-offs between health and economic priorities, highlighting the importance of forging common purpose.

Meeting these twin economic and health challenges has required solidarity at all levels: within our families, with our neighbours and communities, between companies and their employees, suppliers and customers; and between banks and their clients. The effectiveness of actions would have been further reinforced by solidarity and cooperation between countries, but this has been virtually absent. The nation state has been ascendant. Opportunities to share burdens and pool risks, have largely been forgone.

The main economic questions concerned not the depths of near-term recessions but the extent to which the productive capacity of our economies and the livelihoods of our citizens could be preserved. Those objectives explain why central banks and governments launched a series of unprecedented measures designed to bridge to the other side of this enormous – but ultimately temporary – shock, including assuming portions of the salaries of furloughed workers, providing cash transfers to individuals and small businesses and making emergency loans to large corporates.

As we shall see, some familiar value(s) are at the core of how to respond to the Covid crisis:

1) *solidarity* across all strata of society from families to companies and banks;
2) *responsibility* for all of us for each other, and of companies for their employees, their suppliers and clients;
3) *sustainability* because Covid is an intergenerational crisis, with the health consequences skewed towards the old and the economic consequences skewed towards the young;
4) *fairness* in access to healthcare and in bearing the economic costs, and fairness internationally in terms of sharing the burden with emerging and developing economies; and
5) *dynamism* – after the most acute phase of this crisis passed, sustained efforts are now needed to restore dynamism to our economies, given the enormous expansion of the state and increased fragility of the private sector.

These values arise from the answers to some of the critical questions that the crisis raises:

- How could this have happened? Why did so many states fail in their duty to protect?
- What did the response of states and their citizens to the lockdown reveal about the underlying values of societies?
- What can individuals expect from society and what can society expect from each of us?
- Is it just to set economic limits to fighting a disease?
- What does the crisis reveal about how we treat the most vulnerable among us? Do we follow the golden rule (do unto others as you would have them do to you) or pursue the common good?

THE DUTY OF THE STATE

The most fundamental duty of the state is to protect its citizens. In his classic text, *Leviathan*, Thomas Hobbes (1588–1679) described how citizens give up certain liberties in exchange for state protection 'from the invasion of foreigners, and the injuries of one another, and thereby to secure them in such sort as that by their own industry and by the fruits of the earth they may nourish themselves and live contentedly'.[4] Hobbes' conception of the relationship between citizens and the state sprang from his dark view of humanity. Without government, life would be 'nasty, brutish and short' – an ongoing war, with people constantly fearful and in danger of violent death.[5] To limit such strife, citizens submit to the state's rule and are under an obligation to obey the state, at least as long as the state is able to protect them.[6] The state exercises its authority through coercive power and its monopoly on violence.

John Locke (1632–1704) held a more charitable view of human nature and believed life without government could possibly be quite peaceful, filled with goodwill and mutual assistance.[7] Governments were therefore not automatically preferable to the state of nature; their legitimacy depended more fully on the consent of their citizens. This social contract could extend well beyond keeping the peace. Locke agreed with Hobbes that the ultimate duty of the state was to protect its citizens from injury and violence – which to Locke included the protection of property rights – but he believed that additional duties could be bestowed upon the state by agreement of its citizens.[8] Writing after Locke, Jean-Jacques Rousseau (1712–78) espoused similar views, finding agreement to be the 'basis of all authority'.[9]

Such an expansion of state duties has occurred over the centuries. The government's role as protector now extends well beyond shielding citizens from violence and direct injury to cover areas as varied as promoting financial stability, protecting the environment and maintaining data privacy. Much of this growth has been a response to risk-averse populations that expect ever greater protections from government authorities.[10] Moreover, the duties of governments today reach well beyond their traditional roles as protectors to include the provision of basic services, the promotion of welfare and the fostering of culture. As we shall see, in Covid as in monetary policy, the effectiveness of government action depends on its credibility, which in turn rests in part on government's ability to fulfil its many and varied roles.

To both Locke and Rousseau, the duties of the state are products of an exchange whereby citizens accept limitations on their freedoms and obligations in return for benevolent government that works to fulfil its agreed-upon responsibilities. At the heart of their conception of state power is reciprocity.[11] The state has a duty to protect, and citizens have obligations and must work with the state and with each other to achieve satisfactory outcomes. The greater the state's duties, the greater is the imposition on our freedoms and our associated obligations to society. As Rousseau cautioned, we will at times be asked to 'run certain risks on behalf of the source of our security', such as being conscripted into an army or risking financial hardship during an imposed lockdown.[12]

Hobbes, Locke and Rousseau all advanced versions of social contract theory, the idea that we as citizens enter into agreements with each other and with the state that delineate the obligations and rights of all parties. A contractarian model has its limitations in describing reality – people cannot choose to cancel their contract nor do they ever provide express consent to be a party to it – but the concept allows us to reflect on our relationship to the state and to consider what we can expect from government, what government can expect from us, and ultimately what we expect from each other. Those expectations were tested to the extreme in the early months of Covid-19. As with many contracts (see Chapter 14 on corporate purpose), the social contract, even as an abstraction, is not the limit of the relationship. Social capital, a sense of duty and even culture are essential to resilient society.

THE CAPACITY OF THE STATE

To fulfil their duties, states must possess a requisite level of ability or state capacity. State capacity can be broken down into three main components:

1) legal capacity, referring to the state's ability to create regulations, enforce contracts and protect property rights;
2) collective capacity, referring to the state's ability to provide public services; and
3) fiscal capacity, referring to the state's power to tax and spend. These capacities are complementary and any deficiencies in one will impair the others.[13]

The mutually reinforcing nature of the different types of state capacity and how they each contribute to the execution of state duties is evident in the history of government response to infectious disease. When the Black Death hit Europe in the fourteenth century, authorities did not have the capacity to respond effectively to protect their citizens. Populations instead largely turned to the Church for explanations and remedies.[14]

State protection against disease developed slowly over the following centuries as waves of the pestilence returned periodically. Deploying their legal capacity, governments learned to impose quarantines, *cordons sanitaires* and what we would now consider 'social distancing' regulations in order to reduce transmission.[15] By 1700, collective capacity had progressed to the point that boards of health tasked with responding to disease outbreaks had become prevalent across Europe. Special hospitals were erected to isolate infectious patients, and authorities fumigated or destroyed bedding and clothing in order to reduce transmission. Poor families in some cases were provided with government assistance so they could survive forced quarantines.

Through trial and error, regulations and public services were improved, but ignorance of the causes of disease still hindered the effectiveness of the response. Even at the early International Sanitary Conferences of the mid-nineteenth century, competing theories of disease transmission made it difficult to forge accord or develop substantive policy.[16] This would change only with the widespread acceptance of the germ theory of disease a few decades later, an advancement made possible by state investments in knowledge and education.

In the twentieth century, the development of fiscal capacity expanded the ability of the state to protect its population from epidemics. Public funds for disease response in the early modern period were limited. Even in the latter half of the nineteenth century, tax revenue amounted to less than 10 per cent of national income, financing nightwatchman states that could support police forces, court systems, armies and general administration but little else.[17] Today, with taxes on income, consumption and capital gains as well as investments in more effective systems of revenue collection, revenues in advanced economies range from a quarter to a little under half of GDP.[18] This additional fiscal capacity has helped to fund the increase in government spending on healthcare that rose from well under half a per cent of GDP in the nineteenth century to almost 10 per cent by the end of the twentieth.[19]

The goal, of course, is not large states but smart ones that are equipped with the requisite capacity to achieve society's objectives. Effective state capacity is more likely to be built when there is agreement on the long-term priorities to which the resources of the state should be employed, agreements that are possible when states are cohesive and society can engage in a productive exchange of ideas over the responsibilities of government and its citizens.

The state's arms race against bacteria, viruses and other pathogens is a story of expanded duties and capacities, rooted in traditional notions of government as the protector. In this context, the failure of governments to protect their citizens was a failure to perform their first and foremost duty.

But it would be a mistake to pin failure on government as an abstraction. Were inadequate protections caused by how governments make decisions, such as inherent political short-termism? Were they a result of path dependence, where initial failings led to loss of confidence and poor compliance, compounding the problems? And to what extent was pandemic performance more deeply rooted – a consequence of what we value as expressed through our governments?

PANDEMIC PREPAREDNESS AS STATE PROTECTION

Government protection goes well beyond actions against existing threats to preparations against threats that could occur. Standing armies are still maintained, despite the remote risks of invasion in many countries. In contrast, the risk of a pandemic was far from remote. Our globalised, densely populated world is highly conducive to disease transmission, allowing a virus to cross continents before its effects are fully appreciated in its region of origin. Yet our defences were limited.

The severity of a potential pandemic was certainly appreciated by experts, who regularly issued warnings in recent decades. The World Health Organisation's 1999 Influenza Pandemic Plan, for instance, urged governments to create National Pandemic Planning Committees and take responsible action.[20] Modelling by epidemiologists published in the *Lancet* in 2006 found that a modern pandemic could kill between 50 and 80 million people.[21]

Warnings also regularly featured in the media. Newspapers, magazines, cable news, even a Hollywood movie speculated about the effects of a coming global health crisis. In 2015 Bill Gates devoted a TED Talk to promoting the idea of health security in order to replace outdated notions of government protection that focused on threats like nuclear war. The talk took on a new life in

2020 having been largely neglected upon initial release. The media's collective tone in these stories, reports and presentations is perhaps best summarised by a 2017 *Time* magazine cover of ominous microbes accompanied by the headline that stated what is now obvious: 'Warning: We are not ready for the next pandemic'.

Despite the general threat, governments would take significant steps to prepare for a global health crisis only when there were specific, prominent disease outbreaks. After both the SARS and Ebola epidemics, changes were made to improve international coordination. A large component of these improvements related to monitoring and ensuring timely global notification of any outbreak, as prior to SARS countries were under an obligation only to report instances of cholera, plague and yellow fever.[22]

The failure to build national healthcare capacity is another contrast between intensive analysis of the importance of the issue and modest action to address it. Following the Ebola crisis, the WHO identified systemic gaps in the health-crisis response capabilities of countries.[23] By 2018 more than a hundred countries had conducted Joint External Evaluations and Simulation Exercises, and more than fifty had completed an After Action Review.[24] These reviews found that basic healthcare services in many countries were insufficient to combat a novel pathogen.

Identifying gaps is necessary but not sufficient. Action must follow. Unfortunately, just over half of the countries in the WHO's evaluative exercises would develop a National Action Plan for Health Security as recommended by the World Health Organisation, and not a single country had their plan fully financed or implemented by the time Covid-19 struck.[25] Only a third of countries were compliant with the WHO's International Health Regulations that set the standards necessary to safeguard global health.[26]

To take one example, the need for Personal Protective Equipment in a global health crisis is painfully obvious in hindsight, yet few countries had adequate stockpiles or an effective restocking system at the onset of the Covid-19 pandemic. In the UK, vital items, such as visors and gowns, were left out of the national stockpile when it was established in 2009. Six months before Covid-19 began to spread, the government ignored a warning from its own advisory group to buy missing equipment.[27] In Canada, the federal stockpile amounted to less than what one province, Ontario, estimated it needed for one week during the first surge of Covid-19 cases. Moreover, the Public Health Agency of Canada did not have targets for the appropriate levels of equipment to maintain, nor did they know the amount of equipment maintained in provincial stockpiles.[28]

In the US, the Strategic National Stockpile's supply of masks amounted to approximately 1 per cent of what was estimated would be needed in a severe pandemic.[29] The stockpile had been depleted during the 2009 H1N1 pandemic and funds for new equipment had been continually left out of Congressional budgets despite repeated warnings to restock.[30] When asked about the decision not to provide funding to replenish supplies adequately, Denny Rehberg, the congressman who chaired the appropriations committee responsible for overseeing the stockpile in 2011, said that it would have been impossible to predict a public health crisis requiring a more robust stockpile.[31]

Germany and France also suffered from Personal Protective Equipment shortages, and less than two months after emergency measures began to be implemented, healthcare workers in both countries were posting photos to social media of themselves posing naked to protest the equipment shortage and symbolise the vulnerability of working in unsafe conditions.[32]

And these were the advanced economies. The situation was even worse in many developing countries where Personal Protective Equipment was scarce, and even clean running water and soap were perpetually in short supply.[33] Countries with populations of several million had only a handful of ventilators, and ten African countries had none at all.[34]

Inadequate stockpiles could theoretically be augmented in times of crisis by increasing imports or ramping up domestic production, but countries were poorly prepared for the realities of either option. Global supply chains are highly efficient but vulnerable, and reliance on them in times of crisis is risky. During the initial wave of the Covid-19 outbreak, the combination of surges in demand and protectionist measures meant many governments were caught short.

Domestic production capabilities in turn hinge on the presence of a diverse manufacturing sector, increasingly an anomaly in an era of global supply chains and hyper-specialisation. Even if domestic businesses are willing – or compelled – to convert manufacturing plants to production in the national interest, the transition takes time and access to the right materials remains a supply-chain problem. For example, half of the global supply of melt-blown, a type of non-woven polypropylene that is used as a filter in masks, is produced in China.[35]

The investment needed to address the cumulative deficiencies in the world's pandemic preparedness was not a high ask. The World Bank estimated in 2019 that low- to middle-income countries would need to spend an average of less than US$2 per person to improve the core capabilities mandated by the International Health Regulations.[36] A 2016 commission recommended increasing total global spending on pandemic preparation by US$4.5 billion a year, three-quarters of which would be directed towards upgrading national capabilities and the bulk of the rest going to research and development for infectious-disease detection and response.[37]

In the wake of the Ebola crisis, the UN created the Global Preparedness Monitoring Board, an independent panel of experts who report annually on the state of global preparedness for a health crisis. Their first report, released in September 2019, stated that 'The world is at acute risk for [sic] devastating regional or global disease epidemics or pandemics that not only cause loss of life but upend economies and create social chaos.'[38] The report concluded that, although there had been some positive developments since the Ebola epidemic, 'current efforts remain grossly insufficient'.[39] Likewise, the principal finding of the 2019 Global Health Security Index was that 'National health security is fundamentally weak around the world. No country is fully prepared for epidemics or pandemics, and every country has important gaps to address.'[40]

In retrospect, the costs of improving pandemic preparedness were both readily affordable and paltry when compared to the costs of the crisis. Even twice the recommended annual investment in pandemic preparedness would have amounted to about one day of lost global economic output that occurred because inadequate measures had been taken. States had the capacity but failed to deploy it to fulfil their duties.

Why?

VALUES REVEALED: RESILIENCE AND PREPAREDNESS

When I attended my last G20 in Riyadh, South Korea was one of the first countries to have experienced an outbreak of Covid-19. At the end of February 2020, it was behind only China in total number of reported cases. With high case numbers and densely populated cities, it looked to be on its way to becoming a viral hotspot. Yet this did not materialise. Instead of spiralling upwards, new cases dropped precipitously in early March and by the end of April South Korea had one-tenth of the total cases of Spain, despite similar population sizes. It achieved all of this without ever instituting a full lockdown.

South Korea's success in containing the virus is best explained by preparation. The country had struggled with a MERS outbreak in 2015, and subsequently amended its legislation and policies to fight infectious disease. Among other things, these amendments expedited testing and permitted the use of geolocation data in the government response, both of which have been obstacles to efforts in many other countries. With these and other measures in place, South Korea was able to mount an extensive test-and-trace regime that helped the country quickly get the upper hand against the outbreak.[41]

Not all countries had a recent infectious disease outbreak to motivate preparation but, as we have seen, all countries had received ample warnings on the threat that such an outbreak posed. Governments knew of the consequences, but South Korea was an exceptional country that had taken action to prepare. Why were the warnings not acted upon elsewhere?

Put simply, *resilience* was undervalued. The protective responsibilities of the state require planning for failures ranging from managing the collapse of globally systemic banks (see Chapter 8) to preventing Minsky moments in climate change (see Chapter 12) to recognising that health warnings that rise to become the subjects of TED Talks and *Time* magazine covers are likely to become realities.

Our brains often work against us when it comes to making the longer-term investments necessary to withstand catastrophes when they strike. Research in behavioural psychology has established that humans have a host of cognitive biases that mean we undervalue resiliency. We display a present bias and discount problems and benefits that will occur in the future, preferring immediate rewards even if they are lesser in overall value.[42] Our priorities often focus on preventing repeats of recent calamities, even if other threats are greater, so we demand increases in aircraft safety in the weeks following a crash, despite automobile accidents being a far more likely cause of deaths.

In addition, we all, including decision makers, display confirmation biases and focus on the relative successes against SARS, H1N1 and Ebola and ignore the outcomes of the Spanish flu despite clear warnings that a global, fatal outbreak was likely. In these regards, the sorry history of financial crises extends to pandemic preparations, with people being lulled into thinking 'this time is different' and that devastating health crises are things of the past.

These modes of thinking become entrenched in our governing systems through public officials, who harbour these cognitive biases, and by a general population that rewards politicians for delivering immediate benefits but not for pre-emptively solving issues. When resilience is undervalued, funding is diverted elsewhere and National Action Plans for Health Security remain unfinanced.

An infectious-disease outbreak also poses issues of diffused responsibility. For an effective pandemic response, international organisations, all levels of government and a wide range of government agencies need to be coordinated. In peacetime, unclear roles and responsibilities can go unnoticed but such ambiguity and underlap lead to inadequate preparations and then tensions during crises. A 2016 UN report on the Ebola crisis found that 'in the early days of the crisis, there was a lack of clarity over which entities within a national administration were in charge of coordinating the response and which organizations should attend relevant meetings. In isolated cases, decision-making was slowed by interdepartmental rivalries and unclear reporting lines.'[43] In the same vein, a leaked review of a 2019 US simulation exercise found that 'exercise participants lacked clarity on federal interagency partners' roles and responsibilities during an influenza pandemic response'.[44] Governments can also be easily distracted. For example, in the UK Brexit has dominated public discourse and government resources since 2016, while the NHS has remained underfunded. Reporting by *The Times* found that training to prepare key workers for a significant health crisis had been put on hold for two years while contingency planning was diverted to deal with the possibility of a no-deal Brexit.[45]

In the end, cognitive biases and a host of systemic factors resulted in inadequate preparation for a catastrophic health and economically devastating crisis.

COST–BENEFIT ANALYSIS AS A FRAMEWORK FOR HARD CHOICES

Having failed to protect their citizens from the spread of a pandemic, states have concentrated on mitigating the fallout. The complex interrelationships between the twin crises of health and economics have required authorities to weigh the estimated costs and benefits of various restrictions on economic activity and personal liberty. As they have, the crisis has helped reveal what society values. The pandemic has forced society into a series of extremely difficult value judgements.

Decisions around Covid policy represent arguably the most difficult, and undeniably the most significant, weighing of sacred and secular values ever performed. These decisions have applied a tool that has been in widespread use by governments and regulators for a series of micro-decisions over the past few decades (like requiring airbags on cars) to macro-policy decisions of a greater scale, complexity and importance than has been seen before (such as closing and opening entire swathes of the economy). In an effort to help guide these decisions, the initial months of the Covid-19 outbreak brought a wave of cost–benefit analyses on lockdown measures from academic institutions and think tanks,[46] as well as increased public scrutiny of how such decisions are made.[47] Governments were not always forthcoming in how their strategies evolved apart from repeating mantras that they were 'following the science', even if cost–benefit assessments have played important roles in Covid-19 briefings and on occasion in policy determinations.

A major advantage of conducting cost–benefit analyses is that it forces those constructing them to specify the relevant variables and accompanying assumptions. This clarity, however, brings a host of practical challenges. An obvious difficulty is that often the key variables can only be approximated with low degrees of certainty but, once estimated, they can take on an exaggerated authority. For Covid-19, critical determinants such as the mortality rate and the R0 factor were initially challenging to estimate given patchy data, while others, such as the lasting impact of Covid-19 on people's health or the effects of a lockdown on social isolation and domestic abuse, were even harder to assess in real time.

Even if the current value of a variable can be determined with reasonable certainty, its projected future value is a judgement based on a range of assumptions for other variables. R0 will change depending on public compliance with lockdown orders, which in turn is the product of numerous forces that are more or less guaranteed to change over time. Furthermore, decisions need to be compared not against the present state of affairs but against the projected state without intervention. The economic cost of the lockdown also must be compared to the right counterfactual, which is not the full drop in economic activity relative to the pre-Covid economy, because many people would have voluntarily reduced their external activities and therefore consumption to protect their health even if the lockdown had not been implemented. A fully constructed cost–benefit analysis for Covid thus comprises a series of interconnected assumptions. This demands a high degree of caution when interpreting the results.

As we have seen, a fundamental challenge for cost–benefit analysis is how to convert the variables into comparable units so that the net impact of a decision can be calculated. This is particularly difficult when comparing economic costs and the impacts on health and quality of life. An expected decrease in GDP comes with an associated dollar figure, but there is no immediate, obvious numerical value (monetary or otherwise) to represent a lost life. Instead, those constructing a cost–benefit model must insert some estimate to represent the value of a life or the decline in its quality. How this 'monetisation' of life is estimated speaks volumes about our market society. How it was deployed during the Covid crisis underscores the potential shift in values.

Valuations of life – although they have taken on a new importance in the modern regulatory state – are not a new phenomenon. The Prophet Muhammad endorsed compensation of a hundred camels when the life of a free Muslim was taken.[48] Under old Anglo-Saxon law, the perpetrator of a murder owed the victim's family an amount based upon the wealth the victim had accumulated during their life.[49]

In the seventeenth century, Sir William Petty (whom we met as the forefather of GDP in Chapter 1) sought to put a value on life in order to measure England's national wealth. Petty valued the population according to an estimate of average annual labour value multiplied by twenty years.[50] This resulted in a figure of £80 per head, which he noted could be used to estimate national losses from events like plague or a war.[51] His work was an initial foray into valuing lives for the purpose of government decision making, and it remains relevant today as countries regain an interest in measuring wealth and welfare after decades fixated solely on production.

A few centuries after Petty, the Industrial Revolution brought crowded cities and unsafe working conditions, which in turn led to the development of wrongful-death claims and the proliferation of life and accident insurance.[52] As with Petty's calculations of national wealth, the focus of compensation remained on lost earnings. Insurance companies used a policyholder's age and surplus earnings, along with interest rates and standardised mortality tables, to arrive at the value of a life.[53] Courts likewise focused their analysis for punitive damages on lost future earnings.

Valuing lives by labour potential makes sense in instances of civil compensation or insurance where the life in question is already over and the objective is to ensure the deceased's family remains financially secure. The shortcomings of this valuation method, however, became evident as governments in the twentieth century increasingly began to look to value life not to compensate for death but to assess the desirability of preventing death from happening. In these cases, financial security and accounting costs cannot be the only factors to consider, for if they were, money should never be spent to save the lives of retirees and those permanently out of the labour force as no strictly financial loss would be incurred by their death.

But how else to conduct the analysis initially proved elusive. The problem stumped the RAND Corporation in the early 1950s when it tried to determine the value of the lives of air force pilots in order to estimate the total cost of different missions. The value of a pilot to the US Air Force could easily be determined with reference to the cost of training and replacing a new crew member, but, as an internal memo noted, this in itself was insufficient because 'In our society, personnel lives do have intrinsic value over and above the investment they represent.'[54] Even Dr Strangelove could see the difference between intrinsic and replacement value.

These limitations created a desire for a new way to value life, and ultimately led to a shift in the conception of the value of life that has many parallels to the subjective value revolution discussed in Chapter 2, though it has occurred only within the past sixty years.

The advancement that brought the revolution was a seminal 1968 article by future Nobel laureate Thomas Schelling entitled 'The Life You Save May Be Your Own'. One of Schelling's key insights was to shift who was doing the valuing. He contended that for questions of life saving it is not the value to related parties that matters; instead any investment in life saving should be evaluated in terms of the private worth the investment has to the individuals who would be affected. The question Schelling posed was 'Worth to whom?' and his answer was 'To the people who may die.'

Schelling's other critical insight was that calculations did not need to value life but instead needed to value the postponement of death. In particular, the focus was on postponing not a specific death but a statistical death. Presented with imminent and certain death, most people would value their lives at an exorbitantly high level, and thus could not be relied upon for assessments useful to government. However, Schelling realised that people's preferences could be determined by dealing with a reduction in risk. What were people willing to pay to reduce the risk of death by some extremely small amount?

Although 'The Life You Save May Be Your Own' received substantial criticism at the time of publication – and, as we will see, is not free from criticism today – Schelling's work has gone on to form the basis of how policymakers value lives and his term 'value of a statistical life' (VSL) has become the reigning vocabulary.

Schelling's solution to the value-of-life puzzle was to determine people's preferences when it came to accepting risk. To do this he suggested both looking at existing price structures and conducting surveys. Both of these methods are employed today.

The first class of methods, revealed preference, is based on individual behaviour in markets where prices reflect differences in mortality risk. In the hedonic-wage approach, VSL is calculated in reference to the wage premium one receives for working in a dangerous job. As a simplified example, if the risk of death in a certain high-risk job is one in 10,000, and workers received $300 annually in danger pay, the VSL estimate would be $3 million. In an averting-cost approach a VSL is calculated in reference to expenditures people make – such as buying a helmet – to reduce the probability or severity of a bad outcome.

In contrast, stated-preference methods construct a hypothetical market for a given change in mortality risk and ask respondents directly in surveys for their willingness-to-pay to reduce the risk. A contingent-valuation approach typically asks the respondent for their willingness-to-pay for a public programme that would reduce their mortality risk directly. A choice-modelling approach asks respondents to make a series of choices between health risks with different characteristics and monetary costs.

Both revealed-preference and stated-preference methods have their strengths and weaknesses, and both are employed in different circumstances and in different countries. The United States principally uses the hedonic-wage approach, while European countries tend to use some form of stated-preference study, with the choice-modelling approach growing in popularity.[55]

This range of different methods leads to surprising variance in the value of a statistical life across countries. An OECD survey in 2012 showed that, in Canada, estimates ranged from C$3.4 million to C$9.9 million, while in the United States the range was US$1 million to US$10 million.[56] The European Commission meanwhile recommended the value of a statistical life should be somewhere in the range of €1 million to €2 million, and the United Kingdom's Department of Transport used the disturbingly precise figure of £1,638,390. The noticeably lower value of life in Europe is explained principally by European countries not using the hedonic-wage method, which tends to give the highest estimates. It is worth noting that the above values are not static. Government agencies adjust their VSL to account for inflation, and at least in the United States VSL has trended upwards at a rate that rapidly exceeds inflation.[57] In terms of people's estimation of the value of their lives at least, America isn't just great again, it has apparently never been so great.

As an alternative to VSL, it is common in the healthcare sector to employ a cost–utility analysis instead of a cost–benefit analysis. While the latter assigns a monetary value to the benefits through valuing life, cost–utility analyses focus on the added utility per dollar. Depending on the country, public health agencies or insurance companies are likely to approve a treatment if it costs less than a prescribed amount for every year of life that it gives the patient. Cost–utility analyses do not specifically value lives but the results allow decision makers to approve treatments or programmes based on an understood value of a life given budgetary constraints.

Years of life are usually adjusted for quality, so that a year of life in full health is equal to one quality-adjusted life year (QALY) but a year of life with a diagnosable mental illness experience is worth only 0.8 QALY. The impact of a health ailment on quality is determined by surveys of general population, akin to the stated-preference methods of VSL. As an example, the EQ-5D is a questionnaire reflecting five dimensions: mobility, self-care, usual activity, pain and anxiety.[58]

Today the use of VSL and QALY are ubiquitous in policy decision making across the world. VSL is an essential component of what Cass Sunstein has labelled the 'cost–benefit revolution' that has occurred over the past fifty years in the US but also in Canada, Australia, the UK, the Nordic countries and the European Union.[59] QALYs meanwhile form the backbone of health policy in the UK and are used in numerous countries to assess the efficacy of health treatments. The prevalence of these quantification techniques is due to the fact that with clear numbers can come clear decisions. But is this clarity justified and does it reflect the values we should strive for in a society?

A RETURN TO THE PERILS OF RELYING ON SUBJECTIVE VALUE

To Schelling, the intangible qualities associated with life were not that different from other consumer goods. We put a value on pain when, through the market, we set a price for Ibuprofen and a value on pleasure when we set a price for a Pepsi. Following the neo-classicists and their subjective theory of value, Schelling argued that what mattered was that these judgements on the value of intangibles were made by the general population and not by economists.

There are three broad reasons why the value of lives is radically different from that of a typical consumer good for which a market price is used as the measure of its value.

First, unlike most consumer goods, life is what some economists term a non-positional good. That means that no part of a life's value stems from the ownership of comparable goods by others. We do not feel any better off when those around us have less life, though we may feel better off when we have a nicer car. In contrast, drawing on a host of evidence from behavioural trials, Robert Frank posits that the value of many consumption goods is partly based on how they affect the person's actual or perceived position.[60] Positional goods derive their value primarily from their scarcity rather than their absolute characteristics. So in behavioural surveys more people will prefer a smaller house if it is bigger relative to those of their neighbours than a larger house that is smaller in relative terms. This leads to 'expenditure cascades' and the consumer analogue to arms races (spending to be seen to outspend those around us). Evidence shows that workplace safety and risk of death are valued in absolute terms. People will support measures that increase their life expectancy even if it increases the life expectancy of others by more. Frank concludes that life is the one unequivocal non-positional good.

It seems odd to have to state it, but life is different from Pepsi.

Second, serious concerns arise from Schelling's line of reasoning, with its (implicit) faith in the wisdom of crowds. For example, revealed-preference methods to estimate the value of a life depend on a set of strict assumptions about the market and human nature which are seldom, if ever, fulfilled. In particular, the assumption that a person taking on a high-risk job knows the occupational probability of death and rationally analyses this probability against their wage premium while divorcing all other variables from the analysis strains credulity. The surfeit of individual irrationality revealed by advances in behavioural psychology and economics cannot be overcome by the law of large numbers as there is every reason to believe that cognitive biases and inadequate access to information are prevalent market-wide. The questions posed in stated-preference surveys require a rational assessment of probabilities that it is naive to assume.

Evidence that the biases and limited information of respondents may prevent studies from yielding worthwhile results is most apparent when dealing with quality of life. Research has found that the general public tends to overestimate the negative impact of many, though not all, health conditions and that the things we focus on in a preference question are often not what ends up mattering in actual experience.[61] The results of quality-of-life surveys thus speak more to our fears of losing a leg than to the quality of life of someone who has actually lost a leg. Allowing these biases to dictate which healthcare treatments are covered devalues the lives of those who are differently abled or suffering from a manageable health condition.

Third, such systematic devaluing of life speaks to a broader point that transcends methodological flaws. In following a subjective

theory of value, revealed- and stated-preference methods of calculating VSL or determining quality of life find the aggregate value of
individual preferences. They are descriptions of how people value
their life without thought to how we *should* value them. As always,
there are reasons to caution against blind reliance on markets,
particularly those imputed from surveys which rely on a sophisticated understanding of low-risk tail events.

Consider the impact of income inequality. While VSL does not
explicitly take into account either current wealth or future earnings,
such variables are factored in through the preferences of the survey
sample. Thus those in their fifties display a higher VSL than those
in their twenties, and at a national level advanced economies report
higher VSLs than developing economies.[62] But are we comfortable
saying that policy should be made in accordance with these descriptive facts?

This was the topic of a leaked World Bank memo of 1991 that
pointed out the economic logic of directing the dumping of
health-impacting pollution, such as toxic waste, on least developed countries.[63] Impeccable as the logic may be, the memo stirred
a fierce backlash and the memo's author, Larry Summers, subsequently had to make it clear that 'No sane person favours dumping
toxic waste near where anybody lives.'[64] Today the World Bank
recommends countries adjust a VSL estimate in accordance with
their national income, but emphasises that VSL is to be used only
for domestic decision making and not for cross-country
comparisons.[65]

Employing a descriptive measure like VSL can give the appear-
ance of moral impartiality, but this is never actually the case. The
very use of VSL is a moral choice, and numerous critiques have
argued for the use of alternative measures, particularly ones that
more accurately account for welfare.[66] By converting to dollars in a
cost–benefit analysis, we end up selecting the option that maximises
wealth and therefore consumption, but that does not necessarily
mean that welfare has been optimised.[67] A policy that brings large
gains to the wealthy at only a small expense to the poor, for instance,
may optimise wealth but not welfare. To critics, quantifying variables like life into monetary figures ends up trivialising the very

values that make the decision or policy necessary to contemplate in the first place.[68]

VSL also makes a fundamental assumption that lives are the correct unit of analysis as opposed to years of life, which can be measured by a Value of a Statistical Life Year (VSLY). The difference between the two units is immaterial when discussing issues such as traffic regulations, whose effects are not skewed towards any particular age cohort, but can become a matter of considerable controversy in other circumstances. In the case of Covid-19, for instance, the benefits of lockdown measures varied considerably when using VSL or VSLY, as the virus is most fatal to those who have few expected years of life remaining.

The question of which unit to use is one of equality: are all lives equal or are all years of life equal? There are ethical arguments in favour of both approaches, and employing either is a value-laden judgement, whether it is thought of as such or not.

Those constructing a cost–benefit analysis must likewise make a decision on whether to value the nature of dying, and if so, how to do so. A generic VSL assumes that all deaths are equal, but stated-preference studies routinely find that people fear different types of deaths to varying degrees and are willing to pay more to reduce the risk of what they view as unpleasant deaths, for instance dying in a crowded hospital isolated from loved ones in the midst of a pandemic.[69] The decision to augment or discount a VSL to account for the gain or loss of a dignified death – or to forgo either and view differing perceptions of deaths as market distortions to be smoothed out in analysis – remains one guided by morals.

CONCLUSION

Despite their fundamental duty to protect their citizens, governments systematically undervalued resilience in the run-up to the Covid crisis. In the next chapter we will turn to the devastating fallout of this lack of preparedness, including the unequal effects of Covid on the population. And we will see that amid the failures in our pandemic response are numerous successes that can help guide us out of this crisis and inform our preparation and response to future ones.

The role and duties of government are formulated by citizens, yet we increasingly rely on market-based metrics of value to dictate policy instead of societal values driving government action. At the heart of Covid policy decisions have been forms of valuation of life, quality of life and dignity in death, even if those determinations have been implicit. Framing these in terms of cost–benefit analysis immediately brings challenges with estimating monetary values for these sacred values. Policy decisions must also weigh fundamental issues of fairness including the incidence of the disease and of economic hardship as well as the importance of preserving economic dynamism.

Society's response to Covid has revealed much about people's relationship to the state and the values of society. Most fundamentally, when faced with catastrophe, governments and citizens drew on their core values and made decisions based on human compassion and not financial optimisation. Taking our cue from these revealed values to develop a framework for managing the twin crises, let's now turn to how governments have responded, how people have behaved, and what that reveals about the relationship between value and values.

10

Covid Crisis: Fallout, Recovery and Renaissance?

WHAT THE RESPONSE TO THE OUTBREAK REVEALED

On 31 December 2019, China alerted the World Health Organisation to a cluster of cases of an acute respiratory illness in the city of Wuhan. Chinese authorities soon identified the illness as a new type of coronavirus and by the end of January cases were reported across Asia as well as in the Western Pacific, Europe and North America.[1] By the end of February, cases were confirmed on every (inhabited) continent, though China remained the virus's epicentre.[2]

March was the tipping point that moved Covid-19 from one of many stories in a crowded news cycle to an epochal event in the history of the twenty-first century. Over the course of the month, the number of countries experiencing local transmission increased from 18 to over 150, the number of reported cases went from 85,000 to 750,000, and the number of reported fatalities rose from 133 to over 36,000.[3] To billions of people around the world, the virus became a very clear and present danger.

Responding to this threat, governments took drastic actions to limit the spread of the disease. Schools and public spaces were shut down, businesses were ordered to close, people's mobility was restricted, travel bans were imposed and borders were shuttered. Quarantines, curfews and other restrictions were put in place. Executive powers were assumed, the military deployed and elections postponed. Some governments began surveillance operations on their citizens.

Lockdown restrictions had begun in China in January, but for the vast majority of other countries these restrictive measures were implemented rapidly over the course of March. The Blavatnik School of Government at the University of Oxford tracked countries' policy response to Covid-19 over the course of the outbreak, assigning numerical scores out of a hundred for the level of stringency imposed. On 29 February, only five jurisdictions – China, Italy, South Korea, Hong Kong and Mongolia – had containment policies that scored above 50; by 31 March, the number had grown to 158.

Containment policies were accompanied by health policies that increased hospital capacity and funded vaccine research, and economic policies that sought to mitigate the financial devastation. It is the containment policies, however, that permitted governments to assert a level of control over the lives of their populations that surpassed anything seen in modern history. In many countries even leaving your house to exercise or visit immediate family became prohibited activities. People around the world found themselves deprived of their livelihoods, unable to provide for themselves or their families without government assistance.

To ensure compliance with these containment measures many states may deploy their coercive powers. Fines were the most common enforcement tool used – often at sizeable amounts – but countries also threatened jail sentences and detained those found in violation of lockdown restrictions. In the Philippines over 100,000 people were apprehended for violating curfew in the span of one month, while in Malaysia undocumented workers were targeted for arrest in lockdown raids and moved to detention centres.[4] In countries such as China and Hungary, those spreading 'misinformation' about the virus, including doctors and journalists, were investigated and detained.[5]

Furthermore, enforcement officers often resorted to violent tactics. Tear gas, water cannon and rubber bullets were used to disperse crowds. Videos or reports of police officers engaging in violent altercations with citizens in violation of lockdown orders have emerged from dozens of countries including Spain, Israel, the United States, and India.[6] State force was on occasion fatal, with documented cases of deaths related to the enforcement measures in Nigeria, South Africa and El Salvador among others.[7]

To Hobbes, writing amid the tumult of the English Civil War, obedience to the state was the price of protection. Citizens submit to the power of the state, allowing it 'a monopoly on violence' in exchange for the broader security it offers. Unlike Hobbes, however, we do not compare the state's actions to a violent anarchy and gratefully submit. Rather a state's actions are judged for their proportionality and against a standard in which trustworthiness, solidarity and a sense of fairness form the basis of an effective response. States embodying these values can weather crises not by threatening punishment but by relying on the voluntary contributions of their citizens. This is where the soft powers of the state such as legitimacy and reciprocity, as well as broader social capital, matter most, and where the values of government and citizens take on a life-and-death importance.

VALUES REVEALED: LEGITIMACY AND RECIPROCITY

The response of states and their citizens to the lockdown revealed much about the underlying values of societies: undervaluing resilience leading to poor preparation, greater solidarity in the breach, and economic and health inequalities contrasting with importance placed on fairness.

A state's legitimacy derives from the beliefs its citizens hold about the structure of government, its officials and processes. Whether a state's rules and regulations merit compliance depend on how those rules were decided upon and by whom.[8] Behavioural compliance by citizens stems from their sense of obligation and willingness to obey authorities, particularly in cases where compliance is against the citizen's immediate self-interest. This value-based legitimacy stems in turn from judgements and perceptions of the extent of procedural justice present and the general trustworthiness of government, with trustworthiness in government formed by views on government performance, leadership motivations and administrative competence.[9]

Perceptions are formed by the present context, as well as from historical experiences and the beliefs embedded in our culture. As discussed in Chapter 4, part of the enduring importance of Magna Carta is that it embodies the UK's national mythology of the prescribed limits of state power (especially important in the absence of a written constitution). When a newly elected government can rely on generations of constrained power and benevolent governance, it starts from a position of legitimacy. This virtuous circle of governance is a luxury to be prized and carefully guarded, because the opposite – a vicious circle of governance – is always a possibility and too often the reality. Trust in government is diminished by partisanship, self-interest, scandals, incompetence and unjust procedures.

Trustworthiness is founded on process (people are more likely to respect a decision if it was arrived at fairly), while legitimacy is largely about the values embodied in the process. To rule solely by coercive power is possible, but legitimate power makes governing easier and more effective.[10] Even authoritarian regimes do not rely solely on coercion, but often invest substantial resources in attempting to legitimise their rule.[11] Legitimacy is often associated with the belief that government is acting in the interests of the general population's wellbeing.

It can be argued that democracy in itself confers little legitimacy on a state, rather it is the outcomes secured by a high-functioning democracy that confer legitimacy.[12] Established democracies tend to have deeply embedded systems of procedural justice and a better quality of government than authoritarian regimes.[13] Such systems minimise corruption, discrimination and other violations of impartiality and thus foster legitimacy.[14] Fledgling democracies meanwhile have been found to have a lower quality of governance and legitimacy than other systems, as their procedural justice systems are untested and fragile, and it is difficult for politicians to make credible promises.[15] In other words, a symbolic act of voting will not on its own build trust in the state, but the meaningful accountability and fair treatment that democratic institutions can deliver will create legitimacy above what an authoritarian regime is able to achieve.

Political scientists measure legitimacy by looking at compliance or cooperation with acts like voting, volunteer military service or payments of taxes. Such indicators can be supplemented during the lockdown by mobility data published by Apple and Google. For instance, in New Zealand, activity devoted to retail and recreation dropped 90 per cent from the baseline on the first day that a full lockdown was imposed and remained reduced by at least 85 per cent for the entire period of the country's five-week lockdown.[16] Government orders were complied with instantaneously and consistently, suggesting a high degree of legitimacy. The compliance earned by this legitimacy, along with early and decisive government actions in regard to travel restrictions and lockdown orders, meant that New Zealand was able to eradicate the virus entirely by June during the first wave while incurring less than two dozen fatalities.

Reductions in mobility are not exactly comparable across countries, as governments differed in how they defined essential services that were permitted to remain open and took different approaches to activities such as outdoor exercise and the closure of parks. But the speed with which populations complied with government directives and whether compliance was sustained provide evidence of the levels of trust. Lagged compliance suggests the population acted based not on the government's recommendation but on other information such as media reports, social pressure or the virus affecting friends and family. Uneven compliance suggests trust in government was not strong enough to outweigh the inconvenience and hardships of lockdown measures.

Italy's nationwide lockdown that closed non-essential commercial businesses began on 12 March, but the decline in mobility was more gradual than in New Zealand, occurring over the span of four days. In the first two weeks of lockdown daily mobility rates varied by 20 per cent.[17] In New York State, reductions in retail and recreation activity hovered between 50 and 60 per cent in the first two weeks of the state-wide lockdown, and between 50 and 70 per cent after that.[18] In both cases compliance was much less consistent than in New Zealand.

Compliance in New York was representative of the United States as a whole. According to the data company Unacast, on only two days in April did the United States have a drop in mobility between 55 and 70 per cent, despite numerous top officials urging people to stay home and all but five states imposing lockdown measures.[19] On other days in April the mobility decrease was less than 40 per cent, and by mid-May mobility decreases of less than 25 per cent was the norm despite the virus's continued presence.

The US suffered from intense partisanship and high degrees of discord between levels of government during the initial phases of the pandemic, which diminished trust and fed into lower compliance. President Trump openly contradicted health experts and feuded with state governors. Wearing a mask became a partisan issue, resulting in a more than 20 per cent difference between Democrat and Republican compliance with voluntary recommendations.[20] Brazil, under the leadership of President Bolsonaro, faced similar frictions and struggled to contain the virus. In contrast other federalist countries, like Canada, exhibited remarkable levels of cooperation between levels of government led by different political parties, messaging was unified and traditional political animosities were largely set aside for the greater good.

This performance points to the importance of state legitimacy, competence and social capital. Without these factors, preparedness matters little. When the Global Health Security Index released its ranking of countries by preparedness for a health crisis in October 2019, New Zealand ranked 54th, well behind numerous countries that fared poorly against Covid-19 like Brazil, Italy and Spain.[21] The United States and the United Kingdom, which would both struggle to contain the spread of the virus within their borders, ranked first and second respectively, while Singapore, a country that took early and comprehensive action against Covid-19, ranked only 28th. Collectively, the rankings appear to provide at best only a loose correlation of a country's actual performance in a pandemic that would begin shortly after the index's publication. The Global Health Security Initiative's rankings were determined based on six factors: prevention, detection and reporting, rapid response, the health system, compliance with international norms, and risk environment.[22] The index did not consider social trust, current political leadership or the legitimacy of the state.

In contrast, Transparency International's Corruption Perceptions Index is based entirely on the determinants of state legitimacy and is not at all about global health crises. The index is driven by the perceptions of public sector corruption. In the 2019 index, New Zealand ranks as the least corrupt country in the world, and a number of other countries that have been hailed as successful in handling the Covid-19 pandemic crack the top ten including Denmark (which tied with New Zealand for first), Finland, Singapore, Norway and Germany. Iceland, another notable success, ranks 11th.[23] The Corruption Perceptions Index does not track pandemic performance perfectly but the cluster of top pandemic performers at the top of the list emphasises that trust and state legitimacy are crucial factors when dealing with crises and equate to lives saved in such instances.

When citizens stay at home after a government institutes a lockdown or wear a mask after a regulation requiring one is issued, these actions can be viewed as part of the Hobbesian bargain: obedience in exchange for protection. But that misses an important part of the picture. For many, this obedience stems from their willingness to comply with the decrees of a legitimate and trusted power, as well as their desire to help fellow citizens. Compliance is a contribution to society's success, the reciprocal obligations in the social contract rather than a response to Hobbesian state coercion. Coercion might be necessary in the extreme, but it is not the primary means of achieving government ends.[24]

VALUES REVEALED: SOLIDARITY

Compliance is reinforced when policies align with the values of citizens. Once the crisis struck, the values of society were revealed. Citizens across the globe acted as Rawlsians and communitarians not libertarians or utilitarians, broadly supporting lockdown measures and massive government spending even if they perceived little risk to themselves personally.[25] By March 2020, when the majority of stringent measures were implemented, it was widely thought that Covid-19 posed a significant risk only to elderly populations and those with pre-existing health conditions. In this context, the willingness of individuals of all ages and fitness to make personal and financial sacrifices for the benefit of their families, neighbours and the greater good demonstrated a strong sense of solidarity.

Moreover, people went beyond compliance with the law and engaged in mass efforts of community altruism. People sewed masks, delivered food to vulnerable populations and publicly cheered the heroism of frontline workers. As private voluntary groups to address community needs burgeoned, governments started formal volunteer campaigns. In the UK, as we've seen, an appeal for NHS volunteers received over 1 million applicants. Governments encouraged such altruism by emphasising the good that social distancing did for others.

Public reactions to the threat of the virus revealed the values of solidarity and community. The willingness, at times eagerness, of people to help their fellow citizens and fulfil their obligations to society came at great cost. These were actual not theoretical sacrifices. Lockdown measures deepened the economic uncertainty, disrupted social lives and brought incalculable levels of stress and anxiety. These sacrifices, taken in the spirit of community and solidarity, made the deep inequalities that Covid exposed in many societies all the more searing.

Solidarity in a pandemic is an example of positive 'behavioural contagion', in the terminology of the economist Robert Frank. In simple terms, we are influenced by what those around us do. If our friends smoke, we are much more likely to smoke. If those around us observe lockdown rules or wear masks, we are more likely to do so as well. This concept, which can also be termed a social meme, goes back to the moral sentiments of Adam Smith. Frank argues that the existence of important behavioural externalities has implications for public policy. While good ideas and behaviours often triumph, there is no presumption that the marketplace of ideas and behaviours reliably promotes the common good, and therefore 'we

have a powerful and legitimate public policy interest in encouraging
socially beneficial memes and discouraging socially harmful ones'.[26]

VALUES REVEALED: FAIRNESS IN
AN UNEQUAL SOCIETY

Covid is fundamentally unequal in its impact, and its presence has
exposed deep inequalities in our societies. The virus itself targets
older populations – 94 per cent of fatalities are those over the age
of sixty – and those with pre-existing conditions like obesity, hyper-
tension and diabetes.[27] Those who are able to isolate and reduce
contact with strangers are much less likely to catch the virus in the
first place, creating disparities based on occupation and socioeconomic status. Statistics Canada has found that while less than 30
per cent of primary earners with a high-school diploma can work
from home, roughly 66 per cent of their counterparts with a bach-
elor's degree or higher education can do so.[28] The consequence is
that illness is driven by educational attainment. In the UK men in
low-skilled jobs were found to be almost four times more likely to
die from Covid-19 than professionals.[29]

As socioeconomic factors like occupation and income intersect
with race and ethnicity, countries around the world experienced
wide disparities in Covid-19 fatality rates among their domestic
population. In England and Wales, the mortality rates for black,
Pakistani and Bangladeshi people were nearly double that for
Caucasians.[30] In the Brazilian city of São Paulo, people of colour
were 62 per cent more likely to die from Covid-19 than white people,
and in the United States the Covid-19 death rate for African
Americans was reported to be more than double that of other racial
groups.[31] The worst-hit neighbourhoods in Canada's two largest
cities, Toronto and Montreal, were low-income areas with large
immigrant populations.[32]

The impact of containment measures was likewise felt differently
across populations. Lockdowns decimated jobs in the service, hospitality and entertainment industries. In the UK, nearly half the jobs
that were at risk of permanent lay-offs or reduced hours were those

with wages of less than £10 per hour.[33] The increases in unemployment affected the young, minority ethnic communities and women to a materially greater degree than other demographics (see Figures 10.1 and 10.2).[34] Undocumented and temporary foreign workers were left by the wayside when it came to income support programmes.[35]

The closure of primary and secondary schools, a free public good in most countries, had enormous distributional effects that will challenge these schools' contributions to equality of opportunity. Education under lockdown depended heavily on parental guidance and access to a computer and high-speed internet, reinforcing the structural advantages of children coming from high-income households. At the height of the lockdown, the United Nations estimated that approximately half of the 1.5 billion children out of school did not have access to a computer.[36] According to the Center on Reinventing Public Education, wealthy school districts in the United States were twice as likely to provide live teaching over video as low-income districts, and rural students were disproportionately cut off from their teachers when compared to their urban counterparts.[37] Private schools were generally able to transition to video

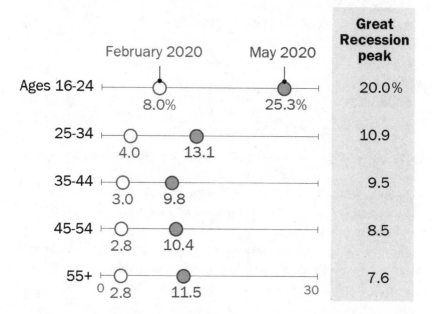

Figure 10.1 Unemployment rate by age group

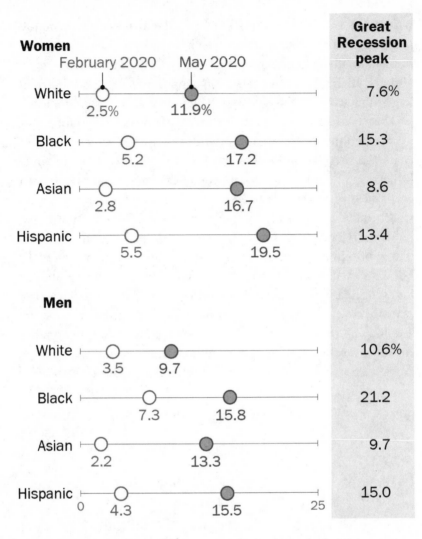

Figure 10.2 Unemployment rate by gender and ethnicity

teaching faster and to offer more regular communication between teachers and students over the course of lockdowns.

Event studies based on past school closures indicate that the inability to access adequate education during the lockdown will lead to undeveloped skills and lower levels of educational attainment.[38] Statistics Norway has estimated that school closures cost $173 per child per day in lost future earnings and lost parental productivity.[39] The end result is that the young, who are much less affected by the disease directly, will likely pay a significant part of the economic price of the pandemic, even before taking into consideration the possibility of higher taxes over their lifetimes to fund current emergency response measures. This is one of the considerations in determining how much of the state's fiscal capacity should be used in the current circumstances, given the potential to reinforce constraints on future generations. This will be discussed more fully in Chapter 16 on the nation state.

A FRAMEWORK FOR THE COMMON GOOD UNDER COVID

One of my mentors when I was starting in finance was Gerry Corrigan. From 1985 to 1993, Gerry was President of the NY Federal Reserve, one of the most powerful positions in global finance (we were all fortunate that Tim Geithner was serving in that role at the height of the global financial crisis). Tough as nails, Gerry was in charge of the NY Fed during Black Monday (19 October 1987), the day when the US stock market crashed by 23 per cent, its largest fall in history. During that dark day and the volatile ones that followed, many clamoured for trading to be halted. The market, it was said, had taken leave of its senses. It needed the equivalent of a child's time out. Gerry would have none of it. In his view, 'the problem with closing the market was that you would have to open it again'. As most military leaders know from a young age, but many politicians have to learn at great cost, starting a war is easy, exiting the field of battle is much harder.

Given the lack of preparations and the slow initial responses to the developing Covid pandemic, by the time most governments acted, they had no choice but to close their economies. It was paramount to reverse what was becoming an explosive contagion of the disease with dire consequence for mortality and human dignity. While it would have been better to have acted earlier and it would have been even better to prepare well in advance, the decisions to lock down were literally the only viable options by the time they were finally taken.

But the problem was, having closed the economy, how could governments open them again? In view of the very real economic costs of the lockdown, many have framed these decisions in terms of trading off the estimated values of health and economic outcomes. President Bolsonaro, for instance, resisted even putting Brazil into lockdown because the country couldn't have a 'wave of unemployment', while President Trump often insinuated that the costs of lockdown measures in the United States were not worth the averted deaths.[40] In the UK, the former Conservative leader Sir Iain Duncan Smith tied the economic recovery directly to health outcomes by arguing that people should go back to work in order to fund the NHS.[41]

This framing of the reopening problem demonstrates in the starkest terms the importance of understanding the relationship between value and values. As we have seen, there are ways to make this a clinical decision. The combination of valuation techniques, such as the Value of Statistical Life, and tools for decision making, such as cost–benefit analysis, can allow policymakers to weigh the current and potential future economic damage against the estimated 'monetary costs' of increased morbidity until, consistent with the marginal revolution discussed in Chapter 2, the marginal costs and benefits of death and commerce are equalised. Such analysis can be made more sophisticated by including estimates of the costs of the lockdown on mental health and forgone education as well as estimates of the benefits of reopening in terms of maintaining the skills of workers and the productive capacity of firms. These extensions would add important considerations to lockdown decisions, albeit in a framework where all factors, including life, have estimated monetary values so that an 'optimal solution' could be found just as in any other economic value-maximisation problem.

Such an approach, however, would have flown in the face of the revealed preferences of people, who, when faced with the prospect of a Covid onslaught, largely embraced efforts to protect the greatest number of their fellow citizens. As we have seen, people's responses to Covid have demonstrated the values of solidarity, fairness and responsibility. The right framework to address the twin economic and health crises wrought by Covid must therefore embody these values in agreed social goals and then assess policies in terms of their impact on them.

In developing a Covid policy framework for the common good, we can take the lessons from climate change (see the next two chapters). In that case, there is an overarching goal – environmental sustainability – that is set by society's values of intergenerational equity and fairness. Environmental sustainability can be achieved through a specific target – limiting greenhouse gas emissions to a carbon budget consistent with global warming of 1.5–2 degrees Celsius. The target is subject to measurement uncertainty as well as uncertainties about how well it maps to exact climate outcomes (feedback loops and so on could mean worse outcomes even if the budgets are respected), but given the starting point it is the best risk-management approach to achieving what society values.

To determine the right policies to address the impacts of Covid, we first need clarity on goals and metrics associated with measuring success in achieving those goals. Ideally, the targets to achieve these outcomes should be set after public discussion of the alternatives, the actions available to achieve them and their relative likelihoods of success. Then, the policies to achieve them should be analysed and implemented.

The economists Tim Besley and Nick Stern have advocated an approach, cost–effectiveness analysis, that examines how to manage and assess the costs of achieving goals in different ways.[42] In cost–effectiveness analysis, the goals – based on society's values – are set first. A clear indicator/measure of those goals is established (the carbon budget consistent with 1.5 degrees for climate, and, as we shall see, a low R0 for Covid), and then alternative policies are examined to determine the most effective way of accomplishing what society wants. Note the differences from cost–benefit analysis. In (admittedly crude applications of) cost–benefit analysis, a series of valuation estimates are made – all of which, including those based on market prices, contain a series of judgements about values. Then the costs and benefits are added up and the decision is taken on the margin. The mixture of values judgements can be obscured in the seductive comfort of 'hard' numbers. Cost–effectiveness analysis explicitly seeks to achieve society's values. In the wrong hands, cost–benefit analysis can determine them.

Let's now put this theory into practice. The standard framing of the policy responses to Covid was outlined in a highly influential blog by the writer, engineer and businessman Tomás Pueyo in which the Covid response was portrayed as comprising:

1) the Hammer, an initial set of extreme restrictions to protect health by controlling the spread of the virus that risks running out of control. This was also the instinctive response of many populations around the world. The Hammer was accompanied in most cases by economic rescue packages to shield firms and households from the negative economic shocks from closing businesses and schools; and

2) the Dance, a trial-and-error process of gradually easing lockdown restrictions (while encouraging social distancing and other containment measures) and gradually restarting economic activity. During this second phase, the pandemic must be kept under control while it is still not completely suppressed.[43]

When Pueyo developed this characterisation, the view among many policymakers was that the lockdown was essential to stop the spread of Covid from overwhelming their health services. The objectives of economic support measures (such as wage furlough schemes and cheap corporate credit) were to maintain the attachment of workers to their jobs to preserve the productive capacity of firms. These policies were designed as bridges, with an implicit assumption that living with Covid would be a temporary experience, an acute rather than a chronic condition. People and governments prioritised health above all and then did what they could to mitigate the economic fallout.

As weeks turned to months and the prospects of a miraculous return to normality receded ever further into the distance, four things changed. First, progress was made containing – but not eradicating – the disease, with the rate of propagation, R0, falling below 1 (the level above which the disease grows exponentially). Second, the economic costs began to mount considerably with government deficits reaching levels not seen since the heights of the Second World War. Third, prolonged inactivity began to erode the productive capacities of workers and many companies. These were spread increasingly unevenly across the economy. As governments worried that support programmes for specific sectors of the economy would amount to picking winners, Covid was busy picking losers in sectors such as hospitality, retail and transportation. Finally, the unequal impacts of the pandemic on different socioeconomic groups – women, minorities and the young – and on the broader health of the population – including mental health, domestic abuse and the non-treatment of other diseases – became increasingly apparent.

In this environment, calls for more explicit trade-offs between health and economic costs and benefits multiplied. All of these assessments required some form of estimates for the Value of Statistical Life (VSL) and then weighed them against the growing economic and social costs of the lockdown. Among the most sophisticated variants was a framework developed by the doyen of happiness Richard Layard and a number of co-authors.[44] Their framework, centred on measures of wellbeing that they termed WELLBYS, balanced a series of social and economic costs and benefits of the lockdown, identifying the cross-over months for reopening.

Even when this is carefully thought through, however, such analyses are fraught with the difficulties discussed in the previous chapter. Assumptions are numerous, methodology is flawed, fairness plays a secondary role while optimisation reigns supreme, and moral stances are embedded into calculations without adequate thought. The exercise of explicitly valuing variables such as life can be corrosive to the values that underpin and sustain our society.

In matters of life, death and health, there are limits to the insights that such quantitative approaches can deliver about both the ethical issues at stake and the practical decisions that must be taken. Too often, the use of a cost–benefit analysis and VSL bestows a degree of authority that is not merited. Schelling's subjective revolution,

while an improvement on valuation of life by labour potential, still
left much to be desired. As many, including the Nobel prize-winning
philosopher-economist Amartya Sen, have argued, life cannot be
distilled into a single figure in dollars, pounds or even WELLBYS.
Tellingly, politicians are reluctant to ascribe a monetary value to
lives in public remarks, likely sensing that such a position will not
sit well with the general public.[45] Indeed, segments of the population have at times been very vocal in their opposition to VSL
estimates when they do not feel their lives have been adequately
weighted in comparison to others'.[46]

More practically, although the economic and health objectives
are often placed in opposition – with economic gains from opening
up traded off against poorer health outcomes – the reality is more
complex. As my colleague at the Bank of England Jan Vlieghe has
documented, there is extensive, cross-country evidence that these
objectives are usually complementary. For example, data from various countries indicate that more than 80 per cent of reductions in
mobility are voluntary as the prevalence of the virus increases.[47]
People won't necessarily come back to work or go out to spend if
they are concerned about their health, so the demand and supply
impacts of lifting lockdown measures prematurely will be limited.
People are less likely to spend on entertainment if they fear higher
risks of infection. Surges in infection rates undermine consumer
and market confidence.[48]

In addition, the prospect of successive waves of the disease will
be more damaging to confidence if people believe they have been
sold false promises of a return towards normality. This underscores
the importance of clear and frank communications about what is
and isn't known about the disease and its propagation. Covid is the
most difficult of challenges: not merely a question of managing risk
but of managing radical uncertainty.[49] There are analogies to the
disease but given the newness of the strain, its asymptomatic propagation and the ever present possibility of mutation, there are no
true precedents. But clarifying what is known and what is not, as
well as updating advice to the public with clear explanations about
why it may have changed, is essential to maintaining state legitimacy and encouraging citizen reciprocity. People need to recognise

why measures make sense if they are to follow them in sufficient numbers for them to be effective.

This is too important a job to be left to public health officials alone. Ultimately, authorities need to 'follow the science' to achieve the fundamental, base objective of R0 less than 1 but then optimise across a range of objectives in order to value truly what society values. There are diminishing returns to following epidemiological advice.

The ideal is to take a comprehensive approach to build the common good by defining the core purpose in terms of the quality of life of all in society, agreed through a process of developing consensus, and then determining the most cost-effective interventions to achieve these goals. Society's choice should be guided by how it values life, the dignity of work and human flourishing today and tomorrow.

As we have seen, the revealed values of the citizens in the midst of the Covid pandemic have been those of solidarity, fairness and responsibility. These values suggest that the overarching objectives of Covid policy should be centred on health and social outcomes – minimising the risks of death and ensuring that the sick have adequate treatment and that the burdens of social distancing and the benefits of any protections provided by the state are shared fairly across society. Once these objectives have been reasonably achieved, policymakers should seek to maximise the benefits to the economy and minimise the threat of a resurgence of the disease by selectively opening up. In pursuing deconfinement, policymakers must pay particular attention to distribution. The scale and distribution of the direct benefits and costs to consumers and workers from relaxing lockdown measures varies widely (in terms of changes in wages, consumption, employment and infection rates).

Authorities need to pursue a risk-management approach: optimising expected outcomes, after having first limited the possibility of extreme negative events in ways that are consistent with the public's priorities. Recognising the public's high valuation of better health outcomes requires controlling the rate of Covid infections under any scenario. This means achieving an R0 well below 1 (the closeness to 0 depends on the prospects of resurgence and the costs of complete elimination). As discussed, there is a useful analogy between the use of R0 and the use of temperature targets in climate change (such as keeping well below 2 degrees Celsius) as part of rational assessments of acceptable risks.

Once the risks of the extremely dangerous scenario of an out-of-control pandemic have been minimised, the relative costs of continued lockdowns on mental health, productive capacity and intergenerational fairness become decisive. Given uncertainties and the compounding costs of full lockdown, the objective cannot be to gamble everything for a vaccine or breakthrough combinations of therapeutics, testing and targeted lockdowns that would allow a return towards the *status quo ante*. The challenge for policy is to minimise the economic costs of keeping the infection rates under control, while paying due consideration to issues of distributional and intergenerational equity. Forfeiting children's education or crippling the future productive potential of the economy would appear too high a price for annihilation of the disease. In other words, equality and dynamism should be added to the values guiding Covid policy decisions.

Targeting a low R0 as the unifying objective to achieve society's values has several benefits. First, by definition, it limits the spread of the disease. Second, by keeping the disease on a non-explosive trajectory, it ensures that existing health capacity is not overwhelmed, maximising the prospects of fair treatment of those who get ill and dignity in death for those who do not survive. Third, it buys time to expand health and testing capacities, to develop new therapeutic treatments that reduce mortality for those who contract Covid, and to increase the possibility that a vaccine could be discovered and administered. Finally, the slow spread of disease could gradually build immunity in the population. Importantly, all of these factors are subject to high degrees of uncertainty given the novel nature of the pandemic.

Focusing on changes in R0 also brings public health and economics together. Relaxation of lockdown can increase R0 with economic, health and social consequences that can be weighed against the potential economic benefits. The core of a strategic policy approach to Covid is the best combination of policies to achieve the desired level of infection control at a minimum economic cost with due respect for distributional and other social consequences. Calculations and calibrations of those costs then provide guidance for the different containment strategies under consideration. As Besley and Stern argue, a major lesson from policy economics is that identifying which combinations of instruments are needed to meet which goal is essential to social decision making.[50] In the case of Covid, that means paying attention to the impact of measures on fairness (in terms of job preservation, social support, health outcomes and so on), the social returns to education, economic incentives, intergenerational equity (education and economic opportunity) and economic dynamism (by limiting scarring and the destruction of productive capacity).

In devising policies, it is important to recognise that Covid is fundamentally asymmetric. It afflicts the old more than the young. The exposure varies widely across economic sectors, hammering certain industries that are particularly prone to spreading disease (entertainment, hospitality and so on), while reinforcing the competitive advantages of those that do not (such as e-commerce, e-learning and e-health). At a minimum, this means that broad-based support programmes need to be supplemented by others targeted at specific sectors of the economy and segments of the population.

In deciding which sectors of the economy to open or close, policymakers must weigh a series of externalities that are not valued in any market. Economic externalities are the spillovers from one activity to other sectors of the economy. For example, a growing auto sector raises demand for steel, aluminium and increasingly software. Infection externalities are the contribution of the economic activity to spreading the disease. Most forms of live entertainment and hospitality have high infection externalities, which are not necessarily fully reflected in their prices.[51]

Taking these dynamics into account, policymakers should tend to restrict economic activities that have weak economic externalities to the rest of the economy but high infection externalities (like live entertainment, closed restaurants and non-essential travel) but tend to open – or even subsidise – those with low infection externalities and high positive economic externalities (like pharmaceuticals and banking). The biggest challenges are in those areas that are essential economically but also highly risky from an infection perspective (healthcare, essential travel and education), though the perspectives on its infection rates have varied over time. Assenza et al. have presented this categorisation diagrammatically (see Figure 10.3), prescribing that all economic activity either be protected, managed, restricted or left alone based on economic externalities and risk of infection.

Even highly sophisticated analyses like that of Assenza et al. with complexities including shadow prices of infection and the equation of marginal rates of substitution across sectors are simplifications of the complex choices that Covid demands of policymakers. For example, most modelling approaches generally do not weight the incidence of either the disease or the economic shocks across different socioeconomic groups. In short fairness is undervalued in them, even though it was both at the heart of the public response and is essential for state legitimacy. And these static trade-offs underweight dynamism by taking for granted that the productive capacity of the economy will not be scarred and diminished by the lockdown.

These additional complexities mean that Covid decision making cannot be reduced to the optimisation of the mathematical expectation of some objective function.[52] The nature of uncertainties, the magnitude of consequences and possible disagreement over values are such that policymakers should choose actions that are robust in the sense that they perform reasonably well relative to other policies over a range of possible scenarios. The ideal would be 'no regret' policies, but given the fog of Covid the best that we can hope for is probably 'low regret' ones.

As discussed in Chapter 16, the use of fiscal capacity is a critical decision. Despite low structural interest rates, the budget constraint is not unlimited. At the same time, the lowest economic cost should not be confused with lowest cost to the public purse. The costs to businesses of regulations can reduce employment or lead to inefficient utilisation of assets, with many of the resulting costs passed on to consumers in the form of higher prices. In this respect, it

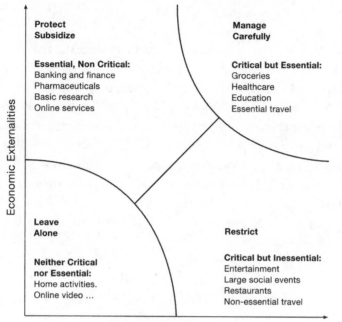

Figure 10.3 Sectoral policy interventions

should be paramount to consider the dynamic capacity of the economy. Policymakers need to consider the impact of policies on the education and skills development of people and the productive capacity of businesses that will be hard to replace. Path dependence matters.

Finally, it should be stressed that, in parallel with these decisions on the path of reopening, fairness in the access to healthcare is essential. If it is compromised, the bounds between legitimacy of the state and reciprocity of citizens will be undermined, feeding back into lower compliance and worse health and economic outcomes. The same goes for perceived fairness in terms of the privations experienced during lockdowns and social distancing. There cannot be one rule for the powerful and another for the rest (as the public outrage over the behaviour during the lockdown of senior government officials and footballers attests).

Managing Covid is a dynamic process. Decisions taken early on when information was limited and fear was rampant should not be set in stone. Policies must be updated and recalibrated with new developments and greater understanding of the risks we face. Improvements in testing and therapeutics change the risk profile of the disease. The economy will adapt to restrictions. The public needs to be brought along with these changes and their implications. Slowing the spread of the disease has meant better health outcomes for those who now get the disease. At the same time, with the build-up of debt, the erosion of skills, the rusting of idle physical capital and the deepening tragedy of inadequate education, the resilience of both the economy and society has diminished. These developments should influence decisions around the nature of reopening, provided the overarching goal of managing R0 continues to be achieved.

VALUE(S) WILL CHANGE

The Covid crisis has revealed the importance of the state and the costs of its failure. Governments had undervalued resilience in the years leading up to the crisis, failing in their duties to protect their citizens. Where governments proved competent, the compliance of their citizens with lockdown orders was reinforced. People across the world rose to the occasion, displaying solidarity and altruism individually and through renewed civil society. At the same time, the Covid crisis has revealed deep strains and injustices. Essential workers have been undervalued, and the contrast between the solidarity with their fellow citizens that so many displayed and the deep inequalities that exist in society is stark. This has rightly raised expectations for fairness and greater equality in all spheres of life.

The question is whether the values revealed during the crisis will be lived in normal times.[53] It will depend in part how value changes in the post-Covid world. Financial market valuations have oscillated with changing perceptions of the length and severity of the pandemic.

Deeper concerns include the extent to which economies are experiencing supply destruction rather than mere disruption. In concrete terms, how many once-viable companies will be permanently impaired? And how many people will lose their jobs and their attachment to the labour force? The answers to these questions – more than the scale of any short-term plunge in GDP – will be the true tests of the effectiveness of the responses of governments, companies and banks.

Attention has turned to the very real opportunities the crisis has already revealed: in teleworking, e-health, distance learning and the acceleration across our economies from moving atoms to shifting bits.

As our digital and local lives expand and our physical and global ones contract, there will be both value creation and destruction. Creativity and dynamism will still be highly valued, but new vectors will shape value: economic, financial, psychological and societal. In ascending order consider the following.

First, the crisis will likely accelerate the fragmentation of the global economy. Until a vaccine has been widely applied, travel restrictions will remain. Even afterwards, local resilience will be prized over global efficiency.

Second, much of the enterprise value of companies will be taken up by lost cash flows and extraordinary financial support. This higher debt – unless it is restructured, extended on concessional terms or forgiven – will increase the riskiness of the underlying equity and weigh on capacity for growth.

More profoundly, the financial relationship between the state and the private sector has already expanded dramatically. How smooth will be the exit? Or will the state remain enmeshed in commerce, restraining private dynamism?

Third, the searing experience of the twin health and economic crises will change how companies balance risk and resilience. We are entering a world where businesses will be expected to prepare for black swans by valuing anti-fragility and planning for failure. The financial sector learned these lessons the hard way during the global financial crisis, which is why banks can now be part of the solution. Going forward, which company will operate with minimal liquidity, stretched supply chains and token contingency plans? Which governments will rely on global markets to address local crises?

Fourth, people's economic narratives will change. After decades of risk being steadily downloaded on to individuals, the bill has arrived, and people cannot even begin to pay it. Entire populations are experiencing the fears of the unemployed and sensing the anxiety that comes with inadequate or inaccessible healthcare. These lessons will not be forgotten quickly. This will have lasting consequences for sectors that rely on levered consumption, a booming housing market and a vibrant gig economy.

This points to a final, deeper issue. In recent decades, subtly but relentlessly, we have been moving from a market economy to a market society. Increasingly, to be valued, an asset or activity has to be in a market; the price of everything is becoming the value of everything.

This crisis could help reverse that causality, so that public values help shape private value. When pushed, societies have prioritised health first and foremost, and then looked to address the economic consequences. We have acted as Rawlsians and communitarians not utilitarians or libertarians. Cost–benefit analyses, steeped in calculations of the Value of Statistical Lives, have mercifully been overruled, as the values of economic dynamism and efficiency have been joined by those of solidarity, fairness, responsibility and compassion.

This crisis has been a test of stakeholder capitalism. When it's over, companies will be judged by 'what they did during the war'. How they treated their employees, suppliers and customers. Who shared, and who hoarded? Who stepped up, and who stood down?

Many leaders have described the current crisis as a war against an invisible enemy. When it is over, we will need to win the peace.

The limited historical experience with such epochal events is that afterwards society's aspirations focus not just on the rate of growth but on its direction and its quality. After the global financial crisis, the goals were to rebalance from financialisation of our economies, to end 'too big to fail' in banking, and more recently to build up stakeholder capitalism. After the Covid crisis, it's reasonable to expect public demands for improvements in the quality and coverage of social support and medical care, for greater attention to be paid to managing tail risks, and more heed to be given to the advice of scientific experts.

It won't be easy to renew our economy and society, not least because the costs of fighting the pandemic will have diminished the capacity of governments, businesses and financial institutions to renew their economies (as well as to tackle the next crisis). How we address climate change will be the test of these new values. After all, climate change is an issue that i) involves the entire world, from which no one will be able to self-isolate; ii) is a fat tail risk today but is predicted by science to be the central scenario tomorrow; and iii) we can address only if we act in advance and in solidarity.

Many leaders have described the Covid crisis as the greatest challenge since the Second World War. After the devastations of the First World War, the Prime Minister Lloyd George rallied the people of the United Kingdom who had been through so much, with a promise to build an 'England Fit for Heroes'. Once this war against an invisible enemy is over, our ambitions should be bolder: 'A planet fit for our grandchildren.' If we come together to meet the biggest challenges in medical biology, so too can we come together to meet the challenges of climate physics and the forces driving inequality.

Let's turn first to the climate crisis before the next Part explores how leaders, companies and countries can step up in crisis and calm.

11

The Climate Crisis

Since the last ice age, the human race has thrived over an 11,000-year era of extraordinary climate stability – the Holocene. Now that stability is shattering. We have created a new era – the Anthropocene – in which our earth's climate is driven, not by the geological rhythms of nature, but by our impacts on the planet.

As the Industrial Revolution spread, the earth's climate began to change. Since 1850, global temperatures have risen at around 0.07° Celsius per decade. In the last three decades, that pace has tripled. Our planet's average temperature is already 1°C warmer since the late nineteenth century.[1]

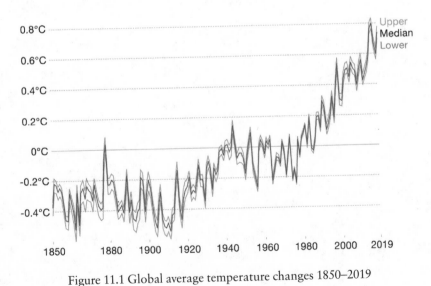

Figure 11.1 Global average temperature changes 1850–2019

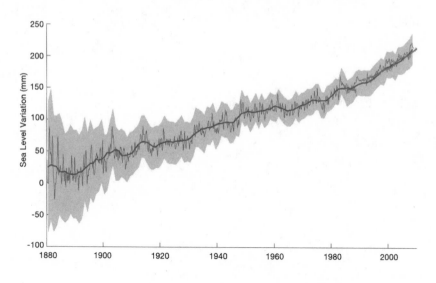

Figure 11.2 Global sea level increases since 1880

The impacts of these changes on our planet's finely tuned ecosystems are intensifying. Our oceans have become 30 per cent more acidic since the Industrial Revolution.[2] Sea levels have risen 20 centimetres over the past century, with the rate doubling in the past two decades.[3] The pace of ice loss in the Arctic and Antarctic has tripled in the last decade.[4] Extreme climatic events – hurricanes, wildfires and flash flooding – are multiplying, with yesterday's tail risk becoming tomorrow's central scenario.

These effects first began to eliminate individual species and then to destroy whole habitats. There have been five mass extinctions in the history of our planet. Now, human activity is driving the planet towards the sixth at an unprecedented rate. Current extinction rates are around a hundred times higher than average over the past several million years. Since I was born, there has been a 70 per cent decline in the population of mammals, birds, fish, reptiles and amphibians.[5]

What had been biblical is becoming commonplace.

Perhaps because they were not formally, financially valued, these losses were initially downplayed and their cause treated as an issue for another day. But now the effects of climate change are beginning to impact assets which have a market price, making the scale of the

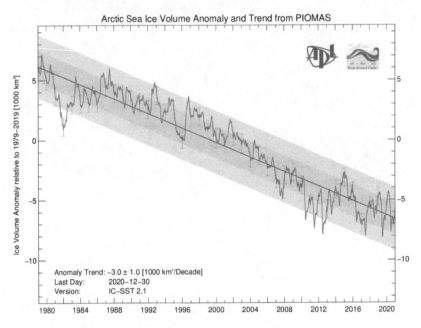

Figure 11.3 Arctic Sea ice volume

looming calamity more tangible. Climate change is setting in train a vicious cycle in which rising sea levels and more extreme weather are damaging property, forcing migration, impairing assets and reducing the productivity of work. And now the Covid crisis has exposed the tragic folly of undervaluing resilience and ignoring systemic risks. As society awakes to these risks, it is beginning to place greater value on sustainability – the precondition to solving the climate crisis.

But, to do so, we must first understand its causes and consequences.

CAUSES: EMISSIONS

The UN's Intergovernmental Panel on Climate Change (IPCC) has concluded that our current warming trend is extremely likely (with greater than 95 per cent probability) to have been caused by human activity.[6] Rapid industrialisation and global growth have increased the level of greenhouse gases (GhG), particularly carbon dioxide

(CO_2), in the atmosphere at an alarming rate. It took 250 years to burn the first half-trillion tons of carbon.[7] On current trends, the next half-trillion will be released into our atmosphere in less than forty years.

Carbon dioxide concentrations have never been so high (Figure 11.4). This is more than an immediate challenge. Among the greenhouse gases (including methane, nitrous oxide and fluorinated gases), CO_2 is the most problematic. It accounts for three-quarters of the warming impact of emissions, and it is the most persistent of the greenhouse gases, with a significant proportion of the carbon emitted today remaining in the atmosphere for centuries.[8]

By analysing the interactions of carbon emissions and temperatures over the past century, scientists have concluded that the pace of global warming is roughly proportional to the amount of carbon dioxide in the atmosphere. Such calculations mean we can estimate our carbon budget – that is, how much carbon dioxide can still be released into the atmosphere before we exceed different temperature thresholds.

The size of the carbon budget depends on (i) the temperature outcome, and (ii) the degree of uncertainty (that is, probability assumed to the outcome). The IPCC reports are the most well-re-

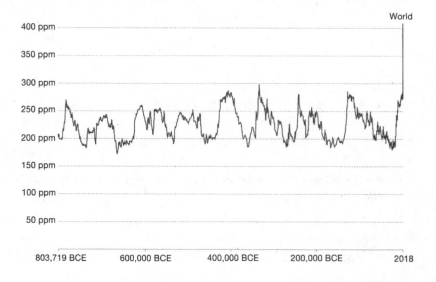

Figure 11.4 Atmospheric CO_2 concentration[9]

spected and commonly cited source on carbon budgets. In 2018, the IPCC estimated a range from 420 Gt (to achieve 1.5°C with 66 per cent probability; this would be exhausted in less than a decade at current emissions) to 1,500 Gt (to achieve 2°C with 50 per cent probability; this would be exhausted in about three and a half decades at current emissions). Limiting temperature increases to 1.5°C from pre-industrial levels keeps the earth's climatic and natural systems from tipping into a dangerous feedback loop. For example, the IPCC projects that if temperatures increase even by 2°C, 1.7 billion people could experience more severe heatwaves, sea levels could rise another 10 centimetres, coral reefs could decline by as much as 99 per cent.

Probability (%)	Degree target (°C)	Carbon budget (Gt remaining, as of report's publication and Q1 2020)[10]	Years remaining at current rate of emissions[11]
66	1.5	420 (at report publication) ~336 (Q1 2020)	~8
50	1.5	580 (at report publication) ~496 (Q1 2020)	~12
66	2	1,170 (at report publication) ~1,086 (Q1 2020)	~26
50	2	1,500 (at report publication) ~1,416 (Q1 2020)	~34

Given the complexity of the ecosystem, it is possible that these budgets could be even smaller, and this is part of the reason for trying to limit temperature increases as much as possible. The earth has a number of feedback loops and tipping points, which could turn from virtuous to vicious and accelerate the process. For example, the polar ice sheets reflect light and reduce warming. As they melt, this effect is lost, making disappearing polar ice both a consequence and cause of a climate catastrophe. Similarly, the permafrost that underpins the land where I was born is now melting, setting in train a process that releases CO_2 and methane and accelerates global warming. The prospect of these feedback loops is becoming more likely as the Arctic has warmed by twice the global mean. And they are not trivial: the IPCC estimates that carbon emissions from thawing permafrost by 2100 could represent as much as *one-third* of the 1.5°C carbon budget.

When the amount of carbon added to the atmosphere is greater than the amount we remove (as has been the case for over a century), the stock of carbon dioxide increases. To stabilise temperature rises below 1.5°C, at 2°C or indeed at any temperature, we must reach net zero – the balance where the carbon emitted and taken out of the atmosphere is equal.

Net zero isn't a slogan, it's an imperative of climate physics.

To get on the path to stabilise temperatures at 1.5°C, emissions need to fall by a minimum of 8 per cent year on year over the next two decades. To put that into context, total CO_2 emissions for 2020 (which incorporated full-scale, Covid-19-induced shutdowns of our economies) decreased by around 5 to 7 per cent. To be clear, even at this crisis-reduced rate, we are continuing to spend our carbon budget, and we are not on track to meet our temperature goals. And to put these efforts in context, a 10 per cent fall in global emissions during 2020 would have still meant 33 $GtCO_2$ were released, a higher total than any year before 2010.

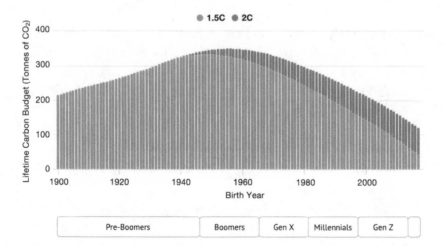

Figure 11.5 Global average lifetime carbon budgets per-capita by birth year for 1.5°C and 2°C scenarios

To limit temperature increases to 1.5°C, the 'average' global citizen born today will have a personal carbon emissions budget over their lifetime equivalent to *one-eighth* of that of their grandparents (Figure 11.5). Think of that next time you hear, 'OK, boomer'.

As it is, if the rise in greenhouse emissions doesn't level off until the latter part of the century, the IPCC estimates that temperatures will rise by 4.0°C (with a 'likely range' of 2.4–6.4°C).

Reducing emissions at the pace and scale required to limit temperature increases to below 2 degrees demands wholesale structural change. The challenges may be unevenly spread across sectors but all must contribute. Even nature will have to turn from a major net emitter of greenhouse gases to a natural carbon sink, removing substantial amounts of excess carbon from the atmosphere.

The biggest contributors to emissions and those with the most distance to travel to get to net zero are:

- Industrial process (32 per cent of current emissions), such as the production of manufactured goods, chemicals and cement. These emissions have increased 174 per cent since 1990.
- Buildings (18 per cent of current emissions), which use energy for electricity and heat generation.
- Transport (16 per cent of current emissions), which includes energy used by cars, heavy goods vehicles and the shipping and aviation industry. Transport emissions alone have grown by 70 per cent in the past two decades.
- Energy generation (11 per cent of current emissions) – the production and supply of energy, not its end use.
- Food and agriculture/nature-based sources (10 per cent of current emissions), of both crops and livestock.

Energy production and consumption is at the heart of climate dynamics, responsible for almost three-quarters of human-caused greenhouse gas emissions worldwide. The energy sector includes transportation, electricity and heat, buildings, manufacturing and construction, 'fugitive' emissions and other fuel combustion. Within

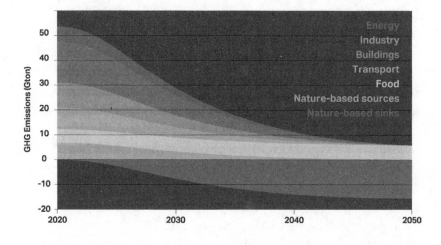

Figure 11.6 Emissions reductions pathways for different sectors to limit global warming to 1.5°C

this, generation of heat and electricity is responsible for most emissions (15 GtCO$_2$e in 2016, or 30 per cent of total emissions), followed by transportation (15 per cent) and manufacturing and construction (12 per cent), residential buildings (11 per cent) and commercial buildings (6.5 per cent). Anywhere between 15 and 40 per cent of the total greenhouse gases generated by petrol, diesel and other transport fuels are generated before they even emerge from the refinery.

To reduce emissions and stabilise the climate, solutions must focus on:

- how we generate energy (by shifting from fossil fuels to renewables);
- how we use energy (for example, by changing from petrol- to electric-powered transport, increasing the energy efficiency of buildings and decarbonising industrial processes); and
- how to increase the amount of carbon we remove from the atmosphere (by mass reforestation and development of carbon capture, use and storage (CCUS) technologies).

Wholesale changes of our energy systems will be required to achieve net zero. That means converting the bulk of energy use to electricity and converting all electricity to renewables. Other technologies which could have decisive roles include hydrogen, particularly for heavy transportation (like trucking, shipping and air travel), and carbon capture and sequestration, although they have a ways to go to become economic.

Some sectors are much harder to decarbonise than others. These 'hard-to-abate' sectors, collectively accounting for over a quarter of all global emissions, include aviation, shipping, long-distance haulage and cement and steel production. Emissions reductions will require efficiencies, new industrial processes and new technologies. In aviation and shipping, biofuels and the potential for hydrogen-powered engines could significantly reduce emissions. In the construction sector for example, 3D printers can now produce entire homes in forty-eight hours, reducing construction waste by a third and emissions by half.

To some calling for further technological innovations is a counsel of despair. To others, the innovators and entrepreneurs, these challenges disguise enormous opportunities. In all cases, speed and scale will be critical. That's why Bill Gates is leading a multi-billion-dollar Breakthrough Energy Fund to help to drive technologies to competitive scale in short order.

Gates's book *How to Solve the Climate Crisis* details the key technologies we need to get to net zero. As he acknowledges, this presents political challenges as well as economic and technological ones. This book outlines ways to do so by aligning financial values with social values. And it underscores the importance of conserving the carbon budget as best we can to create the time and space for the critical technological breakthroughs Bill Gates and others are pursuing.

Just as emissions intensities vary by industrial sector, they vary by geography. Emissions are overwhelmingly urban. While cities occupy 3 per cent of the earth's land mass, they account for 70 per cent of CO_2 emissions. Globally, Asia is the largest emitter (with slightly over half of all global emissions), followed by North America and Europe. Emissions per capita tell a different story,

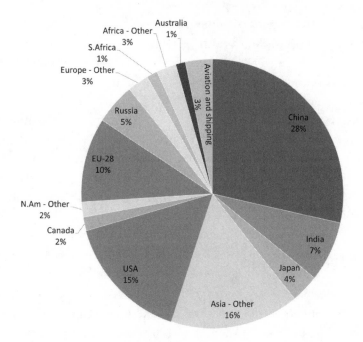

Figure 11.7 Global carbon dioxide emissions by country (2017)

with North America in the lead. Historic cumulative emissions underscore the scale of the (unwitting) contribution of the west to the problem. Trade complicates the picture with some large countries importing emissions. While all of these have implications for relative effort required, they demonstrate the global nature of the problem and the need for ambitious, collective action.

Having rapidly industrialised, China now generates over a quarter of the world's carbon dioxide emissions, followed by the US and the EU. On a per capita basis, there are considerable differences between nationalities. Australian, US and Canadian citizens emit three times the average, while residents of Chad, Niger and the Central African Republic emit 160 times less than these highest emitters, at just 0.1 tonne per capita (Figure 11.8). The EU and the UK fall near the average, partly due to technological and energy-generation choices, as well as their more service-based economies.

Advanced economies had benefited from decades of unregulated emissions, industrialising at pace and growing their economies accordingly. But climate imperatives now require that developing and emerging economies do not follow their lead. It is the global analogue to the need to shift greenhouse gas consumption from the voracious boomers to the sustainable millennials.

In particular, historically the US has emitted about 400 billion tonnes of emissions – a quarter of all global emissions – since the 1750s (Figure 11.9). Europe has emitted just over a fifth. Until 1882, the UK accounted for half the world's cumulative emissions, only to be overtaken by Europe, which was in turn leapfrogged by the US in 1950. In this historical context, Chinese emissions look relatively small, even though today China emits the most carbon into the atmosphere.

Some countries have been able to decouple economic growth from rising emissions. Several large economies (for example, the UK, France, Germany and the US) have done so without relying primarily on offshoring emissions production to countries with less stringent regulations (such that both consumption-based and production-based emissions have fallen). This decoupling reflects structural changes such as increased reliance on non-carbon-intensive sectors (like the service sector), as well as greener policy choices and technologies.

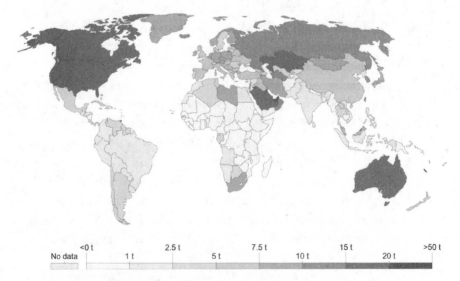

Figure 11.8 Per capita CO_2 emissions in 2018

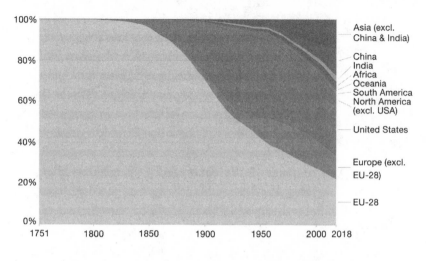

Figure 11.9 Cumulative CO_2 emissions by world region

More broadly, trade in embedded emissions reveals an east–west divide and underscores the global nature of the challenge. Most of western Europe, the Americas and many African countries are net importers of emissions while most of eastern Europe and Asia are net exporters. Asian emissions intensity partly reflects ongoing western emissions appetite.

The world has collectively decoupled the growth of emissions from the growth of GDP since the 1989 fall of the Berlin Wall. However, as noted above, emissions are still growing, even when whole economies were shut down for pandemics. As a consequence, the carbon budget to limit temperature rises to below catastrophic levels is rapidly being exhausted.

By some measures, based on science, the scale of energy revolution required is staggering.

If we had started in 2000, we could have hit the 1.5°C objective by halving emissions every thirty years. Now, we must halve emissions every ten years. If we wait another four years, the challenge will be to halve emission every year. If we wait another eight years, our 1.5°C carbon budget will be exhausted.

The entrepreneur and engineer Saul Griffith argues that the carbon-emitting properties of our committed physical capital mean that we are locked in to use up the residual carbon budget, even if

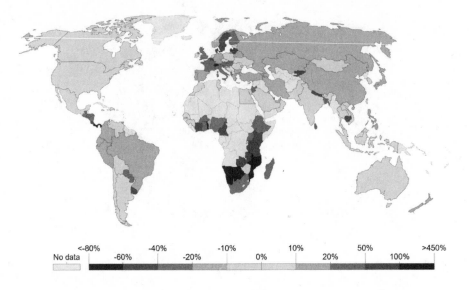

No data | <-80% | -60% | -40% | -20% | -10% | 0% | 10% | 20% | 50% | 100% | >450%

Figure 11.10 CO$_2$ emissions by world region

no one buys another car with an internal combustion engine, installs a new gas-fired hot-water heater or, at a larger scale, constructs a new coal power plant.[12] That's because, just as we expect a new car to run for a decade or more, we expect our machines to be used until they are fully depreciated. If the committed emissions of all the machines over their useful lives will largely exhaust the 1.5°C carbon budget, going forward we will need almost all new machines, like cars, to be zero carbon. Currently, electric car sales, despite being one of the hottest segments of the market, are as a percentage in single digits. This implies that, if we are to meet society's objectives, there will be scrappage and stranded assets.[13]

What's at stake if we don't manage a timely transition? What are the potential costs of climate change? And what value would be preserved if we were to achieve net zero?

THE CONSEQUENCES OF CLIMATE CHANGE

Measuring the consequences of climate change goes to the heart of the challenges of value and valuation. Some costs are immediate, visceral and quantifiable, such as the physical damage from extreme weather events. Others can be estimated through scenarios of the potential impacts of climate change on the standard measure of economic value – GDP. But there are also more fundamental questions of value(s), particularly since much of what climate change destroys, such as biodiversity and communities, is not explicitly (financially) valued. And our assessments of the relative value of policies to address climate change depend crucially on how much we value the future.

Estimates of the costs of climate change and the value of sustainability are subject to a number of uncertainties. These start with how precisely atmospheric concentrations of greenhouse gases affect both average temperatures and the variability of the climate.

The uncertainties around the costs of climate extend to how extreme weather affects the level and rates of change of key economic variables such as GDP growth, employment and wages; and they include uncertainty about the degree to which innovation and adaptation can mitigate some of the impacts on measured economic value. Assessing the value of the lives of species and the livelihoods of people faces familiar challenges with 'monetising' sacred values. And virtually all the estimates of the costs of climate change ignore its potential impact on social capital and institutions, the direct effect of that on wellbeing and the feedback to economic value creation.

To draw out these points, let's begin, as is my wont, with how central bankers view the risks of climate change before building to broader measures of the value that is at risk.

Climate change creates both physical and transition *risks*. Physical risks arise from the increased frequency and severity of climate- and weather-related events (such as fires, floods and storms) that damage property, destroy crops and disrupt trade. When physical risk crystallises it can damage real property, disrupt human and natural systems and impair financial values.

A tangible example of the last is the marked increase in underwriting risk for insurers. Extreme weather events, such as hurricanes, flooding, forest fires and rising sea levels, put the critical infrastructure on which businesses and communities rely at risk. Entire livelihoods could be wiped out as crops fail, homes are destroyed and transport networks buckle.

Since the 1980s the number of registered weather-related loss events has tripled, and the inflation-adjusted losses have increased fivefold. Consistent with the accelerated pace of climate change, the cost of weather-related insurance losses has increased eightfold in real terms over the past decade to an annual average of $60 billion.[14] These trends are set to continue, with coastal flooding projected to rise by 50 per cent over the balance of this century, a development that could threaten assets worth 20 per cent of global GDP.[15]

In contrast to these estimates of the losses for asset values which are measures of the stock of wealth, GDP is a measure of the *flow* – that is, the increase in wealth. Estimates of the potential impact of unaddressed climate change on the level and growth of economic activity are significant, and include not only the costs of disruption from more extreme weather but also the impact of gradual increases in average temperatures. For example, rising temperatures and persistent heatwaves will affect labour productivity, especially of manual and outdoor labourers. Studies show that at 34°C a worker loses 50 per cent of their work capacity.[16] The economic losses due to heat stress at work were estimated to be US$280 billion in 1995. By 2030, this is projected to have risen eightfold to reach US$2.5 trillion. And by 2050 it is estimated that 1.2 billion people, the equivalent of the current population of India, could be living under threat of lethal annual heatwaves.

The Network for Greening the Financial System (NGFS), a coalition of almost eighty central banks, representing countries that generate almost three-quarters of the world's emissions, have developed representative scenarios to show how climate risks might evolve and affect the real and financial economies.[17] One of these scenarios – 'hothouse earth' – models what might happen if there is limited action on climate change, emissions grow and temperatures rise above 3°C (recall that the IPCC's central scenario for unchanged policies is 4°C). In this case, the physical risks of climate change dominate as sea levels rise and more extreme weather events take their toll, resulting in 25 per cent GDP loss by the end of the century. The NGFS judges this to be a conservative estimate.

Although few outside the industry know it, the Bank of England regulates the world's fourth-largest insurance industry. When I became Governor, I soon realised that insurers are on the front line of climate change. With their motives as global citizens sharpened by commercial concerns, insurers have some of the greatest incentives to understand and tackle climate change in the short term. For example, Lloyd's of London underwriters are required to consider climate change explicitly in their business plans and underwriting models. Their genius has been to recognise that past is not prologue and that the catastrophic norms of the future are in the tail risks of today. With such insights, it is perhaps not surprising that the insurance sector has been particularly active in organising itself to address these existential issues.[18]

Property and casualty insurers and reinsurers are already adjusting their business models to the most immediate physical risks – from flood risk to the impact of extreme weather events on sovereign risk. As one of many examples, work done at Lloyd's of London estimated that the 20 centimetre rise in sea level at the tip of Manhattan since the 1950s, when all other factors are held constant, increased insured losses from superstorm Sandy by 30 per cent in New York alone.[19]

Thus far, the combination of sophisticated forecasting, a forward-looking capital regime and business models built around short-term coverage has left insurers relatively well placed to manage physical risks.[20] Insurers have to update their models constantly and adjust coverage prudently. In time, growing swathes of our economies could become uninsurable absent public backstops: $250 billion to $500 billion worth of US coastal property could be below sea level by 2100.[21] Moreover, if coverage is not maintained, the broader financial system would become increasingly exposed to large and variable physical risks.

The second category of climate-related financial risk is transition risk. These risks arise as the result of the adjustment towards a lower-carbon economy. Changes in policies, technologies and physical risks will prompt reassessments of the value of a large range of assets as the costs and opportunities of the transition become apparent. The longer meaningful adjustment is delayed, the more transition risks will increase.

The speed at which the adjustment to a net-zero economy occurs is uncertain and could be decisive for financial stability. There have already been a few high-profile examples of jump-to-distress pricing because of shifts in environmental policy or performance. The combined market capitalisation of the top four US coal producers has fallen by over 99 per cent since the end of 2010, with multiple bankruptcies. To meet the 1.5°C target, more than 80 per cent of current fossil fuel reserves (including three-quarters of coal, half of gas, one-third of oil) would need to stay in the ground, stranding these assets. The equivalent for less than 2°C is about 60 per cent of fossil fuel assets staying in the ground (where they would no longer be assets).

When I mentioned the prospect of stranded assets in a speech in 2015,[22] it was met with howls of outrage from the industry. That was in part because many had refused to perform the basic reconciliation between the objectives society had agreed in Paris (keeping temperature increases below 2°C), the carbon budgets science estimated were necessary to achieve them and the consequences this had for fossil fuel extraction. They couldn't, or wouldn't, undertake the basic calculations that a teenager, Greta Thunberg, would easily master and powerfully project. Now recognition is growing, even in the oil and gas industry, that some fossil fuel assets will be stranded – although, as we shall see later in the chapter, pricing in financial markets remains wholly inconsistent with the transition.

Stranded assets are not limited to fossil fuels. Commercial agriculture is responsible for 70 per cent of tropical deforestation – mainly palm oil, soy, cattle and timber. Some of these agricultural businesses are now becoming untenable as governments restrict deforestation by limiting new land permits and enforcing or declining to renew existing ones.[23] In the EU, it is estimated that up to

€240 billion of assets in the European automotive industry is at risk of being stranded due to three potential disruptions: electric vehicles, driverless vehicles and car-sharing services.[24] Central banks are increasingly focused on how potential risks to financial stability can be managed against the possibility that climate policy could be tightened considerably and suddenly. What can be done to prevent a sudden adjustment and to smooth the transition will be discussed in the next chapter.

The risks from climate change manifest themselves as economic shocks that affect the rate of growth of the economy, the pace of job creation and the increases in wages and inflation. There are two types of economic shocks: demand and supply. Demand shocks affect consumption, investment, government spending and net exports. Demand shocks are often shorter-term in nature, and generally do not influence the longer-term trajectory or productive capacity of the economy. Supply shocks do. They directly impact the drivers of growth – the growth of labour supply and productivity – and their underlying determinants – physical capital, human capital and natural capital, technology and the degree of innovation.

A negative economic shock can affect both the level and rate of growth of GDP (ever the dismal scientists, economists refuse to call an unpredictable event that produces a significant improvement in the economy a positive surprise). Despite there having been a huge sample size of past financial crises, there is no consensus over the effect of this 'conventional' shock on the trend rate of growth, in part because its enduring impact depends on the policy reaction. Predicting the impact of climate shocks is an order of magnitude more difficult.

There have been some estimates of the potential impact of climate change on GDP. These are subject to a number of uncertainties including:

- The mapping of greenhouse gases to climate outcomes
  (subject to scientific uncertainties and the non-linearities of
  climate dynamics). As discussed, the science of climate
  change doesn't proceed in a straight line but is subject to
  feedback loops and non-linear dynamics. Past is not prologue.

– The relationship between temperature and GDP (and how it
could differ depending on the average, the rate of change or
the volatility).
– Determining whether physical climate events have a *level*
effect on GDP or impact trend growth (due to impacts on
labour, production processes and negative feedback from
adverse social impacts).
– The degree of adaptation and innovation that would mitigate
the impact of climate.

Given those fundamental considerations and important caveats,
let's consider the estimates of the potential impact of climate
change on GDP. These generally find that the scale of global GDP
forgone because of climate change could be between 15 and 30 per
cent.[25] In essence, climate change could lead to a full decade of no
economic growth. Moreover, remember that GDP represents a
single year's worth of value added in the economy. In general, estimates of the impact of climate change generally project that what
is lost is likely to stay lost. Climate change is the curse that keeps on
taking.

Importantly, current estimates are incomplete as the impact of
climate change on numerous important issues – water resources,
transport, migration, violent conflict, energy supply, labour productivity, tourism and recreation – has received limited attention, and
no estimate includes them all. These omissions bias downwards the
estimates and strengthen the case for GhG emissions reductions.

These different estimates all suffer from the shortcomings of
what GDP measures and what it does not. In particular, GDP as a
measure of value fails to capture the intangible factors such as relative equality, robust social capital and wellbeing that characterise
happy, healthy and prosperous societies. All will be under strain in
a world ravaged by climate change.

Some factors not modelled in GDP estimates of the impact of
climate change are both fundamental to wellbeing and have direct
economic consequences.

Climate change will increase dislocation and forced migration.
Climate refugees are those impacted by extreme weather events,

water scarcity or rising sea levels. As early as 1990, the IPCC noted that the single biggest impact of climate change on our society and economy could be a mass of climate refugees.[26] In 2017, almost 25 million people were displaced by weather-related disasters, and it is estimated that the figure could rise to 200 million people by 2050.[27] Forced migration has economic consequences, increasing strains on urban areas and health systems, but it also has profound social impacts as communities disband and social capital is destroyed.

Climate change can be expected to increase the incidence of disease. As humans move to climate-resilient areas, overcrowding creates a hotbed for disease. As habitats and food chains are disrupted, disease-carrying hosts move closer to humans. Whether it be malaria-spreading mosquitos or Ebola-carrying bats, the increased incidence of disease carries a huge economic cost.[28] The WHO estimates that the excess risk of various adverse health outcomes as a consequence of human-induced climate change will more than double by the year 2030, driven by the impacts of increased flooding, malaria, malnutrition and diarrhoea. The WHO notes that climate change could increase the risks of global pandemics.[29] Covid is more than a warning about the importance of taking systemic risks seriously. The risk of another pandemic is itself another reason to address climate change.

Last, climate change increases the risk of conflict.[30] As people compete for scarce resources, including water, climate-resilient land and possibly energy, the risk of intra- and inter-state conflict increases. This is especially true in fragile states, where a climatic event, such as a drought or a flash flood, can aggravate tensions and lead to a breakdown of the rule of law.

These scenarios are set to be the lived reality of millions of people around the world. The effects will not fall equally. In virtually all channels of the impact of climate change, the poorest nations and communities are most vulnerable to the economic and social fallout.

For example, as damage to property and infrastructure increases, insurance protection gaps in low- and middle-income countries mean that even greater costs of climate change are being borne by the uninsured. In 2017, the record $140 billion of insured losses were more than eclipsed by an additional $200 billion of uninsured ones. In some of the countries most exposed to climate change – Bangladesh, India, Vietnam, Philippines, Indonesia, Egypt and Nigeria – insurance penetration is under 1 per cent. Decreased productivity is most likely in developing countries, where the economy is dominated by the agricultural and construction sectors, and could respectively account for an expected 60 per cent and 19 per cent of working hours lost to heat stress in 2030. While climate displacement can affect anyone from Louisiana to Lahore, the quality and strength of institutional support for the displaced, as well as the opportunity to migrate, are clearly unequal across the globe.

Similarly, the quality of institutional support and social infrastructure is critical to fighting an increasing incidence of disease, and will once again affect the poorest in society most. A number of studies have found that countries with better institutions, higher per capita income and a higher degree of openness to trade are better able to withstand the initial disaster shock from extreme weather and prevent further spillovers into the macroeconomy.[31]

As imperfect as they may be, the estimates of the economic costs of climate change translate the impact of climate change on the factors of production – physical, human and natural capital – and

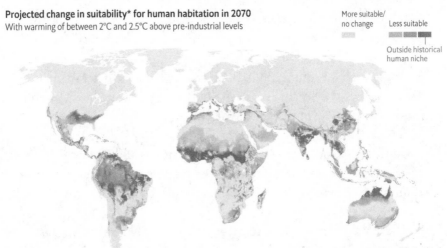

Projected change in suitability* for human habitation in 2070
With warming of between 2°C and 2.5°C above pre-industrial levels

More suitable/
no change   Less suitable

Outside historical
human niche

*Based on temperature and precipitation levels

Figure 11.11 Projected change in suitability for human habitation

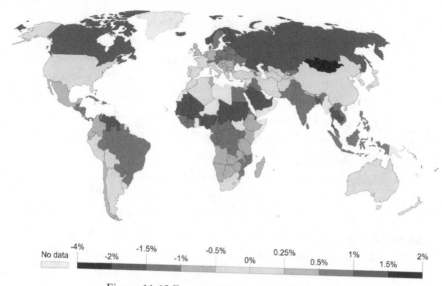

Figure 11.12 Economic impacts of 2°C world

through them and technological change on productivity, investment and income.

There are other factors that are not so readily converted into monetary estimates, however imperfect. So much of what climate change destroys – species, habitats, ways of life, natural beauty – is not formally valued. Recall that the market can estimate the value of the future earnings of Amazon the company, but it doesn't assign a value to the Amazon rainforest until it is stripped and converted to 'productive' use.

For example, the potential destruction of coral reefs is not captured in any GDP scenario of climate change. In 2016, the first study to compare the widespread impacts of climate change at 1.5°C and 2°C of warming warned that 90 per cent of tropical reefs would be 'at risk of severe degradation due to temperature-induced bleaching from 2050 onwards' in a 1.5°C warmer world.[32] For 2°C, this risk increases to 98 per cent of reefs, the study says, indicating that the extra 0.5°C of warming 'is likely to be decisive for the future of tropical coral reefs'.[33]

Widespread loss of coral reefs would be devastating for ecosystems, economies and people. According to the International Union for Conservation of Nature (IUCN), 'despite covering less than

0.1% of the ocean floor, reefs host more than one quarter of all marine fish species'. Coral reefs also 'directly support over 500 million people worldwide, who rely on them for daily subsistence, mostly in poor countries'.[34]

The Dasgupta Review on the Economics of Biodiversity signals that a root cause of our unsustainable engagement with nature is our failure to treat nature as an asset and its loss as an asset-management problem. Like produced capital or human capital, natural assets produce a flow of goods and services over time (that is, ecosystem services). The Review sees biodiversity as a characteristic of nature that plays an important role in the provision of ecosystem services. More diverse ecosystems are more stable, productive, resilient and able to adapt. Just as diversity within a financial portfolio reduces risk and uncertainty associated with financial returns, greater biodiversity reduces risks and uncertainty within a portfolio of natural assets. Policymakers and financial actors can enhance their understanding of these issues through natural capital accounting and assessments. Such frameworks are being developed for use by the public and private sector and communities, for example, through the UN's System of Environmental Economic Accounts (SEEA). Global capital accounts data – from the UN Environment Programme – show that, per capita, our global stock of natural capital has declined nearly 40 per cent since the early 1990s, while physical capital has doubled and human capital has increased by 13 per cent.

To summarise, we are faced with a situation in which the costs which can be quantified (such as the damage to property) are already alarmingly high and expected to grow rapidly. The estimates of the economic impact are significant, with most suggesting the equivalent of more than a decade of lost global growth – a dynamic unprecedented in the modern era. These calculations are highly likely to be underestimated because of the exclusion of climate feedback loops and a host of economic channels. No account is taken of non-market values, such as the value of the species lost in the Sixth Mass Extinction.

With what urgency should we act? I remember about fifteen years ago when Canada hosted a G20 seminar on energy and the environment at the Banff Springs Hotel. Sir Mark Moody-Stuart, then the Chair of Shell, talked about climate change and carbon budgets for 2°C. He acknowledged the uncertainties around the predictions of climate science, but observed that there was over 75 per cent likelihood the risks were at least as great. He then commented that over his career in business he had frequently taken multi-billion-dollar decisions with much lower odds, and that given the risks were existential, the value of acting immediately was clear.

Since then Shell has increased its reserves by 50 per cent, global emissions have increased by almost 7 billion tonnes or 25 per cent, and nine years have been the hottest on record.

CAUSES: INCENTIVES

Climate change is the tragedy of the horizon. Its catastrophic impacts will be felt beyond the traditional horizons of most actors – imposing a cost on future generations that the current generation has no direct incentive to fix. That means beyond the business cycle, the political cycle and potentially beyond the horizons of technocratic authorities, like central banks, which are bound by their mandates.

The horizon for monetary policy extends out to two or three years. The horizon for financial stability is a bit longer, but typically only to the outer boundaries of the credit cycle – about a decade. In other words, once climate change becomes a defining issue for financial stability, it may already be too late. Our 1.5°C carbon budget could already be exhausted.

This paradox is deeper, as Lord Stern and others have demonstrated. As risks are a function of cumulative emissions, earlier action will mean less costly adjustment. One estimate is that acting one year earlier could reduce end-point carbon levels by over 35 $GtCO_2eq$, equivalent to around 5 per cent of 2019 world GDP in net present value terms of carbon. The carbon budget highlights the consequences of inaction today for the scale of reaction required tomorrow. Halving emissions over thirty years is clearly easier than halving them in a decade.

Because greenhouse gases persist in the atmosphere for a century or more, the costs of climate change and the benefits of mitigation must be measured on longer timescales than most other socioeconomic policy issues. The choice of discount rate can be critical to determining whether economic models support investing today to reduce climate risks tomorrow because they determine the weights placed on aggregate costs and benefits that occur at different points in time.[35]

A key determinant of this is how much weight is given to the welfare of future generations. The climate legacy we leave depends on how much we value the future. To paraphrase, are boomers OK with leaving an insoluble mess?

Nick Stern argues for a low discount rate, average of 1.4 per cent (with a pure time-preference rate of 0.1 per cent), which places nearly equal weight on current and future generations.[36] This is based on a prescriptive approach to discounting; since climate impacts are most likely to impact future generations, who don't have a voice in current decisions, Stern argues that it would be unethical to put a high discount rate on the damage done to them. A similar argument is made by young climate activists today.

There is another reason why the tragedy of the horizon is hugely, practically important. Historically, technology adoption follows a relatively predictable life cycle, also known as the technology S-curve. There are three distinct phases: research and development, mass adoption and maturity. The first phase tends to be slow, gradual and expensive, until the new technology reaches an inflection point, becomes more cost effective and adoption increases rapidly.

Typically, reaching the second phase of mass adoption takes forty-five years, which, for climate change, would be too slow to remain within carbon budgets.[37] Moreover, it should be remembered that energy transition take time ... These monumental energy transitions take time. They require huge amounts of infrastructure and economic adjustment. James Watt invented the steam engine in 1769, yet coal did not overtake 'traditional biomass' – wood, peat, dung and the like – until the 1900s. To reach 2°C, we need a much faster and larger-scale energy transition in the next three decades. In the next thirty to fifty years 90 per cent or more of the share of the world's energy now being produced from fossil fuels will need to be provided by renewable-energy sources, nuclear power or fossil-fuel plants that bury their waste rather than exhaling it.

The good news is that newer technology is being adopted much more rapidly now than at any time in the past (Figure 11.13). Since 2000, the short tail of the S-curve – research and development to mass adoption – has shortened to around ten years on average. Even better news is that, in the case of climate change, people are already mapping the exact S-curves we need to hit by sector to achieve our sub 2°C goals.

These S-curves can help show the market where investment may be required and show governments where public policy intervention may be necessary to accelerate technology adoption. For example in electric vehicles governments could help to build the charging infrastructure necessary to increase adoption and introduce policies to incentivise EV purchases, such as reduced road tax rates for EVs and EV-only parking or motorway lanes, or regulation that mandates EV sales by a specific date.

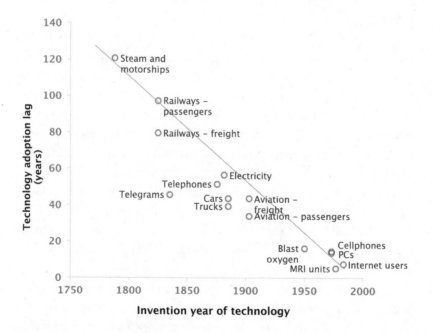

Figure 11.13 Technology adoption rates for new technological inventions

Bringing the future forward will be essential to solving the climate crisis. It is fundamentally a question of how much we value it.

The classic problem in environmental economics is the tragedy of the commons. This arises when individuals, acting independently in their own self-interest, behave contrary to the common good of all users by depleting or spoiling the shared resource through their collective action. There are many examples, including overfishing, deforestation and the original unregulated grazing on the common lands of England and Ireland in the early nineteenth century. The tragedy of the commons is an extreme example of negative externalities: when an action affects third parties who did not directly participate in (nor benefit from) that action. Such is the case with the ultimate global commons – our climate and biosphere, where producers generally do not pay for the carbon dioxide they emit nor consumers for the carbon they consume.

There are three solutions to the tragedy of the commons: pricing the externality, privatisation (through the assignment of property rights) and supply management by the community that uses the commons.

First, the externality can be priced through a user fee or tax to internalise it and incentivise changes in behaviour. To tackle climate change, that would mean putting a price on carbon, so that the polluter (or ultimately the consumer of the polluter) pays. So far this works well in theory but is applied only sparingly in practice. According to the IMF, seventy-four jurisdictions currently put a price on carbon covering about 20 per cent of global emissions with an average price of about \$15/tonne.[38] In comparison, most estimates of the carbon price consistent with achieving the Paris Agreement fall within the range of \$50–\$120/tonne, with the IMF in the midpoint of the range at \$75.[39] As we shall see in the next chapter, both the level and the predictability of a carbon price are important.

The second solution to the tragedy of the commons is privatisation or the assignment of property rights. This was the spirit behind the enclosure movement in which public grazing land was taken into private ownership. While it was managed more sustainably, there

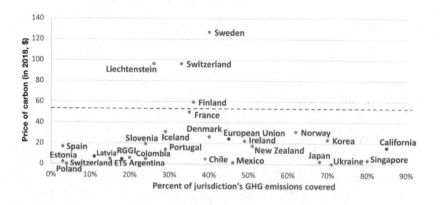

Figure 11.14 Prices for selected carbon initiatives in 2019

were obvious wealth transfers and deep questions of equity in the assignment of ownership. If these decisions are hard at the local level, they are virtually impossible at the global level. The Coase theorem (see Chapter 14) would suggest that one person could gain (or be assigned) the whole world and we wouldn't lose our souls. The experience of Kyoto-style emission-trading permits suggests otherwise.

Both of these conventional economic solutions rely on the price mechanism to internalise the externality and to assign a value to sustainability of the resource. But the question might be asked, why does someone have to be paid not to be a jerk?[40] When companies are *knowingly* on a path inconsistent with net zero, there are echoes of tech companies 'paying all the tax due' while using complex offshore tax shelters to avoid there being any due at all. There are examples of companies which operate with a shadow price on carbon, choosing to internalise the externality in their decision making. For instance, BP has recently introduced a $100/tonne price consistent with what the experts think is required to achieve society's aims.

The third solution to the tragedy of the commons that has been documented by the Nobel economist Elinor Ostrom is for members of a community to cooperate or regulate to exploit scarce resources prudently. This is exactly what efforts by leading companies,

regional governments and countries are trying to achieve – a political consensus that leads to shared management, and *by doing so*
unleashes the private sector dynamism.

Climate change, like a pandemic, is a global problem. No one country or group of countries can solve it on their own. Unlike a
pandemic, no country is an island, like New Zealand, which can get
the lockdown right from the start, then wall itself off from the world
and wait for the vaccine. In climate change, we are not just in the
same storm, we are in the same boat.

Climate change has resulted in international diplomatic efforts
not dissimilar to those in the post-war era. Some of the features of
the Bretton Woods negotiations – national self-interest, historic
debts and new institutions – echo in today's climate diplomacy. It
began in earnest in 1992, at the Rio Earth Summit, where world
leaders agreed to adopt a series of international environmental
agreements under the United Nations Framework Convention on
Climate Change (UNFCCC) to stabilise greenhouse gas concentrations. The Conference of Parties – commonly known as the COP
and comprising representatives from nation states and UN bodies
– meets annually and governs the UNFCCC. The first major agreement was the Kyoto Protocol, agreed at COP 1 and adopted at COP
3 in 1997. This was the first legally binding agreement on emissions
limits but captured only developed countries.

Within a decade, it became clear that the Kyoto Protocol was
flawed. It was binding in name only, and a new alternative framework, which included more countries and encouraged real action,
would be needed. Deep-rooted disagreements on historic emissions
meant that the COP 15 in Copenhagen failed to deliver this much
hoped-for revised framework. The Copenhagen Accord was never
formally adopted by the COP, but the political agreement set out an
important vision, to limit global temperature increases to 2°C and
for countries to pledge action to reduce emissions.

This would lay the foundations for a landmark moment for
collective action to combat climate change in 2015. A total of 195
countries and the EU came together at the COP 21 in Paris to agree
to limit temperature increases below 2°C and to pursue efforts to

limit them even further to 1.5°C above pre-industrial levels. The Paris Agreement was built on each country's Nationally Determined Contribution to limit emissions. Countries agreed to support each other in adapting to the adverse impacts of climate change, and advanced countries pledged to make financial flows consistent with a path to reducing emissions.

This bottom-up approach relies heavily on consensus. Countries are encouraged but not legally bound, with only the process of reporting and reviewing the NDCs in the status of an international legal requirement. COP 21 was also distinguished by engaging a much broader set of stakeholders. COP summits, once the preserve of climate diplomats and scientists, now attract a broad range of civil society groups, the young as well as the old, the world's largest multinational businesses and financial firms, even the occasional central banker.

Although the Paris Agreement was a resounding success for climate diplomacy, its effectiveness depends on implementation not adoption. To date, the NDCs and policy commitments have been insufficient to set us on a course to reach these targets. The world is on track for 2.6°C by the end of the century if all pledges and targets are implemented, but the actual policies that are required to deliver these targets are still lacking (taking the world to 2.9°C), and there is little to suggest at this stage that the planet is not headed for up to 4°C warmer (Figure 11.15).

As we will see in the next chapter, if more countries, like the UK, turn their Paris commitments into legislated objectives and concrete actions, the real economy and financial system will react and amplify the impact of these policies. A credible, time-consistent and committed government policy framework can pull forward sustainable investment and shut down unsustainable activity that is no longer viable in a net-zero world.

The governments that act early will be the ones that can benefit from the proceeds of a green revolution. The UK learned this through the First Industrial Revolution, which brought unimagined domestic progress through new machines and energy sources and could be exported to a receptive global market using the financing capabilities of the City of London. In the same way, the transition

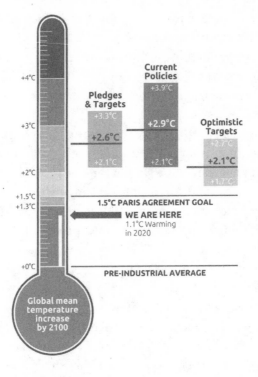

Figure 11.15 Projected increases in global temperatures by 2100

to net zero represents a strategic opportunity to cement leadership in innovative technologies and energy transformations, fuelled by a supporting financial sector, to deliver the sustainable revolution.

Scientists and academics have made a business of forewarning the world of high-impact events, from pandemics to meteor flares to volcanic eruptions. Humanity has made a business of ignoring them. Covid-19 has shown this is an expensive and destructive strategy.

While we cannot fully eliminate these threats, we can think about how to reduce the risks. This can include developing early-warning systems and thinking through playbooks that consider how a scenario evolves if disaster strikes. Recall from the global financial crisis Tim Geithner's refrain 'Plan beats no plan'. A plan provides the necessary clarity of mind by focusing efforts and uniting people around a common goal. Even a strategy that is half-baked but gets you out of immediate danger is better than waiting for the perfect answer and being annihilated.

Our human minds and political systems are woefully ill designed for such long-term planning. We rely on heuristics – go-to reference scenarios – to process information efficiently. The problem is, disasters are characterised by uncertainty, the past is not an accurate reflection of the future. We also tend to be overly optimistic and overconfident. The mind deals in known knowns but rarely considers known unknowns and is oblivious to unknown unknowns. Even if we recognise a risk, we convince ourselves either that it won't happen to us or that we can solve it later. Our political systems often don't overcome these fallacies, but amplify them. Actions to reduce tail risks have no immediate political benefit to a governing party and politicians are elected to represent current not future constituents. But true leaders are stewards of the organisation, system or society they inherit. They recognise that leadership is temporary and that they are custodians.

CURRENT FINANCIAL SECTOR PRICING OF THE TRANSITION

While that purpose and intent is growing, it isn't yet moving fast enough. A broad range of evidence suggests that financial markets are assigning only a modest probability to a transition to net zero consistent with temperature increases remaining below 2°C.

While a carbon price is only one of many policy instruments, it can serve as a useful proxy for the nature of the transition. The NGFS scenarios provide one view on potential paths for overall regulatory effort (proxied by carbon prices) under an orderly transition to net zero, a disorderly, delayed and then abrupt transition to net zero, and a low-effort spiral into 'hothouse earth'.

As can be seen from Figure 11.16, energy companies generally carry a higher shadow carbon price (for their internal planning) than current actual prices, but they do not project price rises in the coming decades. And these are the enlightened energy companies who actually disclose their carbon price assumptions. Only 15 per

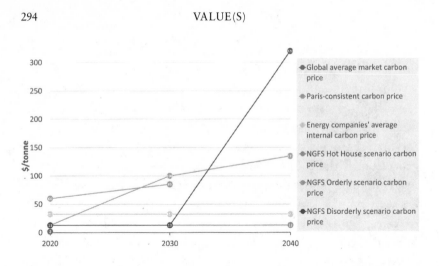

Figure 11.16 Evolution of carbon prices over time under different scenarios

cent of companies that use a carbon price to stress-test capital investment use a forward-looking price that rises over time, the remainder a static price or do not disclose it.

Where companies have disclosed, their prices are well below the minimum $50 per tonne estimated to be needed for net zero, including 90 per cent of utility companies. There are some leaders – BP recently disclosed that it used $100/tonne in its internal models and as a result wrote down $17.5 billion of assets – but they are the exceptions. Only 4 per cent of banks and insurers think that climate risk is being priced correctly.[41] They are not wrong.

Data from the Carbon Disclosure Project shows that companies are using a shadow price in their business (a hypothetical price on carbon of their choosing to reveal risks and opportunities), but the majority of these are still well below the price in the carbon prices in the scenarios above and vary enormously by sector. And only 16 per cent of the sample companies used a dynamic price (one that increases over time).

As mentioned earlier, the concept of stranded assets is gaining traction, but the valuations of existing reserves and the scale of new investments still appear inconsistent with timely attainment of net zero. With the caveat that it depends on the path and the destination

(1.5°C to 2°C have large differences in BTUs (British Thermal Units) of fossil fuels that are burned), market valuations suggest the world is on track for temperature rises of 3–4°C by the end of the century.

Recall that to meet the 1.5°C target, around 80 per cent of remaining fossil fuels would need to remain in the ground. For 2°C, the figure is 60 per cent.

In 2020, Royal Dutch Shell wrote down the value of its oil and gas assets by up to $22 billion. In the second quarter of 2020, BP cut its long-run oil forecast by $20 a barrel and raised its long-run shadow carbon price from $40 to $100 a tonne, three times European benchmark level, as part of its strategic review. These judgements on the pace of the energy transition led to write-downs of £11 billion of assets and highlighted the relative attractiveness to BP of emerging energy sources.

The energy sector has seen other landmark write-downs including Total – $8 billion; Eni – €3.5 billion; Repsol – $1.5 billion; Tullow Oil – $1.7 billion. Assets with high carbon-intensity and long reserve lines have been most at risk. The explanations vary, but the energy transition is an important factor and the decisions have been described as significant first public acknowledgements by these companies of stranded-asset risks.

As well as newly built infrastructure, long-duration assets are generally vulnerable to stranding. For example: stations that generate electricity from fossil fuels, designed to last for forty years or more; heavy industrial assets, such as steel mills or petrochemical plants; and pipelines. Factors that reduce vulnerability include low initial cost, short duration and adaptability (for example, some North Sea infrastructure is moving from oil to wind, some gas pipelines may one day carry hydrogen).

There are signs that the capital costs for high-carbon energy projects have increased significantly. This suggests that the market is pricing in an increasing prospect of a transition, with hydrocarbon assets stranded by a rising cost of capital more than a fall in demand. Goldman Sachs notes that as investors continue to shift capital allocation away from hydrocarbon investments, there is a significant divergence in the cost of capital of oil and gas investments (with hurdle rates of 10–20 per cent) and renewable projects (3–5 per cent for the regulated investments in Europe). Goldman estimates that this divergence in the cost of capital for high-carbon versus low-carbon investments implies a carbon price of US$40–$80/tonne, well above most carbon-pricing schemes.

This is structurally constraining the oil and gas industry's ability to invest. Capital expenditure commitments in new long-cycle oil projects have fallen by more than 60 per cent over the past five years versus the previous five years, reducing oil-reserve life. This could, in Goldman's view, lead to an energy transition through higher oil and gas prices. According to their analysis, the recoverable resources falls dramatically to thirty years in 2020 from around fifty years in 2014.

In parallel, Big Oil is beginning to transition to Big Energy. European Big Oils have reinforced their climate-change commitments since the beginning of 2020. Goldman Sachs estimates that the share of low-carbon energy (mainly renewables, but also biofuels, natural sinks and carbon capture) as a percentage of total capex has increased from 2–5 per cent in 2018–19 to c.10–15 per cent for the group on average in 2020–1. If we were also to include natural gas as a low-carbon fuel (it has half the carbon intensity of coal or oil), Big Oils would be already spending c.50 per cent of their capex on the low-carbon transition, another indication that shareholder climate-change engagement is yielding results.

Goldman projects that renewable power will become the largest area of spending in the energy industry in 2021, surpassing upstream oil and gas for the first time in history. These investments encompass mostly renewables, biofuels and the infrastructure investments necessary to support a new era of electrification (in both grids and charging networks).

As we shall see in Chapter 16, newly developed metrics can show the degree to which an investment portfolio is aligned with the Paris Agreement temperature goals. It takes the emissions by companies in an investment portfolio and calculates the global temperature rise caused by those emissions. This metric could be particularly useful as it is forward looking, easy to communicate and maps to society's goals.

Some of the largest investors are already voluntarily disclosing this information and committing to manage portfolios down in line with Paris Agreement goals by engaging with companies and divesting where absolutely necessary (for example, where it becomes clear that there is no place for that particular industry or technology in a low-emissions world). AXA, one of the world's largest insurance and investment management companies, used this approach to calculate the warming potential of corporate investments and found that, even post-divestment of highly intensive fossil fuel assets, they contributed to over 3°C of warming. Similar results were found by Japan's pension fund, GPIF, Allianz, a major German insurer, and CALPERs, one of the largest US pension funds. All are committed to managing these portfolios down to temperatures aligned with the Paris Agreement over time.

These metrics have only emerged in recent years and there is more work to be done to refine the calculation. The data on emissions by companies is not yet comprehensive, which means a number of assumptions are still baked into the calculation. And there are a variety of approaches to calculating the metric, making comparability difficult. It is however a start, and as disclosures increase and we refine the methodologies, they could become a powerful tool in demonstrating where the capital markets, and by extension the world, are heading on the path to 1.5°C.

Across the financial sector actors are starting to incorporate transition-risk assessments into their activities. Credit-rating agencies are recognising that transition risks can affect cash flow and credit ratings, as demand for high-carbon products decreases or costs of production raise costs. As such, they are increasingly using scenario analysis to assess how resilient companies are to the transition to net zero. Moody's recently identified sixteen sectors with $3.7 trillion of debt with the greatest exposure to transition risk.

The Transition Pathway Initiative (TPI), launched by thirteen leading asset owners and five asset managers in 2019, aims to better understand how the transition to a low-carbon economy impacts investments. The TPI assesses how individual companies are positioning themselves for the transition to a low-carbon economy through a public, transparent online tool.[42] The TPI launched the Financial Times Stock Exchange Transition Pathway Initiative (FTSE TPI) Climate Transition Index, a stock market index that assesses companies on their climate-change targets, tracking their progress and rewarding those with greater levels of commitment and action. The index includes only those companies that have set targets aligned to the 2°C limit agreed at COP 21 in Paris. Stock exchanges are also starting work on transition kitemarks, which assess how a company may be preparing for the transition to net zero.

Transition bonds are another innovation in the sector; as 'brown' companies look to raise funds to support their transition towards the greener end of the spectrum, new transition bonds offer a means to support the transition.

CONCLUSION

The combination of the weight of scientific evidence and the dynamics of the financial system suggest that, in the fullness of time, climate change will threaten financial resilience and economic prosperity. As we shall see in the next chapter, climate change is a risk from which we cannot diversify. Moreover, the window to act is finite and shrinking.

There are three technologies needed to solve the climate crisis. First, engineering where recent progress has been exceptional. If the remaining carbon budgets allowed sufficient time for the capital stock to turn over, much of the challenge would be met. But given the narrow window, investment must be accelerated at a warlike pace, to fight what John Kerry has termed World War Zero.

Two other technologies are needed: political and financial. On politics, we need a consensus to break the tragedies of the horizon and the commons. This is developing. The Paris Agreement and the SDGs set the objectives. Over 125 countries have set net-zero targets. Sub-national governments have made pledges and enacted plans. A variety of industry groups from the Climate Leaders Alliance to the Net Zero Asset Owners Alliance have pledged to do their part. Momentum is building, even if more is required.

We need financial markets to work alongside climate policies in order to maximise their impact. With the right foundations, the financial system can build a virtuous circle of better understanding of tomorrow's risks, better pricing for investors, better decisions by policymakers and a smoother transition to a lower-carbon economy.

A new, sustainable financial system *is* being built. It is funding the initiatives and innovations of the private sector, it has the potential to amplify the effectiveness of the climate policies of governments and it could accelerate the transition to a low-carbon economy. It is within our grasp to create a virtuous cycle of innovation and investment for the net-zero world that our citizens are demanding and that future generations deserve. But the task is large, the window of opportunity is short and the risks are existential.

To bring climate risks and resilience into the heart of financial decision making, climate disclosure must become comprehensive, climate risk management must be transformed and sustainable investing must go mainstream.

The next chapter explains how.

12

Breaking the Tragedy of the Horizon

Efforts to address climate change have been a struggle between urgency and complacency.

The urgency of carbon budgets that could be consumed within a decade. The complacency of adding to the committed carbon in our cars, homes, machines and power plants when those already in place will, over their useful lives, exhaust those carbon budgets.

The urgency of the looming Sixth Mass Extinction. The complacency of not valuing the loss of individual species and the destruction of entire habitats.

The urgency to reorient the financial system to finance the tens of trillions of dollars of investment needed over the next three decades for the transition to a sustainable economy. The complacency of many in finance not knowing their own carbon budgets, not having net-zero transition paths, not understanding their impact on an existential crisis.

Now with society's values being redefined – prioritising solidarity and resilience – these tensions can be resolved. Complacency can be replaced by commitment. Urgency can be turned to opportunity.

Because the challenge of transitioning our economies to net-zero carbon *is* an enormous opportunity. The transition is capital-intensive after a long period when there has been too little investment. Building a sustainable future is job-heavy at a time when unemployment is soaring. It is green when our world is brown. It is global when we are being pulled to the local. It is what the world needs for its future. It is what we need right now.

Solving the climate crisis requires three 'technologies': engineering, political and financial.[1] All are within our grasp.

ENGINEERING TECHNOLOGY: DRIVING SCALE AND INNOVATION

How feasible is the transition to net zero? How economic are existing technologies? What is the role of scale? How reliant is net zero on future innovations? To what extent will we have to change our lifestyles?

The core will be to electrify everything and simultaneously develop green electricity. Achieving net zero will require moving away from fossil fuels to renewables, decarbonising transport and reducing emissions from industrial processes. It will also require novel approaches to manage the hard-to-abate sectors where electrification or decarbonisation of processes may not be feasible even in the medium term, such as long-distance air travel or agriculture.

Let's take each in turn.

The first priority to build a zero-carbon economy is to green the generation of electricity. In a net-zero-carbon economy, electricity's share of total final energy demand could rise from today's 20 per cent to over 60 per cent by 2060. That means total global electricity generation must increase almost *fivefold* by mid-century, while ensuring it is generated by renewables. Greening energy sources is within reach. The technologies – such as solar, wind and hydro power – already exist, and they are increasingly cost effective. In 2013, the UK government estimated that an offshore windfarm opening in 2025 would generate electricity at a levelised (or life-cycle) cost of £140/MWh.[2] By 2016, this was revised down by 24 per cent, to £107/MWh.[3] The latest estimate puts the cost at just £57/MWh, another 47 per cent reduction. Estimates in the US are that the low-end levelised cost of onshore wind-generated energy is $26/MWh and solar energy is $37, below the $59/MWh average levelised cost for coal.[4] Current subsidies in the US push these renewables to highly competitive levels with onshore wind and solar levelised costs of energy of $17/MWh and $32/MWh, respectively.

Some estimate that by 2035 it will be possible to meet almost 90 per cent of power demand with a mix of wind and solar.[5] This will require two things. First, progress on storage and loading challenges for optimisation of the power grids given intermittency issues with renewable power. Second, it will require rapid deployment – doubling capacity every seven years, which, as we shall see in a moment, will depend crucially on the credibility and predictability of public policies.

Alongside the move to renewable sources of electricity, we need to increase significantly the efficiency of power usage. An immediate priority is retrofitting old housing stock, which tends to be particularly energy inefficient.

The second major priority is to decarbonise our transport wherever possible. The solutions lie in electrifying almost all surface transport, and using sustainable fuels including hydrogen for the remainder. Improvements in the volume, usage and electrification of mass transportation is essential. The technology for cars exists, but we need the supporting infrastructure – such as EV charging points – and the right incentives – such as scrappage schemes and potentially EV tax breaks – to increase uptake rapidly. Electrical and plug-in hybrid passenger vehicles could reach close to 100 per cent of new sales by 2030 if they continue on current trends, and

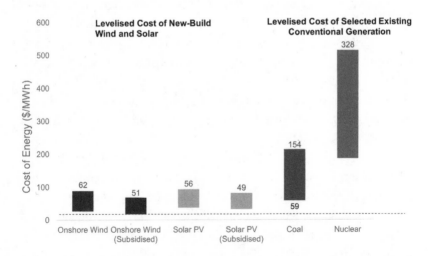

Figure 12.1 Levelised cost of electricity in US

even if growth slows from today's pace of 50 per cent per year to 33 per cent.

Batteries and electricity are not the optimal solution for heavy-goods road transport such as trucks. Hydrogen is much more compatible, but the hydrogen-powered transport economy is much less mature than that for electric-powered infrastructure. Building fuelling stations, funding pilots for heavy-goods trucking fleets running on hydrogen, announcing blended fuel mandates for the future and calibrating vehicle and fuel taxation rules to incentivise the take-up of hydrogen would be effective policy interventions.

Other transport, such as aviation and shipping, falls firmly in the harder-to-abate category. The technologies don't yet exist to decarbonise these sectors, or they are not yet commercially viable. Long-distance aviation will need biojet fuel or synthetic jet fuel, while long-distance shipping will need ammonia or biodiesels. These fuels are more expensive than existing fossil fuels, pushing decarbonisation costs to US$115–$230 per tonne for aviation and US$150–$350 for shipping.[6] For these sectors, not only do we need to reduce demand, for example, by no longer zooming through the skies but zooming through our broadband for business meetings, but we also need to apply on an industrial scale decarbonisation technologies, such as carbon capture and storage, that are not yet economic.

Third, we need to reduce industrial emissions. The industrial sector is responsible for 17 $GtCO_2e$ annually – 32 per cent of the global total. This includes heavy industries such as the manufacturing of cement, plastics, aluminium and chemicals, as well as less energy-intensive industries, such as fashion, furniture and home appliances. The industrial sector is one of the biggest consumers of energy, so moving to renewable energy generation will make a sizeable difference. The energy intensity of this sector could be reduced by up to 25 per cent by 2030 by upgrading or replacing existing equipment with the best available on the market. In reality, however, a lot of the technology does not yet exist. Cement kiln electrification for example may not be commercially ready till 2040, and these actions will only get us so far. Many industrial processes fall into the hard-to-abate category.

There are four generally accepted ways to reduce emissions from industrial processes: increasing the use of hydrogen, electrifying some processes, increasing the use of biomass and utilising carbon-capture technology. These must also be accompanied by being more resourceful with the materials we use, reducing the absolute amount and recycling that which we do use. At the moment, EU countries use an average of 800 kilos of steel, concrete, aluminium and chemicals per person per year. The good news is that the amount of reclaimable material is growing, with accompanied energy savings of up to 75 per cent.[7]

It is technically possible to decarbonise all the harder-to-abate sectors by mid-century at a total cost of less than 0.5 per cent of global GDP,[8] but there is still an open debate on how best to achieve this. For example, there is no current consensus about the necessary scale of carbon capture. Several scenarios for achieving the Paris climate objectives assume that, by 2100, carbon capture and sequestration could account for 18 Gt per annum of emission reductions. There are concerns that carbon capture will be used as a means to justify continued fossil fuel use. The Energy Transition Commission assumes a more modest scale of carbon capture at around 5–8 Gt per year, reserved for the genuinely hard-to-abate sectors.[9] In most cases, carbon-capture technologies will capture about 80–90 per cent of the CO_2 stream, with the remaining 10–20 per cent still released into the atmosphere.

To summarise, existing technologies, particularly when applied at scale, can economically reduce about 60 per cent of emissions, keeping the world on track to net zero consistent with 1.5°C warming provided the capital stock is turned over. The carbon-abatement cost curve for technologies currently available at commercial scale across key industries including power generation, industry, transport, buildings and agriculture is steep, with large investment opportunities in low-cost areas, particularly in power generation, but with rapidly rising costs at higher levels of decarbonisation. At the current costs of commercially available CO_2-abatement technologies, Goldman Sachs estimates that around 60 per cent of current anthropogenic GhG emissions can be abated at an implied CO_2 price of less than US\$100/tonne CO_2 equivalent.[10] Carbon prices of less than

US$100/tonne CO_2eq would transform the power-generation industry from carbon-intensive fuels (coal and oil) to cleaner alternatives (gas, solar, wind), but would make little impact in mobility, industry or buildings, excluding technology-specific incentives.

Most notably, Goldman estimates that around 25 per cent of total current anthropogenic GhG emissions are not abatable under currently available, large-scale commercial technologies. This underscores the need for further technological innovation and greater investment in sequestration technologies. Despite renewed

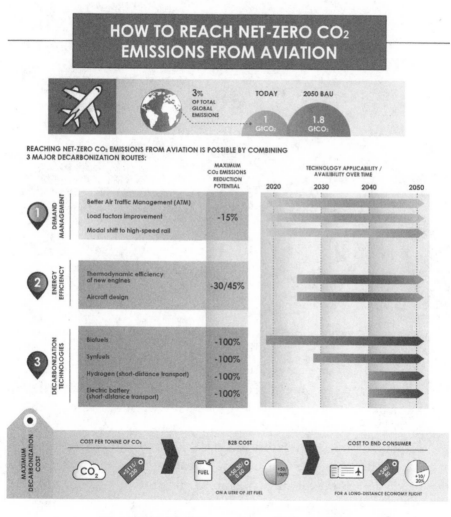

Figure 12.2a Reaching net zero stylised transitions

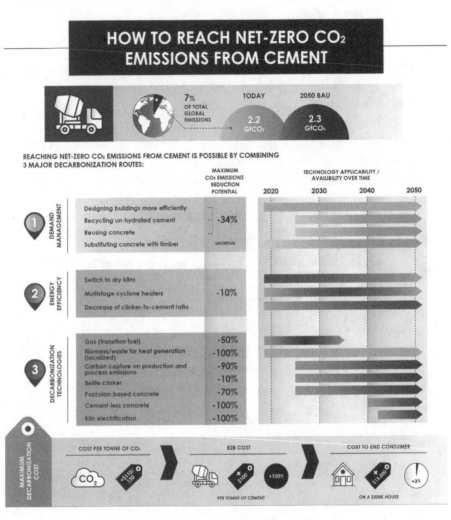

Figure 12.2b Reaching net zero stylised transitions

interest in carbon sequestration, it has not yet reached large-scale adoption and economies of scale that traditionally lead to a breakthrough in cost competitiveness, especially when compared with other CO_2-reducing technologies such as renewables. Investments in carbon capture, use and storage (CCUS) plants over the past decade are less than 1 per cent of the investments in renewable power. In particular, direct air carbon capture and storage (DACCS) has highly uncertain economics, with most estimates in the range $40–$400/tonne (at scale) and only small pilot plants currently in

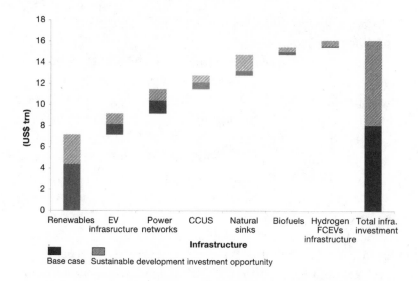

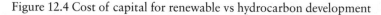

Figure 12.3 Cumulative investment infrastructure opportunities to 2030

activity. The importance of DACCS lies in its potential to be almost infinitely scalable and standardisable, therefore potentially setting the price of carbon in a net-zero emission scenario.

Different sectors of the economy will have different pathways which initiatives such as Mission Possible, SBTI and Race to Zero have each estimated (stylised examples for industry and transport are reproduced in Figures 12.2a and 12.2b). Financial institutions can judge the prospects of individual companies and specific assets

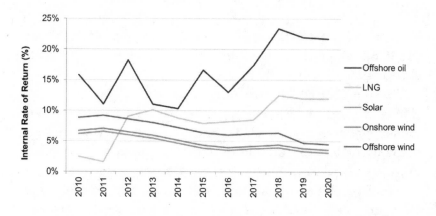

Figure 12.4 Cost of capital for renewable vs hydrocarbon development

against those standards and determine who is on the right and the wrong side of history.

There are assets that will be stranded and embedded capital that must be scrapped. There are sectors that could become obsolete without further technological breakthroughs. Recall from the last chapter how rapid the technology-adoption curves must be in order to achieve net zero in a timely fashion. To some, this presents a counsel of despair, to others enormous possibilities. To the optimistic venture capitalist, the technological choke points that currently prevent the attainment of net zero for industries like air transport or steel are opportunities disguised as intractable challenges.

Critical to the road to sustainability will be achieving scale economies in existing technologies. Some are currently expensive, but their prices should fall substantially with higher volumes of production and adoption. This has been the case in solar-panel production which has followed its version of Moore's law for semi-conductors: Swanson's law (which observes that the price of photovoltaic modules tends to drop 20 per cent for every doubling of cumulative volume shipped). The more credible the path, the more investments will be made in anticipation, and the more the virtuous circle of larger scale and greater efficiency can be put in place.

POLITICAL TECHNOLOGY: SETTING THE RIGHT GOALS

The core political technology we need is to value our future, to care about the generations that come after. That's because climate change is the tragedy of the horizon.

The sooner we act, the easier the adjustment will be. The risk of climate change will be minimised if the transition to a low-carbon economy begins early and follows a predictable path. As we shall see in a moment, breaking the tragedy of the horizon requires a series of measures to make existing markets work better as well as to create new markets. But, most fundamentally, it requires society to set out clearly its values and goals, and then for governments, companies, the third sector – for all of us – to work towards achieving them.

*   *   *

Societies can express their values and goals in a variety of ways and at multiple levels. Internationally, the Sustainable Development Goals – the SDGs – represent the collective view of the 193 UN member states on what is required to 'achieve a better and more sustainable future for all'. The seventeen goals, underpinned by 169 targets, address social and economic challenges, from inequality to responsible consumption, that we need to tackle by the end of this decade to build a more sustainable, prosperous and just world. The Sustainable Development Goals are an economic, as well as a moral, imperative. Achieving the SDGs would mean greater productivity, increased labour supply and ultimately stronger growth. In short, they could pull the global economy out of its current malaise of secular stagnation.

When they were first agreed in 2015 at the Sustainable Development summit in Addis Ababa, the SDGs had an esoteric quality. Many saw them as the province of multilateral development banks and international financial institutions, the latest do-good project of the now derided globalists – those who in a less cynical age were called humanitarians. But as the SDGs have been translated into national objectives and adopted by leading, purpose-driven corporations, they have begun to come alive.

Nowhere is this truer than for climate. Goals to revitalise our planet feature heavily among the SDGs: affordable energy and clean growth, sustainable cities and communities, climate action and life below water. The Paris Agreement in 2015 was a landmark for turning the climate-related SDG goals into tangible targets. World leaders committed to curb carbon emissions and limit the rise in global average temperatures relative to those in the pre-industrial world to less than 2°C, and to pursue efforts to limit the temperature increase to 1.5°C. The Agreement also commits to support countries in adapting to the more immediate impacts of climate change, and to ensure that financial flows support the most vulnerable nation states to build resilience in the face of the climate crisis.

Over the past five years, these international objectives have become embedded at the country level. Over 125 countries, representing more than half the world's GDP, have started to translate their Paris pledges into public commitments to achieve net zero by 2050.[11] Many have interim targets for emissions reductions, and have created decarbonisation plans for different sectors in the economy, supported by public spending on green infrastructure and policy frameworks to incentivise sustainable private investment.

At Paris in 2015, countries outlined their Nationally Determined Contributions or NDCs. These are country-driven pledges to reduce emissions by a particular date to help meet the temperature targets in the Paris Agreement. As the name suggests, NDCs are determined by each country. They are entirely bottom up, and when added up there is no obligation to revise individual country plans if the total exceeds the carbon budget.

The NDCs agreed in Paris and policy commitments that underpinned them were known to be insufficient at that time to meet the agreed global goal of less than 2°C warming; indeed, they were calculated as being sufficient only to keep the world on track for temperatures to rise by 2.8°C by the end of the century compared to pre-industrial levels. In the subsequent years, nations have fallen short of their pledges, and evidence suggests that our planet is headed to between 3 and 4°C of warming by the end of the century.[12]

Up until now, nations have been taking global warming more seriously, but not seriously enough. And so:

> You have stolen my dreams and my childhood with your empty words and yet I'm one of the lucky ones. People are suffering. People are dying. Entire ecosystems are collapsing. We are in the beginning of a mass extinction and all you can talk about is money and fairytales of eternal economic growth. How dare you!
> ... We will not let you get away with this. Right here, right now is where we draw the line. The world is waking up and change is coming, whether you like it or not.

GRETA THUNBERG, speech to the UN Climate Action Summit, 23 September 2019

I sat in the UN General Assembly hall as these words cut through the assembled presidents, prime ministers, business leaders and other 'dignitaries'. People, like me, who were there because they felt they were committed to addressing climate change. To growing high-paying, sustainable jobs in all our economies. We had entered feeling pretty good about ourselves. We weren't the deniers. We had recognised the risks. We were among the vanguard with pragmatic solutions to what we knew was the world's biggest challenge.

And yet there it was in black and white, with the clarity and certainty of youth: we were failing.

In the ensuing months, I would meet Greta Thunberg a few times. Over the years, I have met numerous leaders in politics, business, religion, the arts and philanthropy. It is surprising how 'average' most of them appear, how disappointing the encounters often feel. But sometimes they are exceptional: like the Grand Sheikh of Al Azhar mosque, Bono, Emmanuel Macron. They burst with energy, passion and purpose. They challenge and inspire. This Swedish teenager challenges with a clarity and force of reason that belie her age. She reinforces the remorseless logic of a carbon budget that is rapidly being spent. Her determination lays bare the imperatives of climate physics and the scale of the challenge that we face.

When Greta came into the Bank of England, she interviewed me for a documentary and met our climate team, and afterwards we went down to see the gold in our vaults. That gilded hoard, nominally of great value, lying inert in a basement mocked the earlier conversation about the resources needed to fight climate change. With her, you are always conscious of misplaced priorities, of the time slipping away, of the need to rearrange national priorities and act. Now.

Greta Thunberg and the movement she represents give hope that society won't settle. It won't settle for worthy statements followed by futile gestures. It won't settle for countries having plans for 2.8°C of warming that they then don't even meet. It won't settle for companies that preach green but don't manage their carbon footprints. It won't settle for financial institutions who can't tell whether their investments and loans are on the right or the wrong side of climate history.

Social movements such as hers are giving clarity and urgency to the global SDGs and national commitments to net zero – a purpose that is prerequisite to solving climate change. Given the multi-year nature of the transition, it is essential that climate policies are as credible and as predictable as possible. That requires a broad public consensus, bottom up as well as top down, behind the ultimate goal – a sustainable economy – and it requires endorsing the values that underpin it. The values of solidarity, of fairness and, yes crucially, of dynamism.

This shows the importance of social movements demanding climate action. In recent years, as the scale of the challenge has become increasingly apparent, those demands have moved into the mainstream. Groups such as Fridays for Futures and the People's Climate Movement have demonstrated the strength of public demands for sustainability.

The interest in climate change has moved over the past three decades from corners of the scientific and activist communities to the mainstream media and broader public conscience. It is no longer the preserve of green and environmental parties on the fringes of the political spectrum (Figure 12.5). Today, motivated by fundamental questions about economic wellbeing and intergenerational equity, young and old come together to call for swift, decisive action by governments and businesses to avert the looming climate crisis.

The Global Climate Strike in 2019 mobilised a record 7.6 million people in 185 countries around the world. Greta and her Schools Strike for Climate/Fridays for Future movement demand a safe future for the next generation. Extinction Rebellion puts pressure on businesses conducting, and financial firms funding, activities that are feeding the Sixth Mass Extinction. The People's Climate Movement calls for economic opportunity for all in a low-carbon world, for pollution-free communities and a 100 per cent renewable future to ensure collective wellbeing.

The spread of climate activism from social to mainstream media and street protests to sitting-room debates is reflected in polling of voter interests and voting patterns. As this movement has become more focused on economic wellbeing, it has reached its social tipping point. Against a backdrop of climate protests and children striking to draw attention to their climate fate, an increasing number of voters are ranking climate as a key influence on their vote.[13]

These developments suggest that, in a number of societies, demands for sustainability are reaching tipping points that, while not predestined, can be achieved. Research into social movements shows how they can lead to multiple equilibria. Many social movements that had seemed improbable unexpectedly gain traction due to a combination of factors including preference falsification (what we say publicly diverges from what is inside our heads), diverse thresholds (different people are more willing to speak out before others), interdependencies (what we are willing to say depends on others) and group polarisation (people tend to become more extreme when they come together with like-minded people).[14]

Within a few years, views that were publicly on the fringe become mainstream. Just as de Tocqueville believed that 'no one foresaw the French revolution', John Adams and Thomas Payne were surprised when the American colonies revolted. Yet diary writings at the time in both countries reveal the breadth of private dissatisfaction.[15] What people thought and said were very different, until a focal point emerged and the private became public and was radicalised. Interdependencies – once a critical mass had formed – fanned the rapid spread of the Me Too movement, so that a host of crimes long concealed suddenly came to light. Behavioural science has also shown that, if people learn about a new or emerging social norm, they are more likely to adopt it (for example, the current spread of veganism in some countries).

The economists Tim Besley and Torsten Persson have suggested that similar dynamics could be at work with respect to climate change. The interdependencies between changing environmental values, changing technologies and the changing politics of environmental policy could either create sustainable social change or lock in a 'climate trap'.[16] In their model, values are endogenous – they depend on the paths of technology and government policy. Green nudges in favour of either can drive self-reinforcing cycles where greater consumer demand for sustainable products increases the economic returns to green technologies and the political returns to green policies. Values beget value which reinforces values.

It is reasonable to expect that finance can play a similar role. The more the financial sector focuses on the transition to net zero, the more new technological solutions will be financed in the expectations of climate action, the more savers and investors will be able to track whether their investments are consistent with their values, and, if not, reallocate them accordingly. Sustainable investing can shift from the fringes to the mainstream, greatly increasing the chances of success.

The point is that social movements can move slowly and then with surprising speed. Variously termed social memes, behavioural cascades, moral sentiments, these shifts in values can suddenly drive immense change. Governments are responsible for translating this momentum into actionable policies that are set on credible and predictable paths. One way to do this is to put in place the frameworks so that every financial decision takes climate change into account.

Companies take their cue from what society needs and wants. As the SDGs, the Paris Accord and national objectives have begun to be widely supported through social movements, ESG (that is, a

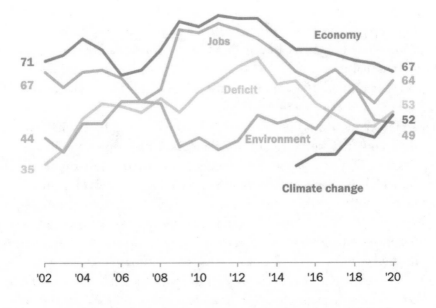

Figure 12.5 Perceived priorities for the president and Congress

focus on environmental, social and governance factors) has moved quickly from a vanguard of enlightened companies rapidly into the mainstream such as the US Business Roundtable. As discussed in Chapters 14 and 15, there is now a social meme of stakeholder value, a purpose-driven approach to business that was long thought but suppressed, which now has a self-reinforcing momentum.

Companies exist to improve our lives, expand our horizons and solve society's problems, large and small. Without a vibrant and focused private sector, we cannot build all the infrastructure we need, drive the innovation required or learn the skills we must have to thrive in the Fourth Industrial Revolution and to address climate change. It is no accident that when more than a hundred of the world's largest companies identified the core environmental, social and governance metrics, they anchored them to the Sustainable Development Goals. As Brian Moynihan, the CEO of Bank of America and the Chair of the International Business Council of the World Economic Forum, declared: 'As CEOs, we want to create long-term value to shareholders by delivering solid returns for shareholders AND by operating a sustainable business model that addresses the long-term goals of society as provided for in the SDG roadmap.'

With their focus on stakeholders including their communities, purpose-driven companies are more likely to internalise negative externalities. They are among the first to assess their contributions to driving to net zero.

The most advanced and forward-thinking companies have strategies to adjust to this new world – some because they astutely recognise changing societal and attitudinal preferences, others in anticipation of government legislation and regulation. These companies do not stop at setting a high-level objective to reach net zero by a given date, but embed it into every business decision, from R&D spending to executive compensation. By doing so, they contribute to and benefit from stakeholder capitalism that creates value for all.

Breaking the tragedy of the horizon and ensuring a smooth adjustment to a low-carbon world requires acting responsibly, fairly and in solidarity. Public, private and third sector will need to work together across borders to create the conditions for economic dynamism to thrive and unleash the investment and innovation we need for strong, sustainable and balanced growth. This will turn climate change from an existential risk into the greatest commercial opportunity of our time, transforming financial peril into moral progress.

This is how values drive value.

With the technologies available for major decarbonisation over the next decade and with the political technology coming into place, here's how to align the financial sector so that value reflects values.

FINANCIAL TECHNOLOGY TO ENSURE THAT EVERY FINANCIAL DECISION TAKES CLIMATE CHANGE INTO ACCOUNT

When I was named the Special Envoy of the UN Secretary General for Climate Action and UK Prime Minister's Adviser for Climate Finance, we formed a small team of experts seconded from the Bank of England and Whitehall and set ourselves a simple but vital task: to have in place by COP 26 in Glasgow all the necessary foundations so that every financial decision takes climate change into account.

This requires a fundamental reordering of the financial system so that all aspects of finance – investments, loans, derivatives, insurance products, whole markets – systemically take the impact of their actions on the race to net zero. The objective is a financial system in which climate change is as much a determinant of value as creditworthiness, interest rates or technology, where the impact of an activity on climate change is a new vector, a new determinant, of value.

So that, as readers of this book will recognise, value reflects values.

Setting the goal that every financial decision takes climate change into account is an example of the power of purpose. This goal is simple but hard. As we will see in a moment, it requires major changes to virtually every aspect of finance – reporting, risk and returns. And it requires the creation of some new markets. But achieving this mission is both essential to accomplishing what society wants – a sustainable future – and a tremendous organising principle for the work required. To ensure that every financial decision takes climate change into account, the COP process has drawn on experts across the private sector, in central banks and regulators and at not-for-profit organisations which have been among the first to identify and advocate some of the necessary changes.

To be clear, while private actions have been part of the problem in the past (ignoring externalities and succumbing to the tragedies of the commons and the horizon), we won't solve climate change in the future without the private sector.

In the first place, the amount of money required is simply too large. For example, the International Energy Agency estimates that the low-carbon transition could require $3.5 trillion in energy sector investments alone every year for decades – twice the rate at present.[17] Climate-resilient infrastructure could reach an estimated $90 trillion of infrastructure investment expected between 2015 and 2030. Smart decisions now can ensure that investment is both financially rewarding and environmentally sustainable. Public investment has a role in building this green backbone. And concessional finance is needed to support adaptation and resilience in developing economies. But only mainstream, private finance can finance investment of this scale. We won't get to net zero in a niche.

And secondly, to solve climate change we need more than the private sector's money, we need its insight and innovation. When society places emphasis on solving a problem, the private sector swings into action, coming up with solutions that public authorities could not have imagined, and implementing them with a speed and competitive zeal that continually surprises.

As we have seen, achieving net zero requires a whole-economy transition – every company, every bank, every insurer and investor will have to adjust their business model. This, in turn, requires a new sustainable financial system to fund private sector innovation, amplify the effectiveness of government climate policies and accelerate the transition. Its building blocks are:

- reporting: disclosure of climate-related financial impacts must become comprehensive;
- risk: climate risk management needs to be transformed; and
- returns: investing for a net-zero world must go mainstream.

REPORTING

Markets require information to operate effectively consistent with the old adage that what gets measured gets managed.

Companies and investors need to understand how extreme weather events (that is, physical risks) and the move to net zero (that is, transition risks) affect business models and financial results. Until recently, information on how companies were anticipating and responding to climate-related risks and opportunities was patchy, inconsistent and fragmented. In recent years, however, there has been a step change in the quantity, quality and comparability of reporting of the risks and opportunities of climate change.

In 2015 at COP 21 in Paris, following a call from the G20, the FSB established the private sector, industry-led Task Force on Climate-Related Financial Disclosures, under the leadership of Michael Bloomberg. The TCFD was charged with developing recommendations for voluntary, consistent, comparable, reliable and clear disclosures around climate-related financial risks. The purpose was to provide the information that investors, lenders, insurers and other stakeholders need to manage these risks and seize the associated opportunities.

Task Force members were drawn from the private sector from across advanced and emerging G20 economies, including major companies, large investors, global banks and insurers, all the major accounting firms and credit-rating agencies. As such, they represented a true cross-section of those who prepare, demand and use climate-related financial disclosures.

The TCFD recommendations are a solution for the market by the market. They were delivered to the G20 leaders' summit in Hamburg in 2018 and have now been adopted by over 1,300 of the world's largest companies from across the G20.[18] They are supported by financial institutions controlling balance sheets totalling over $170 trillion, including the world's largest banks, pension funds, asset managers and insurers. Investors increasingly recognise that climate risk is investment risk, and they want to know every firm's plan for managing these risks. The world's largest asset managers are demanding that all companies disclose in line with TCFD. The International Business Council (IBC) of 140 CEOs agreed a common set of metrics that IBC members signed up to disclose, which included TCFD. And the 2,275 signatories of the UN Principles for Responsible Investment must now make TCFD disclosures or risk ejection from the group.

Suitable for use by all companies that raise capital, the TCFD recommendations encompass a mixture of objective, subjective and forward-looking metrics:

- disclosure of governance, strategy and risk management;
- consistent and comparable metrics applicable across all sectors, as well as specific metrics for the most carbon-intense sectors; and
- use of scenario analysis so as to consider dynamically the potential impact of the risks and opportunities of the transition to a low-carbon economy on strategy and financial planning.

The disclosure recommendations deliver actionable information that will be useful in decision making by a company's management, its investors and its creditors. The recommendations leverage, rather than replace, existing disclosure regimes, so companies can comply more effectively with existing disclosure obligations by disclosing their climate-related financial risks and opportunities in their mainstream financial reports. In turn, this should ensure that consideration of climate-related financial risk and opportunities is embedded properly within, and subject to, firms' corporate governance and risk management. Managing climate risks cannot remain a niche activity.

All firms, from energy giants to consumer goods producers, are encouraged to disclose their direct GhG emissions plus those from their energy consumption, in a consistent manner (that is, scope 1 and 2), complemented by any emission-reduction targets that companies may set for themselves. These can be supplemented, where judged appropriate, with upstream and downstream (that is, scope 3) emissions.

The TCFD recommendations recognise that static disclosures of current carbon footprints will not be sufficient to reveal a company's climate-related financial risks and opportunities. Climate-information needs go beyond the static to the strategic. Markets require this information to assess which companies are well positioned to seize the opportunities the transition to a low-carbon economy brings. Which car manufacturers are leading the way on fuel efficiency and electrification? How are energy companies adapting their mix of energy sources?

For investors to price financial risks and opportunities correctly, they need to weigh firms' strategies against plausible public policy developments, technological advances and evolving physical risks and opportunities. In a ground-breaking innovation, the Task Force recommends that companies explore and disclose the potential impacts of climate-related risks and opportunities on their businesses, strategies and financial planning under different potential future scenarios (known as 'scenario analysis'). Investors need to weigh options against a range of possible transition paths from (the ultimately catastrophic) business-as-usual to a smooth and timely transition to net zero.

Through multi-sector TCFD summits and focused TCFD industry preparer forums, companies should continue to share knowledge on how, what and where they disclose information to give the market the information it needs. This momentum is creating a virtuous circle. As companies apply the TCFD recommendations and investors increasingly differentiate between firms based on this information, adoption is spreading, disclosure is improving and the process is becoming more efficient. We must build on this foundation to enhance both the quantity and quality of disclosures so that TCFD disclosures become as comparable, efficient and decision-useful as possible.

There is however a limit to how far the private sector can push the development of public goods, such as disclosure. The public sector needs to step in to coordinate efforts and ensure consistency. Now is the time for mandatory climate disclosure. There are several complementary routes.

First, financial regulators can embed climate-related financial reporting through their supervisory powers. While I was at the Bank of England, the Prudential Supervisory Authority, the supervisory arm of the central bank, issued a supervisory statement which set out its expectations of how banks and insurers should approach climate change. This included the PRA's expectations for disclosure of climate-related financial risks in line with TCFD, how these risks should be managed and governed, and compulsory tests on the strategic resilience assessments of their investments. Since then, a number of other authorities have issued guidance or started a consultation on climate financial disclosures in line with TCFD. With this information, financial firms across the value chain – and ultimately their customers – can report the climate risk and opportunity on their own balance sheets and in their portfolios.

Second, in order to make climate disclosure truly comprehensive and comparable across all major companies, reporting based on the TCFD framework will need to be made mandatory. International standard setters, such as International Financial Reporting Standards (IFRS), who are responsible for establishing common rules for financial statements, and the International Organisation of Securities Commissions (IOSCO), the group of organisations that regulate securities and futures markets, must agree how to turn the TCFD recommendations into reporting standards. If these organisations can align around a common disclosure regime, it will help the market assess climate risks and opportunities with less room for fragmented, complex and inconsistent debate.

Third, national jurisdictions can mandate climate-related disclosures through different routes. Over 106 regulators and government organisations from around the world are TCFD supporters, including the governments of Canada, Belgium, France, Sweden and the UK. They have taken different approaches to implementing TCFD disclosures. In the EU, the European Commission is embedding climate reporting through a Non-Financial Reporting Directive (NFRD) aimed at listed companies across the EU. France and New

Zealand have introduced TCFD reporting on a comply-or-explain basis. The UK has committed to TCFD disclosure for all listed companies by 2025, with progressive interim targets for large companies.

RISK MANAGEMENT

The second building block of a more sustainable financial system is effective risk management.

As discussed in the last chapter, climate change creates both physical and transition risks. Physical risks arise from extreme weather events such as floods, droughts and heatwaves, which destroy property, damage communities and disrupt livelihoods. These are the high-profile risks that we are facing with increased frequency and ferocity. Transition risks result from the adjustment towards a lower-carbon economy. Changes in climate policies set by governments, technologies and the price of carbon will prompt a reassessment of the value of a large range of assets. For example, for banks the nature of the transition will affect the riskiness of their exposures to carbon-intensive sectors (such as in energy where large swathes of assets could become stranded), consumer finance (where for example certain vehicles will lose their residual values under new emissions standards) and mortgage lending (where some properties won't be rentable under new energy-efficiency requirements).

More fundamentally, climate risks differ from conventional risks in several critical respects, including:

- Their unprecedented nature. Past experience and historical data are not good predictors of the probabilities in the future. Indeed, as the insurance industry has learned, yesterday's tail is becoming today's central scenario.
- Their breadth and magnitude. They will affect every customer in every sector in every country. Their impact will likely be correlated, non-linear, irreversible and subject to tipping points. They will therefore occur on a much greater

scale than the other risks financial institutions are used to managing.

- That they are both foreseeable, in the sense that we know some combination of physical and transition risk will occur, and uncertain, in that the timing and scale are path dependent. It is difficult to say now exactly what combination of physical and transition risks we will experience, but it is certain that some combination of these risks will materialise. Either we continue on our current emissions pathway and face enormous physical risks or we change course and large face transition risks.[19]

- Finally, although the time horizons for physical risks are long – not the usual three-to-five-year business planning horizon, but over decades – addressing major climate risks tomorrow requires action today. Indeed, actions over the next decade – probably in the next three to five years – will be critical to determining the size and balance of future risks.[20]

It is self-evident that the financial system cannot diversify its way out of this risk. As the pandemic has revealed, the interconnections between the real economy and the financial system run deep. And just like Covid-19, climate change is a far-reaching, system-wide risk that affects the whole economy, from which the financial system is not immune.

As my colleague at the Bank of England Sarah Breeden observed,

> For the same reason, while individual investors can divest, the financial system as a whole cannot. Indeed, seemingly rational individual actions that delay the transition make our collective future problems much bigger. Given the scale of change required, we will simply not be able to divest our way to net-zero.[21]

Rather, if financial risk is to be reduced, the underlying climate risks in the real economy must be managed. And fixing this collective-action problem is a shared responsibility across financial institutions and regulators. The public and private sectors need to work together to solve it, and that means developing the necessary risk-management expertise rapidly.

That expertise is needed because it is challenging to assess financial risks in the normal way. As emphasised by the TCFD, it means that disclosures need to go beyond the static (that is, what a company's emissions are today) to the strategic (that is, what their plans are for their emissions tomorrow and the associated financial impact). That means assessing the resilience of firms' strategies to transition risks. The TCFD recommends the use of scenario analysis, but this is a developing field, where there is an urgent need to upskill.

The Bank of England has recognised the need to catalyse these risk assessments, consistent with its financial stability and prudential regulatory mandates. As the supervisor of the world's fourth largest insurance industry, the Bank knows that general insurers and reinsurers were on the front line of managing the physical risks from climate change. Insurers responded by developing their modelling and forecasting capabilities, improving exposure management and adapting coverage and pricing. In the process, insurers learned that yesterday's tail risk is closer to today's central scenario. Banks meanwhile had begun to consider the most immediate physical risks to their business models – from the exposure of mortgage books to flood risk to the impact of extreme weather events on sovereign risk. And they began to assess exposures to transition risks in anticipation of climate action. This included, for example, exposures to carbon-intensive sectors, consumer loans secured on diesel vehicles and buy-to-let lending given new energy-efficiency requirements.

To further develop and embed this risk-management capability, the Bank of England will stress-test the UK financial system against different climate pathways, including the catastrophic business-as-usual scenario and the ideal – but still challenging – transition to net zero by 2050 consistent with the UK's legislated objective. In response, banks will need to establish how their borrowers are managing current and future climate-related risks and opportunities. Those assessments will reveal which firms have strategies for the transition to a net-zero economy, which are gambling on new technologies or government inaction and which haven't yet thought through the risks and opportunities. The test will help develop and mainstream cutting-edge risk-management techniques, and it will make the heart of the global financial system more responsive to changes in the climate and to government climate policies.

To capture fully the distinctive nature of climate risks, climate stress tests will differ from normal stress tests. Climate stress tests will include climate outcomes as well as more traditional macro and financial impacts aspects. Specifically, they need to assess physical and transition risks together – because businesses and our economies will face both.

The precise combination of physical or transition risks that materialises depends largely on the policy responses to climate change. For example, a decisive shift in policy will limit the size of physical risks but create some transition risks, while a business-as-usual scenario will be dominated by more severe physical risks. Given the horizons, the stress test must look at the risks over decades to the transition end state in 2050. Finally, modelling must be bottom up, requiring firms to gather information from their clients and counterparties to identify those that are managing the transition.

In the end, climate stress tests are as much about strategy and governance as they are about developing climate risk-modelling skills. They are certainly not conventional pass-or-fail stress tests that could lead to a capital charge at their end. Banks do need to assess the impairment of assets and revalue their trading books under different climate scenarios, but there will be no hurdle rate and no associated capital charges. There will be an assessment of whether their strategies are consistent with managing to net zero, and if not, questions will be asked about what is going to change.

Most fundamentally, climate stress tests will help stretch the horizons of financial actors as well as the businesses they lend to, insure or invest in. The stress test will help improve risk-management capability, building knowledge and expertise in an incipient field. The stress test will also show policymakers and the market how far behind we are on the transition to net zero. By establishing how many companies have transition plans, the sophistication of

these plans and the exposure of the financial sector to these companies, policymakers will develop a better understanding of the
outstanding economy-wide actions that are required. The results
from the tests could also help develop a more accurate estimate of
the macroeconomic impacts of climate change, which in turn could
inform policy action.

As with climate disclosure, such strategic assessments will need
to go global if the world is going to stabilise temperatures below
2°C. The coalition of central banks and supervisors, the Network
for Greening the Financial System (NGFS), shares experience and
best practice for stress-testing and is playing a critical role in developing climate risk-management expertise in the public and private
sectors. In parallel, the FSB has started to map the risk-transmission
channels of climate change. The IMF has started embedding climate
risks into its assessments of country preparedness.

RETURNS

Addressing climate change is about much more than managing
risks. Ultimately, it is about delivering what society wants, valuing
what it values. This means that the transition to a green economy
can be the greatest commercial opportunity of our time. Over the
next three decades, the total required investments in the energy
sector alone will be $3.5 trillion per year. Another $50 to $135
billion per year will be needed to develop and scale carbon capture
and biofuel technology.[22] And more than 6 billion people will live in
urban areas. Some 400 million homes are expected to be built in the
next decade alone, all of which will require green technology and
infrastructure to align with a net-zero, resilient transition.

While green investment products, such as green and transition
bonds, are important catalysts to developing a new financial
system, they will not be sufficient to finance the transition to a
low-carbon future. We need to mobilise mainstream finance to help
support all companies in the economy to adjust business models to
align with net-zero pathways. Value will be driven by identifying
the leaders and laggards, as well as the most important gener-

al-purpose technologies that will overcome choke points in the transition.

That means having a more sophisticated understanding of how companies are working to transition from brown to green, not just where they are at a single point in time. Thus far, the approaches to doing so have been inadequate. Scores that combine E, S and G to give a single ESG metric – while worthy – are dominated by the S and the G.[23] Carbon footprints are not forward-looking. And the impact of shareholder engagement is hard to measure. Moreover, a whole-economy transition isn't about funding only deep green activities or blacklisting dark brown ones. We need fifty shades of green to catalyse and support all companies towards net zero and enable us to assess collectively whether we're 'Paris aligned'.

That means investors need to be able to assess the credibility of company transition plans. Transition planning is nascent and of varying quality. Some companies have a stated net-zero objective but are yet to set out a credible strategy or credible tactics to achieving it. Others have fully integrated climate strategies, governance and investments. Emerging best-practice transition plans include:

- defining a net-zero objective in terms of scope 1, 2 and 3 emissions;
- outlining clear short-term milestones and metrics that senior management uses to monitor progress and gauge success;
- board-level governance; and
- embedding metrics in executive compensation.

Initiatives such as the Science Based Targets and Transition Pathways are already supporting companies to develop transition plans and certifying them when they meet appropriate thresholds. But as discussed in Chapter 15, the investment community will need to develop its own expertise rather than outsource these critical judgements.

A framework for assessing the efficacy of transition plans will arm investors with the questions to ask of their portfolio companies. But as an increasing number of firms disclose their assessment of climate risks, investors should have the opportunity to opine on the quality of these disclosures and transition plans. As with 'say on pay', where investors get to vote on executive compensation levels, there are growing calls for investors to have a 'say on transition': a vote on the adequacy of a company's preparedness for the transition to a net-zero world. This mechanism would embed the critical link between responsibility and accountability.

Over time, investors will not just judge company transition plans, they too will be judged. Investors should be obliged to assess the alignment of their portfolios with the transition and disclose their position in a readily understandable manner. There are several ways to do this. At the most basic end of the spectrum, investors could calculate the percentage of assets that have a net-zero target. As disclosures improve in the real economy, a more sophisticated option is to calculate the warming potential of assets in a portfolio. As we will see in more detail in Chapter 15 on values-based investing, a 'warming potential' calculation – or Implied Temperature Rise – calculates a global temperature rise associated with emissions by the companies in any given investment portfolio.

Rating the warming potential of assets and portfolios has a number of ancillary benefits. It will signal to governments the transition path of the economy, and therefore the effectiveness of their policies. It will empower consumers, giving them more choice in how to invest to support the transition. After all, with our citizens, particularly the young, demanding climate action, it is becoming essential for asset owners to disclose the extent to which their clients' money is being invested in line with their values. A temperature calculation also helps show how investment management decisions impact our planet.

CROSS-BORDER FINANCIAL FLOWS AND GLOBAL CLIMATE EQUITY

The previous chapter underscored historic inequities of climate change and the responsibility of the largest historic emitters to help lead the transition. The UK, the cradle of the Industrial Revolution, must lead the sustainable revolution as President of COP 26.

Developing countries face twin challenges of climate change and development. They suffer some of the greatest harms from the physical impacts of climate change and, as we have seen, have enormous gaps in their abilities to build resilience and to adapt their economies to a more volatile climate. Moreover, green technologies are capital intensive, and the cost of capital in developing countries is higher due to a combination of political and regulatory uncertainties, less liquid and less developed financial markets and the economic impacts of climate risk itself.

Developed countries committed to a goal of jointly mobilising US$100 billion a year in climate finance by 2020 to address the needs of developing countries for climate mitigation and adaptation. This commitment came out of the Copenhagen Accord in 2009, was formalised in the Cancún Agreements in 2010 and was reaffirmed in the Paris Agreement in 2015. This funding is noted to come from a wide variety of sources, public and private, bilateral and multilateral, including alternative sources of finance. In Paris, it was decided that this collective mobilisation goal would be continued through 2025 and that by that point there would be a new collective quantified goal under the Paris Agreement from a floor of US$100 billion a year, taking into account the needs and priorities of developing countries.

There are three ways that the new sustainable financial system is helping emerging and developing economies.

First, by financing investments in sustainable infrastructure, the new finance will drive scale efficiencies in critical technologies that can then be applied globally. This is a bigger advantage in those economies with a smaller installed base of fossil fuel power generation. Significant investment – around US$90 trillion – is needed over the next fifteen years. This includes ageing infrastructure in advanced economies and higher growth and structural change in emerging-market and developing countries, especially due to rapid urbanisation. Emerging and developing economies will account for roughly two-thirds of global infrastructure investment (or about US$4 trillion per year). This new infrastructure offers a great opportunity to leapfrog the inefficient, sprawling and polluting systems of the past.

Second, comprehensive reporting by companies in advanced economies of their scope 1, 2 and 3 emissions will encourage them to minimise climate risks and maximise opportunities across their supply chains. With companies addressing sustainability across the breadth of their operations, including those of their suppliers, distributors and retailers, substantial green investment in developing countries will be encouraged since this is where many scope 3 emissions are generated or outsourced.

Third, the transition to net zero will require new market structures that could substantially increase capital flows to developing and emerging economies. As companies commit to net zero or net negative and investors seek out companies with credible transition plans, companies will need to show how they plan to meet their net-zero targets through the appropriate mix of emissions reductions and credible carbon offsets (including nature-based solutions such as reforestation and offsets generated by the switch from brown to green). This will create substantial demand with some estimates of annual volumes quickly scaling to the tens of billions of dollars.

At the moment, buying offsets is an opaque, cumbersome and expensive process. In 2019, only 98 million tonnes of carbon dioxide ($MtCO_2e$) were traded for a total market value of $295 million. The marketplace is fragmented, with many local, sector-specific or offset-specific (such as a nature-based offset) markets without central coordination. Uniform standards for carbon credits and offsets don't yet exist. This makes it hard to compare a credit bought for a forest in Brazil to one bought in India, which in turn causes price variability. Prices for similar-sounding offsets can range from $0.1/mtCO_2e$ to just over $70/mtCO_2e$. This opacity creates trust issues and friction in a market that is critical to helping us reach net zero. The lack of assurance that the offset has been enacted and lack of transparency of ownership of an offset further compounds the trust issues.

To unlock this market, which could be worth up to $100–$150 billion per annum, we need the right infrastructure to connect demand from companies with net-zero goals with supply in countries that need to finance decarbonisation initiatives. This should be a particularly attractive proposition to developing and emerging economies, as activities and projects in these countries will most likely provide the most cost-effective of these offsets.

The financial sector has the experience and resources to develop this market. It is not unprecedented. A decade ago, over-the-counter (OTC) derivative trades were largely unregulated, unreported and bilaterally settled. When Lehman fell during the financial crisis, uncertainty about such exposures sparked panic. Post-crisis, the FSB worked with the sector to make derivative markets that were safer and more transparent by requiring trade reporting and by encouraging central clearing of OTC trades. For COP 26, we are working to harness this expertise, under the leadership of Bill Winters, CEO of Standard Chartered, once more to develop a blueprint for a carbon market in the hope that we can move rapidly to developing this market so that companies can purchase carbon credits and investors can be assured of their authenticity.

Finally, with proper structuring we can turn billions of public investment into trillions of private investment. That requires public–private partnerships, pipelines of projects and new market structures to make opportunities for sustainable investment commercially viable. Multilateral and National Development Banks (MDBs and NDBs) and Development Finance Institutions will have important roles derisking projects and providing technical assistance in new markets to fund climate-resilient infrastructure and invest in adaptation, as well as aligning their lending and investments with climate goals.

Development banks can also help increase the liquidity of local markets, including by working with local governments to develop a pipeline of sustainable projects, providing technical assistance to create investment frameworks and increasing transparency. In this process, development banks should commit to fully integrating climate risks into their operations and lending, and communicating comparable, robust and bank-wide Paris-alignment implementation plans. They should commit to working collectively to help implement ambitious climate targets in relevant countries through the Nationally Determined Contribution (NDC) enhancement and implementation cycle. The IMF has already signalled a strong commitment to addressing climate change and assisting countries in reducing emissions and increasing climate resilience.[24]

THE INTERACTION BETWEEN POLICY AND CLIMATE ACTION

Public policies, company transition plans and the disclosures of climate-related risks and opportunities are the building blocks for transitioning to a net-zero economy (Figure 12.6).[25] The combination of policy credibility and a sustainable financial system will accelerate and amplify these efforts.

Public policy provides the foundation for the transition to net zero. The tragedies of the commons and the horizon mean that private companies and financial institutions will not fully take into account the impact of their actions on the climate. Although leading businesses will anticipate future climate policies and adapt to them today, ultimately catalysing a critical mass of private sector actions requires effective, predictable and credible public policies.

Through fiscal measures (such as prices on pollution and support for R&D and specific sectors) and regulatory initiatives (such as

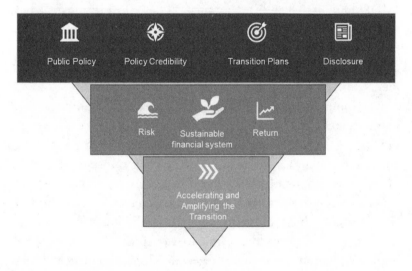

Figure 12.6 The public and private sectors' role in shaping the transition to a net-zero economy

clean fuel mandates and pathways for climate efficiency), government policies can do more than provide targeted support. When these measures form part of a credible and predictable track record of climate policies, they create a framework for private investment that will pull forward climate action creating a virtuous cycle to break the tragedy of the horizon.

Meaningful carbon prices are a cornerstone of any effective policy framework. An explicit price for the right to emit GhGs helps ensure that more sustainable businesses are not put at an unfair disadvantage and encourages higher-carbon businesses to adjust. To support an effective, orderly and fair adjustment, carbon prices should increase in a gradual and predictable manner, and they should be designed equitably, including by using proceeds to support lower-income households.

But the scale of the challenge means that carbon prices alone are not enough. Policymakers need to align public spending with the needs of the transition including investments in low-carbon infrastructure, as well as loans and grants to support sustainable R&D. Targeted environmental regulations can catalyse change in industries that are subject to significant collective-action problems and that may be less responsive to carbon pricing.

In order to support an efficient global response to climate change, the level of ambition of national strategies will need to converge over time. In the meantime, carbon border adjustments (a form of tariff linked to relative climate effort) would allow leading countries to pursue more ambitious targets, while avoiding carbon leakage. These adjustments should be designed in a way that is fully consistent with World Trade Organisation rules.

The more predictable and credible are public climate policies, the greater their impact on private investment. In this respect, it is important to recognise that climate policy can suffer from the same type of credibility problems that beset monetary policy in the past (as discussed in Chapter 4).

From a political perspective, the temptation to change interest rates to support short-term employment to the detriment of long-term inflationary stability has always been high. To overcome this problem, governments around the world adopted explicit inflation

targets, which allowed voters to hold them to account more easily
for any failure to deliver on promises of low and stable inflation. In
addition, they restricted their own role to formulating the long-term
goals of monetary policy, and delegated the use of the instruments
necessary to meet these goals (for example, the setting of interest
rates) to independent central banks that are less exposed to the
temptations of boosting short-term growth.

A similar type of time inconsistency has frequently undermined
the credibility of the climate strategies of governments. The benefits
of climate policies will not be fully visible until long after the next
elections, but any short-term costs will be felt immediately. Once
elected, politicians are thus tempted to pursue environmental efforts
that are more soundbite than substance. This can make it difficult
for businesses to predict the future direction of climate policy,
delaying or muting the necessary climate action. Even if politicians
ultimately do end up adopting the measures necessary to avoid a
climate catastrophe, a lack of *ex ante* credibility means missing out
on the benefits of an early, unambiguous commitment to act.

In contrast, if climate policy is decisive, the financial system will
anticipate future policies and encourage companies to start adjust-

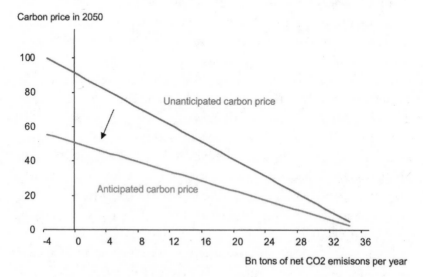

Figure 12.7 Credible policy frameworks can reduce the carbon prices
necessary to achieve a given goal

ing to them today. Policymakers will need to intervene less forcefully to achieve a given climate target and the stock of stranded assets will be substantially reduced. If ambitious climate targets are credible, businesses will limit investments in brown technologies, thereby reducing the stock of fully depreciated high-carbon machines to compete against green alternatives in the future. As a result, carbon prices will need to be raised less aggressively to achieve a given reduction in GhG emissions (Figure 12.7). This can reduce any unintended consequences of high carbon prices, including the risk of carbon leakage.

The idea that credibility allows policymakers to achieve a given target more easily is not limited to climate policy. My predecessor at the Bank of England, Lord King, once brilliantly drew an analogy to football in the 'Maradona theory of interest rates'. Inspired by the great Argentinian player's goal, scored once he'd evaded five England players despite running in a more or less straight line, King argued that credible central banks need to adjust interest rates less aggressively to keep inflation close to its target.

In addition, starting to cut emissions to net zero earlier can significantly reduce the ultimate end-point carbon concentrations.[26] However, using plausible estimates of the 'social costs of carbon', analysis in the G30 Report (2020) suggests that the benefits could be very large. Bringing forward the achievement of net zero by even one year would reduce end-point carbon levels by over 35 $GtCO_2e$ and be worth around 5 per cent of 2019 world GDP in net present-value terms.[27]

Finally, credible policy frameworks reduce the risk of adding to the existing stock of stranded assets. Credible policy frameworks reduce the risk that businesses form wrong expectations about future policies and continue to invest in obsolete technologies. By setting out clear strategies, politicians can provide forward guidance on the policies they plan to put in place. Such predictability of climate policy helps companies start adjusting to the reality of a net-zero world today, and ensures that this adjustment is orderly.

There are several ways to establish credible and predictable climate policies.

First, the experience with inflation targeting demonstrates that, in order to address a time-inconsistency problem, the objective must be acknowledged by politicians across the political spectrum. Knowing that opposition parties are likely to implement similar policies also gives businesses the certainty that they need in order to invest in green infrastructure that has economic lifespans of several decades. This means that credible climate policies require broad political and public support.

Second, actions speak louder than words. Credible climate policies don't delay, but rather cut emissions from day one to reduce the end point in carbon concentrations. And they provide an objective assessment of the scale of the challenge and the effectiveness of the measures. Specific climate policies should be linked to estimates of the greenhouse gas reductions expected to be achieved. And the overall climate strategy should be assessed as to whether it is consistent with a smooth transition to net zero – the national equivalent of an investors' implied temperature warming that was mentioned earlier. The evidence around climate change is unequivocal as are the imperatives of climate physics, including those of a carbon budget and the need to achieve net-zero emissions. Too often, these basic truths have been obscured. The more that progress towards net zero is transparently and reliably reported, the more that authorities can be held to account.

Third, credible policy frameworks make clear that certain activities will not be viable in a net-zero world and it creates strong incentives to support alternatives.

Fourth, a climate-policy track record is required to cement credibility. Just as in fiscal policy, monetary policy and company performance, track records are built through the identification and achievement of intermediate goals that are consistent with their long-term strategies and objectives. If credibility is low, the experience with fiscal and monetary policy provides ample evidence that it can take years to establish, and may require more stringent policies in order to build a reputation for being responsible. Governments need to formulate intermediate goals consistent with their long-term strategies and formulate policy for specific sectors, such as emissions targets for steel production, and with cross-cutting initiatives, such as setting appropriate carbon prices.

In a variety of areas, such as monetary policy, governments have established credibility by delegating certain limited responsibilities to independent, technocratic bodies. Setting the goals of climate policy, such as the commitment to reach net zero by 2050, requires full democratic accountability and can be done only by elected governments. But governments can delegate certain aspects of the calibration of specific instruments necessary to achieve this target to Carbon Councils in order to improve the predictability, credibility and impact of climate policies. In ascending order, these delegations could entail:

- assessments of whether climate policies are consistent with the government's short- and long-term objectives;
- comply-or-explain recommendations to the government for the setting of these instruments or
- deciding the calibration of a limited number of instruments in a manner analogous to central bank policy setting to achieve the inflation target.

Even if a government were to delegate fully calibration decisions to a Carbon Council to ensure that they are taken on the basis of objective, scientific evidence, the government should still retain full control over how any proceeds are used. This ensures that elected governments shape the distributional consequences of carbon prices. In the case of most climate policy levers, governments may want to retain control because they have substantial distributional implications that are more difficult to offset than in the case of carbon prices. These tools might include introducing enhanced environmental standards for manufacturing firms, or accelerating the phase-out of the internal combustion engine.

Chapter 16, which addresses the nation state, will discuss the pros and cons of various approaches.

* * *

The policy frameworks with the greatest impact will be time consistent (not arbitrarily changed), transparent (with clear targets, pricing and costing) and committed (through treaties, nationally determined contributions (NDCs), domestic legislation and consensus). As countries build their track records and their credibility grows, the market will allocate capital to deliver the necessary innovation and growth and pull forward the adjustment to a low-carbon future.

The more prolific the reporting, the more robust the risk assessment and the more widespread the return optimisation, the more rapidly this transition will happen, breaking the tragedy of the horizon.

The power of Greta Thunberg's message lies in the way she drives home both the cold logic of climate physics and the fundamental unfairness of the climate crisis. Our current lifestyles are rapidly exhausting a limited (and non-renewable) carbon budget and come at the direct expense of future generations. Like many, I am persuaded by the force of her logic and her cry for intergenerational justice. We diverge, however, on how to solve this immense problem.

As this book has made clear, I am not a market fundamentalist in that I do not reflexively think that the market is *the* answer to everything. At the same time, I have seen the market's immense power in multiple situations, and I know that the market is a critical part of the solutions to many of humanity's greatest challenges. We won't achieve the Sustainable Development Goals without growth; and we won't get to net zero without innovation, investment, purpose and profit. My experience has made me a profound believer in the market's ability to solve problems. I have seen day in and day out the very human desire to grow and progress, of people's yearning to make better lives for themselves and their families.

Continued growth isn't a fairy tale; it's a necessity.

But not just any growth. The power of the market needs to be directed to achieving what society wants. That requires measures of income and welfare that reflect our values. Measures that count natural and social capital as well as economic capital. We need a world where we are no longer guided solely by measures like GDP, that were devised a century ago when the earth seemed immortal and when the social norms of the market felt immutable.

The policies for achieving our climate goals should be designed to encourage the economic adjustments and technological innovations at the least possible cost, while sharing the burden of adjustment as fairly as possible within countries and across nations. The critical success factors are the establishment of a broad social consensus, the use of clear, consistent communications and the building of credible and predictable track records for government and regulatory policies. The more that these conditions are fulfilled, the more likely that markets will pull forward adjustment and smooth the transition to a net-zero carbon economy.

A market in transition to less than 2°C is being built on the foundations of reporting, risk management and returns. It will reveal how the valuations of companies could change over time as climate policies adapt and carbon intensity declines. It will allow feedback between the market and policymaking, with policymakers learning from markets' reactions, and markets internalising policymakers' objectives, strategies and instruments. It will expose the likely future cost of doing business, of paying for emissions and of tighter regulation. It will help smooth price adjustments as opinions change, rather than concentrating them in a climate Minsky moment. It will open up the greatest commercial opportunity of our time.

The next Part outlines action plans for leaders, companies, investors and countries to seize it as part of a broader initiative to reclaim our values.

PART III

RECLAIMING
OUR VALUES

13

Values-Based Leadership

Reflecting on leadership and values is somewhat dangerous territory, and certainly one that creates a target-rich environment for critics who can spot gaps between preaching and practising. Indeed, a newspaper review of a recent book on leadership and values suggested that its very publication signalled overconfidence – the complacency before the storm – and cautioned that CEOs and investors ought to be wary of the 'curse of authorship'.[1]

There are certainly countless examples of pride coming before the fall in finance. Think of those who dubbed the period before the global financial crisis the 'Great Moderation'. Or the four most expensive words in the English language, 'This time is different.' But I will forge ahead not only because we must learn from experience but also because such leadership across society is at the heart of how we can refound our values.

LEADERSHIP MODELS

People have long been interested in leadership. There are voluminous writings on the subject, drawing on countless examples of success and failure over the millennia. Some, particularly generals, go back to Plutarch for lessons from the age of Caesar and Pompey, while others are drawn to charismatic leaders, such as Gandhi, who inspired entire nations.

Although the theory and practice of leadership is now a huge branch of management science, formal leadership theories emerged only in the last century. The earliest analysis concentrated on the qualities of leaders before attention turned to the importance of situational factors. An influential, early formulation by Max Weber (in 1947) identified three types of leaders: charismatic, traditional and legal/bureaucratic.[2] Even though this taxonomy is primarily of interest to students of history and sociology, it is instructive because it hints at the limits of institutional power in this twilight of elites, and it sets the basis for later work on the importance of emotional intelligence for transformational leadership.

Weber actually focused more on authority than leadership, by profiling the progression of societies from charismatic leaders whose authority grew out of force of personality or 'the extraordinary gift of grace (charisma)'. Once the charismatic leader dies or moves on, the system must evolve into 'traditional' or 'legal-rational' models in order to be sustained. In traditional systems, such as monarchies, legitimacy comes from 'the authority of the eternal yesterday', whereas in legal-rational systems, such as modern democracies, individuals and institutions hold power by virtue of their office. This power is defined, constrained and accountable. The delegated authority given to central banks for certain specific tasks is a classic example of legal-rational authority.

But as the discussion in Chapters 4, 7 and 8 reveals, authority is not leadership and institutional authority is not sustainable without maintaining social licence. No one would accuse central bankers of being charismatic, but even they need to do more than merely occupy their offices to inspire the confidence and trust that is needed for their policies to be most effective. They must engage, explain and emote. And if that is demanded of those atop what, in many respects, are the quintessential technocracies, it also applies to leaders of companies, of communities and of teams, particularly at times of great economic and social change.

To begin to suggest how leaders can continually earn their legitimacy and maximise their effectiveness, it can be helpful to distinguish between models of leadership. I will grossly simplify the many carefully crafted leadership models into three major categories.

The first type, Great Person theories, identify the inherent traits of leaders throughout history and contend that great leaders are born with those attributes – particularly charisma, confidence and intelligence – that make them effective. These theories often portray great leaders as heroic, mythic and predestined to greatness. This 'great man theory' (as it was then known) became popular during the nineteenth century, drawing on the mythology behind leaders such as Alexander the Great, Julius Caesar and Abraham Lincoln. It is typified by the writings of the influential historian Thomas Carlyle, who concluded that 'The history of the world is but the biography of great men.'[3]

While there undoubtedly have been exceptional individuals who have bent the arc of history, countless others have made differences in organisations large and small. General Stanley McChrystal, who has made the study of leadership his vocation following his highly successful military career, decries what he terms the 'Atlas/formulaic myth' under which a specific set of leadership traits automatically yield success. In his experience there were many great leaders who displayed none of them.[4]

Moreover, the examples on which great-leader theories are based tend to attribute the successes of an organisation entirely to the leader, when a range of factors play important roles. Indeed, since most challenging decisions that a leader makes are taken under enormous uncertainty, it is more than possible for someone who is lucky to be judged as good. In addition, if leadership were simply the product of inherent qualities, why don't all who possess those traits eventually become leaders?

Research finds that, rather than leadership being preordained, numerous factors influence the success of a particular leader, including the characteristics of the group and the situation that calls for their leadership.[5] For these reasons, the observations in this chapter are more consistent with two other schools of leadership theory: behavioural and participative.

Behavioural theories of leadership contend that leaders are made not born and that leadership is a process not a gift. Behavioural theories are rooted in the idea that all behaviours can be developed through conditioning[6] – or what we have been referring to as moral sentiments. Behavioural theories focus on the actions of leaders, not on their mental qualities or internal states, and they offer hope to us mere mortals by suggesting we can all learn highly effective leadership through observation and teaching. As we shall see, internal attributes of leaders are important to their authenticity and to developing the virtues needed for sustained excellence in leadership.

Participative leadership theories suggest that the ideal leadership style draws on the input of others, and focuses on the connections formed between leaders and colleagues. Participative leaders encourage contributions from group members, making them feel both more relevant to making decisions and more committed to the successful execution of those decisions. Such transformational leaders can motivate and inspire by helping group members see how tasks connect to the higher purpose of the organisation.

In my experience, behavioural and participative forms of leadership underscore the extent to which leadership is less about what leaders achieve themselves and more about both the sense of purpose they impart to their colleagues and the actions they catalyse in pursuit of that objective.

Effective leadership is clearly situational. This means much more than Shakespeare's 'Cometh the hour, cometh the man.' Managerial styles should vary depending on the nature of the challenge, the context and the type of people being led.[7] Different leadership approaches are more effective for defence and offence, for siege or strategy, for transactional or transformational tasks. Good leaders assess the needs of their followers, take stock of the situation and adjust their behaviours accordingly. For example, in a situation where the leader is the most knowledgeable and experienced member of a group, a more formal style (also called authoritarian) might be most appropriate. In instances where group members are skilled experts, a more participative or democratic approach would work better.

In these respects, leadership theory often differentiates between transactional and transformational leadership. The former, also known as managerial leadership, concentrates on the achievement of specific tasks and uses rewards and punishments to motivate follow-ers.[8] Transactional leaders operate within the existing systems such as bureaucracies or large corporations, using their knowledge, or legal authority, to achieve results. Often deployed in sports, as well as busi-ness, transactional leadership relies on supervision, organisation, rules and procedures. The better transactional leaders set expecta-tions and standards, give constructive feedback on the performance and fairly distribute rewards and recognition. This creates a construc-tive, reciprocal relationship between leaders and their colleagues. Research finds that transactional leadership is most effective in situa-tions where problems are straightforward and can be clearly defined.[9]

Transformational leadership inspires positive changes in colleagues, organisations and – through a shared purpose – the leader themselves. Transformational leaders are generally energetic, enthusiastic and passionate. Through the strength of their vision and personality, they inspire colleagues to change expectations, perceptions and motivations to achieve common goals.

The concept of transformational leadership was popularised by the US political biographer James MacGregor Burns who built on Weber's analysis of a charismatic leader. According to Burns, in transformational leadership 'leaders and followers help each other advance to a higher level of morale and motivation'. Following on from Burns, Bernard Bass identified four components of transfor-mational leadership:

1) Intellectual stimulation. Transformational leaders not only challenge the status quo; they also encourage creativity among colleagues.
2) Individualised consideration. Transformational leaders support and encourage individual followers by keeping lines of communication open so that colleagues feel free to share ideas and receive direct recognition of their unique contributions.
3) Inspirational motivation. Transformational leaders articulate a clear vision and inspire passion to fulfil these goals.
4) Idealised influence. The transformational leader serves as a role model, encouraging colleagues to emulate and internalise the leader's ideals.

Effective transformational leaders often possess high emotional intelligence, or emotional quotient (EQ), as an essential complement to their intelligence quotient (IQ). The concept of emotional intelligence was first developed by Peter Salovey and John Mayer who defined it as 'the ability to perceive emotions, to access and generate emotions so as to assist thought, to understand emotions and emotional knowledge, and to reflectively regulate emotions so as to promote emotional and intellectual growth'.[10] The science journalist Daniel Goleman popularised the importance of emotional intelligence ranging from self-awareness to empathy to effective leadership.[11] Leaders know that they must recognise, understand and manage their own emotions, and recognise, understand and *influence* the emotions of those with whom they work.

Being a transformational leader requires a strong, positive vision of the future. It is not enough for the leaders to believe in the vision themselves; they must inspire others to buy into it. Being authentic, passionate, supportive and trustworthy are key characteristics that will help motivate followers to support your goals for the group.

Groups led by transformational leaders tend to be both successful and loyal, with low turnover and strong commitment. Evidence shows that these groups have higher levels of performance, satisfaction and wellbeing, not least because members feel inspired and empowered.[12] In their classic text *Transformational Leadership*, Bernard Bass and Ronald Riggio explain that:

> Transformational leaders ... stimulate and inspire followers to
> both achieve extraordinary outcomes and, in the process,
> develop their own leadership capacity. Transformational leaders
> help followers grow and develop into leaders by responding to
> individual followers' needs by empowering them and by aligning
> the objectives and goals of the individual followers, the leader,
> the group, and the larger organization.[13]

In practice, both transactional and transformational leadership approaches are important. Transactional execution matters hugely for its own sake and because a track record builds trust in the leader's competence. At the Bank of England, we recognised that everything we did could affect people's confidence in our ability to fulfil our mission. At present, the forces of transformation are immense: we are living in a time of great economic, technological and social change. Whole industries (like retail) are being disrupted and new ones invented (like carbon capture and storage). The global economy is simultaneously fragmenting (due to trade barriers) and integrating (through social networks). As systemic biases are being exposed, we face an imperative to choose inclusion as part of our common humanity or allow existing social cleavages to become chasms.

In this age of machines, the leadership of technology must be both transactional and transformational. Artificial intelligence is a general purpose technology with widespread applications, whose productivity benefits depend on re-engineering processes to achieve a common purpose.

Artificial intelligence can be thought of as 'prediction machines' which can make better forecasts about the future than humans, and whose accuracy improves with use.[14]

Machine learning (ML) works generally best in situations where transactional leadership is required. That is, where there is a clearly defined question, the future is expected to behave like the past and there is sufficient data to compute the problem. Examples in finance include identifying fraud or money laundering or evaluating common risk factors in insurance or default risks of small and medium-sized companies. AI can be particularly effective in games with set rules, such as arbitrage in financial markets, where algorithms can spot and take advantage of opportunities that humans cannot see. In this last respect, AI's ability to see the unseeable can occasionally lead to transformative insights such as the famous game of Go between DeepMind and Kim Jayeol which was transformed when the machine discovered another local maximum that dominated the area in which the world's finest Go players had been operating for years.

Part of managing machines involves determining when an objective prediction can be improved by combining it with human judgement. This requires understanding the strengths and limitations of AI. Machines can perform initial screens on credit assessments or loan extensions particularly for retail consumer lending because there is so much data available. While AI and ML can compute more data than the human brain, reducing the probability of placing too heavy a weight on a single factor, AI's ability to eliminate human biases depends of course on whether they are present in the historic data the machine uses to learn.

Sometimes decision making needs to be quick not perfect, especially in a complex world. Where humans cannot find an optimal solution, we 'satisfice' – adopting a pragmatic approach by settling with the option that reaches a satisfactory threshold. AI is also dominated by human intuition when there is simply not enough data from which to learn. When past is not prologue, the ability of humans to think laterally has enormous value.

AI can be particularly challenged by transformational leadership issues. AI struggles to spot and understand long-run structural shifts such as climate change, ageing population and AI itself. AI obviously struggles when there is too little data to infer conclusions. When there is not enough data to compute, AI can't fill in the blanks as it doesn't recognise or cannot compute the known unknowns in the same way humans do.

AI models can also be hard to interpret. Model parameters are usually known by the developers (though not always in the case of neural networks), but the large number of parameters and non-linear form of models makes them hard for humans to grasp. For example, Amazon's AlexNet, used for natural language processing, has 60 million estimated parameters. And even more narrowly focused credit-rating models can have thousands of parameters that are non-linear or non-parametric, making it hard to explain how they work.

In finance stability, AI could make it more difficult for humans at financial institutions and regulators to understand behaviour in tail events, including how decisions, such as those for trading and investment, have been formulated. It is hard to fix a problem without knowing its cause. Increased dependency on third parties creates an operational risk and a risk of a single point of failure, with interoperability meaning that the consequences of an action may be amplified.

*   *   *

In what follows I will assume readers are not leading by either divine right or autocratic fiat, that in your leadership challenges, whether large or small, you require at a minimum the consent – and ideally the enthusiasm – of your colleagues, boards, shareholders and stakeholders. Irrespective of the scale of your organisation, remember that consent extends to broader society. When tested, we all need social licence to operate effectively.

That's why, in this age of disruption, we need to focus on a form of the values-based leadership described in this chapter. To be successful that approach begins with a recognition that the current 'crisis of trust' is as much as anything a crisis of leadership.[15]

LEADERSHIP AND THE CRISIS OF TRUST

It is fashionable to speak of the loss of trust in many societies, and longitudinal social surveys do show a general downward trend over recent decades in the public's confidence in a number of institutions.[16]

This loss of trust is often described as a disillusionment with 'experts', but that is overly simplistic. The population today, when asked, is in fact relatively trusting of scientific expertise,[17] directing instead most scepticism towards government and the media. The Edelman Trust Barometer for 2020 finds that, in approximately two-thirds of the countries sampled, trust in government and the media to do what is right was below 50 per cent.[18] Trust in the very wealthy and – as discussed in Chapter 7 – the financial sector is also quite low.[19] The response to this lack of trust in institutions has been to look elsewhere. 'A person like yourself' is now as credible as a technical expert and far more credible than a CEO or a government official – reflecting a shift in trust towards family and friends apparent on social media.

The mistrust of institutions has multiple origins. Some is grounded in poor performance. Competence matters, and incompetence breeds suspicion and derision. In the financial sector, the turning point was undoubtedly the failure of the mainstream economics profession to foresee how the failings of the light-touch, market-fundamentalist financial system could lead to crisis. Public scepticism was reinforced by a series of eurozone crises, which laid bare the inadequacies of the institutional architecture of the single currency,[20] something that had been widely seen as an elite project. Financial conduct scandals like Libor then added to the disillusionment.

Although the medical profession has fared better than financiers, it has seen a continual decline in public confidence since the 1970s and its missteps demonstrate how trust can be diminished. An infamous failure of expert systems for quality control was a 1998 study published in the prestigious, peer-reviewed journal the *Lancet* which claimed a link between the MMR vaccine and autism. Uptake of the vaccine in the UK subsequently dropped to under 80 per cent nationally, prompting a mumps epidemic by 2005. The lead author was later struck off the medical register, and the *Lancet* retracted the article (which had been based on study of just twelve children) as subsequent studies failed to establish a credible link between vaccines and autism.

During the Covid crisis, public health officials occupied centre stage and in many respects wielded *de facto* power over the day-to-day life of whole populations (the logical implication of government commitments to 'follow the science'). The pressures of providing real-time advice under enormous uncertainty led to a series of judgements that drew down the reservoir of trust in the profession. Over the course of the pandemic, scientists were encouraged to give and then forced to reverse clear advice on issues as varied as the impact on the transmission of the disease by asymptomatic patients, wearing masks, the two-metre rule and quarantining inbound travellers. Not surprisingly given the novelty of the virus, mortality proved difficult to estimate, and counterfactuals such as preventable deaths were taken as fact. While each of these developments can be characterised as learnings, they can also be perceived as errors, eroding confidence in the lockdown strategy and splitting the population into those who felt the threat had been overstated and those who feared that scientific advice was bending to economic and political objectives.

Such polarisation of opinion around issues is typical and is fed by the revolution in information technology. The digitisation of knowledge and free access to it has been hugely democratising and empowering.[21] At the same time, the news and opinions we receive are increasingly targeted by self-reinforcing search engines and social media algorithms. These feed our confirmation biases and remove the space for nuanced, risk-based judgements. Who needs experts when we can rely on our Facebook friends or those we follow on Twitter to validate our opinions?

As the Director of LSE Dame Minouche Shafik concludes, 'In a world where information is plentiful, the future of education will be about critical thinking and creating citizens with an ability to learn and make judgements.'[22] As she notes, assessing the quality of that information can be difficult when algorithms create echo chambers of the like-minded; fake news distorts reality; 'post-truth' fosters cynicism; and online anonymity bestows power on to individuals and countries that can abuse it. According to the Reuters Institute for the Study of Journalism at Oxford University, half of people with online access use social media as a news source (the number having doubled in the US since just 2013).[23] This reliance on news delivered by algorithms which guess users' preferences based on content they have previously read and liked increases the risk of living in an informational echo chamber. These risks are compounded in a world in which clicks mean revenue. This can reward the shrillest voices and promote the most extreme views.

The mistrust of experts and expertise is being stoked by the rise of populist politics. Populism is a specific form of identity politics that makes a moral claim to representation of the 'true people'.[24] It is by nature anti-pluralist and anti-elite, promoting an 'us versus them' mentality that places all wisdom in 'the people' who can be identified by their support for the populist policies. An example of this approach occurred during the Brexit referendum by the UK cabinet minister Michael Gove who asserted that people 'have had enough of experts'. Apparently, the sentiment was short lived for him: within a couple of years he was a member of a government whose response to the Covid crisis was to 'follow the science'.

*　　*　　*

There are a variety of colourful metaphors for the dynamics of trust. In finance, trust is said to arrive on foot and leave in a Ferrari. A senior Indian government official, Montek Singh Ahluwalia, once told me that trust grows at the rate of the coconut tree and falls with the speed of the coconut. The lesson is the same: trust can take ages to build and moments to destroy.

Leaders in all organisations can clearly learn from the types of measures that experts need to take to rebuild public trust. Six steps are particularly relevant.

First, improved transparency can help when the public has insufficient information to understand how and why decisions have been taken. However, transparency has become an easy default, and it can be ineffective in an age overwhelmed with information. As Onora O'Neill has stressed, carpet bombing the public with all available information is not the solution ('it seems no information about an institution or a profession is too boring or routine to remain unpublished'[25]). Transparency serves little purpose if the information is inaccessible to stakeholders because of language or cannot be assessed by them because of complexity or context. Stakeholders need effective transparency, with information provided in ways that empower individuals to judge trustworthiness for themselves by assessing its quality and differentiating facts from falsehood.[26] That's what we strove to achieve at the Bank of England following the Warsh Report on transparency and accountability, by providing all information related to a single decision in layers suited to the interest level and expertise of our stakeholders. The general public could assess the clarity and intent of the top-line message, financial market experts and academics could pore over and debate the significance of every phrase and data point, and the media could judge the consistency of the package.

Second, establish the facts. As the late US Senator Daniel Patrick Moynihan said, 'You are entitled to your own opinion, you are not entitled to your own facts.' To provide them, some traditional institutions have created public information services, like NHS Direct and the National Institute of Health Protection. Non-traditional judges of the quality of information have emerged such as fact-checking websites that appraise claims made by public figures.

Fact checkers have even developed a code of conduct to enable users to assess the veracity of their own work.[27]

The fundamental importance of fact checking has even resonated with the social media giants. Companies like YouTube and Twitter were founded on values of free expression and the decentralisation of information control but have increasingly taken action against misinformation, employing thousands of content moderators and experimenting with appropriate procedures and governance models.

An interesting governance advancement is Facebook's oversight board, which will make final determinations on controversial content and will have the power to overturn decisions made by Facebook's leadership. The board is composed of distinguished individuals from around the globe, and includes a former prime minister, a Nobel laureate and constitutional law experts. The deliberate similarities to a judicial body – including an appeals process and the publishing of the board's decisions – suggests a genuine attempt to balance issues of free speech and accuracy in a transparent and fair manner.

The publishing of decisions, models and underlying data is one way experts and organisations can seek to maintain public trust, as others can then test the reliability of their arguments and results. In a similar fashion, governments would ideally publish sensitivities and give stakeholders the ability to vary them in order to assess the robustness of the conclusions (and at a minimum familiarise themselves with the uncertainty of results). At the Bank of England, we would occasionally publish sensitivities and different scenarios around our projections. Our objective was to allow people to try to determine how we would react to different economic circumstances if they arose (technically our reaction function).[28]

A third popular prescription to improve trust is for experts to embrace uncertainty.[29] As Bertrand Russell once lamented, 'The whole problem of the world is that fools and fanatics are always so certain of themselves, but wiser people so full of doubts.' There are good reasons for doubt in a complex world. As the experience of the Covid crisis underscored, uncertainty can lead to wildly different outcomes arising from apparently small changes in the assumptions of epidemiological models. Experts are uncertain not only about the calibration of their models, but also about whether their models are even the right ones.

So, rather than professing false certainty and risk being wrong, it is argued that being candid about uncertainty could build the credibility of experts over the long term. As André Gide said, 'Trust those who seek the truth but doubt those who say they have found it.'[30] A classic example of this approach is the use of 'fan charts' in economic forecasts produced by the Bank of England's MPC. These show the wide range of possible outcomes for inflation, growth and unemployment for a given set of initial circumstances.

However sound this advice appears on paper, it has its limitations. It is naive to think that this uncertainty will always be conveyed by the media or, even if it is, that it will be understood by the public. I frequently observed that the Bank of England's worst-case scenarios that we used to stress-test the banks were described as forecasts, predictions, even promises. Moreover, conveying uncertainty increases the complexity of a message, something that's tough to do in 280 characters.

To try to meet Minouche Shafik's challenge, experts need to make judgements about no-regret communications. I would rather be accused of being too pessimistic when preparing for risks than being caught unprepared when bad things happen. Consider the Bank of England's experience with worst-case scenarios used for Brexit preparations being misconstrued as dire predictions of what would happen. As my colleague Sam Woods once said, 'We have been called merchants of doom, which I take as a compliment.' Sam was right because the worst-case scenarios served their purpose which was to ensure that UK banks would be strong enough to withstand the worst possible economic circumstances following the UK's *de facto* (not *de jure*) departure from the Single Market. As discussed in Chapter 8, by planning for failure, we could help ensure success. As a consequence, we were confident that the financial sector was the one area of the economy that was ready for a no-deal Brexit. Moreover when Covid hit, the Bank of England had the necessary credibility when we said that the banks were part of the solution. We were trusted.

This leads to the fourth common solution to improving trust: better communications. Certainly, in the deluge of social media and media which measures balance by quantity not quality, experts are just one of many voices. And these voices often use inaccessible language when they speak. For example, a 2017 study by Bank of England staff compared the linguistic complexity of our publications to other sources of information to find that they require a level of reading comprehension which makes them accessible to only one in five people.[31]

In response, we began rating all internal memos and external speeches by their Flesch scores to encourage plainer talk, and created layers of communications so that people could access our core messages easily, giving them the option of drilling down into the data and detail if they wished. We have learned that talking about 'prices and jobs' is far more effective than the economic jargon of inflation and employment.

But this approach is not without its challenges. Speaking plainly strips out nuance and that sense of uncertainty we were advised to embrace. When asked about the outlook for the economy, 'we have no idea' might be clear but it is neither very helpful nor likely to engender trust given that the Bank is required to have a view of the likely economic outcomes in order to set monetary policy. In the end, the Bank has to make a call about the most likely outlook and then explain what changed when actual performance turns out differently. The second challenge with speaking plainly is that the language of jobs and growth is the language of politicians. This raises the risks that people conclude that the Bank can do more than it can, and that they conflate an independent technocratic institution with the political process.

This leads to the fifth strategy for building trust, as advocated by the Chair of the Federal Reserve Jay Powell: staying in your lane. As discussed in Chapter 4, central banks operate under carefully constrained discretion. Power comes from the people and is delegated to expert bodies or institutions to achieve specific tasks. Staying in our lane was why we at the Bank of England were always exceptionally careful when asked about fiscal policy, even though we had more than enough information and expertise to offer a view, and the stance of fiscal policy always matters for the conduct of monetary policy. But fiscal policy wasn't our responsibility, and the flexibility of monetary policy meant that the Bank can adjust policy quickly to the slower-moving changes in fiscal policy. Moreover, the Bank commenting on fiscal policy would invite comments on the conduct of monetary policy by politicians, confusing the public and blurring the lines of accountability in ways that could ultimately undermine trust in both.

The breadth of the Bank of England's remit meant there were contentious areas where the combination of threats to UK financial stability and democratic accountability required us to comment. The Scottish referendum raised fundamental questions of monetary sovereignty and financial stability.[32] The proposal that Scotland would move quickly to independence while keeping the pound without any form of fiscal union or shared financial safety net risked destabilising the very large financial services sector headquartered there. As a precaution, the Bank undertook extensive contingency planning to protect the system – precautions that we had to reveal when we testified to parliamentary hearings on the subject. The Bank's powers devolve from the people and we are accountable to them when we exercise them.

In a similar vein, it would have been inconceivable for the Bank either not to prepare for the potential financial stability consequences of Brexit or to remain quiet about those preparations since they involved wholesale changes to how banks were funding themselves and could have resulted in the Bank lending hundreds of billions of pounds to the financial sector. Any losses on that lending would ultimately have been borne by the taxpayer. Not to have acted would have been a political decision, and to have kept it quiet, again in the face of parliamentary questioning, would have been unconscionable. As the Chair of the Treasury Committee, through which the Bank of England is accountable to Parliament, said, 'a vow of Omertà from the Bank of England on this subject would have resulted in a bumpy hearing or two for you and your colleagues in front of this Committee in the face of a decision or an event of this type'.[33]

There was no doubt among any of the committee members regarding their responsibility to assess the implications of the UK's

EU membership for the Bank's ability to achieve its statutory objectives. The Bank also has a statutory duty to report our evidence-based judgements to Parliament and the public. For example, the Remit for the Monetary Policy Committee stipulates that 'the Committee should promote understanding of the trade-offs inherent in setting monetary policy'. Moreover, when inflation deviates from the 2 per cent target by more than 1 percentage point, as was the case the month before the referendum, it requires that the Governor write an open letter to the Chancellor that sets out, among other things, a description of 'the trade-off that has been made with regard to inflation and output variability in determining the scale and duration of any expected deviation of inflation from the target rate' and of 'how this approach meets the Government's monetary policy objectives'. Given that in the view of all nine independent members of the MPC the 'most significant risks to the MPC's forecast concern the referendum' and that the implications of a vote to leave the EU 'could lead to a materially lower path for growth and a notably higher path for inflation' and therefore the Committee 'would face a trade-off between stabilising inflation on the one hand and output and employment on the other', it would have been clearly contrary to our remit not to comment on this in our publications.[34]

Similarly, the Bank's Financial Policy Committee was quite clearly meeting its statutory remit when it reported that in agreeing its view on the outlook for financial stability and, on the basis of that, its intended policy actions, it 'assessed the risks around the referendum to be the most significant near-term domestic risks to financial stability'.[35] As I testified to the House of Lords Economic Affairs Committee in April 2016, 'This is the fundamental standard of an open and transparent central bank. Assessing and reporting major risks does not mean becoming involved in politics; rather, it would be political to suppress important judgments that relate directly to the Bank's remits and which influence our policy actions.'[36] As I also explained in my testimony to the House of Commons' Treasury Committee in May 2016, if 'we are changing policy, as the Bank of England has – we have changed our liquidity policy, we have changed our supervisory policy, and we might have to change our monetary policy in pursuit of our remit – we have an obligation to disclose that'.[37]

In the event, those preparations meant that the morning following the Leave vote in the referendum – a result on which financial markets had placed a less than one-in-five probability the day before – it was credible when I declared on behalf of the Bank, 'We are well prepared for this.' Markets calmed, banks lent money and we were able to provide the stimulus the economy needed. We were trusted when it mattered most.

Finally, and most fundamentally, experts need to listen to all sides. Within your organisation, this goes to the heart of participative leadership. As we will discuss in the next chapter on fulfilling corporate purpose, reaching out to all stakeholders is essential to maintain social licence and to improve performance. When you engage widely, you will find some sharp, firmly held but often lightly researched differences of opinion about fundamental issues. As NYU Professor Jonathan Haidt argues, that is in part because humans are prone to 'groupish righteousness' when it comes to how people reach moral judgements about important issues. This tendency is exacerbated by social media, which provides the ability to communicate exclusively among the like-minded.

At the end of the day, even when all of the facts are established, differences of opinion can legitimately exist, even among experts. This is why the process of coming to a decision matters. That has been my experience across a range of complex issues in diverse settings. When I was chairing the Financial Stability Board in the wake of the global financial crisis, authorities from more than twenty of the world's largest countries grappled with how to solve highly complex problems that would affect billions of people for decades to come. There were always strongly held, well-reasoned differences of opinion. But with shared purpose and open, fact-based discussion we consistently came to consensus because honest efforts were made by all parties to understand each other's viewpoints. In my experience working for two ministers of finance in Canada the same was true for whenever solutions could be found to thorny federal–provincial issues. It's the same for negotiations within European institutions, and in the Glasgow Climate negotiations among 195 countries. It is true for how companies engage with their stakeholders, and organisations with their wider community.

Making decisions by seeing the world from the perspective of others can be messy and time consuming, but it is essential. Leadership increasingly comes in forging consensus, not pre-empting conclusions.

Arguably we need such inclusive processes in all parts of society more than ever. All of us as individuals have a responsibility to be more open and to engage respectfully with different views if we want constructive political debates and to make progress on important issues.

Many of the ways to rebuild trust in experts resonate with what is required of effective leaders. Humility, candour about the limits of expertise, effective transparency and clearer communication. Engaging widely and seeing issues from the perspectives of others.

In the end, however, not all experts are leaders. Many make expert judgements, but they are important observers and influencers rather than vital actors. Leaders are different in that they *have* to decide. In the end, to lead is to choose. Just because something is uncertain is not reason enough for a leader to throw their hands up and sit on the sidelines. If leaders can't make the call, there will be consequences from that inaction. And over time, if they can't decide, someone else will.

When you do take decisions as leader, it will obviously help greatly if they are the right ones. It is inescapable that your trustworthiness will be affected by the track record of your team, division, department or organisation. People will respect a leader who has integrity and is benevolent, but they won't always follow them if they are not deemed to be competent. As we will discuss in the next chapter, business leaders must keep their businesses going while they are benevolent. Purpose must be accompanied by profit.

What should you do to make sure that those decisions are likely to be the best possible ones?

WHAT LEADERS DO

It's important to distinguish between what leaders do and who they are. Of the many things leaders must do, three are particularly important:

1) finding and developing the right people;
2) setting priorities; and
3) catalysing action.

This starts with recruiting widely. Leaders who search out the like-minded will build on a narrow foundation.

The Bank of England has embraced the perspectives of those such as the leading venture capitalist Sir Ken Olisa, who stresses that 'Tackling diversity is a business imperative not an HR policy.' Ten years ago the Bank's graduate intake was comprised largely of economists drawn from just eleven universities. By the time I left, we hired from over forty post-secondary institutions with half of the intake having studied sciences, business, law and the humanities. Of the 700 experienced professionals we hired in 2017, almost half were women and a quarter came from BAME backgrounds.

Covid has accelerated another approach to increasing diversity. Leading technology firms like Stripe are rapidly expanding remote working, and Shopify is even going 'digital by default', opening up a huge global talent pool. The important thing will be to ensure that talent is not merely geographically diverse. As Christine Lagarde told me when she became head of the IMF there was tremendous diversity at the Fund, with over 150 nationalities, the only problem was that they all had a PhD in economics from MIT.

Once the right people are through the door (even if it is virtual) they need to be developed. That includes identifying a pipeline of future leaders with a diverse and broad set of experiences and pushing them in order to prepare them for bigger roles. At the Bank, we not only recruit widely but also encourage colleagues to collaborate across the organisation and spend time in different areas to develop the varied skills required of a modern central banker.

In large organisations, developing future leaders requires discipline. For example, when he was the CEO of Vodafone, Vittorio Colao and his top management team would review the company's top 200 executives annually to assess performance, set development actions and manage those who were having difficulties. The Executive Committee at Vodafone then discussed the progress of a different subset of their leaders at each Executive Meeting, making the process transparent and rigorous. The Bank of England has adopted a similar approach.

Developing the right people also requires a culture of inclusion that values diverse ideas, encourages open debate and empowers people at all levels to take the initiative.

Finally, for leaders, having the right people also means being able to draw on trusted outside perspectives such as an external advisory board or informal contacts with other leaders. I was fortunate that as Governor I could regularly share experiences with a wide range of leaders in diverse fields. Of these, the most important sounding boards were my fellow central bankers. In this circle of trust, we had regular, frank discussions of issues that we either didn't understand (but couldn't admit as much publicly) or that were particularly sensitive.

I recall my first such dinner on a dark, cold February evening, high atop Basel's BIS Tower. It was early March 2008, and the American investment bank Bear Stearns was on the ropes. Among many other messes, Bear was tangled up in the derivatives and money markets that were dragging down the nonsensical ABCP complex described in Chapter 7. No one knew what would happen if Bear Stearns suddenly collapsed. Time was of the essence as Asian markets would open shortly, but the President of the ECB Jean-Claude Trichet who chaired the meeting took his time to welcome me. He explained the unique setting, the candid nature of the discussions and the circle of trust. After about ten minutes, once he'd finished, he said, 'Now, if we don't act in the next hour, all is lost.' Within an hour we had agreed to supply the at that time unheard-of $200 billion of liquidity to markets, helping to bridge the bank until it was rescued by a competitor.

* * *

The second critical thing that leaders do is to set the priorities for their organisation. Before they do so, a good leader assesses the context in which their organisation operates. That process starts with discussions with all stakeholders, including clients, senior managers and, via roundtables and surveys, colleagues at all levels.

Understanding context requires developing intuitions about global developments and shifting technologies. This has always been second nature to central banking in open economies like the UK and Canada where global events quickly affect local conditions. But there are few organisations today that are not affected by the mega-trends of shifting demographics, the accelerating pace of technological disruption and the demands for a more inclusive capitalism.

The priorities that leaders set should be ambitious. Not ambitious for themselves but ambitious for their organisation. As we will see in a moment, ambition must be grounded in the purpose of the organisation.

When she was Vice-Chancellor of Cambridge University, Alison Richard would ask, 'Who will be ambitious on our behalf if we are not ambitious for ourselves? We cannot take Cambridge's greatness for granted even after 800 years. We must tend it with care and energy, and ambition must translate into tasks.'[38] If this message applies to a venerable institution such as Cambridge, it certainly applies to the Bank of England at a little more than three centuries, and to the latest start-up on Silicon Roundabout at a little more than three months.

So run towards the sound of gunfire. Seek to solve your clients' biggest problems. Take on complex situations, set clear agendas for resolving them and get on them fast.

The third thing leaders do is to catalyse action. Specific catalysts vary with an organisation's structure and culture, but in all cases they require the full and visible commitment of the leader before devolving power to colleagues. Catalysing action means engaging with and empowering colleagues, who are more likely to follow a new direction if they have been consulted during its development. Once again, this underscores the importance of a clear purpose to the organisation and to tying strategic initiatives to its fulfilment. If this is accomplished, colleagues will anticipate, innovate and execute with authority.

Amazon's remarkable success has popularised the concept of 'feeding the flywheel' that was first coined by management theorist Jim Collins. The premise is simple. A flywheel is a mechanical device specifically designed to store energy efficiently (rotational or kinetic energy).[39] Keep pushing and the flywheel builds momentum. A company goes from good to great when the flywheel acts as a self-reinforcing loop fed by a few key initiatives that are in turn driven by each other, building a long-term business in the process.

Such empowerment means that leaders then need to get out of the way. In a quote often attributed to Teddy Roosevelt, 'The best executive is the one who has sense enough to pick good people to do what [the leader] wants done, and self-restraint enough to keep from meddling with them while they do it.'[40] Such delegation has traditionally been anathema for central banks. But when following the crisis the Bank of England doubled in size and tripled in responsibilities, we knew our rigid hierarchy had to change.

To start that process, we surveyed widely and met with colleagues across the Bank in order to develop our new strategy. We then slashed the number of internal committees by two-thirds and instituted a policy that the author of every analysis had to be in the room whenever it was discussed. We devolved decisions to the right level, changed the way we met and made the Bank more permeable to the outside world by multiplying our channels of communications and the number of our spokespeople.

But we knew we also had to change the way we made decisions, so we decided to make decisions more like Amazon. That didn't mean asking Alexa (machine learning still has a way to go yet), but it did mean trying something that I had heard from people who worked at Amazon. My understanding was that Amazon had a very structured way of making decisions: whether by machines, by people with the aid of machines or by people alone. On one level it's obvious their decision-making process must be consistent and efficient because Amazon literally makes millions of decisions every day deciding which items to profile on their website or to suggest to consumers.

But Amazon apparently makes every strategic decision in the same manner, even their strategic plan for the year. To learn how this worked, Andrew Hauser, the Executive Director running our Markets area, and I walked the few blocks from the Bank of England to Amazon's European headquarters and sat with its leader Doug Gurr and his team. I had met Doug a few times and had always been impressed by his detailed knowledge, strategic acumen and focus. All were on display in his comprehensive response to my asking: 'How does Amazon make decisions?'

From that conversation, Andrew and I had everything we needed to change how we made decisions at the Bank. The essence of the new approach is straightforward:

— Define the purpose of the meeting, including whether it is for decisions, discussions and brainstorming or debriefs.
— Include everyone necessary in the meeting and identify who needs to be informed of the outcome. Be as inclusive as possible.
— Ensure everyone has all the necessary information beforehand, that they read it and that they all expect to participate.
— Take clear decisions and ensure immediate follow-up.

If you are preparing for a decision meeting, identify the reader and write for them. Think about: why is the issue relevant now? What should the reader do and by when? The paper should be focused, clearly written and no more than six pages. This is hard work; as Steve Jobs said, 'Simple can be harder than complex. You have to work hard to get your thinking clean to make it simple.' Put all the crucial information upfront. A (typical) inattentive reader will remember two or three things from your paper at most. Tell a linear story and avoid repetition. And use your judgement to make clear recommendations, while giving the reader enough information to interrogate them to decide whether they agree.

The author must be in the room with other experts to answer questions. Everyone should have read the materials and be ready to contribute. Amazon even ensures the former by reserving the first fifteen minutes of the meeting for people to read the memo. The chair should set out the purpose of the meeting, ensure that everyone has a chance to contribute, that no one dominates or derails the discussion, and keep the meeting on time. The decision should be clearly communicated at the meeting, and any follow-up actions assigned immediately.

There was understandable pushback on some of these points – the experts in the Bank highlighted the complexity of their issues and the challenges in boiling them down to clear recommendations. There was merit in both points, but they were also what had contributed to a tendency to have 'on the one hand, on the other hand' inconclusive recommendations with key information buried in footnote 17 in the third annex.

These concerns were initially overcome by two considerations. First, as we've seen, this was how Amazon made decisions up and down the organisation. Given the range of new initiatives for the 'everything store', it is compelling that it can be done. Second, it was clear to everyone that this approach could be more inclusive and impactful. People were at the Bank for its mission and wanted to know how their work was contributing to it. Getting decision making right is hugely empowering.

This quickly became apparent at the Bank. The quality of our discussions and the impact of colleagues were immensely improved. Moreover, if policymakers took a different direction from the recommendation coming into the meeting, colleagues could learn from the reasons why. This meant they were more likely to implement it, not least because it seemed less arbitrary. Empowered colleagues were more motivated, and by making clear recommendations they were practising leadership. You become a follower when you have a personal commitment to the project. If followers and leaders are mutually committed then levels of trust are very high and the prospects of success are magnified.

THE ATTRIBUTES OF VALUES-BASED LEADERSHIP

Finding and developing the right people, setting priorities and cata-lysing action are things that all leaders must do, but what ultimately most determines a leader's effectiveness is who they are. In my expe-rience, leadership qualities are not inherent, they can be developed. The attributes are not finite goods that are exhausted by use but are like muscles that grow with regular exercise. They are virtues that can be nurtured.

There are five essential and universal attributes of leadership:

1) Purpose
2) Perspective
3) Clarity
4) Competence
5) Humility

As discussed in more detail in the next chapter, purpose is what an organisation stands for; why it does what it does; and what it should be trusted to deliver. Purpose is always broader than a simple bottom line. An organisation's purpose can be for the client, such as Shopify's 'making commerce better for everyone', for a higher purpose such as Google's 'to organise the world's information', or for the greater good, such as the World Bank's mission 'to end extreme poverty'.

When I joined the Bank of England, I went around to meet colleagues to learn what they did, what they thought we should change and (implicitly) what they expected of me. I wandered the corridors, not because I was lost, but because I was in search of purpose. The first question I would ask my new colleagues was why had they chosen to work at the Bank? I was quickly surprised by the wide range of the answers I received from 'public service' to 'path dependence' (a summer internship leading to a series of jobs) to the intellectual challenge, the work environment and the people. There was even one colleague who had watched a TV programme about a financial crisis and identified with the bank supervisor rather than the swashbuckling masters of the universe (I am pleased she is now one of the Bank's top supervisors).

To my surprise, no one mentioned the Bank's mission. Since I didn't know precisely what it was, I began to ask them, only to find they didn't know either. This was in stark contrast to the German Bundesbank's historic mission 'to protect the integrity of the Deutschemark', which their former Chief Economist Otmar Issing assured me everyone there would recite (even today!). So when we sat down to develop our initial strategy, our first priority was to agree a mission. As a source we dragged out the vellum Charter of the Bank and took inspiration from its first sentence that the Bank's founders were 'desirous to promote the publick good and benefit of our people'. We modernised it to add our current responsibilities and agreed that the Bank of England's mission is to 'Promote the good of the people of the United Kingdom by maintaining monetary and financial stability'.

Even though this book isn't about the Bank *per se*, you may recall coming across that mission several times already in it. After all, the leader's job is to ensure that the purpose of their organisation is always present and anchors its goals, values and strategy.

Like diversity, purpose is not a 'nice to have'. Evidence shows that purposeful companies have higher employee engagement, greater customer satisfaction, tighter supplier linkages and better environmental stewardship. The pay-offs to purposeful business are superior share-price performance, better operational performance, lower costs of capital, smaller regulatory fines and greater resilience in the face of shocks.

A sense of purpose is closely connected to trust because our trust in someone is based in part on understanding what they are trying to achieve and what guides them. For a leader of an organisation, that purpose is their compass. To be effective, purpose requires integrity. Your integrity as a leader will be tested by some, and they will need to discern whether the stated purpose is the actual purpose. That requires openness and time to build a track record, including addressing the inevitable mistakes that will happen along the way.

True understanding of purpose means always remembering that leaders are stewards of the purpose of their organisations. In this sense, leadership is the acceptance of responsibility rather than the assumption of power. True leadership is not an end in itself but rather a means to accomplishing a worthwhile goal.

It is easy to be swept away by the trappings of leadership. There are two possible reactions to the grandeur of the Governor's office: to believe that it signals the holder's importance or to feel the weight of history and expectations that it imparts. I would often remind myself where I had come from and that I was merely the 120th Governor of the Bank of England. To remind me of my background, I hung at eye level by the door a small map of County Mayo in Ireland. It's a place of breathtaking beauty and charm, but it was also the poorest county in one of the poorest countries in Europe when my grandfather emigrated to Canada almost a century ago to find a better life. And if the map didn't do the trick, I would tell myself that there would be scores of governors to come after me. My job was to preserve and if possible improve the legacy that I had inherited.

If I was ever in any doubt about my own importance, a visit to one of Britain's many cathedrals would put me in my place. Cathedrals that were destined to be finished beyond the lifetime of their creators are always good for individual humility. Westminster Abbey did more than that, it put whole professions in their place. The scene of coronations since 1066, this magnificent 'Royal Peculiar' is also the final resting place for Britain's greatest poets (from Chaucer to Tennyson), scientists (from Newton to Darwin) and politicians (from Prime Ministers Pitt the Younger to Clement Attlee). That would be the Pitt who, during the French crisis of 1797, famously assaulted the Old Lady of Threadneedle Street for her reserves and the Attlee who nationalised us in 1946.

I'm not suggesting there's an animus against the Bank of England, but I did note that only two economists merit the glories of being buried in Westminster. And they enjoy them incognito because 'economics' is not one of the thirty-one 'professions' represented at the Abbey. 'Socialist' is – which is how the founders of the LSE, Sidney and Beatrice Webb, are listed. There are no capitalists, and not one of the 118 dearly departed Governors of the Bank of England lies in the Abbey. Now that is as it should be – after all, the work of central banking is to create the conditions for others to take risks, to create and to improve the state of the world. In contrast, central bankers' most dramatic contributions are when they get things wrong, such as in the response to the Great Depression. The financial sector destroyed its reputation for competence in the global financial crisis and is climbing the long road back to rebuild trust. Disaster doesn't command a decent burial nor is competence a recipe for immortality.

Discussion of mortality is a good reminder for a leader not to confuse their leadership role with themselves or become addicted to the status and privileges of power. Rather, recognise that all leadership is temporary, that you will be custodians of your institutions and keepers of their flames. And if possible, take a cue from Cincinnatus and Washington, and leave before you are asked.

Leaders must have perspective. Consistent with purposeful ambition, leaders must assess the landscape to determine how their organisation can plan the future. Note the distinction from planning *for* the future. Ambitious leadership means helping to shape the future rather than just reacting to it. Organisations need both to be resilient against storms and to make the weather.

The perspective of leaders cannot be limited to the horizon. True leaders must also take in the periphery. Pope Francis emphasises that we perceive a situation most accurately when we look at it from the standpoint of those on the edge rather than those in the centre. The state of the economy looks different to the unemployed. The political structure looks different to someone who is powerless, the community to the excluded or the security forces to the persecuted.

Addressing simplistic populist solutions can only be accomplished through perspective. Jan-Werner Müller argues against conflating populism with 'irresponsible politics' or equating it with the fears or anger of voters. Such condescending psychological analyses expose elites that are 'unable to live up to their own democratic ideals by failing to take ordinary people at their word'.[41] Populism can only be addressed by engagement. As Müller argues, 'One can take their political claims seriously without taking them at face value.'[42] Thus politicians and the media should address the issues raised by populists but challenge their framing and how best to resolve them.

Improving our ability to see from the periphery was one of the many values of school visits, of visits to town halls in the regions, of the outreach sessions with third-sector groups which we initiated at the Bank of England. Even though central banking is ultimately about macroeconomic outcomes, it is essential to understand the experiences behind the numbers. It makes us better at communicating with people. Better at listening. And it motivates us to do what we can to bring everyone up together, leading to such initiatives as the educational charity econoME and new ways to bridge the gap in SME lending through fintech.[43]

When leaders design initiatives, thinking of these examples from the periphery can make them most likely to support the common good which has at its heart the interests of the most marginalised:

- during the financial crisis, the working poor who were most concerned about their savings;
- during the climate crisis, the young, the unborn and those who live in vulnerable island states; and
- during the Covid crisis the elderly, the vulnerable and the essential workers who faced the highest personal risks for often meagre wages.

The Covid crisis teaches us that we are all in the same storm but not necessarily in the same boat. That we need to act as an interdependent community not as independent individuals. Can anyone 'unmeet' their neighbour? Once workers are revealed to be essential can our value of them be the same?

Such a change in perspective is possible when companies engage with all their stakeholders and understand their needs, hopes and fears. Or if we strive to improve the common good of society (so it is only as successful as the most vulnerable) rather than seek the greatest prosperity of the greatest number, which can leave many behind.

*   *   *

The third essential quality of leadership is clarity. Clarity starts with the clarity of mind and sound judgement that arise from emotional awareness and control. A good leader is contemplative, meaning they can be present in the moment and find meaning in experience. Like many others, I have found the practices of meditation and the daily examen to be effective disciplines for a more contemplative approach to life and, as a consequence, leadership. That is to say I find them effective when I practise them and I notice their absence once the errors and misunderstandings pile up after I determine that I am 'too busy'. A stitch in time.

Leadership always has an element of power even when it is grounded solely in the powers of persuasion, but the quest for power over others quickly becomes dangerous, especially if it is divorced from the moral authority that effective leaders require. Leaders need to renounce power for its own sake and discern the power of service. The daily practice of meditation is a simple way to realise this paradox – letting go of power (over others) in order to use it (in the service of others).

When I worked at the Bank of England, I would remind myself each morning of Marcus Aurelius' phrase 'arise to do the work of humankind'. Even when I would occasionally forget, I would be reminded as I entered the Bank of England by the verse from Virgil that framed the doorway into Parlours: *sic vos non vobis*, 'for you but not yours'.

The sense of emptying and ensuing clarity that comes with meditation is helpful because leaders will always find themselves facing multiple problems at the same time. They have to be careful not to bring all those problems with them during every interaction because part of a leader's job is to absorb the stress so that the rest of the organisation can focus. Leaders also need to remember that each of their (many) meetings each day is probably the most important for the others involved. These individuals will carry the experience forward, sharing and even amplifying the values that they discern the leader demonstrating. These tests of authenticity and trust can set in train positive or negative dynamics.

An essential part of clarity is to simplify the complicated, to reduce complex problems to their essentials and then communicate them to your team so that they can be addressed. Say it straight. Say it simply. Say it over.

This was a lesson that it took me years to absorb. My nature is to take a deep dive into analysis to understand an issue. This requires reading widely, speaking to lots of different people and then attempting to synthesise conflicting viewpoints or data. But then having done so, I would be tempted to dump the lot on the audience in an attempt to convince by analytic volume rather than reasoned argument and anecdote. I found over time that while the homework was still essential for trying to come to the right conclusions, people would at best remember the anecdote not the analysis. And I came to admire leaders like Christine Lagarde or Jamie Dimon, who would consistently communicate extremely complex issues with clarity and purpose, but could also act like hyperlinks if you ever wanted to drill down more deeply on a subject.

The best leaders treat their audience with respect. It is particularly important to talk to people, not to be perceived as talking down to them. This was never more important than during the Covid crisis when such fundamental issues were at stake and uncertainty was paramount. Leaders like Jacinda Ardern and Angela Merkel would lay out the information, options and risks as they were then known.

Shortly after imposing a lockdown order, Jacinda Ardern held a Facebook Live event where she clarified points about her government's response and answered questions directly from the audience. She set the tone for the event when she opened by stating that she just wanted 'to check in with everyone'. A month later when easing up lockdown restrictions in Germany, Angela Merkel described how slight increases in the R0 would translate to hospitals quickly becoming overcrowded. Her explanation of the likely consequences of different actions came across as someone sharing insights on the importance of compliance with the remaining regulations as opposed to demanding blind obedience. Neither Ardern nor Merkel went for easy narratives which could later imprison them; instead both highlighted current uncertainties. And they showed empathy with the difficulties people were having and the anxieties that they were experiencing.

When leaders speak, they get the balance right between realism and optimism. They acknowledge uncertainty, mistakes and difficulties, but then give hope that these can be overcome. The engineer of America's Great Society in the 1960s, John Gardner, struck this difficult balance when he said: 'What we have before us are some breathtaking opportunities disguised as insoluble problems.'[44]

Leaders often use narratives to inspire people to act. Consider the difference between an exhortation 'to implement COP 21's Nationally Determined Contributions in a determined fashion' with Emmanuel Macron's simple statement, 'Make no mistake on climate: there is no Plan B because there is no Planet B.' Or the succinct reply of the head of Morgan Stanley, James Gorman, to a question in Congressional testimony about whether climate change really was a risk to financial stability: 'It's hard to have a financial system if you don't have a planet.'

When leaders strike the balance between realism and optimism, the combination of purpose, hope and clarity inspires, unleashing the talent and energy of the organisation. Inspiration is essential because it is impossible for leaders to meet every challenge, see every opportunity or manage every situation by themselves. The highest-performing organisations are those with the highest number of people who are empowered to think as leaders themselves.

During the financial crisis the need for clarity of mind, thought and communication was paramount. In its depth, panic took hold as 'Firmly held truths [were] no longer relied upon. Articles of faith [were] upended. And the very foundations of economies and markets [were] called into question.'[45] The only goal in a panic is to stop it. Leaders do this by, as Napoleon would demand of his generals, 'march[ing] towards the sound of gunfire'. This requires mobilising quickly.

In this spirit, as discussed in Chapter 7, Tim Geithner's refrain was 'Plan beats no plan.' A plan provides the necessary clarity of mind by focusing efforts and uniting people around a common goal. Even a strategy that is half-baked but gets you out of immediate danger is better than waiting for the perfect answer and being annihilated. In my last few weeks at the Bank of England, I gathered our financial stability team to debrief on the disturbing news we had learned at the Saudi Arabian G20 meeting about Covid-19 and to discuss what it could mean for markets and banks. To give a sense of the gravity of the situation, I asked them 'What beats no plan?' I was relieved to hear the resounding response, 'A plan!' And then I asked, 'What beats a plan?' Again, they came straight back, 'A plan that's well executed!' From that point, I knew that at least from the perspective of the financial system, we would be ready for the virus.

Part of the plan to end the financial panic had to include reducing uncertainty over objectives. During the global financial crisis, some fretted that actions to save a crumbling system would encourage reckless behaviour in the future. But Ben Bernanke was clear that invoking moral hazard in the middle of the US financial crisis was misguided and dangerous. Using the power of narrative, he challenged the arguments of the 'moral hazard fundamentalists' in his oft cited and simple hypothetical example: do you let the man who smoked in bed die in the burning house to teach him a lesson? Or do you save him, stop the risk of surrounding houses catching fire and then reprimand him for reckless behaviour?

No discussion of leadership should overlook the importance of competence. Plan beats no plan, but a plan well executed is best of all. Competence doesn't mean getting everything right, but it is important to get more right than wrong. Strategy is an important part of leadership but execution is vital. You need to be able to do what you intend, and your colleagues will remember your deeds more than your words. The leadership expert Veronica Hope Hailey puts it simply: 'you won't be trusted if you are not competent'. And you won't be competent unless you get hard decisions more right than wrong.

Making hard decisions isn't easy by definition. Churchill had many sleepless nights. President Obama observed that decisions wouldn't come to him as President if they weren't difficult. Moreover, there will be strongly held views on many sides of an issue. Process can help reconcile those, but in the end it is important that leaders don't overcompensate and seek to be liked by everyone.

It was President Kennedy's ability to question the received wisdom of his generals that helped resolve the Cuban missile crisis.

Kennedy had read Barbara Tuchman's masterful account *The Guns of August*, which depicted the way European nations, caught up in battle plans and railway timetables, marched straight into the carnage of the First World War. Kennedy saw the parallels with how blockades and threats of pre-emptive military action could easily lead to a nuclear escalation.

Leaders need to be guided by expertise rather than outsource decisions to experts (except in carefully defined spaces consistent with the principles of constrained discretion described in Chapter 4). The intersections of health, social and economic factors during the Covid crisis argued for decision-making processes which brought together a range of different viewpoints. And when you do so, keep in mind where the expertise lies. For example, since everyone communicates, most people, myself included, think they are experts in communications. But it is really only exceptional communications people, like my colleague at the Bank Jenny Scott, who are the experts, as I would be reminded to my benefit when I listened and to my cost when I didn't.

A leader who is focused on achieving their objective under uncertainty or fast-changing circumstances knows they need to be intensely adaptive. As General McChrystal put it, leadership is 'an emergent property that is the product of interactions between leaders and followers, set amidst a range of contextual factors'. Leaders must have the ability to be quiet and to listen in order to recognise that they do not have the right answer. By doing so, they are better able to transfer leadership from one situation to another.

The final essential leadership quality is humility. Recall what I said about this chapter being a target-rich environment?

Good leaders combine personal humility, self-knowledge and the ability to learn. That means admitting mistakes, seeking and accepting feedback and sharing the lessons. When leaders become overconfident (or turn to writing books), they stop learning.

Over time I have learned more than a few lessons (in other words made a lot of mistakes). For example, it is important to admit when you don't know something, especially in finance. Remember, 'If something doesn't make sense, it doesn't make sense.' In the run-up to the financial crisis, I was one of the chorus of economists who worried about 'global imbalances', the combination of a large current account deficit in the US and large surpluses in Asia, particularly China. But while I had identified a symptom, I didn't follow through to the source of the problem. I was worried about the prospect of a sharp move in the US dollar. I didn't follow the money to see how cross-border flows of capital were building up the enormous risks in subprime mortgages and the shadow banking system described in excruciating detail in Chapter 7.

Second, I've learned that it pays to ask what could go wrong, even if steps have been taken to make bad outcomes less likely. Once the financial crisis broke out, a number of authorities came up with a range of explanations for why subprime would be contained. They didn't ask the relevant question about the implications if it wasn't. I still find I need to devote more time to stepping back to imagine different possibilities. In this spirit, policymakers must remain humble as they work to build a more resilient financial system. We must remember that, although we can make financial crises less likely to happen and less severe when they do occur, we cannot abolish them. Something will go wrong again even if we do not know exactly what or precisely when. As discussed in Chapter 8, accepting this means our best strategy is to create an anti-fragile system that can withstand potential shocks when they happen.

Third, I have worked with colleagues, such as Jan Vlieghe on the MPC, who are incredibly disciplined about regularly reviewing their decisions and comparing these assumptions to new information received before taking a fresh decision. This is an excellent practice as it both leans against confirmation biases and promotes continuous learning. But it takes time and a sense of discipline which I haven't always mastered. At the Bank we institutionalised this approach for our forecasts by conducting and publishing an annual assessment of forecast performance and detailing what we got right and what we got wrong, while trying to draw broader lessons.

Leaders need to be humble about success and honest about failure. Admitting mistakes and publicly learning lessons are important parts of being authentic. Being authentic means doing what you say, and letting people know who you are – including what you believe in, what drives you, as well as your strengths and, importantly, your weaknesses. Authenticity is intimately connected with trust. People may not agree with every decision, but they deserve to know why those decisions are made. And decisions will be easier to follow, indeed easier to anticipate, if people know what the leader stands for.

When a leader admits their weaknesses, they recognise that they are on a path of continuous learning and self-improvement. Becoming a leader does not mean the person has made it and has nothing left to learn. Rather leadership is a discipline that involves deliberate practice and continuous learning.

Purpose. Perspective. Clarity. Competence. And humility. Not all of these qualities are ever visible in any leader, certainly never at the same time.

But if you keep them in mind, they will be seeds that the exercise of leadership will germinate. And their growth will benefit both you as the leader and those you lead.

VALUES-BASED LEADERSHIP IN A DISRUPTIVE AGE

Leaders today operate in the face of enormous challenges from a combination of the strains of the ongoing health crisis and the associated economic shock, with longer-term structural challenges from climate change and the Fourth Industrial Revolution. Disguised within each challenge is an enormous opportunity. Leaders today have a chance to plan the future. A decade or so ago, transformative leadership in the UK was to 'make the weather'. Now leaders can literally change the climate. Such ambition is the best of purpose-driven capitalism.

Today's young will assume the mantle of leadership at a time when globalisation of trade and capital is reversing and the Fourth Industrial Revolution is dawning. And at a time when we are learning of the power of networks to divide as well as to connect.

How to lead in such a world?

First, define your purpose and stick to it obsessively. And remember that purpose, including the purpose of business, must be grounded in the objectives of clients, society and humanity. As John Kay has observed, 'Profit is no more the purpose of business than breathing is the purpose of living.' As we will see in the next chapter that means measuring both financial returns and social impact, working with all stakeholders and helping them to succeed.

Second, in a world of division, fusion will bring breakthroughs. Select your teams wisely and recognise that while diversity is a reality, inclusion is a choice. Take it by recruiting widely, set targets for diversity and then exceed them by pursuing deliberate strategies to develop your teams and empower them. How you make decisions is an essential element of building inclusion and maximising impact.

Third, while you should always marshal your facts, you must engage people's intuitions and win their trust in order to convince them. We must all resist the slide into a 'post-truth' society. But while evidence matters hugely, it is seldom enough. Building trust, creating followership and engagement require empathy – the antidote to righteousness. Be open to dialogue and remember Henry Ford's advice that 'if there is any one secret of success, it lies in the ability to get the other person's point of view'. A leader in this disruptive age must not only be able to set their eyes on the horizon, they must see from the periphery. Being able to take the perspective of those on the edge of your organisation, of society, will drive inclusive capitalism.

This underscores that good leadership isn't just effective but ethical. It leads to human flourishing. And that isn't surprising because real human progress is moral progress. Moral progress requires not only values but also virtues. Virtues are elements of character. They are absolutes, not relatives. They occupy the golden mean between two extremes, with the virtue of courage as the middle way between rashness and cowardice.

There are almost as many different schools of virtue as there are of leadership. For example, Aristotle divided virtues into the moral (those that had to do with character) and the intellectual (those that had to do with the mind), whereas Aquinas distinguished the four cardinal virtues on which all other virtues hinge – justice, wisdom, courage and moderation – and theological virtues – faith, hope and charity – through which 'grace perfects nature'.

What virtues have in common is that they can be built through pattern formation, repetition and development. They are like muscles, which grow with their exercise. The Oxford scholar Ed Brooks stresses three familiar virtues as particularly important to moral leadership:

- humility, which points to our intellectual limits and the sometimes radical uncertainty in which we live;
- humanity, which aspires to a feeling of solidarity with those on the periphery; and
- hope, which raises our ambitions for the future.

What should that ambition entail? The next chapter examines how the purpose of companies can be to develop solutions to help achieve what society values, all while helping its employees, suppliers and clients to flourish.

And the penultimate chapter outlines national strategies to achieve society's objectives. The purpose of society can be human flourishing, to have a good life, and to build the common good. The common good should not be confused with the good of the greatest number, but it is rather the good from which no one is excluded. Achieving the common good requires a shared sense of purpose, including the perspective of those on the periphery. With that sense of solidarity we then determine how best to accomplish those goals. The goals, our values, are not priced, but decisions regarding the tools, the mechanisms, to achieve them may well be.

Determining where society wants to go and how to get there will take the type of values-based leadership described in this chapter, the purpose-driven companies outlined in the next and the national strategies outlined in the penultimate chapter.

14

How Purposeful
Companies Create Value

When we work at an organisation, we should be able to answer
some fundamental questions. What is its purpose? Who
owns it? To whom is it responsible? Over what horizon? How
dependent is it on its operating environment? And what contribution does it make to the communities in which it operates?

As we saw in the last chapter, successful leadership imparts a
shared sense of purpose and catalyses action in pursuit of that
objective. Values-based leaders generate the enthusiastic engagement of their colleagues, boards, shareholders and other
stakeholders to achieve a common goal. Their organisations earn
the consent of society, a social licence, to operate.

Purpose is what an organisation stands for, why it does what it
does and what it should be trusted to deliver. Underlying purpose is
a set of values and beliefs that establish the way in which the
company operates. And so it is that the purpose of companies is
always broader than a simple bottom line. Companies have stakeholders – their shareholders, employees, suppliers and customers.
And companies *are* themselves stakeholders. They have a deep
interest in and share responsibility for the economic, social and
environmental systems in which they operate.

Purpose is fundamentally a question of value and values. Is it the
responsibility of a company to create value for its shareholders
alone? Or its stakeholders together? If the latter, how should value,
particularly that which is not priced in any market, be measured?
Through outcomes, processes or a combination of the two? To

what extent does stakeholder value maximisation ultimately lead to the maximisation of returns to shareholders – a divine coincidence of cake and eating? Or should it be recognised (and celebrated) that by honouring society's values some of a company's contributions will accrue to stakeholders other than shareholders and to broader society?

This chapter will examine how purposeful companies measure and create value for their stakeholders and for society. A company with true corporate purpose drives engagement with a broader set of stakeholders by being a *responsible* and responsive employer; through achieving honest, fair and lasting relationships with suppliers and customers across the supply chain; and by being a good corporate citizen making full contributions to society. Corporate purpose embeds solidarity at local, national and, for the largest companies, global levels. And it recognises the need for sustainability across generations.

Companies exist to improve our lives, expand our horizons and solve society's problems, both large and small. Without a vibrant and focused private sector, we cannot build all the infrastructure we need or innovate to solve today's seemingly intractable problems, learn the skills needed to thrive in the Fourth Industrial Revolution or address climate change. To be successful, companies must make our lives better in ways that earn a fair return for their innovation, drive and dynamism. As already noted, John Kay's essential insight is that 'Profit is no more the purpose of business than breathing is the purpose of living.' But just as breathing is essential to living, profit is vital to the delivery of purpose over time. Purpose therefore requires balancing the core values of dynamism, responsibility, fairness, solidarity and sustainability.

And that is never more important than at times of great change.

PURPOSE IS REVEALED AND REINFORCED DURING TIMES OF DISRUPTION

There are many contemporary examples of purpose-driven companies, but to draw out the concept let's cast our minds back a few centuries to the remarkable life of Josiah Wedgwood, a life that testifies to what purpose can accomplish.

Born in 1730 into a family of potters, Josiah Wedgwood was the Steve Jobs of his day, bringing unparalleled innovation and design brilliance to the field of pottery and in the process transforming business practices across all industries. Originally trained as a pottery thrower, Wedgwood contracted polio as a teenager, leaving him unable to operate the throwing wheel and forcing him to concentrate on other aspects of pottery production, in particular the composition of clays and glazes. He took a scientific approach to his work and his notebooks document over 5,000 experiments he conducted searching for optimal production conditions.[1] Later in his life, troubled by the unreliability of oven temperature, he invented a pyrometer that got him elected a member of the prestigious Royal Society.[2]

Wedgwood's experiments resulted in superior products, and he scored lucrative contracts and became a favourite of Queen Charlotte. He could have had a successful business catering to England's elites, but recognising that his innovations had also improved the reliability of production and lowered costs, he expanded his business into new markets.[3] By the end of his life, he had brought fine pottery products to the emerging middle class in England and overseas. In doing this he revolutionised factory production as well as marketing and sales.

All of this would have been enough to establish Wedgwood as one of history's great entrepreneurs, but he was more than that. Wedgwood operated his business at the beginning of the Industrial Revolution. Technological changes were leading to greater prosperity but also gave rise to inhumane and dangerous working conditions. At a time of minimal government regulation, Wedgwood looked after his workers. He built a village alongside his factory,

Etruria, with housing for employees that exceeded standards prevailing at the time.[4] Amenities included a bowling green, public houses and eventually a school where members of the Wedgwood family taught elements of their trade. Wedgwood implemented a sick club scheme at his factory, where employees paid a small portion of their weekly wages into a fund that could be used to support those who had to miss work due to ill health or accident. He was a fierce opponent of foreign outsourcing, and publicly advocated national production despite potential higher costs.[5]

Beyond caring for his workers and community, Wedgwood was a social activist, involved particularly in the movement to end the transatlantic slave trade. In 1787, he produced a medallion for the Committee for the Abolition of the Slave Trade that depicted a slave in chains accompanied by the text 'Am I not a man and a brother?' Wedgwood bore the cost of producing the medallion, and it would go on to become an iconic symbol in the British abolitionist movement.[6]

Wedgwood's example, grounded in his outstanding success as a businessperson, underscores the importance of purpose in an age of tectonic change. We are currently living through a series of transformations that are as far-reaching and disruptive as those in Wedgwood's day, ranging from the new technologies of the Fourth Industrial Revolution to shifting geopolitics that are reshaping the nature of global integration, to the worsening climate crisis and the rapidly changing social norms bringing renewed imperatives for social justice and equity. These changes are influencing virtually every company's strategy, and they will increasingly prompt the question 'what is your company for?'

Into this mix, the Covid crisis has been a major test of stakeholder capitalism. Once the crisis passes, people will judge which companies supported their employees, engaged with their suppliers and customers and pivoted to help society weather this unprecedented shock. To the extent that the Covid crisis reduced the perceived tensions between maximising shareholder value and stakeholder value, it is consistent with the experience of prior crises. These experiences can teach us much about how the values underpinning true corporate purpose can help solve the problems of people and planet.

Consider five lessons from previous financial crises and their relevance today.

Throughout history, crises call into question both how we value and what our values are. Indeed, the first lesson of past crises (as this book has argued) is that they often have value, or rather misvaluation, at their heart.

As we saw in Chapter 7, the global financial crisis was caused in part by the underpricing of risks and the surrendering of supervisory judgement to the perceived wisdom of the market. As reviewed in Chapter 9, the Covid crisis arose partly as a result of years of undervaluing resilience. States failed to protect their citizens from a known risk despite ample and varied warnings. The annual cost of these preparations would have been about one day's worth of the economic output we have lost. As discussed in Chapter 11, the climate crisis is growing because, in the tragedy of the commons, we are not pricing the externalities of pollution and we are effectively ignoring the environmental degradation and species loss, while in the tragedy of the horizon we are undervaluing the future, leaving a tragic legacy for future generations.

Second, crises change strategies. The question is for whose benefit? The joint responsibilities of companies to their stakeholders and as stakeholders in their communities are brought to the fore at times of great change – changes that have been intensified by the Covid crisis. The Covid crisis is leading to a reappraisal of value and values, prompting strategic resets by companies and social resets by countries. A strategic reset because of the accelerated move to e-commerce, e-learning and e-health, the reorientation of supply chains from global and just-in-time to local and just-in-case, the greater consumer caution and the widespread financial restructuring. And a social reset because the crisis forced an appraisal of our values.

During the crisis, we have acted as interdependent communities not independent individuals, with the values of economic dynamism and efficiency, joined by those of solidarity, fairness, responsibility and compassion. The realities of inequality have been exposed, including low-paid key workers, the unequal incidence of the disease, the burdens of unpaid care work and the tragedy of unequal education when it is conducted online. We are all in the same storm, but we are not all in the same boat.

To build a better future, we must learn from our current predicament. The Covid tragedy proves we cannot wish away systemic risks and that we need to invest upfront to avoid disaster down the road. And so it is with climate change, a crisis that involves the entire world, from which no one will be able to self-isolate. Resilience is now highly valued.

Given the shift in economic and social drivers of value, it will be rare for a company's pre-crisis strategy to remain optimal. Covid is demanding a strategic reset for business, with new strategies grounded in purpose to address the most pressing issues for people and planet. Purposeful corporations recognise that the strategic and social resets must be aligned. Their actions will determine whether society can achieve its goals, including a net-zero carbon economy.

The third lesson from past crises is they catalyse efforts to improve reporting of systemic risks. In other words, valuing both risks and resilience. Following the 1929 Wall Street Crash, alongside the sweeping social reforms in Roosevelt's 'New Deal', the Securities and Exchange Commission (SEC) was created with a clear purpose: to protect investors, to maintain fair, orderly and efficient markets and to facilitate capital formation.[7] At the core of delivering its mission was the first common disclosure standard (at the federal level) so that investors could receive 'truthful and uniform' financial data about public securities. By 1936, GAAP accounting was born.

In the immediate aftermath of the global financial crisis, there were several initiatives to improve the disclosure of the types of risks that were its cause. To make derivative markets safer and more transparent, requirements to report trades of OTC derivatives were introduced. To help eliminate risky securitisation and opaque shadow banking, new rules for securitisation and accounting standards now ensure that if a bank has an ongoing relationship with any aspect of the transaction the risk stays on its balance sheet. And a new accounting standard – IFRS 9 – was developed to recognise expected losses, giving a more accurate picture of bank resilience while reducing pro-cyclicality in the system.

If the climate crisis crystallises, we will not get a second chance to put in place the right reporting framework. In this spirit, authorities are acting in advance to ensure stakeholders know the climate-related financial risks that companies are facing and how they are working to manage them. The TCFD, a private-sector-led initiative for disclosure, has become the go-to standard for consistent, comparable and decision-useful information on climate-related financial risks. The push now is to make it mandatory for all public companies.

The fourth common response to crises is to increase resilience. After all, once a crisis reveals vulnerabilities and exposes fragilities, it is only natural to want to come back stronger. Before the global financial crisis, major banks were woefully undercapitalised, with complex business models that relied on the goodwill of markets and, ultimately, the support of taxpayers. Large global banks can now stand on their own with common equity requirements, and buffers are now ten times higher than the pre-crisis standard. Regulation has made banks less complex and more focused. Trading assets have been cut in half, interbank lending is down by one-third and liquidity has increased tenfold since the crisis. And a series of steps are helping to ensure that banks can fail without systemic consequences.

We did not build this strength for its own sake. It's there to be used when needed. This is prudence with a purpose. Resilience with a reason. The resilience of the financial sector has meant finance can be part of the solution to the economic shock associated with Covid.

Now authorities need to apply these lessons to the climate crisis by stress-testing banks and insurers against different climate pathways from a smooth transition to net zero to the catastrophic business as usual. Critically, this will help banks think through potential risks associated with both the transition to net zero and continuing business as usual. With three-quarters of the world's known coal reserves, half of gas reserves and one-third of oil unburnable if we want to keep emissions below 2°C,[8] uncovering information about company exposures to stranded assets will be critical. Climate stress-testing will reveal the financial firms – and by extension the companies – that are preparing for the transition. And it will expose those that have not.

The final lesson from crises past is the need to embed responsibility by re-establishing a sense of purpose in business. The global financial crisis showed what happens when the sense of purpose is lost.

Without a sense of purpose, finance lost track of its core values of fairness, integrity, prudence and responsibility, which eroded the social licence on which markets need to innovate and grow. It is a gross understatement to say this is not a solid foundation for future prosperity and sustainable growth. After the financial crisis, the industry has worked to rediscover its purpose. To move to a world that once again values the future, bankers need to see themselves as custodians of their institutions, improving them before passing them along to their successors. And they have to be grounded in strong connections to their clients and their communities.

Regulations, codes and compensation have their place, but ultimately integrity can neither be bought nor regulated. It must come from within; it must be grounded in values.

As with crises past, the Covid crisis has laid bare failings of the old approach. More positively, it has demonstrated the value of solidarity in our local communities and, largely because of its absence, across the global community. Now as every business is resetting their strategy, their energy, imagination and capital can launch a common approach for sustainable growth.

For companies, that means focusing on measurement, resilience and responsibility to achieve their corporate purpose. For investors it means using this information to identify the leaders and laggards, and to invest money consistent with the values of their clients. And for governments, it means stepping in to turn these nice-to-haves into must-haves by implementing mandatory, comprehensive frameworks where appropriate.

The breadth of these initiatives underscores how purpose-driven companies operate in an ecosystem, where the boundaries of the firm and its relationship with its clients, suppliers, investors, creditors and communities are more complex and permeable than depicted in traditional economics. These realities are critical to how purpose-driven companies can create value. Just as no person is an island, no company can realise its full potential alone.

THE FIRM AS A SERIES OF CONTRACTS VERSUS PURPOSE-DRIVEN COMPANIES AT THE HEART OF AN ECOSYSTEM

The company is a legal structure designed to bring together the different parties to the firm – its employees, investors, customers and suppliers – in the delivery of its corporate purpose. Corporations are institutions with autonomous lives as self-standing legal entities independent of those who work, finance and manage them. The corporate personality is both a legal concept and a lived reality.

The traditional economic view of the firm is that it comprises a series of contracts. The firm is owned by its shareholders. Its purpose is to maximise shareholder value. To do so, shareholders delegate responsibility to professional management, but this creates a principal–agent problem in which the shareholders must monitor management to ensure they are acting in their best interests. An array of governance mechanisms and incentive structures are employed to promote this alignment. The boundary of the firm itself is determined by the trade-off between operating in the market through contracts and within the firm through hierarchies.

Like much of economic theory, each component of this view is satisfyingly simple, the product of a reductionist modelling exercise that makes important insights (such as those around the incentive challenges arising from the principal–agent problem). But the whole is less than the sum of its parts. The view of a company as a 'nexus of contracts' is an incomplete depiction of how companies operate in practice, and, if taken as a guide, it risks forgoing economic value. Over time such a view will undercut social values, including those on which fair and effective markets depend.

Purpose can be used to build trust and motivate employees well beyond monetary incentives. Moreover, this sense of purpose and trust can extend well beyond the boundaries of the firm. As we shall see, companies operate as part of an ecosystem. Their boundaries are permeable and interconnected. And in these connections lies the opportunity to create tremendous value.

Who owns a firm? The answer appears straightforward: shareholders. But shareholders are not owners in the classic sense of ownership. They have no rights of possession or use. They have no more right than other customers to the services of the businesses they 'own'. The company's actions are not the shareholders' responsibilities under limited liability.

Even though English shareholders have more rights than their counterparts in many other jurisdictions, they are not owners; as the Court of Appeal declared in 1948, 'shareholders are not, in the eyes of the law, part owners of the company'.[9] In 2003, the House of Lords reaffirmed that ruling, in unequivocal terms.[10]

As John Kay concludes, 'Who owns a company? The answer is no one does, any more than anyone owns the River Thames, the National Gallery, the streets of London, or the air we breathe. There are many different types of claims, contracts, and obligations in modern economies, and only occasionally are these well described by the term ownership.'[11] And as the management theorist Charles Handy wrote, when we look at the modern corporation 'The myth of ownership gets in the way.'[12] We must look beyond ownership towards the company's objects and purpose.

Shareholders may not be owners in the classic sense but they are the residual claimants in a company. Simply put, they get paid after everyone else – creditors, employees, suppliers and governments (in the form of taxes). This position in the hierarchy has underpinned much of the legal approach to entrenching shareholder primacy.

Whether the shareholders take the most risk is a more open question. As Martin Wolf has argued, employees cannot diversify their exposure to a company.[13] The same truth can hold for key suppliers or communities in which a company is dominant. When this is combined with the doctrine of shareholder primacy, there are incentives for firms and management (if their compensation is heavily weighted towards short-term equity incentives) to take excessive risks.[14]

There is an incentive for shareholders to take on greater risk since their downside is limited (they cannot lose more than all of their money under limited liability), but their upside is unlimited. This shifts risk to other claimants, notably employees and creditors.[15] A similar dynamic holds for externalities, such as pollution.

Purpose was at one time an essential element to corporate formation. When business corporations began in the sixteenth and seventeenth centuries, they were incorporated for an express purpose, such as an infrastructure project or foreign exploration, and were to be dissolved upon completion of their stated task.[16] Incorporation was a privilege not a right, and occurred only when the government or monarch approved of the objective and granted the corporation a charter or other such instrument. The company was conceived as a device to ensure long-term commitment to shared goals and risks, with reciprocal obligations on those engaged in them. For example, the East India Company, England's earliest public company to issue shares to the public as permanent capital, was given the monopoly of English trade in Asia with reciprocal obligations to protect trade along its routes. Early business corporations were thus imbued with a purpose of serving the public good and were in many respects public agencies.[17] Adam Smith believed corporations should be formed only under stringent criteria, including that there was the 'clearest evidence' that they would bring greater utility than ordinary common trade.[18]

Prior to – and for the most part throughout – the Industrial Revolution, a shareholder bought shares in a corporation with an understanding that the money would be directed towards the corporation's stated purpose, and that returns on their investment would come only after the purpose had been realised.[19] This system did not always guarantee ethical outcomes – foreign trading corporations like the East India Company and the Hudson Bay Company were far from moral actors, and corruption and bribery often influenced who received corporate charters – but the corporation's purpose did unite all of a corporation's stakeholders behind an explicit larger goal.

The Industrial Revolution brought profound changes to this system. With more projects to finance and more people with savings to finance them, governments felt pressure to facilitate easier access to capital.[20] In 1844, the UK government passed the Joint Stock Companies Registration and Regulation Act which allowed for incorporation through registration without approval President Andrew Jackson had implemented general inc in the United States the decade before, and France and would follow suit in the decades following.[22] By the begin twentieth century, purpose was not a prerequisite to existence.

To many corporations this change was largely immate they operated. The ease of corporate registration had incorporation of small businesses that resembled partner than large, complex and heavily capitalised ventures.[23] T held entities could operate with the limited number of sl finding common agreement on corporate direction. Pu remained at the heart of many private companies with who owned and controlled them, such as Wedgwood, interest in wider social purpose beyond pure financial larger corporations, which increasingly had hundreds or sands of shareholders, did not have the luxury of forging agreements. And so, with freedom of incorporation in the middle of the nineteenth century, the focus on public purpose gave way to private interest. For many industrial firms in the early twentieth century, family control was diluted by public market capital. Capital-intensive industrial growth was financed, but new challenges from the separation of ownership from the control of firms would emerge.

One such corporation was the Ford Motor Company, founded at the beginning of the twentieth century in Detroit, Michigan. In 1908, Ford released its famous Model T automobile, revolutionising transportation and bringing the company a handsome profit that by 1916 had accumulated and become a $112 million surplus on its balance sheet.[24] Shareholders of the company pushed for a special dividend in order to share in the company's success, but Henry Ford, President of company, instead planned to invest the profits in further expansion of the business. As he declared publicly, 'My ambition is to employ still more men, to spread the benefits of this industrial system to the greatest possible number, to help them build up their lives and their homes. To do this we are putting the greatest share of our profits back in the business.'[25] This rationale did not stop shareholders from pursuing their legal action against Ford Motor Company, asking the courts to order the distribution to shareholders of at least 75 per cent of the accumulated surplus.[26]

While Ford's professed benevolence was at least partially a public relations strategy, it pitted public aims against private gains and resulted in a judicial verdict on the purpose of a corporation. The Michigan Supreme Court sided with the shareholders, going so far as to conclude that 'A business corporation is organized and carried on primarily for the profit of the stockholders. The powers of the directors are to be employed for that end.'[27] The Ford Motor Company was ordered to distribute dividends to its shareholders, though only a fraction of the requested amount, as management retained a degree of discretion as to how to operate the business.

The case of *Dodge v. Ford* is today foundational to the conception of a corporation as being for the primary benefit of the shareholders. The Great Depression and the Second World War would slow the adoption of the shareholder-primacy conception – crises reminding businesses that they do not operate in a vacuum – but it would become the dominant mindset and governing law in Anglo-Saxon countries by the 1970s.[28] Economists associated with the University of Chicago were principal advocates of shareholder primacy, and part of the appeal of the conception is in its economic simplicity. If corporations have a broad public duty it is difficult to measure corporate performance quantitatively. If, however, their duty is to maximise shareholder wealth, performance can be better measured and in turn optimised.[29]

This doctrine is reinforced by the 'agency' problem that arises from the separation of ownership (the shareholders) and control (the company's managers). The risk is that the managers will optimise their personal preferences – including empire building, corporate perquisites, even a quiet life – all at the expense of share-holder returns. The solutions lie in monitoring and alignment of incentives between shareholders and managers via equity grants and stock options. The concerns about the separation of ownership and control were expressed most forcefully by Adolf Berle and Gardiner Means in *The Modern Corporation and Private Property*. Their insights spurred many innovations that have vastly improved the governance and management of companies.

However, when taken to the extreme of shareholder value *über alles*, the alignment of control and shareholder value maximisation can diminish stakeholder value creation while corroding the values of society. Indeed, a truth largely forgotten is that Berle and Means' argument was embedded in a larger vision that 'wanted economic and political power in all its guises to be exercised to benefit the community at large. This pluralist frame of reference subsequently fell out of view, with consequences that reverberate today.'[30] This has included a steady strengthening of shareholder rights.[31]

Shareholder primacy is premised on the idea that shareholders were the owners of the corporation. As Milton Friedman, the most prominent economist of the Chicago school, famously wrote half a century ago:

> a corporate executive is an employee of the owners of the business. He has direct responsibility to his employers. That responsibility is to conduct the business in accordance with their desires, which generally will be to make as much money as possible while conforming to the basic rules of the society, both those embodied in law and those embodied in ethical custom.[32]

Friedman's doctrine has been hugely influential, but its absolutism is based on two false premises. First, in the passage above, Friedman gives himself an out with the addendum that money making should conform 'to the basic rules of the society, both those embodied in law and those embodied *in ethical custom* [emphasis added]'. As we have seen, those ethical customs are not immutable. Indeed, many of the customs necessary to support good market functioning are corroded when financial return becomes disembodied from stakeholders. Friedman only implicitly and tragically acknowledges the importance of such moral sentiments when observing that a company might devote resources to provide amenities to its community (in expectation of returns on attracting employees), and that it could engage in 'hypocritical window dressing' by calling this social responsibility, lest it 'harm the foundations of free society' to admit that this 'fraud' was all in the pursuit of profit alone. This is how corrosion happens and did happen in the ensuing decades.

The second false premise is that shareholders are owners of a corporation rather than its residual claimants. If, as we have seen, shareholders are not owners in the conventional sense, the limits to shareholder primacy become apparent. Lynn Stout, professor at Cornell Law School, pointed out that what shareholders own are the shares themselves, which are a type of contract that gives them specific and limited legal rights.[33] They thus have a contractual relationship with the corporation that in many ways parallels the corporation's relationship with bondholders, suppliers, employees and consumers.[34] They are no more than a corporation's residual claimants – they get paid after everyone else. In taking on this risk, they rightly expect a return, but they are not entitled to one above all else. Shareholders are one of many stakeholders and the duty of directors to maximise shareholder wealth cannot be sustained under an idea of ownership.

Corporations own themselves, and central to British company law (since the nineteenth century) and American company law is the doctrine of corporate personality. The company is an entity independent of its managers, shareholders, employees and creditors. Its directors thus serve *its* interests; they are not merely agents working on behalf of shareholders.

Due in part to these realities, the Supreme Court of Canada rejected shareholder primacy in two prominent cases in the early 2000s, instead holding that the duties of directors were to uphold the best interests of the corporation, which can be determined in relation to the interests of a broad range of stakeholders.[35] France never adopted shareholder primacy, and a 2018 report commissioned by its government reaffirmed this position and recommended reinvigorating corporate purpose beyond mere wealth generation.[36]

The report led to meaningful legal reforms that, among other changes, require French corporations to consider the social and environmental implications of business activity.[37] In Germany, up to 50 per cent of a corporation's supervisory board is elected by employees of the corporation not the shareholders, embedding a stakeholder conception into corporate structure.

Yet shareholder primacy remains deeply rooted in conceptions of corporate law in the UK and in the state of Delaware – where the majority of large US corporations are registered. In the UK, the Companies Act 2006 reflects a shareholder-centric perspective by stating (in Section 172) that the duty of the director is 'to promote the success of the company for the benefit of its members'.[38] These are defined elsewhere in the Act as consisting almost entirely of shareholders.[39] In Delaware, judges have formulated directorial duty in similar terms to the UK law.[40] Summarising the state of Delaware law in 2015, the then Chief Justice of the Delaware Supreme Court wrote that 'directors must make stockholder welfare their sole end'.[41] A corporation's purpose in both jurisdictions is maximisation of shareholder wealth.

Describing how the purpose of a corporation is conceived, however, is an attempt to hit a moving target. While shareholder primacy is vital to understanding how the law in the UK and Delaware has been formulated over the past century, it has begun to lose its influence. Companies are realising that the value of a corporation comes from a comprehensive balancing of a variety of interests and not a narrow-minded focus on share price. This view, often referred to as enlightened shareholder value, holds that shareholder wealth is maximised when other stakeholders are considered and the corporation works with a defined purpose that goes beyond profit. As both UK and Delaware law afford management substantial deference in the business decisions they make, enlightened shareholder value permits purpose-driven companies to operate within the confines of corporate law as all acts are still ultimately for the benefit of the shareholder. But the emphasis is increasingly being placed on serving the corporation generally, and with it the interests of a broader set of stakeholders more immediately and clearly.

For example, the concept of enlightened shareholder value was central to the reforms of the UK Companies Act in 2006. As mentioned above, the duties of directors are to serve the interests of shareholders, first and foremost, but also to 'have regard' to wider interests, including those of employees, customers, suppliers and the wider community. The precise role of the 'have regard' provision has been left open to interpretation. With time, it has increasingly been supported by public accountability, with annual reporting (through sustainability or impact reports) on how companies were meeting their wider interests. This process, arguably reinforced by the crises of value(s) that this book has chronicled, is helping rebalance corporate purpose in the interests of broader stakeholders.

In recent years, the idea has reached a tipping point and is becoming dominant. In 2019, a total of 181 CEOs from some of America's largest and most influential corporations endorsed a statement by the Business Roundtable rejecting the idea that corporations had any one principal aim. The statement acknowledged that generating long-term value to shareholders was a commitment, but placed it alongside four other commitments to different stakeholders, in addition to each business's specific corporate purpose. In the weeks following, several prominent US law firms released public memos cautiously supporting the legality of the statement by relying on enlightened shareholder value and deference to managerial decisions.[42] The memo issued by Wachtell, Lipton, Rosen & Katz LLP – often cited as the most profitable law firm in the world – boldly stated that 'Delaware law does not enshrine a principle of shareholder primacy.'[43]

Several Delaware judicial decisions say otherwise, but this inconsistency with decades of case law is perhaps not surprising. Corporate law is not an inviolable truth, but rather a delayed reflection of how we in society conceive of corporate purpose. William T. Allen, Chancellor of the Delaware Court of Chancery in the early 1990s, expressed this idea eloquently when he wrote:

> in defining what we suppose a public corporation to be, we implicitly express our view of the nature and purpose of our social life. Since we do disagree on that, our law of corporate

entities is bound itself to be contentious and controversial. It will be worked out, not deduced. In this process, efficiency concerns, ideology, and interest group politics will commingle with history ... to produce an answer that will hold for here and now, only to be torn by some future stress and to be reformulated once more.[44]

We are once again in a period of tearing and reformulation, brought on by the stresses of cumulative crises and the prospects of seizing new opportunities. The rising doctrine is enlightened shareholder value, and there is pressure for even greater change. Enlightened shareholder value allows for consideration of other stakeholders, but it is still a form of shareholder primacy. Corporate law continues to prohibit directors from acting at the ultimate expense of shareholders for achievement of corporate purpose. The legality of the varying commitments pledged by the CEOs in the Business Roundtable statement rests on the assumption that what is good for the corporation, one stakeholder group or society more broadly will always end up being good for the shareholder (in divine coincidence, as discussed in the next chapter). As will be discussed, this is often the case, but it will not necessarily always be the case. At times, large positive gains could accrue to society if small sacrifices were made on behalf of shareholders.

Because of this many advocate changes in UK and US corporate law that would better balance profit and purpose as dual aims of a corporation.[45] Such changes would align the law with society's growing expectation of corporations to care for more than maximisation of profit, and acknowledge the multifaceted nature of a firm, its relationship with its stakeholders and how those relationships could be developed to mutual advantage.

Every company operates in an ecosystem. The boundaries between the firm and its suppliers, customers and community are both real and permeable. Purpose can leverage these relationships to mutual advantage. Not only can purpose create a common cause and values that bind a firm together,[46] it can inspire and invigorate all members of its community. A clear purpose, commonly understood, can help convince stakeholders that their interests are being served in the trade-offs and the distribution of investments and returns that are needed to create value.[47] Such trust can help create the perspective needed for long-term value creation.

Purpose, values and trust are not natural concepts for economists. The classic economic view, developed by Nobel laureate Ronald Coase, is that a company is a network of contracts in which everyone – owners, managers and workers – responds rationally to incentives. According to Coase's *The Nature of the Firm*, the boundaries of the firm are defined by the differences in costs of providing a good or service through the market or a firm.[48] Market transactions bear the costs of searching and gathering information, as well as of bargaining, policing and enforcement. Internalising these transactions within firms saves cost but at the expense of span of control, complexity and diseconomies of scale. The boundary of the firm is determined by the balance of these factors, with those activities that can be performed more efficiently and best done by command and control occurring within firms and the rest mediated through markets.

A strict interpretation of this approach misses how shared purpose can reduce transaction costs allowing activities outside the firm to become shared investments that advance the firm's purpose, reinforcing its profitability and creating shared value. Shared purpose can alter the boundary of the firm (while increasing its ability to create value) by lowering transaction costs in market relationships as well as by making larger and more complex corporate entities possible. Confidence in shared purpose reduces the need for costly, fully complete contracts with suppliers and customers. At the same time, clarity of purpose within organisations, reinforced by strong internal culture, can lead to a type of continuous innovation that turns good companies into great ones.

This is important because, not for the first time, simple theoretical economic models can be poor guides to business in practice. A contractual model is only as good as the contracts, which in practice can be incomplete, difficult to enforce and subject to default. The assumption that human incentives will be solely guided by contractual terms is belied by the realities of people's behaviours in a wide range of economic circumstances. Moreover, different parties have different time horizons and interests, which frustrate the achievement of optimal outcomes. As Martin Wolf argues, 'If the rationale for the corporation is to substitute relational contracts, and so trust, for explicit contracts, and so enforcement, one cannot ignore this in deciding what businesses are for and who should control them.'[49]

The crucial insights of principal–agent theory are not limited to the need to align incentives of shareholders and management but extend to similar challenges between directors, management and employees as well as between companies and their suppliers and communities. When time horizons differ, there will always be incentives for one party to promise one thing and then renege. As we saw in Chapter 4, this is one of the classic motivations for delegated authority to central banks. And even that elegant solution has its limitations, underlining the importance of a shared mission and values.

A strong corporate culture is part of the solution to the problems of incomplete contracts and imperfect incentives. A strong corporate culture encourages stakeholders to internalise the behaviours firms want to create and sustain. In particular, purpose is indispensable to a culture of integrity. As we have seen, trust cannot be achieved merely by asserting rules and following protocols, but rather it is earned by multiple social interactions that reinforce behaviours and values. What are variously termed moral sentiments, social memes or behavioural cascades matter.

Thus purpose operates on a number of planes. First, internally, it creates the necessary social capital within the firm to underwrite foundations of value creation: tightly functioning teams, and high employee participation and engagement. Second, externally, it operates as a means of generating focus on customer service and alignment. The company's external focus relates to the traditional purpose of a company: to serve its customers.[50] If a firm does this well, it generates customer loyalty, and with time the consumer will become a stakeholder, reinforcing trust, good faith and fair dealing. Third, purpose operates as a social narrative, in communities and societies beyond the firm, helping to create and sustain the firm's social licence to operate. At the highest level, purpose captures the moral contribution of companies to the betterment of the world now and in the future.

The economy does not comprise simple islands of profit-maximising individuals who come together temporarily through a web of contracts. Companies are the engine of value creation in a modern economy. They are complex organisations. Companies bring people together to act collectively, with their motives empowered and their actions coordinated by their companies' purpose.

That purpose is not simply to maximise value for one of the stakeholders – the shareholders. Profit is essential but it must be achieved in a manner that creates shared value for all stakeholders. Nor is the purpose of business to maximise the returns to any other stakeholder group, such as employees. A company's highest purpose is to provide solutions, in a profitable manner, and contribute in its own way to the betterment of society.

To be successful, a company needs purpose and to deliver that purpose it must balance competing interests among stakeholders, just as an individual must in the pursuit of Aristotle's good life.[51] A firm is more than a nexus of contracts. It is a real corporate personality. The successful firm adds value in an economic sense because it is more than the sum of its parts. The extent to which the firm succeeds depends on its distinctive set of capabilities that generate its competitive advantage. And those advantages rest importantly on the firm's stakeholders, a foundation that can be strengthened by shared purpose and the creation of social value. As we shall see, these links are at the core of successful impact investing.

DELIVERING CORPORATE PURPOSE AND SUSTAINABLE VALUE CREATION

Having settled on a defined and motivating purpose, the essential question is how to deliver it. The short answer is that purpose must be integrated into every aspect of a company. Achieving a company's purpose starts with the right governance and flows through to strategy, the alignment of management incentives, the empowerment of employees and full engagement with all stakeholders.

The fundamental challenge for modern corporate governance is to translate purpose into practice. That means creating a strategy that integrates shareholder and stakeholder value, aligns managerial interests with the company's core purpose and establishes accountability to a range of stakeholders through appropriate board structures. Boards and management should agree the set of values necessary to deliver purpose and embed them in their company culture.

Once it is recognised that maximising (short-term) shareholder returns is no longer the sole aim of a corporation, management and directors need to reformulate how they measure success. Value creation must be assessed relative to the company's stated purpose. To be effective, the relevant environmental, social and governance (ESG) factors (described in the next chapter) must be fully integrated and internalised into governance, strategy, operations and performance management rather than segmented and *de facto* subordinated as matters of corporate social responsibility (CSR). Every board committee should have the relevant ESG factors integrated into their work, and the full board should be informed on how ESG issues affect the company's risk management.[52]

For example, the Anglo-Dutch food conglomerate Unilever launched its Sustainable Living Plan (USLP) in 2010, one that included goals and specific targets related to improving health and wellbeing, reducing environmental impact and enhancing livelihoods. These specific targets are measured and reported each year in annual reports – overseen by the board's Disclosure Committee – with select indicators verified by a third-party accounting firm overseen by the board's Audit Committee.[53] Progress and developments related to the USLP are tracked by the board's Corporate Responsibility Committee, which additionally monitors potential risks and works to protect and enhance the Unilever brand.[54] The Compensation Committee meanwhile has integrated USLP targets into the executive bonus pay structure.[55] Through these mechanisms board oversight becomes centred around ensuring the company's operations are in line with its corporate purpose.

Additionally, a critical aspect of a board's supervisory role is challenging and supporting management to allocate capital to intangible drivers of long-term value such as research and innovation, respect for human rights, employee wellbeing, talent development, reinforcing corporate culture, strengthening external stakeholder relationships and building public trust.[56] These efforts should be tracked, and their effectiveness assessed through appropriate metrics and over sufficiently long time horizons.

The composition of the board and the agenda of board meetings need to reflect this commitment to the corporate purpose.[57] This may require an overhaul of board nomination criteria to ensure adequate representation of diverse viewpoints and disciplines. In adapting to a purpose-oriented structure, boards must rigorously reassess their capabilities and priorities for oversight and governance. Many necessary changes will go against decades of established norms, and boards need to think critically about the way they are structured and why.

Pursuing corporate purpose when there is clear and complete alignment with shareholder value creation is, of course, straightforward. And so it is under enlightened shareholder value where management pursues purpose – provided there is a reasonable belief that value to the shareholder will eventually accrue. This would sensibly take into account the maintenance of public trust and social licence as well as the ability of the company to attract, retain and empower the best people over time. In these cases, purpose is prominent in internal and external communications and integrated in company governance, strategy and performance management.

Some companies take steps to commit to purpose more fundamentally by embedding it in their legal structure. The easiest way to do so is by including purpose within their governing documents, namely their articles of association (UK and most of the Commonwealth) or articles of incorporation (US and Canada). These are the constitutions of a company, laying out crucial information like the company's name, share structure and voting rights. Some jurisdictions, like Delaware, still require articles of incorporation to include the purpose of the corporation, a relic from the days when incorporation was dependent on the corporation's larger social contribution, although this requirement has been watered down to the point it has become a meaningless exercise. While Facebook's stated mission for instance is 'to build community and bring the world closer together', its much less compelling legal purpose is 'to engage in any lawful act or activity for which corporations may be organized under the Delaware General Corporation Law'.[58]

More in the spirit of the law, many companies have adopted more specific purpose within their Articles. Patagonia, for instance, a world leader in CSR, amended its Articles in 2012 to include six specific benefit purposes, including giving 1 per cent of its net revenue to promote environmental conservation and sustainability, building the best product with no unnecessary harm and providing a supportive work environment to its employees.[59] These commitments are now part of the company's constitution and set the agenda for management decision making. Governing documents are established at the time of incorporation but can be amended at any time, usually requiring the approval of a supermajority of shareholders.[60]

Companies can go further by enshrining their purpose explicitly in their corporate structure. In the United States, many state governments have facilitated this trend by creating different types of corporations beyond the standard for-profit entity. These corporate types, including benefit corporations, social purpose corporations and flexible purpose corporations, signal to shareholders and other stakeholders about the balance of the corporation's objectives and allow management more latitude in considering factors beyond maximising shareholder returns. In 2019, France followed suit and created a new corporate type, allowing corporations to become *entreprises à mission*. Different corporate types have not generally been the preferred solution in the Commonwealth, although the Canadian province of British Columbia has created a benefit corporation designation.

Changing the corporate structure, through altering the type of corporation or adding a specific purpose in core governing documents, rises above the legal debate about the general purpose of corporations and enables corporations to pursue broader public aims. They allow companies to go beyond divine coincidence or enlightened shareholder value doctrines in which all stakeholder benefits are deemed worthy if and only if they ultimately enhance shareholder value.

This clarity is why such an explicit change in corporate structure is a requirement of many third-party auditing systems that focus on social benefit, the best known of which is the B Corp certification organised by the non-profit B Lab. B Corps are businesses that meet verified metrics in social and environmental performance, public transparency and legal accountability, and which, in doing so, balance purpose and profit. In order to become certified, a B Corp must alter its legal structure to acknowledge this balancing, with B Lab specifying the changes that must be made for each jurisdiction. At a minimum, B Lab usually requires a corporation's Articles to state that the purpose of the corporation is to have a positive impact on society and the environment. The B Lab assesses companies on a wide variety of indicators before certifying and then reassesses them every three years.

There are currently over 2,500 B Corp certified entities in over fifty countries and many more working to join this group.[61] A recent, prominent example is Danone, the multinational food corporation with revenue of US$30 billion. Over the past few years Danone has taken steps to define its corporate purpose beyond shareholder value. In 2017, for instance, it unveiled its new corporate signature, 'One planet. One health', and made a commitment to nurturing healthier and more sustainable eating habits across the globe.[62] The company is focused on regenerative agriculture and soil health and has made substantial efforts to package its products in materials that are reusable, recyclable or compostable.[63] Danone has enshrined its purpose in its corporate structure, subsidiary by subsidiary. For instance, Danone Canada's articles of incorporation now require consideration of employees, community and the environment, while Alpro, a European plant-based food subsidiary, has a governance structure that requires stakeholder consideration.[64] In June 2020, the parent corporation itself altered its legal structure, to become the first large listed company in France to adopt the *entreprise à mission* designation. As part of the change, Danone's corporate by-laws now include a corporate mission of bringing 'health through food'.[65] Speaking to the 99 per cent of shareholders who voted for the change, CEO Emmanuel Faber praised the outcome as having 'toppled the statue of Milton Friedman'.[66]

While a company's strategy will evolve with new information and shifting competitive forces, its reason for being, the company's purpose, should remain constant. For purpose to have meaning it has to connect directly to strategy and the difficult choices a company needs to make to meet the challenges and seize the opportunities during this period of great change. As the Enacting Purpose Initiative observes, there is often too much purpose as culture and not enough purpose as strategy.[67]

It is the responsibility of management and boards to ensure that their strategic priorities and capital allocation support the key drivers of sustainable, long-term value creation. In the context of rapid technological and social change, this requires determined focus on intangibles such as corporate culture, talent development, research and development, and branding.

Stakeholders, particularly shareholders, need to be able to judge whether this alignment of strategy with purpose exists. In his annual letter to CEOs, Larry Fink, the CEO of the world's largest asset manager, emphasised that BlackRock expects companies to issue an annual strategic framework to shareholders that has been approved by the board.[68] Such a framework should include how the business 'is navigating the competitive landscape, how it is innovating, how it is adapting to technological disruption or geopolitical events, where it is investing and how it is developing its talent'.[69] It should set out the metrics that management uses to gauge progress and detail how these influence management incentives and compensation.

Like a growing number of investors, BlackRock has expressly made the connection between purpose and profit, stating that as an investor it expects the management of companies to be able to explain how the company's strategic framework connects to the broader corporate purpose.[70] As Fink emphasises:

> when a company truly understands and expresses its purpose, it
> functions with the focus and strategic discipline that drive long-
> term profitability. Purpose unifies management, employees, and
> communities. It drives ethical behavior and creates an essential
> check on actions that go against the best interests of
> stakeholders.[71]

To be clear, in creating value for stakeholders, that strategy must be profitable over time. Profits and purpose are inextricably linked. Profits are essential if a company is to serve all of its stakeholders over time – not only shareholders, but also employees, customers and communities. Once again, the value of dynamism is essential for value creation.

The horizon and sustainability of profits, of course, matter. Long-term strategies will, by definition, avoid any actions that seek temporary gains to the detriment of future value. They are a bridge between an overarching purpose and day-to-day operations, helping guide management in resisting the siren call of maximising the next quarter's results.

Those who lead a company should reap the rewards – and bear the consequences – of their actions. However, as we have seen, the separation of ownership and control of modern corporations makes this difficult.

To overcome this, boards have developed complex performance-based metrics and bonus structures for executive management that seek to align incentives with value creation. One challenge is that existing compensation packages often incentivise the wrong type of actions. Most prominently, the common timeframe for performance-based vesting in executive compensation packages is one to three years, yet research indicates that the market may take five years to incorporate fully information about intangible investments into the share price.[72] Executives therefore who seek to invest in research and development or improved employee working conditions may well be acting against their narrow self-interest.

The strong links between bonuses and other variable pay structures and short-term revenue gains have been widely recognised as contributing to the 2008 financial crisis.[73] As explained in Chapter 8, the compensation rules in UK financial services now align risk and reward, with a significant proportion of variable compensation deferred for a period of seven years to ensure it can be clawed back over the timescales it generally takes for undisclosed risks or conduct issues to come to light. This alignment has been reinforced through linkages to industry standards and good governance under the Senior Managers Regime.

Executive compensation needs to be reconfigured to align incentives with long-term and sustainable value creation. Annual performance-based bonuses should be replaced by – or play a secondary role to – equity and debt packages that through vesting structure and sales restrictions extend the executive's interest in the company over a period of at least five to seven years – with the specific timeframe tailored to the industry.[74]

Where performance-based metrics are used, they should align with corporate purpose and be based on both financial and non-financial metrics, avoiding excessive focus on a sole dimension of performance.[75] Incentives should be adjusted to account for the types of risk the company faces – including reputational and compliance risk.[76] Any annual monetary bonuses should be tied to a diverse scorecard, and such metrics should be incorporated into malus and clawback clauses that allow boards to reduce incentives prior to vesting or demand the return of other compensation in cases where the executive did not meet defined expectations or engaged in misconduct.

Incorporating non-financial metrics into executive compensation is at present not a common practice, with only 9 per cent of the companies contained in the Financial Times Stock Exchange All-World Index linking executive pay to ESG criteria.[77] Unilever's compensation committee has integrated non-financial indicators into the company's remuneration structure through its Management Co-Investment Plan, with sustainability factors measured by the company's Sustainability Progress Index and weighted at 25 per cent.[78] The aluminium producer Alcoa has been lauded for linking 30 per cent of its annual incentive compensation to non-financial metrics, though this is somewhat less than meets the eye. Half of this 30 per cent is related to workplace safety – as measured by fatalities and serious injuries – and just 5 per cent linked to the company's environmental targets.[79] Five per cent is modest for an extractive company whose societal impact is by and large environmental. Moreover, executives can score above 100 per cent in certain categories and so compensate for poor performance in sustainability. Thus while in 2019 the company failed to meet its emissions targets – costing executives 5 per cent of their bonus – they more than made up for this by scoring 148 per cent in the 'free cash flow' category.[80] The company also failed to meet even the minimum threshold for its diversity targets, but in the end executives received over 90 per cent of their incentive compensation for the year.

These examples underscore that to be a driver of change executive compensation structures need to rise above superficial incorporation of ESG factors and create meaningful incentives.

Companies must define the measures of performance that they use to evaluate their success in delivering their purpose. These should be published and their attainment should be material to the measure of management performance and their compensation. Non-financial metrics need to be treated by boards as sales, cash flow or returns metrics. Internally, balanced scorecards and non-financial metrics should help determine executive performance appraisals.

Alignment of compensation is part of a broader need to assign responsibility. The management of a company should feel personal responsibility for the impacts of the corporation on its stakeholders. Boards are responsible for internalising material ESG factors in enterprise risk management in recognition of their link to material operational, financial, reputational and regulatory risks that a company may face. There should be clear lines of accountability for managing these risks, with specific senior managers reporting to the relevant board committees.

Executive management is ultimately only a fraction of a corporation's workforce. For purpose to be embedded within a corporation and its operations, employees need to align their performance with the broader goals of the corporation and conduct their roles with professionalism and engagement. This is easiest when employees can focus on their jobs because they are compensated fairly, have adequate resources and a constructive work environment. The particulars of a good work environment will look different for every company and position, but the basics will not; all employees should be treated with dignity and respect and be free from intimidation and harassment.

Companies should reward such professionalism. High-performing employees should be recognised, and a company should have a strong record of internal promotions. To assist with internal advancement, career development opportunities should be available for all employees regardless of where they fit within the company's structure. Management at all times should be asking, 'What skills are we going to need in future and how can we invest in them now?'

Through fair treatment and work connected to a meaningful corporate purpose, employees will be motivated and see themselves as custodians of the corporation who have a responsibility towards it and its success. The transition of Danone and its subsidiaries to benefit corporation structures, for instance, has in part relied on employee volunteers who were willing to take the time and energy to pioneer the benefit transition process within Danone.[81]

In turn, this energy and motivation translates to corporate value. Toyota's rising success in the late 1980s, as an example, has been attributed to an engaged workforce who were treated as valuable members of the corporate team.[82] By developing vocation, workers feel a sense of duty to understand and uphold the ethics of their profession. These ethics may be codified in standards or even regulations or may be described in a voluntary industry code or internal employer policy. The point is not whether the standards are legally binding, but whether workers look to them for guidance in difficult situations. This is more likely when people take pride in where they work. Engaged employees can help a company address issues proactively and crowdsource solutions. Being a responsible and responsive employer prevents small problems from festering into firm-wide crises.

*   *   *

Engaging all stakeholders is critical in ensuring that performance is aligned with purpose and that unintended consequences or unexpected events are taken into account in decision making. Suppliers and customers need to be engaged with honestly and fairly, with an emphasis on developing a sustainable business model. Understanding how corporate purpose can serve customers can drive innovation and keep the company competitive.[83]

Companies should engage in cooperative efforts to strengthen the communities in which they operate, both geographically and at an industry level. Good corporate citizens make a full contribution to society, and at the very least avoid causing harm by being aware of their impacts and responding accordingly. Large corporations will need to have an eye to the global community as well, and should live up to the power that they possess in acting as a guardian of the global commons.

Companies also need to act with consideration to future generations, who will always be underrepresented in engagement but whose needs will often be the most at risk. In doing so companies need to internalise that they have a duty to protect the natural world, and invest in developing skills, knowledge and understanding, not just within their company but within wider society.

Finally, purposeful companies need to practise smart transparency to open up a constant, two-way flow of information between them and stakeholders. Transparency enables stakeholders to assess performance, forecast its trajectory and critically evaluate when outcomes have deviated from stated intentions.

Where possible information disclosure should be standardised and allow for ease of comprehension and comparison. Commitment to standardised reporting reduces the likelihood of corporations attempting to exclude or obfuscate unfavourable information. Such a user-centred approach to disclosure acknowledges that stakeholders care about access to information, but do not necessarily have the time or resources to undertake a complex analysis.

There is a growing imperative to prepare a company's mainstream financial reports in an integrated fashion by combining standard financial reporting with reporting on material ESG risks and opportunities. The increased materiality of these factors requires well-governed companies to reflect them in mainstream disclosures and to ensure greater public transparency and accountability to investors and other stakeholders by setting public targets, providing independent assurance on performance against these targets and analysis of relevant risks and opportunities. Such an approach is at the heart of the TCFD recommendations on climate (discussed in Chapters 11 and 15). A major initiative of the International Business Council of the World Economic Forum working in concert with the major accounting firms is broadening this approach to a core set of ESG metrics.

DOING WELL BY DOING GOOD: EVIDENCE ON PERFORMANCE AND INVESTING FOR PURPOSE

There is a growing body of evidence that indicates purpose and a commitment to values will help and not hurt a company's bottom line. A 2015 meta-analysis of over 2,200 studies published since the 1970s found that 90 per cent of studies reported a non-negative relationship between environmental, social and governance criteria and financial performance, with 63 per cent reporting a positive relationship.[84]

In particular, there is evidence that strong financial performance is aided by a focus on ESG criteria that are material to the business industry. When resource companies care about the environment and financial institutions care about governance, positive effects are realised. A 2016 study found that when companies had high investment in the issues material to their industry and low investment in issues immaterial to their industry, they outperformed the market by 4.83 per cent.[85] In contrast, companies that failed to invest significantly in material ESG issues fared worse than the market.

Furthermore, the evidence suggests that companies must meaningfully tackle the issues relevant to their industries in order to see benefits. Values advertised by businesses on their website or in annual reports have not been shown to contribute to firm performance, but the values noticed by employees – who work for the company day in and day out – do matter. Companies whose employees report that management's actions matched its words and that management was honest and ethical in its business practices are more profitable.[86] Likewise, companies whose mid-level employees can identify a strong clarity of purpose in the company's work have been shown to experience better financial performance.[87]

An obvious reason for purpose to translate into profit is the reduction of risk. Resource companies, for example, that are environmentally conscious reduce the likelihood of costly mistakes like oil spills and litigation concerning environmental damage. By investing in the issues material to their industry, companies are more likely to maintain their social licence to operate and avoid boycotts that stem from egregious corporate practices. ESG factors when mismanaged can destroy reputation and value, leaving a previously well-performing company suddenly in the red. A study from 2015 found that a one-standard-deviation increase in a firm's CSR score was associated with a firm beta – a standard measure of a stock's volatility – that was 4 per cent lower than the sample mean.[88]

Another reason is that strong commitment to a socially driven purpose attracts and retains top talent. Patagonia gives 1 per cent of its revenue to the planet and prioritises sustainable consumerism and in return it gets 9,000 applications for every internship position it offers, and high retention rates in permanent positions.[89] Furthermore, those showing up for work are less likely to coast on autopilot when they are motivated by intrinsic value and not merely financial gain. As explained by Rebecca Henderson, 'The sense of being part of something greater than yourself can lead to high levels of engagement, high levels of creativity, and the willingness to partner across functional and product boundaries within a company, which are hugely powerful.'[90] This effect can be material. Companies listed in the 100 Best Companies to Work For in America generated returns 3.8 per cent above the benchmark between 1984 and 2011 when controlling for market performance and other risk factors.[91]

Earned social capital also helps corporations weather – and perhaps sometimes thrive in – times of crisis. An analysis of performance during and in the wake of the 2008 financial crisis found that high-CSR firms had crisis-period stock returns 4 to 5 per cent higher than low-CSR firms.[92] In addition, companies can leave a crisis period having increased their social capital by focusing on purpose over profit. Questions will be asked post-Covid about which companies stepped up and which stepped back? Who hoarded and who acted in solidarity with their stakeholders?

Finally, a sense of purpose is crucial to innovation. A study by the *Harvard Business Review* analysed the purpose of hundreds of corporations and defined them as either prioritisers (which already had a clearly articulated and understood purpose), developers (which do not yet have a clearly articulated purpose but are working to develop one) and laggards (which have not yet begun to develop or even think about purpose).[93] The 39 per cent deemed to be prioritisers not only reported higher sales growth, but also reported expanding more readily into new markets and a focus on continuous transformation. Half of prioritisers said their organisation had made a change in strategy development over the past three years based on purpose, and a third said purpose had propelled shifts in the business model as well as product and service development. Conversely, 42 per cent of laggards reported flat or declining revenue over the past three years, and only 13 per cent reported being successful at innovation and transformation.

Corporate purpose thus reduces risk, inspires employees, provides guidance in uncertain times and spurs innovation. In a comprehensive review of the existing literature, the Big Innovation Centre's interim report on 'The Purposeful Company' found 'impressive empirical support – even allowing for qualifications and unanswered questions – for the proposition that purposefulness has beneficial effects across the spectrum of business outcomes'.[94] The report's authors concluded that the evidence suggests that investment in purposefulness could be worth up to 6 to 7 per cent, or up to £130 billion a year in increased stock market capitalisation in the UK.[95]

CONCLUSION: BUILDING
DYNAMIC PURPOSE

In promoting corporate purpose, the quest for profit must not be relegated to a secondary role but must be one of equal import. Profit is vital to companies and essential for societies. Profits allow companies to function and to build. The prospect of a return helps incentivise people to invest their money and time in new ventures. Capital is put to work, innovating and building a better tomorrow. Good ideas flourish while bad ideas are tested and then discarded.

When this 'creative gale' is anchored in purpose, in solving problems of people and planet, this pursuit of profit improves lives at an astonishing rate. Dynamism manifests as the continual pursuit for the faster, the better, the more affordable, the more sustainable.

This dynamism must continue. Many of the problems in society today – from our searing inequalities to our continued, destructive dependence on fossil fuels – are the result of a misplaced acceptance of the status quo. More fundamentally, they are the result of not first expressing and then pursuing our values. With our challenges laid bare by the triple crises of credit, Covid and climate, now is the time for companies to define and pursue their purpose.

As the American entrepreneur Marc Andreessen has argued, the solution to the problems we face is to create and build.[96] We need new infrastructure, new modes of learning, new manufacturing systems, new medicines and new forms of energy. The public sector will provide the foundations to much of this development, but the private sector's ability to finance, explore and operationalise will be the driving force. To build a better tomorrow, we need companies imbued with purpose and motivated by profit. Their activities will produce a shared value that accrues to the shareholders as well as to employees, customers, suppliers and the wider community. If Josiah Wedgwood could manage this balance in the eighteenth century, surely his modern successors can too with even greater impact.

Investors have a critical role to play in this dynamic. They too need to define and pursue their purpose. Nowhere is that more important than with respect to climate change. Let's now turn to how investors can measure, invest and build value(s).

Investing for Value(s)

THE RISE AND RISE OF ESG

This book has argued that a common cause of the three crises of credit, climate and Covid is how we measure value. Indeed, responses to past crises have usually included improvements in the way we measure the impacts of companies and the risks that they face. Following the crash of 1929, standardised accounting practices, US GAAP, were created. In the wake of the global financial crisis, there have been a series of measures to improve the reporting of risks and exposures of banks. It is now imperative that mandatory reporting of climate-related financial risks is instituted so capitalism can help solve the climate crisis. In parallel, the spread of impact investing could prove decisive in achieving the Sustainable Development Goals.

As the previous chapter explained, companies have stakeholders and they are stakeholders. Their actions influence – and sometimes determine – a wide range of sustainability outcomes, commonly referred to as environmental, social and governance (or ESG). To measure these impacts, there have been a flurry of initiatives to eval-uate the sustainability performance of companies. There is, pardon the pun, value in all of these approaches in isolation, but the sheer volume of different methodologies – ranging from ESG ratings to impact accounting – threatens to turn into a cacophony of meas-urement that obscures more than it illuminates.

To rebalance value and values, we must develop and embed comprehensive and transparent approaches to measuring stakeholder value creation by companies. Finance is a utility, a means to an end with the ends determined by society. For investors to align with the values of their clients requires informed and careful applications of ESG factors. These providers of capital – investors, pension funds, banks and insurers – need to be more transparent about their objectives, including their investment horizons and where they are placed on the continuum between maximising value for shareholders and doing the same for stakeholders.

The rapid rise of ESG measurement and investing is the most promising contribution to the creation of stakeholder value. ESG investing grew out of philosophies such as Socially Responsible Investing (SRI) that developed in the 1960s. The early SRI models used value judgements and negative screening to identify which companies to avoid, such as those that were involved in tobacco or active in apartheid-era South Africa. The considerations have broadened since then, and while there is no agreed list of ESG factors, the types of issues generally included are set out below:

Environmental Impacts	Social Contributions	Governance and Management
Climate change and GhG emissions	Customer satisfaction	Board composition
Air and water pollution	Data protection and privacy	Audit committee structure
Biodiversity	Gender and diversity	Bribery and corruption
Deforestation	Employee engagement	Executive compensation
Energy efficiency	Community relations	Lobbying
Waste management	Human rights	Political contributions
Water scarcity	Labour standards	Whistleblower schemes

Investors and creditors are increasingly considering ESG factors alongside traditional financial ones in their decision-making processes. Modern ESG investing and analysis places more emphasis on finding value in companies (through higher risk-adjusted returns over time), opting in to purpose-driven firms that are making positive impacts in the three ESG areas. For example, from a climate perspective, the distinction is between divesting all energy companies and selecting those that have net-zero targets and credible strategies to achieve them. In other words, avoiding those which are part of the problem and supporting those which are finding solutions. As we shall see, as society places greater value on sustainability, this form of capital allocation has the potential to create a new asset class that could be critical to driving the whole-economy transition we need to solve climate change.

Sustainably managed assets totalled over $30 trillion at the start of 2018, with the approach covering about half of the assets in Europe and one-third in the US. The sector has grown very rapidly since then with the latest estimates putting ESG assets under management now at over $100 trillion. Relatedly, fully one-third of large asset owners globally have signed up to the UN's Principles for Responsible Investment (PRI). The health crisis has reinforced this trend.[1]

There are signs that this surge of interest is creating a self-reinforcing cycle that is typical of new developments in finance where more widespread adoption of an innovation initially comes at the price of uneven quality. As financial market participants develop the necessary expertise, this naturally leads to wider variation in performance. There is also some evidence that ESG kitemarks, such as membership of the PRI, have been sought for their role in gathering assets, or reducing the risk of losing client mandates, rather than reflecting improvements in managing towards ESG objectives.[2] If that is the case, the PRI's new strategy of ejecting members who don't follow its principles will expose them.

Whatever the motivations and quality of execution, it is clear that there is real momentum behind sustainable investing, and that it can be a powerful tool to create value and advance social goals, such as the attainment of the United Nations Sustainable Development Goals. This chapter is about how this approach can be applied to maximum effect.

HOW ESG CAN GUIDE STAKEHOLDER VALUE CREATION

Compared to traditional investing (which either ignores ESG factors or does not systematically take them into account), there is a broad continuum of ESG investing. The vast majority of ESG assets seek to 'do well by doing good' by using ESG criteria to identify common factors that support risk management and value creation in order to enhance long-term risk-adjusted returns in a form of divine coincidence. These strategies encompass both responsible investing, which largely uses ESG for risk mitigation, and sustainable investing, which adopts progressive ESG practices that are expected to enhance long-term economic value. Impact investing seeks to support positive social or environmental benefits alongside financial returns. It is distinguished by measuring social and environmental outcomes as rigorously as financial outcomes, and by pursuing additionality which means concentrating on investments that catalyse social or environmental change. So an impact strategy focused on accelerating the transition to a net-zero economy would not simply invest in existing green assets but rather develop new renewables projects or help companies invest to reduce their carbon footprint.

At one end of the impact spectrum, finance first strategies seek to generate competitive financial returns, while at the other end impact first strategies accept below-market returns. Finally, values-based investing aligns portfolios with the moral values or beliefs of the individual or organisation. These are often (but not always) philanthropic, investing in the expectation of partial if not complete loss of capital to advance broader social goals.

The continuum of ESG investing strategies is described in Figure 15.1 from the Impact Management Project.

Unless otherwise specified, this chapter will concentrate on finance first impact investing strategies, those that seek to do well by doing good. In essence, these approaches are premised on the view that companies that create stakeholder value will create greater shareholder value over time than those that do not.

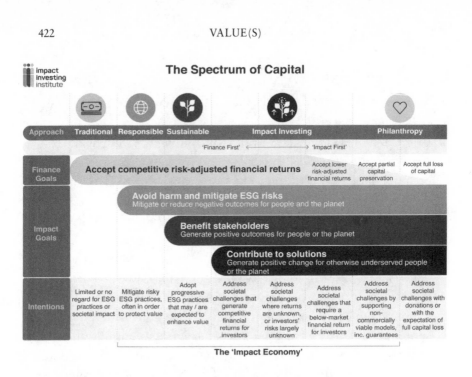

Figure 15.1 The spectrum of capital: choices and strategies for investors

That superior performance could be for a variety of reasons. These companies could be better managed in general and good ESG performance serves simply as a proxy for that superior management. In addition, companies that balance the interests of all stakeholders could be more likely to create greater long-term value for all parties, shareholders included. Most fundamentally, the broad alignment of shareholder value and stakeholder value could occur when the purpose and competitive advantage of a company both depend on the achievement of a specific social or environmental value (as will be discussed below, this is termed shared value).

In this context, impact strategies are a class of sustainable investing that explicitly evaluates the social impact of a company's activities, calculating a social return on investment. Impact strategies seek a balance of financial and social returns that align with the values of their end investors. Some will trade off a degree of financial returns to achieve greater social returns, while others target divine coincidence. In the latter case, the difference with generic sustainable investing is that the social 'good' that is targeted is explicitly calculated, tracked and reported.

As we will review in a moment, there is considerable evidence that purpose-driven companies which score well on ESG metrics outperform those that do not. There are, however, some nuances. For example, not all ESG factors are created equal when it comes to creating shareholder value. Some may be immediately, directly relevant to creating shareholder value. Others may be longer-term, indirect drivers of competitiveness, including maintaining social licence, and improving a company's ability to attract and retain the best people. The prospect of these higher future cash flows could explain why a strong ESG company trades at a valuation premium today.

But it should not be assumed it will always be the case that strong ESG performance will translate fully over time into higher cash flows nor – obviously – should society's values be determined solely by whether the stock market gives companies credit for helping to achieve them. There are some things that money cannot buy but over which companies can have enormous influence, such as species loss or inequality. Typically, the value of these accrues to broader society. They will not always be 'in the price' of companies.

In a phrase often attributed to Albert Einstein, 'Not everything that counts can be counted, and not everything that can be counted counts.' As we shall see, there is a proliferation of methods to expand the universe of what is counted, to determine whether society believes it counts.

To draw out some of these distinctions, consider a series of issues around climate change. For some companies, energy efficiency is closely tied to competitive advantage. Walmart is a classic example as superior logistics are a core competency of that retailer. Thus an improved environmental footprint – a social good – and corporate efficiency – a financial good – are closely aligned in divine coincidence. At the other extreme is a company that takes action to help protect an endangered species, does not receive a direct financial gain and may well incur considerable costs. It has placed a higher weight on a social value as part of being a good corporate citizen. There may be indirect financial benefits such as attracting employees and maintaining social licence, but the company may not necessarily capture all of the positive social benefits of saving a species through improved financial performance via these other channels. The withdrawal of social licence can be hugely damaging to a company's prospects, but the tipping point for this to happen is hard to predict (in some ways akin to the earlier discussion of social movements in the climate chapter and the discussion below of 'dynamic materiality').

PERFORMANCE

There is considerable evidence of outperformance of sustainable investing strategies (divine coincidence) over traditional ones. This outperformance continued during the intense market volatility experienced in the first half of 2020 when the Covid crisis struck hard. As Morgan Stanley Capital Investment observes:

> The positive contribution from the ESG factor, though over a limited period, supports our previous research where we found certain high ESG-rated companies were less exposed to systematic risks such as exogenous shocks. The coronavirus crisis is a recent example of such a shock.[3]

Consistent with their better ability to manage such episodic downside risks, ESG funds are more likely to survive. Morningstar found that, on average, over three-quarters of sustainable funds available to investors ten years ago have survived, compared with less than half (46 per cent) of traditional funds.[4] Examining large global and US funds, they find consistently higher average returns of around 1pp per annum across various time horizons over the past five to ten years.[5]

Part of the reason for ESG outperformance may be that ESG factors provide new information about company performance. Research by Mozaffar Khan of Causeway Capital, George Serafeim of Harvard and Aaron Yoon of Northwestern University finds that, when companies focus their sustainability efforts primarily on material social and environmental factors, they significantly outperform the market, with 'alpha' (outperformance relative to a market median) of 3 to 6 per cent annually.[6] They also outperform peer companies that concentrate sustainability efforts on non-material factors. Mining ESG information for specific drivers of value creation is a process of shared value discussed below.[7]

There is also evidence that the financial valuations of strong ESG performers increase as the values of society move in their direction. In theory, the more that society values the transition to net zero, the more valuable companies that are part of the solution will be because of greater demand for their products as well as because of developments in regulation and carbon pricing that support society's objectives. In this spirit, Serafeim finds evidence of outperformance for ESG stocks with positive ESG sentiment factors, with the valuation premiums paid for companies with strong sustainability performance increasing over time and the premium increasing as a function of positive public sentiment momentum.[8] The evidence suggests that public sentiment influences investor views about the value of corporate sustainability activities and thereby both the price paid for corporate sustainability and the investment returns of portfolios that consider ESG data.

Morningstar observes that firms' ESG risks are likely growing and becoming more correlated over time, if for no other reason than these issues are receiving more attention from consumers, regulators and investors. Portfolios that pay attention to those risks and manage them better will outperform all else equal.

In this regard, some of the valuation premiums on ESG assets reflect the expectation that their outperformance on ESG factors will ultimately translate into higher profitability in divine coincidence. As noted above, this outperformance can occur through a variety of channels from changing consumer preferences to new supportive regulations, as well as the realisation of shared value opportunities across the value chain with suppliers, customers and communities, and the maintenance of social licence to operate.[9]

Although many of the factors that drive ESG outperformance could translate into higher future cash flows, directly or indirectly, they will not necessarily explain the entire valuation premium.

Companies can also be valued for being good corporate citizens, with their corporate personalities leading the equivalent of a balanced 'good life'. Moreover, social licence as well as the ability to attract, motivate and retain the best people is critical to corporate flourishing. There are many 'second-order' financial benefits that will come from first-order social improvements.

Overall, the studies of the performance of ESG investing are encouraging for the existence of divine coincidence between the creation of sustainable and economic value. There is, however, a need for longer track records through several market cycles to be more fully confident of outperformance. Moreover, caution is warranted because ESG is a large, varied and rapidly growing field. As we shall see in a moment, different providers can make very different judgements. It is obviously not the case that all ESG strategies will outperform, and, as discussed below, investors should be wary of formulaic application of ESG ratings or kitemarks. The equation is not simply that ESG equals alpha. Judgements about value and values take work.

Moreover, and this is a crucial point, in the fullness of time, if ESG mainstreams, then overall market performance, risk-adjusted returns, should improve, but relative performance will not. Broad, societal improvements to workforce diversity and inclusion across the board won't differentiate specific companies that have helped make it happen, except during the transition to a more equal and inclusive society. These shifts will create 'social alpha', or what people would colloquially refer to as progress.

FIDUCIARY DUTY

The degree to which investors weigh ESG factors depends ultimately on how they fulfil their fiduciary duties to their clients. This is an area in which it is essential to have both the clarity of objectives of an investment vehicle and a deep understanding of the divine coincidence between stakeholder and shareholder value.

Fiduciaries are those who have been given a special level of trust to look after the interests of another party as well as the power to act on their behalf. Fiduciaries are required to act not out of personal interest but in the interests of the beneficiary and comply with their duties in this regard as stipulated by law. Corporate directors, for instance, are fiduciaries of the corporation and, as discussed in the previous chapter, must act in its best interest, whether that is framed as maximising shareholder value or balancing a range of stakeholder interests. Institutional investors (from pension funds to unit trusts) owe a fiduciary duty to those whose money they manage. Thus with investing, we return to the same dilemma posed within corporate law: is the fiduciary duty solely about generating profit for the beneficiary (you and I) or is there something more?

Clearly, taking social factors into account in investment decisions when they have a direct influence on a company's future economic performance does not violate fiduciary duty; in fact it is mandated by it. As we have seen, there is growing evidence that improving stakeholder value often generates shareholder value while reducing extreme or tail risks, suggesting that the scope for taking into account ESG factors is very wide. Indeed, EU policy actually emphasises that failure to consider the multifaceted relationship between ESG factors and risk and return might create a risk of liability for fiduciaries.

The argument that full alignment between stakeholder and shareholder value is the only possible interpretation of fiduciary duty hinges on assumptions about the preferences of beneficiaries. The narrowest interpretation is that these preferences are solely for financial returns. But a trustee's role is to act in the interest of the beneficiary, which means maximising their welfare, not merely their financial returns. While all beneficiaries in investment activities seek monetary gain, this does not suggest that they are indifferent to how such returns are realised.

Recent polling and evidence in consumer trends from larger asset managers reveal that owners of capital do care about more than profit and would like investment decisions to be made with regard to ESG considerations.[10] As but one of many examples, a recent survey of savers undertaken by the UK FCDO (Foreign, Commonwealth & Development Office) found that over half were interested in investing sustainably now or in the future, with almost a third being willing to accept a lower return provided they knew the investment was making a difference to something about which they cared.[11] In the area of pensions, we have learned (unsurprisingly) that UK cancer researchers do not want their retirement savings financing tobacco companies, nor do Ontario teachers want theirs financing immigration detention centres in the United States.[12] This is regardless of how profitable promoting a cancer-causing activity or locking up children may be.

A fiduciary duty that adequately accounts for the interests of beneficiaries must therefore move beyond mere financial considerations and require consideration of ESG factors when making investment decisions. If performed transparently, based on a well-articulated framework with expressed principles, beneficiaries will be able to select the investment manager that best represents their priorities and will be more likely to maximise their welfare. In cases where participation in a fund is required – as is the case with mandatory pension plans – and 'voting with their feet' is not possible, beneficiaries should be able to vote on social responsibility resolutions and major investment decisions in order to ensure decisions are in line with their interests.[13] Just as beneficiaries can specify their risk appetites, they could also specify the degree by which they wish to prioritise non-financial values.

Governments have a role in clarifying the scope of the duties of investors and encouraging clear communication with beneficiaries. This is beginning to be more systematic. EU rules coming into effect in 2021 will require financial market participants and financial advisers to consider sustainability risks in assessing financial performance.[14] In addition, they will be required to publish information about how they integrate these considerations into their decision making.[15] The new rules thus clarify how investment managers should conceive of their fiduciary duty to their clients, mandating a focus on long-term and sustainable value creation.

The new EU rules are a bold step towards a more comprehensive view of fiduciary duty. Smaller steps are occurring in other jurisdictions, most often in the area of pension funds because of their mandatory contribution requirements. Since 2016, for instance, the Canadian province of Ontario has required pension funds to issue an investment policy that indicates 'whether environmental, social and governance factors are incorporated into the plan's investment policies and procedures and, if so, how those factors are incorporated'.[16]

The guidance from the UK Law Commission to trustees of defined contribution pension schemes is that trustees can take into account non-financial factors when two conditions are met.[17] First, when trustees have good reason to think that scheme members share the concern. This does not need to be unanimous agreement, but a balancing of interests that takes into account the intensity of views. For example, it may be sufficient if a majority are opposed to an investment while the rest remain neutral. On the other hand, if a majority oppose but a sizeable minority are strongly in favour, the trustees will be expected to focus on financial factors. Second, trustees must ensure they are not risking significant financial detriment in prioritising ESG factors, and they should receive professional financial advice to this effect.

Against this grain, fiduciary duty and its relationship to ESG investment strategies has come under increased scrutiny in the US, where the Department of Labor took a number of specific actions in 2020, including stating that 'It is unlawful for a [pension plan] fiduciary to sacrifice return or accept additional risk to promote a public policy, political, or any other nonpecuniary goal.'[18] Thus, under the proposed rules, the interests of plan participants are assumed to be strictly financial. Specific measures include plans for a new rule that requires private pension administrators to prove that they are not sacrificing financial returns by investing in ESG-focused investments, and in some instances asking some asset managers to produce support for investment decisions dating back five years, regardless of their financial performance. The additional administrative burden could put ESG funds and investments at a competitive disadvantage. Given the growing track record of ESG in creating shareholder value, it is perhaps no surprise that the vast majority (95 per cent) of responses to the Department of Labor consultation are opposed to the policy.[19]

How then should we envision the modern fiduciary duty for investors? The United Nations Environment Programme Finance

Initiative has suggested reformulating the traditional fiduciary duty
of loyalty and the related duty of care in a manner that accounts for
both the importance of beneficiary interests and the value offered
by ESG consideration.[20] In this reformulation, the duty of loyalty
would be broadened so that investors would have the responsibility
to understand the sustainability preferences of their beneficiaries
and incorporate this understanding into their decision making,
whether or not these preferences are financially material. The duty
of care meanwhile is modernised to acknowledge the role of ESG
factors in identifying long-term value and reducing risk. To act
prudently and with due care, investors must incorporate financially
material ESG factors into their investment decision making consistent with the timeframe of the obligation. In addition, investors
must be active owners, encouraging high standards of ESG performance in the companies in which they invest.

Overall, the direction of travel for regulation is generally towards
this form of responsible investment, as evidenced by the acceleration globally in responsible investment regulation and policy since
the turn of the millennium (Figure 15.2).

Despite this progress, in most jurisdictions there is still more
work to be done to move the law towards this modern formulation
in which investment managers must make efforts to understand

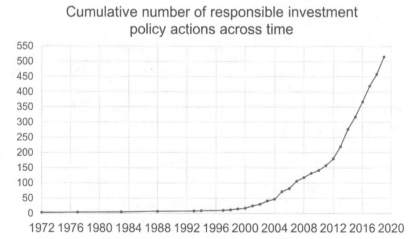

Figure 15.2 Growth in responsible investment

their clients' sustainability preferences while also understanding the impact of ESG factors on long-term value and risks. In the meantime, investors will need to work within the parameters of their legal duty. The increased understanding of the value added of ESG considerations creates a valid financial reason for investors to look beyond immediate financial indicators. Moreover, the promising legal reforms mentioned above, and recent initiatives such as the Make My Money Matter campaign in the UK (that aims to stimulate individual investors to express their views) underscore the responsibilities of fiduciaries to understand and maximise their clients' welfare by considering their values alongside value.

THE INVESTING ECOSYSTEM FOR STAKEHOLDER VALUE CREATION

The investing ecosystem for stakeholder value creation is complex and rapidly evolving, and as a result can appear confusing. It is helpful to clarify up front the principal actors involved, the information they need and the actions they take.

The main actors are:

- Companies which receive the investments and put that money to work to create economic value and social impacts. The latter can be deliberate or unwitting, positive or negative.
- Investors who provide capital to companies to support their activities. As we have seen, they can pursue strategies ranging from traditional investing that does not take into account ESG factors to integrated and impact strategies that systematically do.
- Other stakeholders which include the employees, suppliers, customers and communities that are affected by the actions of both companies and investors.
- Governments and regulators which oversee the system, set the rules and are responsible for addressing the systemic consequences of the actions of companies and investors.

All of these actors want information to assess the economic and social impacts of companies. Some of that information will be drawn directly from companies and others from third-party sources. The information from companies – corporate reporting – is governed by a combination of regulation and market convention. Corporate reporting is the means by which stakeholders, including investors, can understand and evaluate a company's performance. Financial reporting has developed significantly over the past century (not least due to lessons learned during past crises) and is codified in internationally recognised accounting and disclosure standards that bring transparency, accountability and efficiency to financial markets. Sustainability reporting is younger, less mature and more complex due to a number of factors discussed below.

Actions. Once information is disclosed the question is what to do with it. As we shall see, many investors use raw sustainability information from companies and other sources to make their own assessments of a company's impact, while others rely on third-party ESG ratings providers to aggregate ESG information and assess a company's ESG performance.

Investors will place different weights on different ESG factors. They will also weigh societal trends, including the evolving standards of social licence and the implications of collective actions of companies on systemic risks. The pursuit of divine coincidence, of doing well by doing good, includes both improving returns and reducing exposure to tail risks. These risks can include the withdrawal of a company's social licence and improving a company's resilience to systemic shocks. Like all systemic risks, it is not clear when these will crystallise in a new pandemic, a climate Minsky moment or the withdrawal of social licence.

Critically, the users of sustainability disclosure are broader than financial intermediaries and include all stakeholders who have an interest in the impact of companies. These stakeholders look at social value as well as economic value, and take into account societal trends and priorities. As a consequence, they want a broader set of information than that which can be expected to impact a company's financial value over time. This is a reminder that ESG reporting is part of a company's responsibilities to society.

With this context, let's now turn to a series of issues around information and analysis that help determine impact.

INFORMATION AND DISCLOSURE

The information set for stakeholder value creation has three elements. The first, traditional financial reporting, has evolved over many decades. As noted, financial reporting is relatively mature and has a robust governance structure that is rooted in the private sector and overseen by public authorities. There are recognised bodies which set corporate reporting standards, in particular, the two main accounting standards boards the IASB and FASB and the securities regulators who oversee disclosure. And the system has formal mechanisms to adapt to new learnings such as those from the financial crisis which led to the adoption of new standards (like IAS39 for the valuation of financial instruments and IAS9 for expected losses on loans).

In contrast, sustainability reporting is new and rapidly evolving. In response to the demands of both investors and society for systematic and decision-useful sustainability information, many public companies now produce some form of sustainability reports. In parallel, a number of bodies have developed (largely over the past two decades) to set voluntary standards for sustainability disclosure. These include the GRI (Global Reporting Initiative), the SASB (Sustainability Accounting Standards Board) and the TCFD. As we shall see, one issue is how the guidance from these initiatives can be rationalised and their coverage be made comprehensive so that all companies report sustainability disclosure as consistently and fulsomely as they do financial disclosure. Figure 15.3 depicts the relationship between these standards.

Finally, there is a wealth of public information from social media to scientific analysis which informs views of both the current state of sustainability and public expectations for its evolution.

All stakeholders are users of sustainability information from employees, suppliers, customers, local communities, regulators, governments, financial institutions and investors. Their interests

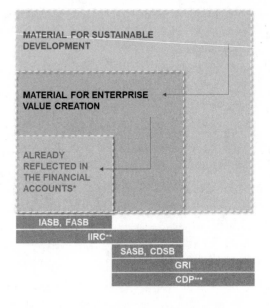

Figure 15.3 The corporate reporting system

will differ by topic and will vary over time, but all matter. Investors will make judgements about which sustainability factors will influence long-term enterprise value creation by companies: in effect, what determines the creation of economic capital. Other stakeholders will place greater emphasis on sustainability value creation – some of which creates economic capital but some of which creates social capital. Stakeholders will also consider the aggregate impacts of all companies across different sectors on sustainability. After all, there are no externalities at the global level.

These broader considerations mean that what companies may need to report is broader than 'just' those sustainability factors that drive economic value. And it underscores that they have to be mindful of how the requirements of social licence may evolve. No company is an island. For example, before the carbon budget had been set, issues of environmental sustainability were principally concerns for energy companies and very heavy polluters. Now that the carbon budget is on the verge of being exhausted, environmental sustainability is an issue for everyone. For the Fridays for Futures school strike movement this is an existential crisis. For corporate reporting this is an example of dynamic materiality,[21] how the importance of sustainability issues for corporate performance can shift, sometimes rapidly. (These changes are represented by the arrows in Figure 15.3 above.)

Following a period of huge innovation in sustainability reporting, it is now time to consolidate and rationalise these various standards. To that end, there are three types of efforts: private, standard setters, public sector.

The first major effort to consolidate sustainability reporting was launched by the International Business Council of the World Economic Forum. As part of their commitment to stakeholder capitalism, this collection of 140 leaders of the world's largest companies have worked with the Big Four accounting firms (Deloitte, EY, KPMG and PwC) to develop a framework for corporate reporting and a minimum set of recommended disclosures. The goal is to agree common metrics and disclosures tied to the UN's SDGs across the broad topics of People, Planet, Prosperity and Principles of Governance, with these recommendations to be implemented by companies on a disclose-or-explain basis. The agreed standards are drawn wherever possible from existing standards and disclosures (such as the GRI, the SASB, the TCFD, and so on) and include both core and expanded metrics:

- *Core metrics.* A set of twenty-two well-established metrics and reporting requirements. These are primarily quantitative metrics for which information is already being reported by many firms or which can be obtained with reasonable effort. Core metrics are primarily focused on activities within an organisation's own boundaries.
- *Expanded metrics.* These additional thirty-four metrics tend to be less well established in existing practice and standards and have a wider value chain scope or convey impact in a more sophisticated or tangible way, such as in monetary terms. They represent a more advanced way of measuring and communicating sustainable value creation, and companies are encouraged to report them as well, when material and appropriate.

Impact Management Project or IMP convenes a number of climate reporting initiatives to align their standards and frameworks, with a view to agreeing a consolidated global sustainability reporting architecture that uses management commentary and integrated reporting to connect the front and back end of accounts.

Specifically the IMP is building a framework that accommodates different layers of materiality covering:

– what is already reflected in financial accounts (IASB),
– information material for enterprise value creation (SASB/ CDSB/IIRC) and
– information material for sustainable development (GRI).

Figure 15.4 shows the interrelationship between the three.

Financial accounting and sustainability disclosure should be connected via integrated reporting and should recognise that materiality may change over time as risks change and societal norms

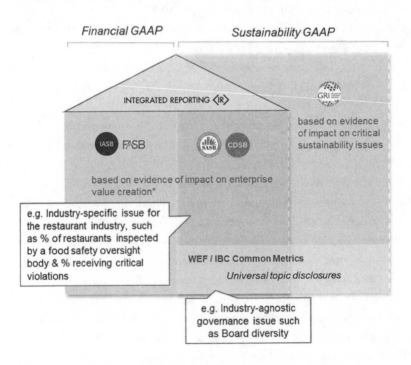

Figure 15.4 Standard setting reporting framework

evolve. Integrated reporting is a principles-based framework produced in 2013 (and currently in the process of being revised) for reporting by an organisation on its value creation over time, including human, social, intellectual, manufactured and broader natural capital. An integrated report communicates how an organisation's strategy, governance, performance and prospects, in the context of its external environment, lead to the creation of value in the short, medium and long terms. IIRC is working with IASB, GRI and SASB to create a cohesive interconnected reporting system (through the IMP work). The intention is that this integrated reporting framework would be combined with the Impact Management Proposal, and act as the link between financial disclosure and accounts and information material for enterprise value creation.

For several years the European Union has been at the vanguard of non-financial reporting, notably with the publication of the Non-Financial Reporting Directive (NFRD) in 2014. As part of the European Green Deal, the European Commission is now reviewing the NFRD; considering the need for standards to improve the comparability and reliability of non-financial reporting in Europe, including on measures beyond those solely material for financial impact; and is expected to put forward a final legislative proposal on the matter in due course.

At the global level, the IFRS Foundation, which sets the basis for corporate disclosure standards in most countries outside the United States, has been called upon by many to incorporate non-financial reporting within its remit. The IFRS's deep expertise in the development of robust reporting standards and its broad geographical coverage place it in an excellent position to take on this role. To that end, the IFRS Foundation is currently working on how it could incorporate climate-related financial disclosures into financial statements and how to create global standardisation in non-financial reporting.

In order to achieve their objectives, investors pursue different strategies such as positive screening for best-in-class performance on ESG factors; negative screening for those that perform poorly; and momentum investing in companies that are improving aspects of their ESG performance. Deeper analytics can support systematic approaches to shared value that identify the social impacts that are closely tied to a company's competitive advantage.

Within these strategies, there are three main approaches to applying ESG factors:

- ratings-based where assessments of ESG performance are outsourced to a third-party provider;
- fundamental value in which raw ESG data is analysed, as part of an integrated assessment of the relationship between the creation of sustainable and enterprise value; and
- impact assessments which measure and report the wider impacts on society while targeting specific positive social impacts alongside financial returns.

RATINGS-BASED APPROACHES

In the ratings-based approach, investors outsource assessments to ESG data providers who use their own methodologies to aggregate objective and subjective data covering all ESG segments into comprehensive indices or ratings. The data starts with publicly available information (including sustainability disclosures), and then combines it with questionnaires, company interviews and in some cases in-house analysis of the ESG rating provider.[22] Providers of capital use these ratings as simple screens or factors in their decision making.

There are a large number of ESG ratings and data providers, offering a wide array of data. These range from specialised providers that calculate metrics on specific ESG components, such as scores on carbon and gender diversity, to providers that rate companies based on hundreds of ESG-related metrics. In early 2020, around seventy different firms provided some sort of ESG ratings data.[23] This does not include investment banks, government organisations and research organisations that conduct ESG-related research that can be used to create customised ratings.

The rise of ESG investing coupled with the growing popularity of passive investing has made the quality and availability of systematic ESG ratings data ever more important. Unfortunately, ESG ratings data can fall short due to incomplete coverage and a dependence on self-reporting by companies. In addition, the methodologies used by ESG data providers vary widely and can lead to materially different outcomes when constructing a portfolio. Even within ESG, all factors are not created equally. Recent MSCI analysis of the relative impact of E, S and G issues on companies' financial fundamentals and stock-price performance between December 2006 and December 2019 found that the G score was the most significant in measuring exposure to financial factors, while the S score was the weakest.

The rating systems of data vendors can vary dramatically, leading to substantially different ratings of the same company. For example, a 2020 study found that the correlation between the overall ESG ratings of six rating providers is about 0.46, so only about half the time would a rating provider come up with the same assessment.[24] The average correlation is lowest for the governance (0.19) and highest for the environmental factors (0.43). More profitable firms are subject to lower ESG rating disagreements, while firms without a credit rating have higher disagreements. A 2019 study found the level of ESG disagreement for a given firm has increased over the same period.[25] Methodologically, Berg, Koelbel and Rigobon find that these differences are primarily driven by measurement (that is, what metrics are used to assess different ESG attributes), followed by differences in scope (that is, what attributes are being assessed) and lastly by weight (that is, the level of materiality the ratings provider assigns to each attribute).[26]

Whatever the cause, these differences matter. Given the large number of providers and the wide range of ESG approaches, different ESG ratings providers will yield different results – in some cases, substantially different. This means that, depending on the ESG approach followed, ESG investments could yield very different returns, in effect because investors are supporting different ESG outcomes, and ultimately values.

To give a sense of the magnitude, Research Affiliates analysed two model US and European portfolios using two leading ratings providers (with coverage of over 95 per cent of the respective market capitalisations). Over an eight-year period, the difference in the annual performance of the two portfolios was 70 basis points (bps) in Europe and 130 bps in the United States. Over the full period, the cumulative performance difference was around 10 per cent and 25 per cent respectively. The performance dispersion is even greater with portfolios constructed using the environmental, social and governance subcomponent scores, with differences ranging from 70 bps a year to 220 bps a year, with the biggest dispersion coming from the governance-based strategies in both the US and EU.

These differences highlight the subjective nature of many of the judgements of ESG ratings providers. ESG ratings consider hundreds of metrics, with many of them qualitative in nature. Different ESG raters include different metrics, translate qualitative metrics into a numerical quantity based on their own algorithms and weigh them according to their views of their relative importance. In all cases, they are making value judgements.

This demonstrates that it is not always straightforward to value the outcomes that we value. The ability to do so should improve with time and effort, but there will always be an element of subjectivity. What's important is that those judgements are exposed, so that investors apply their own judgement (even if it is through a conscious decision to accept the judgements of others). Investors should thus study carefully the methodologies of various ESG ratings providers to select the one whose ratings align more closely with the investors' own views on ESG. Alternatively, they should screen in and use the raw data to determine the most decision-useful metrics themselves.

Putting values to work is hard work, but as with virtue, it should become easier with sustained practice.

FUNDAMENTAL SUSTAINABLE VALUE

Such an approach is at the heart of strategies of investors using raw or fundamental ESG data across the broad range of criteria. This data is usually collected from publicly available information (from company filings, company websites, NGOs and social media), and then disseminated to end users in a systematic way. The users of this data determine the materiality of the information and deploy their own methodologies when making investment and lending decisions. Examples of these data providers include IHS Markit, Refinitiv and Bloomberg.

An important subset of fundamental sustainable value investing is a 'shared value' approach which concentrates on a subset of broader ESG factors that are specific to a company's purpose and strategy. Shared-value strategies tie social impact directly to competitive advantage and economic performance. As advocated by Michael Porter, George Serafeim et al., creating shared value is fundamentally distinct from making incremental improvements to a broad range of ESG factors that the authors argue 'tend to converge over time in any given industry' (remember that's a good thing for society!).

Shared-value companies make a different set of choices from their competitors, building a distinctive social impact into their business models. Shared value can affect strategy on three mutually reinforcing levels: (1) creating new products that address emerging social needs or open currently unserved customer segments; (2) enhancing productivity in the value chain, whether by finding new efficiencies or by increasing the productivity of employees and suppliers; and (3) investing to improve the business environment or industry cluster in the regions where the company operates.[27] Note the contrast to a ratings-based approach which leads many investors either to adopt a mechanistic index strategy or to use a company's overall ESG performance as a final screen to reduce risk.

A shared-value approach to investing will help both companies and investors grasp opportunities to align social purpose with investing, while offering a focused way for companies to contribute to a better world at the same time as improving shareholder returns. It is not, however, a comprehensive approach to rebalancing value and values. It runs the risk of undervaluing broader sustainability improvements that have second-order effects on the future performance of companies, as well as general improvements in ESG performance which, while not contributing to a specific company's outperformance, are part of broader social and economic progress.

And it explicitly excludes broader environmental and social progress that is not priced in the market.

For these reasons, impact-investing approaches that look at the general as well as the specific may be more effective in creating economic and social value in the medium to long term. There is a growing list of social factors that were once not material but which have rapidly become so (think about the intense scrutiny of companies' efforts to increase diversity and inclusion). Investors have a responsibility to assess and manage systemic risks, which will affect absolute performance more than relative performance of specific companies. In this vein, Porter et al. recognise that broader ESG focus can improve industry- and economy-wide performance.

> Regulators, NGOs, and sustainability-minded investors will, of course, continue to focus on overall ESG performance.
> Companies will need to continue to improve and report on their performance across the broader set of ESG factors, even though most will not confer any sustainable competitive advantage.

As corporate and investor understanding of the connectivity between value and values evolves, integrated reporting provides a framework for companies to highlight and communicate their purpose and what they view as the drivers of value creation.

The proliferation of what some might perceive as competing interests of different investors and stakeholders, combined with growing data sources (well beyond company-sourced information) and new analytical approaches, has created a landscape of competing narratives around company performance. Companies are still best suited to tell their own value creation 'story'. Historically, they told that story through different channels to different audiences. This has resulted in fragmented messages at best and contradictory ones at worst, leaving the various users of information ill-equipped to piece it all together. This has contributed to the view that sustainability reporting can sometimes be more about branding and public relations than about value creation.

Providing the wide range of users of corporate reporting information with a common 'integrated' framework helps companies communicate not only how their business strategy is driven by financial and sustainability considerations, but also how they work across functions to execute that strategy. And now, with the rise of impact investing, integrated reporting provides a conceptual framework for accommodating evolving impact measurements and considerations.

IMPACT, MONETISATION AND VALUE

Impact investment strategies do more than simply incorporate ESG considerations. They are outcome oriented, focusing on how a company's products and services advance specific impact goals, such as the Sustainable Development Goals. In doing so, impact strategies concentrate on a company's purpose – what it is trying to achieve, how it measures success – as well as on its broader impact on society.

Impact strategies make investments with the intention of generating positive, measurable social and environmental impact, alongside a financial return. Impact strategies manage this 'double bottom line' along a continuum between financial and social returns. Some trade off some of the former in pursuit of the latter, while a number of other impact managers seek to deliver financial outperformance alongside social contributions.

Impact strategies require that managers have ways to evaluate, track and communicate social impact. While advancing the UN SDGs provides a framework for anchoring impact objectives, managers use additional qualitative and quantitative methods and frameworks to track and report the social and environmental benefits their investments create. Industry standards are beginning to emerge for impact management practices including the IFC Operating Principles, the Impact Management Project Dimensions of Impact, and the Global Impact Investing Network's (GIIN's) IRIS+ metrics. Many large sophisticated investors incorporate multiple frameworks to measure and manage impact using these standards.

In parallel, a growing number of companies are including impact assessments (of varying degrees of comprehensiveness) in their corporate sustainability reports or in dedicated impact reports. For example, a review by PwC finds that almost one-third of FTSE100 companies do so.[28] A number of organisations – including GRI, the Impact Management Project, the Impact Weighted Accounts Initiative, SDG Impact, Social Value International and the Value Balancing Alliance – are working to build impact disclosure standards, which will streamline production of these statements and facilitate comparability. More ambitious efforts to develop comprehensive impact accounting standards with estimates of the ESG impacts of companies should be embedded in company profit and loss and balance sheet statements. This project is the equivalent of a financial moonshot.

Some impact strategies rely heavily on impact monetisation, an analytic process to convert ESG impacts to monetary values. Impact monetisation can be applied to specific investments as part of a blended assessment of their attractiveness alongside financial returns, as well as applied to ambitious efforts to develop impact-weighted accounts.

Monetisation quantifies the positive and negative impacts of a firm, including the externalities they create. It puts prices on those impacts that are not in the market. The extent to which these estimates influence investment decisions should depend on a fully informed understanding of their merits and robustness. After all, these impact assessments are calculated on the basis of a combination of objective and subjective information, with the calculations relying heavily on the judgements and values of those making them.

Sometimes monetisation calculations are straightforward. The financial impact of a solar company is the price of the panel sold minus the costs of production. Its broader social impact includes the breadth of impact – for example, household solar arrays installed (arrays are the group of panels installed on a typical house) – multiplied by its depth (for example, each array reduces CO_2 emissions by about 12 tonnes per year), and then multiplied by a value factor (for example, the price per tonne of CO_2, say $17). The result is a monetary value of the social impact for this activity.

This can then be used to model risk, test sensitivities to various assumptions and generally be analysed as any other business or financial measures. In this example, it could be that investors place a higher value factor on CO_2 averted either because they think that the carbon price is going to rise (consistent with some stated government policy) or that it *must* rise (a value judgement) on a path consistent with achieving net zero (for example, the NGFS orderly scenario uses $100/tonne by 2030 and Canada's carbon price path which reaches C$170 per tonne by that date). The depth and breadth are objective factors determined by the success of the company, and the value factor could be either objective (the current price) or subjective (what the investor thinks it could become or ought to be). Depending on the investor's values, it will assess and act accordingly.

The most ambitious approaches to impact measurement involve the development of comprehensive and robust impact accounting standards. These will take time, but they are useful to consider because they illuminate the advantages and potential limitations of monetisation of social and environmental outcomes.

The potential of Harvard Business School's impact-weighted accounts initiative led by George Serafeim and chaired by Sir Ronald Cohen is revealed by the following examples:

> What if you compared the total environmental cost created by 1,800 companies? You might find for instance that the operations of Sasol and Solvay, two chemical companies with sales of around $12bn each, created environmental damage of $17bn and $4bn a year respectively, while another, BASF, with $70bn of sales, created $7bn.
>
> What if you did the same for the social cost of deficient diversity in the workforce? Take Intel. It pays its 50,000 US employees more than $7bn a year and promotes employee wellbeing and diversity. But if you measure its diversity relative to local demographics then you might find Intel's positive employment impact on communities falls to about $2.5bn.[29]

The Harvard Impact Accounting Project has published estimates of the environmental impact of more than 1,800 companies, based on public information. In 2021, they will add employment and product impacts, providing a more complete picture of the effects that companies have. The ultimate objective is to create 'generally accepted impact principles', and to reflect them in financial accounts that show impact-weighted profits.

The advocates of impact accounting caution not to let the best be the enemy of the good. After all, as Greg Fischer of Y Analytics puts it, financial accounting standards 'continue to evolve, and notes to financial statements provide essential detail for myriad nuanced calculations underlying income statements, balance sheets and statements of cash flows. We should embrace similar sophistication in our approach to impact accounting.' He adds, 'We should also abandon any fantasies about living in a fully certified world. We [already] understand this for forward-looking statements.'[30]

There is much to commend in these efforts, particularly because the analytic rigour required to develop impact-weighted accounts will undoubtedly advance our understanding of social and environmental impacts. But there are also a number of challenges which urge caution, particularly the risks of being drawn into adding financial and social values to yield 'one true number' – a dollar figure – that is optimised in a mixture of the secular and the sacred.

The core challenge to value activities not priced in markets is a familiar one (to the reader) but no less difficult for that. What is the value of reduced mortality due to the displacement of electricity generated by fossil fuels? What is the value of maintaining the Amazon rainforest? Or of preserving a species of newt? As we saw in the decisions around Covid, options for how to make these calculations include revealed preference (using real-world examples of related transactions like how much someone pays for an air filter or side-impact airbags, and infer their value for the underlying non-market good – clean air or a reduced chance of injury).[31] The alternative is to use stated preferences, which are calculated by asking individuals how they value the good. As revealed during the Covid crisis, these methods often fail to capture the 'full' value of an outcome such as mortality. These challenges are reinforced when markets are imperfect, as observed behaviours will not capture, for example, the value of biodiversity or even education when poverty and broken credit markets can lead us to mistake ability to pay for willingness to do so.[32]

Converting social and environmental outcomes into monetary values requires a comprehensive understanding of relevant research and evidence. For example, the various calculations of quality-adjusted life years that we saw in Chapter 9 in relation to the Covid crisis or different estimates of the diminishing marginal utility of income are also relevant to calculating the impact value of switching from fossil fuel to renewable power generation. Given the variety of assumptions that often feed into these estimates and the uncertainty around them, it is often better to calculate ranges and to highlight which assumptions or judgements are particularly important. Indeed, a major danger with monetisation approaches is the risk that users will forget the careful assumptions that have been used, ignore the dangers of uncertainty and luxuriate in false precision.

While examining ranges and sensitivities and then debating assumptions can be effective for specific impacts, things get more complicated quickly when there are a series of ranges for a series of inputs that all determine net valuation. Aggregating positive and negative impacts to one net number may obscure the trade-offs and assumptions involved in their preparation. As Greg Fischer of Y Analytics observes, by collapsing a series of trade-offs into what could be seen as 'one true number', impact measurement doesn't just overlook but obliterates nuance.

> Used carelessly, monetization can cloud rather than clarify. But used correctly, monetization forces us to spell out our values, making trade-offs explicit, highlighting negative impacts and distributional issues, and allowing us to express risk, uncertainty, and how we weigh future costs and benefits against the present. Ultimately, this allows enterprises and investors to make better decisions about impact and to effectively communicate the drivers of those decisions to their stakeholders.

To summarise, despite the attractions of comparing apples with apples (or dollars with dollars), monetisation is not without its challenges, including the need to grapple with uncertainty, the danger of false precision, the difficulty of comparing impacts across different sectors or geographies and the challenge of valuing outcomes that are not naturally monetised, like healthier children. Of course, monetisation does not create these issues. Used correctly it can make them more transparent, and by doing so support better decisions about impact. But the risk is that the more broadly it is applied, such as in full impact-weighted accounts, the more monetisation could obscure rather than illuminate.

Converting non-market outcomes into monetary values inescapably involves subjective judgement. Reasonable people can disagree, and different stakeholders will value outcomes differently. This can be particularly difficult when examining trade-offs that involve the secular (the economy or profits) and the sacred (biological species or human lives). Monetisation has the advantage of making these differences transparent and providing a medium for decision making, comparability and accountability. But the more these highly subjective, but seemingly precise, numeric judgements are combined, the greater the risks that nuance and sensitivity could be lost and financial optimisation dominate the pursuit of the greater good.

Given these challenges, there are attractions in tailoring monetisation for specific investments or in using consistent assumptions, transparently disclosed, across a portfolio designed to achieve a specific impact, such as reducing child poverty or addressing climate change. In many cases, these outcomes can be better measured by metrics tied to the precise objective sought, without an artificial translation into 'dollars' that, on the margin, could corrode the values that are to be supported.

SECURING CLIMATE IMPACT: THE TRANSITION TO NET ZERO AS A MAJOR NEW ASSET CLASS

As we saw in Chapter 12, the most promising approach to solving climate change involves engineering, political and financial technologies. In a broad sense, the necessary engineering technologies either exist or are emerging; certainly, existing technologies are sufficient to secure the first decade of the energy transition. The challenge is that these technologies must be deployed across the whole economy at great scale and at tremendous speed. This requires political technology to build a broad consensus around the right goals. A broad consensus is now coalescing in many countries around the Paris objective to keep temperature rises below 2°C. Now it is time for financial technology to orient (impact) investing towards this goal, a goal agreed by society and made increasingly possible by scientists and engineers.

Given that the transition to net zero is both an imperative of climate physics and highly valued by society, it is likely that sustainable, and ultimately mainstream, investors will focus on how well companies are positioned to manage the associated risks and opportunities.

Companies and assets will increasingly be viewed through the lens of the climate transition. Who is on the right and who on the wrong side of history? Which companies have momentum? And which could be climate roadkill? With over 125 countries having net-zero objectives, it is reasonable to expect that all major companies will have to publish their transition plans, and that the providers of capital – asset owners like pension funds, asset managers, banks and insurers – will have to use that information to direct their company engagement strategies, to assess and disclose how well they are positioned for the move to net zero. This will create a new cross-cutting asset class, with investment (and ultimately lending and underwriting) portfolios judged by their roles in warming the atmosphere. The more rapidly investors can help portfolio companies and assets move to net zero the lower the implied temperature rise.

The new transition asset class can reinforce the emerging engineering and political momentum, creating an impact that doesn't just 'make the weather' but literally 'changes the climate'. Its foundations are:

- societies that are increasingly valuing stabilising the climate as the early destructive, physical manifestations multiply;
- the imperative of net zero to stabilise the climate at whatever temperature;
- that the necessary adjustments will require a whole-economy transition, involving every sector of the economy (we won't get to net zero in a niche); and
- the objective of the private finance initiatives for the Glasgow COP to ensure that 'every financial decision takes climate change into account'.

Bringing these together, sustainable impact investing should focus on advancing the transition to net zero, in the tradition of impact investing that requires measurement relevant to that clear objective. There are several ways to track and disclose progress including reductions in GhG emission by asset and portfolio and alignment relative to Science-Based Targets when available.

Investors need to demonstrate how their clients' investments are aligned with the transition. Any such measure of portfolio alignment needs to be:

- forward looking, giving appropriate credit to efforts by companies to decarbonise;
- anchored in real-world climate targets; and
- dynamic, to show progress over time and accommodate new technologies.

Following these criteria will encourage investor engagement with companies across the economy. We won't get to net zero in a niche nor will divestment alone deliver the whole economy transition that we need.

Existing climate-related metrics serve useful roles, but aren't best suited to a whole economy transition. Carbon footprints and CO_2 emissions per dollar invested aren't forward-looking. ESG metrics are inconsistent, poorly correlated, and their 'E' is not benchmarked to net zero. And taxonomies capture a small proportion of business activity, cannot chart progress through fifty shades of green, and are not sufficiently dynamic.

There are several possible ways for the providers of capital to assess the position of companies and investment portfolios along the transition path. To support their assessments, providers of capital could measure and disclose a range of metrics. In increasing order of sophistication, these include:

- the percentage of assets that have a net-zero transition plan;
- a percentage of portfolio that is net-zero-aligned or Paris-aligned (for example, based on an external taxonomy);
- percentage deviation from a target (for example, relative to EU benchmarks, or the pathways of the Net Zero Asset Owners or Science Based Target Initiative); and
- portfolio warming, a forward-looking metric to assess the potential global temperature rise associated with GhG emissions from a given company or portfolio. Firms such as GPIF, AXA and Allianz have already voluntarily disclosed this information. And some of them are now feeding into a TCFD working group for COP 26 that is considering whether the degree warming or any other metric is the best way to measure the potential risks and opportunities in the transition.

Whatever approach is used, as with all impact assessments it will be important to be transparent about the data inputs and methodology, as well as to perform sensitivity analysis of the results. The current assessments of portfolio warming conduct in financial markets are sobering but not surprising, suggesting that the markets are financing a world in which temperatures rise by more than 3°C.

Exposing this gap should help close it. A leading group of investors managing over $5 trillion in assets, under the Net Zero

Asset Owners Alliance, are setting specific carbon reduction targets for their portfolios and committing to align their portfolios over time with a 1.5°C world. I have joined Brookfield, a major alternative asset manager, in order to pursue a similar strategy of relentlessly focusing on decarbonisation across the economy while achieving commercial returns for investors. These efforts will make a difference in and of themselves, but they will also create momentum that makes the transition to net zero an asset class, encouraging more and more investors to back companies that have plans to decarbonise.

THE SOCIAL PURPOSE OF INVESTING

Sustainable investing is developing into an essential tool for bringing the values of investing into line with those of society. It improves the measurement of what society values from workplace diversity to the Sustainable Development Goals. It can be used to increase the shareholder value of companies through multiple channels by helping them attract and retain the best people, increase resilience, improve efficiency, align better with stakeholders and maintain social licence.

To put values into value, investors can pursue a variety of strategies. They can progress macro sustainability through broad ESG approaches that lead to general improvements in environmental, social and governance standards. They can be more closely targeted by pursuing shared value to align the purpose of a company, its competitive advantages and its social impacts. By concentrating on specific, material ESG factors, investors can generate alpha while solving specific problems.

And investors can target specific impacts across people and planet. Developing the climate transition as an asset class is arguably the largest opportunity. The potential investible universe is every company. The targets are the ones which are developing actionable, profitable strategies to transition to net zero. Progress can be measured by the contribution of the portfolio to the warming of the planet. The social return is a future for all. The economic return is potentially enormous because, remarkably, this existential societal objective is not yet in the price.

While ESG is a powerful tool, it needs to be used wisely and transparently. Investors should take their cue from William Blake: know their values rather than be enslaved by those of another. Every sustainable investing approach makes judgements even if they are outsourced to an ESG ratings provider. In all cases, it is critical that users of ESG data understand the assumptions, trade-offs and limitations so that they can apply their judgements to align portfolio allocation with their objectives and values.

These challenges of developing sustainability reporting must be weighed against the status quo of ignoring the full impacts of a company's activities. What is the point of having purpose but not measuring whether it is being achieved? How can a company be a true stakeholder if it does not track its positive and negative spillovers to its community and broader society? And how can investors and creditors judge a company's prospects if they are blind to its internal governance, including governance of the factors that drive its social and environmental impact? Why would people – if they hold certain values strongly – put their savings in ethical blind pools where they don't know how they are being invested?

Investing in companies that contribute profitably to social progress and withdrawing capital from those that do not can create a virtuous cycle. It improves the welfare of customers, employees and communities, while generating growth and opportunities for people. Investing in dynamic companies that innovate to meet society's needs is core to capitalism's power. When a social need can be tackled with a profitable business model, the magic of capitalism is unleashed, and the answers to the many deeply rooted problems we face become self-sustaining and scalable.

The power of these solutions can be multiplied by national strategies for strong, sustainable and balanced growth. The next chapter shows how.

How Countries Can
Build Value for All

During the last quarter-century, a series of profound disruptions to the way we work, trade and live helped lift more than a billion people out of poverty, made the sum of human knowledge available to 4 billion people and raised global life expectancy. These changes were made possible by the combination of transformative information and communication technologies at the heart of the Third Industrial Revolution and the increasingly free movement of trade, capital and ideas.

Now we are on the cusp of what some have called a Fourth Industrial Revolution (the 4IR). Applications of artificial intelligence are spreading due to advances in robotics, nanotechnology and quantum computing. Our economies are reorganising into distributed peer-to-peer connections across powerful networks – revolutionising how we consume, work and communicate. Enormous possibilities are being created by the confluence of advances in genetic engineering, artificial intelligence, nanotechnology, materials science, energy storage and quantum computing.

The nature of commerce is changing. Sales are increasingly taking place online and over platforms, rather than on high streets. The value of intangible capital (like software and intellectual property) now dwarfs that of physical capital (like factories and real property).[1] We are entering an age when anyone will be able to produce anything anywhere through 3-D printing, where anyone can broadcast their performance globally via YouTube or sell to China whatever the size of their business via Tmall or Shopify.

But for many people measures of aggregate progress bear little relation to their own experiences. Rather than a new golden era, globalisation and technological advance are associated with low wages, insecure employment and striking inequalities. They are losing trust in a system that doesn't appear to give them and their children a fair chance of sharing in this bright future.

The ten years following the global financial crisis marked the first lost decade for real incomes in the UK since the middle of the nineteenth century. Substitute platforms for textile mills, machine learning for the steam engine, and Twitter for the telegraph, and current dynamics echo those of that era. Then, Karl Marx was scribbling the *Communist Manifesto* in the reading room of the British Library. Today, radical viral blogs and tweets voice similar outrage.

I could feel it when I went out to the union conferences in Canada or in the UK (where the theme was 'Britain deserves a pay rise'). When I visited Hamilton or Liverpool, I felt the strains of a frenetic modern life and the undercurrents of extreme uncertainty. Stagnant income growth focused greater attention on its distribution. Inequalities, which had been tolerated during generalised and rising prosperity, began to be felt more acutely as hope began to fade.

These emotions were particularly raw in the UK. Was that because it was more exposed or just ahead of the curve?

As a central banker I had a unique (but frustrating) vantage point. Armed with reams of data, brilliant colleagues and access to people from all walks of life domestically and globally, I could see much, but do relatively little, in the face of these big forces. As we have seen, central banks provide part of what's needed for prosperity: sound money, a financial system that works in bad times and good. In these respects, central banks are responsible for some basic aspects of the state's duty to protect. This work is necessary, important and foundational. It is what people should expect. But it is far from sufficient to achieve sustainable growth.

Sustainable growth can be undercut on a number of dimensions:

- through the build-up of excess debts of households, companies and banks;
- by governments squandering their future fiscal capacity on current spending, robbing the (future) Peter to pay the (current) Paul;
- through the rapid exhaustion of the carbon budget and the associated assault on biodiversity; and
- by devouring the social capital necessary for markets to function and for everyone to thrive.

And now we face enormous forces that could intensify these vulnerabilities. The Covid crisis has exposed deep fissures in many of our societies. The Fourth Industrial Revolution, while bringing great promise, is likely to widen inequalities further and increase social strains if left to run its course. The climate transition, while essential and fundamentally positive, will involve enormous structural changes in a short period of time.

THE PROMISE AND CHALLENGE OF THE FOURTH INDUSTRIAL REVOLUTION

The fundamental challenge is that alongside the great benefits that every technological revolution ultimately brings, it mercilessly destroys jobs and livelihoods – and therefore identities – well before new ones emerge. This was true of the eclipse of agriculture and cottage industry by the Industrial Revolution, the development of the production line and the displacement of manufacturing by the service economy. The same forces are now in train, possibly on a greater scale and at a faster pace, through machine learning and global sourcing.

Some economists wonder what all the fuss is about. They argue that there has been little evidence, over the long term, of technological unemployment. After all, average employment and unemployment rates today are similar to those in the eighteenth century (Figure 16.1).

The catch is that, although equilibrium will eventually be restored, such big transitions take time. Workers cannot move seam-

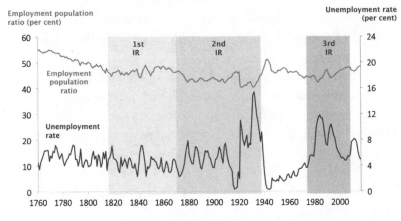

Figure 16.1 Technological unemployment 1760–2000

lessly into new jobs, whether because of the mismatches of skills or location. The benefits of the First Industrial Revolution, which began in the latter half of the eighteenth century, were not felt fully in productivity and wages until the second half of the nineteenth. This meant that generations of workers knew little more than wrenching adjustments and persistent fragility.

At the start of the nineteenth century, wage growth stalled and the labour share fell – a period dubbed 'Engels' pause' (Figure 16.2). What economists euphemistically call frictions can wipe out regional jobs and sharply increase national inequality.[2] Similarly, it could be generations before the gains of the Fourth Industrial Revolution are

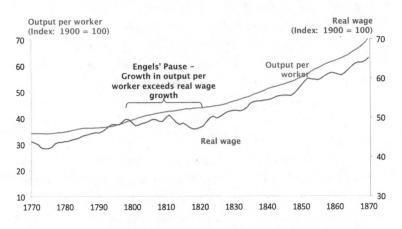

Figure 16.2 Real wages vs. Productivity in the First Industrial Revolution

widely shared. In the interim, there could be a long period of technological unemployment, sharply rising inequalities and intensifying social unrest. In parallel, the values captured and propagated by algorithms could frame social choice in unintended ways.[3]

Historically, over the medium term, technological change tends to reduce labour's share of total income relative to capital, as the returns to workers from higher productivity are not enough to counteract the destruction of jobs. Over the longer term, a third effect – the creation of new tasks for labour[4] – when combined with the ongoing productivity boosts counterbalances the displacement effects of technology and boosts wages while leaving employment unaffected.

The Fourth Industrial Revolution could be more intense than its three predecessors in terms of scope, scale and speed. Moreover, it comes hard on the heels of the Third Industrial Revolution, which generally reinforced inequality and widened polarisation. Thus far, each wave of technological change has increased the importance of cognitive tasks relative to non-cognitive ones. In other words, machines have largely substituted for human hands not heads. Workers have been able to improve their skills and take on newly created sets of cognitive, higher-value tasks – tasks beyond the cognitive limits of machines.

Rapid improvements in computing power, the greater availability of big data and advances in artificial intelligence and machine learning all mean smarter machines are already replacing a broader range of human activities than before, reaching well into the realm of heads. New technologies may increasingly provide intelligence, sensory perception and reasoning that previously only human labour could provide. Technological optimists[5] believe future automation will move beyond substituting for the 'routine-manual' human tasks technology performed in the late twentieth century to almost the entire spectrum of work.[6]

Estimates of the potential number of jobs affected span a very wide range of 10–50 per cent of all employment.[7] Evidence increasingly suggests that, while large parts of many jobs will be subject to automation, relatively few will be completely automated.[8] Edward Felten, Manav Raj and Robert Seamans show that recent advances in technology can be used to predict future changes in the task structure of occupations, lending further support to the argument that technological advancement will likely change the nature of many jobs rather than eliminate them entirely.[9] The more extreme estimates are often based purely on the technical feasibility of automation with limited consideration of economic feasibility.[10]

Taking these additional considerations into account reduces the share of jobs at high risk of automation to some 10–15 per cent in most advanced economies.[11] That is comparable with the three previous technological revolutions, which saw the share of aggregate employment accounted for by the most exposed industries fall by between 10 and 20 per cent over long periods.

There are at least four areas where new jobs will be created. First, people will continue to provide the hearts – that is, performing tasks that require emotional intelligence, originality or social skills such as persuasion and caring for others. Second, an ageing population will also lead to greater demand for care and a straight decrease in labour supply. Third, if new forms of bespoke mass creativity are made possible by the new global economy, human hands may once again take over (a form of cottage industry going full circle). Finally, there will be new roles that we don't imagine. After all, when the smartphone was invented, no one immediately thought, 'There goes the taxi industry.'

Despite these offsetting forces, there are several reasons why the 4IR could substantially increase inequality. Most fundamentally, the more that new technology substitutes for labour rather than complements it, the more that the gains would accrue to the owners of capital. An unequal distribution of capital means that the higher returns to capital from increasing automation will push up inequality. Second, during the transition as new technologies are adopted, what economists euphemistically call frictions can lead to depressed local labour markets or boost inequality in national ones. Third, if education is unable to keep pace with the changing demand for skills, those who already have them will earn even higher premiums, and job polarisation will increase the supply of labour competing for lower-skilled jobs.[12] Finally, greater global interconnectedness will reinforce these dynamics.

If this world of surplus labour comes to pass, Marx and Engels could again become relevant.

Prior to the Covid crisis, evidence suggested that, on balance, automation had not yet reduced employment in aggregate, but had led to substantial compositional changes. There were also signs that recent technological advances had boosted inequality. Globally, labour's share of income fell over the two decades in the run-up to the pandemic with evidence suggesting that technology had been the biggest contributor. The UK and Canada are outliers: countries where income inequality has been generally stable – if relatively high – since the late 1980s.[13]

Moreover, there is strong evidence that advanced-economy labour markets have been polarising since the 1980s – a structural shift that has generally been attributed to technological displacement of mid-skilled jobs resulting from the early stages of automation and digitisation of tasks. Employment growth has been strongest at the high- and low-skilled ends of the jobs spectrum, resulting in a hollowing out of mid-skilled employment (Figure 16.3). The polarisation of the labour market has also been evident in the returns to skilled labour, with earnings growth for those with higher levels of education far outstripping those with less schooling.

In sum, if the 4IR is similar to past technological revolutions, the overall effect will *eventually* boost productivity and wages, while

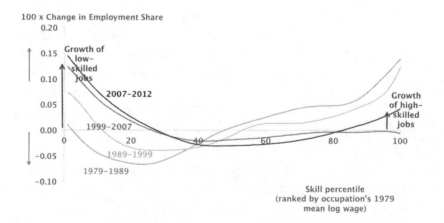

Figure 16.3 Employment changes by occupational skill percentile, 1979–2012

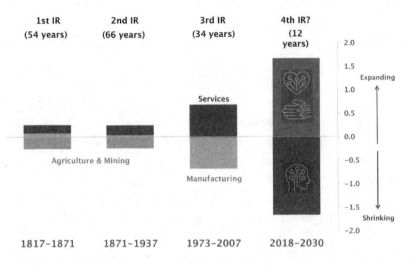

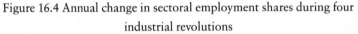

Figure 16.4 Annual change in sectoral employment shares during four
industrial revolutions

creating enough new jobs to maintain or even increase overall employment. But that is in the long run. In the interim, if the transformation that is just beginning is similar to those experienced in previous industrial revolutions, there will be a long period of technological unemployment, large dislocations of workers and rising inequalities.

Given that the accelerating technology adoption cycles could mean that these changes could happen more rapidly, the challenges could be significant (Figure 16.4). Moreover, unlike in the previous industrial revolutions, the more rapid pace of adjustment and longer working lives means workers may not have the option of retiring. This raises the risks of substantial skills mismatches, much higher long-term structural unemployment and rising social pressures.

THE MACROECONOMIC CHALLENGES OF COVID

Covid has intensified the pace of the 4IR. With invention and application born of necessity, the changes to work made possible by new technologies are happening more rapidly than previously envisioned. The economy is shifting from moving atoms to moving bits with the rise of e-health, e-learning and e-commerce. For example, the share of online retailing which had grown to about one-fifth of UK sales in 2018 almost doubled at the height of the lockdown in the spring of 2020 and was settling at around one-third as restrictions were eased. The nature of work for the one-third of all workers who can work remotely has been transformed into a web of almost exclusively digital communications. Global supply chains are being reconfigured moving from 'just in time' to 'just in case' in the pursuit of greater resilience, sustainability and security.

We are living Lenin's observation that there are 'decades when nothing happens and weeks when decades happen'. Covid has already lasted decades. The nature of work and commerce has changed dramatically for many. Entire populations are experiencing the fears of the unemployed and the anxieties of inadequate or inaccessible healthcare. Following decades in which risk has been downloaded on to individuals, the bill has arrived, and many cannot think of how to begin to pay it.

Notwithstanding my normal caution against the temptation to think that we always live in interesting times, this time really *is* different. Most recessions are the consequence of the build-up of imbalances during what is suddenly revealed to have been a period of unsustainable growth. Aggregate demand – the spending by households, companies and governments – then goes into reverse, plunging the economy into recession. Eventually, as the excesses are purged, the combination of supportive monetary and fiscal policies and renewed confidence starts the recovery.

This time the shock is a massive contraction in aggregate supply. The disease has decimated large segments of the economy (hospitality, bricks-and-mortar retail, transportation, international education), threatening widespread bankruptcies and throwing huge numbers of people out of work. It has stalled international trade, and its spectre haunts business investment.

Demand has fallen with supply, with total world output collapsing by an average of 10 per cent by the middle of 2020. In some countries such as the UK and Spain the drop was more than twice as large. Although growth picked up as some lockdown measures were eased, economies will be fortunate to return to their size at the end of 2019 within a few years. Even if they do, the composition of activity will be very different.

The disease struck as I was finishing my term as Governor of the Bank of England. At that time, the judgement of health authorities was that it would be possible to have the pandemic under control by the autumn. As a consequence, the decision was taken for unprecedented fiscal and monetary support to bridge households and businesses through a difficult but temporary period. The goal in the UK, Europe and Canada was to maintain as much of the productive capacity of their economies as possible, and especially to keep as many people attached to their jobs as possible. The US government chose a different route, accepting a large increase in unemployment while paying enhanced benefits. The US approach would break the attachments of workers with their employers but speed adjustment, particularly if the disease lasted longer than expected.

Everywhere, central banks, drawing on past efforts to strengthen the resilience of the banking system, acted swiftly and effectively to minimise risks to financial stability. Fiscal policy was both generous and effective. At the height of the lockdown, average US household disposable income was growing at its strongest rate since 2000. The combination of markedly higher uncertainty and physical limitations on spending (such as on hospitality and travel) led to sharp rises in household savings rates (Canadian households paid down substantial debt).

As spring turned to autumn with no respite from the virus in prospect, the question rapidly became how much longer to bridge workers and firms. Not only were the costs becoming enormous (with fiscal deficits rivalling the worst in wartime), the support schemes also risked preventing difficult but necessary closures of failing businesses and openings of new ones. Governments had to ask themselves when bridges could become piers or whether they could instead be turned into slip roads. Although the disincentive of enhanced support measures was initially blunted by their perceived temporary nature,[14] the more they appeared as a form of permanent and generous universal basic income.

The longer social distancing and the isolation economy persist, the more difficult it will be for unemployed workers to retain their skills, develop new ones and find fulfilling jobs. More fundamentally, Covid has intensified the transitions of the 4IR. Many jobs will be replaced sooner by the efficiencies of remote working and the accelerated automation of tasks. In parallel, concerns over health may reverse the decades-long trend of older workers staying longer in the workforce.

The overall environment is one of rising risks. Household spending is being weighed down by extreme uncertainty, high unemployment and weak income growth. Business investment is under similar pressures. Foreign trade is being held back by a combination of physical restrictions, geopolitical tensions and weak investment. Global interest rates remain exceptionally low due to a combination of extreme uncertainty (investors take solace in buying the safest assets), weak investment, high savings and low productivity.

After having failed in their most basic duties to protect their citizens, governments must now act to restore confidence. The economy has needed support; it increasingly needs direction. That is one crucial reason why our fiscal capacity must be used wisely. It is often observed that interest rates are exceptionally low, but just because high spending is possible does not make it optimal. Current spending can help maintain activity today, but it doesn't grow the economy tomorrow. And simple debt dynamics must still be respected. With time, living beyond our means is unsustainable, even if the exact moment when higher interest rates crystallise and drive brutal spending cuts is uncertain. What is clear is that, if theses risks are ignored, the reckoning will come sooner.

Budget choices are often talked about in abstract terms of sustainability of debts or dictates of amorphous markets. But they are really about the sustainability of people's livelihoods. People know that spending only on the present will not deliver a better future for them and their children. Both fiscal consolidation (reducing deficits) and a shift from current to capital spending (investing in the future) are questions of economic welfare and intergenerational fairness.

The following conclusions of Tharman Shanmugaratnam, Singapore's Senior Minister, put these trends into a disturbing longer-term context:

There has been a drift in fiscal policy, in a whole range of countries, towards individuals rather than public goods and towards the short term or the next electoral cycle rather than the long term. For instance, in the 1960s 75% of the US budget went into public goods of one form or another – infrastructure, schools, hospitals, transport and so on. And 25% went in some form of benefits to individuals. Today it's exactly the other way around – 75% to individuals, and 25% on public goods. That is inherently short term. It sometimes solves immediate problems – but it doesn't lead to a better long-term future and it doesn't lead to optimism. If you don't invest in public goods, and people can't see that you're investing for the long term, then it's very hard to get a more optimistic society. You get a society where people are constantly concerned about 'how much do I get compared to someone else'.[15]

My advice to governments that have asked has been that they should divide their expenditures into three categories: Covid (emergency), Current (basic ongoing programmes like childcare benefits or spending on defence) and Capital (measures to boost the long-term productive capacity of the economy). Their task is to transition from the first category of spending to the last category of investment as quickly and as transparently as possible. Once the acute phase of the health crisis passes, it's time to move from fighting fear to fuelling optimism.

Government initiatives need to take into account new realities. It is increasingly obvious that the economy is not bridging back to where it was before. Recall my distant predecessor at the Bank of England advising Winston Churchill to go back to the old certainties of the gold standard. Montagu Norman's instinct was fatally flawed because a great tragedy, the First World War, had accelerated changes that were already underway: the rise of US power, the unwillingness of increasingly organised labour to sacrifice their wages to support an artificial currency peg, the advent of new technologies and real-time trading that speeded up decision making.

Similarly, we are not going back to the pre-Covid economy. That has multiple implications. First, in the process of accelerating the

Fourth Industrial Revolution, Covid is using up the buffers of business, households and governments – buffers that would have helped cushion the wrenching changes that transformative technologies will bring. Workers are more exposed sooner than we would have previously thought possible. Second, the Covid crisis has underscored the importance of resilience in all its forms. Third, Covid is compelling strategic resets by most companies. Fourth, new company strategies will not be complete unless they outline the company's plans for net zero. Finally, populations that have made enormous sacrifices for the common good expect solidarity in return.

In the response, central banks will continue to have an important foundational role. They must continue to provide the twin anchors of monetary and financial stability under radically changed circumstances. Deflationary pressures intensified during the acute phases of the health crisis. With the challenges of the zero lower bound on interest rates ever more pressing, greater clarity about the target pathways for inflation add policy flexibility and help ensure that the challenges of the massive leveraging of all sectors of the economy can be addressed. In these regards, the Federal Reserve's adjustment to its mandate to pursue Flexible Average Inflation Targeting is timely and welcome. Reflation of the economy in the medium term is essential.

At the same time, authorities need to recognise that inflation will return, particularly because Covid represents a major negative supply shock. Significant capacity has been destroyed, and a tough adjustment is underway. The twin risks of fiscal dominance – where central bank policies are dictated by the spending priorities of the state – and financial dominance – when central bank policies are driven by a perceived need to support financial markets – will rise over the coming years. In this environment, it is more important than ever that independent authorities assess and address risks to monetary and financial stability. In an environment where many assume that interest rates will stay low for ever and that authorities will always bail out markets under stress, a more active and holistic approach to managing risks in market-based finance is imperative. The lessons of Magna Carta live on (see Chapter 4).

To move from where we are to where we need to go, governments should follow a ten-point plan:

1) Set a clear goal to move from emergency support of the old economy to building the new one in which everyone can thrive. We need mission-oriented capitalism that works to solve our current problems rather than perpetuates them, and that creates the future rather than tries to preserve the past.

2) Set rules and guidelines on spending and borrowing that will discipline them while encouraging greater focus on a brighter future for all.

– The combination of Current and Covid spending should be back in balance over the medium term.

– Investments in capital should be separately identified and subject to independent assessments to establish whether they add to the nation's balance sheet. Independent budget authorities (like the Office for Budget Responsibility in the UK) should publish these assessments of whether the returns to the economy over time will be greater than the upfront investments.

– A new debt service to revenue test to ensure that while governments take advantage of low interest rates they aren't seduced by them.

3) Taper the emergency Covid support measures to transition from supporting jobs to supporting workers. German-style *Kurzarbeit* schemes with partial wage support are well suited to this task. Extraordinary supplements to unemployment insurance should be tied to retraining programmes, especially to building the digital skills needed for the new economy. Support for companies should be targeted at regenerating the most affected industries rather than expensive, blanket support for all.

4) Maximise government investment both to support short-term economic activity and to build the physical, digital and natural capital we need.

5) Concentrate new budget measures on green activities that are job heavy and capital intensive (as detailed below).

6) Use regulatory policy to frame the future direction of the economy (such as explicit timetables to phase out internal combustion engines and hydrogen fuel mandates). These measures are critical to provide the certainty and predictability to drive private investment.

7) Pursue financial sector policies that provide the foundations so that the financial system can help drive the transition towards net zero.

8) Institute a disciplined approach to building resilience by assigning clear responsibilities, transparent actions and public accountability.

9) Develop intergenerational accounts that track the sustainability of current spending with demographics and track natural capital through a new natural capital balance sheet.

10) Develop the new institutions needed for how we will work tomorrow, including quaternary education and new employment insurance schemes for workers in the gig economy (as detailed below). Focus relentlessly on increasing inclusion of all socioeconomic groups in the workforce.

A sustainable recovery is not a slogan. It's what the next generation deserves, and it is what we need now. It is job heavy (heavier than conventional 'shovel-ready' building of roads and bridges), capital intensive (at a time when interest rates are low and household spending is subdued) and fair (to all socioeconomic groups, to those in the most affected regions and industries today and to those who will come after). A sustainable recovery favours regeneration over redistribution.

A sustainable recovery must be built on solid foundations and the right values.

INSTITUTIONS AND MARKETS: THE FOUNDATIONS OF OPPORTUNITY FOR ALL

Strong institutions and fair and effective markets are the foundations of opportunity for all. Institutions are, in the definition of the Nobel laureate Douglass North, 'humanly devised constraints that structure political, economic and social interactions'.[16] They are social infrastructure, which includes formal institutions – like parliaments, judiciaries, central banks, social safety nets and schools – and informal associations and groups, such as trade unions, guilds and charities.

There are several institutions that are critical to market economies. Most fundamentally, property rights allow people to own and generate capital without undue fear of theft, expropriation or rent seeking. The prospect of owning the fruits of their labours incentivises people to strive and innovate. Recorded ownership allows people to secure credit by borrowing against the value of their property. Without the protection of contract rights, commercial business would be limited to instantaneous transactions and those enforceable through personal relations.

Other key institutions determine the ease of establishing, running and winding down a business. They set the terms for obtaining permits, accessing finance, paying taxes, trading across borders and managing insolvency. Such economic institutions make possible the 'gale of creative destruction' of new ideas and new firms.

Although institutions provide the framework for how markets should function, they are meaningless if citizens don't comply. Thus those who study institutions often concentrate on the informal constraints that guide our behaviour, such as customs, conventions and taboos – what Smith would have termed 'moral sentiments'. When complementary to formal structures, these norms ensure compliance and fill in legal cracks. When they are out of sync, they place outsized – and often unrealistic – pressures on legal structures to rein in private actors. In these regards, values are not just fundamental to the health of institutions, they are institutions themselves.

Institutions have been found to be more important than either geography or international trade in explaining economic growth.[17] Good institutions encourage productive activity, lower transaction costs by establishing norms, reduce uncertainties and discourage behaviours which impair economic growth. Bad institutions lead to a culture of corruption and rent seeking. As North explains, 'If [the] institutional matrix rewards piracy (or more generally redistributive activities) more than productive activity, then learning will take the form of learning to be better pirates.'[18]

The effectiveness of institutions depends on how they adapt. Institutions will drift with social currents over time, and at critical junctures newly established norms and structures emerge.[19] These come into being for a variety of reasons, including as a response to pressing financial and social needs arising from periods of technological disruption that leave large swathes of society worse off. Such a time is just beginning.

History teaches that smoothing this transition and realising the gains of the 4IR will require the overhaul of virtually every institution, from education to finance. During the first three industrial revolutions, the skills of workers were fundamentally transformed by the advent of primary, secondary and tertiary education. New insurance institutions supported those left behind in the transition, including unemployment insurance and universal healthcare. New labour market institutions – cooperatives, trade unions, the introduction of a minimum wage and private company pensions – plugged gaps in provisions. And new market structures, such as limited-liability companies and markets in international telephony, were developed for a globalising economy.

We need to remember that economies built solely on formal institutions and markets, directed by invisible hands without purpose, are like mansions built on sand. They affect how value is derived, not which values are expressed. They are blind to the forces of inequality as well as to the very real, growing fragilities of our societies. They promise to increase aggregate, measured value rather than people's wellbeing. But they will forfeit both over time, because they will undercut the social institutions of the market.

Markets are essential to progress, to finding solutions to our most pressing problems and to seizing our largest opportunities. But they don't exist in a vacuum. Markets are social constructs, whose effectiveness is determined partly by the rules of the state and partly by the values of society. If left unattended, they will corrode those values.

Achieving inclusive prosperity will require both foresight and will. Will we anticipate or react? Do we possess the values to prevent machines from gaining the whole world while humanity loses its soul? Building social capital requires a sense of purpose and common values among individuals, companies and countries. The book has therefore emphasised the imperatives of developing these by building vocation for individuals, instilling purpose in companies and appealing to patriotism over nationalism within countries. The following pages provide examples of how to put these principles into action.

RECLAIMING THE VALUES TO CREATE VALUE FOR ALL

Given the deficits accumulated over recent decades, we must concentrate on rebuilding social capital to make markets work. To do so, individuals and their firms must rediscover their sense of responsibility for the system. More broadly, by rebasing valuation on society's values, we can create platforms of prosperity for all that focus on solving our biggest problems.

These are not naive aspirations, and they are not 'anti-market'. The action plans in this book for leaders, companies and countries unabashedly recognise that the dynamism of markets is essential to our prosperity and wellbeing. But markets too need purpose. Through shared understanding and values, we can channel the dynamism of markets to create value for all.

To do so, we need to reinforce the core values that have been emphasised throughout this book:

- solidarity
- fairness
- responsibility
- resilience
- sustainability
- dynamism, and
- humility.

The following illustrates some concrete examples of how to live and grow these values to everyone's benefit.

SOLIDARITY

Solidarity has been at the heart of effective responses to Covid. Solidarity is critical to a just transition to a net-zero economy. And it will determine the success of the 4IR, where the need for new institutions that live the value of solidarity is the greatest.

Solidarity connects companies and their stakeholders: employees, suppliers, customers and communities. Solidarity extends across regions. Solidarity is international. Ultimately, solidarity is about people. How to help people acquire new skills so that they have varied and fulfilling careers. How to help people transition into new industries. How to ensure economic change benefits everyone.

To do so, we need to support workers not jobs. Companies should guarantee employability not employment. Governments need to redesign labour market and educational institutions so that new ways of working respect the enduring values of dignity and purpose in work.

Earlier in this chapter, we reviewed the potential scale of job losses in the 4IR. The pandemic appears to have accelerated the adoption of automation and exposed how many workers are vulnerable. For example, in a study of 1,100 micro labour markets, McKinsey found growing mismatches between skills and job growth and decline, and a big overlap between the workers who are vulnerable during Covid and those that will be affected by technology.[20] In the US, these tend to be low-wage jobs, which employ a larger proportion of minorities, raising huge issues of inclusion and fairness.

As noted above, in past industrial revolutions, the actions of public, private and third-party institutions helped shrink the duration, impact and costs of the transition for workers.[21]

Building on the past, what could be done this time?

First, everyone can contribute to a better understanding of the new skills that will be required. That includes granular reviews by firms of the mismatches between their current talent and future needs; estimates by the creators of general-purpose technologies of the breadth of their potential applications; and reporting by public institutions on trends in the labour market, the pace of automation.

Second, the tax system should support skilled (and fulfilling) employment. We cannot keep on subsidising capital at the expense of labour when we know that there is a labour shock coming. At present, in most countries it is more attractive to invest in machines or software than it is to invest in people. Changing that is a part of a broader need to assess the relative tax treatment for investment in tangible capital (plant and machinery), intangible capital (ideas and processes) and people (known to economists as human capital). Nowhere is that clearer than with respect to developing employee skills.

Why should it be advantageous to invest in a physical plant when it's the mental plant that increasingly matters in a creative and caring economy? And why does it make sense for the average tax rate on labour in the US to be around 25 per cent (combining payroll and federal income taxes) compared to mid-teen to single-digit rates for software, structures and equipment? Surely, with an understanding of what we value, we will expand the development and use of technologies that are complementary to the creation of well-paying jobs.

Third, employers should take greater responsibility for building the employability of their workers. This is in employers' collective interest as the speed of technology adoption is often limited by the existing skill sets of employees. Taking responsibility for those people whose tasks and jobs are being replaced should be part of

business plans and social licence. For example, a few years ago
AT&T determined that 100,000 of the company's jobs probably
wouldn't exist in the next decade. Rather than fire them and hire
others, AT&T invested $1 billion in training these employees for
jobs of the future.

Fourth, the providers of new general-purpose technologies have
a responsibility to explore how they can develop their products and
services in ways that maximise job creation or broader social benefits. It isn't globalisation and technology that have led to increased
inequality but our response to them. We have assumed a rising tide
would lift all boats, ignoring the lessons of history that transformative technologies lead to decades-long adjustments. We need to
focus now on how technologies can be deployed to upskill existing
jobs rather than replace them, and how to build the skills in anticipation of the jobs of the future. For example, DeepMind, a leading
artificial intelligence company established an Ethics and Society
Research Unit to help technologists put ethics into practice, and to
help society anticipate and direct the impact of AI so that it works
for the many.

We will end up with 'digital by default' unless we choose 'digital
by design'. We shouldn't view technology through the lenses of Big
Tech where the role of algorithms is to replace humans, and interactions are organised to feed business models centred on big data.
We should start by valuing the outcomes that we want technology
to help achieve such as reducing carbon and improving the returns
to labour. This can be helped by carbon taxes and other incentives
for more human-capital-intensive sectors to expand. Professor
Daron Acemoglu of MIT argues that we should go further by redi-
recting technological change itself whose path is not 'preordained'.
If technology is biased against labour with huge economic and
social costs, then it is imperative to think about how it can be redi-
rected through changing how we regulate companies, how we
regulate technology and how government interfaces with technology providers and leaders.

Fifth, we need to focus on the skills development of junior to
mid-level workers. Those at the top end of skills are engaged in
continuous learning through their roles and contacts. For inclusive

growth, there need to be determined efforts to develop skills across the social spectrum. A particular emphasis should be given to adjacent skills, or those that build on existing skill sets.

Sixth, it should go without saying that all-pervasive, affordable broadband is a right. Inclusive growth demands nationwide coverage at affordable rates. General service obligations of broadband providers and competition policy should be designed to encourage universal not just mass adoption. Uneven access to broadband during Covid was one of the biggest scandals of inequality, with direct knock-on effects on educational outcomes and job prospects across social strata. All options should be explored from increased foreign competition to ambitious Low Earth Orbit satellite systems that leapfrog existing technologies. In a world where remote working is increasingly possible, the geographic levelling possibilities of the revolution in information and communications technology may finally be realised.

Seven, new labour market institutions will be needed to facilitate labour mobility and encourage appropriate protection of workers in the new forms of employment that emerge in industries. The UK Taylor review of modern working practices[22] suggested that the existing (conceptual and legal) definitions of work are inadequate. In the gig economy, there is a third class of worker that is neither self-employed nor an employee, more of a 'dependent contractor'. The responsibilities of 'employers'/platform providers for these types of workers need to be clearly defined. These workers should enjoy comparable protections in terms of their rights and safety nets. It was telling that many Covid support packages bypassed the fastest-growing class of workers entirely. The Taylor review suggested that platform workers should continue to enjoy flexibility, but also earn at least the national minimum wage, enjoy a baseline level of protection (holiday and sick pay) and be given routes to progress at work. Other issues range from technology solutions to improve the matching of applicants and jobs to new frameworks of data portability (including reputational histories).

Finally, there needs to be a radical rethink of education for true lifelong learning. Each industrial revolution has eventually been accompanied by major innovations in enabling or educational institutions. What can be done at different levels of education (primary, secondary and tertiary and vocational) to meet future skills needs in a job market where jobs are no longer for life?

It has become a truism – but it is true – that early-childhood education is critical. This isn't about sending infants to school, but about involving them in their communities, and in building communities with people of diverse backgrounds and achievements. The public school system must become the route for social mobility and excellence. A parallel system for the elites is economically, socially and morally disastrous. Great public education requires recruiting, training and regenerating teachers, including giving sabbaticals to primary and secondary teachers as they do in Singapore. It requires differentiated learning pathways for different strengths of students, but with flexibility so they can move between cohorts. It will require major investment and constant experimentation.

A major issue in a world where life expectancy could approach a century is how to institutionalise retraining in mid-career and to integrate it with the social welfare system. The time is coming for a system of quaternary education, founded on the same principle of universality as primary, secondary and tertiary education. Social welfare schemes need to be developed to support such mid-career training, since workers will be more likely to have a partner, possibly children and a mortgage during this essential period of formal reskilling. With more than half the population moving into tertiary and quaternary education over time, the need for vocational training will become paramount.

In parallel, there is a role for mass retraining schemes, such as the UK's Flexible Learning Fund and Singapore's SkillsFuture programme, which offers all its citizens aged twenty-five and over £250 credit to pay for approved work-skills-related courses. Generous subsidies, of up to 90 per cent for Singaporeans aged forty and over are available on top of this credit. According to SkillsFuture's chief executive, the returns on that spending matter less than changing the mindset around continuous reskilling.

The general orientation of these policies should be to give everyone the opportunity to thrive. Solidarity is about working together. It is about regeneration more than redistribution; teaching someone to fish rather than giving them a fish. The test should be that every-one sees their real earnings and prospects grow over their lifetimes. An extension of the long period of wage stagnation for huge swathes of people in many societies is neither morally justified nor politically sustainable. This is a high bar, but it is one that compa-nies, communities, governments and families must all strive to meet.

FAIRNESS AND RESPONSIBILITY

Two of the core lessons that I learned as a central banker were the primordial importance that markets are fair and that fairness will endure only if market participants take responsibility. Fairness and responsibility go together in markets from finance to employment.

It is distressingly easy for institutions to develop in ways that undercut fairness. Daron Acemoglu and James Robinson attribute bad institutions in developing nations to colonial rule that put in place structures for the purpose of extracting wealth from the popu-lation.[23] As institutions reflect the accumulated learning of society, these systems continue to have influence despite legal, economic and political reforms. When corruption is endemic, it cannot be rooted out by formal laws alone. North also cites such path depend-ency as the main culprit in the vitality of bad institutions.

In his Reith Lectures, Niall Ferguson focused his attention on how previously strong institutions fall into decline. To Ferguson, stagnation in western nations can be attributed to institutions which protect the status quo and inhibit growth.[24] His examples include banks that were overregulated and too big to fail, and US public schools captured by teachers' unions. To Ferguson, western busi-nesses suffer, not from a culture of unofficial rent seeking, but from onerous regulation and expensive legal fees that restrict economic activity. Ferguson's argument is in the spirit of Mancur Olson, who believed that over time in stable societies interest groups would form and grow in power, leading to institutional sclerosis and weak economic growth.[25]

The same cure – inclusiveness – is prescribed for path depend-ency and institutional sclerosis. Acemoglu and Robinson emphasise the importance of building institutions that encourage economic participation by the great mass of people through political engagement. Ferguson suggests that institutions need to be constructed by a country's citizens and not its lawyers. In both accounts, the economic depends on the political. This echoes the sentiments of North, who in his 1993 Nobel Prize acceptance speech stressed that ensuring fair and open markets was 'a complex process because it not only entails the creation of economic institutions but requires that they be undergirded by appropriate political institutions'.

To maintain legitimacy, institutions must tend towards the inclusive and away from the extractive. It requires eternal vigilance to ensure they benefit society as a whole and do not fall under the influence of the powerful.

As we have seen, institutions are the rules of the game, the constraints that structure our political, economic and social interactions. Fairness is fundamental to their legitimacy.

It is critical that laws, rules, codes and conventions are equally applied and are seen to be so. There cannot be one set of rules for insiders and elites and another for the rest. That's why violations of Covid restrictions by those in positions of authority were generally cause for resignations. And it is why a series of inequities and scandals in the financial system that were revealed in the wake of the global financial crisis proved so damaging to the legitimacy of finance and, to some degree, of markets themselves.

Though markets are generally a force for good, markets can go wrong. Left unattended, they are prone to instability, excess and abuse. We need real markets for sustainable prosperity. Not the types of markets that developed in the run-up to the financial crisis: markets that collapsed when there was a shock from abroad, markets where transactions occurred in chat rooms, markets where no one appeared accountable for anything.

Following the global financial crisis, many supposedly rugged markets were revealed to have been either cosseted or corrupt:

-   major banks were too big to fail, operating in a privileged 'heads I win, tails you lose' bubble;

- there was widespread rigging of benchmarks for personal gain; and
- equity markets demonstrated a perverse sense of fairness, blatantly favouring the technologically empowered over the retail investor.[26]

Real markets are professional and open, not informal and clubby. Real markets compete on merit rather than collude online. Real markets are resilient, fair and effective. They maintain their social licence.

Real markets don't just happen; they depend on the quality of market infrastructure. Robust market infrastructure is a public good, one in constant danger of under-provision because the best markets innovate continually. This inherent risk can be managed only if all market actors, public and private, recognise their responsibilities for the system as a whole.

To maximise the impact of markets and to maintain the social capital they need to operate, we must take measures to make markets both effective and fair. This requires the right hard infrastructure (such as fair, open-market trading and settlement platforms) and soft infrastructure (such as rules and regulations). It means promoting competition. It requires transparency, including the publication of all relevant information and ensuring equal access to it. As outlined in Chapter 9, in order to guide that understanding, the Bank of England helped develop principles of fair and effective markets for FICC markets.[27]

One way to instil greater responsibility in market participants and – with it – greater fairness is to ensure that they had 'skin in the game'; in other words, to ensure that failure had personal consequences. For example, as we have seen in Chapters 7 and 8, the reality of too-big-to-fail banks, seen by many as a scandal of 'heads I win, tails you lose' capitalism, was a major contributor to the growing mistrust in finance, the elites and the market system. The reforms to end too-big-to-fail banking thus take on enormous importance, particularly when combined with massive changes to the structure of the compensation of senior management.

A key lesson of the crisis was that compensation schemes that delivered large bonuses for short-term returns encouraged individuals to acquire too much long-term and tail risk. It was a time when the present counted for everything and the future for nothing. To align better incentives with the long-term interests of the firm – and, more broadly, society – compensation rules in the banking industry now align risk and reward by deferring a significant proportion of compensation for up to seven years. This allows bonuses to be reduced in the future if evidence emerges of employee misconduct, error or failure of risk management by an individual, their team or company.

The scandals of Libor and FX fixes are practical examples of how economic institutions can be captured by special interests and then reformed for general social benefit. Libor is a public good, one of the most important interest rates in the world, serving as the reference for trillions of dollars of mortgages, corporate loans and derivative contracts. So it was a shock in 2012 when it became apparent that some banks were colluding with each other, and that a similar cheating occurred in corners of foreign exchange markets.

As we have seen, there have been two classes of initiatives to reinstil fairness in these markets. First, the hard infrastructure was reformed (including the benchmarks, the trading platforms and monitoring systems) in order to make it more difficult to cheat. Equally important have been changes to the soft infrastructure – the rules and codes that govern markets. Drawing on the principle of inclusive institutions, the new codes and standards have been designed by the private sector to bring to life the principles of fair markets. Authorities have encouraged market participants to develop standards of market practice that are well understood, widely followed and, crucially, that keep pace with market developments.[28]

As emphasised in Chapter 9, codes are of little use if nobody reads, follows or enforces them. This is where measures like the UK Senior Managers Regime (SMR) come in. The SMR gives teeth to voluntary codes by incentivising firms to embed them and by re-establishing the link between seniority and accountability.

Ultimately, as this book has emphasised, social capital is not contractual. While compensation packages can better align rewards and risks, none can fully internalise the impact of individual actions on systemic risks, including on trust in the system. Integrity can neither be bought nor legislated. Even with the best possible frameworks of codes, principles, compensation schemes and market discipline, business people must constantly challenge themselves on the standards they uphold. Market participants need to become true stakeholders, recognising that their actions do not merely affect their personal rewards, but also the legitimacy of the system in which they operate.

All market participants should recognise that market integrity is essential to a sustainable system. To build this sense of solidarity, business ultimately needs to be seen as a vocation, an activity with high ethical standards, which in turn conveys certain responsibilities. This begins by asking the right questions. For example, whom does finance serve? Itself? The real economy? Society? And to whom is the financier responsible? Herself? His business? Their system?

The answers start with recognising that financial capitalism is not an end in itself but a means to promote investment, innovation, growth and prosperity. Banking is fundamentally about intermediation – connecting borrowers and savers in the real economy. In the run-up to the crisis, banking became about banks not businesses, transactions not relations, counterparties not clients.

When bankers become detached from end users, their only reward becomes money, ignoring the satisfaction from helping a client or colleague succeed. This reductionist view of the human condition is a poor foundation for ethical financial institutions needed to support long-term prosperity. To help rebuild that foundation, financiers, like all of us, need to avoid compartmentalisation – the division of our lives into different realms, each with its own set of rules. Home is distinct from work, ethics from law, the individual from the system.

To end the divided life, boards and senior management must define the purpose of their organisations, channelling the dynamism of the company to improve some aspect of the world. They must promote a culture of fairness and responsibility within their organisations.

Employees must be grounded in strong connections to their clients
and their communities (that is, solidarity). To move to a world that
once again values the future, bankers need to see themselves as custodians of their institutions, improving them before passing them along
to their successors.

The need to tend to institutions is not limited to the risks of regulatory capture or decay. Institutions also require care because society
evolves as technology changes. Property rights were not new even in
Aristotle's time, let alone when John Locke stressed their importance in the seventeenth century. The first modern patents were
issued in Venice in the fifteenth century during a time of intense
innovation in instruments and glass making. The first modern copy-
right law was introduced in 1710 in the UK, in belated response to
the spread of printed works in the fifteenth and sixteenth centuries.
Today we face novel issues of ownership stemming from the growth
of social media and markets for personal data. Advancements in
biotechnology, meanwhile, confront us with proprietary concerns
about our DNA, and the creation of deep fake videos questions our
ability to control our likenesses.

We can draw from existing structures in responding to these novel
issues – for example, treating legal liability for a malfunctioning
autonomous car the same way we would a belligerent horse
– but this can lead to economically inefficient and societally harmful outcomes. The gig economy has transformed many workers
from employees into independent contractors – a distinction well
settled in law but inconsistent with the power relationships between
the contractor and their platform. Moreover, at a societal level, the
rapid growth of 'dependent contractors' leads to more people
deprived of insurance schemes, sick days, pensions and career development opportunities, and thus the legal regime may need to be
adapted for economic and social good.

There is reason to worry that leading technology companies
could decide how institutions evolve, thereby locking in their advantages and discouraging creative destruction. Nations – not
companies – must set these ground rules for markets to be fair and
for market participants to take their responsibilities. States need fair

rules enacted and maintained by fair processes, held together by both formal structures and informal conventions, resistant to capture and adaptable to changing circumstances.

RESILIENCE

The state has been failing in its fundamental duty to protect. A pandemic has been allowed to run rampant, leading to the wholesale withdrawal of personal liberties and entire populations facing risks of unemployment and inadequate healthcare. These twin crises arrived only a decade after people's savings and jobs were imperilled by the implosion of global finance. Meanwhile, governments struggle to protect their media and electoral commons from foreign interference.

Countries must pursue a more disciplined approach to building resilience so that people can withstand shocks when they appear, and the economy can recover quickly from them. We have suffered

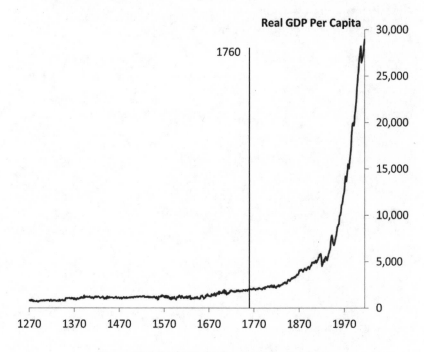

Figure 16.5 Real UK GDP per capita over time

through too much fragility, with shocks cascading through the system, magnifying destruction along the way. Moreover, as the scandal of too-big-to-fail banks demonstrated, when those responsible for failure can simply walk away from its consequences, market incentives are warped and social capital corrodes.

Resilience makes growth possible. Consider that estimates of the size of western economies show that there was no growth in income per capita between the Middle Ages and the dawn of the Industrial Revolution in 1760. Thereafter a miracle occurs (Figure 16.5).

Those aggregates hide the real story. The economic historians Steve Broadberry and John Wallis have shown that period averages conceal large, long-lasting swings in growth over time (Figure 16.6). Their revised measures suggest growth did not flat-line prior to 1750, even though it averaged zero. Rather, growth oscillated wildly, with long periods of strong growth followed by sharp contractions which gave it all back. Their estimates for the UK (which broadly match the pattern in the major European countries at the time) show that, between 1300 and 1700, GDP expanded slightly more than half the time, with growth averaging 5.3 per cent per year. These expanding periods were almost exactly offset by

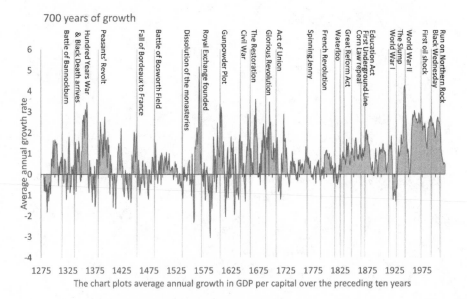

700 years of growth

Labels (left to right): Battle of Bannockburn · Hundred Years War & Black Death arrives · Peasants' Revolt · Fall of Bordeaux to France · Battle of Bosworth Field · Dissolution of the monasteries · Royal Exchange founded · Gunpowder Plot · Civil War · The Restoration · Glorious Revolution · Act of Union · Spinning Jenny · French Revolution · Waterloo · Great Reform Act · Corn Law repeal · First Underground Line · Education Act · World War I · The Slump · World War II · First oil shock · Black Wednesday · Run on Northern Rock

The chart plots average annual growth in GDP per capital over the preceding ten years

Figure 16.6 700 hundred years of UK growth

contracting periods, during which growth averaged *minus* 5.4 per cent per year.

As my colleague at the Bank of England Andy Haldane emphasised, since the Industrial Revolution growth during expansion periods is relatively little changed, but the frequency and cost of GDP contractions have fallen significantly. Recessions have occurred only one-third of the time since 1700 and only one-sixth of the time since 1900. During these periods, growth has averaged minus 2.2 per cent per year since 1700 and minus 3.4 per cent per year since 1900. It is the avoidance of deep recessions – resilience – that 'differentiates the Golden Era [since the dawn of the Industrial Revolution] from its Malthusian predecessor'.[29]

To build resilience we must recognise the unique nature of systemic risks. Systemic risks are not bolts from the blue. Systemic risks arise from interconnections and feedback loops in our economy, financial system, climate and biosphere. These characteristics of the system take bad triggers and make them worse. Many shocks cannot be prevented, but the damage they cause can be significantly reduced.

Most systemic risks have at their heart a fallacy of composition – that is, the sum of individual actions is both damaging and self-reinforcing. For example, a recession can be propagated by the paradox of thrift in which the collective impact of individuals (rationally) saving more for fear of higher unemployment becomes self-fulfilling. These dynamics can be amplified by banks which become belatedly prudent, choking the economy of credit when it needs it the most. This is what happened when the losses from US subprime mortgages cascaded through the global financial system. Systemic risks and amplification meant that the cumulative economic hit was more than five times the ultimate losses on subprime mortgages.

Feedback loops from the melting of the permafrost or the bleaching of coral reefs are magnifying the damage of temperature rises and accelerating the climate emergency. These tipping points are rapidly consuming carbon budgets and could force bigger, quicker adjustments in the economy. These interconnections could bring forward the climate Minsky moment when markets hastily reprice the value of stranded assets and those who are exposed to them.

The essential health measures to protect against the pandemic have triggered a series of knock-on economic effects with parents unable to work because they have been forced to stay home with their children. The resulting loss of income and heightened uncertainty have triggered a paradox of thrift among households and companies as (understandable) spending caution by individuals collectively reinforces the sharp economic slowdown that they fear.

At the highest level, we have been living through the systemic risks from unfettered capitalism. In the abstract, it might be individually rational to pursue shareholder value maximisation to the exclusion of other stakeholders but eventually it proves socially disastrous. As we have seen, there are several channels through which market fundamentalism undermines the social foundations of markets themselves. This can crystallise in systemic risks ranging from corruption of markets to the destruction of asset values from rapid withdrawal of social licence. It will be increasingly important for companies to be part of a credible transition to net zero. When there is existential risk, 'jump to default' social licence is always a possibility.

Actions can be taken to build resilience. First, authorities should be given specific responsibilities for identifying systemic risks and taking the necessary actions to mitigate their impact, while being held accountable to explain what progress has been made and which gaps remain. The structure of the Bank of England is the model in the financial sector, with its clear responsibilities for identifying and mitigating risks to the financial system and macroeconomy, wide-ranging powers to address them and the ability to make recommendations to other authorities to take actions when necessary.

Countries need to develop a more rigorous approach to assessing systemic risks and public processes to building resilience. They would do well to consider examples set by the Nordic countries.[30] Finland's focus on preparedness is grounded in a law which explicitly references pandemics. To instil joined-up thinking and improve preparations, Finland selects leaders from across society to participate in its National Defence Centre course to review how different areas – logistics, food, energy, banking and defence – work in a crisis. Other Nordic countries involve their citizens in contingency planning, in contrast to most advanced economies where such strategies are kept at arm's length. For example, Sweden sent a pamphlet to all households a few years ago detailing how they should act in case of war or a cyber-attack. The idea was to promote self-reliance among the able so that the government could concentrate on the vulnerable. These inclusive approaches can improve decision making and increase the legitimacy of crisis-fighting measures when they are put into action.

Second, authorities and companies must plan for failure. As we have seen, people are bad at predicting systemic risks because of various biases including disaster myopia, hyperbolic discounting and recency bias. Financial markets can be particularly vulnerable because of the temptations of liquidity illusion, and the reliance on a strategy of being able to get out before the greater fool. For example, asset-management vehicles that promise daily liquidity to their clients while investing in fundamentally illiquid assets (like corporate loans) were prone to fire sale risk and were saved only by the prospect of massive Fed intervention in the spring of 2020. I know from experience that a booming economy can give the illusion of lower risk, feeding beliefs that potential growth is both stronger and more sustainable than it is. Risks are often the greatest when they seem the least.

A critical part of building resilience is creating an anti-fragile system that is robust. Tangible examples include completing the measures to end too-big-to-fail in banking, building cyber resilience, pursuing climate stress tests and creating social safety nets for those in new forms of work. And, of course, it means maintaining pandemic preparedness, national defence and anti-terrorism capacity.

Third, planning for failure includes conducting stress tests and war games. Authorities need to think about what would happen when something goes wrong, don't spend time justifying why it will never happen. Ask not what you can do to the market but what the market can do to you. Then examine the consequences. The results of these stress tests and war games should be made public, with specific follow-ups to boost resilience, and someone else to mark your homework (as the IMF does for the Bank of England in relation to stress tests of financial institutions).

Of course, when disaster strikes, it won't follow the exact scenario for which you have prepared. As Eisenhower emphasised, 'plans are worthless, but planning is everything'. For example, the Bank of England's preparations for Brexit built buffers, reserves and contingency plans across the financial system. These were quickly repurposed and then deployed when the pandemic struck.

This leads to the fourth measure, to build buffers and then use them. Following the financial crisis, all banks have had to carry much more capital and liquidity, and the largest, most interconnected ones have had to hold even more (in a form of a 'Pigouvian' tax that internalises their contribution to systemic risks). But buffers are useless unless they can be implemented under stress. It is part of the job of central banks to prevent the collective-action problem of the bankers' paradox of thrift when risks spike and fear is the greatest. That's what the Bank of England did post-referendum and at the start of the pandemic by cutting capital requirements and releasing massive liquidity.

As I said in a televised address to the nation on the morning after the Brexit referendum, 'we are well prepared for this' – a result that financial markets had assigned a 10 per cent probability to just hours before. Preparations must be made whether or not you think something will happen on your watch.

In healthcare, prudential buffers include PPE stockpiles and testing capacity. In cyber, they include backup systems and contingency plans. Sadly, there are no buffers that can insure against climate risks; the only protection now is to catalyse early action, in part through a credible path for carbon pricing.

Finally, promote diversity in all its forms. A more diverse system is more resilient. Systemic risks punish mono-strategies and groupthink. It is critical therefore to promote diversity of institutions, strategies, people and processes in assessing risks. In finance, different firms have different load-bearing capacities under stress. This is essential to limit fire sales (there need to be willing buyers for sellers). From healthcare to climate engineering, diverse approaches are essential to innovation.

SUSTAINABILITY

Sustainable development meets the needs of the present generation without compromising the ability of future generations to meet their own needs. Its pillars are economic, environmental and social. It is an understatement to say that we have been eroding them all. The burdens – from mounting government debts, underfunded pensions, inadequate health and social care to environment calamity – that we are pushing on to the next generation are unfair, inequitable and irresponsible.

Sustainability requires thinking beyond the here and now, further than the news cycle, past the political cycle. At its best, sustainable policy pulls the future into the present in ways that improve both.

The pillars of sustainability are interdependent; none stand on their own. Consider the climate crisis, which is consistently the top priority of the next generation. Its solutions are intimately tied to our fiscal, economic and social wellbeing. We need to leverage the social coalition that has formed for climate action, but that coalition won't, and shouldn't, hold if we don't have a just transition. We cannot achieve environmental sustainability if we sacrifice our economy and, with it, people's livelihoods. Similarly, we won't devise all the necessary solutions or implement them with sufficient speed without market forces.

This is why we need to channel the power of markets to missions that society values. As Chapter 12 explains, addressing climate change requires a clear goal – net zero – that can be attained only by comprehensive efforts from across society. To be properly grounded, efforts to address climate change must be:

– tangible (by helping people to make their homes and workplaces energy efficient, making it easy to drive electric vehicles, plant trees and preserve our natural heritage);

- predictable (by building a track record of credible climate policies that emphasise investment in solutions in order to crowd in private investment); and
- equitable (by supporting just transitions for regions and sectors that will undergo wrenching adjustments).

The green investment opportunity – amounting to tens of trillions of dollars over the next decade – brings together a unique combination of factors:

- potential consumer caution, pressures on employment and weaker export markets could all mean that investment will determine the strength of most economic recoveries;
- the low-for-long interest rate environment means large-scale public investment is possible, despite record fiscal expenditures to fight the Covid crisis (provided the transition from Covid to Capital begins soon);
- the largest investment opportunities for the next decade all involve accelerating the transition to a net-zero economy; in parallel, these investments will create high-paying jobs across the country while advancing competitiveness in the industries of the future; and
- the global private financial sector increasingly sees the transition to net zero as the future of finance.

These factors create a win–win–win: stronger growth and better jobs, greater export competitiveness in industry, services and finance, and the prospect of meeting climate goals. This green investment opportunity can be seized by using government fiscal capacity to support targeted investments and set out a clear strategic direction for the transition, supported by carbon pricing, appropriate regulation and financial disclosure in order to unleash private investment at lowest possible cost.

Our approach to sustainability should also draw on the wisdom of indigenous traditions. In my native Canada, the First Nations know that environmental and economic considerations are not independent factors to be weighed against one another. They are intrinsically linked. In many parts of Canada, like our Pacific coast and rivers, the environment is the economy. And our First Nations traditions teach that we are not apart from nature but are integral to it. We are just one small – and humble – element of an integrated ecosystem and have to earn our right to take from the environment, while always respecting and nourishing it.

Similarly, as the Nobel laureate Partha Dasgupta describes in his Review of the Economics of Biodiversity for the UK government, sustainability means accepting that our economy is embedded in nature – not external to it. This forces us to recognise the limits nature places on the economy, shaping our understanding of sustainable development and growth. This recognition begins to reveal the value of our natural capital, including biodiversity. Natural capital which on a per capita basis has fallen by an estimated 40 per cent in the past few decades while our produced capital has almost doubled.[31]

Given rapidly depleting carbon budgets and eroding fiscal capacity, the next few budgets will be critical to national efforts to achieve sustainability. This will require using all levers of public policy, or the 3 Fs: fiscal, framing and finance.

FISCAL

The government balance sheet must be used to maximum effect to balance short-term growth and long-term sustainability. Governments need to invest in the necessary public goods while setting the longer-term direction for the economy in order to catalyse the private investment needed. They will accelerate the transition towards proven, economic zero-carbon solutions, as well as take calculated risks in new solutions from hydrogen to CCUS and the bio-revolution. The problem is simply too large and urgent to be solved otherwise.

A decade on with the carbon budget rapidly depleting, we cannot repeat the mistakes of the aftermath of the global financial crisis when spending was 'shovel-ready' and backward-looking. At that time, across advanced economies, green measures and investments amounted to around 16 per cent of total fiscal stimulus spending. A handful of countries such as China (one-third of spending), Germany (one-fifth) and South Korea (three-quarters) spent with a longer-term, green orientation. As a consequence, these countries materially improved the competitiveness of their economies.

The early signs today are promising, with budgets of the EU, France and Germany all dedicating about one-third of resources to a green recovery when measured on the basis of euros of spending. More to the point, as will be described below, the life-cycle impact of many of the measures announced is substantially greater. That is because they change the 'shadow price of carbon' and have the potential to create economies of scale and complementarities within energy systems that improve their competitiveness and adoption rates. On this basis, Eurasia Group finds that for a hundred different stimulus measures between February and July 2020 more than two-thirds ($500 billion) could be classified as green, and would result in estimated net emissions savings of 413 million metric tonnes of carbon dioxide (CO_2) on a peak annual basis (approximately equivalent to the annual emissions of Poland), and just over 400 million metric tonnes of CO_2 on a life-cycle basis.[32]

Some of the most promising areas for investment include:

- Home retrofits to improve energy efficiency through better insulation, conversion from gas to electric heating, installation of heat pumps and solar.
- Sustainable power. To build a zero-carbon economy we must electrify as much as possible and produce all our electricity in a zero-carbon manner. That includes completely electrifying surface transport and a large share of building heating, and using electricity to make hydrogen which can then be used in multiple industrial processes and fuels. This is more than simply getting rid of fossil fuel generation. In many economies it will require doubling the total energy production within a few decades to meet much higher demand.

- Building charging networks to ease the transition to zero emission vehicles (ZEV). The key issue is that this relatively modest investment needs to be front loaded in order to overcome any initial range anxiety and to encourage rapid take-up of green cars and trucks.
- Developing hydrogen and Carbon Capture Use and Storage (CCUS). Hydrogen will be a crucial building block of a zero-carbon economy, potentially playing a major role in the decarbonisation of long-distance trucking, steel production, petrochemical processes, shipping (in the form of ammonia) and aviation (converted into a synthetic jet fuel). CCUS will likely also play a major role in the power sector, steel and synthetic fuel and petrochemicals processes (where hydrogen and CO_2 can be synthesised together to create multiple products).
- A deeply electrified economy will automatically be more efficient, and even more so if advanced digital capabilities enable the optimal management of electricity across the day, week and year. This requires smart grid software and business model innovation that builds on a hardware platform of high-speed interconnectivity, delivered by optical fibre and 5G networks.

The last example underscores the synergistic relationship between the pillars of sustainability. Digitisation is required to make the most of green investments. It also by definition improves social sustainability by bridging the digital divide that Covid has so cruelly exposed.

One of the biggest synergies is the job-creation potential of sustainable investment. On average sustainable investments in renewable and energy efficiency create about five jobs more per $1 million spent than traditional spending on conventional energy.[33]

Investing in housing-stock refurbishment is the best job-creating policy because most of the spending required is to pay workers doing the home insulation and equipment installation, minimising the danger that expenditure generates imports of equipment from overseas.

Investing in zero-carbon electricity generation and networks will create fewer jobs per dollar spent than building retrofits, but the numbers will still be material and many of the jobs will be high skill and highly paid, they can be spread across regions and can help create industrial clusters and competitive strengths in technologies and jobs of the future.

The focus on achieving net zero can catalyse enormous private investment, underscoring the fundamental importance of framing policies.

Framing policies are regulations, rules, mandates, prohibitions, taxes and subsidies that set the direction towards a low-carbon economy. Their effectiveness is reinforced by clear strategies for the energy transition, including timetables and milestones that build credibility and predictability. In these ways, framing policies set the terms for longer-term private investment, and can pull forward action.

A clear strategic vision of the transition to a zero-carbon economy could significantly reduce its costs. The more certain private investors are of the direction of travel, the scale of future investment opportunities and the legal and contractual framework in which they will operate, the lower the expected rate of return they will require to invest. Similarly, the more certain companies are about the pace and nature of future technology deployments, the more they will invest in the development of technologies and supply chains, and the faster capital equipment and operating costs will come down as a result of the economy of scale and learning-curve effects.

Over the last ten years, these effects have helped reduce the costs of onshore wind, solar photovoltaics and batteries by 60, 90 and 85 per cent respectively. Public policy must use several levers to unleash further progress in these and in a widening set of other technologies. These levers include:

- A clear carbon price path for the next decade to create investor certainty that high-carbon technologies will become uneconomic and that low-carbon ones will be increasingly profitable.

- Regulation to spur specific transitions. For instance, rising minimum fuel efficiency standards and commitments to phase out all internal combustion engine (ICE) passenger-vehicle sales spur companies to accelerate investments in electric engines and batteries, and investors to support the auto companies which had the most ambitious electrification strategies. Private investment in sustainable aviation fuels would be encouraged by a carbon price and a regulatory mandate for a rising percentage of jet fuel from zero-carbon sources.
- Reinforcement of the financial disclosure regime, which forces companies and investors to formulate and disclose their transition strategies.

Carbon pricing. One of the most important initiatives is carbon pricing. The best approach is a revenue-neutral, progressive carbon tax. That is, the average proceeds should be returned to individuals so that incentives to spend on lower-carbon projects are in place but less well-off households benefit from rebates.

Meaningful carbon prices are a cornerstone of any effective climate policy framework. By charging an explicit price for the right to emit greenhouse gases, policymakers ensure that green businesses are not put at an unfair disadvantage relative to their polluting competitors. In addition, carbon prices can induce existing high-carbon businesses to adjust to net zero in whatever way is most efficient. Carbon prices should increase in a gradual and predictable way to support an orderly adjustment to a net-zero carbon economy, and they should be designed equitably – for example, by using proceeds to support low-income households.

If policymakers make clear the direction and speed of the shift towards a low-carbon economy the financial system will pull forward future policies and ensure that the economy starts adjusting to them today. Every year that we gain on the path to net zero can have significant benefits – around 5 per cent of 2019 world GDP in net present value terms. A credible commitment to act also avoids the risk of adding trillions to the stock of stranded assets, and means that policymakers will need to intervene less forcefully in the future.

Climate policies need broad political support to be credible. The experience with inflation targeting demonstrates the value of politicians across the political spectrum recognising a common problem. Backtracking on ambitious climate agendas is more difficult if politicians share the same goals and expect to be held to account. Such a broad-based consensus needs to be supported by clear communication and advocacy.

Countries can cement credibility by building a climate-policy track record. Governments need to formulate intermediary goals that are consistent with their long-term strategies and demonstrate that they are taking steps to achieve these intermediary goals – for example, by setting appropriate carbon prices.

One way that governments could gain credibility is by delegating some decisions to independent Carbon Councils. To be clear, the goals of climate policy, such as the commitment to reach net zero by 2050, can only be decided by elected governments. Governments can, however, delegate to Carbon Councils the calibration of the instruments, such as carbon prices, that are necessary to achieve these targets. Delegating responsibilities helps insulate decisions with significant long-term implications from short-term political pressures, and allows countries to gain credibility more quickly and more effectively. Such an institutional set-up mirrors the design of monetary policy frameworks. And in the same way that some central banks are subject to supervisory authorities, Carbon Councils could supervise companies' emissions and their reduction targets as they align to these national climate goals.

Such an approach should be accompanied by appropriate accountability mechanisms. It is for elected governments to formulate the mandates of Carbon Councils, enshrine them in legislation and determine appropriate accountability mechanisms. This is particularly important as climate policy can have significant distributional implications, which puts a premium on political accountability.

The amount of direct control that governments should delegate to Carbon Councils will differ across the different areas of climate policy. At one end of the spectrum, governments could grant them the direct power to calibrate policy tools independently. This would maximise the Councils' independence and would be most likely to insulate the calibration of climate policies from short-term politics. At the other end, Councils could only issue comply-or-explain recommendations and leave the decision to accept or reject them with the government. While such a set-up would stop short of full independence, it would help address valid concerns around leaving important distributional decisions to unelected officials. In the area of macroprudential policy, comply-or-explain recommendations have proven to be an effective way of combining flexibility with political oversight and democratic legitimacy.

A host of other fiscal and regulatory policies made by governments can be highly effective in setting out the contours of a net-zero economy including:

- measures to address the structural issues that could hold back the expansion of renewable energy (for example, investments and regulations that promote grid interconnections, storage and smart charging);
- initiatives to raise the demand for electric vehicles (for example, through differentiated subsidies and cash for clunkers) and regulations to phase out the sale of new internal combustion vehicles in the next decade;
- mandates for fuel and energy use (for example, maritime/ aviation hydrogen blends by 2025);
- instituting new residential and commercial building codes (with associated support programmes in retrofits and green mortgages); and
- requirements for climate disclosure and net-zero transition plans from large companies.

The financial system can play a decisive role in accelerating and amplifying the effectiveness of public policies. By factoring a forward-looking assessment of future climate policies into today's insurance premiums, lending decisions and asset prices, the financial system pulls forward the adjustment to a net-zero economy.

By assessing the impact of policies in a systematic way, finance can ensure that climate policies inform the allocation of capital across all sectors of the economy. Finance is already starting to factor climate-related risks. Insurance companies have long incorporated the physical risks of climate change into their risk models. Many of the largest banks have decided to stop lending to high-carbon industries, and financial markets are starting to price in the risks associated with transitioning to a net-zero economy.

To manage these risks and seize the associated opportunities, financial institutions need to take a strategic, forward-looking approach. Static information such as the carbon emissions of companies that financial institutions are lending to, insuring or investing in is a natural starting point, but it may reveal little about the prospects for a company going forward. Financial institutions need to consider companies' transition plans and their strategic resilience to new climate policies and technologies.

Diligent readers of this book will be familiar with the '3R' agenda – to improve approaches to climate reporting, risk management and return optimisation – that will ensure that every decision takes climate change into account (as discussed in detail in Chapter 12). Authorities are putting in place the right market frameworks so the private sector can do what it does best: to allocate capital to manage risks and seize opportunities across all of our economies.

DYNAMISM

Dynamism – what Schumpeter famously termed the 'creative gale of destruction' – is essential for growth. The cycle of new firms and ideas overtaking the old is at the heart of the market economy, but dynamism is not self-perpetuating. Countries must jealously guard and actively nurture the conditions that promote it.

Many remember Schumpeter's phrase 'creative destruction' but forget its context. The core of his voluminous writings was his view that capitalism was prone to ossification. In 'the treason of the clerks', large companies tend to become self-perpetuating bureaucracies. When coupled with the natural tendencies of incumbents towards rent seeking – seeking the rewards of value created by other people – the treason of the clerks can quell the creative gale.

This is more likely to happen if public policy is pro-business rather than pro-market – that is, if it concentrates on the needs of incumbent firms to the detriment of new entrants. An economy is more dynamic the more decentralised it is, and, by definition, the more that the leaders in economic sectors change as good new ideas come to market. In contrast, concentration leads to rent seeking and efforts to entrench existing advantages.

As John Kay has emphasised, part of the genius of capitalism is the 'process of discovery'. Managed economies tend to be hostile to innovation, while market economies thrive on it. Most ideas fail, but the 'continuous supply of unreasonable optimism' produces the odd successes which bring new solutions, solutions that are quickly imitated and widely disseminated. This is why ease of entry and exit are essential. Disruptive innovations usually come from new entrants – such as Amazon in retail or Uber in transport. Just as importantly, bad ideas that arise outside of established incumbents are quickly starved of funds and fade away before they consume too many resources.

There are six strategies that are critical to promote dynamism.

First, robust competition policy is essential. It has become largely about defining a market and estimating the impact of mergers or corporate actions on price. In technology, where services are often provided for 'free' (or more precisely in exchange for advertising and the collection of personal data), a series of acquisitions have been waved through because there is no discernible price impact. But there is a detrimental impact on experimentation and another one on the concentration of economic power. And with them, on dynamism.

In his rigorously researched work *The Great Reversal*, the economist Thomas Philippon argues that such a process has occurred in the United States. To Philippon, American markets, once a model for the world, are giving up on healthy competition. Sector after economic sector is more concentrated than it was twenty years ago, dominated by fewer and bigger players who lobby politicians aggressively to protect and expand their profit margins. This drives up prices while driving down investment, productivity, growth and wages, resulting in more inequality. Meanwhile, Europe – long dismissed for competitive sclerosis and weak antitrust – is beating America at its own game. Europe is now leading the thinking and action on pro-competitive policies from finance to tech.

Countries would do well to heed this cautionary tale. It is a gentle slope towards cosy oligopolies. The costs of this quiet life are not immediately apparent, but they grow with time through lost innovation, stilted ideas and growing rent seeking. Eternal vigilance in the name of competition is essential. The future will be made by entrepreneurs we do not yet know.

Given the nature of the 4IR, this vigilance is particularly important for digital competition. In 2019, Professor Jason Furman of Harvard chaired an expert panel for Her Majesty's Treasury to Unlock Digital Competition. Its core conclusions should guide policy, particularly:

- Instead of just relying on traditional competition tools, countries should take a forward-looking approach that creates and enforces a clear set of rules to limit anti-competitive actions by the most significant digital platforms while reducing structural barriers that currently hinder effective competition.
- These rules should be based on generally agreed principles and developed into more specific codes of conduct with the participation of a wide range of stakeholders. It should be made easy for consumers (and small businesses) to move their data across digital services, to build systems around open standards and to make data available for competitors, offering benefits to consumers and facilitating the entry of new businesses.
- Existing competition tools also need to be updated to address the changing economy more effectively. 'Ensuring that competition is vibrant requires ensuring that there are competitors.' Merger control has long had this role and in the context of the digital economy it needs to become more active with an approach that is more forward-looking and more focused on innovation and the overall economic impact of mergers. Even with clearer *ex ante* rules, *ex post* antitrust

enforcement will remain an important backstop – but it needs to be conducted in a faster and more effective manner for the benefit of all parties.

Second, in an increasingly intangible economy, where ideas and processes are at the heart of competitiveness, a solid intellectual property framework is critical. Many intangibles are 'highly contested' in that they can be easily appropriated and copied. To maintain incentives to invest in intangibles, companies must have a reasonable expectation that they will obtain the benefits of their labours.

Third, we need a tax system that supports true dynamism. Individuals who invest their time and money in creating new solutions should be rewarded fairly. And given that many of the best ideas will come from the smallest beginnings, it is sensible to encourage enterprise investment. Tax arrangements like the UK's Enterprise Investment Scheme do this by allowing tax relief on investments in start-ups of all types provided the capital is held for a three-year period. Many of these investments will be unsuccessful, in which case the investor will be able to offset a portion of their investment against their income tax. The result is to encourage an ecosystem of investment, creation, destruction and reinvestment. We want experimentation, particularly during a period of great change. The winners, those who master the power of new technologies, will be very successful. Consideration should also be given to deferral of capital gains that are rolled over into new investments.

It may be unfashionable to support wealth creation but it is essential if we are to address our many challenges. This book has clearly argued that wealth creation should not be viewed in isolation. It is complementary to the other elements of the action plan: aggressive competition policy that discourages rent seeking, enhanced corporate purpose that creates value for all stakeholders, individual responsibility and a commitment to fairness that respects and builds the social capital of markets.

Fourth, an essential part of a dynamic business environment will be new forms of financing for small and medium-sized businesses.

Big data is opening up new opportunities for more competitive, platform-based finance of SMEs. This has the potential to yield enormous benefits for households and businesses by developing new lines of credit, providing greater choice, better-targeted products and keener pricing. Putting data to work is critical to closing one of the biggest funding gaps in our economies. In the UK, SMEs generate more than half of private sector employment and private business turnover, yet they face a £22 billion funding gap.[34] Almost half of all SMEs do not plan to use external finance, citing the hassle or time associated with applying. Of those that have approached their bank, two-fifths have been rejected.[35]

Part of the problem is that the assets that SMEs are seeking to borrow against are increasingly intangible – the value of a brand or user base – rather than physical assets, like buildings or machinery. SMEs that have not borrowed lack the historic data required for credit scoring. And legal requirements to prevent money laundering and Know Your Customer make the process especially burdensome for a small business with limited resources.

This should not be the case in a data-rich world. Lenders should be able to access a broader set of information on which to base credit decisions. Already, search and social media data are supplementing traditional metrics to unlock finance for smaller enterprises whose assets are increasingly intangible, including e-commerce platforms like Shopify and payment providers like Stripe and PayPal.

To make real inroads, SMEs must be able to identify the data relevant to their businesses, incorporate it into their individual credit files and easily share these files with potential providers of finance through a national SME financing platform. This is how to extract value from data and promote competition. The Bank of England developed an open platform for SME lending that would enable open banking and empower SMEs. It would help avoid lock-in on existing platforms and enable providers of finance to compete for SME lending, helping to broaden the products available to companies and offer more competitive rates, making access to finance quick, easy and cost effective.[36]

Fifth, successful countries will be centres of excellence and hubs in global supply chains. As will be discussed in the globalisation section below, these connections must be based on values to create platforms of prosperity, including safe data portals and platforms that facilitate free trade for SMEs.

Sixth, social cohesion is the new competitiveness. Businesses increasingly want to operate in jurisdictions that are on a path to sustainability. A progressive society that truly celebrates diversity and brings its strength to the fore is vital. Social resilience breeds economic resilience, making stakeholder capitalism anchored in truly purpose-driven companies essential.

A core message of this book has been that dynamism is most effective if it is channelled towards what society values. This mission-oriented capitalism can use the market to achieve larger social goals from net zero to disease control (a low R), regional solidarity and social equity. As we saw in the last chapter, impact investors are usually anchored to making progress towards one or more of the SDGs. As discussed in previous chapters, countries can take a number of tangible steps to promote corporate purpose including:

- Set company law and governance standards so that companies state their specific purpose clearly in their articles of association and their directors have regard to the interests of all stakeholders. Regulation should expect alignment of managerial interests with corporate purpose and establish clear reporting and accountability mechanisms.

- Allow new corporate forms, like B Corps and *entreprises à mission*, to enshrine principles that go beyond the standard for profit corporate entity. These corporate forms signal to shareholders and all stakeholders the balance of the corporation's objectives and allow management more latitude in considering factors beyond maximising shareholder value.

- Require companies to report on stakeholder outcomes as measured by sustainability reporting standards in their main financial reports. Set formal reporting requirements and comply-or-explain disclosure obligations.

– Modernise fiduciary duties so that investors have an
   obligation to understand the sustainability preferences of
   their beneficiaries and incorporate these preferences into
   their decision making whether or not these are financially
   material. Investors' duty of care should be clarified to
   acknowledge the role of ESG factors in identifying long-term
   value and reducing risk.

VALUES-BASED GLOBALISATION

The globalisation of the production of goods and services has deepened the interdependence of countries. Since 1995, foreign trade has
increased from around 45 per cent of global GDP to about 70 per
cent today and cross-border holdings of financial assets from 75 per
cent of global GDP in 1995 to over 200 per cent. This process has
been driven in part by policy choices, but primarily by technological
progress with businesses capitalising on advances in transportation,
telecoms and computing to make it easier to build global value
chains and trade globally. Indeed, fully 30 per cent of foreign value
added is now created through global supply chains.[37]

Globalisation has simultaneously brought great prosperity and
caused tremendous misery. As a consequence, the principles of
international integration are being challenged, and the institutions
that underpin it are losing their relevance. This is happening while
the forces of integration through technological change continue
unabated. We run the risk of haphazard and uncontrolled integration that compromises our values. Therefore, a defining challenge
of this generation is to build a more inclusive, resilient and sustainable globalisation as it enters its fourth phase.

The first phase of globalisation was in the period leading up to
the First World War when immigration and cross-border capital
flows were largely unrestricted and substantial even by recent standards (Canada ran current account deficits averaging 10 per cent of
GDP for three decades during which time its population doubled).
The global institutional architecture was limited to a handful of
international institutions such as the International Telegraph

Union. The gold standard was a convention, not a treaty. International property rights were enforced by gunboat.

The inter-war years witnessed the disastrous breakdown of these informal conventions for trade and capital flows. Indeed, as we have seen, it was clinging to them that would prove the UK's undoing. Globalisation re-emerged from the ashes of the Second World War grounded in a new rules-based architecture for trade, capital and development aid flows centred on the Bretton Woods institutions. By the 1980s, domestic economic liberalisation accelerated the pace of global integration.

Several factors turbocharged globalisation's third phase. The fall of the Berlin Wall and the reforms initiated by Deng Xiaoping led to the integration of a third of humankind into the global labour force. The establishment of the WTO and China's formal accession into the international trading system transformed global commerce. In parallel, an explosion of technological innovations has brought access (at the click of a virtual button) to the sum of human knowledge to 4 billion people. The deepening of the symbiotic relationship between global markets and technological progress has lifted more than a billion people out of poverty, while a series of technological advances have fundamentally enriched our lives.

But of course all was not well under the surface. Severe fault lines would emerge in the financial system leading to a financial and economic crisis as serious as any in Montagu Norman's times. Only by learning the lessons of that era has catastrophe been averted.

The result was 'much better than it could have been', but counterfactuals are very hard to sell. 'You could've had it a lot worse' doesn't have quite the ring of 'you've never had it so good'. Indeed, many citizens in advanced economies are facing heightened uncertainty, lamenting a loss of control and losing trust in the system. To them, measures of aggregate progress bear little relation to their own experience. Instead of a new golden era, globalisation is associated with low wages, insecure employment, stateless corporations and striking inequalities.

A belief in free trade may be totemic among economists, but while trade makes countries better off, it does not raise all boats within them. Rather, the benefits from trade are unequally spread across individuals and time.

As a consequence, the rules-based architecture to which every small and medium-sized power attaches is under strain. The WTO is no longer mentioned in polite company, currency manipulation is now defined by the US Treasury rather than the IMF, invasions are denied with doublespeak worthy of Orwell, and climate policies are unmade with a tweet.

It would be a mistake to put this down to the rogue actions of a few individuals. The causes are deeply rooted and in some cases institutional. As stated earlier, common rules and standards are required for trade in goods, services and capital, but those rules cede or, at best, pool sovereignty. To maintain legitimacy, the process of agreeing those standards must be rooted in democratic accountability.

Global trade integration tends to reduce that capacity, because as production fragments through value chains there is a greater need for countries to agree on common standards. Those standards are mostly set not within the World Trade Organisation but by large economies with dominant positions in the value chain. Smaller economies tend to end up as rule-takers in the international system.[38]

Using a values-based approach, it is possible to build a more inclusive, resilient and sustainable globalisation. Though we cannot agree binding global rules to tackle the challenges we face, multilateralism can still be powerful. We can build on the lessons from how the international community responded to the financial crisis, which saw the development of robust standards and deeper cooperation without binding rules.

This experience points to a form of cooperative internationalism that is more compatible with the complexities of the problems we face and the valid demands of the electorates. Cooperative internationalism:

- is outcomes-based not rules-based, seeking to advance values like resilience, sustainability and dynamism;
- involves multiple stakeholders and has a flexible geometry (rather than universal);
- is interoperable (works with multiple political systems rather than assuming a Fukuyamesque convergence towards liberal democracy and open markets); and
- is inclusive in that it focuses on the impact on the lives of all of our fellow citizens.

The response to the financial crisis provides the best example of this approach. It clearly reinforced the sovereign obligation for cross-border financial stability – resilience – while respecting national differences in approach to achieving it. The emphasis was on achieving solidarity through an inclusive outcome-focused process. I know from personal experience as the Chair of the body responsible for these reforms, the Financial Stability Board or FSB, that it was time consuming, analytically intensive hard work but ultimately enormously rewarding.

As its performance during the Covid crisis demonstrated, the financial system today is safer, simpler and fairer. This didn't just happen. It was a direct consequence of hundreds of reforms agreed at the global level over the past decade. The challenges were set by G20 leaders. The solutions were developed, debated and decided by reaching consensus at the FSB, and then implemented in national jurisdictions not because of any treaty obligations but through a sense of common ownership and mutual reliance.

As described in Chapter 9, the FSB has succeeded when others, from trade to peacekeeping, have struggled because it has a clear mission with political backing, has the right people around the table, and has built consensus and instilled ownership of decisions.

The experience of the FSB provides a model for successful international cooperation: an outcomes-based approach guided by standards whose ownership is created by shared development not by treaty obligation. They offer broad guidance not absolute prescriptions as it is recognised that they will be tailored to work with different systems.

The FSB reforms are goods in themselves because they promote financial stability in the countries that adopt them. As we will see in a moment, they also create a platform for greater integration between those countries that wish to do so.

To be clear, integration in a G0 world will be partial and fragmented. That is less than the textbook ideal but it is grounded in sovereignty that it is grounded in values. Moreover, the best platforms should gain critical mass (just as they do in social media due to network effects) and could, in time, dominate.

The opportunity is to apply a similar approach to address some of the main challenges wrought by globalisation, including trade, technology and temperature.

Cross-border trade – commercial value – could increasingly be determined by whether countries share values most relevant to the area such as privacy, inclusive growth, workers' rights or climate change. By pursuing cooperative internationalism to develop platforms with other nations who share their values, nations can build a more inclusive, resilient and sustainable globalisation.

Financial services reforms provide the platform for a new outcomes-based approach to trade in services. Leveraging this would not only help address trade imbalances but also help make growth more inclusive given the much larger share of female employment in services. At the same time, the combination of new financial technologies and e-commerce platforms can be used to promote freer trade for small and medium-sized enterprises. After decades of multilateral trade deals, opening seamless cross-border trade for companies from Sheffield to Shanghai to Saskatoon would be truly inclusive globalisation.

One cause of current large trade imbalances is the uneven playing field between trade in goods and services, with barriers to services trade currently up to three times higher than for goods. Most of the world's major surplus countries, like Germany and China, are net exporters of goods and therefore benefit from this asymmetry. Conversely countries with a comparative advantage in services, like the US and UK, are more likely to run current account deficits.

Levelling up offers a way to make trade work for all. Reducing barriers to services trade would enable service-oriented economies to capitalise on their areas of comparative advantage. Reducing restrictions on services trade to the same extent as they have been on goods trade in recent years could halve global imbalances. And doing so can help make growth more inclusive. Services account for a 10pp larger share of women's employment than men's. In fact, the entire (net) rise in female hours over the past few decades (from 37 per cent of men's hours in the UK in 1968 to 73 per cent in 2008) took place in the services sector.

Of course, liberalising services is not straightforward, as barriers are typically not tariffs but 'behind the border' differences in regulatory standards and trading conditions. That is precisely why the experience with financial services is so relevant. It shows that we can make significant progress in addressing concerns about cross-border protections through non-binding global standards and regulatory cooperation, even absent a formal harmonisation and enforcement mechanism such as exists in the EU.

One of the main tasks that has occupied bodies such as the FSB has been how to maintain financial market openness by giving national authorities the confidence that their financial stability will not be undermined by spillovers from poor regulation or risk management elsewhere. Common standards, open information sharing and good supervisory cooperation can create a level playing field and provide the trust needed to allow authorities to recognise and defer to each other's approaches when they achieve comparable outcomes.

This provides a platform for free trade in financial services, building a more open, integrated and resilient financial system where capital can move freely, efficiently and sustainably between jurisdictions, driving investment and innovation. And this platform for free trade in financial services can serve as a template for broader services trade liberalisation. An example of this approach is the recent derivatives accord between the UK and the US, covering up to two-thirds of global activity.

Freer services trade on such a model would have broader benefits beyond addressing external imbalances, including improved consumer choice and lower prices. It is likely to result in widespread increases in productivity, not least because services such as IT, R&D, transport, communications and finance are integral to the manufacture of a wide range of products. And freer trade in services could help rebalance Rodrik's trilemma from prescriptive supranational rules to more differentiated, national approaches to achieve common outcomes (see Chapter 8).

Freer trade in services can help make growth more inclusive, since it is SMEs that stand to gain the most from the lower costs of complying with diverse regulations across countries. SMEs are the engine rooms of most economies. Yet they account for only a fraction of exports. In the UK, for example, SMEs ship only a third of total exports despite accounting for two-thirds of value added. A large part of this underrepresentation reflects the much higher costs of doing business across borders – from complying with diverse regulations across countries to the cost of transferring money internationally. These sunk costs are more burdensome for smaller companies.

Arguably after decades of 'multinational' trade deals, the time has come for free trade for SMEs. This would be truly inclusive globalisation. To do so, countries can leverage the SME platforms, like Shopify, tMall, Etsy, Amazon, that are at the heart of the new economy. These platforms give smaller-scale businesses direct stakes in local and global markets, allowing them to bypass big corporates and engage in a form of artisanal globalisation – a revolution that could bring cottage industry full circle.

Apart from lowering tariffs and recognising product standards (through a focus on outcomes), freer trade for SMEs requires:

- lowering the cost of cross-border payments which can be ten times more expensive than domestic ones, and
- improving SMEs' access to finance, in part by using the broader data and the sociographic footprint of companies as discussed above.

New technologies open the potential to transform retail payments. These include the possibilities that could be created by the development of central bank digital currencies. These could be exchanged between users on messaging platforms and with participating retailers. If properly designed, they may substantially improve financial inclusion and dramatically lower the costs of domestic and cross-border payments.

Unlike social media platforms for which standards and regulations are being debated well after they have been adopted by billions of users, the terms of engagement for innovations in payments and currencies must be adopted in advance of any launch. They must meet the highest standards of prudential regulation and consumer protection, and address issues ranging from anti-money laundering to data protection to operational resilience, while being pro-competitive with open platforms that new users can join on equal terms.

This is why Christine Lagarde and I set up a working group of major central banks to explore the development of CBDCs. We share common values – resilience, universality and dynamism – and a pragmatic approach to ensuring that this promising technological avenue can be developed in the service of citizens, not of tech companies. Expect the solution to be outcomes-focused (on customer service and protection and by enhancing financial stability), resilient, developed by stakeholders, with an open platform that others can join in the future.

A common objective of the initiatives is to spread opportunity to all strata of society. Initiatives include mandatory workforce training, universal skills measures, tax incentives to promote an enterprise society, effective regulation of markets, the balancing of rights of all stakeholders, and free trade for small and medium-sized enterprises. A core challenge is to develop opportunities in a globally integrated economy while reinforcing the values of society.

The nation serves an essential economic role, but it is much more than a collection of marketplaces or a trade negotiator. The state embodies collective ideals such as equality of opportunity, liberty, fairness, regional solidarity and caring for future generations. It can set national goals, such as a just transition to a net-zero economy or universal training so all can reap the rewards of the Fourth Industrial Revolution.

In recent years, both globalists and nationalists have too often devalued these ideals, and in the process reinforced a narrow, trans-action-based sense of nationhood in which nations either cede sovereignty to join larger markets or take it back to win trade wars, respectively. Patriotism is the opposite of such egotistical national-ism. As Emmanuel Macron stressed, 'By putting our own interests first, with no regard for others, we erase the very thing that a nation holds dearest, and the thing that keeps it alive: its moral values.'

As the President of the European Union, Donald Tusk, said at the UN on the same day that Greta Thunberg spoke there:

> History shows how easy it is to transform the love of one's homeland into a hatred towards one's neighbours. How easy it is to transform pride for one's culture into a contempt for the culture of strangers. How easy it is to use the slogans of one's own sovereignty against the sovereignty of others.

And how easy it is to confuse independence with sovereignty. A central challenge is to address the inherent tension between the clear gains of economic integration and the cooperation that is necessary to bring it about, which can be difficult to achieve or explain. In many cases, this tension is illusory because rather than taking away countries' sovereignty, international cooperation offers a way to regain it.

When I used to take the bus between Oxford and London as a student, I would always look out for a landmark. Not the dreaming spires of the university town or Marble Arch in the capital, but rather a terraced house off Headington high street a few miles from my college. To the dismay of his neighbours, a man had constructed a giant sculpture of a shark attacking his roof on an otherwise nondescript street. Catalysed in part by the Chernobyl nuclear disaster, the sculpture expressed his feelings of 'impotence, anger and desperation' at how existential challenges from abroad could quickly become local. Over the years, I have thought back to the shark because it isn't just nuclear fallout that spreads across borders, but financial instability, cyber-crime and climate chaos. To what extent can a country wall itself off from these sharks? And for those that try, what opportunities in trade and investment, ideas and creativity do their citizens forfeit?

We must not confuse independence with sovereignty. As Mario Draghi stresses, 'True sovereignty is reflected not in the power of making laws – as a legal definition would have it – but in the ability to control outcomes and respond to the fundamental needs of the people: what John Locke defines as their "peace, safety, and public good".'[39] Addressing the challenges we face will prove difficult even for those with the will and the authority to act alone. And many of the challenges require internationally coordinated action, which is even more difficult to achieve. In many cases, countries need to find ways to cooperate with like-minded nations to advance common values.

We should take heart from the example of finance, which demonstrates that cooperative internationalism can succeed through:

- a focus on outcomes based on values;
- a willingness to work across boundaries with multiple stakeholders;
- greater use of soft forms of cooperation short of legally binding global standards; and
- mechanisms to help national approaches develop in way that is as aligned as possible.

International cooperation is solidarity at its best when it pursues pragmatic solutions to concrete challenges. Challenges like building the resilience, fairness and responsibility in the financial system, so that capital can flow across borders to create jobs, opportunity and growth. Challenges like creating dynamism through free trade for small businesses so growth can be more inclusive. Challenges like advancing sustainability through like-minded approaches to mainstreaming sustainable finance and comparable national efforts to combat climate change.

Advancing patriotism by re-instilling common purpose, ideals and values in global affairs is integral to country strategies that build opportunities for all. We need a new form of international integration, one that is focused on outcomes, that maintains values and preserves sovereignty in its truest sense. That is the highest example of institutions adapting to achieve their purpose.

There should be no doubt. These adjustments to institutions will have to be as deep as the phenomena that revealed the fragility of the existing order and as vast as the reordering of the geopolitical landscape currently underway. Nations can only navigate and prosper in these cross-currents if they are grounded in values. Nations cannot sustain global integration without the kind of domestic initiatives that this chapter has detailed to reinforce the values of fairness, responsibility, resilience, sustainability, dynamism and, above all, solidarity.

It is essential that the process of agreeing, developing and acting on those initiatives is as inclusive as possible. It is a task which should be approached with ambition, and the seventh value, humility.

And it is with humility that this book will now conclude.

CONCLUSION

Humility

RESET

Whenever I wake up, I get up. Usually, it's dark, so I try to slip downstairs, avoiding the squeaky second step. As I grab a glass of water, I think of my friend Nikolai who once told me that this was the most important thing for cognitive functioning (increasingly I feel like I must not be drinking enough of it). If I'm particularly busy, I meditate (trust me, it creates time) and then go to work. There is no schedule, no impediment to starting. After all, I have taken to sleeping in the office.

Like hundreds of millions of others, my commute changed over the past year. There is no car, tube, bus, ride, run or walk to the office. The transition from home to work involves only a few steps from bed to computer. I lift my screen and go anywhere. Usually, it's into someone else's home. A few people sit in front of a corporate banner, and the more technically inclined disappear into their virtual backdrops whenever they lean back.

But most are content for their home to be their studio, their workstation. I prefer that. I see an Australian cat walk across the keyboard. Glimpse the snow falling in Edmonton. Hear an Argentine boy ask for his lunch. Clock the Billy bookshelves just like mine. And wait while the home deliveries interrupt the conversation. They all level, connect, humanise.

The world is being reset. This book has argued for a direction in which values drive value.

HUMILITY

The attentive reader will have noticed one of the seven values wasn't explored in the last chapter: humility. This wasn't an oversight. Humility wasn't overlooked because it's awkward, although campaigning for a national humility strategy might be challenging – 'to be clear, that's national humility not national humiliation …' And yes, I have much to be humble about.

Humility matters. It matters because it is an attitude to leading and governing. Not an impediment to acting. Humility is recognising that there will be surprises. I have learned that it is worth asking what could happen if things go wrong, even when you think it unlikely. What if subprime isn't contained? What if a cyber-attack is successful? What if there is no deal? Humility admits the limits of our knowledge, that there are unknown unknowns which make resilience and adaptability imperative. The humble can plan for failure, even if they don't know how or when it will happen.

Humility allows us to set goals before we know all the answers. If we are humble, we don't think we can make a map of the whole world to chart our course or try to put a price on every value so we can optimise. If we are humble, we can recognise that answers can be found through processes that will bring them out through debate, considering different perspectives and forging consensus.

The humble recognise the limits of meritocracy. Humility admits the role of good fortune and the responsibilities that success brings – the duties that should be put into the service of purpose. Being humble is recognising that we are custodians of our companies, communities and countries. And that all are equal within. That the common good trumps utilitarianism.

UNCERTAINTY

A few years back, I met some students at the University of Alberta. The UofA was where my father used to teach and my mother and sister studied. Feeling that I should offer some career advice, I began by telling the students that, from my experience, the road ahead would not be straight. That it is entirely unrealistic to try to map out the decades ahead, especially since many of the jobs and even the industries of tomorrow do not yet exist. To make my advice seem more accessible, I noted John Lennon's observation that 'Life is what happens to you while you're busy making other plans.'[1] They nodded slowly but looked a bit puzzled, so I added the clarifier: 'John Lennon was a member of the Beatles.' And just in case, some colour, 'The Beatles were a British rock band.'

I ploughed on. My point was that, whenever I would meet my high-school or university friends – friends old enough to remember the Beatles – they were often surprised by where their careers have taken them. Whether they were happy usually depended on whether they had continued to pursue their interests, given back to their communities and stayed true to their values.

With this context, I advised the students to be flexible and adventurous as they began their careers, to pick opportunities that gave them a chance to learn new things and grow as a person; and to think of every job not only as being worthwhile in itself, but also as being an experience that will prepare them for the next opportunity that comes along. In those ways, they would build adaptability, enjoy themselves and be more likely to succeed.

Such adaptability is especially important for those graduating into a world of tectonic shifts. From G7 to G20 to G0. From the Third to the Fourth Industrial Revolution. From, it can be hoped, diversity to inclusion. Amid this uncertainty lie great opportunities to build the new economic and social engines of our shared prosperity. In the coming years, we will determine how well the world commercialises fundamental breakthroughs in areas such as renewable energy, biotech, fintech and artificial intelligence. We will decide whether they serve the many or the few.

And we will determine whether we rebuild the social capital, the moral sentiments, for the shared prosperity consistent with our values.

CHANCE

Finally, I suggested to the students that, when success comes – I meant more success because after all they had already made it quite far – it will be important to remember the role that chance plays in all of our lives and the responsibilities that come with that good fortune.

I should know since it is a total accident of history that I became Governor of the Bank of England. Indeed, many in the UK are still wondering how it happened. I had studied economics because I had wanted to understand how the world worked – not realising for decades that the economics of the subjective revolution was changing the very world it purported to describe.

I had never set out to be a central banker. I worked for years as an investment banker moving jobs every eighteen months or two years across three continents. While the variety was stimulating, I found that I most enjoyed working on issues where the public and private sectors intersected, from post-apartheid South Africa to pre-privatisation Ontario.

So when the opportunity to join the Canadian public service arose, I leapt at it. Fortunately, by pursuing what had interested me the most, I'd acquired just enough experience of markets and quasi-public policy to get through the Bank of Canada's big brass doors. There I learned from exceptional colleagues including my predecessor, David Dodge, and my successor, Tiff Macklem. I was pleased to be able to give something back to the great country which had educated me, inspired me and, yes, given me my chance.

When I was appointed Governor of the Bank of Canada, I thought that, for the first time since Grade Five, I knew what I'd be doing for the next seven years. My predecessors had left the economy in great shape. There were only eight, regularly scheduled interest rate decisions a year. All I had to do was set the cruise control and not mess it up.

Oops. Remember what I said about humility. The global financial crisis began almost immediately, putting paid to my idea that central banking would mean a quiet life, away from the sound and fury of the private sector. Through those harrowing years, I was privileged to learn from a remarkable group of people on how to address complex problems under enormous uncertainty and great pressure.

By following my passion, by partnering with exceptional people and by chance encounters – being in the right place at the right time – I ended up at the Bank of England during a time of great consequence. It was a total, improbable fluke.

As Michael Lewis once said, 'This isn't just false modesty, it's false modesty with a point.'[2]

RESPONSIBILITY

The point is that we are all fortunate. My luck is obvious. The students I met were fortunate to have studied at the University of Alberta, to be young in Canada at this time, and to have had family, friends and mentors who had inspired them to learn and develop. Their future would be down to them. To define their purpose and to create the future they want. That plan, like life's plan, wouldn't unfold seamlessly, but if they stayed true to their interests and values, their careers, with purpose, would grow like an oak through the ages.

Today, those who are given talent and opportunity can reap tremendous rewards. Success is magnified in a global marketplace. The Covid crisis has only made that easier. A few steps. The opening of the computer. Digital – and dominant – by default. Now is the time to be famous or fortunate. But (as Luke records) of those to whom much is given, much is expected. Recognising that none of us truly succeeds entirely on our own points to our responsibility for improving the systems in which we work and live. It is the first mark of humility.

As this book has detailed, economic and political philosophers have long espoused the importance of values, beliefs and culture to a vibrant economy. Values such as responsibility, fairness, integrity, dynamism, solidarity and resilience. It is our responsibility to reinforce these values and to pass them on. Pass them on until they are bred in the bone. By building a sense of vocation, we can be custodians who improve our institutions and communities before passing them along to the next generations.

By living purpose, companies can work to find solutions to society's challenges, while being responsible and responsive employers, with honest, fair and lasting relationships with suppliers and customers, and engaging in their communities as good corporate citizens.

And by advancing patriotism, nations can spread opportunity across society without exception and embody the ideals of equality, liberty, fairness, dynamism and solidarity across regions and generations.

In these ways, we can rebuild the ethical foundations necessary for long-term prosperity. We all need to avoid compartmentalisation – the division of our lives into different realms, each with its own set of rules. Home is distinct from work, ethics from law, the individual from the system. Reinstilling higher purpose, ideals and virtues can help end this divided life and, by broadening the range of values in value, it can spread the rewards of the market more widely.

We have a choice. We can continue to let financial valuation narrow our values or we can create an ecosystem in which society's values broaden the market's conceptions of value. In this way, individual creativity and market dynamism will be channelled to achieve society's highest goals.

RENEWAL

A few months before I finished my term at the Bank of England, I attended the City New Year Service at St Michael's Cornhill. This gathering is always a welcome opportunity after the revelry of Christmas to reflect before a new year of work begins. As had been the case for the past six years, I was seated next to a new Lord Mayor of London. This year was special because the latest, William Russell, was a long-time friend. William had been a highly capable banker, who was now devoting his time to charity and family and brimming with ideas to make the City more sustainable.

William's term of office was just beginning as mine was coming to an end. That morning, in keeping with my reflective mood, I had re-read some of Marcus Aurelius' *Meditations* and was struck by his reminders of our mortality, such as:

> This mortal life is a little thing, lived in a little corner of earth;
> and little too, is the longest fame to come – dependent as it is on
> a succession of fast-perishing little men who have no knowledge
> even of their own selves, much less of one long dead and gone.[3]

In his sermon, to my surprise, the Rev. Charles Skrine picked up the theme, drawing first on the tragedy of the horizon before broadening his lesson to address perspectives on immortality and how we live today. Speaking directly to the first pew, he observed:

> Some of us are in jobs where we know where we come on a list
> ... in our front rows we have the 120th Governor and 692nd
> Lord Mayor. Governors last longer than Lord Mayors and you
> will see from the back of the church that organists do the same
> thing to priests.
>   How many of the distinguished Governors of the Bank can
> we name? Of the 120? Or Lord Mayors? ... I can do seven of my
> predecessors without cheating, and even then I don't get all the
> first names. People who went to the horizon of their death
> feeling like they were the heroes of their own story.

Then, drawing on the readings, he set our transience in two opposing perspectives:

> Let us eat and drink for tomorrow we die. If you set the horizon
> for your performance review at the moment you die, life is
> short, and pressured, and the pressure degrades selflessness and
> service of others.
>   If the horizon goes beyond the grave, and goes beyond for
> immortal amounts of time, and without all the corruption of
> death that blights the world, then there is a horizon that puts
> our life here into the right perspective.

He meant a life not easily moved by the day-to-day 'crises' of home and work, a life of purpose, a life that can achieve lasting benefit.

In my view, that is a life of moral, not market, sentiments. A life that seeks to advance the trinity of distributive justice, equality of opportunity and fairness across generations. And even if those efforts fail, it is a life which recognises that in pursuing virtue we help build it in ourselves and in others. We expand its practice and give it life.

Arise for the work of humankind. Be humble. However grand you are today or may become tomorrow, you too will be forgotten. There are no places for us in the crypt of Westminster Abbey. Even if there were, with the centuries, our accomplishments would be forgotten and our names become puzzles. But our moral sentiments can live on as memes that multiply through values in the service of others. A worthy past sedimented into a better future.

That is how grappa turns back into wine.

Appendix

COMPARATIVE ADVANTAGE IN TRADE

The law of comparative advantage is true but not obvious. Suppose Portuguese workers can produce one bottle of wine with four hours of labour and one bolt of cloth with eight hours. And suppose that English workers are more productive in both: they produce a bottle of wine with three hours of labour and a bolt of cloth with one hour. One might think at first that because England requires fewer hours to produce either good, it has nothing to gain from trade. Not so.

Portugal's cost of producing wine, although higher than England's in terms of hours of labour, is lower in terms of cloth. For every bottle produced, Portugal gives up half of a bolt of cloth, while England has to give up three bolts of cloth. Therefore, Portugal has a comparative advantage in producing wine. Similarly, for every bolt of cloth it produces, Portugal gives up two bottles of wine, but England gives up only a third of a bottle. Therefore, England has a comparative advantage in producing cloth.

If they exchange wine and cloth one for one, Portugal can specialise in producing wine and trading some of it to England, and England can specialise in producing cloth. Both England and Portugal will be better off than if they had not traded. For example, by shifting eight hours of labour out of producing cloth, Portugal gives up the one bolt that this labour could have produced, but that labour now produces two bottles of wine, which Portugal can trade for two bolts of cloth. England also gains. By shifting three hours out of producing wine, England cuts wine production by one bottle but increases cloth production by three bolts. It trades two of these bolts for Portugal's two bottles of wine, leaving England with one more bottle of wine than it had before and an extra bolt of cloth.

MARXIAN SURPLUS VALUE

What are the types of capital identified by Marx? First, constant capital (c) that is held in machines and other non-labour means of production. Marx makes clear that the underlying value of those machines is the embedded labour used in their production. Indeed, according to him, the values of 'all commodities are only definite masses of congealed labour time'. Constant capital earns a return as this embedded labour is gradually realised as the means of production is depreciated or otherwise used up.

Second, variable capital (v), which is used to hire workers and pay their wages.

Third, interest-bearing capital (i) which is supplied by banks who earn interest on loans that industrialists take out to expand production.

Finally, Marx distinguished between productive and commercial capital (cc). The former own the means of production and produce the goods and services. The latter circulates these products in the economy and makes money available to production capital to buy the means of production. Industrial capital creates surplus capital, commercial capital 'realises' it.

So the overall value of a product, W (or its worth), can be expressed in two ways. First, the sum of the amount necessary to restore labour power, Ln, and the surplus value, s.

$Ln + s = W$

And second, as the division of proceeds across labour, profits/ surplus (p) and the various forms of capital:

$$v + c + i\,cc + p = W$$

The value of labour power is expressed to workers as wages and to capitalists as profits. The size of the average profit in the economy is the total surplus value divided by the total variable capital (the capital used to hire labour) and constant capital (capital is invested in other means of production – machinery, land, buildings and raw materials).

List of Figures

California, Oregon, and Washington: Past, Present, and Future', National Research Council, *National Academy of Sciences*, 250 pp, ISBN:978-0-309-25594-3, http://www.nap.edu/catalog.php?record_id=13389, 2012)

Figure 11.3 Arctic Sea ice volume. (Polar Science Centre, PIOMAS data, A. Schweiger, R. Lindsay, J. Zhang, M. Steele, H. Stern, 'Uncertainty in Modeled Arctic Sea Ice Volume'. *J. Geophys. Res.*, doi:10.1029/2011JC007084, 2011)

Figure 11.4 Atmospheric CO_2 concentration. (EPICA DOME C CO_2 record (2015) and NOAA (2018) OurWorldInData.org/co2-and-other-greenhouse-gas-emissions • CC BY)

Figure 11.5 Global average lifetime carbon budgets per-capita by birth year for 1.5°C and 2°C scenarios. ('Younger Generations will have much lower lifetime Carbon Budgets', based on historical emissions data from the Global Carbon Project, historical and future projected population from the United Nations and global emission projections from MESSAGE-GLOBIOM. Generation birth years shown at the bottom from the Pew Research Center. Chart by Carbon Brief using Highcharts)

Figure 11.6 Emissions reductions pathways for different sectors to limit global warming to 1.5°C. Sectoral emission reduction pathways (through avoiding emissions and sequestering greenhouse gases) for halving global emissions every decade during 2020–2050 (Carbon Law). The pathways on the positive y-axis indicate emissions avoidance whereas on the negative y-axis they indicate ramping up natural sinks for greenhouse gas sequestration. According to this scenario, net-zero greenhouse gas emissions is achieved in 2039, and after that, greenhouse gas sequestration is greater than emissions. The energy sector's emissions address only emissions related to the process of energy production (energy supply) and do not include electricity- and heat-related emissions in buildings, industry and the transport sector, which are instead allocated to those sectors. In the food sector, solutions draw down emissions from 5.6 Gt in 2020 to 5.0 Gt (planetary boundary for food) in 2050. (J. Falk, O. Gaffney, A. K. Bhowmik, P. Bergmark, V. Galaz, N. Gaskell, S. Henningsson, M. Höjer, L. Jacobson, K. Jónás, T. Kåberger, D. Klingenfeld, J. Lenhart, B. Loken, D. Lundén, J. Malmodin, T. Malmqvist, V. Olausson, I. Otto, A. Pearce, E. Pihl, T. Shalit, Exponential Roadmap 1.5.1. *Future Earth*. Sweden (January 2020) www.exponentialroadmap.org)

Figure 11.7 Global carbon dioxide emissions by country (2017). Shown are national production based emissions in 2017. Production-based emissions measure CO_2 produced domestically from fossil fuel combustion and cement and do not adjust for emissions embedded in trade. (Global Carbon Project (GCP) and Our World in Data: https://ourworldindata.org/annual-co2-emissions)

Figure 11.8 Per capita CO_2 emissions in 2018. Carbon dioxide emissions from the burning of fossil fuels for energy and cement production. Land use change is not included. CO_2 emissions are measured on a production basis, meaning they do not correct for emissions embedded in traded goods. (Our World in Data based on data from: the Carbon Dioxide Information Analysis Centre (CDIAC); Global Carbon Project; Gapminder; and the United Nations, https://ourworldindata.org/co2-emissions#year-on-year-change-in-global-co2-emissions)

Figure 11.9 Cumulative CO_2 emissions by world region from the year 1751 onwards. Emissions are based on territorial emissions (production-based) and do not account for emissions embedded in trade. This measures CO_2 emissions from fossil fuels and cement production only – land use change is not included.

Notes

Introduction

1. The First Industrial Revolution (1760–1840) saw the mechanisation of the textile industry with the introduction of steam power, moving people from home-based to urban factories. The Second Industrial Revolution (1860–1914) was driven by the introduction of electricity to manufacturing, extending mechanised, assembly-line mass production to broader industries. The Third Industrial Revolution (1970–2000) was defined by the move from mechanical and analogue to digital, with widespread adoption of electronics at home and at work.

1: Perspectives of Value – Objective Value

1. Richard Layard, Andrew Clark, Jan-Emmanuel De Neve, Christian Krekel, Daisy Fancourt, Nancy Hey and Gus O'Donnell, 'When to Release the Lockdown: A Wellbeing Framework for Analysing Costs and Benefits', Centre for Economic Performance, Occasional Paper No. 49 (April 2020).
2. *The New Oxford American Dictionary.*
3. Exceptions include the canonists, as discussed in this chapter.

4. Walton Hamilton, 'The Place of Value Theory in Economics', *Journal of Political Economy* 25(3) (March 1918), p. 217.
5. Mariana Mazzucato, *The Value of Everything* (London: Allen Lane, 2018), p. 6.
6. Foster argues that Aristotle anticipated the content and rationale of most subsequent theories of value. Aristotle states the bullion-wealth idea of the mercantilists but disavows it. He gave the physiocrats their cue about land as the source of values. His condemnation of usury was used by the canonists. John Fagg Foster, 'John Dewey and Economic Value', *Journal of Economic Issues* 15(4) (December 1981), p. 882.
7. Aristotle, *Politics*, trans. Benjamin Jowett (Oxford: Clarendon Press, 1908), p. 41.
8. Fagg Foster (1981), p. 882.
9. Bede Jarrett, *S. Antonino and Medieval Economics* (London: The Manresa Press, 1918), p. 65.
10. As Hamilton (1918) cautions, this creates a dilemma: 'To abstract the economic is to sever the tentacles which bind it to mediaeval thought and which bring to economic concepts, principles, and ends their very life.' If, instead, the whole of the medieval ecclesiastical scheme is studied, however, then the

economic melts away into 'shadowy nothingness' (pp. 223–4).

11. Ibid., p. 224.

12. Thomas Mun, Director of the East India Company, as quoted in Mazzucato (2018), p. 25.

13. Bernardo Davanzati, 'A Discourse Upon Coins', trans. John Toland (1588): https://quod.lib.umich.edu/e/eebo/A37157.0001.001/1:3?rgn=div1;view=fulltext (accessed 15 December 2020).

14. Robert B. Ekelund Tr. and Mark Thornton, 'Galileo, Smith and the Paradox of Value: The "Connection" of Art and Science', *History of Economic Ideas* 19(1) (2011), pp. 85–6.

15. In algebra, 'solving for' is the method of isolating x or the variable on one side of the equation.

16. Sir William Petty, 'The Political Anatomy of Ireland – 1672', in *A Collection of Tracts and Treatises Illustrative of the Natural History, Antiquities, and the Political and Social State of Ireland*, vol. II (Dublin: Alex. Thom & Sons, 1861), p. 50.

17. Mazzucato (2018), pp. 25–6.

18. Petty's work was complemented by that of his contemporary Gregory King (see ibid.).

19. See Hamilton (1918), p. 224, and Fagg Foster (1981), p. 884.

20. Hamilton (1918), pp. 225–6.

21. He argued that only nature could produce new things: grain out of small seeds for food, trees out of saplings for wood, mineral ores from the earth from which houses and ships and machines could be built. Humans could only *transform* value: bread from seeds, timber from wood, steel from iron.

22. Mazzacuto (2018), p. 23.

23. 'Who were the Physiocrats?', *The Economist*, 11 October 2013.

24. The term 'classicist' is a conscious echo of the status given to writers and thinkers of the ancient Greek and Roman worlds, whose works were still the bedrock of education when the term 'classical' economists began to be used in the later nineteenth century.

25. Mazzucato (2018), p. 33.

26. Jesse Norman, *Adam Smith: What He Thought, and Why it Matters* (London: Allen Lane, 2018), pp. 21–2.

27. As Norman concludes, 'the real Adam Smith was not an advocate of self-interest, did not believe rational behaviour was constituted solely by the pursuit of profit, was not a believer in *laissez-faire* and was not pro-rich. Nor was he anti-government ... Smith did not think that all markets behaved the same way ... or that markets form a kind of self-regulating system that might obviate the need for the state.' (Ibid., p. 241)

28. Norman (2018), pp. 286–9.

29. Adam Smith, *An Inquiry into the Nature and Causes of the Wealth of Nations* (1776; digital edn MetaLibri, 2007), I.ii.16.

30. Norman rightly stresses this point.

31. As Smith wrote, 'It is the great multiplication of the production of all the different arts, in consequence of the division of labour, which occasions, in a well-governed society, that universal opulence which extends itself to the lowest ranks of the people. Every workman has a great quantity of his own work to dispose of beyond what he himself has occasion for; and every other workman being exactly in the same situation, he is enabled to exchange a great quantity of his own goods for a great quantity, or, what comes to the same thing, for the price of a great quantity of theirs. He supplies them abundantly with what they have occasion for, and they accommodate him as amply with what he has occasion for, and a general plenty diffuses itself through all the different ranks of society' Smith (1776/2007), I.i.10.

32. 'In any particular branch of trade or manufactures, is always in some respects different from, and even opposite to, that of the public ... The proposal of any new law or regulation of commerce which comes from this order, ought always to be listened to with great precaution, and ought never be adopted till after having been long and carefully examined, not only with the most scrupulous, but with the most suspicious attention.' Smith (1776/2007), I.xi.9

33. Ibid., I.v.1.

34. Ibid., I.v.7.

35. Ibid., I.vi.1.

36. Ricardo also invented comparative statics, one of the core analytic techniques of economics, and he made his reputation as an economist by promoting the quantity theory of money.

37. David Ricardo, 'Chapter 1: On Value', in On the Principles of Political Economy and Taxation (1817): https://www.marxists.org/reference/subject/economics/ricardo/tax/ch01.htm (accessed 15 December 2020).

38. Despite these improvements, Ricardo was forced to accept that there were other forces affecting value which prevented a pure theoretical labour theory of value. Nevertheless, he still believed that it was the quantity of labour to produce goods that was crucial to determining value. In the end, Ricardo's value theory applies to freely reproducible goods (or commodities) in competitive markets.

39. Hamilton (1918), 'There is no explicit part of the book, stretching away on the one hand to general material well-being and on the other toward technique, organization, and arrangements, to which the title "production" can be given. On the contrary the institutional matter of the older treatise is omitted, is made to serve the purposes of an economics of currency and fiscal reform, or is irrelevantly inserted to give a seeming unity and symmetry to an academic treatise' (p. 238).

40. Another way to put this might be as follows: if I bought a factory, I wouldn't expect to make back all my investment in the first month, but rather over several years. However, if I worked in a factory, I would expect the pay packet for my wages to show up every week. The horizon of the worker is much shorter than that of the capitalist.

41. Karl Marx, Critique of Political Economy, 1857, I.3: https://www.marxists.org/archive/marx/works/1859/critique-pol-economy/appx1.htm#193 (accessed 15 December 2020). 'The categories which express its [bourgeois society's] relations, and an understanding of its structure, therefore, provide an insight into the structure and the relations of production of all formerly existing social formations the ruins and component elements of which were used in the creation of bourgeois society.'

42. Recall that, in their efforts to reduce intrinsic value to one factor of production, previous value theorists all struggled with how to account for the others in terms of their chosen core factor. For example, Cantillon posited that land was worth two units of the land required to sustain the worker, enabling him to substitute the $2x$ for land in any production function (he didn't have one). Ricardo recognised three factors of production – land, labour and capital. He also used a subsistence wage (effectively substituting $1x$) and he substituted for capital the accumulated labour required to make the machine. So far so good, but as we have seen his theory

came a cropper once he realised
the differing time dimension of the
returns to capital and labour.
Adjusting for labour quality was
not enough.

2: Perspectives of Value – Subjective Value

1. Frances Morris, 'On Tate
   Modern's 20th anniversary,
   director Frances Morris says we
   must assert the value of culture',
   Financial Times, 11 May 2020.
2. The term was later coined by
   Thorstein Veblen.
3. Morris (2020).
4. William Stanley Jevons, *Theory of
   Political Economy* (London:
   Macmillan, 1871), p. 2.
5. Nicholas Barbon, *Of the Quantity
   and Quality of Wares*, cited in
   Elgin Williams, 'Nicholas Barbon:
   An Early Economic Realist',
   Southern Economic Journal 11(1)
   (July 1944), p. 50.
6. John Stuart Mill, *The Principles of
   Political Economy* (Batoche Books,
   1848/2000), p. 517.
7. Carl Menger, *Principles of
   Economics*, trans. James Dingwall
   and Bert F. Hoselitz (Auburn, Ala.:
   Ludwig von Mises Institute, 2007),
   pp. 120–1.
8. William David Anthony Bryant,
   *General Equilibrium: Theory and
   Evidence* (World Scientific
   Publishing Company, 2009),
   ProQuest Ebook Central, p. 119.
9. Alfred Marshall, *Principles of
   Economics* (London: Macmillan,
   1920), V.iii.7: https://www.econlib.
   org/library/Marshall/marP.
   html?chapter_num=31#book-
   reader (accessed 15 December
   2020).
10. Jeremy Bentham, *An Introduction
    to the Principles of Morals and
    Legislation*, vol. 1 (London: W.
    Pickering, 1823), p. 3.
11. John Stuart Mill, 'Bentham',
    London and Westminster Review
    (August 1838), accessed at
    Classical Utilitarianism website

https://www.laits.utexas.edu/
poltheory/jsmill/diss-disc/
bentham/bentham.html.

12. Cass R. Sunstein, *The Cost-Benefit
    Revolution* (Cambridge, Mass.:
    MIT Press, 2018), pp. 23–4.
13. Layard et al. (2020).
14. Mazzucato (2018), pp. 11–12.
15. Ibid., p. 74.
16. That is, all final products and
    services. The distinction between
    productive and unproductive of
    yore is gone.
17. Diane Coyle, *GDP: A Brief but
    Affectionate History*, revised and
    expanded edn (Princeton:
    Princeton University Press, 2015),
    p. 108.
18. Commission on the Measurement
    of Economic Performance and
    Social Progress (Stiglitz–Sen–
    Fitoussi Commission), *Report*
    (Paris, 2009).
19. Sunstein (2018), pp. 60–1.
20. This is part of the reason why
    distributional impacts are
    explicitly taken into account in
    cost–benefit analysis conducted by
    the US federal government, and has
    spawned the doctrine of
    prioritarianism in which the social
    goal is to maximise welfare subject
    but with priority given to the most
    disadvantaged. See ibid.

3: Money, Gold and the Age of Consent

1. The famous convention speech of
   Democratic presidential candidate
   William Jennings Bryan in July
   1896 ended with the crescendo,
   'Having behind us the producing
   masses of this nation and the
   world, supported by the
   commercial interests, the laboring
   interests, and the toilers
   everywhere, we will answer their
   demand for a gold standard by
   saying to them: "You shall not
   press down upon the brow of labor
   this crown of thorns; you shall not
   crucify mankind upon a cross of
   gold."'

2. This is an abbreviation of Adam Smith's famous quote from *The Wealth of Nations*. It appeared on the £20 note that bore his likeness. The full quote is 'This great increase of the quantity of work which, in consequence of the division of labour, the same number of people are capable of performing' Smith (1776/2007), I.i.5.

3. 'It is not from the benevolence of the butcher, the brewer, or the baker that we expect our dinner, but from their regard to their own interest' (ibid., I.ii.2).

4. For this reason, some economists consider the operation as a unit of account to be the most important characteristic of money. Indeed, it is commonly argued that a defining feature of monetary policy lies in central banks' control of the unit of account. See Robleh Ali, John Barrdear, Roger Clews and James Southgate, 'The economics of digital currencies', *Bank of England Quarterly Bulletin* (2014) Q3.

5. Agustín Carstens, 'Money in the Digital Age: What Role for Central Banks?', lecture given at the House of Finance, Goethe University, Frankfurt, 6 February 2018.

6. The data are for 2016. Banknotes accounted for 45 per cent of transactions in 2015, and as such there was a 5-percentage-point fall year on year which may be related to increased use of cards and online payments.

7. See Michael McLeay, Amar Radia and Ryland Thomas, 'Money Creation in the Modern Economy', *Bank of England Quarterly Bulletin* (2014) Q1. They note that the reality of how money is created often differs from that found in standard textbooks and, rather than banks receiving deposits when households save and then lending them out, bank lending creates deposits.

8. For a detailed description of the money-creation process see ibid.

9. Although Ronald Reagan is often credited with the quote 'Trust, but verify', it is an old Russian proverb cited by Gorbachev at their Reykjavik arms control talks in 1986.

10. Although it does not target monetary aggregates *per se*, the Bank of England conducts monetary policy to ensure that the amount of money creation in the economy is consistent with low and stable inflation. In normal times, the Bank implements monetary policy by setting the interest rate on central bank reserves. In exceptional times when interest rates cannot be lowered further, the Bank implements monetary policy by purchasing assets, which has the by-product of increasing the central bank reserve holdings of private banks.

11. The ownership history of the Yap stone is recorded through oral history, a form of modern consensus mechanism.

12. For a detailed description of debasement see Niall Ferguson, *The Cash Nexus: Money and Power in the Modern World, 1700–2000* (London: Allen Lane, 2001), Chapter 5: 'The Money Printers: Default and Debasement'.

13. Ernest Hemingway, *The Sun Also Rises*, (New York: Scribner's, 1926), as quoted by Agustín Carstens (2019).

14. Isabel Schnabel and Hyun Song Shin, 'Money and Trust: Lessons from the 1620s for Money in the Digital Age', BIS Working Paper No. 68 (February 2018), p. 2.

15. And in many respects represent the precursors to central bank money in that they also facilitated wholesale transactions between other banks.

16. Carstens (5 December 2019).

17. See G. Dwyer, 'Wildcat banking, banking panics, and free banking

in the United States', *Federal Reserve Bank of Atlanta Economic Review* 8(3) (1996), pp. 1–20; Arthur J. Rolnick and Warren E. Weber, 'New evidence of the free banking era', *American Economic Review* 73(5) (December 1983), pp. 1080–91; and Charles W. Calomiris, 'Banking crises yesterday and today', *Financial History Review* 17(1) (2010), pp. 3–12.

18. Niall Ferguson, *The Ascent of Money: A Financial History of the World* (London: Allen Lane, 2008), p. 24.

19. Ibid., p. 26.

20. P. G. M. Dickson, *The Financial Revolution in England: A Study in the Development of Public Credit, 1688–1756* (London: Macmillan; New York: St Martin's Press, 1967); David Omrod, *The Rise of Commercial Empires: England and the Netherlands in the Age of Mercantilism, 1650–1770* (Cambridge: Cambridge University Press, 2003); John David Angle, 'Glorious Revolution as Financial Revolution', *History Faculty Publications* 6 (2013), https://scholar.smu.edu/hum_sci_history_research/6.

21. The bank could issue a limited amount of currency (the *fiduciary issue*) backed not by gold but by government securities.

22. Ferguson (2008), p. 56.

23. Under the 1844 Bank Charter Act, the Bank of England's note-issuance responsibilities were formalised and the rights of others to issue notes in England and Wales began to be phased out.

24. Some historians also point to the influence of major silver discoveries in the 1850s in the US, e.g. Barry Eichengreen, *Globalizing Capital* (Princeton: Princeton University Press, 1996), pp. 17–18.

25. Ibid., p. 7. 'Its [the gold standard's] development ... owed much to

Great Britain's accidental adoption of a de facto gold standard in 1717 ... With Britain's industrial revolution and its emergence in the nineteenth century as the world's leading financial and commercial power, Britain's monetary practices became an increasingly logical and attractive alternative to silver-based money for countries seeking to trade with and borrow from the British Isles' (pp. 5–6, 2019 edn).

26. This did not necessarily hold for central banks in the periphery of the system.

27. What was essential was not that exchange rates were fixed, as some have asserted, but that governments did not feel pressure to trade exchange rate stability for other goals: Eichengreen (2019 edn), p. 7.

28. Ibid., p. 128.

29. B. R. Mitchell, *International Historical Statistics, Europe 1750–1988* (New York: Stockton Press, 1992), p. 840.

30. Ferguson (2008), p. 332.

31. Eichengreen (1996), pp. 34–5.

32. Ibid., p. 30.

33. Angus Maddison, *Contours of the World Economy, 1–2030 AD: Essays in Macro-economic History* (Oxford: Oxford University Press, 2007), p. 379.

4: From Magna Carta to Modern Money

1. See Paul Tucker, *Unelected Power* (Princeton: Princeton University Press, 2018).

2. For an excellent summary, see N. Vincent, *Magna Carta: A Very Short Introduction* (Oxford: Oxford University Press, 2012).

3. His allies were finally defeated in 1214 at the Battle of Bouvines, which ended the Anglo-French War which had started in 1202.

4. Paul Latimer suggests that the inflation was concentrated in the first six years or so of the thirteenth century: see 'The

English inflation of 1180–1220 reconsidered', *Past and Present* 171 (2001), pp. 3–29.

5. P. D. A. Harvey, 'The English inflation of 1180–1220', *Past and Present* 61 (1973), pp. 3–30.

6. They were responsible for collecting the fixed farms from the king's assets. In normal years, they made an enormous profit, paying only a small fixed farm to the king, yet raking in a great deal more in terms of the real income of the counties. They were accustomed to keeping this surplus. Any attempt to reform this system, by reducing the imbalance between real income and fixed farm, threatened to destabilise relations between the king and the vitally significant administrative class of sheriffs and other royal officials upon whom the king's political stability depended. As a result, each king's preference was to find other ways of raising the cash.

7. As Latimer (2001) says, 'Between 1198 and 1206, sheep prices, wine prices and the price paid by the exchequer for its regular supply of cloth all indicate a steep and sustained increase' (p. 4).

8. Harvey (1973), p. 13. Henry II had paid his knights 8d per day: King John was handing over 2s or 3s, an increase of about 275 per cent.

9. Less directly, one can infer from evidence on the exercise by manorial lords of their options to take cash payments from their villeins (peasants), instead of forcing them to work the land, that the going rate for unskilled farm labour must also have increased.

10. Assuming those increases occurred over the six years Latimer (2001) identifies as the period of significant inflation.

11. In very crude terms, the supposition here has been that we can extrapolate from the quantity of coins found in modern times the number of moneyers and mints that were in operation in the thirteenth century. With this information, we can then work out how many coins each moneyer struck (the only coin in circulation at this time being the silver penny), and then calculate the total money supply.

12. Latimer (2001), pp. 11–12.

13. R. C. Palmer, 'The Economic and Cultural Impact of the Origins of Property: 1180–1220', *Law and History Review* 3(2) (Autumn 1985), pp. 375–96.

14. Ben Bernanke, Mark Gertler and Simon Gilchrist, 'The financial accelerator and the flight to quality', *Review of Economics and Statistics* 78(1) (February 1996), pp. 1–15.

15. Latimer (2001), pp. 15–16.

16. It is perhaps for this reason – a thirteenth-century manifestation of Gresham's Law – that archaeological finds of coin hoards are often thought to contain suspiciously high proportions of freshly minted coins.

17. John had restored himself to favour from excommunication and placed himself under the protection of Innocent by pronouncing himself a papal vassal, and England a papal fief, in 1213 and subsequently by 'taking the cross' in March 1215 – that is, declaring himself a crusader.

18. The coronation charter of Henry I issued in 1100 (which was also endorsed by Henry II at his own coronation in 1154) is a pertinent example because it was effectively the draft on which Magna Carta was later based, containing several of the clauses now regarded as the most significant. The original text was written in one continuous flow. Its division into clauses is a modern construct.

19. Moreover, it came after a lacuna of sixty years during which the House of Plantagenet had issued no similar conciliatory charters; its

actions in the meantime had caused sufficient damage to the relationship between nobility and monarchy as to make an uprising inevitable.

20. Even the 'fish weirs' clause (33) can be read, in hindsight, as a protection both of the public good (in Roman law terms, *res publica*) and of the freedom of navigation: the same principle for which the English entered into the Seven Years War of 1756–63, whose costs, in turn, brought about the American Revolution of 1776.

21. Tucker (2018) addresses these challenges in the context of central banks.

22. Other banks were restricted to partnerships of up to six members.

23. During the 1866 and 1878 crises the Bank lent freely to the system but allowed the insolvent Overend Gurney and City of Glasgow Bank to fail. And in 1890 it used a 'lifeboat' approach to rescue Barings, which was perceived to be solvent. Note however that there is no definitive evidence that an explicit set of lender of last resort (LOLR) principles was accepted by the senior staff of the Bank and its directors. The emergence of the Bank's LOLR role in this period is discussed in Rudiger Dornbusch and Jacob Frenkel (1984) 'The Gold Standard and the Bank of England in the Crisis of 1847', National Bureau of Economic Research. *A Retrospective on the Classical Gold Standard*. 1821–1931, pp. 233–76.

24. In the late nineteenth century the banking system was relatively unregulated (and partly self-regulated) – the Bank did not have an explicit supervisory infrastructure or system of prudential control until 1979. Nevertheless, the scope of the Bank's responsibilities was arguably as broad then as it is now, albeit that the mix was different.

25. Eddie George, 'Central bank independence', speech given at the SEANZA Governors' Symposium, 26 August 2000.

26. The Bank operates the Real-Time Gross Settlement (RTGS) service and infrastructure that holds accounts for banks, building societies and other institutions. The balances in these accounts can be used to move money in real time between these account holders. This delivers final and risk-free settlement.

27. In the UK, from 1971 to 1992, inflation was high, averaging 9 per cent, and volatile, with a standard deviation of 5.4 per cent.

28. The inflation target rose from the ashes of the ERM debacle in 1992, marking the point when price stability became the unambiguous objective of UK monetary policy. The new framework was a success, though only a partial one. That's because, with interest rate decisions continuing to be made by the Chancellor, it still wasn't fully credible. Welfare could be further improved if governments first chose the preferred rate of inflation and then delegated operational responsibility to the central bank to achieve it. Constrained discretion would be introduced by the Chancellor Gordon Brown in 1997 and enacted the following year.

29. Mervyn King, 'Monetary policy: theory in practice', speech given at the joint luncheon of the American Economic Association and the American Finance Association, Boston, 7 January 2000. King attributes the 'constrained' versus 'unfettered' distinction originally to Ben Bernanke and Frederick Mishkin.

30. The inflation target is symmetric (meaning the MPC cares as much about returning inflation to target from below as from above), and it applies at all times. Subject to

achieving the target, the MPC is also required to support the government's economic policy objective, currently strong, sustainable and balanced growth.

31. For further information, see Mark Carney, 'Lambda', speech given at the London School of Economics, 16 January 2017, and 'A framework for all seasons?', speech given at the Bank of England Research Workshop on The Future of Inflation Targeting, 9 January 2020.

32. In addition to the MPC, FPC and PRC, the Bank is responsible for the issuance of banknotes, provides the foundations of the payments system through RTGS, regulates systemic financial market infrastructure and has powers and facilities to provide a wide range of liquidity to banks and other financial institutions in order to promote the continuous functioning of the financial system during shocks. Other institutions that support confidence in the currency include legal tender status (meaning that you cannot be sued for non-payment of debts if you offer sterling to meet them) and the insurance of deposits of up to £85,000 at banks and building societies backed by the government.

33. In 1946, King George VI appointed Turing an Officer of the Order of the British Empire for his wartime services, although the details of his work remained secret for many years.

34. Alan Turing, 'On Computable Numbers, with an Application to the Entscheidungsproblem', *Proceedings of the London Mathematical Society* 42(1) (1936), pp. 230–65.

35. When he was working first at the National Physical Laboratory in London and later at the Computing Machine Laboratory at Manchester University, his insights led to the creation of the Automatic Computing Engine (ACE) in 1950 and the program for Ferranti Mark 1, the world's first commercially available electronic computer.

36. See Alan Turing's interview in *The Times* newspaper (11 June 1949). Turing's interests in neurology and physiology led him to ask whether computing machines might be capable of mimicking the faculties of the human mind, including the ability to learn. His work prefigured the neural networks that are used today in applications such as cancer diagnosis and self-driving cars and as yet undiscovered new technologies of tomorrow. And the Turing Test, a method for determining whether a computer can exhibit intelligent behaviour indistinguishable from a human being, remains the benchmark for judging true artificial intelligence.

5: The Future of Money

1. Especially the balance between inside money (created by commercial banks) and outside money (created by central banks).

2. John Maynard Keynes, *The Economic Consequences of the Peace* (London: Macmillan, 1920), p. 11.

3. For a broad exposition see Niall Ferguson, *The Square and the Tower* (London: Allen Lane, 2017).

4. When I was at the Bank of England there were several ways in which we changed our hard infrastructure to equalise access. Until recently only commercial banks had direct access to RTGS (the banks' wholesale payments system), and alternative payment service providers (or PSPs) had to route through them. That made sense in the old financial world arranged around a series of hubs and spokes, but it was increasingly anachronistic in the new, distributed finance that is emerging. So the Bank made it

easier for a broad set of firms to plug in and compete with more traditional providers. Responding to demands from fintech providers, the rebuild of RTGS will provide API access to read and write payment data. In July 2017, the Bank of England became the first G20 central bank to open up access to our payment services to a new generation of non-bank PSPs. Wider access will improve services to UK households and businesses and it will bring financial-stability benefits by increasing the proportion of settlement in central bank money, diversifying the number of settlement firms and driving innovation.

5. Agustin Carsten, 'Money in the digital age: what role for central banks', speech given at House of Finance Goethe University, 6 February 2018.

6. Though it is not in gold but in new banknotes, their value is institutionally backed.

7. Hyman P. Minsky, *Stabilising an Unstable Economy* (New York: McGraw Hill, 1986).

8. Agustín Carstens, 'Data, technology and policy coordination', speech given at the 55th SEACEN Governors' Conference and High-level Seminar on 'Data and technology: embracing innovation', Singapore, 14 November 2019.

9. They are also funded by borrowing in wholesale money and capital markets but that doesn't change the core economics that concern this inquiry.

10. In the words of the General Manager of the BIS, Agustín Carstens (2018), 'Novel technology is not the same as better technology or better economics. That is clearly the case with Bitcoin: while perhaps intended as an alternative payment system with no government involvement, it has become a combination of a bubble, a Ponzi scheme and an environmental disaster. The volatility of bitcoin renders it a poor means of payment and a crazy way to store value. Very few people use it for payments or as a unit of account. In fact, at a major cryptocurrency conference the registration fee could not be paid with bitcoins because it was too costly and slow: only conventional money was accepted.'

11. Asli Demirgüç-Kunt, Leora Klapper, Dorothe Singer, Saniya Ansar and Jake Hess, 'The Global Findex Database 2017: Measuring Financial Inclusion and the Fintech Revolution' (2017), pp. 4–5, 11, 35, 92.

12. Benoît Cœuré, 'Fintech for the people', speech given at 14th BCBS-FSI high-level meeting for Africa on strengthening financial sector supervisión and current regulatory priorities, Cape Town, 31 January 2019a.

13. Carstens (2019).

14. See Ben Broadbent, 'Central Banks and Digital Currencies', speech given at the LSE, 2 March 2016, https://www.bankofengland.co.uk/speech/2016/central-banks-and-digital-currencies.

15. As quoted in Carstens (2018), Curzio Giannini, *The Age of Central Banks* (Cheltenham: Edward Elgar, 2011), observes that 'The evolution of monetary institutions appears to be above all the fruit of a continuous dialogue between economic and political spheres, with each taking turns to create monetary innovations … and to safeguard the common interest against abuse stemming from partisan interests.'

6: The Market Society and the Value of Nothing

1. Joel Waldfogel, *Scroogenomics: Why You Shouldn't Buy Presents for the Holidays* (Princeton: Princeton University Press, 2009)

and 'The Deadweight Loss of Christmas', *American Economic Review* 83(5) (1993), pp. 1328–36.

2. Waldfogel (2009), p. 67.

3. Even better, and more rational to the economists, if they had perfect foresight and promised to give the money, they could have not only saved the deadweight losses of the transactions but also not bothered getting the money in the first place; after all life is a finite game and that would be a subgame perfect equilibrium.

4. Michael Sandel, *What Money Can't Buy: The Moral Limits of Markets* (London: Penguin, 2012), p. 124.

5. O. Henry, *The Four Million: The Gift of the Magi and Other Short Stories* (Minneapolis: Lerner Publishing Group, 2014), p. 16.

6. See Federico Cingano, 'Trends in Income Inequality and its Impact on Economic Growth', OECD Social, Employment and Migration Working Papers No. 163 (2014); Joseph Stiglitz, 'Inequality and Economic Growth', in Michael Jacobs and Mariana Mazzucato (eds), *Rethinking Capitalism* (Oxford: Wiley Blackwell, 2016), pp. 148–69; Andrew G. Berg and Jonathan D. Ostry, 'Inequality and Unsustainable Growth: Two Sides of the Same Coin?', IMF Staff Discussion Note (April 2011); Roberto Perotti, 'Growth, income distribution and democracy: what the data say', *Journal of Economic Growth* 1(2) (1996), pp. 149–87; Philip Keefer and Stephen Knack, 'Polarization, politics and property rights: Links between Inequality and Growth', World Bank Policy Research Working Paper No. 2418 (August 2000).

7. Cingano (2014).

8. Jonathan D. Ostry, Andrew Berg and Charalambos G. Tsangaride, 'Redistribution, Inequality, and Growth', IMF Staff Discussion Note (April 2014).

9. Berg and Ostry (2011).

10. Ibid., p. 9. The Gini index, or Gini coefficient, is a measure of the distribution of income across a population developed by the Italian statistician Corrado Gini in 1912. It is often used as a gauge of economic inequality, measuring income distribution or, less commonly, wealth distribution among a population.

11. Kristin Forbes finds a positive relationship between income inequality and economic growth in the short to medium term ('A Reassessment of the Relationship between Inequality and Growth', *American Economic Review* 90(4) (2000), pp. 869–87); Daniel Halter, Manuel Oechslin and Josef Zweimüller find an increase in inequality has a positive impact on the average growth rate of GDP per capita for the subsequent five-year period followed by a negative impact for the following five years ('Inequality and growth: the neglected time dimension', *Journal of Economic Growth* 19(1) (March 2014), pp. 81–104). Also see Abhijit Banerjee and Esther Duflo, 'Inequality and Growth: What Can the Data Say?', *Journal of Economic Growth* 8(3) (2003), pp. 267–99, who argue that the relationship between economic growth and inequality is likely non-linear.

12. In addition to note 6, see Alberto Alesina and Dani Rodrik, 'Distributive Politics and Economic Growth', *Quarterly Journal of Economics* 109(2) (1994), pp. 465–90; Torsten Persson and Guido Tabellini, 'Is Inequality Harmful for Growth?', *American Economic Review* 84(3) (1994), pp. 600–21; William Easterly, 'Inequality Does Cause Underdevelopment: Insights from a New Instrument', *Journal of Development Economics* 84(2) (2007), pp. 755–76.

13. For example, Persson and Tabellini (1994); Perotti (1996); Alesina and Rodrik (1994).

14. Forbes (2000); and Banerjee and Duflo (2003).

15. Describing the human capital accumulation theory formalised by Oded Galor and Joseph Zeira, Federico Cingano writes that 'lower-income households may choose to leave full-time education if they cannot afford the fees, even though the rate of return (to both the individual and society) is high. In turn, under-investment by the poor implies that aggregate output would be lower than in the case of perfect financial markets.' (2014), p. 11.

16. Shekhar Aiyar and Christian Ebeke, 'Inequality of Opportunity, Inequality of Income, and Economic Growth', IMF Working Paper No. 19/34 (15 February 2019). The authors found that the effect of intergenerational mobility is economically very meaningful: 'To give a flavour of the magnitudes: an increase in income inequality by one standard deviation in the pooled sample (corresponding to 10 units of Gini expressed in percentage points) will knock 0.5 percentage points off average growth in the next five-year period for a level of intergenerational income elasticity set at the 25th percentile (roughly where Japan is situated in the distribution) as opposed to 1.3 percentage points reduction at the 75th percentile (roughly where Brazil is situated in the distribution).'

17. See Alberto Alesina, Rafael Di Tella and Robert MacCulloch, 'Inequality and Happiness: Are Europeans and Americans Different?', *Journal of Public Economics* 88 (2004), pp. 2009–42; Richard Wilkinson and Kate Pickett, 'Income Inequality and Social Dysfunction', *Annual Review of Sociology* 35 (2009), pp. 493–511.

18. Richard Layard, *Can We be Happier? Evidence and Ethics* (London: Pelican Books, 2020), pp. 44–54.

19. Daniel Kahneman and Angus Deaton. 'High Income improves evaluation of life but not emotional well-being'. *Proceedings of the National Academy of Sciences of the United States of America* 107(38) (2018), pp. 16489–93

20. See Branko Milanović, *Capitalism, Alone: The Future of the System that Rules the World* (Cambridge, Mass.: Belknap Press, 2019), and Layard (2020).

21. In thirty-one of the thirty-nine countries surveyed by Pew Research in 2013, half or more of the population believed inequality to be a 'very big problem' in their societies (Pew Research Center, 'Economies of Emerging Markets Better Rated During Difficult Times', *Pew Research Center* (23 May 2013) p. 20).

22. Steven Levitt and Stephen J. Dubner, *Freakonomics* (William Morrow and Company, 2005), p. 11. As quoted in Michael J. Sandel, 'Market Reasoning as Moral Reasoning: Why Economists Should Re-engage with Political Philosophy', *Journal of Economic Perspectives* 27(4) (2013), p. 122.

23. A. B. Atkinson, 'Economics as a Moral Science', *Economica* 76 (2009) (issue Supplement S1), pp. 791–804.

24. Cass R. Sunstein, *The Cost-Benefit Revolution* (Cambridge, Mass.: MIT Press, 2018).

25. Ibid. p. 22.

26. See Chapter 2.

27. Douglass C. North, Nobel Prize Lecture (9 December 1993).

28. Milanović (2019), p. 2.

29. Paul Mason, *Postcapitalism: A Guide to Our Future* (London: Allen Lane, 2015).

30. John Micklethwait and Alan Wooldridge, *The Fourth Revolution: The Global Race to Reinvent the State* (London: Penguin, 2014).

31. Thomas Hobbes, *Leviathan* (1651; reissued Lerner Publishing Group, 2018), 1.xiii.4, p. 115.

32. Thomas Hobbes, *Hobbes' Verse Autobiography* (Cambridge: Hackett Publishing Company, 1994), II.liv.25.

33. John Micklethwait and Alan Wooldridge, 'The Virus Should Wake Up the West', *Bloomberg Opinion*, 12 April 2020.

34. Tommaso Padoa-Schioppa, 'Markets and Government Before, During and After the 2007–20XX Crisis', Per Jacobsson Foundation lecture, Basel, 27 June 2010, p. 8.

35. Ibid., pp. 13–14

36. Milanović (2019), pp. 190–1.

37. Ibid., p. 112.

38. In contrast, globalisation acts as a counterweight to inequality in developing economies, which have seen a rise in relative productivity in sectors such as agriculture that traditionally employ low-wage workers. 'World Economic Outlook: Globalization and Inequality', IMF (October 2007), ch. 4, 'Globalization and Inequality', pp. 31–65.

39. In the classical capitalism of Marx and Ricardo there were three distinct classes – landlords, workers and capitalists – and they all did only one thing. Therefore in Marx/Ricardo there was inequality between classes but not interpersonal inequality. Now people have both capital and labour income; therefore they look at distribution between individuals. The rich now have a greater proportion of their income from capital than from labour. Richer societies have more income/ GDP. For example, this ratio is *8x* in Switzerland versus *3x* in India.

40. Michael Lewis, Princeton University's Baccalaureate Remarks (3 June 2012).

41. Miles Corak, 'Income Inequality, Equality of Opportunity, and Intergenerational Mobility', *Journal of Economic Perspectives* 27(3) (2013), pp. 79–102.

42. Padoa-Schioppa (2010), p. 8: 'I have myself observed the impervious reluctance of a generation of economists to use basic economic concepts such as equilibrium exchange rate, core inflation, neutral interest rate, output gap, or structural deficit. They were putting forward difficulties in the measurement and definitional controversy, but the root of their reluctance was the self-cancellation of the policymaker's judgment: only the market knows, only credibility counts, and if you speak against the market, your credibility is destroyed.'

43. Milanović (2019), p. 177.

44. In the spirit of Tom Wolfe. See Joel Best. '"Status! Yes!": Tom Wolfe as a Sociological Thinker', *American Sociologist* 32(4) (Winter 2001), pp. 5–22.

45. Milanović (2019), p. 104.

46. Ibid., p. 106.

47. Max Weber, *The Protestant Ethic and the Spirit of Capitalism*, trans. Talcott Parsons (London and New York: Routledge/Taylor & Francis e-library, 2005), pp. 115–16.

48. Ibid., p. 116.

49. The internalisation of desirable behaviour which, in John Rawls' words, reaffirms in its daily actions the main beliefs of society, was possible thanks to the constraints of religion and the tacit social contract' Milanović (2019), p. 179.

50. See Rabbi Jonathan Sacks, *Morality* (London: Hodder and Stoughton, 2020); Archbishop Justin Welby, *Dethroning*

Mammon: Making Money Serve Grace (London: Blomsbury, 2017); Pope Francis' Encyclical, *Laudato Si* (24 May 2015).

51. Jonathan Sacks, 'Morals: the one thing the markets don't make', *The Times*, 21 March 2009.
52. Milanović (2019), p. 105.
53. Ibid.
54. Sandel (2012), p. 9.
55. As Sandel observes, even those who oppose the buying and selling of kidneys cannot argue that the market in kidneys would destroy the good being sought (Ibid., p. 95).
56. Uri Gneezy and Aldo Rustichini, 'A Fine is a Price', *Journal of Legal Studies* 29(1) (2000a), pp. 1–17.
57. Uri Gneezy and Aldo Rustichini, 'Pay Enough or Don't Pay at All', *Quarterly Journal of Economics* 15(3) (2000b), pp. 791–810.
58. Sandel (2012), pp. 19–20 cross-references 128 studies.
59. Richard Titmuss, *The Gift Relationship: From Human Blood to Social Policy* (1971).
60. Sandel (2012), p. 128.
61. Aristotle, *Nicomachean Ethics*, in Christopher Rowe and Sarah Broadie (eds), *Aristotle: Nicomachean Ethics* (Oxford: Oxford University Press, 2020), II.i.35, p. 111.
62. As quoted in Sandel (2012), p. 128.
63. Fagg Foster (1981), p. 895.
64. Atkinson (2009). The many cases when none of these assumptions hold make economics on its own a poor guide to deciding whether a good should be allocated by market or non-market principles.

7: The Global Financial Crisis: A World Unmoored

1. Often also referred to as a special purpose vehicle, or SPV, the term SIV is more directly associated with the vehicles in the run-up to the crisis that were tied to banks, and integral to the story of the meltdown.
2. AAA is the highest possible rating that can be assigned by independent credit rating agencies. It means that the risk of default is very, very low. That did not prove the case for some of these highly structured and untested products.
3. See Mark Carney, 'What are Banks Really For?', Bank of Canada. Speech given to University of Alberta School of Business, 30 March 2009.
4. Figures from Bank of International Settlements. After a small decline following the financial crisis, debt securitisation has only continued to climb and in 2019 hit a new high of over $25 trillion.
5. Miguel Segoviano, Bradley Jones, Peter Lindner and Johannes Blankenheim, 'Securitization: Lessons Learned and the Road Ahead', IMF Working Paper (2013), pp. 8–9.
6. Testimony of Secretary Timothy Geithner before the House Financial Services Committee, 20 April 2010.
7. Figures from the Bank for International Settlements. 'Over-the-counter' derivatives are traded directly between parties without going through an exchange or intermediary.
8. Larry Summers, 'Beware Moral Hazard Fundamentalists', *Financial Times*, 23 September 2007.

8: Creating a Simpler, Safer, Fairer Financial System

1. The South Sea Company was initially forecast to be quite profitable, as the government had granted it a monopoly on trade with Central and South America. However, when Spain – which controlled the ports in Latin America – limited the company to one ship per port per year, the South Sea Company's business plan was effectively crippled.

Undeterred, the company's leadership continued to advertise the riches of the Americas and used generous share-purchase incentives and other questionable tactics to drive the share price from £128 to £1,050 within half a year. The public, enthralled by the ease of gaining money, started investing in ever more speculative businesses, often on credit. The growth was fuelling itself and was completely divorced from operational prospects.

2. See, for example, the Leaders' Statements issued after the G20 meetings, from Washington in 2008 and London and Pittsburgh in 2009 through to the Hamburg G20 meetings in 2017.

3. The Edelman Trust barometer finds that in two-thirds of countries less than half the population trusts mainstream institutions of business, government, media and NGOs to 'do what is right'. Edelman, *2020 Edelman Trust Barometer*, Global Report (19 January 2020).

4. Remarks during a visit to the London School of Economics in 2008.

5. Tim Besley and Peter Hennessy, 'The Global Financial Crisis: Why Didn't Anyone Notice?', British Academy, 2009.

6. Dani Rodrik, *The Globalization Paradox: Democracy and the Future of the World Economy* (New York and London: W. W. Norton, 2012).

7. Jamie Dimon, CEO of JP Morgan, Testimony to the Financial Crisis Inquiry Commission, 9 January 2010.

8. For an extensive survey, see Carmen M. Reinhart and Kenneth S. Rogoff, *This Time is Different: Eight Centuries of Financial Folly* (Princeton: Princeton University Press, 2009).

9. Raghuram Rajan, *Fault Lines: How Hidden Fractures Still Threaten the World Economy* (Princeton: Princeton University Press, 2010), p. 21.

10. This emphasis on the endogenous tendency of financial systems to become unstable is reminiscent of Hyman Minsky's 'financial instability hypothesis' (Hyman P. Minsky, 'The Financial Instability Hypothesis', *Levy Economics Institute* Working Paper No. 74 (May 1992), pp. 1–9).

11. In a July 2016 article, *The Economist* noted that Minsky had been referred to only once in their publication during his working life from the 1950s through to 1996 when he died, but that he had been mentioned around thirty times since the crisis broke in 2007 ('Minsky's Moment', *The Economist*, 30 July 2016).

12. See also Adair Turner, 'Market efficiency and rationality: why financial markets are different', Lionel Robbins Memorial Lectures, London School of Economics, 2010.

13. More nuanced economists pointed out as far back as the 1950s the flaws in this logic. See R. G. Lipsey and Kelvin Lancaster, 'The General Theory of the Second Best', *Review of Economic Studies* 24(1) (1956), pp. 11–32.

14. Kenneth J. Arrow and Gérard Debreu, 'Existence of an equilibrium for a competitive economy', *Econometrica* 22(3) (1954), pp. 265–90.

15. The bankers who played a leading role in developing the credit derivatives market declared that 'Credit derivatives are a mechanism for transferring risk efficiently around the system' and that defaulted loans that would have knocked a hole in a bank's balance sheet ten years ago were 'now hits that we have spread around the system, and represent tiny blips on the balance sheet of hundreds of financial institutions'. See Gillian

Tett, *Fool's Gold* (London: Little, Brown, 2009), p. 99.

16. Frank H. Knight, *Risk, Uncertainty, and Profit* (Boston and New York: Houghton Mifflin, 1921; reissued Orlando, Fla.: Signalman Publishing, 2009).

17. F. A. Hayek, 'The pretence of knowledge', Nobel prize speech, 1974.

18. John Maynard Keynes, *The General Theory of Employment, Interest and Money* (London: Palgrave Macmillan, 1936).

19. Ibid., ch. 12.

20. FICC Markets Standards Board, 'Behavioural Cluster Analysis: Misconduct Patterns in Financial Markets' (July 2018).

21. Ibid.

22. Mark Carney, 'Turning Back the Tide', speech given to FICC Markets Standards Board Conference, 29 November 2017.

23. Alison Park, Caroline Bryson, Elizabeth Clery, John Curtice and Miranda Phillips (eds), British Social Attitudes 30, *NatCen* (2013).

24. See Abigail Haddow, Chris Hare, John Hooley and Tamarah Shakir, 'Macroeconomic Uncertainty: What Is It, How Can We Measure It and Why Does It Matter?', *Bank of England Quarterly Bulletin* (2013) Q2. See also Nicholas Bloom, Max Fleototto, Nir Jaimovich, Itay Saporta-Eksten and Stephen J. Terry, 'Really Uncertain Business Cycles', *Econometrica*, 86(3) (May 2018), pp. 1031–65.

25. Mark Carney, 'What a Difference a Decade Makes', speech given at the Institute of International Finance's Washington Policy Summit, 20 April 2017.

26. Illiquid assets are those that require a material price discount for a quick sale, or equivalently those that require a significant period for sales to avoid a material price discount. For discussion, see the chapter on 'Vulnerabilities in open-ended funds' in the Bank of England's 'Financial Stability Report', December 2019.

27. Committee on the Global Financial System, 'Structural Changes in Banking After the Crisis' CGFS Paper No. 60 (January 2018).

28. 'In a panic the holders of the ultimate Bank reserve (whether one bank or many) should lend to all that bring good securities quickly, freely and readily.' (Walter Bagehot, *Lombard Street: A Description of the Money Market* (Cambridge: Cambridge University Press, 2011), p. 173).

29. Macroprudential policy is distinct from microprudential policy. Microprudential policy concentrates on promoting the safety and soundness of individual institutions. Macroprudential policy addresses risks arising from interactions between institutions and sectors within the financial system, and interactions between the financial system and the real economy.

30. Deferral of variable compensation is not mandatory in the US, but it is recommended for senior executives in agency guidance and used in a number of institutions.

31. Bank of England. PRA Supervisory Statement SS28/15, 'Strengthening Individual Accountability in Banking' (May 2017).

32. Bank of England, HM Treasury and Financial Conduct Authority, 'Fair and Effective Markets Review: Final Report' (June 2015).

33. See, for example, FMSB's 'Reference Price Transactions standard for the Fixed Income markets' (November 2016); 'New Issue Process standard for the Fixed Income markets' (2017); 'Surveillance Core Principles for FICC Market Participants: Statement of Good Practice for Surveillance in Foreign Exchange

Markets' (June 2016). All standards and publications available at https://fmsb.com/our-publications/.

34. Financial Stability Board, 'Strengthening Governance Frameworks to Mitigate Misconduct Risk: A Toolkit for Firms and Supervisors' (April 2018).

9: The Covid Crisis: How We Got Here

1. Municipal lockdowns had been in place for several days and a national lockdown would follow in little more than a week.

2. World Health Organisation, 'Coronavirus disease 2019 (COVID-19) Situation Report – 40' (February 2020).

3. With the sole exception of the US restrictions on people recently in China.

4. Thomas Hobbes, *Leviathan* (1651; reissued Lerner Publishing Group, 2018), II.xvii.7 p. 160.

5. Ibid., p. 115.

6. Ibid., p. 97.

7. John Locke, *Two Treatises of Government*, in Ian Shapiro (ed.), *Two Treatises of Government and A Letter Concerning Toleration*, (1689; reissued New Haven: Yale University Press, 2003), II.iii.19, p. 108.

8. John Locke, *A Third Concerning Toleration*, in Ian Shapiro (ed.), *Two Treatises of Government and A Letter Concerning Toleration*, (1689; reissued New Haven: Yale University Press, 2003), III, p. 227.

9. Jean-Jacques Rousseau, *The Social Contract*, in Susan Dunn and Gita May (eds.), *The Social Contract and The First and Second Discourses* (1762; reissued New Haven: Yale University Press, 2002), I.iv., p. 158.

10. As Lord Sumption has written, we have developed an 'irrational horror of death' that led us to protect lives at exorbitantly high costs that previous generations did not contemplate incurring. See Jonathan Sumption, 'Coronavirus lockdown: we are so afraid of death, no one even asks whether this "cure" is actually worse', *The Times*, 4 April 2020.

11. Timothy Besley, 'State Capacity, Reciprocity and the Social Contract', *Econometrica* 88(4) (2020), p. 1309.

12. Rousseau (1762/2002), II.iv., p. 176.

13. Timothy Besley and Torsten Persson, 'The Causes and Consequences of Development Clusters: State Capacity, Peace, and Income', *Annual Review of Economics* 6 (2014), pp. 932–3.

14. Paul Slack, 'Responses to Plague in Early Modern Europe: The Implications of Public Health', *Social Research* 55(3) (1988), pp. 436–40.

15. Ibid., pp. 441–2.

16. Howard Markel, 'Worldly approaches to global health: 1851 to the present', *Public Health* 128 (2014), p. 125.

17. Thomas Piketty, *Capital in the Twenty-First Century* (Cambridge, Mass.: Harvard University Press, 2014), pp. 474–9.

18. OECD, 'Revenue Statistics 2019' (2019).

19. In 2017, domestic general government health expenditures ranged between 7 and 9 per cent of GDP among the G7 countries; see the World Health Organisation's Global Health Expenditure Database. For historical analysis of the rise in public spending see Vito Tanzi and Ludger Schuknecht, *Public Spending in the 20th Century: A Global Perspective* (Cambridge: Cambridge University Press, 2000).

20. World Health Organisation, Department of Communicable Disease Surveillance and Response, 'Influenza Pandemic Plan. The Role of WHO and Guidelines for National and Regional Planning', 1 April 1999.

21. Christopher J. L. Murray, Alan D. Lopez, Brian Chin, Feehan Dennis and Kenneth H. Hill, 'Estimation of potential global pandemic influenza mortality on the basis of vital registry data from the 1918–20 pandemic: a quantitative analysis', *Lancet* 368(9554) (2006), pp. 2211–18.

22. The World Health Organisation, 'Frequently Asked Questions about the International Health Regulations' (2005).

23. The World Health Organisation, 'Country Implementation Guide: After Action Review & Simulation Exercise Under the International Health Regulations 2005 Monitoring and Evaluation Framework' (2018), pp. 7–9.

24. Global Preparedness Monitoring Board, 'A World at Risk: Annual Report on Global Preparedness for Health Emergencies' (September, 2019), p. 19.

25. Ibid., pp. 19 and 33.

26. Ibid., p. 20.

27. 'Coronavirus: UK failed to stockpile crucial PPE', BBC, 28 April 2020.

28. Marieke Walsh, Grant Robertson and Kathy Tomlinson, 'Federal Emergency Stockpile of PPE was Ill-Prepared for Pandemic', *The Globe & Mail*, 30 April 2020.

29. 'New Document Shows Inadequate Distribution of Personal Protective Equipment and Critical Medical Supplies to States', Press Release from the Office of Carolyn B. Maloney, Chairwoman of the House Committee on Oversight and Reform, Department of Health and Human Services, 8 April 2020.

30. Beth Reinhard and Emma Brown, 'Face masks in national stockpile have not been substantially replenished since 2009', *Washington Post*, 10 March 2020.

31. Yeganeh Torbati and Isaac Arnsdorf, 'How Tea Party Budget Battles Left the National Emergency Medical Stockpile Unprepared for Coronavirus', *Propublica*, 3 April 2020.

32. 'Stripping Naked for Masks: German Doctors Protest Lack of Protective Gear', Reuters, 28 April 2020.

33. UNICEF, *Progress on household drinking water, sanitation and hygiene 2000–2017* (New York: United Nations Children's Fund (UNICEF) and World Health Organisation, 2019), pp. 36–7.

34. Ruth Maclean and Simon Marks, '10 African Countries Have No Ventilators: That's Only Part of the Problem', *New York Times*, 18 April 2020.

35. Jane Feinmann, 'PPE: what now for the global supply chain?', *British Medical Journal* 369(1910) (May 2020).

36. World Bank Group, 'Pandemic Preparedness Financing – Status Update' (September 2019).

37. Commission on a Global Health Risk Framework for the Future, 'The Neglected Dimension of Global Security: A Framework to Counter Infectious Disease Crises', National Academy of Medicine, (Washington: National Academies Press, May 2016).

38. Global Preparedness Monitoring Board (2019), p. 11.

39. Ibid., p. 16.

40. Global Health Security Index, 'Global Health Security Index: Building Collective Action and Accountability' (October 2019), p. 9. The average overall score for the 195 countries the index assessed was 40 out of 100.

41. Derek Thompson, 'What's Behind South Korea's COVID-19 Exceptionalism?', *Atlantic*, 6 May 2020.

42. Richard Thaler, 'Some empirical evidence on dynamic inconsistency', *Economics Letters* 8(3) (1981), pp. 201–7; Jess Benhabib, Alberto Bisin and Andrew Schotter, 'Present-bias,

quasi-hyperbolic discounting, and fixed costs', *Games and Economic Behavior* 69 (2010), pp. 205–23.

43. United Nations General Assembly, 'Protecting Humanity from Future Health Crises: Report of the High-level Panel on the Global Response to Health Crises' 17th Session, Agenda Item 125 (February 2016), p. 40.

44. US Department of Health and Human Services, 'Crimson Contagion 2019 Functional Exercise Key Findings: Coordinating Draft' (October 2019), p. 1, available via David E. Sanger, Eric Lipton, Eileen Sullivan and Michael Crowley, 'Before Virus Outbreak, a Cascade of Warnings Went Unheeded', *New York Times*, 22 March 2020.

45. Jonathan Calvert, George Arbuthnott and Jonathan Leake, 'Coronavirus: 38 days when Britain sleepwalked into disaster', *The Times*, 19 April 2020. According to the article, 'An equally lengthy list of recommendations to address the deficiencies was never implemented. The source said preparations for a no-deal Brexit "sucked all the blood out of pandemic planning" in the following years.'

46. See e.g. Michael Greenstone and Vishan Nigam, 'Does Social Distancing Matter?', *Becker Friedman Institute for Economics* Working Paper No. 2020-26 (March 2020); Richard Layard, Andrew Clark, Jan-Emmanuel De Neve, Christian Krekel, Daisy Fancourt, Nancy Hey and Gus O'Donnell, 'When to release the lockdown: A wellbeing framework for analysing costs and benefits', Centre for Economic Performance, Occasional Paper No. 49 (April 2020); Linda Thunström, Stephen C. Newbold, David Finnoff, Madison Ashworth and Jason F. Shogren, 'The Benefits and Costs of Using Social Distancing to Flatten the Curve for COVID-19', *Journal of Benefit-Cost Analysis* 11(2) (2020), pp. 179–95; Paul Dolan and Pinar Jenkins, 'Estimating the monetary value of the deaths prevented from the UK Covid-19 lockdown when it was decided upon – and the value of "flattening the curve"', London School of Economics and Political Science (April 2020).

47. See e.g. Chris Conover, 'How Economists Calculate the Costs and Benefits of COVID-19 Lockdowns', *Forbes Magazine*, 27 March 2020; Amy Harmon, 'Some Ask a Taboo Question: Is America Overreacting to Coronavirus?', *New York Times*, 16 March 2020; Sarah Gonzalez and Kenny Malone, 'Episode 991: Lives vs. The Economy', *Planet Money – NPR*, 15 April 2020; David R. Henderson and Jonathan Lipow, 'The Data Are In: It's Time for a Major Reopening', *Wall Street Journal*, 15 June 2020; W. Kip Viscusi, 'What is a life worth? COVID-19 and the Economic Value of Protecting Health', *Foreign Affairs*, 17 June 2020.

48. This practice of Diyah remains present in many modern Islamic legal systems, though both the method of valuation and currency have evolved over time.

49. A. E. Hofflander, 'The Human Life Value: An Historical Perspective', *Journal of Risk and Insurance* 33(1) (1966), p. 381.

50. 'The mass of mankind being worth twenty years purchase': Sir William Petty, *Political Arithmetick* (London: Printed for Robert Clavel, 1690), I, p. 31.

51. Hofflander (1966), p. 382.

52. Ibid., p. 386; Wex S. Malone, 'The Genesis of Wrongful Death', *Stanford Law Review* 17(6) (1965), pp. 1043–76.

53. Hofflander (1966), pp. 386–7.

54. H. Spencer Banzhaf, 'Retrospectives: The Cold-War

Origins of the Value of Statistical Life', *Journal of Economic Perspectives* 28(4) (2014), pp. 214–18. In the end, RAND avoided assigning a dollar figure to the lives of pilots by offering optimal strategies for a range of fixed fatality counts, essentially offloading the calculation of the value of human life to military command.

55. OECD, 'Mortality Risk Valuation in Environment, Health and Transport Policies' (OECD Publishing, 2012), pp. 22, 29.

56. Ibid., pp. 24–8.

57. Dave Merrill, 'No One Values your Life More Than the Federal Government', *Bloomberg*, 19 October 2017.

58. EQ-5D is an index of health status for use in health care evaluation and developed by research experts at the EuroQol foundation – https://euroqol.org/support/terminology/.

59. Cass R. Sunstein, *The Cost-Benefit Revolution* (Cambridge, Mass.: MIT Press, 2018); OECD (2012), p. 55.

60. Robert H. Frank, *Under the Influence: Putting Peer Pressure to Work* (Princeton: Princeton University Press, 2020).

61. Paul Dolan, 'Using Happiness to Value Health', Office of Health Economics (2011), summarising the research of: David A. Schkade and Daniel Kahneman (1998), 'Does living in California make people happy? A focusing illusion in judgments of life satisfaction', *Psychological Science* 9(5) (1998), pp. 340–6; Daniel T. Gilbert and Timothy D. Wilson (2000), 'Miswanting: Some problems in the forecasting of future affective states', in Joseph P. Forgas (ed.), *Feeling and Thinking: The Role of Affect in Social Cognition* (New York: Cambridge University Press, 2000), pp. 178–97; G. A. De Wit, J. J. Busschbach and F. T. De Charro,

'Sensitivity and perspective in the valuation of health status: Whose values count?', *Health Economics* 9(2) (2000), pp. 109–26.

62. Joseph E. Aldy and W. Kip Viscusi, 'Age differences in the value of statistical life', *Review of Environmental Economics and Policy* 1(2) (2007), pp. 241–60; Ted R. Miller, 'Variations between countries in values of statistical life', *Journal of Transport Economics and Policy* 34 (2000), pp. 169–88.

63. The Lawrence Summer World Bank Memo (excerpt) (12 December 1991), https://www.uio.no/studier/emner/sv/oekonomi/ECON2920/v20/pensumliste/summers-memo-1991-%2B-nytimes.pdf.

64. Noam Scheiber, 'In Defense of Larry Summers', *The New Republic*, 7 November 2008.

65. The World Bank and Institute for Health Metrics and Evaluation, 'The Cost of Air Pollution: Strengthening the Economic Case for Action' (2016), pp. xii, 48–50.

66. See e.g. John Bronsteen, Christopher Buccafusco and Jonathan S. Masur, 'Well-being analysis versus cost-benefit analysis', *Duke Law Journal* 62 (2013), pp. 1603–89; Matthew D. Adler, *Well-Being and Fair Distribution: Beyond Cost-Benefit Analysis* (New York: Oxford University Press, 2011).

67. Bronsteen, Buccafusco and Masur (2013), pp. 1666–7.

68. Frank Ackerman and Lisa Heinzerling, *Priceless: On Knowing the Price of Everything and the Value of Nothing* (New York: New Press, 2004).

69. See e.g. W. Kip Viscusi, Joel Huberb and Jason Bel, 'Assessing Whether There Is a Cancer Premium for the Value of a Statistical Life', *Health Economics* 23(4) (2014), pp. 384–96.

10: Covid Crisis: Fallout, Recovery and Renaissance?

1. World Health Organisation, 'Coronavirus disease 2019 (COVID-19) Situation Report – 11', 31 January 2020.
2. World Health Organisation, 'Coronavirus disease 2019 (COVID-19) Situation Report – 40', 29 February 2020.
3. Ibid.; World Health Organisation, 'Coronavirus disease 2019 (COVID-19) Situation Report – 71', 31 March 2020.
4. Emma Farge, 'U.N. raises alarm about police brutality in crackdowns', Reuters, 27 April 2020; Rozanna Latiff, 'Malaysia seizes hundreds of migrants in latest lockdown raid', Reuters, 12 May 2020.
5. Stephanie Hegarty, 'The Chinese doctor who tried to warn others about coronavirus', BBC, 6 February 2020; Andras Gergely and Veronika Gulyas, 'Orban Uses Crisis Powers for Detentions Under "Fake News" Law', Bloomberg, 13 May 2020.
6. See e.g. Farge (2020); 'Coronavirus: Police officers in Spain suspended for violent lockdown enforcement', ASTV, 6 July 2020; Josh Breiner, 'Violence between Israeli Police and Public Rises with Coronavirus Enforcement, Source Says', Haaretz, 7 July 2020; Chas Danner, 'Philly Police Drag Man from Bus for Not Wearing a Face Mask', New York Magazine, 10 April 2020; 'Indian police use force against coronavirus lockdown offenders', Al Jazeera, 30 March 2020; 'Covid-19: Tear Gas Fired at Kenya Market', Bloomberg, 25 March 2020.
7. 'Nigerian security forces killed 18 people during lockdowns: rights panel', Reuters, 16 April 2020; 'Court orders suspension of South African soldiers over death of man in lockdown', Reuters, 15 May 2020; 'El Salvador: Police Abuses in Covid-19 Response', Human Rights Watch, 15 April 2020.
8. Margaret Levi, Audrey Sacks and Tom Tyler, 'Conceptualizing Legitimacy, Measuring Legitimating Beliefs', American Behavioral Scientist 53(3) (2009), p. 354.
9. Ibid., p. 356.
10. Ibid., p. 355.
11. Christian von Soest and Julia Grauvogel, 'Identity, procedures and performance: how authoritarian regimes legitimize their rule', Contemporary Politics 23(3) (2017), pp. 287–305.
12. Bo Rothstein, 'Creating Political Legitimacy: Electoral Democracy Versus Quality of Government', American Behavioral Scientist 53(3) (2009), pp. 311–30.
13. Ibid.; Nicholas Charron and Victor Lapuente, 'Does democracy produce quality of government?', European Journal of Political Research 49(4) (2010), pp. 443–70.
14. Rothstein (2009), p. 325.
15. Philip Keefer, 'Clientelism, Credibility, and the Policy Choices of Young Democracies', American Journal of Political Science 51(4) (2007), pp. 804–21.
16. Google, COVID-19 Mobility Reports, Retail and Recreation Mobility Data for New Zealand, https://ourworldindata.org/covid-mobility-trends (accessed 9 December 2020).
17. Google, COVID-19 Mobility Reports, Retail and Recreation Mobility Data for Italy, https://ourworldindata.org/covid-mobility-trends (accessed 9 December 2020).
18. Google, COVID-19 Mobility Reports, Retail and Recreation Mobility Data for New York State.
19. 'Social Distancing Scoreboard', Unacast, unacast.com/covid19/social-distancing-scoreboard (accessed 26 June 2020).
20. Ruth Igielnik, 'Most Americans say they regularly wore a mask in

stores in the past month; fewer see others doing it', Pew Research Center, 23 June 2020.

21. Global Health Security Index, 'Global Health Security Index: Building Collective Action and Accountability' (October 2019).

22. Ibid., p. 36.

23. Transparency International, 'Corruption Perceptions Index' (2019).

24. Timothy Besley, 'State Capacity, Reciprocity, and the Social Contract', *Econometrica* 88(4) (July 2020), p. 1309–10.

25. John Authers , 'How Coronavirus Is Shaking Up the Moral Universe', *Bloomberg*, 29 March 2020.

26. Robert H. Frank, *Under the Influence: Putting Peer Pressure to Work* (Princeton: Princeton University Press, 2020), p. 6.

27. F. Natale, D. Ghio, D. Tarchi, A. Goujon and A. Conte, 'COVID-19 Cases and Case Fatality Rate by Age', European Commission, Knowledge for Policy Brief, 4 May 2020.

28. Derek Messacar, René Morissette and Zechuan Deng, 'Inequality in the feasibility of working from home during and after COVID-19', Statistics Canada, 8 June 2020.

29. 'Coronavirus (COVID-19) related deaths by occupation, England and Wales: deaths registered up to and including 20 April 2020', Office for National Statistics, 11 May 2020.

30. Michelle Bachelet, 'Disproportionate impact of COVID-19 on racial and ethnic minorities needs to be urgently addressed', Office of the UN High Commissioner for Human Rights, 2 June 2020.

31. Ibid.

32. Alan Freeman, 'The unequal toll of Canada's pandemic', *iPolitics*, 29 May 2020.

33. Tera Allas, Mark Canal and Vivian Hunt, 'COVID-19 in the United Kingdom: Assessing jobs at risk and the impact on people and places', McKinsey & Company, 11 May 2020.

34. Rakesh Kochhar, 'Unemployment rose higher in three months of COVID-19 than it did in two years of the Great Recession', Pew Research Center, 11 June 2020; 'Coronavirus: "Under-25s and women financially worst-hit"', BBC 6 April 2020.

35. See e.g. Andy Uhler, 'With no federal aid, undocumented immigrants look to states, philanthropy for support', *Marketplace*, 1 May 2020; Elise Hjalmarson, 'Canada's Emergency Response Benefit does nothing for migrant workers', *The Conversation*, 6 May 2020.

36. 'Startling disparities in digital learning emerge as COVID-19 spreads: UN education agency', *UN News*, 21 April 2020.

37. Betheny Gross and Alice Opalka, 'Too Many Schools Leave Learning to Chance during the Pandemic', Center on Reinventing Public Education (June 2020).

38. See 'Closing schools for covid-19 does lifelong harm and widens inequality', *The Economist*, 30 April 2020).

39. Ibid.

40. Flora Charner, Shasta Darlington, Caitlin Hu and Taylor Barnes, 'What Bolsonaro said as Brazil's coronavirus cases climbed', CNN, 28 May 2020; Maggie Haberman and David E. Sanger, 'Trump Says Coronavirus Cure Cannot "Be Worse Than the Problem Itself"', *New York Times*, 23 March 2020; Peter Baker, 'Trump's New Coronavirus Message: Time to Move On to the Economic Recovery', *New York Times*, 6 May 2020.

41. Iain Duncan Smith, 'We must speak about the threat coronavirus poses to our economy', *Sun*, 17 May 2020.

42. Daniel Kahneman, *Thinking, Fast and Slow* (London: Allen Lane, 2011).

43. Tomas Pueyo, 'Coronavirus: The Hammer and the Dance', *Medium*, 19 March 2020.

44. Richard Layard, Andrew Clark, Jan-Emmanuel De Neve, Christian Krekel, Daisy Fancourt, Nancy Hey and Gus O'Donnell, 'When to release the lockdown?: A wellbeing framework for analysing costs and benefits', Centre for Economic Performance, Occasional Paper No. 49 (April 2020).

45. When faced with the decision about how to reopen New York, Governor Andrew Cuomo did not publish a summary of the relevant cost–benefit analysis but tweeted that 'There is no dollar figure to a human life. New York will reopen (by region) when it is safe to do so' (@NYGovCuomo, 10:27am 5 May 2020). The Ontario Premier Doug Ford has also said: 'We all have to ask ourselves, what is the cost of a life? Is a life worth a picnic in a park? Is a life worth going to the beach? Is a life worth having a few cold ones with your buddies in the basement? The answer is no' ('Doug Ford's latest coronavirus update: "You have saved thousands of lives" (Full transcript)', *Maclean's*, 3 April 2020).

46. See e.g. the United States Environmental Protection Agency's 2003 'senior death discount' controversy and the significant opposition the agency faced from senior interest groups.

47. Gertjan Vlieghe, 'Assessing the Health of the Economy.' Speech given at Bank of England. 20 October 2020.

48. Tiziana Assenza, Fabrice Collard, Martial Dupaigne, Patrick Fève, Christian Hellwig, Sumudu Kankanamge and Nicolas Werquin, 'The Hammer and the Dance: Equilibrium and Optimal Policy during a Pandemic Crisis', *Toulouse School of Economics Working Paper* (May 2020).

49. In cases of managing risk, the possible outcomes are generally known and probabilities can be determined. In cases of radical uncertainty on the other hand, we have a limited ability even to describe what might occur and probabilistic assessment is impossible.

50. Timothy Besley and Nicholas Stern, 'The Economics of Lockdown', *Fiscal Studies* 41(3) (October 2020), pp. 493–513.

51. To the extent to which demand for these services suffers because of the public's concern of catching the disease there would be some internalisation of the externality.

52. Besley and Stern (2020), p. 504.

53. Mark Carney, 'The World After Covid-19: on how the economy must yield to human values', *The Economist*, 16 April 2020.

11: The Climate Crisis

1. Global Annual to Decadal Climate Update from the World Meteorological Organisation (WMO), 8 July 2020. A good introduction to this subject can be found in David Wallace-Wells' *The Uninhabitable Earth* (Penguin, 2019).

2. 'What is Ocean Acidification', PMEL Carbon Program. http://www.pmel.noaa.gov/co2/story/What+is+Ocean+Acidification%3F.

3. R. S. Nerem, B. D. Beckley, J. T. Fasullo, B. D. Hamlington, D. Masters and G. T. Mitchum, 'Climate-change-driven accelerated sea-level rise detected in the altimeter era', *PNAS* 115(9) (February 2018). 10.1073/pnas.1717312115.

4. 'Ramp-Up in Antarctic Ice Loss Speeds Sea Level Rise', NASA Jet Propulsion Laboratory, California Institute of Technology (June 2018). https://www.jpl.nasa.gov/news/news.php?feature=7159.

5. WWF Living Planet Report 2020: https://livingplanet.panda.org/en-gb/ (accessed 9 December 2020). The Dasgupta Review – Independent Review on the Economics of Biodiversity. Interim Report (April 2020).

6. IPCC, Fifth Assessment Report (October 2014).

7. Myles R. Allen, David J. Frame, Chris Huntingford, Chris D. Jones, Jason A. Lowe, Malte Meinshausen and Nicolai Meinshausen, 'Warming caused by cumulative carbon emissions towards the trillionth tonne', *Nature* 458 (April 2009), pp. 1163–6.

8. Carbon dioxide is also the most prominent gas, constituting approximately three-quarters of all greenhouse gas emissions. Methane, nitrous oxide and fluorinated gases make up the remaining quarter. Their potency – how much heat each molecule traps and how long it stays in the atmosphere – however, is markedly different. For example, methane is a better heat trapper than CO_2, but remains in the atmosphere for only ten years. Still, methane is significantly (eighty-six times) more potent than carbon dioxide. Nitrous oxide is more powerful still, with almost 300 times the warming potential of carbon dioxide and remains in the atmosphere for about a century. There is one common thread in greenhouse emissions: human activity has contributed to an increase in atmospheric concentrations of all these potent gases at a rate faster than their removal.

9. This graph, based on the comparison of atmospheric samples contained in ice cores and more recent direct measurements, provides evidence that atmospheric CO_2 has increased since the Industrial Revolution. D. Luthi et al. (2008); D. M. Etheridge et al. (2010); Vostok ice core data/J. R. Petit et al.; NOAA Mauna Loa CO_2 record. See Dieter Lüthi, Martine Le Floch, Bernhard Bereiter, Thomas Blunier, Jean-Marc Barnola, Urs Siegenthalerm Dominique Raynaud, Jean Jouzel, Hubertus Fischer, Kenjiy Kawamura and Thomas F. Stocker, 'High-resolution carbon dioxide concentration record 650,000–800,000 years before present', *Nature* 453 (May 2008), pp. 379–82; Mauro Rubino, David M. Etheridge, David P. Thornton, Russell Howden, Colin E. Allison, Roger J. Francey, Ray L. Langenfelds, L. Paul Steele, Cathy M. Trudinger, Darren A. Spencer, Mark A. J. Curran, Tas D. van Ommen and Andrew M. Smith, 'Revised records of atmospheric trace gases CO_2, CH4, N2O, and δ13C-CO2 over the last 2000 years from Law Dome, Antarctica', *Earth System Science Data* 11 (2019) pp. 473–92; J.R. Petit, J. Jouzel, D. Raynaud, N.I. Barkov, J.-M. Barnola, I. Basille, M. Bender, J. Chappellaz, M. Davis, G. Delaygue, M. Delmotte, V.M. Kotlyakov, M. Legrand, V.Y. Lipenkov, C. Lorius, L. Pépin, C. Ritz, E. Saltzmanand M. Stievenard, 'Climate and atmospheric history of the past 420,000 years from the Vostock Ice Core, Antarctica', *Nature* 399(6735) (1999), pp. 429–36; NOAA Mauna Loa CO_2 record: https://www.esrl.noaa.gov/gmd/obop/mlo/ (accessed 9 December 2020).

10. IPCC, Special Report: Global Warming of 1.5°C (2018). The report used a carbon budget as of end 2017. The current rate of depletion is about 42 ± 3 GtCO2 per year (based on 2019 rates).

11. Assuming emissions stay at the same rate. For a smooth and realistic transition scenario, the

IPCC estimates that we'll need to start reducing CO_2 emissions now and reduce them by 45 per cent (vs 2010 levels) by 2030 to reach the 1.5°C target (IPCC, 2018).

12. Saul Griffith, *Rewiring America*, e-book (2020). See also *The Ezra Klein Show* podcast, 'How to decarbonise America and create 25 million jobs', 27 August 2020.

13. Carbon Tracker, 'Decline and Fall Report: The Size & Vulnerability of the Fossil Fuel System' (June 2020).

14. Bank of England internal estimates.

15. Ebru Kirezi, Ian R. Young, Roshanka Ranasinghe, Sanne Muis, Robert J. Nicholls, Daniel Lincke and Jochen Hinkel, 'Projections of global-scale extreme sea levels and resulting episodic coastal flooding over the 21st century', *Scientific Reports* 10(11629) (July 2020).

16. International Labour Office, 'Working on a warmer planet: The impact of heat stress on labour productivity and decent work' (2019), p. 13.

17. Network for Greening the Financial System 'NGFS Climate Scenarios for Central Banks and Supervisors' (June 2020).

18. The Insurance Development Forum was formed in 2015 as a public–private partnership between the United Nations Development Programme, the World Bank and the insurance sector to use the industry's expertise to insure people in developing countries who are unprotected but vulnerable to climate-change risk. This protection gap currently represents 90 per cent of the economic costs of natural disasters that are uninsured.

19. See Lloyd's of London, 'Catastrophe Modelling and Climate Change' (2014).

20. As described in Prudential Regulation Authority, 'The impact of climate change on the UK insurance sector' (2015).

21. Risky Business, 'The Economic Risks of Climate Change in the United States' (2014).

22. Mark Carney, 'Breaking the Tragedy of the Horizon', speech given at Lloyd's of London, 29 September 2015.

23. Some 28 per cent of Indonesia's land (over 6 million hectares) has become stranded since its government stopped issuing new palm-oil licences and started a moratorium on licences for forest and peatland. And 29 per cent of Indonesia's palm-oil concessions cannot be developed without violating buyers' policies on deforestation and peatland use, meaning ninety-five Indonesian palm-oil companies each have at least 1,000 hectares of stranded land on their books. (https://chainreactionresearch.com/report/28-percent-of-indonesias-palm-oil-landbank-is-stranded/ (accessed 14 December 2020))

24. Stockholm Environment Institute, 'Framing stranded asset risks in an age of disruption' (March 2018).

25. One of the most comprehensive assessments of the possible impacts of climate change on the economy, the Stern review in 2006, found that if left unaddressed it could reduce by 20 per cent by the end of the century (Nicholas Stern, 'Stern Review: The Economics of Climate Change', (2006)). Stern has recently updated his numbers to find that an impact would be potentially nearer to 30 per cent. Burke et al. (2015) have found that relative to no change in the climate, GDP could be about one-quarter lower relative to trend by 2100. (Marshall Burke, Solomon M. Hsiang and Edward Miguel, 'Global non-linear effect of temperature on economic production', *Nature* 526 (October 2015) pp. 235–9).

26. The World Bank estimates that by 2050 Latin America, sub-Saharan Africa and South-east Asia will generate 143 million more climate refugees. (The World Bank, 'Climate Change Could Force Over 140 Million to Migrate Within Countries by 2050: World Bank Report' (March 2018)).

27. Norman Myers, 'Environmental Refugees: An Emergent Security Issue', *Oxford University* (May 2005).

28. A 10 per cent increase in deforestation was associated with a 3.27 per cent increase in malaria cases (Andrew MacDonald and Erin Mordecai, 'Amazon deforestation drives malaria transmission, and malaria burden reduces forest clearing' PNAS 116(44) (2019) pp. 22212–8).

29. WHO survey article, https://www.who.int/globalchange/climate/summary/en/index5.html.

30. Climate change increases the risk of conflict, according to Burke et al. (2014) (Marshall Burke, Solomon M. Hsiang and Edward Miguel, 'Climate and Conflict', NBER Working Paper No. 20598 (October 2014), which surveys fifty-five econometric studies of the connections between climate and conflict. By synthesising the results of the prior research, this study concludes that there are statistically significant linkages between climate and conflict.

31. Sandra Batten, 'Climate Change and the Macro-Economy – A Critical Review', Bank of England Staff Working Paper No. 706 (January 2018).

32. Carl-Friedrich Schleussner, Tabea K. Lissner, Erich M. Fischer, Jan Wohland, Mahé Perrette, Antonius Golly, Joeri Rogelj, Katelin Childers, Jacob Schewe, Katja Freiler, Matthias Mengel, William Hare and Michiel Schaeffer, 'Differential climate impacts for policy-relevant limits to global warming: the case of 1.5°C and 2°C', *Earth System Dynamics* 7 (2016) pp. 327–51.

33. Ibid., p. 327.

34. International Union for Conservation of Nature, 'Issues Brief' (November 2017).

35. As Batten (2018) summarises, 'The Ramsey formula … decomposes the discount rate r into two components: $r=\delta+\eta g$. The first component, δ, is the pure rate of time preference; the second component represents aversion to inequality in consumption between generations: it determines how much weight is given to the welfare of future generations, and is expressed as the product of the elasticity of marginal utility η and the rate of economic growth g. Estimating the discount rate therefore involves both positive uncertainty in the forecasts of the future economic growth rate g, and normative uncertainty of the subjective welfare parameters δ and η. In practice, most of the debate around the choice of discount rate in climate models has been focused on the choice of δ, considered by most authors an ethical parameter.'

36. Stern (2006).

37. Using data on the diffusion of fifteen technologies in 166 countries over the last two centuries. Results reveal that, on average, countries have adopted technologies forty-five years after their invention. There is substantial variation across technologies and countries. Newer technologies have been adopted faster than old ones. (See Diego A. Comin and Bart Hobijn, 'An Exploration of Technology Diffusion', *American Economic Review* 100(5) (April 2008) pp. 2031–59)

38. IMF, 'The Economics of Climate' (December 2019).

39. These vary depending on a number of factors, including the temperature outcome (1.5 or 2 degrees), assumptions on technological advances, fossil fuel prices, the speed of the transition, country conditions and other policy choices.

40. Ryan Avent, 'Greed is good isn't it?', American Spirit, 18 April 2020.

41. Jo Paisley and Maxine Nelson, 'Second Annual Global Survey of Climate Risk Management at Financial Firms', GARP (2020).

42. https://www.transition pathwayinitiative.org/.

12: Breaking the Tragedy of the Horizon

1. I am borrowing this taxonomy from Ezra Klein (podcast with Saul Griffith, 'How to decarbonize America', The Ezra Klein Show, 27 August 2020).

2. Department of Energy and Climate Change, 'Electricity Generation Costs' (July 2013).

3. Department for Business, Energy and Industrial Strategy, 'Electricity Generation Costs' (November 2016).

4. Department for Business, Energy and Industrial Strategy, 'Electricity Generation Costs' (August 2020).

5. The Exponential Roadmap Initiative, 'Exponential Roadmap Report' version 1.5 (2020).

6. Energy Transitions Commission, 'Mission Possible: Reaching Net-Zero Carbon Emissions from Harder-to-Abate Sectors by Mid-Century', Sectoral Focus: Shipping (2020).

7. The Exponential Roadmap Initiative (2020).

8. Energy Transitions Commission (2020).

9. Ibid.

10. Goldman Sachs, 'Carbonomics: Innovation, Deflation and Affordable De-carbonization', Equality Research (October 2020).

Ton of carbon dioxide equivalent, including the impact of other greenhouse gases, such as methane and nitrous oxide, converted in terms of the amount of CO_2 that would create the same amount of warming.

11. See Energy and Climate Intelligence Unit, 'Net Zero Tracker: Net Zero Emissions Race 2020 Scoreboard': https://eciu.net/netzerotracker.

12. Climate Action Tracker, 'Warming Projections Global Update' (December 2019).

13. In the UK, in the run-up to the general election in 2019, polls found that climate change ranked above the economy, education and immigration on a list of voter issues, fifth only to Brexit, the NHS, crime and care for the elderly (See Sarah Prescott-Smith, 'Which issues will decide the general election?', YouGov, 7 November 2019). Similarly in the US, climate change is rising up the ranks, as Americans are starting to rank climate change above other pertinent issues such as employment and more so than at any other time in the past few decades (See Robinson Meyer, 'Voters Really Care About Climate Change', The Atlantic, 21 February 2020). And in the last Canadian elections, just under a third of citizens considered climate change a critical issue influencing their vote – breaching the coveted 'top three' for the first time in voter polls (See Jessica Murphy, Robin Levinson-King, Tom Housden, Sumi Senthinathan and Mark Bryson, 'A Canadian Election Looms – Seven Charts Explain All', BBC News, 18 October 2019).

14. Cass Sunstein, How Change Happens (MIT Press: Cambridge, MA, 2019).

15. Cass Sunstein, 'How Change Happens' podcast. London School of Economics Public Lectures and Events, 14 January 2020.

16. Tim Besley and Torsten Persson, 'Escaping the Climate Trap? Values, Technologies and Politics', unpublished manuscript (February 2020).

17. International Energy Agency, 'Deep energy transformation needed by 2050 to limit rise in global temperature' (20 March 2017).

18. It extends well beyond the G20 to over seventy countries. See Task Force on Climate-Related Financial Disclosures, 'Final Report: Recommendations of the Task Force on Climate-Related Financial Disclosures' (June 2017).

19. Of course, at the end of these paths we would face very different worlds.

20. UN Environment Programme, 'Emissions Gap Report, 2019' (26 November 2019).

21. Sarah Breeden, 'Leading the Change: Climate Action in the Financial Sector', speech given at Bank of England, 1 July 2020.

22. Stern Review: The Economics of Climate Change: https://webarchive.nationalarchives.gov.uk/20100407172955/ or http://www.hm-treasury.gov.uk/d/Executive_Summary.pdf

23. MSCI, 'Is ESG All About the "G"? That Depends on Your Time Horizon', (15 June 2020).

24. See Kristalina Georgieva, 'Statement by Kristalina Georgieva on Her Selection as IMF Managing Director', (25 September 2019) and Kristalina Georgieva, 'IMF Managing Director Kristalina Georgieva's Opening Press Conference, 2020 Annual Meetings' (14 October 2020).

25. This section draws heavily on the report of the G30 which Janet Yellen and I co-chaired (Group of Thirty, 'Mainstreaming the Transition to a Net-Zero Economy' (October 2020)). Particular thanks to core team of Caspar Siegert, Jacob A. Frenkel, Maria Ramos, William R. Rhodes, Adair Turner, Axel A. Weber, John C. Williams, Ernesto Zedillo, Debarshi Basu, Jennifer Bell, Carole Crozat, Stuart Mackintosh and Sini Matikainen.

26. An alternative assumption is that an early adjustment will lead to less mitigation in later years, resulting in the same end-point carbon concentrations. The IPCC's 'Fifth Assessment Report' demonstrates that in this scenario pulling the adjustment forward can still have material benefits. This is because emission reductions in early years reduce the need to reduce emissions drastically in the future by relying on expensive technologies such as carbon capture and storage. The precise economic benefits of reductions in end-point carbon concentrations are highly uncertain and depend on a number of assumptions. In addition, the impact of carbon concentrations on physical losses are estimated to be highly non-linear. So the benefits of any additional reductions in emissions depend in part on how sharply emissions are expected to fall in the baseline.

27. This assumes a (discounted) social cost of carbon of $115 (in 2010 US dollars). The estimate of the social cost of carbon is based on Nordhaus (2018) and uses a discount factor of 2.5 per cent to discount future physical risks. This discount factor is lower than the baseline assumption in Nordhaus (2018), resulting in a higher social cost of carbon (See William Nordhaus, 'Projections and Uncertainties About Climate Change in an Era of Minimal Climate Policies', *American Economic Journal: Economic Policy* 10(3) (2018) pp. 333-60)). Stern (2006) sets out reasons why in the context of climate change it is appropriate to use low discount factors. The benefits of an earlier

adjustment do not consider any
costs of transitioning more quickly,
and aiming for a lower end-point
carbon concentration. However, as
explained transitioning to a given
end-point more quickly tends to be
cheaper, which may offset the cost
of pursuing a stricter end-point
target. The estimate does not
consider the benefits of reducing
GHGs other than CO_2.

13: Values-Based Leadership
1. Peter Atwater, 'CEOs and investors
   should beware the curse of
   authorship', *Financial Times*, 17
   September 2017.
2. Max Weber, *The Theory of Social
   and Economic Organisation* (New
   York: Oxford University Press,
   1947).
3. Thomas Carlyle, *On Heroes, Hero-
   Worship, and the Heroic in History*
   (1841; reissued New Haven: Yale
   University Press, 2013), p. 30.
4. Stanley McChrystal, Jeff Eggers
   and Jason Mangone, *Leaders:
   Myth and Reality* (New York:
   Portfolio Penguin, 2018).
5. See for example Gary Yukl,
   'Effective Leadership Behavior:
   What We Know and What
   Questions Need More Attention',
   *Academy of Management
   Perspectives* 26(4) (2012),
   pp. 66–85.
6. Technically rooted in the branch of
   psychology known as
   behaviourism.
7. Philip V. Hodgson and Randall
   P. White, 'Leadership, Learning,
   Ambiguity and Uncertainty and
   Their Significance to Dynamic
   Organisations', in Randall S.
   Peterson and Elizabeth A. Mannix
   (eds), *Leading and Managing
   People in the Dynamic
   Organization* (Hillsdale, NJ:
   Lawrence Erlbaum, 2003),
   pp. 185–99.
8. St Thomas University, 'What is
   transactional leadership? Structure
   leads to results', 25 November 2014.
9. Umme Salma Sultana, Mohd
   Ridzuan Darun and Liu Yao,
   'Transactional or transformational
   leadership: which works best for
   now?', *International Journal of
   Industrial Management* 1 (June
   2015), pp. 1–8.
10. J.D. Mayer and P. Salovey, 'What is
    Emotional Intelligence?', in P.
    Salovey and D. Sluyter (eds.),
    *Emotional Development and
    Emotional Intelligence:
    Implications for Educators* (New
    York: Basic Books, 1997),
    pp. 3–31.
11. See Daniel Goleman, *Emotional
    Intelligence: Why It Can Matter
    More Than IQ* (London:
    Bloomsbury, 1996).
12. Ronald E. Riggio, 'Are You a
    Transformational Leader?',
    Psychology Today, 24 March 2009;
    Christine Jacobs et al., 'The
    Influence of Transformational
    Leadership on Employee Well-
    Being: Results from a Survey of
    Companies in the Information and
    Communication Technology
    Sector in Germany', *Journal of
    Occupational Environmental
    Medicine* 55(7) (2013), pp. 772–8.
13. Bernard M. Bass and Ronald E.
    Riggio, *Transformational
    Leadership* (New Jersey: Lawrence
    Erlbaum Associates/Taylor &
    Francis e-Library, 2006), pp. 2–3.
14. Ajay Agrawal, Joshua Gans and
    Avi Goldfarb, 'The Simple
    Economics of Machine
    Intelligence', *Harvard Business
    Review* (November 2016).
15. A point emphasised by Robert
    Phillips of Jericho Chambers
    (Robert Phillips, 'The Banality of
    Talking Trust', *Jericho*).
16. See e.g. NORC, 'General Social
    Survey 2012 Final Report: Trends
    in Public Attitudes about
    Confidence in Institutions' (May
    2013); The National Centre for
    Social Research 'British Social
    Attitudes 35: Key Findings: Trust,
    Politics and Institutions' (2018).

17. Katharine Dommett and Warren Pearce, 'What do we know about public attitudes towards experts? Reviewing survey data in the United Kingdom and European Union', *Public Understanding of Science* 28(6) (2019), pp. 669–78.

18. Edelman Trust Barometer 2020.

19. Ibid.

20. See for example European Commission, 'The Five Presidents' Report: Completing Europe's Economic and Monetary Union' (June 2015); Mark Carney, 'Fortune Favours the Bold', speech given at Iveagh House, Dublin, 28 January 2015.

21. Zizi Papacharissi, 'The Virtual Sphere: The Internet as a Public Sphere', *New Media & Society* 4(1) (2002), pp. 9–27.

22. Minouche Shafik, 'In experts we trust?' speech given at Oxford Union, 22 February 2017.

23. Nic Newman, Richard Fletcher, David A. L. Levy and Rasmus Kleis Nielsen, *Reuters Institute Digital News Report 2016*, Reuters Institute for the Study of Journalism (2016).

24. Jan-Werner Müller, *What is Populism?* (Philadelphia: University of Pennsylvania Press, 2016).

25. Onora O'Neill, 'Lecture 4: Trust and Transparency', Reith Lectures 2002: A Question of Trust.

26. Onora O'Neill, 'Questioning Trust', in Judith Simon (ed.), *The Routledge Handbook of Trust and Philosophy* (New York and London: Routledge, 2017), pp. 17–27.

27. The International Fact-Checking Network's code of principles includes a commitment to non-partisanship, transparency, openness about funding sources, methodology and honest corrections. See https://www.ifcncodeofprinciples.poynter.org/.

28. Mark Carney, 'Guidance, Contingencies and Brexit', speech given at the Society of Professional Economists, 24 May 2018.

29. See Shafik (2017), John Kay and Mervyn King, *Radical Uncertainty: Decision Making for an Unknowable Future* (London: The Bridge Street Press, 2020).

30. André Gide, *Ainsi soit-il ou Les jeux sont faits* (Paris: Gallimard, 1952).

31. Jonathan Fullwood, 'A cat, a hat and a simple measure of gobbledygook: How readable is your writing?', *Bank Underground* (2016).

32. See Mark Carney, 'The Economics of Currency Unions', speech given to the Scottish Council for Development & Industry, Edinburgh, 29 January 2014.

33. Oral evidence on the Bank of England inflation report, 24 May 2016. Chris Giles, 'Mark Carney defends BoE stance on Brexit recession danger.' *Financial Times*. 24 May 2016.

34. Monetary Policy Summary and minutes of the Monetary Policy Committee meeting ending on 11 May 2016, http://www.bankofengland. co.uk/ publications/minutes/Documents/ mpc/pdf/2016/mav. pdf.

35. Record of the FPC's March 2016 meeting: http://www.bankof england.co.uk/publications/ Documents/records/fpc/pdf/2016/ record1604.pdf.

36. Mark Carney, Opening Statement to the House of Lords Economics Affairs Committee. 19 April 2016. https://www.bankofengland.co. uk/-/media/boe/files/about/people/ mark-carney/mark-carney-opening-statement-2016.pdf.

37. Oral evidence on the Bank of England inflation report, 24 May 2016.

38. Alison Richard, Report to the Regent House, 1 October 2004.

39. They are often used to provide continuous power output in systems where the energy source is not continuous (like crankshafts in reciprocating engines).

40. John C. Maxwell, *The 21 Irrefutable Laws of Leadership* (Nashville: Thomas Nelson Publishers, 1998), p. 79.
41. Müller (2016), p. 16.
42. Ibid., p. 84.
43. Bank of England, 'Review on the Outlook for the UK Financial System: What it Means for the Bank of England', Future of Finance Report, June 2019.
44. John Gardner, speech accepting President Johnson's offer to serve as US Secretary of Health, Education, and Welfare, 27 July 1965.
45. Kevin M. Warsh, 'The Panic of 2008', speech given at the Council of Institutional Investors 2009 Spring Meeting, Washington, DC, 6 April 2009.

14: How Purposeful Companies Create Value

1. Andrea Sella, 'Wedgwood's Pyrometer', *Chemistry World*, 19 December 2012.
2. Ibid.
3. Derek Lidow, 'How Steve Jobs Scores on the Wedgwood Innovation Scale', *Forbes*, 3 June 2019.
4. 'Etruria Village', Wedgwood Museum, http://www.wedgwoodmuseum.org.uk/archives/archive-collections-/story/the-etruria-factory-archive/chapter/etruria-village.
5. See e.g. Josiah Wedgwood, *An Address to the Workmen in the Pottery, on the Subject of Entering into the Service of Foreign Manufacturers. By Josiah Wedgwood, F.R.S. Potter to Her Majesty* (Newcastle: Printed by J. Smith, 1783).
6. Mary Guyatt, 'The Wedgwood Slave Medallion: Values in Eighteenth Century Design', *Journal of Design History* 13(2) (2000), p. 97.
7. US Securities and Exchange Commission, 'What We Do', 10 June 2013.
8. Chris McGlade and Paul Eakins, 'The geographical distribution of fossil fuels unused when limiting global warming to 2 Degrees C, *Nature* 517 (2015), pp 187–90.
9. *Short v. Treasury Commissioners* [1948] SVC 177, *Croner-i*.
10. *Inland Revenue v. Laird Group* [2003] BTC 385, *Croner-i*.
11. John Kay, 'Shareholders Think They Own the Company – They are Wrong', *Financial Times*, 11 November 2015.
12. Ibid.
13. Martin Wolf, 'Shareholders Alone Should Not Decide on AstraZeneca', *Financial Times*, 9 May 2014.
14. Andy Haldane, 'Who Owns a Company?', speech given at the University of Edinburgh Corporate Finance Conference, 22 May 2015.
15. In an influential 1974 paper, Robert Merton showed that, under limited liability, the equity of a company can be valued as a call option on its assets, with a strike price equal to the value of its liabilities. The value of this option is enhanced by increases in the volatility of asset returns because under limited liability this increases the upside return to shareholders, without affecting their downside risk. So for a firm seeking to maximise shareholder value, an expedient way of doing so is simply to increase the volatility of company profits. This risk does not, however, disappear, but is shifted on to other stakeholders in the company. There is therefore – as shown by Jensen and Meckling – an incentive for the management of a limited liability company to shift risks from shareholders to debtors, by increasing company-specific risk. Robert C. Merton, 'On the Pricing of Corporate Debt: The Risk Structure of Interest Rates', *Journal of Finance* 29(2) (1974), pp. 449–70; Michael C. Jensen and

William H. Meckling, 'Theory of the Firm: Managerial Behavior, Agency Costs and Ownership Structure', *Journal of Financial Economics* 3(4) (1976), pp. 305–60.

16. Samuel Williston, 'History of the Law of Business Corporations before 1800: I', *Harvard Law Review* 2(3) (1888), pp. 110–12; David Ciepley, 'Wayward Leviathans: How America's Corporations Lost their Public Purpose', *Hedgehog Review* 21(1) (2019), p. 71.

17. Williston (1888), pp. 110–12.

18. Adam Smith, *An Inquiry into the Nature and Causes of the Wealth of Nations* (1776; digital edn MetaLibri, 2007), IV.viii.2.

19. Ciepley (2019), p. 70.

20. John D. Turner, 'The development of English company law before 1900', QUCEH Working Paper Series No. 2017–01 (2017), p. 16.

21. Ibid., p. 17.

22. Peter Muchlinski, 'The Development of German Corporate Law until 1990: An Historical Reappraisal', *German Law Journal* 14(2) (2013), pp. 348–9.

23. Turner (2017), p. 22.

24. *Dodge v. Ford Motor Co.* [1919] 204 Mich 459.

25. Ibid.

26. Ibid.

27. Ibid.

28. Ciepley (2019), pp. 76–7. Continental Europe for its part never adopted shareholder primacy to the extent Anglo-Saxon countries did, following more stakeholder-centric models. These are best exemplified by the German law of *Mitbestimmung*, which allows workers to elect representatives to sit on the supervisory board of directors.

29. Lynn A. Stout, 'The Shareholder Value Myth', *Cornell Law Faculty Publications*, Paper 771 (2013).

30. Big Innovation Centre, 'The Purposeful Company: Interim Report' (2016), p. 42. See also Leo

E. Strine Jr, 'Can We Do Better by Ordinary Investors? A Pragmatic Reaction to the Dueling Ideological Mythologists of Corporate Law', *Columbia Law Review* 114(2) (2014), pp. 449–502; Dalia Tsuk Mitchell, 'From Pluralism to Individualism: Berle and Means and 20th-Century American Legal Thought', *Law & Social Inquiry* 30(1) (2005), pp. 179–225.

31. Big Innovation Centre (2016), 'The Purposeful Company: Interim Report' p. 43, adapted from 'The Law, Finance and Development Project' (University of Cambridge).

32. Milton Friedman, 'A Friedman Doctrine: The Social Responsibility of Business is to Increase its Profits', *New York Times Magazine*, 13 September 1970.

33. Stout (2013).

34. Ibid.

35. *Peoples Department Stores Inc. (Trustee of) v. Wise*, 2004 SCC 68; *BCE Inc. v. 1976 Debentureholders*, 2008 SCC 69.

36. Nicole Notat and Jean-Dominique Senard, 'L'Entreprise Objet d'Intérêt Collectif', Rapport aux Ministres de la Transition Écologique et Solidaire, de la Justice, de l'Économie et des Finances du Travail, 9 March 2018.

37. Jean-Philippe Robé, Bertrand Delaunay and Benoît Fleury, 'French Legislation on Corporate Purpose', Harvard Law School Forum on Corporate Governance, 8 June 2019.

38. UK Companies Act 2006, s. 172(1).

39. Ibid., s. 112.

40. See e.g. *eBay Domestic Holdings, Inc. v. Newmark*, 16 A.3d 1, 34 (Del. Ch. 2010), which states that the duty of a director is 'to promote the value of the corporation for the benefit of the stockholders'.

41. Leo E. Strine Jr, 'The Dangers of Denial: The Need for a Clear-Eyed Understanding of the Power and

Accountability Structure Established by the Delaware General Corporation Law', *Institute for Law and Economics*, Research Paper No. 15-08 (2015), p. 10.

42. See e.g. Sullivan & Cromwell LLP, 'Business Roundtable "Statement on the Purpose of a Corporation" Proposes New Paradigm', 20 August 2019; Davis Polk & Wardwell LLP, 'The Business Roundtable Statement on Corporate Purpose', 21 August 2019; Wachtell, Lipton, Rosen & Katz LLP, 'Stakeholder Governance and the Fiduciary Duties of Directors', 24 August 2019.

43. Wachtell, Lipton, Rosen & Katz LLP (2019).

44. William T. Allen, 'Our Schizophrenic Conception of the Business Corporation', *Cardozo Law Review* 14(2) (1992), p. 281.

45. See e.g. the British Academy's 2019 'Principles for Purposeful Business' report which advocates a change to UK corporate law to change the duty of corporate directors, and Senator Elizabeth Warren's 2018 proposed Accountable Capitalism Act which would require directors of US corporations with revenue greater than US$1 billion to consider all relevant stakeholders when making decisions, and operate the corporation in a manner that seeks to create a general public benefit.

46. Big Innovation Centre (2016), p. 19.

47. Thomas Donaldson and James P. Walsh, 'Towards a theory of business', *Research in Organizational Behaviour* 35 (2015), pp. 181–207.

48. Ronald Coase, 'The Nature of the Firm', *Economica* 4(16) (1937), pp. 386–405.

49. Martin Wolf, 'We Must Rethink the Purpose of the Corporation', *Financial Times*, 11 December 2018.

50. Elizabeth Anderson, 'The Business Enterprise as an Ethical Agent', in Subramanian Rangan (ed.), *Performance and Progress: Essays on Capitalism, Business, and Society* (Oxford: Oxford University Press, 2015), pp. 185–202.

51. John Kay, *The Truth about Markets: Their Genius, their Limits, their Follies* (London: Penguin, 2003).

52. See 'Integrated Corporate Governance: A Practical Guide to Stakeholder Capitalism for Boards of Directors', World Economic Forum, White Paper (June 2020), pp. 30–3.

53. Unilever, 'Purpose-Led, Future-Fit: Unilever Annual Reports and Accounts 2019' (2020), p. 55; Unilever, 'The Governance of Unilever', 1 January 2020, p. 24.

54. Unilever, 'Purpose-Led, Future-Fit', p. 56.

55. Ibid., p. 40.

56. 'Integrated Corporate Governance', pp. 18–19.

57. Ibid., pp. 30–3.

58. Mark Zuckerberg, 'Bringing the World Closer Together', Facebook, 22 June 2017; 'Eleventh Amended and Restated Certificate of Incorporation of Facebook, Inc.', available through EDGAR, US Securities and Exchange Commission.

59. Patagonia Works, 'Annual Benefit Corporation Report, Fiscal Year 2013', pp. 7–11.

60. Former Chief Justice of the Delaware Supreme Court Leo E. Strine Jr has advocated reducing the supermajority requirement and other 'unreasonable barriers' to becoming a benefit corporation as a way of facilitating better corporate governance in the United States. See Leo E. Strine Jr, 'Toward Fair and Sustainable Capitalism', *Roosevelt Institute* (2020), p. 13.

61. B Corporation, 'About B Corps', https://bcorporation.net/

faq-categories/about-b-corps (accessed 7 September 2020).

62. Danone, 'Our Vision', https://www.danone.com/about-danone/sustainable-value-creation/our-vision.html (accessed 7 September 2020).

63. Danone, 'Regenerative Agriculture', https://www.danone.com/impact/planet/regenerative-agriculture.html (accessed 7 September 2020); Danone, 'Circular Economy of Packaging', https://www.danone.com/impact/planet/packaging-positive-circular-economy.html (accessed 7 September 2020).

64. Danone Canada, 'Transparent Assessment', 4 July 2017; Alpro, 'Transparent Assessment', 20 September 2020.

65. Leila Abboud, 'Danone adopts new legal status to reflect social mission', *Financial Times*, 26 June 2020.

66. Ibid.

67. Rupert Younger, Colin Mayer and Robert G. Eccles, 'Enacting Purpose within the Modern Corporation', Harvard Law School Forum on Corporate Governance, 2 September 2020.

68. Larry Fink, 'Larry Fink's 2016 Letter to CEOs' (2016), https://www.blackrock.com/corporate/investor-relations/2016-larry-fink-ceo-letter.

69. Ibid.

70. Larry Fink, 'Larry Fink's 2019 Letter to CEOs: Purpose and Profit' (2019), https://www.blackrock.com/corporate/investor-relations/2019-larry-fink-ceo-letter; Larry Fink, 'Larry Fink's 2018 Letter to CEOs: A Sense of Purpose' (2018), https://www.blackrock.com/corporate/investor-relations/2018-larry-fink-ceo-letter.

71. Fink (2019).

72. Big Innovation Centre (2016), pp. 11–12.

73. Bank of England, HM Treasury and Financial Conduct Authority,

'Fair and Effective Markets Review: Final Report' (June 2015), p. 79.

74. Big Innovation Centre (2016), pp. 11–12.

75. Ibid., p. 86.

76. Bank of England, HM Treasury and Financial Conduct Authority (2015), p. 79.

77. 'ESG Spotlight – The State of Pay: Executive Remuneration & ESG Metrics', Sustainalytics, 30 April 2020.

78. Unilever, 'Statement on the implementation of Unilever's Remuneration Policy for 2020', 11 February 2020.

79. Alcoa, 'Notice of 2020 Annual Meeting of Stockholders and Proxy Statement', 19 March 2020, p. 54.

80. Ibid.

81. Cassie Werber, 'Danone is showing multinationals the way to a less destructive form of capitalism', *Quartz at Work*, 9 December 2019.

82. Rebecca Henderson, *Reimagining Capitalism in a World on Fire* (New York: Hachette Book Group, 2020), ch. 4.

83. Henderson (2020), ch. 2.

84. Gunnar Friede, Timo Busch and Alexander Bassen, 'ESG and Financial Performance: Aggregated Evidence from More than 2000 Empirical Studies', *Journal of Sustainable Finance & Investment* 5(4) (2015), pp. 210–33.

85. Mozaffar Khan, George Serafeim and Aaron Yoon, 'Corporate Sustainability: First Evidence on Materiality', *Accounting Review* 91(6) (2016), pp. 1697–1724.

86. Luigi Guiso, Paola Sapienza and Luigi Zingales, 'The Value of Corporate Culture', *Journal of Financial Economics* 117(1) (2015), pp. 60–76.

87. Claudine Gartenberg, Andrea Prat and George Serafeim, 'Corporate Purpose and Financial Performance', Harvard Business School Working Paper No. 17-023 (2016).

88. Rui Albuquerque, Art Durnev and Yrjö Koskinen, 'Corporate Social Responsibility and Firm Risk: Theory and Empirical Evidence', *Management Science* 65(10) (2015), pp. 4451–69.

89. Nell Derick Debevoise, 'Why Patagonia Gets 9,000 Applications for an Opportunity to Join their Team', *Fortune*, 25 February 2020.

90. Ernst & Young, 'Why Business Must Harness the Power of Purpose', 26 April 2018, https://www.ey.com/en_gl/purpose/why-business-must-harness-the-power-of-purpose.

91. Alex Edmans, 'The Link between Job Satisfaction and Firm Value, with Implications for Corporate Social Responsibility', *Academy of Management Perspectives* 26(4) (2012), pp. 1–19.

92. Karl V. Lins, Henri Servaes and Ane Tamayo, 'Social Capital, Trust, and Firm Performance: The Value of Corporate Social Responsibility during the Financial Crisis', *Journal of Finance*, European Corporate Governance Institute (ECGI), Finance Working Paper No. 446/2015 (2016).

93. 'The Business Case for Purpose', Harvard Business Review Analytic Services Report (2015).

94. Big Innovation Centre (2016), p. 25.

95. Ibid.

96. Marc Andreessen, 'It's Time to Build', Andreessen Horowitz, 18 April 2020, https://a16z.com/2020/04/18/its-time-to-build/.

15: Investing for Value(s)

1. Hortense Bioy, 'Sustainable Fund Flows Hit Record in Q2', Morningstar, 4 August 2020.

2. Soohun Kim and Aaron S. Yoon, 'Analyzing Active Managers' Commitment to ESG: Evidence from United Nations Principles for Responsible Investment', SSRN (2020).

3. Morgan Stanley Capital Investment, 'MSCI ESG Indexes during the coronavirus crisis', 22 April 2020.

4. Hortense Bioy, 'Do Sustainable Funds Beat their Rivals?', Morningstar (June 2020).

5. Hortense Bioy and Dimitar Boyadzhiev, 'How Does European Sustainable Funds' Performance Measure Up?', Morningstar Manager Research (June 2020).

6. Mozaffar Khan, George Serafeim and Aaron Yoon, 'Corporate Sustainability: First Evidence on Materiality', *Accounting Review* 91(6) (2016), pp. 1697–1724, https://ssrn.com/abstract=2575912 or http://dx.doi.org/10.2139/ssrn.2575912.

7. Michael E. Porter, George Serafeim and Mark Kramer, 'Where ESG Fails', *Institutional Investor*, 16 October 2019.

8. George Serafeim, 'Public Sentiment and the Price of Corporate Sustainability', *Financial Analysts Journal* 76(2) (2018), pp. 26–46, https://ssrn.com/abstract=3265502 or http://dx.doi.org/10.2139/ssrn.3265502.

9. As Porter et al. (2020) state, 'However, without examining the actual link between social impact and profitability, there is little economic justification for this premium.' This implicitly assumes that all social values must be priced in the market to be captured in cash flows.

10. Robert G. Eccles and Svetlana Klimenko, 'The Investor Revolution', *Harvard Business Review* (May–June 2019); 'The True Faces of Sustainable Investing: Busting the Myths Around ESG Investors', Morningstar (April 2019); John G. Ruggie and Emily K. Middleton, 'Money, Millennials, and Human Rights: Sustaining "Sustinable Investing"', Harvard Kennedy School's Corporate Responsibility

Initiative Working Paper No. 69 (June 2018).

11. UK Department for International Development, 'Investing in a Better World: Result of UK survey on Financing the SDGs' (September 2019).

12. Sarah Boseley, 'Revealed: cancer scientists' pensions invested in tobacco', *Guardian*, 30 May 2016; Nicole Brockbank, 'Ontario Teachers' Pension Plan had shares in company that runs controversial U.S. migrant detention centres', CBC News, 11 July 2019.

13. Oliver Hart and Luigi Zingales, 'Companies Should Maximize Shareholder Welfare Not Market Value', *Journal of Law, Finance, and Accounting* 2(2) (2017), pp. 264–6.

14. Regulation (EU) 2019/2088 of the European Parliament and of the Council of 27 November 2019 on sustainability-related disclosures in the financial services sector (text with EEA relevance).

15. Ibid.

16. Ontario Pensions Benefits Act, Regulation 909, s. 40(v)(ii).

17. Law Commission, 'Pension Funds and Social Investment: Summary', Law Com No. 374 (June 2017), p. 2.

18. Employee Benefits Security Administration, Department of Labor, 'Financial Factors in Selecting Plan Investments', *Federal Register* 85(220) (2020), pp. 72854–5.

19. Carlos Tornero, '"Premised on an assumption – unsupported by any cited facts – that ERISA fiduciaries are misusing ESG": Investors slap back DoL plans', *Responsible Investor* (August 2020).

20. 'Fiduciary Duty in the 21st Century: Final Report', United Nations Environmental Programme Finance Initiative (2019).

21. 'Dynamic Materiality: Measuring What Matters', Truvalue Labs (January 2020).

22. Examples of the providers of these ratings include MSCI, Sustainalytics and Truvalue Labs.

23. Feifei Li and Ari Polychronopoulos, 'What a Difference an ESG Ratings Provider Makes!', *Research Affiliates* (January 2020).

24. Rajna Gibson, Philipp Krueger, Nadine Riand and Peter S. Schmidt, 'ESG rating disagreement and stock returns', ECGI Finance Working Paper No. 651/2020 (January 2020).

25. Dane Christensen, George Serafeim and Anywhere Sikochi, 'Why is Corporate Virtue in the Eye of the Beholder? The Case of ESG Ratings', Harvard Business School Working Paper 20-084 (2019).

26. Florian Berg, Julian F. Kölbel and Roberto Rigobon, 'Aggregate Confusion: The Divergence of ESG Ratings', MIT Sloan School of Management Working Paper 5822-19 (May 2020).

27. Porter et al. (2019), p. 7.

28. PwC, 'Purpose and Impact in Sustainability Reporting' (November 2019).

29. Ron Cohen FT Op Ed (July 2020)

30. https://yanalytics.org/research-insights/monetizing-impact

31. Greg Fischer, 'Monetizing Impact', Y Analytics (January 2020), p. 4.

32. Ibid.

16: How Countries Can Build Value for All

1. In the UK, intangible investment rose above tangible investment in the early 2000s, and stood at 11 per cent as a share of output in 2014 compared with 10 per cent for tangible investment. Investment in intangibles also exceeded that in tangibles in the US, Sweden and Finland (on average over 1999–2003), but not in other European countries including Germany, Italy and Spain. See Jonathan Haskel and Stian Westlake, *Capitalism without Capital: The Rise of the*

Intangible Economy (Princeton: Princeton University Press, 2017); and Peter R. Goodridge, Jonathan Haskel and Gavin Wallis, 'Accounting for the UK Productivity Puzzle: A Decomposition and Predictions', *Economica* 85(339) (2016), pp. 581–605.

2. This process has been well documented for the China Shock in the US (Autor, Dorn and Hanson (2015)) and the collapse of local housing markets (Mian and Sufi (2015)).

3. The following is based on Daron Acemoglu and Pascual Restrepo, 'Artificial Intelligence, Automation and Work', NBER Working Paper No. 24196 (2018). To understand such dynamics it helps to have a common conceptual framework. The impact of technological change on employment and wages can be depicted as the sum of three major effects: destruction, productivity and creation. The *destruction effect* is the focus of most alarmist accounts: the replacement of labour by technology, with an associated reduction in labour demand, wages and employment. Less commonly acknowledged are the positive effects on aggregate demand of new technologies, what can be termed the *productivity effect*. This effect is analogous to the classic Say's law in which supply creates its own demand. Technology makes those in work more productive, in time boosting wages and increasing the returns to those who own capital. This greater income boosts aggregate demand and leans against the destruction effect. When technological change is disruptive and widespread, the productivity effect is generally insufficient to counteract completely the destruction effect, partly because of the time it takes for the full potential of new technologies to be realised, and partly because of the phenomenon of greater job polarisation – to which we will turn in a moment.

4. This creation effect need not be fully exogenous to the technological change, for example because the new technologies allow new jobs to emerge that wouldn't otherwise be possible – though of course factors like education and skills are important in determining how quickly and smoothly these gains come about.

5. For example, Erik Brynjolfsson and Andrew McAfee, *The Second Machine Age: Work, Progress, and Prosperity in a Time of Brilliant Technologies* (New York and London: W. W. Norton, 2014). The most extreme view of this is put forward by Daniel Susskind, who highlights the possibility that in the future machines can perform all tasks leading to technological unemployment (Daniel Susskind, 'A model of technological unemployment', University of Oxford, Department of Economics Series Working Papers No. 819 (2017)).

6. The question at the heart of this debate is whether we can overcome 'Polanyi's Paradox' – that we can know more than we can tell (Michael Polanyi, 'The Logic of Tacit Inference', *Journal of the Royal Institute of Philosophy* 41(155) (1966) pp. 1–18.). Our inability to detail these tasks (such as social interactions) in a formulaic manner currently makes them difficult to encode and automate.

7. Carl Benedikt Frey and Michael A. Osborne, 'The future of employment: How susceptible are jobs to computerisation?', *Technological Forecasting and Social Change* 114 (2017), pp. 254–80. These authors estimate that up to half of jobs could be affected.

8. For example, McKinsey Global Institute, 'A Future that Works: Automation, Employment and Productivity' (2017), suggest that 60 per cent of occupations could see over 30 per cent of their tasks replaced by technology, based on O*NET analysis.

9. Edward W. Felten, Manav Raj and Robert Seamans, 'A Method to Link Advances in Artificial Intelligence to Occupational Abilities', *AEA Papers and Proceedings* 108 (2018), pp. 54–7.

10. For example, it may be possible to automate the pouring of drinks in bars, but doing so may not present a cost saving over hiring bar staff to do the job, let alone the ancillary benefit of being able to tell them your troubles.

11. Ljubica Nedelkoska and Glenda Quintini, 'Automation, skills use and training', OECD Social, Employment and Migration Working Papers No. 202 (2018). Similarly, McKinsey argue that across advanced economies 15 per cent of the workforce in total will need to shift occupational categories because of digitisation, automation and AI.

12. Analysis by the IMF indicates that the extent of job polarisation depends far more on the ease of substitution between labour and technology than it does on the relative price of technology.

13. The low level of automation in the UK – which Hal Varian has suggested could be linked to the size of the automobile and electronics sectors – may be one reason why the UK labour share has remained resilient (https://www.youtube.com/watch?v=VLcnN3kLUKI&app=desktop).

14. In the US, people with high replacement rate of earnings are just as likely to take jobs as those with low ones.

15. Tharman Shanmugaratnam, 'Making the Centre Hold: Keynote Speech', Institute for Government (July 2019).

16. Ibid.

17. Dani Rodrik, Arvind Subramanian and Francesco Trebbi, 'Institutions Rule: The Primacy of Institutions over Geography and Integration in Economic Development', *Journal of Economic Growth* 9(2) (2004), pp. 131–65.

18. Douglass C. North, 'The New Institutional Economics and Third World Development', in John Harriss, Janet Hunter and Colin M. Lewis (eds), *The New Institutional Economics and Third World Development* (London: Routledge, 1995), p. 17.

19. Daron Acemoglu and James A. Robinson, *Why Nations Fail: The Origins of Power, Prosperity, and Poverty* (New York: Crown, 2012). There are parallels to the dynamics of social movements detailed in Chapter 12.

20. Tera Allas, Marc Canal and Vivian Hunt, 'COVID-19 in the United Kingdom: Assessing jobs at risk and the impact on people and places', McKinsey & Company (11 May 2020).

21. See Mark Carney, 'The Future of Work', Whitaker Lecture, given at the Central Bank of Ireland, 14 September 2018. My colleague Andy Haldane has also discussed these issues. See 'Ideas and Institutions – A Growth Story', speech given at the Guild Society, Oxford, 23 May 2018.

22. Available at https://www.gov.uk/government/publications/good-work-the-taylor-review-of-modern-working-practices.

23. Acemoglu and Robinson (2012).

24. Niall Ferguson, *The Great Degeneration: How Institutions Decay and Economies Die* (London: Penguin, 2014).

25. Mancur Olson, *The Rise and Decline of Nations: Economic Growth, Stagflation, and Social*

Rigidities (New Haven, Conn.: Yale University Press, 1984).

26. See Michael Lewis, *Flash Boys: A Wall Street Revolt* (New York and London: W. W. Norton, 2014), and Roger L. Martin, 'The Gaming of Games & the Principle of Principles', Keynote Address to the Global Peter Drucker Forum, Vienna, 15 November 2012.

27. Bank of England, HM Treasury and Financial Conduct Authority, 'Fair and Effective Markets Review: Final Report' (June 2015).

28. See, for example, FMSB's 'Reference Price Transactions standard for the Fixed Income markets' (2016); 'New Issue Process standard for the Fixed Income markets' (2017); 'Surveillance Core Principles for FICC Market Participants: Statement of Good Practice for Surveillance in Foreign Exchange Markets' (2016). All standards and publications available at https://fmsb.com/our-publications/.

29. Andy Haldane, 'Ideas and Institutions – A Growth Story', speech given at the Oxford Guild Society, 23 May 2018.

30. Helen Warrell and Richard Milne, 'Lentils and War Games: Nordics Prepare for Virus Lockdown', *Financial Times*, 20 March 2020.

31. Dasgupta (2020).

32. Eurasia Group, *Climate Monthly* (August 2020).

33. Heidi Garrett-Peltier, 'Green versus Brown: Comparing the employment impacts of energy efficiency, renewable energy, and fossil fuels using an input-output model', *Economic Modelling* 61 (February 2017), pp. 439–47.

34. NAO report, 'Improving access to finance for small and medium-sized enterprises', Department for Business, Innovation and Skills and HM Treasury (November 2013).

35. British Business Bank, 'Small Business Finance Markets Report' (2019).

36. See https://www.bankofengland.co.uk/research/future-finance.

37. UNCTAD, 'World Investment Report 2018: Investment and New Industrial Policies' (2018).

38. See K. Blind, A. Mangelsdorf, C. Nichol and F. Ramel (2018), 'Standards in the global value chains of the European Single Market', *Review of International Political Economy* 25:1, 28-48; K. Nadvi (2008), 'Global standards, global governance and the organization of global value chains', *Journal of Economic Geography*, 8(3): 323–343.

39. Mario Draghi, 'Sovereignty in a Globalised World', speech as President of ECB at University of Bologna, 22 February 2019.

Conclusion: Humility

1. John Lennon worked this line into the song 'Beautiful Boy' but the observation was first made by the cartoonist Allen Saunders in *Readers Digest* in 1957.

2. Michael Lewis, 'Commencement Address', Princeton University (June 2012).

3. Marcus Aurelius, *Meditations* (Penguin: 2004. Translated Maxwell Shaniforth, 1964). Book 3: 10.

Acknowledgements

T his book draws impressions, perspectives and lessons gathered over many years. Its influences are multiple. I owe much to my experiences in public policy, and I am deeply grateful to those who gave me that chance, including David Dodge, Jim Flaherty and George Osborne. While in public service I learned from a number of remarkable colleagues about the importance of resilience, innovation and responsibility including Andrew Bailey, Jean Boivin, Sarah Breeden, Ben Broadbent, Agathe Cote, Jon Cunliffe, Brad Fried, Charlotte Hogg, Mike Horgan, Anil Kashyap, Don Kohn, Tiff Macklem, Nick Macpherson, John Murray, Tom Scholar, Minouche Shafik, Richard Sharp, Martin Taylor, Jan Vlieghe and Sam Woods. I am particularly indebted to Jenny Scott whose dedication to the common good transformed my thinking on purpose and leadership as well as my commitment to action.

During my time in central banking, I worked with a number of economists who understood both models and morals, including Nicola Anderson, David Aikman, Alina Barnett, Jamie Bell, James Benford, Alex Brazier, Jon Bridges, Paul Brione, Alice Carr, Ambrogio Cesa-Bianchi, Bob Fay, Jeremy Harrison, Andrew Hauser, Shoib Khan, Clare Macallan, Daisy McGregor, Alex Michie, Tom Mutton, Ben Nelson, Jen Nemeth, Cian O'Neil, Caspar Siegert, Kate Stratford, Tim Taylor, Greg Thwaites, Jill Vardy, Thomas Viegas, Matt Waldron, Anne Wetherilt and Ian de Weymarn. Professor Nicholas Vincent provided critical scholarship on the history and importance of the Magna Carta.

Many colleagues contributed to the initiatives to reform global finance including Tobias Adrian, Svein Andresen, Ben Bernanke, Benoît Cœuré, Bill Dudley, Mario Draghi, Tim Geithner, Christine Lagarde, Jean-Claude Trichet, Axel Weber and Kevin Warsh.

The chapters on climate change reflect ongoing dialogue with those leading the mainstreaming of sustainable finance, particularly Frank Elderson, Christiana Figueres, Yi Gang, Kristalina Georgieva, Sylvie Goulard, Christine Lagarde, Hiro Mizuno and Laurence Tubiana. The insights on the relationship between finance and climate policy sprung from a G30 working group led by Janet Yellen with the research formed by Caspar Seigert and Sini Matikainen. The Private Finance Hub for COP 26, led by Steve Field, Yasmine Moezinia and Jen Nemeth, has been at the forefront of many of the most important developments, under the determined leadership of Secretary-General António Guterres, Deputy Secretary-General Amina Mohammed, and COP President Alok Sharma.

Those who are closing the gap between what is counted and what counts have greatly influenced my thinking on the future of value, particularly Mike Bloomberg, Mary Schapiro and Curtis Ravenel – the pioneers of the TCFD – Clara Barby of the Impact Management Project, Brian Moynihan and Bill Thomas at the IBC, George Serafeim and Ronald Cohen of the Impact Weighted Accounts Project at Harvard, and Lucrezia Rechlin and Erkki Likkanen at the IFRS Foundation.

My thinking on the imperative of action on climate change has been shaped by Richard Curtis, Partha Dasgupta, Jamie Drummond and Greta Thunberg. My confidence in the art of the possible has been inspired by Bill Gates, Jeremy Oppenheim, Nick Stern, Adair Turner, Lance Uggla, and my colleagues at Brookfield including Bruce Flatt, Sachin Shah, Connor Teskey and Natalie Adomait.

The chapters on Covid drew on important conversations with, and the research of, Nick Stern, Tim Besley, Gus O'Donnell and Daisy McGregor.

Deeper issues of values were informed by discussions with Oliver Baete, Thomas Buberl, Edward Burtynsky, Emerson Czorba, Roger Ferguson, Lynn Forester de Rothschild, Laurence Freeman, Antony Gormley, Paul David Hewson, Philipp Hildebrand, Michael

Ignatieff, Father Augusto Ocampo, Jenny Scott, Tharman Shanmugaratnam, Ng Kok Song, John Studzinski, Cardinal Peter Turkson and Archbishop Justin Welby.

The book would not have been possible without the creativity, dedication and range of Jen Nemeth. R.J. Reid, Tim Krupa and Eliza Baring provided invaluable research assistance, and Gerry Butts kindly reviewed the draft manuscript and provided essential insights.

Caroline Michel believed in this project from the outset, encouraged me to stretch my thinking, expand my horizons and get on with the work. Caroline, Rebecca Wearmouth and their colleagues at Peters Fraser Dunlop helped get the book into the hands of my editor, Arabella Pike, who has shaped it into something far better than it would have been. I also am grateful to the team at HarperCollins, including Peter James (who did a fine job copyediting the book) and Eve Hutchings. I also benefited from the active and focused engagement (and good humour) of my Canadian editors, Doug Pepper and Jenny Bradshaw. Some of the core themes of the book were sharpened by the process of preparing and giving the Reith lectures. I am grateful to Mohit Bakaya, Jim Frank and Hugh Levinson for their challenge and guidance.

During the most intense phases of the writing, I was blessed by the gifts of food, shelter and friendship by Nez and Hassan Khoshrowshahi, Bill and Anda Winters, Sean and Mimi Carney and the incomparable Ruthie Rogers.

My wife, Diana, has been with me throughout, debating, criticising, and always encouraging. My children forced me from complacency and have constantly challenged my thinking. My siblings have, as always, been supportive, and I thank my mother every day for the childhood she and my father gave me and the values they imparted.

Despite such enormous support and resources, the book is rife with errors and omissions. They remain my own.

Index

Mark Carney is an economist and banker. He is currently serving as the UN Special Envoy on Climate Action and Finance. From 2013 to March 2020, he served as the governor of the Bank of England and chair of the Monetary Policy Committee, Financial Policy Committee, and the Board of the Prudential Regulation Committee. He lives in Ottawa, Canada.